Lecture Notes in Computer Science 14037

Founding Editors

Gerhard Goos
Juris Hartmanis

The series Lecture Notes in Computer Science (LNCS), including its subseries Lecture Notes in Artificial Intelligence (LNAI) and Lecture Notes in Bioinformatics (LNBI), has established itself as a medium for the publication of new developments in computer science and information technology research, teaching, and education.

LNCS enjoys close cooperation with the computer science R & D community, the series counts many renowned academics among its volume editors and paper authors, and collaborates with prestigious societies. Its mission is to serve this international community by providing an invaluable service, mainly focused on the publication of conference and workshop proceedings and postproceedings. LNCS commenced publication in 1973.

Norbert A. Streitz · Shin'ichi Konomi
Editors

Distributed, Ambient and Pervasive Interactions

11th International Conference, DAPI 2023
Held as Part of the 25th HCI International Conference, HCII 2023
Copenhagen, Denmark, July 23–28, 2023
Proceedings, Part II

 Springer

Editors
Norbert A. Streitz
Smart Future Initiative
Frankfurt am Main, Germany

Shin'ichi Konomi
Kyushu University
Fukuoka, Japan

ISSN 0302-9743 ISSN 1611-3349 (electronic)
Lecture Notes in Computer Science
ISBN 978-3-031-34608-8 ISBN 978-3-031-34609-5 (eBook)
https://doi.org/10.1007/978-3-031-34609-5

Foreword

Human-computer interaction (HCI) is acquiring an ever-increasing scientific and industrial importance, as well as having more impact on people's everyday lives, as an ever-growing number of human activities are progressively moving from the physical to the digital world. This process, which has been ongoing for some time now, was further accelerated during the acute period of the COVID-19 pandemic. The HCI International (HCII) conference series, held annually, aims to respond to the compelling need to advance the exchange of knowledge and research and development efforts on the human aspects of design and use of computing systems.

The 25th International Conference on Human-Computer Interaction, HCI International 2023 (HCII 2023), was held in the emerging post-pandemic era as a 'hybrid' event at the AC Bella Sky Hotel and Bella Center, Copenhagen, Denmark, during July 23–28, 2023. It incorporated the 21 thematic areas and affiliated conferences listed below.

A total of 7472 individuals from academia, research institutes, industry, and government agencies from 85 countries submitted contributions, and 1578 papers and 396 posters were included in the volumes of the proceedings that were published just before the start of the conference, these are listed below. The contributions thoroughly cover the entire field of human-computer interaction, addressing major advances in knowledge and effective use of computers in a variety of application areas. These papers provide academics, researchers, engineers, scientists, practitioners and students with state-of-the-art information on the most recent advances in HCI.

The HCI International (HCII) conference also offers the option of presenting 'Late Breaking Work', and this applies both for papers and posters, with corresponding volumes of proceedings that will be published after the conference. Full papers will be included in the 'HCII 2023 - Late Breaking Work - Papers' volumes of the proceedings to be published in the Springer LNCS series, while 'Poster Extended Abstracts' will be included as short research papers in the 'HCII 2023 - Late Breaking Work - Posters' volumes to be published in the Springer CCIS series.

I would like to thank the Program Board Chairs and the members of the Program Boards of all thematic areas and affiliated conferences for their contribution towards the high scientific quality and overall success of the HCI International 2023 conference. Their manifold support in terms of paper reviewing (single-blind review process, with a minimum of two reviews per submission), session organization and their willingness to act as goodwill ambassadors for the conference is most highly appreciated.

This conference would not have been possible without the continuous and unwavering support and advice of Gavriel Salvendy, founder, General Chair Emeritus, and Scientific Advisor. For his outstanding efforts, I would like to express my sincere appreciation to Abbas Moallem, Communications Chair and Editor of HCI International News.

July 2023   Constantine Stephanidis

HCI International 2023 Thematic Areas and Affiliated Conferences

Thematic Areas

- HCI: Human-Computer Interaction
- HIMI: Human Interface and the Management of Information

Affiliated Conferences

- EPCE: 20th International Conference on Engineering Psychology and Cognitive Ergonomics
- AC: 17th International Conference on Augmented Cognition
- UAHCI: 17th International Conference on Universal Access in Human-Computer Interaction
- CCD: 15th International Conference on Cross-Cultural Design
- SCSM: 15th International Conference on Social Computing and Social Media
- VAMR: 15th International Conference on Virtual, Augmented and Mixed Reality
- DHM: 14th International Conference on Digital Human Modeling and Applications in Health, Safety, Ergonomics and Risk Management
- DUXU: 12th International Conference on Design, User Experience and Usability
- C&C: 11th International Conference on Culture and Computing
- DAPI: 11th International Conference on Distributed, Ambient and Pervasive Interactions
- HCIBGO: 10th International Conference on HCI in Business, Government and Organizations
- LCT: 10th International Conference on Learning and Collaboration Technologies
- ITAP: 9th International Conference on Human Aspects of IT for the Aged Population
- AIS: 5th International Conference on Adaptive Instructional Systems
- HCI-CPT: 5th International Conference on HCI for Cybersecurity, Privacy and Trust
- HCI-Games: 5th International Conference on HCI in Games
- MobiTAS: 5th International Conference on HCI in Mobility, Transport and Automotive Systems
- AI-HCI: 4th International Conference on Artificial Intelligence in HCI
- MOBILE: 4th International Conference on Design, Operation and Evaluation of Mobile Communications

List of Conference Proceedings Volumes Appearing Before the Conference

1. LNCS 14011, Human-Computer Interaction: Part I, edited by Masaaki Kurosu and Ayako Hashizume
2. LNCS 14012, Human-Computer Interaction: Part II, edited by Masaaki Kurosu and Ayako Hashizume
3. LNCS 14013, Human-Computer Interaction: Part III, edited by Masaaki Kurosu and Ayako Hashizume
4. LNCS 14014, Human-Computer Interaction: Part IV, edited by Masaaki Kurosu and Ayako Hashizume
5. LNCS 14015, Human Interface and the Management of Information: Part I, edited by Hirohiko Mori and Yumi Asahi
6. LNCS 14016, Human Interface and the Management of Information: Part II, edited by Hirohiko Mori and Yumi Asahi
7. LNAI 14017, Engineering Psychology and Cognitive Ergonomics: Part I, edited by Don Harris and Wen-Chin Li
8. LNAI 14018, Engineering Psychology and Cognitive Ergonomics: Part II, edited by Don Harris and Wen-Chin Li
9. LNAI 14019, Augmented Cognition, edited by Dylan D. Schmorrow and Cali M. Fidopiastis
10. LNCS 14020, Universal Access in Human-Computer Interaction: Part I, edited by Margherita Antona and Constantine Stephanidis
11. LNCS 14021, Universal Access in Human-Computer Interaction: Part II, edited by Margherita Antona and Constantine Stephanidis
12. LNCS 14022, Cross-Cultural Design: Part I, edited by Pei-Luen Patrick Rau
13. LNCS 14023, Cross-Cultural Design: Part II, edited by Pei-Luen Patrick Rau
14. LNCS 14024, Cross-Cultural Design: Part III, edited by Pei-Luen Patrick Rau
15. LNCS 14025, Social Computing and Social Media: Part I, edited by Adela Coman and Simona Vasilache
16. LNCS 14026, Social Computing and Social Media: Part II, edited by Adela Coman and Simona Vasilache
17. LNCS 14027, Virtual, Augmented and Mixed Reality, edited by Jessie Y. C. Chen and Gino Fragomeni
18. LNCS 14028, Digital Human Modeling and Applications in Health, Safety, Ergonomics and Risk Management: Part I, edited by Vincent G. Duffy
19. LNCS 14029, Digital Human Modeling and Applications in Health, Safety, Ergonomics and Risk Management: Part II, edited by Vincent G. Duffy
20. LNCS 14030, Design, User Experience, and Usability: Part I, edited by Aaron Marcus, Elizabeth Rosenzweig and Marcelo Soares
21. LNCS 14031, Design, User Experience, and Usability: Part II, edited by Aaron Marcus, Elizabeth Rosenzweig and Marcelo Soares

47. CCIS 1836, HCI International 2023 Posters - Part V, edited by Constantine Stephanidis, Margherita Antona, Stavroula Ntoa and Gavriel Salvendy

https://2023.hci.international/proceedings

Preface

The 11th International Conference on Distributed, Ambient and Pervasive Interactions (DAPI 2023), an affiliated conference of the HCI International Conference, provided a forum for interaction and exchanges among researchers, academics, and practitioners in the field of HCI for DAPI environments. The DAPI conference addressed approaches and objectives of information, interaction, and user experience design for DAPI Environments as well as their enabling technologies, methods, and platforms, and relevant application areas.

The DAPI 2023 conference covered topics addressing basic research questions and technology issues in the areas of new modalities, immersive environments, smart devices, etc. On the other hand, there was an increase in more applied papers that cover comprehensive platforms and smart ecosystems addressing the challenges of cyber-physical systems, human-machine networks, public spaces, smart cities, and nature preservation. The application areas also include education, learning, culture, art, music, and interactive installations.

Two volumes of the HCII2023 proceedings are dedicated to this year's edition of the DAPI Conference. The first volume focuses on topics related to designing and evaluating intelligent environments, user experience in intelligent environments, and pervasive data. The second volume focuses on more applied topics related to smart cities and environment preservation, media, art and culture in intelligent environments, and supporting health, learning, work, and everyday life.

Papers of these volumes are included for publication after a minimum of two single–blind reviews from the members of the DAPI Program Board or, in some cases, from members of the Program Boards of other affiliated conferences. We would like to thank all of them for their invaluable contribution, support, and efforts.

July 2023
Norbert A. Streitz
Shin'ichi Konomi

11th International Conference on Distributed, Ambient and Pervasive Interactions (DAPI 2023)

Program Board Chairs: **Norbert A. Streitz**, *Smart Future Initiative, Germany*, and **Shin'ichi Konomi**, *Kyushu University, Japan*

Program Board:

- Pedro Antunes, *University of Lisbon, Portugal*
- Kelvin Joseph Bwalya, *University of Johannesburg, South Africa*
- Morten Fjeld, *Chalmers University of Technology, Sweden*
- Nuno Guimarães, *Instituto Universitário de Lisboa - ISCTE, Portugal*
- Kyungsik Han, *Hanyang University, South Korea*
- Jun Hu, *Eindhoven University of Technology, The Netherlands*
- Eiman Kanjo, *Nottingham Trent University, UK*
- Nicos Komninos, *Aristotle University of Thessaloniki, Greece*
- Maristella Matera, *Politecnico di Milano, Italy*
- H. Patricia McKenna, *AmbientEase/UrbanitiesLab Initiative, Canada*
- Tatsuo Nakajima, *Waseda University, Japan*
- Guochao (Alex) Peng, *Sun Yat-sen University, P.R. China*
- Elaine M. Raybourn, *Sandia National Laboratories, USA*
- Carsten Röcker, *TH OWL, Germany*
- Tomoyo Sasao, *University of Tokyo, Japan*
- Reiner Wichert, *Darmstadt University of Applied Sciences, Germany*
- Chui Yin Wong, *Intel Corporation, Malaysia*
- Woontack Woo, *KAIST, South Korea*
- Takuro Yonezawa, *Nagoya University, Japan*
- Chuang-Wen You, *National Tsing Hua University, Taiwan*

The full list with the Program Board Chairs and the members of the Program Boards of all thematic areas and affiliated conferences of HCII2023 is available online at:

http://www.hci.international/board-members-2023.php

HCI International 2024 Conference

The 26th International Conference on Human-Computer Interaction, HCI International 2024, will be held jointly with the affiliated conferences at the Washington Hilton Hotel, Washington, DC, USA, June 29 – July 4, 2024. It will cover a broad spectrum of themes related to Human-Computer Interaction, including theoretical issues, methods, tools, processes, and case studies in HCI design, as well as novel interaction techniques, interfaces, and applications. The proceedings will be published by Springer. More information will be made available on the conference website: http://2024.hci.international/.

General Chair
Prof. Constantine Stephanidis
University of Crete and ICS-FORTH
Heraklion, Crete, Greece
Email: general_chair@hcii2024.org

https://2024.hci.international/

Contents – Part II

Media, Art and Culture in Intelligent Environments

Supporting Health, Learning, Work and Everyday Life

Contents – Part I

User Experience in Intelligent Environments

Pervasive Data

Smart Cities and Environment Preservation

Methodology for Functionalization of "Living Lab" Under Concept of Smart Cities

Case through Service Design Development Workshops Using Frailty Prevention AI Technology

Yuki Igeta[1]([⊠]), Tomoyo Sasao[1] [iD], Haruka Kitamura[1], Mitsuharu Tai[2], Takuya Kurita[1], and Atsushi Deguchi[1] [iD]

[1] Graduate School of Frontier Sciences, The University of Tokyo, 5-1-5 Kashiwanoha, Kashiwa City, Chiba, Japan
`igeta.yuki@edu.k.u-tokyo.ac.jp`
[2] Hitachi, Ltd., 6-6, Marunouchi 1-Chome, Chiyoda-Ku, Tokyo, Japan

Abstract. This study focuses on the Living lab as one of the methods of co-creation. The main objectives are to identify the goals from Living lab in smart cities and to propose the methodology for functionalization of Living lab in smart cities. In practice, this paper defines the Living lab in smart cities as "a series of co-creation activities in which multi-stakeholders and citizens through experiments and trials in real-life environments in the processes of identifying issues and establishing a vision, designing ideas, implementing in real life environment for common goals such as solving regional issues". Second, goals of co-creation through Living lab are categorized into seven types in "Ideation", "Feedback on testing", "Market intelligence", "Networking", "Raising awareness", "Social acceptance", and "Other". Third, the effect of manipulations and process for goals which are expected in Frailty Prevention AI Living lab is evaluated, through the participant observation method. As a result, it is clarified that four goals; 1) specific service ideas using the technology (Ideation), 2) feedback on them (Feedback on testing), 3) clarifying of key factors for services to work (Market intelligence), 4) citizen acceptance (Social acceptance), are achieved in the Living lab. And the manipulations and process for these goals are presented. Finally, the remaining issues and how to improve them are proposed as the methodology of functionalizing the Living lab under the concept of smart cities.

Keywords: Living lab · Smart Cities · co-creation

1 Introduction

1.1 Research Background

Smart Cities are cities and regions which are developed to solve various problems such as inclusiveness and environment and improve people's quality of life and well-being using cutting-edge technologies or information technologies [1, 2]. OECD proposes

N. A. Streitz and S. Konomi (Eds.): HCII 2023, LNCS 14037, pp. 3–17, 2023.
https://doi.org/10.1007/978-3-031-34609-5_1

smart city indicators, and mentions that involvement of stakeholders in smart cities, such as city/local government, city's residents and private sectors, is important for achieving smart city's objectives [3]. Especially, the importance of citizen participation is emphasized in academic field [4]. Smart cities in Japan also focus on citizen participation. "Smart city guidebook [5]", a guide book for smart city's organizations that was published by Japan cabinet office in 2021, picks up a participation by diverse entities as an effective process in a preparatory stage in a smart city.

There is a Living lab methodology as one of citizen participation, which leads smart city services to implementation, connecting citizens who use smart city services and smart city organizations who have technology seeds and provide smart city services. Now, Living lab programs are practiced all over the world. These goals spread to a lot of types; service development [6], mixing together personalities and activities [7], combating the digital divide [8], grasp needs and prototyping survey [9]. Therefore, enterprises and organizations that want to start the new Living lab program find it hard to imagine its effects and align recognition.

When Living lab is used in smart cities, themes are often difficult to imagine for citizens. For example, cutting-edge technologies such as autonomous vehicles and artificial intelligence and unfamiliar fields such as energy and infrastructure. Based on the difference between general Living lab and Living lab in smart cities, clarifying the effect of manipulations for expected goals in Living lab in smart cities as methodology, Living lab in smart cities will spread widely.

1.2   Living Lab Concept and Definition of Living Lab in Smart Cities

William J. Mitchell from MIT proposed the Living lab concept in the late 1990s for the first time [10, 11]. At that time, Living lab meant an experimental living place for researchers to observe, analyze, and evaluate the uses and effects of technology in user's daily life [12, 13]. After that, the concept went around to Europe. ENoLL (European Networks of Living Labs), it is the large Living lab network in Europe founded in 2006, defines Living lab as "open innovation ecosystems in real-life environments using iterative feedback processes throughout a lifecycle approach of an innovation to create sustainable impact [14]". It shows that the new concept; community, co-creation, and innovation was added to the primary definition. Furthermore, according to Botnia Living Lab, the first Living lab in Europe, there are three iterative steps "Concept Design", "Prototype Design", and "Innovation Design" in Living lab process [15].

Co-creation, one of the Living lab's key factors, is defined as "creative activity for realizing the common goals and dreams together sharing with multi background people [16]". SIG-CCI (Special Interest Group on Crowd Co-creative Intelligence) mentions "multi background people", "common goals and issues", and "creative activity" as definition of co-creation [17].

Therefore, in this paper, Living lab in smart cities is defined as "a series of co-creation activities in which multi-stakeholders and citizens through experiments and trials in real-life environments in the processes of identifying issues and establish a vision, idea design, implement in society for common goals such as solving regional issues". And the diagram representing this definition is shown below (Fig. 1).

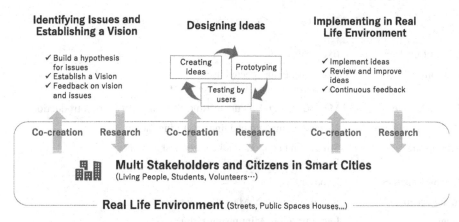

Fig. 1. A diagram representing the definition of Living lab in Smart City

1.3 Previous Study on Living Lab Goals in Smart Cities

There are some studies about Living lab in smart cities. Tran et al. [18] propose a collaboration framework with multi-stakeholders including citizens for sharing decision making processes in smart city Living lab. According to Alam et al. [19], using the Living lab methodology is an important factor for developing sustainable smart services. However, the methodology for achieving outcomes in smart city Living lab is still not mentioned enough.

There are also some studies about goals in general Living lab. Ballon et al. [20] show as the goals of Living lab, "bring digital innovation processes and outcomes more in line with user preferences and practices, discover unexpected uses, identify potentially sound business and revenue models, stimulate cooperation between stake-holders, enable specific stakeholder groups to influence design features, increase acceptance, understand and tackle inhibiting factors, minimise failures, or study effects of introduction." Katharina [21], analyzing 14 Living lab projects, shows measurable outcomes, "Market acceptance, Price Acceptability, Exposure, Product Testing, Market Intelligence, Legitimisation, Method Testing, Networking." Moreover, Leminen et al. [22] show five factors that influence outcomes in smart city Living labs, strategic intention, passion, knowledge and skills, other resources, and partners in the Living lab network.

Based on the above, it is said that the achievements of Living lab include outputs such as some ideas and effects such as improvement of social acceptance. Therefore, outcomes in general Living lab are sorted out as seven goals of co-creation through Living lab (Table 1). While these are expected in general Living lab, this thought should be adopted into the smart city Living lab and clarified if it functions at that.

1.4 Objectives

This paper defines the Living lab in smart cities and sorts out the goals of general Living lab. Then methodology for the functionalization of Living lab in smart cities is proposed through the case of Living lab in Kashiwanoha, Japan.

Table 1. Goals of Co-creation through Living lab

Types of goals	Examples
Ideation	Discovering unexpected uses, Identifying business and revenue models
Feedback on testing	Method testing, Product testing, Studying effects of introduction
Market intelligence	Understanding and tackling inhibiting factors
Networking	Stimulating cooperation between stakeholders, Involving of specific stakeholder groups
Raising awareness	Exposure
Social acceptance	Social acceptance, Market acceptance
Other	Legitimisation, Minimising failures

The first objective is to evaluate the effects of manipulation to gain four of the seven goals of general Living lab; "Ideation", "Feedback and Testing", "Market Intelligence", and "Citizen Acceptance". Second, this paper aims to clarify the issues through Frailty Prevention AI Living lab in Kashiwanoha. Consequently, processes and manipulations to improve these issues is proposed as a methodology for achieving goals in smart city Living lab.

1.5 Method

This paper targets "Frailty prevention AI Living lab" which has been organized as a Living lab in Kashiwanoha Smart City located in the northwestern part of Kashiwa City, Chiba Prefecture in Japan. This Living lab expects four goals; 1) specific service ideas using Frailty Prevention AI (Ideation), 2) feedback on these ideas (Feedback on Testing), 3) clarifying of key factors for a service to work (Market Intelligence), and 4) citizen acceptance for that technology and future services (Social acceptance). It is the reason why this paper treats this Living lab.

Specifically, the participant observation method is chosen, which means the author participates in the Living lab program as a workshop organizer and obtains outputs from each workshop and answers from questionnaire surveys for workshop participants and other organizers. Using these outputs, the effect of manipulations and processes for goals which are expected in Living lab in smart cities is evaluated.

2 Outline of Frailty Prevention AI Living Lab

"Frailty Prevention AI", a core technology for this Living lab program, is healthcare technology that makes use of big data and is developed by H-UTokyo Lab [23]. Frailty Prevention AI has a mission to estimate risks of becoming in need of care in the future by analyzing answers to questionnaires about oral, nutrition, exercise, and social participation and big data from the National Health Insurance database. When creating a service using the technology, careful consideration for handling personal data, the management system, and social acceptance are essential.

This chapter explains the specific details of the Frailty Prevention AI Living lab program.

2.1 Operation Structure

The operation structure of Frailty Prevention AI Living lab was composed of Living lab Organization which planned and organized the whole Living lab program and each workshop, Program Participants who participate in each workshop (Fig. 2).

Living lab Organization was comprised of UDCK (Urban Design Center Kashiwanoha), the area management hub in Kashiwanoha area, UDCKTM (UDCK Town Management) which supported urban planning in Kashiwanoha area with UDCK, Living lab Working Group and Smart Aging Working Group in H-UTokyo Lab. Also, UDCK, UDCKTM and Living lab Working Group composed the Living lab Project "Urban Design Studio for everyone in KASHIWA-NO-HA [21]", and it held other Living lab programs in Kashiwanoha. Public Intelligence Japan (PI), Denmark enterprise which organized health care Living lab and demonstration experiments, joined as an advisor for planning the whole program and facilitator in workshops each session.

Program Participants were estimated users such as the elderly whom Frailty Prevention AI targeted, elderly families, and healthcare and nursing care professionals. Living lab Organization recruited widely using flyers and SNS, the number of participants in each workshop was 9 to 12, and the age of participants was 40s to 80s. The four people of authors participated as members of the Living lab Working Group.

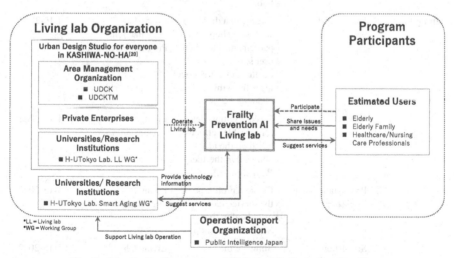

Fig. 2. The Frailty Prevention AI Living lab Operation Structure.

2.2 Program

Frailty Prevention AI Living lab was held from November 2021 to July 2022. The program was designed following the process in Fig. 1. Specifically, the vision was established and shared among stakeholders. Then, issues related to frailty prevention were identified with citizens. After these activities, ideas using Frailty Prevention AI were designed and prototypes were made, and feedback was gathered from participants. Finally, some key factors were found. Each session in each workshop was designed to refer to PI's methodology. Citizens participated in a series of workshops, Idea Workshop, Simulation Workshop, and Trial Action Design, and provided feedback through dialogs with each other and touching ideas and prototypes (Table 2).

Table 2. Living Lab Program Overview

Phase	Workshops in each phase	Purpose	Participants	Date
Identifying Issues and Establishing a Vision	Workshop 1	Identify issues to be targeted in the Living lab program; identify stakeholders	Living lab Organization	10-12-2021
	Workshop 2	Explore the causes of the issues and set goals	Living lab Organization	10-18-2021
	Workshop 3	Set up a dimension and build a structure and workshop tools for the Trusted User Lab	Living lab Organization	10-25-2021
Designing Ideas	Idea Workshop	Engage in a dialogue with workshop participants based on user stories, and obtain cues for service ideas from this dialogue	Living lab Organization, Program Participants	4-16-2022
	Service Workshop	Discuss initial ideas for possible services based on the ideas obtained in the Idea Workshop	Living lab Organization	4-16-2022
	Prototyping Workshop	Create a prototype of the service ideas discussed in the Service Workshop	Living lab Organization	5-13-2022
	Simulation Workshop	Simulate the prototype and gauge the workshop participants' reactions	Living lab Organization, Program Participants	5-15-2022

(*continued*)

Table 2. (*continued*)

Phase	Workshops in each phase	Purpose	Participants	Date
	Trial Action Design	Refine the prototype based on participants' reactions and conduct a small-scale test in an environment similar to real life	Living lab Organization, Program Participants	7-23-2022

3 Goals of Frailty Prevention AI Living Lab

In this chapter, four goals of ideas, feedback, key factors, and citizen acceptance through Frailty Prevention AI Living lab are shown.

3.1 Specific Service Ideas Using Frailty Prevention AI and Feedback on These Ideas

From Service Workshop and Prototyping Workshop in Idea Design Phase, three ideas using Frailty Prevention AI technology and brief prototypes were output. Ideas and prototypes were designed by Living lab organization members. Furthermore, in Simulation Workshop and Trial Action Design, program participants touched ideas and used prototypes, and various feedback such as real voices and reactions of program participants was obtained (Table 3).

Table 3. Summary of service ideas and reactions of program participants.

	Summary of service ideas	Reactions of program participants
Idea 1	**Frailty Prevention App:** During a waiting time at the hospital, the smartphone app receives a notification that presses patients to answer the Frailty questionnaire. After their answering, Frailty Prevention AI analyzes the answers. The results were shown on the smartphones with the previous results and recommended Frailty prevention activities can be shared with their doctors. Also, the app connects to point cards in that area, so the points will be earned if some activities were done	Supporting Opinions • It's good to make effective use of the waiting time at the hospital • It may be good not only at the hospital but also at the pharmacy Suggestions for Improvement • Smartphone apps may be unfamiliar to the elderly • There are only burdens and no merits for medical professors and government offices

(continued)

Table 3. (*continued*)

	Summary of service ideas	Reactions of program participants
Idea 2	**GIFT-from child to parents:** Children ask their parents to answer the Frailty questionnaire. After their answering, Frailty Prevention AI analyzes the answers. The results were shown to the children. According to the result, the children choose and give a gift to their parents to make them start Frailty prevention activities. (e.g. If the result shows that their father was lack of exercise, children choose and give walking shoes or travel tickets.)	Supporting Opinions • It is very probable to start some activities because of the recommendation from the children and relatives • Each parent has their own preferences, so it may be better if there are some options that parents can choose the gifts by themselves • It may be a merit for medical professors if it can screen the risk of Frailty widely Suggestions for Improvement • This service needs both good relationships and IT literacy
Idea 3	**Recommendation at Medical check-up site:** Attendees answer the Frailty questionnaire at the medical check-up site. After their answering, Frailty Prevention AI analyzes the answers on the spot. Administrative hygienist tells them the result and proposes the recommended Frailty prevention activities. (e.g. "regional walking map" for exercise)	Supporting Opinions • It was a good idea to be told the results by not AI but person (administrative hygienist) • Introduction at the place and the advanced information may be effective Suggestions for Improvement • It is difficult to care for all attendees because medical check-ups are busy for doctors • There are high hurdles to joining the regional activities even if it is recommended

3.2 Clarifying of Key Factors for Services to Work

The key factors which were found through co-creation and research with program participants were below,

1. Be a service that can get answers to frailty questionnaires.
2. Be a service that can continuously get answers to frailty questionnaires.
3. Be a service that connects starting frailty prevention activities.
4. Be a service that promotes continuing frailty prevention activities.

At first, Smart Aging Working Group which proposed the theme as a Living lab program had a simple concept; "a service that can realize continuous frailty prevention activities". Through brushing ideas up in Prototyping Workshop, these four key factors were drawn as more detail factors and were shared among Living lab organization members and program participants.

In Trial Action Design, touching three ideas and prototypes and observing how others used prototypes, program participants rated on a five-point scale whether ideas meet these factors. All ideas relatively meet the first and second factors, so these ideas could be said to promote answering the frailty questionnaire. On the contrary, it was revealed that more ingenuities were required for the third and fourth factors; connecting frailty prevention activities and promoting continue activities (Fig. 3). In addition to the five-point scale, feedback was gathered from free text comments and interactive question-and-answer sessions. Because there were many types of participants, someone preferred writing free comments and someone preferred interactive communication.

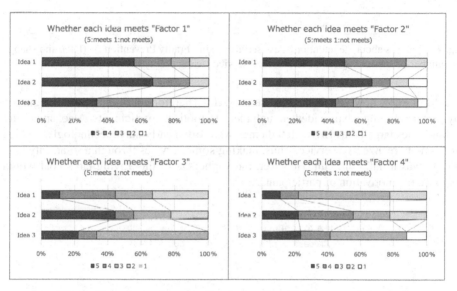

Fig. 3. Percentage of answers to whether three ideas meet each factor.

3.3 Citizen Acceptance for the Technology and Future Services

The attitude survey, intention to use services and opinion about providing services that use Frailty Prevention AI, was conducted before and after three workshops in which Program Participants were. As a result, both the intention to use raised and the answer to agree to provide services increased after workshops (Fig. 4). Due to the small sample size, it was difficult to generalize, but the potential of Living lab to change participants' attitudes and increase the likelihood of acceptance of services was shown.

3.4 Intention to Participate in Frailty Prevention AI Living lab

As above, Frailty Prevention AI Living lab brought four effects to the Living lab organization. On the other hand, it was wondered if program participates also get some outcomes. Actually, their intention to participate in this Living lab decreased after the third workshop (Fig. 5). Also, someone commented, "I couldn't see the goal of this Living lab through these workshops", and "the workshop was vague a little bit for me,

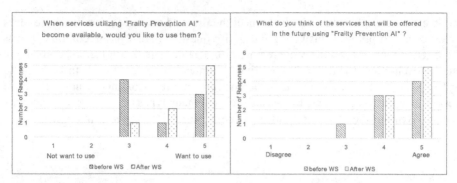

Fig. 4. Changes about the intention to use services using Frailty Prevention AI (left), and change the number of answer "agree" to be provided services using Frailty Prevention AI (right).

I couldn't know how you wanted to use this AI." Therefore, it might be challenging to say that this Living lab provided enough merit to motivate participants. Also, smart city technologies targeted as Living lab themes were often early-stage technologies, which take time to realize as a service. Thus, making some services through a smart city Living lab was usually difficult. However, the vagueness of this Living lab's goal would decrease the motivation of participants.

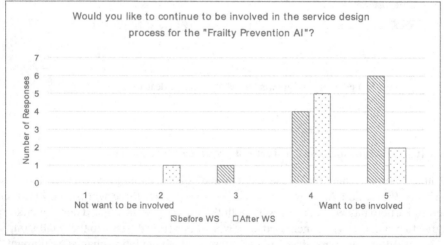

Fig. 5. Changes about the intention to participate in Frailty Prevention AI Living lab.

4   Evaluation the Effect of Manipulation, Issues, and Proposal for Improvement

The prior chapter showed that Living lab in smart cities could also get some outcomes, such as specific service ideas and feedback, clarifying key factors, and citizen acceptance for the technologies and service itself. In this chapter, the reasons and issues to improvement was discussed, and the knowledge was proposed as possible methods to utilize for the new Living lab programs.

4.1 How to Get Some Specific Service Ideas, and Feedback from Participants

In the Living lab, the Smart Aging Working Group participated, which has developed the Frailty Prevention AI technology, as a member of creating ideas. Thus, other members could get opportunities to ask questions about that technology frequently and to touch the prototypes of that technology directly. Usually, cutting-edge technologies often became black-box and were grasped as almighty, in Frailty Prevention AI Living lab, all members understood what it could and couldn't do, and could create highly feasible ideas based on the actual state of the technology.

On the other hand, some issues emerged because of the absence of the important roles; service providers and the program owner. Frailty Prevention AI technology developer had a business model to sell the technology and service model to some companies which wanted to provide the service. However, a future service provider was neither clarified nor participated as a member of the Living lab. As a result, the issue that no one could receive the three ideas from the Living lab emerged. Also, there were no program owners who decided the direction of whole Living lab program. As a result, after Prototyping Workshop, the idea to be focused on was not decided though the agendas; focusing on one idea and moving to the next phase to brush up on some functions and user experiences.

To solve these problems, making sure carefully that any important roles were missed at the beginning of the program was an essential point. For example, the following figure was the ideal structure for Frailty Prevention AI Living lab (Fig. 6).

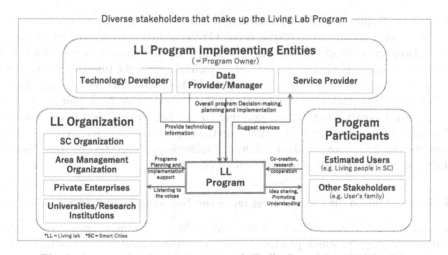

Fig. 6. An example of an ideal structure in Frailty Prevention AI Living lab.

Living lab organization undertakes the role of planning and management as sustained functions in smart cities and also gets engaged in launching various Living lab programs.

Living lab program implementing entities is comprised of technology developers, data providers/managers, and service providers, and they are also program owners. As pointed out in the first issue, service providers are important roles, however they are almost unclear at the beginning of the Living lab programs. Therefore, service providers should be involved in the Living lab program as soon as the candidates appear. Program owner, which was pointed out in the second issue, makes important decisions throughout the whole Living lab program. Program participants are mainly comprised of citizens and estimated service users. They participate in each workshop, bring information about their own problems and needs, create some ideas, provide feedback on some ideas, and test some prototypes.

It is important to assume such a relationship among various stakeholders in advance and check whether important roles are not absent from the beginning to the end of the program. Especially, the importance increases in smart cities because of the many and complicated stakeholder relations.

Also, various feedback was gained from Program Participants through the three workshops. Because there were multiple ways to get feedback such as observing reactions of touching prototypes, having dialogs about questions and thoughts, and writing down score evaluations and free comments on the paper. Especially, the main target people for Frailty Prevention AI technology were the elderly, and participants were relatively old. Therefore, the workshop questionnaire was devised to be prepared both on sheet and on the website. In the other words, it was important to devise according to the characteristics of the participants, for example, to design the way of receiving feedback carefully and to use both analog and digital on the situation.

4.2   How to Clarify the Key Factors for Services to Work

The previous chapter showed the presence of the technology developers as a reason for the first output; creating three possible ideas. On the contrary, the reason why the goal was to clarify the key factor for services was the presence of non-engineers who didn't know about the detail of Frailty Prevention AI technology. At the time of idea creation, some non-engineer members said, "I want some hints or requirements to create ideas", and "what is the validation point of this prototype?". As a result, these four key factors were shown. In other words, it was said that Living lab, in that various stakeholders did co-creation together, required spelling out the important factors for services even if it was obvious and it went without saying for technology developers or specialists in Frailty Prevention. This was a fine example of co-creation.

4.3   How to Obtain the Citizen Acceptance for Technologies and Services

There were some devices to generate two-way dialogue, not presentation nor hearing in three workshops in which program participants participated. For example, in Idea Workshop, there was a talking session about the elderly's problems using some pictures which showed a day in the life of an elderly person. During the session, participants of the workshop were divided into small groups of 4–6 people and Living lab organization members devoted themselves completely to hearing from participants. It was said that drawing out the voice of participants and reflecting on ideas carefully affected the citizen acceptance positively. Also, it was expected that active dialogue shortened the distance between Living lab organization members and program participants. As a result, participants became to have feelings of closeness to technology.

The next challenge was how to expand this effect in smart cities. In other words, the acceptability of only a few people who participated in the Living lab changed in this case, thus it wasn't said to be accepted by smart cities. Although this was a limit of the method of Living lab, which couldn't serve many citizens at once, it was needed some devices to increase the number of people who can participate, using a hybrid of online and offline tools, opening the results of each workshop to the public with highly transparent.

4.4 Challenges in Creating Merits for Program Participants

When a Living lab was designed, it tended to focus on only goals for Organization. Previous studies often offered goals for the organizations and technology developers as outcomes of Living Labs. However, it was essential to design the programs considering the merits for citizens and to make participants understand the significance and the positioning of that activity for ensuring citizens' continued participation in Living labs.

It was important to present both the goals of the Living lab itself and the goal realized beyond the service implementation after the Living lab was completed for citizens to understand the positioning of the Living lab activity. At the launching stage of the Living lab, it could be effective that conduct hearing for program owners using the diagram (Fig. 7). Also, the examples of merits for participants through the Living lab were the building of community and networking with others, self-growth through the opportunity of touching cutting-edge technologies and expertise and contributing to the improvement of their own city. These messages should have been sent when recruiting.

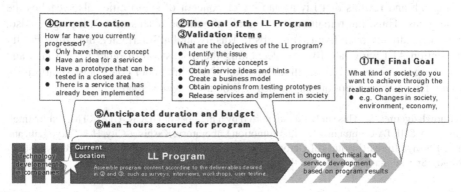

Fig. 7. A diagram to be used when hearing program owners who brought in a theme at the beginning of the Living lab program.

5 Conclusion

The background of this paper is that the image of the goals is difficult and the method to reach these goals are not sure in Living lab. The objectives are to identify the goals of Living lab in smart cities and to propose an appropriate methodology. The seven goals of general Living lab are "Ideation", "Feedback on testing", "Market intelligence", "Networking", "Raising awareness", "Social acceptance", and "Other". Then, the four goals; 1) specific service ideas using the technology (Ideation), 2) feedback on them (Feedback on testing), 3) clarifying of key factors for services to work (Market intelligence), and 4) citizen acceptance (Social acceptance), are focused on at the participant observation method in Frailty Prevention AI Living lab in Kashiwanoha Smart City in Japan. The effects of manipulations are evaluated, the issues are clarified, and the improvement of these issues is proposed.

For Ideation and Feedback on testing, co-creation by multi-stakeholders is effective. On the other hand, it should not forget to confirm the existence of some roles, such as program owners and service providers. Also, when getting feedback from participants, various devises according to the characteristics of the participants should be provided. For Market intelligence, co-creation of multi-background people is effective. Especially, communication with specialists and non-specialists are good for clarifying some factors for services. Active dialogue and reflecting participants' voice on ideas carefully contribute to social acceptance. On the other hand, there are still issues to motivate participants. The goals of the Living lab itself and the goal realized beyond the service implementation after the Living lab is completed should be presented. Also, some merits such as community building and networking with others, self-growth through the opportunity of touching cutting-edge technologies and expertise and contributing to improving their own city should be shown.

For further research, since this study only focuses on four of seven goals in general Living lab and reveals that Living lab under concept of smart cities also reaches the same goals. Thus, the remaining three goals should be discussed continuingly. Also, there have already been five Living labs in Kashiwanoha Smart City, including Frailty Prevention AI Living lab. By also deepening the discussion of other Living labs and proposing the goals and the methodology for Living lab under concept of smart cities, Living lab under concept of smart cities will be more widespread.

Acknowledgements. This study was supported by a member of UDCK, UDCKTM, Public Intelligence, A-SHI-TA Community Health Promotion Laboratory, Kashiwa-City, H-UTokyo Lab, and Prof. Katsuya Iijima (Institute of Gerontology, Institute for Future Initiatives, The University of Tokyo). Special thanks are given to them for their valuable input to this research.

References

1. ITU-T: Y. 4900/L.1600 (2016)
2. EU et al.: CITYkeys indicators for smart city projects and smart cities (2017)
3. OECD: Measuring Smart Cities' Performance (2020)

4. Simonofski, A., Asensio, E.S., Wautelet, Y.: Citizen participation in the design of smart cities: methods and management framework. In: Smart Cities: Issues and Challenges, pp. 47–62 (2019)
5. Japan Cabinet Office: Smart City Guidebook Apr.2021 ver. 1.01 (2021)
6. Veeckman, C., Schuurman, D., Leminen, S., Westerlund, M.: Linking Living lab characteristics and their outcomes: towards a conceptual framework. Technol. Innov. Manage. Rev. 3(12), 6–15 (2013)
7. Liberté Living Lab. https://enoll.org/network/living-labs/?livinglab=liberte-living-lab#description. Accessed 2023/2/10
8. Manda Lab. https://enoll.org/network/living-labs/?livinglab=manda-lab#description. Accessed 2023/2/10
9. Matsumoto Health Lab. https://m-health-lab.jp/about. Accessed 2023/2/10
10. Mulvenna, M., Martin, S., et al.: TRAIL Living Labs Survey 2011: A Survey of the ENOLL Living Labs. Ulster University (2011)
11. Eriksson, M., Niitamo, V., Kulkki, S., Hribeinik, K.: Living labs as a multi-contextual R&D methodology. In: 2006 IEEE International Technology Management Conference (ICE), pp. 1–8 (2006)
12. Hossain, M., Leminen, S., Westerlund, M.: A systematic review of Living lab literature. J. Clean. Prod. 213, 976–988 (2019)
13. Schuurman, D., De Moor, K., De Marez, L., Evens, T.: A Living lab research approach for mobile TV. Telemat. Inform. 28(4), 271–282 (2011)
14. European Networks of Living Labs: What are Living Labs? https://enoll.org/about-us/what-are-living-labs/. Accessed 2023/2/6
15. Botnia Living Lab: The Living Labs Methodology Book (2012)
16. Shimizu, H., Kume, T., Miwa, Y., Miyake, Y.: Ba and Co-creation, 1st edn. NTT Publishing Co., Ltd., Japan (2000)
17. Horita, R., Mitsui, M., Ito, T., Shiramatsu, S., Fujita, K., Fukuta, N.: A new academic workshop to generate co-creation between researchers and citizens. Jpn. Soc. Artif. Intell. 34(4), D-192_1-D–192_8 (2019)
18. Giang, T.T.H., Camargo, M., Dupont, L., Mayer, F.: A review of methods for modelling shared decision-making process in a smart city living lab. In: 2017 International Conference on Engineering, Technology and Innovation (ICE/ITMC) (2017)
19. Alam, M.T., Porras, J.: Architecting and designing sustainable smart city services in a living lab environment. Technologies 6(4), 99 (2018)
20. Ballon, P., Van Hoed, M., Schuurman, D.: The effectiveness of involving users in digital innovation: measuring the impact of living labs. Telemat. Inform. 35(5), 1201–1214 (2018). https://doi.org/10.1016/j.tele.2018.02.003
21. De Vita, K., De Vita, R.: Expect the unexpected: investigating co-creation projects in a living lab. Technol. Innov. Manage. Rev. 11(9/10), 6–20 (2021)
22. Leminen, S., Westerlund, M., Kortelainen, M.: A recipe for innovation through living lab networks. In: The XXIII ISPIM Conference (2012)
23. H-UTokyo Lab. http://www.ht-lab.ducr.u-tokyo.ac.jp/en/summary/. Accessed 2023/2/6
24. Public Intelligence. Introduktion til Public Intelligence's INNOVATIONSMETODIK. https://publicintelligence.dk/metode/. Accessed 2023/2/6

Toward Supporting Baggage-Free Walk-Arounds at Travel Destinations: Issues of the Hassle of Baggage During Travel

Fumika Kaburagi[1] and Kenro Aihara[1,2]([✉]) (iD)

[1] Tokyo Metropolitan University, Hachioji, Tokyo 192-0397, Japan
kaburagi-fumika@ed.tmu.ac.jp, kenro.aihara@tmu.ac.jp
[2] National Institute of Informatics, Chiyoda-ku, Tokyo 101-8430, Japan
https://behavior.ues.tmu.ac.jp/

Abstract. Luggage is a hassle for travelers. In recent years, various services related to luggage have emerged, as people are increasingly interested in how to handle luggage during travel. Luggage-free is expected to be beneficial for both businesses by expanding their business opportunities, and for travelers by freeing them from their luggage. Previous research on luggage has often focused on limited subjects, such as public transportation. Therefore, this research aims to propose a methodology that allows travelers and other visitors to leave their baggage behind and ease their behavioral restrictions and effectively promote their behavior at their destination. To analyze the influence of luggage, this paper dealt with distances from key stations by using individual behavior logs. The results suggested that tourists' activities may be affected by various constraints such as physical limit, location, temporal, and transportation when they carry luggage. Therefore, carrying luggage may not only restrict one's mobility but also restrict one's choice of places to stay and activities to enjoy. To achieve more freedom in tourism, it is important not only to increase fixed services such as coin lockers but also to improve services such as delivery.

Keywords: Carrying luggage · Hassle-free travel · Behavior change

1 Introduction

1.1 Luggage for Travelers

Baggage is a universal problem for travelers. For many people, the carrying of bags can be a big pain point of the travel experience. According to one article of BBC News, losing luggage at the airport is called "lost baggage" and is a source of frustration for air travelers [3]. It also states that Delta Airlines confirmed that there were about 25 million cases of lost baggage in 2018. Handling of baggage is ranked among the top complaints of airlines, and is typically a very slow process, which has been suggested as a cause of traveler dissatisfaction [7]. The

N. A. Streitz and S. Konomi (Eds.): HCII 2023, LNCS 14037, pp. 18–34, 2023.
https://doi.org/10.1007/978-3-031-34609-5_2

issue of baggage extends beyond just airline passengers. According to a survey conducted by Transport Focus in 2020, it was found that about 20% of the UK railway customers showed dissatisfied views towards the space for luggage on existing trains and metro cars [17]. This means that baggage is perceived as a hassle for air and rail travelers, and the influence of baggage is expected to be far-reaching, with many travel problems caused by it.

1.2 Services Developed in Response to Concerns About Luggage

As a result of this awareness, various services related to baggage have emerged in recent years. In fact, baggage delivery services such as Luggage Free[1] and Airportr[2] are being developed to help travelers avoid the hassle of carrying, checking, and picking up their luggage. Other innovative new baggage services are being offered at Zurich Airport by Swiss International Airlines (SWISS), which is expanding its partnership with Airportr and Swissport[3] in 2022. In addition, SWISS has expanded its successful collaboration with AirPortr and Swissport to offer innovative new baggage services at Zurich Airport [10].

On the other hand, in Japan, efforts are being made to address the inconvenience of baggage in response to the increasing demand from inbound travelers. The Japanese government has incorporated the promotion of "Hands-Free Travel" using delivery services as part of its policy to improve the reception of foreign visitors to Japan. "Hands-Free Travel" is a service that visitors can check in their luggage at the reception counters of airports, stations, and business facilities during their stay in Japan that the heavy bags will soon be delivered to their accommodation like hotels, inns, even their home in overseas countries, or to any other location of their choice [16].

In recent years, various luggage-free services have been proposed and offered in response to the needs of travelers seeking freedom from the hassle of luggage.

1.3 Travelers' Need for Luggage Storage Services

According to Chang [8], non-business travelers tend to be more willing than business travelers to pay more for luggage service and daytime arrival. It appears that there is a demand for innovation in the air travel industry, as consumers have expressed a need for it. Even though many consumers were not familiar with the concept of luggage delivery services, the service received favorable feedback [7]. Based on these studies, it can be anticipated that there is a high demand among travelers for luggage services.

From the above, in recent years there has been an increasing interest in how to handle baggage during travel. For travelers, checking their baggage provides a sense of freedom, and for businesses, it presents an opportunity to expand their business by providing baggage storage services. Therefore, it is expected that baggage-free services will be beneficial for both parties.

---

[1] Luggage Free. https://www.luggagefree.com/, accessed on 2023-01-29.
[2] Airportr. https://airportr.com/, accessed on 2023-01-29.
[3] https://www.swissport.com/.

In this paper, the authors aim to support the expansion of baggage-free travel and clarify the influence of carrying baggage by using tourists' behavior logs.

2   Related Works

2.1   Luggage and Passengers in Public Transportation

A study based on individual experiences has made it clear that "transport disadvantage" individuals, experienced by various groups in society, are a socially relevant issue that should be a priority target for public policy. Among the accounts of "transportation disadvantaged" individuals, some expressed that they feel fatigued and stressed when traveling with their hand luggage on public transportation [12].

In a study on the effect of step height on train boarding and alighting time, it was found that the heavier the luggage of the passengers, the longer the train boarding and alighting time. Additionally, younger people are relatively less affected by the presence of luggage, while the presence of luggage is a hindrance for elderly people and affects the boarding and alighting time for them as well [14].

2.2   Influence of Luggage on the Choice of Public Transportation Options

The study investigating air traveler choice of mode for access to the airport in the San Francisco Bay Area revealed that the number of pieces of baggage played an important role as a variable in mode choice [11]. A similar study has been conducted on travelers' ground access modes choice to King Khalid International Airport. This survey also revealed that the number of pieces of luggage significantly influences mode choice, and as the number of pieces of luggage increases, travelers are more likely to choose a private car over a taxi [2]. In a study investigating whether older air passengers exhibit different mode choice behavior for airport ground access, it was revealed that improving the convenience for storing luggage is necessary and that older people tend to use private cars more often when they have a lot of luggage [9].

Among the personal accounts of "transport disadvantage" individuals, there were opinions emphasizing that trips involving large shopping should avoid traveling by public transportation [12].

Based on detailed interviews, luggage carriage is identified as a major obstacle to train travel. Additionally, it is suggested that providing additional services such as luggage carriage for free may help alleviate existing obstacles to train travel [4].

The result obtained was that people who perceive the use of public transport modes as difficult, because they feel they have low control over its use, due to the presence of other people or the difficulty of traveling with shopping or luggage items, are more likely to use their car than public transport modes [6].

In a study that investigated how interchange is perceived and how this perception deters public transport use amongst car users or limits public transport use amongst public transport users, one benefit of car usage mentioned was that it makes it easier to carry luggage. In addition, one of the factors associated with poor interchanges is the need to transport luggage over long distances [13].

A paper aimed at presenting the results of a stated choice experiment to model P&R choice reveals that car drivers with heavy luggage are more likely to use both P&R and the car than are car drivers without luggage. The authors explain that this result can be explained by the fact that car drivers prefer to use the car for (a part of) the trip when they have to carry heavy luggage [5].

While many existing studies have focused on the impact of travelers' luggage on the choice of public transportation, this study focuses on how it affects tourism behavior itself, such as travel range and length of stay.

2.3   Influence of Luggage on Walking Itself

A study investigating the impact of luggage on pedestrians examined luggage-laden pedestrian movement (with bag and trolley case) through a series of individual and a single-file pedestrian experiment. The analysis revealed that while the luggage has little impact on individual walking speed, pedestrian carrying luggage took longer to accelerate and decelerate. The study also showed that the greatest impact of luggage on pedestrian flow was the spacing distance between individuals [15].

This study analyzes the effects of hand luggage in a real tourist destination as a field, rather than a narrow range.

3   Our Approach

This paper aims to propose a methodology that allows travelers and other visitors to leave their baggage behind and ease their behavioral restrictions and effectively promote their behavior at their destination. This paper provides an overview and presents experimental results on how baggage carrying affects traveler behavior. This reveals that baggage is one of major behavioral constraints in travel behavior, and that freedom from baggage may a key to facilitate behaviors of travelers and visitors.

Specifically, this paper shows the results of a survey of attitudes toward checked baggage and a behavioral survey of how people's behavior changes when they can leave their baggage, to capture the impact of baggage on behavior from multiple perspectives.

Here, three conditions were set for the subject: that the baggage was travel baggage, that each traveler had one carry-on bag, and that each traveler was not traveling in a self-owned vehicle.

While there are studies showing that luggage can influence people's behavior and choices, their focus is often limited, such as to public transportation. In contrast, this study is innovative in analyzing and discussing how luggage and its hassle transform tourist behavior, delving into actual sightseeing activities.

Table 1. Subjects of awareness surveys

characteristic		%
gender	male	50
	female	50
age	20 s	20
	30 s	20
	40 s	20
	50 s	20
	60 s	20

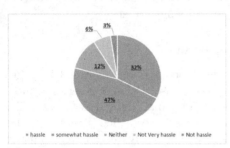

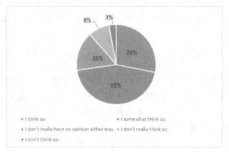

(a) How much of a hassle do you consider your carry-on luggage to be while traveling?

(b) Do you feel that carrying your luggage around is actually restricting your movements?

Fig. 1. Answers of awareness surveys

4   Behavioral Surveys

4.1   Preliminary Surveys on Awareness

Prior to the behavioral survey, the authors conducted an online survey of travelers' luggage during their trips to clarify their attitudes toward luggage. The survey was conducted through a web-based questionnaire from November 29th to December 2nd, 2022. It targeted individuals who have traveled within the past year. 960 valid responses were received (Fig. 1).

Results. Firstly, about 79% of the respondents who felt bothered by their luggage during travel answered that it was either hassle or somewhat hassle (Table 1).

About 73% of respondents felt that their movements were restricted by carrying their luggage. Furthermore, 66% of the respondents reported having experienced searching for coin lockers, while 67% reported experiencing delays in their movements due to carrying their luggage.

These results not only confirm the perception of travelers that luggage is a hassle, but also the perception that it restricts their movements. Therefore, the next survey will reveal the impact of luggage on travelers' actions.

4.2   Overview of Behavioral Survey

The authors used a smartphone application with a behavior logging function to obtain travel logs of users and conducted a survey as a follow-up. The purpose was to understand how hassle affects the tourism behavior of travelers by observing their actual behavior.

Assumptions. In this paper, it was assumed that luggage, such as suitcases, would be hassle mainly on the first and last days of a trip, unless there were any specific reasons related to transportation to the accommodation. Therefore, this survey focused on the last day of the trip. The survey was conducted under the assumption that the checkout time at the hotel was 10:00 am and that the respondents would start their journey home from the terminal station at 3:00 pm.

Procedure. The experiment was conducted on December 22nd, 2022. To record and collect data on the participants' behavior during the experiment, an application called "Zap Sapporo" [1] was used. Prior to the experiment, participants were instructed to install this application on their smartphones. On the day of the experiment, we confirmed that the application was always acquiring location information. Participants began free activities from Koshigoe at 10:00 am and gathered around the facilities near Fujisawa Station at 3:00 pm. After the gathering, the participants answered the post-survey questionnaire regarding the places they visited and where they stored their luggage. There were 14 participants, of whom 9 carried a carry-on suitcase with 5kg load. The remaining 5 participants carried foldable eco-bags that were empty.

Location. The experimental site was set in Kamakura, a tourist destination in Tokyo. Kamakura is located near the metropolitan area and is a famous tourist spot in Japan, popular for strolling and other activities. It was chosen as the experimental site because it attracts many young people who visit as a "sacred place" for anime, as well as having numerous temples and shrines, making it a tourist destination that can be enjoyed by a wide range of age groups.

Origin and Destination. Assuming the final day of the trip, we set the starting point a little away from the hotel, and a little away from the station (Koshigoe), and not too close to the destination. Since many travelers are expected to return from the terminal station on the last day of the trip, we set the terminal station as Fujisawa Station. To reproduce the movement with luggage from the accommodation to the terminal station, we set the start and finish points in different locations (Fig. 2).

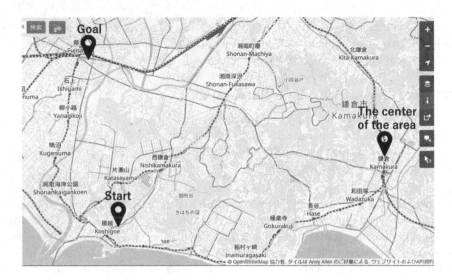

Fig. 2. Information about the meeting place

Cautions. There were five cautions to be taken during the experiment.

First, while participants were generally free to move around, they were advised to refrain from wasting time on activities such as watching movies, going to game centers or amusement parks, or visiting fast food chains and family restaurants without any special reason. This was to encourage them to engage in "sightseeing" activities around Kamakura, assuming that they were on a trip to the area that day. Of course, if such activities were part of their usual travel routine, there was no problem.

Second, participants who engaged in the same activities were counted as one person. They were asked to avoid contacting each other during the trip, even if they were friends or acquaintances. They were informed to prevent participants from influencing each other's actions that day.

Third, they were given a task to purchase a "Kamakura-like" souvenir, which helped them to be conscious of their role as tourists.

Fourth, they were allowed to use rental cars or taxis without any issue during their sightseeing activities.

Fifth, participants were instructed to carry all the luggage and items given to them at the departure point, and to gather at the finish line near Fujisawa Station at 3:00 pm.

4.3   Experimental Methods

The authors obtained activity logs by using the smart city app service "Zap Sapporo" [1]. By utilizing a data collaboration platform to integrate content from various information sources, this system provides a one-stop service for various content held by Sapporo City and tourist associations, as well as transportation provider information. In addition to traffic information, it also collects crowd conditions during event times through crowdsourcing for immediate information provision. This application is publicly available on the official website for distributing smartphone applications and can be used free of charge. This application has a function to acquire the location information of the installed smartphone even in background mode and send the acquired position data to the server with the user's permission. In this paper, the authors used this application as a tool for behavior measurement. The acquisition of position data follows the guidelines of Apple and Google, the vendors of smartphone operating systems, and the application is implemented to record and transmit the location information that is notified by the OS at the timing of "sufficient movement detected by the OS". Although there is no official explanation for "sufficient movement", it is generally considered to be finer timing than the movement of switching between mobile base stations (typically several hundred meters).

The log data collected by Zap Sapporo is saved in a cloud-based database as data that includes the following items:

- ID assigned to each device
- device time, time obtained by GPS
- latitude, longitude, altitude, horizontal accuracies, vertical accuracies
- move speed (m/s), move course (angle relative to true north)
- device information (manufacturer, model name, version)

In addition, the following information, which is considered useful for later analysis and visualization, is added when saved to the cloud:

- day of the week
- time zone
- weekday/holiday flag

Furthermore, the trajectory data, which represents a sequence of points that denote continuous movements of an individual, is aggregated from the logged data as point data. In this process, the point data, which is arranged in chronological order for each individual, is filtered by excluding data with low positioning accuracy[4]. Then, the trajectory is segmented by applying a cutting process when the distance between two consecutive points is beyond a specified distance threshold, or when there is a leap greater than a certain distance regardless of time interval. This process ensures that the trajectory becomes a coherent sequence of points.

Furthermore, by converting the point data into trajectory data, it is possible to detect dwell time (act of staying within a certain range for a certain period of time) and stop locations during movement. Here, if a stay of 300 s or more is detected in the same grid in the 1/4 mesh of Japan grid square code (JIS X 0410)[5], it is considered a "stop" and extracted.

The trajectory data and stopping points obtained in this way are represented as geographic objects in GeoJSON format and visualized on a map using

---

[4] In this paper, with an error of 1000 m or more.
[5] approximately 250m square.

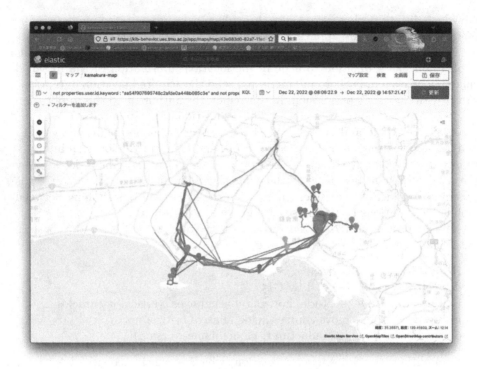

Fig. 3. Behavioral survey in Kamakura

Kibana[6], which is a interactive tool for Elasticsearch DB. Figure 3 shows an example of the visualization of the trajectory and stop-off points using Kibana. The line indicates the trajectory and the pin represents the stop-off points. The size of the pin is proportional to the duration of the stay. The authors conducted an analysis of behavioral measurement data using these apps and visualization tools.

4.4   Analysis Methods

Considering the location relationship between tourist facilities near the stopping points, destination, and stations at the center of this area is believed to be a useful perspective in the analysis. The data was loaded into the PostgreSQL database management system[7] with GIS functionality extended by PostGIS[8]. Using the MAPPLE POI Data[9] version 3.1 for Points of Interest (POI), such as tourist facilities, the nearest neighbor POIs and distance to them can be

---

[6] https://www.elastic.co/kibana/.
[7] https://www.postgresql.org/.
[8] https://postgis.net/.
[9] https://mapple.com/products/data-poi/.

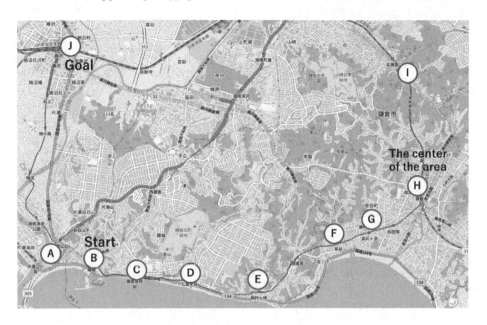

Fig. 4. Locations of visit

Table 2. Participants of behavioral survey

age	male	female	total
10 s	0	1	1
20 s	4	4	8
30 s	0	0	0
40 s	0	1	1
50 s	1	2	3
60 s	0	0	0
over 60 s	0	1	1
total	5	9	14

calculated. By using these functions, the places visited along the routes and the distances to the center of the area and the destination for each point were obtained. The authors used these findings to confirm and examine each subject's behavioral range. To indicate the locations visited by the participants, the stations they visited were alphabetized as follows (Fig. 4):

- Location B is Koshigoe Station, the starting point.
- Location H is Kamakura Station, the center of the area.
- Location J is the terminal station, Fujisawa Station (Table 2).

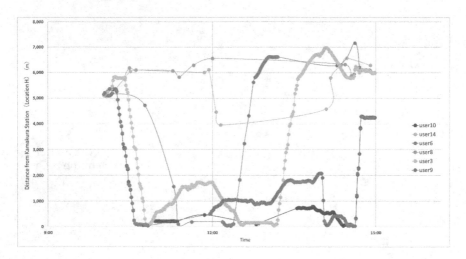

Fig. 5. Distance from the central station (Kamakura Station, Location H), hold luggage.

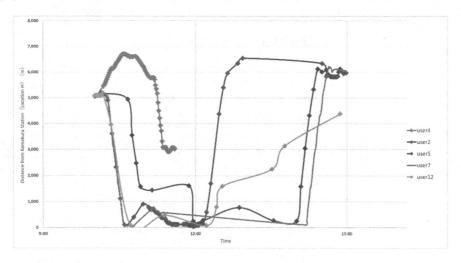

Fig. 6. Distance from the central station (Kamakura Station, Location H), no luggage

4.5 Analysis Results

Overall Results. Looking at the relationship with Kamakura Station, which is the center of the area, for those with luggage (Fig. 5), those who did not leave their luggage were not bound to Kamakura Station. Those with luggage had a narrow margin for leaving Kamakura Station. Also, those who deposited their luggage at Kamakura Station were relatively close to the station.

For those without luggage (Fig. 6), there were sightseeing activities after leaving Kamakura Station. In addition, since they were not bound by their luggage, the time of departure from Kamakura Station was diverse.

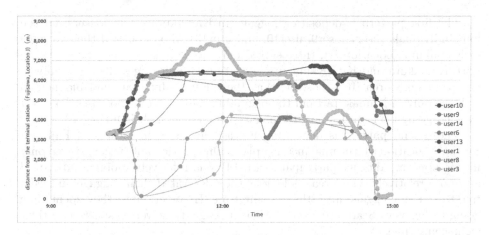

Fig. 7. Distance from the terminal station (Fujisawa station, Location J), hold luggage

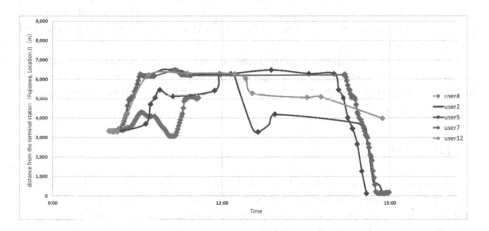

Fig. 8. Distance from the terminal station (Fujisawa station, Location J), no luggage

Next, looking at distances from the terminal station (Fujisawa Station) in Fig. 7 and 8, people who left their luggage at Fujisawa Station tended to have a range of activities relatively closer to Fujisawa. It is also possible that they left their luggage in Fujisawa because they planned to move around in that area originally (Table 3).

Individual Results. Two participants (user6 and user11) carried their luggage with them and were not limited to sightseeing only in Kamakura. However, their comments indicate that they faced physical limitations such as avoiding areas with many stairs and difficulties in walking.

There were three patterns of behavior observed when using coin lockers.

The first pattern is depositing luggage in Kamakura's coin lockers. Of the four individuals (user7, user9, user10, and user13) who deposited their luggage in Kamakura (Location H), three stayed only in Kamakura, and one stayed in both Kamakura and Kita-Kamakura (Location I), enjoying sightseeing only in the Kamakura area. It is possible that these four individuals had planned to sightsee only in Kamakura from the beginning, but it is also possible that they avoided going far from Kamakura to consider retrieving their luggage.

The second pattern is depositing luggage at the coin lockers of Fujisawa Station (Location J), the final meeting place. One participant (user8) stayed only in one station. Another participant (user14) was relatively mobile and moved around a relatively wide area, as long as they deposited their luggage and were free from their luggage until the meeting time. However, since they spent time going to Fujisawa Station to deposit their luggage, they were restricted by their sightseeing time.

The third pattern is depositing luggage at Enoshima (Location A). Although they did not stay in only one station, it is possible that they faced physical limitations (specifically, restrictions on train use) because they could not use a different line than the station where they deposited their luggage, as indicated in their comments.

Looking at the five participants without carry-on luggage, two (user1 and user5) stayed in one station, but it was found that the other three (user2, user4, and user6) stayed in relatively different stations without limiting themselves to a single location.

5   Discussion

In this paper, it was found that tourists' behaviors may be constrained by having luggage. It became apparent that having luggage can result in physical constraints, constraints on places to stay, constraints on tourist time, constraints on railway use, and so on. In particular, it was suggested that travelers carrying luggage may be tied to a place to deposit their luggage. Even if they can release their luggage, if they deposit it in a fixed location such as a coin locker, users will need to return to that location, and travelers may need to consider this in their travel plans. Therefore, this study has shown that not only increasing the number of storage locations, but also enhancing delivery services, is important to achieve a stress-free trip.

Table 3. Details of behavioral survey

participant	carrying	checking	locker	visit	comment
user1	no			A	
user2	no			A, H	
user3	yes	yes	A	A, H	I had to retrieve my luggage at Enoshima Station, so I couldn't take the Odakyu train from Katase-Enoshima
user4	no			A, E, F, H	
user5	no			H	
user6	yes	no		A, B, C, H	I toured the area, avoiding stairs by taking a route that accommodated my carry-on luggage
user7	yes	yes	H	H, I	
user8	yes	yes	J	A	
user9	yes	yes	H	H, I	
user10	yes	yes	H	H	
user11	yes	no		G, H	Due to the short duration of the trip and the fact that the starting and ending points were somewhat ambiguous, I decided not to check my suitcase this time. It was quite cumbersome to carry it around everywhere, and especially at the precincts of Tsurugaoka-Hachimangu Shrine, the pavement was uneven and difficult to walk on with a suitcase, particularly after the rain
user12	no			E, F, H	
user13	yes	yes	H	H	
user14	yes	yes	J	A, D	

Although existing studies have clarified the importance of the number of luggage, it was also possible to show the importance of the destination for luggage storage in this study. However, although it is important to enhance delivery services for luggage, the recognition rate of such services during travel was only 46% in our awareness surveys, which is less than half, and the awareness level is low at present. Furthermore, 27% of the respondents stated that they did not know about such services but would like to use them, and particularly these people have a high potential to use such services. Therefore, to achieve a high degree of freedom in tourism, it is necessary to first increase the awareness of luggage delivery services during travel.

In addition, even among those who knew about such services, 61% have never used them. From this, it can be inferred that there are some barriers to using such services, such as the price or the possibility that travelers cannot secure time to complete the service procedures due to the uncertainty of their travel schedule.

Besides, in services such as luggage delivery, the issue of trust must also be important. While many people have positive opinions about luggage delivery services, such as not having to carry their baggage, a major disadvantage is that it is not reliable [7]. In this survey, 85% answered that trust in depositing luggage is important or somewhat important. Therefore, it may be important to increase the reliability to promote lug-gage delivery services, among other things.

6 Conclusion

This paper aims to propose a methodology that allows travelers and other visitors to leave their baggage behind and ease their behavioral restrictions and effectively pro-mote their behavior at their destination. To analyze the influence of luggage, this paper used distances from various stations and detailed individual behavior data. The results suggest that tourists' sightseeing activities may be restricted by physical constraints, location constraints, time constraints, and transportation constraints if they carry luggage.

From the above, carrying luggage can be a burden not only for the luggage itself, but also for the places where the luggage is stored. To achieve a more free and enjoyable tourism experience, it is necessary to not only increase the availability of fixed services like coin lockers, but also to enhance services such as delivery. In recent years, Japan has seen an increase in inbound demand, and solutions for improving the reception of foreign visitors to Japan are needed. Therefore, it can be said that it is necessary to enhance services beyond coin lockers to meet these needs.

The issue with behavioral surveys in this study is its small sample size, which made it difficult to quantitatively demonstrate the impact of having or not having luggage on travelers. To gain further insights into the effects of luggage, it is necessary to consider the following points. For example, when investigating the effects of luggage in a small-scale experiment, it may be effective to conduct within-subject comparisons. While conducting experiments with many participants can make between-subject comparisons easier, it is difficult to measure the behavior of many travelers at once in reality, and therefore, this study remained limited to a small number of participants. However, conducting behavioral surveys in actual tourist destinations can reveal realities that cannot be captured by surveys on awareness, so it is considered significant to observe the real behavior of tourists.

Studying travelers from different nationalities regarding their awareness and behavior towards luggage, as they may vary depending on the country of origin is also one of future issues. In addition, while this study focused on the Kamakura area, it may be beneficial to compare various locations to understand the overall influence of luggage on travelers.

Acknowledgments. The authors would like to thank NPO Airport RFID Technology Alliance (ARTA), and Central Japan International Airport Co., Ltd. for their cooperation with this research.

This work was supported by JSPS KAKENHI Grant Number JP22H03856.

References

1. Aihara, K., Takasu, A.: Development of one-stop smart city application by interdisciplinary data linkage. In: Streitz, N., Konomi, S. (eds.) HCII 2020. LNCS, vol. 12203, pp. 379–390. Springer, Cham (2020). https://doi.org/10.1007/978-3-030-50344-4_27
2. Alhussein, S.N.: Analysis of ground access modes choice king khaled international airport, riyadh, saudi arabia. J. Transport Geography **19**, 1361–1367 (2011). https://doi.org/10.1016/j.jtrangeo.2011.07.007
3. BBC News: Why do airlines still mislay 25 million bags a year? https://www.bbc.com/news/business-48437262. Accessed on 2023-02-20
4. Böhler, S., Grischkat, S., Haustein, S., Hunecke, M.: Encouraging environmentally sustainable holiday travel. Transp. Res. Part A Policy Practice **40**, 652–670 (2006). https://doi.org/10.1016/j.tra.2005.12.006
5. Bos, I.D.M., Van der Heijden, R.E.C.M., Molin, E.J.E., Timmermans, H.J.P.: The choice of park and ride facilities: an analysis using a context-dependent hierarchical choice experiment. Environment and Planning A: Economy and Space **36**, 1673–1686 (2004). https://doi.org/10.1068/a36138
6. Bouscasse, H., de Lapparent, M.: Perceived comfort and values of travel time savings in the rhône-alpes region. Transp. Res. Part A Policy Practice **124**, 370–387 (2019). https://doi.org/10.1016/j.tra.2019.04.006
7. Ceregeiro, M.M.S.d.A.d.S.: The future of the air travel industry: the concept of door-to-door luggage delivery service. dissertation, Management with Specialization in Strategic Marketing, the Universidade Católica Portuguesa (April 2021)
8. Chang, L.Y., Sun, P.Y.: Stated-choice analysis of willingness to pay for low cost carrier services. J. Air Transp. Manage. **20**, 15–17 (2012). https://doi.org/10.1016/j.jairtraman.2011.09.003
9. Chang, Y.C.: Factors affecting airport access mode choice for elderly air passengers. Transp. Res. Part E Logist. Transp. Rev. **57**, 105–112 (2013). https://doi.org/10.1016/j.tre.2013.01.010
10. Future Travel Experience: SWISS and AirPortr expand smart baggage services to zurich airport. https://www.futuretravelexperience.com/2022/07/swiss-and-airportr-expand-smart-baggage-services-to-zurich-airport/. Accessed on 2023-01-29
11. Harvey, G.: Study of airport access mode choice. J. Transp. Eng. **112**, 525–545 (1986). https://doi.org/10.1061/(ASCE)0733-947X(1986)112:5(525)
12. Hine, J., Mitchell, F.: Better for everyone? travel experiences and transport exclusion. Urban Studies **38**(2), 319–332 (2001). http://www.jstor.org/stable/43100394
13. Hine, J., Scott, J.: Seamless, accessible travel: users' views of the public transport journey and interchange. Transp. Policy **7**(3), 217–226 (2000). https://doi.org/10.1016/S0967-070X(00)00022-6. https://www.sciencedirect.com/science/article/pii/S0967070X00000226
14. Holloway, C., et al.: Effect of vertical step height on boarding and alighting time of train passengers. Proc. Inst. Mech. Eng. Part F J. Rail Rapid Transit **230** (2015). https://doi.org/10.1177/0954409715590480
15. Huang, S., Wei, R., Lo, S., Lu, S., Li, C., An, C., Liu, X.: Experimental study on one-dimensional movement of luggage-laden pedestrian. Phys. A Stat. Mech. Appl. **516**, 520–528 (2019). https://doi.org/10.1016/j.physa.2018.09.038

16. Japan National Tourism Organization: Enjoy the freedom and luxury of "hands-free" travel. https://www.japan.travel/en/plan/getting-around/luggage-storage/. Accessed on 2023-02-21
17. Transport Focus: National rail passenger survey spring 2016 main report. https://d3cez36w5wymxj.cloudfront.net/wp-content/uploads/2016/06/29162541/TF-NPRS-Spr16-pages-ALL-WEB-v4.pdf. Accessed on 2023-01-29

Platform Urbanism for Sustainability

Aikaterini Katmada[(✉)], Garyfallia Katsavounidou, and Christina Kakderi

School of Spatial Planning and Development, Aristotle University of Thessaloniki, Thessaloniki, Greece
{akatmada,gkatsavou,kakderi}@plandevel.auth.gr

Abstract. Digital transformation has brought about significant changes in nearly all aspects of urban life, including mobility, energy, economy, and governance. In recent years, many cities have pursued smart city initiatives in order to address emerging urbanization and sustainability issues. However, the existing top-down approaches to smart city initiatives have resulted in decreased citizen participation, which, in turn, can lead to decision-making processes that lack inclusivity, diversity, trust, and accountability. As such, there is a growing interest in the potential of digital platforms for enhancing citizen participation in sustainable urban planning and development. This paper delves into the concept of platform urbanism and examines the capabilities of urban digital platforms in facilitating co-creation and innovation for sustainable and livable cities. Furthermore, it provides a number of select case studies, in order to explore how digital platforms can enhance public participation and contribute to more democratic and inclusive urban planning processes. Finally, critical questions and considerations related to the use of urban platforms are highlighted, and corresponding conclusions and insights about the future of urban platforms are discussed.

Keywords: Digital Platforms · Platform Urbanism · Sustainable Urban Development · Citizen Engagement

1 Introduction

Over the last decades, as digital Information and Communication Technologies (ICTs) become more ubiquitous and permeate nearly all aspects of everyday life, cities are increasingly becoming the scene for techno-urban experimentation and transformation [1]. Furthermore, a growing number of cities have implemented policies and programmes intended to transform them into smart cities, in an attempt to tackle emerging issues of urbanization, and to achieve economic and environmental sustainability. Being a prominent urban digitalisation model, smart cities reconfigure urban space production and governance through data-driven systems and the increasing influence of IT corporations, as well [1]. Additionally, the phenomenon of platform urbanism, which refers to the integration of platform services and their underlying logic within "the fine-grain of cities" [2], is also gaining increasing attention. In general, even though the more specific characteristics of smart cities vary greatly, there is a common thread permeating most of them and that would be the reliance on ICTs and digital tools as their foundation.

© The Author(s), under exclusive license to Springer Nature Switzerland AG 2023
N. A. Streitz and S. Konomi (Eds.): HCII 2023, LNCS 14037, pp. 35–52, 2023.
https://doi.org/10.1007/978-3-031-34609-5_3

This proliferation of digital tools and smart city applications, as well as the digital transition of urban societies, have created further opportunities for citizen participation and, consequently, a better chance of solving complex urban problems such as that of sustainability. Examples of this urban twin transition include, among others, cooperative, automated and connected multimodal mobility systems, as well as energy systems integration and management in order to lower emissions in the so-called circular city. Digital transformation has disrupted all urban domains from mobility to energy, economy, and governance, with different intensity each one. Digital tools play an increasingly important role in the traditional urban processes, such as urban planning, since they allow planners to make more informed decisions, by providing data, visualizations, and simulations that can help them understand complex urban systems better [3].

To this end, some of the most commonly used digital tools in urban planning include: (a) platforms with embedded Geographic Information System (GIS) tools that allow planners to comprehend the spatial patterns and relationships within urban areas, and make knowledge-based planning decisions; (b) Building Information Modelling (BIM) that facilitates the analysis of the potential impact of different planning decisions, and test the feasibility of different designs before they are built; (c) visualization tools that aim to support dialogue in urban planning by focusing on visual aspects and experiences of the environment [4]; (d) urban dashboards that consolidate urban information into a single view to efficiently monitor the performance of urban systems [5]; and (e) simulation models that help planners understand how different factors, such as transportation, demographics, and economic conditions, interact to shape the urban environment, and therefore, to identify potential problems and opportunities and make more informed decisions about how to respond to these challenges [6].

Nonetheless, most of these tools are used in the planning process following a rather top-down approach, where citizens are rarely included [7]. So far, urban planning is a domain in which digital technologies have not yet been utilized to their full potential so that they could also fully support, as well as incentivize, public participation. Recently, the focus is increasingly shifting on new opportunities that could enable the active participation of citizens, through digital platforms. These include, among others, platforms for crowdsourcing knowledge, as well as digital games that can change urban planning towards a more agile, data and user-driven direction, empowering citizens to share resources, collaborate and co-create solutions. MinStad, BlockByblock, CityLab010, VisitTheMayor, and NextCampus are a few examples of such platforms intended to create planning and design solutions; yet, their development is usually detached to the formal planning procedures and routines embedded in cities and regions.

As the effects of today's urban sustainability problems are increasing, the need to take various measures in order to address them is becoming more and more apparent. It is argued that the integration of digital technologies, and, especially, digital platforms in urban planning could facilitate the twin transition (i.e. green and digital transition). In addition, there is a growing interest in the roles of grassroots and digital social innovation in the transition to more sustainable cities and societies. While there is an abundance of literature on smart cities (e.g. [8–12]), this paper focuses on a more recent development of the smart city notion, that of platform urbanism (see Sect. 3 for definition), and explores the use of digital platforms beyond the "platform-as-company" paradigm (which generates private value), but rather as open, participatory online spaces facilitating two-way interactions between city stakeholders.

To this end, this paper aims to conduct an overview of collaborative urban (digital) platforms that facilitate the co-creation of innovative solutions for sustainable and livable cities. It is structured as follows: first, we provide a concise overview of citizen participation in urban planning and development, focusing on the various types of public participation in the context of planning and how participation relates to urban sustainability (Sect. 2). In Sect. 3, we present the theoretical framework of platform urbanism, as well as participatory urban platforms, alongside several examples of platforms. For these purposes, we conducted a systematic review in the pertinent academic and practitioner literature, using Scopus and ScienceDirect. We performed our search queries between December 2022 and February 2023, using keywords such as "citizen participation", "participatory urban planning", "platform urbanism", "platformization", etc. We then performed a manual selection based on publication date, type, and focus, and we analyzed interesting documents further, which led us to select 70 documents. Additionally, we conducted a thorough online search in order to find and examine digital platforms that were then categorized according to their attributes (Sect. 3). Afterwards, in Sect. 4, through the presentation of select case studies addressing the creation of urban open/green spaces, we explore the capabilities of digital platforms in enhancing public participation, the level of participation they currently support, and their role in facilitating more democratic and inclusive urban planning processes. Finally, corresponding conclusions, critical questions, and ideas about the future of urban platforms are discussed in Sect. 5.

2 Public Participation in Urban Planning and Development: An Overview

The city, a complex system of social, economic, and environmental forces at play, is a place viewed quite differently, by various stakeholders, from the individual to the collective level, based on their needs, values, and aspirations. Planning, as a process of shaping a city's future, cannot be achieved without conflict, and planners cannot be viewed as skilled technocrats with the expertise to produce 'good' plans, without involving the people for whom they are planning in the process [13]. This relationship between participation and planning might sound almost axiomatic in our days, as around the world "citizens push for substantive inclusion in decision making" [14] (p. 295). It is noteworthy, nonetheless, that public participation was hardly an issue during the early years of the planning profession, during which, as [15] points out, planners were considered a privileged elite, holders of superior knowledge, producing plans to be gratefully accepted by local officials and the public. It was in the 1960s and 1970s that the planning profession started to realize the deficiency of such an approach, especially in view of the racial and class conflicts in cities at that time. With ground-breaking work by liberal academics such as Paul Davidoff [25] and Sherry Arnstein [26], the planning profession started to acknowledge the importance of the engagement of the public in the decision-making process and of confronting the conflicts that different planning choices evoke, for individuals and stakeholders [16]. In the realm of planning theory, public participation has been a crucial constituent in the communicative model, which emerged during the 1980s and 1990s [17]. Since then, the body of knowledge of what Healey [18] calls "collaborative planning" has been growing exponentially, a growth that coincided with a general turn in public policy, as government was replaced by governance [19].

Research on public participation in urban planning and development is today extensive and multifaceted. Any attempt to include the public brings to the fore "the more conflictual, structural factors that underpin city making" (p. 377) [20]. At the same time, however, participation is based upon and at the same time cultivates effective communication, empathy, and shared responsibility among citizens. If done appropriately, participatory processes can benefit conflict resolution, development of partnerships, transparency, and empowerment [21]. In relation to planning, in specific, participation is affected by the planning task, the nature of the planning environment and the decision-making system in which it takes place [19]. More and more it is acknowledged that efforts of scaling up the participation of residents and their associations in planning process have to take into account issues of inclusion of marginalized groups [22] of challenging localism and of formalization of participatory processes [14]. Last but not least, the concept of e-democracy and the use of ICT tools has been a driver of change in participation processes related to planning and development [23].

For this overview of this vast and interdisciplinary field, we will focus on three key aspects of how participation and planning can be viewed in tandem: first, the degree of citizens' participation in planning as an index of how democratic a city is; second, the various types and categorisations of public participation in the context of planning; and third, how participation relates to urban sustainability and resilience. According to the World Bank, participation is "a process through which stakeholders influence and share control over development initiatives and the decisions and resources which affect them" (p. xi) [24]. From this definition alone, it is clear that participation and distribution of power are closely linked. Arnstein [26] defines public participation as "the redistribution of power that enables the have-not citizens to be deliberately included in the future" (p. 216) [26]. She proposes a hierarchy of eight different forms of participation, in the well-known diagram called "a ladder of citizen participation". At the first, lowest rung of the ladder, she ranks 'manipulation', followed by 'therapy', 'informing', 'consultation', 'placation', 'partnership', 'delegate power' and 'citizen control' at the very top. Arnstein's ladder has been persistently reviewed and updated by other academics. [27] stresses that this categorisation fails to take into account that there is no single "point of decision" in a planning process. Instead, there are many stages during which contributions can come: from setting the agenda, defining problems, collecting information and analyzing it, identifying and selecting possible options, to formal decision, implementation and evaluation. Therefore, if the level of participation is only determined by the degree of power over "who makes the decision", it ignores the benefits of other forms of influencing the outcome, such as dialogue and information exchange, which can be instrumental in the informal policy-making arena [19], and a sound pillar of democratic society.

A host of studies attempt to propose a typology of public participation, which can be valuable in understanding the scope and assessing the available methodologies or participation techniques [28, 29]. [30] propose a comprehensive five-level scheme of "intensity of participation", which can be adapted for the scope of planning as a practice. At the lowest level there is 'information', which is one-directional and aims at public outreach. It provides the background necessary for setting the agenda and on raising awareness of the problem. One step up lies 'consultation' (still one-directional), which seeks the input of participants, their knowledge and data, through surveys, interviews, discussions. On the third step we find 'cooperation', which is bi-directional, and involves the participants in a dialogue with each other to formulate common approaches, define issues, and select from available options. One level up there is 'collaboration', in which the scope is to co-design and co-develop in equal terms (eye-to-eye), in a democratic context. And, finally, there is 'empowerment' which aims at assisting participants to formulate their own ideas and carry out their own projects. Figure 1 shows this five-level scheme.

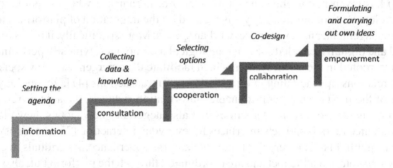

Fig. 1. Diagram 1. Five levels of intensity of public participation in urban planning and development. Based on [30].

Participatory planning, as a process that involves thinking about the common future, is an important tool for achieving sustainability, in all aspects: economically, socially, and environmentally. Participation in urban planning and management is included in the 17 Sustainable Development Goals, as part of Goal 11, Sustainable Cities and Communities. Target 11.3 specifies that, by 2030, the goal is to "enhance inclusive and sustainable urbanization and capacity for participatory, integrated and sustainable human settlement planning and management in all countries" [31]. The engagement of citizens and communities may also contribute to improving urban governance and ensuring more resilient responses to complex urban problems [32]. Through information and citizen participation, communities can build their capacity for environmental management in terms of local sustainability, while also contributing to global sustainable development [33]. The complexity of global problems we face today call for coordinated action at the local level. In view of the climate crisis, which is a result of human actions and choices, expansion of participatory budgeting into climate change mitigation and adaptation [34] is an important driver towards a more sustainable and resilient future urban development.

3 Platform Urbanism and Participatory Urban Platforms

Having discussed public participation in urban planning and development, we move forward to an overview of commercial and community digital platforms and the ways they (can) support collaborative urban design processes. In general, digital platforms constitute virtual environments that enable the delivery of digital products, services, and experiences. Typically, they comprise a set of technologies and tools that support digital interactions and transactions. Additionally, they provide an open, participative infrastructure for these interactions and they set governance conditions, in order to facilitate matchmaking, as well as the exchange of goods, services, or social currency [35]. Leveraging advances in technology, such as cloud computing, big data analytics, and artificial intelligence (AI), digital platforms deliver more personalized, efficient, and effective services. Lastly, especially with the advent of Web 2.0, digital platforms have been increasingly providing new opportunities for innovation and the creation of new business models.

The widespread use of platforms in different domains and functions of the city (e.g. [36–40]) has given rise to the concept of 'platform urbanism', which – as one of the latest developments of the smart city – is focused on the integration of platforms into the design, management, and governance of urban spaces. More specifically, it refers to data-centered and digitally-enabled socio-technological assemblages, typically performed on a platform, rooted in the urban system, which facilitate the emergence of new social and material relationships including intermediations and transactions [41]. Technology is at the core of the urban ecosystem: it enables information richness, capable of revealing the complex natures of urban interactions, but also negotiates new tactics, new players, new governance models and new interfaces for everyday interaction [2]. The 'ecosystem approach' highlights the diversity of multiple actors (governance, individuals, technology providers, etc.) that interact and are coordinated through the platform but, also, their constant evolution and adaptation across time and space, since platforms are never fixed entities [42]. Although urban platforms constitute generic templates that can be applied across various geographical scales and multiple urban environments, platform urbanism is deeply spatially configured. As the authors in [41] mention, "platforms function across space but are rooted in place", as they are built in specific urban realities and involve connections between spatially specific nodes.

Urban platforms can be defined as digital software and hardware-based interfaces that: (a) allow multiple users to interact; (b) support transactions being carried out in real time or near-real time; (c) are focused on the analysis, manipulation and (oftentimes) monetisation of digital data; and (d) affect the way urban life is conducted [43]. Examples of platform urbanism include smart city initiatives, for example, the Chinese CityBrain AI platform for urban planning and management [43]; corporate platforms, such as property rental and ride-sharing/-hailing platform services; and platform-based systems for urban governance and decision-making, where citizens can access and inform governance-related information and decisions. Overall, smart cities and platform urbanism can be considered complementary approaches to urban planning and management. Smart cities typically use technology such as sensors, Internet of Things (IoT) devices, and big data analytics to gather and process information about city operations, in order to improve decision-making and optimize resource allocation, whereas platform urbanism is more focused towards utilizing digital platforms to support collaboration between city stakeholders. It is also proposed that while smart city initiatives are mainly focused on optimizing oversight of city systems through state procured "solutions," platform urbanism aims to transform the operations of city services that are usually geared to consumers or the market [44].

As already mentioned, smart city initiatives most often follow top-down approaches, with critical questions related to the role of citizens and the ownership of public and private data, arising. Indeed, researchers are increasingly pointing out the potential drawbacks of such approaches; for example, according to [45], citizens are frequently excluded from being meaningfully involved in the design, use, or appropriation of civic technologies, even though they are their main beneficiaries. Often, the "black-box" technology of smart cities reinforces a "a status-quo" where citizens remain outsiders [46]. In addition, it is also argued that smart city projects typically consist of only government, knowledge production and industry actors, often overlooking the role of citizens as equally important agents, and not only as "end-users" [47]. Furthermore, when citizens are only expected to contribute data to companies developing smart city solutions, they are transformed from participants to the *objects of control* of the strategies developed by smart city technologies [48]. On the other hand, citizens themselves are gradually becoming more informed and participatory on their own initiative; they claim democratic representation in policy making and governance and they generate innovative ideas [49]. In addition, they often demand direct participation as co-designers and active decision makers in urban development projects [50].

Ongoing discourse and scientific research have introduced new concepts regarding the active participation of citizens in spatial planning, policy-making, and service development. Such concepts include grassroots and open innovation, co-design and co-creation, and crowdsourcing, among others [49]. As mentioned in [51], under the umbrella term of "bottom-up urbanism", citizens all around the world carry out activities that can be considered as drivers for urban innovation; for example, "they revive an unused building into a community cinema, or organize street festivals". As cities around the world are facing a wide range of pressing challenges, such as climate change, public health in the face of the COVID-19 pandemic, socio-economic disparities, and aging infrastructure that has to accommodate growing populations, there is a need for more integrated, flexible, and adaptive urban planning strategies. Urban citizen projects, which are initiatives led or co-created by citizens in order to shape the design of their urban environments and create more livable, equitable, and sustainable cities, can be important tools for engaging communities and fostering innovation. Examples of such projects include: (a) parklets: small park-like public spaces built by communities to serve as gathering places; (b) community gardens: public spaces where people can engage in urban agriculture, created and maintained by communities; (c) placemaking projects: the creation, redesign or revitalization of public spaces so that they are attractive and usable for the community; and (d) pop-up projects: temporary initiatives that transform public spaces and promote community engagement. Such projects also play an important role in the sustainable development of cities, given the fact that urban open spaces improve quality of life by offering multiple social, ecological, spatial, economic and health benefits [52].

In cases where urban platforms are concerned, the trend towards applying participatory design processes is growing, as cities seek to harness the collective wisdom of their citizens. Based on the pertinent literature, we categorized digital platforms that support participatory urban planning and decision-making in the following broad areas:

- Urban crowdsourcing platforms: Digital platforms that engage citizens in the planning and design of their cities, based on crowdsourcing, which constitutes a *distributed online problem-solving process that requires the participation of the crowd for the accomplishment of specific tasks* [39]. For example, there are urban design crowdsourcing platforms (e.g. Neighborland, Commonplace, Streetmix) and crowdfunding platforms (e.g. Spacehive, Voor je Buurt, Ioby). Citizens can gather and contribute data, e.g. by identifying city areas that need improvement, they can provide feedback, suggestions, and ideas on urban design projects, or support initiatives by investing in the urban projects that matter most to them.
- Urban data platforms: Digital platforms that gather, process, and visualize big data about city activities, such as mobility and transportation patterns, energy usage, air quality, and waste management, to inform urban decision-making. These can be urban analytics platforms, city dashboards, and city data portals. Examples include CitySense, Ride Report, Urban Footprint, and Urban Open Platform.
- Collaborative governance platforms: Digital platforms that support collaboration and decision-making between city stakeholders, such as participatory budgeting and citizen engagement platforms, where citizens can discuss and co-create urban initiatives, as well as directly participate in budget allocation decisions by voting on proposed projects (e.g. CitizenLab, Décider pour Paris, Decide Madrid, Decidim Barcelona); and smart city governance portals, which are online platforms that provide citizens with access to information and data about their cities (e.g. Open Data Barcelona, London Datastore, Helsinki Region Infoshare).

4   Presentation of Related Case Studies

In what follows, we present in more detail a few examples of digital platforms from the categories mentioned in Sect. 2, which are used as tools for: (a) informing stakeholders and increasing public awareness on various issues, and (b) engaging citizens and communities in co-creating more livable and sustainable cities. Afterwards, we suggest how they support the five levels of intensity of public participation in urban planning and development, as described in Sect. 2.

4.1   Urban Crowdsourcing Platforms

So far, crowdsourcing platforms have already been used in many diverse areas, from business projects to non-profit initiatives, and it has also been suggested that they could motivate and facilitate citizen participation in urban projects [39]. Indeed, there are many noteworthy examples of crowdopinion, crowdfunding, crowdcasting, and open innovation platforms. In this section we focus on two case studies harnessing the collective intelligence of the crowd for eliciting citizens' perspectives on important urban issues, as well as devising innovative solutions.

Spacehive[1]: a community fundraising platform in the UK and Ireland. It works by allowing individuals, groups, and organizations to create a page about their project on the Spacehive website, set a fundraising goal, and invite the community to contribute funds. Projects can be related to various categories, including public spaces, community centers, and parks. If the fundraising goal is met, the project can move forward, and the funds are released to the project's creator. According to its website, Spacehive has helped crowdfund over 2,000 ideas and raised nearly £30 million to support local projects, which include climate change initiatives, new public places to improve mental and physical health, and spaces for young people. The platform has a partner network that includes councils, foundations and businesses that assist in funding projects that local communities want, so that they can reach their fundraising goals faster, and mitigates the risks and rewards that come with crowdfunding public projects by having publicly accessible projects and the involvement of public officials [53]. One important benefit of Spacehive is that smaller organizations (e.g. local initiatives, charitable projects) with limited budgets also gain access to significant marketing and networking possibilities [54]. Furthermore, on a crowdsourcing platform such as Spacehive, citizens and communities are given the opportunity to express their local viewpoint and propose projects which they believe that would benefit their neighborhoods, something that, in accordance with [55], can lead to citizen empowerment, by enabling the crowd to contribute to the definition of the problem and complement top-down urban governance.

Some examples of projects funded on Spacehive include the following: the Thames Head Energy, a community energy initiative aiming at helping residents reduce their energy costs and carbon footprint, and ultimately achieving NetZero, while raising money for the community[2]; the Peckham Coal Line, a community-led project to reconnect Peckham's neighborhoods with a new linear park, connecting communities, opening up business possibilities and creating new green space[3]; as well as an initiative to raise the money for a new, more environmentally friendly wind turbine for the Kielder Observatory[4].

Block by Block[5]: The Block by Block project is a partnership between the United Nations Human Settlements Programme (UN-Habitat) and the video game company Mojang (creator of the computer game Minecraft), and Microsoft (corporate parent of Mojang), aiming at integrating Minecraft into public space planning to get community members more involved. The idea of using digital games for developing community engagement has gained attention in the last decades, and "serious" games that aim to provide an engaging environment combined with pedagogical principles have emerged [56]. However, these tools are usually limited in their use in space and time and tailored for specific urban contexts [56]. On the other hand, the Minecraft platform provides an endless virtual world that players can appropriate according to their imagination. Further,

---

[1] https://www.spacehive.com/
[2] https://www.spacehive.com/thames-head-energy-community-project
[3] https://www.spacehive.com/peckhamcoalline
[4] https://www.spacehive.com/kielder-observatory-wind-turbine
[5] https://www.blockbyblock.org/

being a very efficient and cost-effective way to visualize a three-dimensional space, in a format designed for rapid iteration and idea-sharing, it allows people to visualize and create models of their local environments, allowing for more effective and inclusive urban planning.

So far, the Block by Block Foundation has funded and activated dozens of public space projects in more than 35 countries around the world. The foundation's committee members evaluate proposed projects based on a range of detailed criteria addressing financial sustainability, partner capacity, and suitability for Minecraft, as well as project design, accessibility, economic impact, etc., and they select a wide range of projects incorporating diverse themes such as gender equality, climate change, accessibility, cultural heritage, social inclusion, etc. After, using GIS and satellite data, as well as photographs of the proposed work area, the workshop facilitators create models in-game that workshop participants can edit as they please [57].

For instance, the Municipality of Pristina was one of the first sites in Europe selected by UN-Habitat to test the Block by Block Methodology for upgrading public space[6]. The initial project focused on revitalizing a former green market in one of Pristina's largest neighborhoods and creating a multifunctional public space. The site's temporary market structures had been removed, leaving an abandoned, concrete-covered space that was rarely used by the community's 4,000 residents. More than 70 Pristina residents participated in a Block by Block Workshop to redesign the former marketplace. After initial discussions on urban design and the importance of public space, the participants formed small teams to model different solutions and co-create the final designs on a multiplayer Minecraft server. The final concept featured a range of facilities addressing the needs of various groups, including gardens, comfortable resting places, a playground, and a skatepark. The 17 team proposals and the final concept were used as the basis for detailed architectural designs.

Several other projects have been implemented across the globe, including the use of Minecraft to crowdsource ideas for the redesign of Plaza Tlaxcoaque in Mexico City, in which 7,429 young people participated and 1,438 ideas were submitted[7]; a workshop in which residents designed a park in Jianghan district, one of the most populous industrial regions in Wuhan, China[8]; and a three-day workshop involving 50 resident youth in the design of a community garden in Wadi al-Joz, East Jerusalem, Palestine[9].

4.2 Urban Data Platforms

Urban data platforms crowdsource data and provide insights into various aspects of urban life, such as transportation, housing, environment, energy usage, air quality, and more, in order to inform decision-making around urban planning and policy. A common way to showcase this data is with city dashboards, which provide access to data visualizations from public or private service providers, relevant to a city's performance against selected indicators [2].

---

[6] https://www.blockbyblock.org/projects/kosovo

[7] https://www.blockbyblock.org/projects/mexico

[8] https://www.blockbyblock.org/projects/wuhan

[9] https://www.blockbyblock.org/projects/palestine

There are many urban data platforms, which typically collect, process, and analyze big data from a variety of sources to provide insights into urban systems. An example of such platform would be UrbanSim[10], an open source platform supporting land use, transportation, and environmental planning and analysis. It integrates a range of data sources allowing users to customize models and parameters to match local conditions. UrbanSim has been used to model and simulate urban development patterns, assess the impact of proposed policies, generate forecasts for future scenarios, as well as engage the local communities by making models more tangible. It has been applied to cities and regions around the world, including cities in the United States, Europe, Asia, and Australia. Another urban data platform is UrbanFootprint[11], a proprietary web-based urban planning software that helps city officials, developers, and designers make informed decisions about the built environment. The platform provides data-driven insights and visualizations for urban design, land use planning, transportation, and sustainability. Users can access a variety of data sets, including demographic, economic, and environmental data, to help inform their decisions. The platform also provides collaborative tools for sharing and analyzing data, making it a useful resource for public engagement and community involvement in the planning process.

Regarding any urban data platform research projects, an earlier example would be the 'CityDashboard'[12] platform, which was developed by the CASA research lab at the University College London (UCL). It aggregates simple spatial data for cities around the UK and then displays this data on a dashboard and a map. Lastly, the Urban Open Platform (UoP) is a research initiative originating from the European Innovation Partnership on Smart Cities and Communities (EIP SCC). It comprises a collection of smart city services that communicate internally and externally with harmonized APIs, using open standards and widely used technologies and software, which make it easy to develop and integrate with. Its aim is to support not only data acquisition but also various types of data processing: data is aggregated, processed, manipulated and extended within the city context. The platform was validated with 10 real-life urban use cases in two European capital cities, Helsinki and Tallinn [58].

4.3 Collaborative Governance Platforms

Digital platforms for urban democracy facilitate citizens in: (a) expressing their opinions about developments, plans and policies to city authorities, (b) debating urban issues, and, (c) taking part in participatory city budgeting [59]. It is argued that these platforms have been introduced and advanced within a discourse which contrasts the notion of the smart city, by promoting open-source, commons-based democratic approaches instead of using closed and proprietary software services for e-participation [59]. Two prominent examples of such platforms are Decide Madrid and Decidim Barcelona, which are described in more detail in what follows.

---

[10] https://www.urbansim.com/
[11] https://urbanfootprint.com/
[12] https://citydashboard.org/

Decide Madrid[13]: Decide Madrid is a collaborative governance platform launched in 2015 by the Madrid City Council in order to engage the public in decision-making. Built on the "Consul" open source software, it aims at ensuring the transparency of government proceedings and to increase public participation in council decision-making and spending processes. Currently, Consul is being used by over 130 institutions in 33 countries, mostly cities and regions [59].

The citizens of Madrid can engage with the local government through the platform, in the following ways:

- Participatory budgeting – citizens can make spending proposals for city projects
- Proposals – citizens can shape government actions by directly proposing and supporting ideas for new legislation
- Consultations – citizens can vote on council proceedings
- Debate – citizens can deliberate on various issues so that the local government has access to the public opinion

An important aspect of the platform is the support for local participatory budgeting: citizens can submit proposals (which are analyzed by city council officials), support by voting the proposals they like (both for city-wide projects and for district-level projects), and vote on final projects after they are presented with estimated costs and overall budgets. According to [59], the first budget in 2016 opened €60 million to citizen proposals; it attracted 5,184 proposals, on which 22,389 participants cast 168,111 votes. Further evaluation and voting led to 206 selected projects that were funded, including tree-planting in the city, facilities for recycling, green routes interconnecting the city, etc. Another successful Decide Madrid project was the remodeling of the city's Plaza de España in 2017, in which 26,961 citizens actively participated by making and voting on proposals[14]. The winning project, named "Welcome Mother Nature, Goodbye Mr. Ford" was voted by more than 52% of the participants[15]. The main focus of the winning proposal was to prioritize cyclists and pedestrians, reduce car traffic around the square by diverting it underground, and increase greenery, by planting over 1200 new trees. The remodeled square also includes children's playgrounds, a park for the elderly and routes to view the archaeological finds that have come to light during the work.

Decidim Barcelona[16]: Similar to Decide Madrid, Decidim Barcelona is a collaborative governance platform built on open source software. It launched in 2016 aiming at elaborating Barcelona's municipal strategic plan, which defines objectives and actions to be carried out by the local government during the current legislature, with the participation of the citizens [60]. Using the platform citizens can (among others):

- Consult the open participatory processes
- Take part in debates (make new proposals, debate/comment on existing proposals, support or share through social media)

---

[13] https://decide.madrid.es/
[14] https://involve.org.uk/resources/case-studies/decide-madrid
[15] https://decide.madrid.es/proceso/plaza-espana-resultados
[16] https://www.decidim.barcelona/

- Track proposals (those that began on the platform and those generated at face-to-face meetings)

According to [61], the platform increased the transparency of information leading to better accountability and result monitoring, and also managed to incentivize citizens to collaborate around key issues. There has also been an increase in participation and proposal deliberation towards the municipal strategic plan of Barcelona [61]. During a two-month process of co-production, more than 40,000 citizens discussed and supported proposals made by the government, and also made their own proposals for the strategic city plan [60]. The Decidim Barcelona platform has been used to crowdsource citizen proposals and opinions on a number of projects[17], such as the design of the new green area in Bon Pastor's "Cases Barates", the development of the Action Plan for the Parc de Montjuïc, the development of the strategic plan for the city's coastal areas, etc.

As already mentioned, urban platforms are developed as generic "socio-technical assemblage templates", with the capability of using them across different local contexts [41]. As with Decide Madrid, several other platforms were also built on the Decidim open-source platform for participatory democracy used by Decidim Barcelona. An example is OmaStadi[18], a participatory platform in Helsinki, Finland, which allows residents to propose and vote on ideas for urban development and improvement. The first round of the OmaStadi project was piloted between 2018–2020 by the city of Helsinki, as part of its efforts to increase citizen participation and engagement in decision-making processes related to urban planning and development. The platform was open to all residents of Helsinki as it was designed to make the city's decision-making processes more transparent and accessible to the public. The evaluation results of the project were rather positive, as it emphasized direct participation and online democracy [62]. According to the Omastadi website, the platform has been used to crowdsource over 6,000 ideas from citizens and has been successful in promoting collaboration and participation in the planning process. The city government has also been supportive of the platform and has incorporated citizen ideas into the urban planning process. The implemented projects range from using renewable energy sources for illuminating parks and streets, to planting more trees and flowers in the city, and adding more benches, lamps, and bins to prevent littering.

So far, we have presented a number of cases where participatory urban platforms have been used along with formal planning procedures and routines embedded in cities. We argue that these platforms hold significant potential for engaging citizens and communities in co-creating more livable and sustainable cities, by providing feedback on urban design projects, supporting various initiatives, or even proposing their own solutions; thus, they should not only be viewed as ecosystems of value extraction but also as tools with a great potential for connectivity, exchange of knowledge, and for raising awareness on important issues. Additionally, acting as generic templates, they can be (re)used in multiple urban contexts and environments (as in the case of the Consul software) and be iteratively improved.

---

[17] https://ajuntament.barcelona.cat/digital/en/digital-empowerment/democracy-and-digital-rig
hts/decidim-barcelona

[18] https://omastadi.hel.fi/

However, the level of citizen engagement varies according to the platform's architecture and capabilities, as well as the level of integration of the platform into the formal planning procedure. Concerning the levels of public participation in urban planning, as described in Sect. 2, we suggest that urban data platforms, such as urban analytics platforms, city dashboards, and city data portals, correspond to the lowest level ("information" level), providing one-directional information aiming at public outreach, or at the "consultation" level, as they gather big data in order to inform policies and to increase public awareness and engagement with urban data. Participatory governance platforms that support collaboration between city stakeholders can be categorized in the third level ("cooperation" level), as this level involves the participants (e.g. citizens and city authorities) in a dialogue with each other in order to define issues, formulate approaches and decide on solutions, or, in certain cases, in the "collaboration" level, as all involved stakeholders co-create solutions in equal terms, following democratic processes. Crowdsourcing platforms, such as Spacehive, where citizens identify local problems, propose their own ideas on urban design projects, or support initiatives by investing in urban projects, can be placed in the "collaboration" level. Finally, concerning the last level of participation, ("empowerment" level), we believe that initiatives such as Block by Block could have the potential to support participants in formulating their own ideas and projects. Nonetheless, we argue that the empowerment level in the urban platform context would mean that citizens themselves can self-organize in order to develop open, neutral, and transparent urban technologies, or appropriate technological tools to meet their needs, by following genuine bottom-up approaches [1].

5 Conclusions

In this paper, we argued that the introduction of digital technologies in urban planning processes and the use of digital platforms under the platform urbanism framework could facilitate the twin transition of urban areas. This can be done by dealing with three main drawbacks of urban planning; first, urban planning is an urban policy domain that is relatively rigid, embedded in the institutions of each area. This creates obstacles to the development of scalable solutions, leaving room only for softer retrofitting solutions, sometimes with the addition of a digital layer. Second, although citizen participation in urban planning has been discussed for quite a while, it has not been practiced. As shown in our analysis, digital platforms are mostly used for relatively simple activities and functions, such as information-exchange, consultation, cooperation, etc. and much less for more complex ones such as co-design. Third, there is a significant time lag between urban planning formulation and implementation.

However, green transformation and response to environmental crises urge us to view urban planning as a mission-oriented strategy, that allows the participation of different actors, enables bottom-up experimentation and seeks societal transformation. The emergent complex and co-generative dynamics between platforms and the urban space can lead to the transformation of place- and space-based social worlds and provides a great opportunity to renegotiate the "urban" and to shape new visions of the city. Platform urbanism is characterized by dynamic networks involving different actors [41] which are hybrid and ephemeral; they can appear out of nowhere when there is a specific need but can also withdraw when the demand has fallen. We also believe that platform urbanism could be a useful framework for shaping urban planning towards the goals of the New European Bauhaus Initiative, an EU launched, creative and transdisciplinary movement that aims to connect the European Green Deal with the living spaces based on mission-oriented innovation, participation and creative contestation [63].

Furthermore, we explored the role of participatory urban platforms in effectively disseminating knowledge, engaging citizens, and raising public awareness. Even though these platforms contribute significantly in bringing people together, they are still challenged by various issues and critical questions. For instance, an important issue, also common in smart city initiatives, is participation bias and the platform's accessibility and inclusivity with regard to the digital skills of users [64]. Also, the discussion regarding platform urbanism often revolves around the notion of the *platform-as-a-company*, which generates private value from coordinating different networked actors [65]. As profit-driven, commercial platforms mediate main activities of daily life, many concerns regarding the politics and accountability of these socio-technical systems, arise [66]. Based on the findings of this paper, we argue that participatory urban platforms can support and engage citizens in co-creating more fair, livable, and sustainable cities. Nonetheless, there is a need for further research into the platform technology and attributes (e.g. openness, transparency) that can lead to citizen empowerment, as well as into frameworks and methodologies that could facilitate the successful incorporation of such platforms in bottom-up, citizen-led initiatives, and, subsequently, connect these to effective urban policy.

References

1. Vadiati, N.: Alternatives to smart cities: a call for consideration of grassroots digital urbanism. Digit. Geogr. Soc. **3**, 100030 (2022)
2. Barns, S.: Platform Urbanism: Negotiating Platform Ecosystems in Connected Cities. Springer Nature (2019)
3. Münster, S., et al.: How to involve inhabitants in urban design planning by using digital tools? An overview on a state of the art, key challenges and promising approaches. Procedia Comput. Sci. **112**, 2391–2405 (2017)
4. Billger, M., Thuvander, L., Wästberg, B.S.: In search of visualization challenges: the development and implementation of visualization tools for supporting dialogue in urban planning processes. Environ. Plan. B: Urban Analyt. City Sci. **44**(6), 1012–1035 (2017)
5. Lock, O., Bednarz, T., Leao, S.Z., Pettit, C.: A review and reframing of participatory urban dashboards. City Cult. Soc. **20**, 100294 (2020)
6. Schwarz, N., Haase, D., Seppelt, R.: Omnipresent sprawl? A review of urban simulation models with respect to urban shrinkage. Environ. Plan. B: Plan. Des. **37**(2), 265–283 (2010)
7. Hasler, S., Chenal, J., Soutter, M.: Digital tools as a means to foster inclusive, data-informed urban planning. Civil Eng. Architect. **5**(6), 230–239 (2017)
8. O'grady, M., O'hare, G.: How smart is your city? Science **335**(6076), 1581–1582 (2012)
9. Yin, C., Xiong, Z., Chen, H., Wang, J., Cooper, D., David, B.: A literature survey on smart cities. Sci. China Inf. Sci. **58**(10), 1–18 (2015). https://doi.org/10.1007/s11432-015-5397-4
10. Albino, V., Berardi, U., Dangelico, R.M.: Smart cities: definitions, dimensions, performance, and initiatives. J. Urban Technol. **22**(1), 3–21 (2015)

11. Chamoso, P., González-Briones, A., Rodríguez, S., Corchado, J.M.: Tendencies of technologies and platforms in smart cities: a state-of-the-art review. Wirel. Commun. Mobile Comput. **2018**, 1–17 (2018). https://doi.org/10.1155/2018/3086854

12. Silva, B.N., Khan, M., Han, K.: Towards sustainable smart cities: a review of trends, architectures, components, and open challenges in smart cities. Sustain. Cities Soc. **38**, 697–713 (2018)

13. LeGates, R., Stout, F.: The City Reader, 6th ed. Routledge (2016)

14. Mitlin, D.: Editorial: citizen participation in planning: from the neighbourhood to the city. Environ. Urban. **33**(2), 295–309 (2021). https://doi.org/10.1177/09562478211035608

15. Hall, P.: Cities of Tomorrow: An Intellectual History of Urban Planning and Design in the Twentieth Century, 3rd edn. Blackwell (2002)

16. Forester, J.: Planning in the face of conflict. J. Am. Plan. Assoc. **53**(3), 303–314 (1987)

17. Fainstein, S.S.: New directions in planning theory. Urban Affairs Rev. **35**(4), 451–478 (2000). https://doi.org/10.1177/107808740003500401

18. Healey, P.: Collaborative Planning: Shaping Places in Fragmented Societies. Macmillan Press (1997)

19. Lane, M.B.: Public participation in planning: an intellectual history. Aust. Geogr. **36**(3), 283–299 (2005). https://doi.org/10.1080/00049180500325694

20. de Carli, B., Frediani, A.A.: Situated perspectives on the city: a reflection on scaling participation through design. Environ. Urban. **33**(2), 376–395 (2021). https://doi.org/10.1177/09562478211028066

21. Kelly, E.D.: Community Planning: An Introduction to the Comprehensive Plan, 2nd edn. Island Press (2010)

22. Vuksanović-Macura, Z., Miščević, I.: Excluded communities and participatory land-use planning: experience from informal Roma settlements in Serbia. Environ. Urban. **33**(2), 456–477 (2021). https://doi.org/10.1177/09562478211024095

23. Rotondo, F.: The U-City paradigm: opportunities and risks for e-democracy in collaborative planning. Future Internet **4**(2), 563–574 (2012). https://doi.org/10.3390/fi4020563

24. The World Bank: The World Bank Participation Sourcebook (1995)

25. Davidoff, P.: Advocacy and pluralism in planning. J. Am. Inst. Plan. **31**(4), 331–338 (1965). https://doi.org/10.1080/01944366508978187

26. Arnstein, S.R.: A ladder of citizen participation. J. Am. Inst. Plan. **35**(4), 216–224 (1969). https://doi.org/10.1080/01944366908977225

27. Painter, M.: Participation and power. In: Munro-Clarke, M. (ed.) Citizen Participation in Government, pp. 21–36. Hale & Ironmonger (1992)

28. New Economics Foundation: Participation Works! 21 Techniques of Community Participation for the 21st Century (1998)

29. Wilcox, D.: Guide to Effective Participation. Partnership Books (1994)

30. Stauffacher, M., Flüeler, T., Krütli, P., Scholz, R.W.: Analytic and dynamic approach to collaboration: a transdisciplinary case study on sustainable landscape development in a Swiss Prealpine region. Syst. Pract. Action Res. **21**(6), 409–422 (2008). https://doi.org/10.1007/s11213-008-9107-7

31. UN-Habitat: SDG Indicator 11.3.2 Training Module: Civic Participation. United Nations Human Settlement Programme (UN-Habitat) (2018)

32. Almansi, F., Motta, J.M., Hardoy, J.: Incorporating a resilience lens into the social and urban transformation of informal settlements: the participatory upgrading process in Villa 20, Buenos Aires (2016–2020). Environ. Urban. **32**(2), 407–428 (2020). https://doi.org/10.1177/0956247820935717

33. Menegat, R.: Participatory democracy and sustainable development: integrated urban environmental management in Porto Alegre, Brazil. Environ. Urban. **14**(2), 181–206 (2002)

34. Cabannes, Y.: Contributions of participatory budgeting to climate change adaptation and mitigation: current local practices across the world and lessons from the field. Environ. Urban. **33**(2), 356–375 (2021). https://doi.org/10.1177/09562478211021710
35. Parker, G.G., Van Alstyne, M.W., Choudary, S.P.: Platform Revolution: How Networked Markets are Transforming the Economy and How to Make Them Work for You. WW Norton & Company (2016)
36. Kakderi, C., Psaltoglou, A., Fellnhofer, K.: Digital platforms and online applications for user engagement and collaborative innovation. In: The 20th Conference of the Greek Society of Regional Scientists (2018)
37. Komninos, N., Kakderi, C. (eds.): Smart Cities in the Post-algorithmic Era: Integrating Technologies, Platforms and Governance. Edward Elgar Publishing (2019)
38. Panori, A., Kakderi, C., Komninos, N., Fellnhofer, K., Reid, A., Mora, L.: Smart systems of innovation for smart places: challenges in deploying digital platforms for co-creation and data-intelligence. Land Use Policy **111**, 104631 (2021)
39. Katmada, A., Komninos, N., Kakderi, C.: The landscape of digital platforms for bottom-up collaboration, creativity, and innovation creation. In: Streitz, N.A., Konomi, S. (eds.) Distributed, Ambient and Pervasive Interactions. Smart Environments, Ecosystems, and Cities: 10th International Conference, DAPI 2022, Held as Part of the 24th HCI International Conference, HCII 2022, Virtual Event, Proceedings, pp. 28–42. Springer International Publishing, Cham (2022). https://doi.org/10.1007/978-3-031-05463-1_3
40. Komninos, N., Kakderi, C., Collado, A., Papadaki, I., Panori, A.: Digital transformation of city ecosystems: platforms shaping engagement and externalities across vertical markets. In: Sustainable Smart City Transitions, pp. 91–112. Routledge (2022)
41. Caprotti, F., Chang, I.-C.C., Joss, S.: Beyond the smart city: a typology of platform urbanism. Urban Transform. **4**(1), 4 (2022)
42. Van Dijck, J., Poell, J., De Waal, M.: The Platform Society: Public Values in a Connective Society. Oxford University Press, Oxford (2018)
43. Caprotti, F., Liu, D.: Emerging platform urbanism in China: reconfigurations of data, citizenship and materialities. Technol. Forecast. Soc. Change **151**, 119690 (2020). https://doi.org/10.1016/j.techfore.2019.06.016
44. Sadowski, J.: Cyberspace and cityscapes: on the emergence of platform urbanism. Urban Geogr. **41**(3), 448–452 (2020)
45. Saunders, T., Baeck, P.: Rethinking Smart Cities from the Ground Up. Nesta, London (2015)
46. Gleeson, D., Dyer, M.: Manifesto for collaborative urbanism. In: Certomà, C., Dyer, M., Pocatilu, L., Rizzi, F. (eds.) Citizen Empowerment and Innovation in the Data-Rich City, pp. 3–18. Springer International Publishing, Cham (2017). https://doi.org/10.1007/978-3-319-47904-0_1
47. De Lange, M., De Waal, M.: Owning the city: new media and citizen engagement in urban design. In: Etingoff, K. (ed.) Urban Land Use: Community-Based Planning, pp. 87–110. Apple Academic Press, 3333 Mistwell Crescent, Oakville, ON L6L 0A2, Canada (2017). https://doi.org/10.1201/9781315365794-5
48. Keymolen, E., Voorwinden, A.: Can we negotiate? Trust and the rule of law in the smart city paradigm. Int. Rev. Law Comput. Technol. **34**(3), 233–253 (2020)
49. Angelidou, M., Psaltoglou, A.: Digital social innovation in support of spatial planning. An investigation through nine initiatives in three smart city programmes. Spatium 7–16 (2018)
50. Stelzle, B., Jannack, A., Noennig, J.R.: Co-design and co-decision: decision making on collaborative design platforms. Procedia Comput. Sci. **112**, 2435–2444 (2017). https://doi.org/10.1016/j.procs.2017.08.095
51. Abel, P., Miether, D., Plötzky, F., Robra-Bissantz, S.: The shape of bottom-up urbanism participatory platforms: a conceptualisation and empirical study. In: BLED 2021 Proceedings, 32 (2021). https://aisel.aisnet.org/bled2021/32

52. Smaniotto Costa, C., Bahillo Martínez, A., Álvarez, F.J., Šuklje Erjavec, I., Menezes, M., Pallares-Barbera, M.: Digital tools for capturing user's needs on urban open spaces: drawing lessons from cyberparks project. In: Citizen Empowerment and Innovation in the Data-Rich City, pp. 177–193. Springer International Publishing, Cham (2017)
53. Treutel, E.: Crowdfunding Community Projects (2014)
54. Hollow, M.: Crowdfunding and civic society in Europe: a profitable partnership? Open Citizenship **4**(1), 68–73 (2013)
55. Certomà, C., Rizzi, F.: Crowdsourcing processes for citizen-driven governance. In: Certomà, C., Dyer, M., Pocatilu, L., Rizzi, F. (eds.) Citizen Empowerment and Innovation in the Data-Rich City, pp. 57–77. Springer International Publishing, Cham (2017). https://doi.org/10.1007/978-3-319-47904-0_4
56. Bashandy, H.: Playing, mapping, and power: a critical analysis of using "minecraft" in spatial design. Am. J. Play **12**(3), 363–389 (2020)
57. McDaniel, T.: Block by Block: The Use of the Video Game "Minecraft" as a Tool to Increase Public Participation (2018)
58. Soe, R.M., Ruohomäki, T., Patzig, H.: Urban open platform for borderless smart cities. Appl. Sci. **12**(2), 700 (2022)
59. Smith, A., Martín, P.P.: Going beyond the smart city? Implementing technopolitical platforms for urban democracy in Madrid and Barcelona. In: Sustainable Smart City Transitions, pp. 280–299. Routledge (2022)
60. Aragón, P., et al.: Deliberative platform design: the case study of the online discussions in Decidim Barcelona. In: Ciampaglia, G.L., Mashhadi, A., Yasseri, T. (eds.) Social Informatics: 9th International Conference, SocInfo 2017, Oxford, UK, September 13–15, 2017, Proceedings, Part II 9, pp. 277–287. Springer, Cham (2017). https://doi.org/10.1007/978-3-319-67256-4_22
61. Peña-López, I.: Decidim, Barcelona, Spain (2017)
62. Rask, M., Ertiö, T.P., Tuominen, P., Ahonen, V.L.: Final evaluation of the City of Helsinki's participatory budgeting: OmaStadi 2018–2020 (2021)
63. Bason, C., Conway, R., Hill, D., Mazzucato, M.: A New Bauhaus for a Green Deal (2020). https://www.ucl.ac.uk/bartlett/public-purpose/publications/2021/jan/new-bauhaus-green-deal. Accessed 23 Feb 2023
64. Chiappini, L., de Vries, J.: Civic crowdfunding as urban digital platform in Milan and Amsterdam: don't take pictures on a rainy day! Digital Geogr. Soc. **3**, 100024 (2022)
65. Richardson, L.: Coordinating the city: platforms as flexible spatial arrangements. Urban Geogr. **41**(3), 458–461 (2020)
66. Fields, D., Bissell, D., Macrorie, R.: Platform methods: studying platform urbanism outside the black box. Urban Geogr. **41**(3), 462–468 (2020)

Experiences with Using Diverse Evaluation Methods for Extracting Insights via Experience Prototyping in Ambient and Civic Computing

Risa Kimura[✉] and Tatsuo Nakajima

Department of Computer Science and Engineering, Waseda University, Tokyo, Japan
{risa.kimuratatsuo,tatsuo}@dcl.cs.waseda.ac.jp

Abstract. In this paper, we report our experiences with using diverse evaluation methods in our recent studies to develop some ambient and civic computing services. Extracting insights from doing researches is essential in our daily research activities, and we usually use diverse research methods for finding new opportunities from our research activities. In our current researches, we examined to use diverse research methods so we like to report our insights extracted from using the research methods. The most important contribution of this paper is to show the importance to use multiple research methods to extract various insights from the diverse angles in conducted researches.

Keywords: Research Methods · Ambient Intelligence · Rapid Prototyping · Ambient and Civic Computing

1 Introduction

The relationship between research and design has been investigated due to recent advances of designerly ways of working in innovative digital technologies [1, 4, 12, 14, 18, 28, 33, 36, 37, 43, 44]. In particular, researchers in ambient and civic computing engage in design practices to create digital services that can be explored in their use contexts, and reflect on new use cases and design perspectives revealed through the practices, services, or their use. Some approaches explore various forms of intermediate knowledge, such as annotated portfolios, strong concepts, design programs, manifestos, concept-driven designs, and bridging concepts [2, 10, 13, 19–21, 30, 34, 45]. For example, Löwgren emphasizes intermediate knowledge forms, which are meta-knowledge representations to guide how to design rather than what to design [31]. Gaver states that textual descriptions of artifacts, including theoretical declarations about them are considered as annotations in portfolios [15].

Research methods are essential to extract knowledge from doing researches so that typical academic researches adopted various and diverse research methods to extract insights and validate hypotheses in their researches. In this paper, based on our experiences with designing and evaluating some ambient intelligence services [22–27], we

N. A. Streitz and S. Konomi (Eds.): HCII 2023, LNCS 14037, pp. 53–66, 2023.
https://doi.org/10.1007/978-3-031-34609-5_4

present diverse insights to extract potential opportunities of the researches' future directions. In the researches, we adopted diverse research methods including usability evaluation, paper prototyping, user centered design, user enactments, design fiction/speculative design, practice-based researches, annotated portfolio, and non-human perspective. One essential issues common in our researches is that to develop prototypes to allow participants to offer proper experiences to extract diverse voices from them. The approach is known as "Experience Prototyping" [5]. We present several examples to use diverse research methods based on experience prototyping in our researches, then we show some comparisons of these methods. In our research projects, the extracted insights were usually used to refine existing services and develop new services based on the insights, then extracting opportunities and pitfalls is more important than validating the quantitative effectiveness of the proposed services.

The contribution of the paper is that the discussions described in the paper show the importance to use multiple research methods to extract diverse insights from multiple angles since one single research method adequately cannot extract diverse insights.

2 Experience Prototyping

Buchenau and Suri [5] coined the term experience prototyping. Experience prototyping aims to get a sense of the actual experience through prototypes and to let the designer reflect upon them before the product or service exists. In recent advanced digital service, it is hard to develop complete prototypes to investigate various aspects of the target digital services. The tools and techniques used for experience prototyping reinforce the attitude of actively experiencing the sometimes subtle differences between different design solutions. For example, paper prototyping [46] is a celebrated example of low-fidelity prototyping, but it can also benefit a lot from advanced technologies such as augmented reality [38], as it can provide a cheaper alternative without developing expensive systems.

Rather than deciding between low-fidelity and high-fidelity prototyping, both can be combined to explore different dimensions of design consideration, as shown in [35]. In [29], the authors said that "the best prototype is one that, in the simplest and most efficient way, makes the possibilities and limitations of a design idea visible and measurable". One promising approach is to construct multiple fragments of user experiences and to investigate respective experiences by developing different prototypes for them. We can develop respective prototypes that are suitable for investigating the respective experiences. This is because fidelity of the prototype remains an important issue, and fidelity is a matter of cost.

For investigating opportunities from respective experiences, we may also consider to use different evaluation methods to use different prototypes. In this paper, we show our experiences to use diverse evaluation methods used to investigating potential opportunities for exploring CollectiveEyes and CollectiveEars [22–27]. In the researches, we have mainly developed minimum prototypes for extracting potential opportunities. The most important factors of the prototypes are to offer proper experiences to participants that experience the prototypes. Thus, the prototypes have carefully developed for offering proper experiences, but avoided to complete to develop full functions. In some cases, we may use the Wizard-of Oz method to similar to some functionalities manually or to use limited contents to offer partial but essential experiences to the participants.

3 Practice-Based Research I: User Enactment

Practice-based research or research through design is a practice-based form of inquiry that is now widely adopted in humanities-based research cultures and beyond. The aim of practice-based research is to foreground the materiality of design research, placing the artifacts of research practice in a center stage [16, 48].

User Enactments (UEs) is a widely used practice-based research method developed as a design approach to help design teams better investigate fundamental changes in the role, form, and behavior of technology in an unknown design space [40].

Fig. 1. Immersive Environments for User Enactments [23]

In our project, we usually used the user enactments method for extracting diverse opportunities from prototype services because our aim is not to compare our approach with other approaches and we like to explore diverse opportunities of our approach. When using the method, we usually created some scenarios that we asked participants to perform [23–25]. We consider that the following two aspects are important for us to adopt the user enactments method. The first aspect is to develop a prototype service partially. The aspect is essential because developing a prototype service is costly so we like to omit to implement some inessential features in the prototype service. The scenarios allows us to implement only necessary functions appeared in the scenarios so that the unused features in the scenarios does not need to be implemented. The second aspect is to offer immersive experiences when performing scenarios. In our project, we usually took various videos to visually present scenarios as shown in Fig. 1. The videos simulated people's eye sights in the prepared scenarios. We may use a head-mounted display and little interactivity to make participants feel their autonomy in the experiments. The approach is promising to extract diverse opportunities without requiring heavy human and monetary resources.

4   Practice-Based Research II: Annotated Portfolio

In our project, we have develop a family of services. By comparing these services, we may extract new insights, but it is not easy to comparing the services without using a better tool. We considered annotated portfolio is a promising tool for the purpose [27].

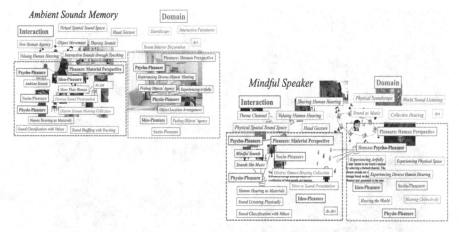

Fig. 2. Annotations for Ambient Sound Memory and Mindful Speaker [27]

The annotated portfolio method is one of research through design approach and is a collection of designs, represented in an appropriate medium, and combining the design representations with brief annotations [3, 9]. The method describes the context to design artifacts for their designers and researchers and provides an understanding of the research outcomes, successes and failings at each stage of the design process. The purpose of the research methods is to extract knowledge from the design process of actual artifacts and document the knowledge. The knowledge is essential to extract new insights from the design process and refine existing artifacts and new innovative artifacts.

In our approach, we created a new approach to structurally document annotations for the services. Figure 2 presents two examples of the annotations. The annotations present various interactive features of the services and possible user experiences. Therefore, it is easy to find missing features and hidden opportunities in respective services. We found that documenting diverse features of services is a promising direction to learn somethings from the experiences to develop other services.

5 Practice-Based Research III: Experience Prototyping Portfolio

For exploring potential opportunities of a new service, it is hard to extract effective insights from simple user studies. In particular, a laboratory study is not suitable for increasing knowledge about the service. In Experience Prototyping Portfolio, several key user experiences are extracted and reflective insights are documents as annotations. The annotations of respective user experiences are collected as a portfolio. The annotations are coded under several themes for representing key opportunities in respective fragmented user experiences.

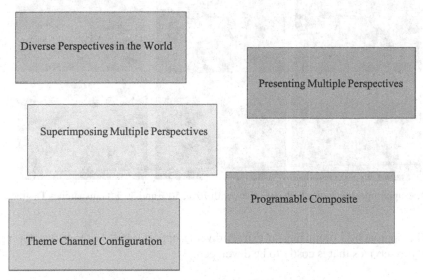

Fig. 3. Experience Prototyping Portfolio

Figure 3 presents an example to use Experience Prototyping Portfolio in CollectiveEyes. In the example, five typical user experiences are extracted from analyzing use cases of CollectiveEyes. Then, diverse insights from multiple user studies conducted on CollectiveEyes are classified according to respective user experiences. The insights are documented as annotations based on several themes. Finally, a portfolio containing annotations for the respective user experiences is holistically analyzed for extracting the potential opportunities of CollectiveEyes.

6 Paper Prototyping

In human-computer interaction, paper prototyping is a widely used technique in the user-centered design process, a process for developing software that satisfies user expectations and needs, and in this case is particularly suitable for testing [46].

Developing a prototype service is usually expensive. However, we need to investigate some opportunities before developing actual prototype services. In our project, as shown in Fig. 4, we used a paper prototype service for investigating some opportunities of the main features of the service [25]. In the service, the scenes dynamically created according to other persons' current eye sights. In the prototype, some scenes are created statically and show the scenes based on scenarios that participants perform. The participants of the experiment can experience the service sufficiently because the scenes in the scenarios were shown immersively through the head mounted displays.

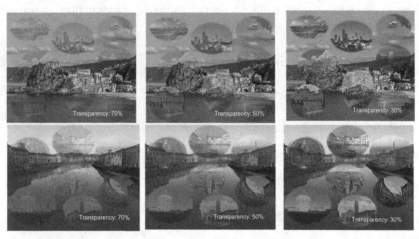

Fig. 4. Superimposing Multiple Perspectives with 70%, 50% and 30% Transparency Degree [25]

The approach is promising to extract diverse opportunities without developing a prototype services that is costly to be developed.

7   Human Centered Design

Similar Sounds in the Different Place Scenario   *Different Sounds in the Same Place Scenario*

Random Sounds Scenario   *Speaking sounds in streets Scenario*

Fig. 5. User Centered Design based on Scenarios [24]

Human-Centered Design (HCD) is a design methodology that focuses on usability goals, user demographics, real-world environments, tasks, and workflows in the design of products and services [39]. The approach is extremely important to extract complex requirements in digital platforms and services. Scenario-based analysis is one poplar techniques in HCD to extract the requirements for designing products and services.

In our project, for using human centered design, we created some scenarios shown in Fig. 5 [24]. The scenarios represent typical use cases of CollectiveEars. From the scenarios, we identified several typical functions that require to be implemented in the prototype service. The approach is effective to develop prototypes for extracting opportunities because the extracted functions are essential functions for constructing desirable experiences during the experiments.

8 Speculative Design and Design Fiction

Speculative Design is to describe work that uses design (products, services, scenarios) to address challenges and opportunities of the future [11, 47]. The canonical definition of speculative design is that it is an approach to design that does not seek solution-oriented projects. Instead, it attempts to probe alternative futures. Design fiction, which is certainly the most commonly used genre in the development pf speculative context, is a design practice aiming at exploring and criticizing possible futures by creating speculative, and often provocative, scenarios narrated through designed artifacts [36]. Design fiction typically uses fictional scenario including imaginary artifacts that do not exist in the current real world to investigate the possibilities of the artifacts, and it is different from speculative design in terms of the strongly focus on artifacts, where the suspension of disbelief of the artifacts is the most essential when using design fiction.

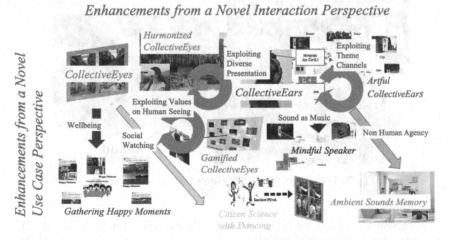

Fig. 6. Speculative Design in Our Projects [20, 26]

In our project, we used design fiction and speculative designs from several perspectives [23, 26]. In the first perspective, we used design fiction for imagining promising new services. In typical design fiction based researches, fictional technologies may be assumed with fictional scenarios. However, in our cases, our fictional technologies should me implementable, but the cost to implement complete functionalities may be reasonable. In the second perspective, we investigate promising services in the future and consider their potential use cases. As shown in Fig. 6, our project discusses a family of services that collectively shares human eyes and ears. During the investigation, we have proposed some new services for speculating some features of existing services. Then, we considered potential use cases by speculating these features. The approach is promising to expand the current scope of our imagination about the services.

9   Usability Evaluation

Usability evaluation focuses on the extent to which users are able to learn and use the product to achieve their goals [32]. Also important is how satisfied users are with the process. To gather this information, practitioners use a variety of methods to gather feedback from users about existing sites and plans related to new sites. Usability refers to the quality of the user's experience in interacting with a product or system, such as a website, software, device, or application. Usability refers to effectiveness, efficiency, and overall user satisfaction.

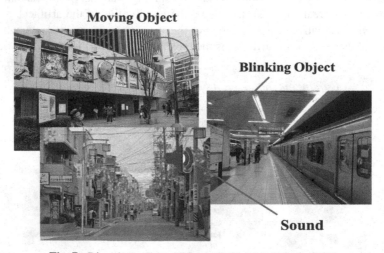

Fig. 7. Directing a Selected Person's Head Orientation [23]

In our research projects, we typically used usability evaluation to discuss the effectiveness of multiple approaches. In CollectiveEyes, we mainly investigated the tradeoffs of two features [23]. The first feature as shown in Fig. 7 is to direct a selected person's head orientation for watching the scenes that a user wants to see. There are several alternatives in the features so we conducted an experiments to reveal the tradeoffs among the alternatives by asking several participants to answer questionnaires and to interview with them after experiencing the alternatives. The second feature shown in Fig. 8 is to present multiple eye sights that a user wants to see. After using the two presentation methods, we conducted the interviews with the participants to extract their findings when using both methods.

Fig. 8. Spatial and Temporal View [23]

When using usability evaluation, it is important to hire a sufficient number of participants. However, we found that there are two different aspects in terms of the number of participants. For answering questionnaires, the reliability of the score is important so the number of participants is essential, where the distribution of the score needs to be small in this case. On the other hand, for conducting interviews, the most essential issues is to extract sufficiently diverse opinions. In this case, the diversity of the participants is more important than the number of participants.

10 Exploiting Mon-Than-Human Perspectives

Building on definitions of technology through a large number of researchers' perspectives and thinking has given birth to debates about technology-in-use and sociomateriality with its groundings [41, 42]. Sociomateriality denotes the enactment of a specific set of practices that combine materiality with institutions, norms, discourses, cultures, and other social phenomena. Introducing the world model in CollectiveEyes is heavily influenced by some basic concepts in sociomateriality. Investigating services from the material perspective is promising because the approach broaden our scope to reveal hidden aspects of the service [27].

In our project, we offer multiple visual perspectives to offer new insights from multiple angles [25]. For example, in Fig. 9, multiple viewpoints are simultaneously shown in one visual perspective. A user may be aware of unnoticed aspects from the non-human perspective. It is also helpful to consider to play a role that is not human in scenarios [7, 8]. For example, in [6], participants are asked to play a role of a scooter and they consider some insights from the scooter's point of view.

When we use the research methods introduced in the paper, we usually created scenarios, and a participant is asked to play a role of a person in the scenarios, but we also consider to play a role of non-human in scenarios. The approach is promising to extract more diverse opportunities from the experiments with various research methods.

Fig. 9. Observing from Multiple Angles [25]

11 Discussions

In the above sections, we presented how we have used various research methods in our research projects. Figure 10 summarizes the discussions presented in the section. Before starting to develop actual prototype services, we usually created paper prototypes of target services. We created several videos to demonstrate our target services. For creating the videos, we usually created very simple user interfaces that users can investigate how they can use the services. User centered design is useful to determine necessary functions in target digital services. In our projects, user centered design used scenarios to extract necessary functions. Also, design fiction and speculative design is a promising approach to analyze opportunities of target digital services. In our project, as shown in Sect. 4, design fiction/speculative design has been used to investigating various opportunities of a family of digital services, where these services are designed through the refinement or customization of the services. These services may not be actually implemented, but these features are explored by comparing their features. These research methods have been used for revealing potential opportunities and determine necessary functions in prototype systems.

After starting to implement prototype services, our main aims are to find potential opportunities of the services. We usually used the user enactments method. The method can be used with partially implemented prototype services that implements necessary functions to perform scenarios. Therefore, we do not need to implement complete functions in target services. The approach is useful to reveal diverse opportunities before implementing more complete prototype services. We also used annotated portfolio to investigate opportunities among a family of digital services. The annotated portfolio method is useful to find new opportunities by comparing among the services. For investigating diverse opportunities, the most important issue is to expand our eyes to find these opportunities. The research method like annotated portfolio is promising to find the opportunities by comparing multiple services, but the most important approach is to hire various people to investigate the opportunities because different people may find more opportunities based on their diverse experiences and backgrounds. In this case, hiring people who have different experiences and backgrounds are the most essential strategy for successful investigation.

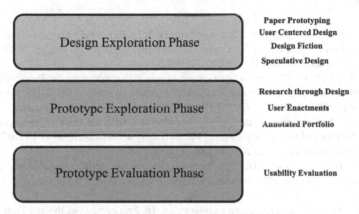

Fig. 10. A Summary of using Research Methods

While developing more complete prototype services, we usually need to investigate several difference in the approaches. In Sect. 9, we presented two examples to analyze the tradeoff among multiple strategies in our project. The method is essential, but for validating the tradeoff, it is important to hire sufficient people to join to the usability evaluation.

One of the most important finding in our researches is that developing proper prototype is significant to extract desirable opportunities. For reducing the cost to develop the prototypes, only necessary functions to offer proper user experiences during the experiments should be implemented. For offering desirable experiences, we should focus on the interaction between users and services. User-centered design based on scenarios is promising to identify essential functions for offering proper experiences during the experiments. A Promising future direction is to investigate a guideline to develop prototypes for extracting from researches.

12 Conclusion

In this paper, we presented research methods used in our projects and showed some insights to use the methods. The contribution of the paper is to emphasize the importance to use multiple research methods in different service development phases to extract diverse opportunities from the services.

In the paper, we focused on the design process before starting to investigate prototype services in field studies. A field study is another important research method to find actual problems by deploying the services in actual environments [28]. In [17], authors reported to use virtual reality technologies to simplify a field study. In our user enactments, we already adopted virtual reality technologies to offer immersive environments to find more realistic opportunities so we like to extend the approach to be used in a field study.

References

1. Bates, O., et al.: Towards a innovation agenda for HCI. In: Extended Abstracts of the 2019 CHI Conference on Human Factors in Computing Systems (CHI EA 2019), pp. W24:1–W24:8 (2019). https://doi.org/10.1145/3290607.3299017
2. Beck, J., Ekbia, H.R.: The theory practice gap as generative metaphor. In: Proceedings of the 2018 CHI Conference on Human Factors in Computing Systems (CHI 2018), pp. 620:1–11 (2018). https://doi.org/10.1145/3173574.3174194
3. Bowers, J.: The logic of annotated portfolios: communicating the value of "research through design". In: Proceedings of the Designing Interactive Systems Conference (DIS 2012), pp. 68–77 (2012). https://doi.org/10.1145/2317956.2317968
4. Brown, T., Wyatt, J.: Design Thinking for Social Innovation (SSIR). Stanford Social Innovation Review (2010). http://www.ssireview.org/articles/entry/design_thinking_for_social_innovation/
5. Buchenau, M., Suri, J.F.: Experience prototyping. In: Proceedings of the 3rd Conference on Designing Interactive Systems: Processes, Practices, Methods, and Techniques, pp. 424–433. ACM (2000)
6. Chang, W.-W., Giaccardi, E., Chen, L.-L., Liang, R.-H.: "Interview with things": a first-thing perspective to understand the scooter's everyday socio-material network in Taiwan. In: Proceedings of the 2017 Conference on Designing Interactive Systems (DIS 2017), pp. 1001–1012. Association for Computing Machinery, New York, NY, USA (2017). https://doi.org/10.1145/3064663.3064717
7. Coulton, P., Lindley, J.G.: More-than human centred design: considering other things. Design J. 22(4), 463–481 (2019). https://doi.org/10.1080/14606925.2019.1614320
8. Cruickshank, L., Trivedi, N.: Beyond human-centred design: supporting a new materiality in the internet of things, or how to design when a toaster is one of your users. Design J. 20(5), 561–576 (2017). https://doi.org/10.1080/14606925.2017.1349381
9. Culén, A.L., Børsting, J., Gaver, W.: Strategies for annotating portfolios: mapping designs for new domains. In: Proceedings of the 2020 ACM Designing Interactive Systems Conference (DIS 2020), pp. 1633–1645. Association for Computing Machinery, New York, NY, USA (2020). https://doi.org/10.1145/3357236.3395490
10. Dalsgaard, P., Dindler, C.: Between theory and practice: bridging concepts in HCI research. In: Proceedings of the SIGCHI Conference on Human Factors in Computing Systems (CHI 2014), pp. 1635–1644 (2014). https://doi.org/10.1145/2556288.2557342

11. Dunne, A., Raby, F.: Speculative Everything: Design, Fiction, and Social Dreaming. The MIT Press (2013)
12. Fallman, D.: Why research-oriented design isn't design-oriented research: on the tensions between design and research in an implicit design discipline. Knowl. Technol. Policy **20**(3), 193–200 (2007). https://doi.org/10.1007/s12130-007-9022-8
13. Frauenberger, C.: Entanglement HCI the next wave? ACM Trans. Comput. Hum. Interact. **27**(1), 1–27 (2019). https://doi.org/10.1145/3364998
14. Gaver, W.: What should we expect from research through design? In: Proceedings of the SIGCHI Conference on Human Factors in Computing Systems (CHI 2012), pp. 937–946 (2012). https://doi.org/10.1145/2207676.2208538
15. Gaver, W., Bowers, J.: Annotated portfolios. Interactions **19**(4), 40–49 (2012). https://doi.org/10.1145/2212877.2212889
16. Giaccardi, E., Stappers, P.J.: Research through design. In: Chapter 43: The Encyclopedia of Human-Computer Interaction, 2nd ed. Interaction Design Foundation (2017)
17. Gushima, K., Nakajima, T.: Virtual fieldwork: designing augmented reality applications using virtual reality worlds. In: Chen, J.Y.C., Fragomeni, G. (eds.) HCII 2021. LNCS, vol. 12770, pp. 417–430. Springer, Cham (2021). https://doi.org/10.1007/978-3-030-77599-5_29
18. Hassenzahl, M.: User Experience and Experience Design, In the Encyclopedia of Human-Computer Interaction. The Interaction Design Foundation (2013)
19. Hauser, S., Oogjes, D., Wakkary, R., Verbeek, P.-P.: An annotated portfolio on doing postphenomenology through research products. In: Proceedings of the 2018 Designing Interactive Systems Conference (DIS 2018), pp. 459–471 Association for Computing Machinery, New York, NY, USA (2018). https://doi.org/10.1145/3196709.3196745
20. Höök, K., Löwgren, J.: Strong concepts: intermediate-level knowledge in interaction design research. ACM Trans. Comput. Hum. Interact. **19**(3), 1–18 (2012). https://doi.org/10.1145/2362364.2362371
21. Höök, K., et al.: Knowledge production in interaction design. In: Proceedings of the 33rd Annual ACM Conference Extended Abstracts on Human Factors in Computing Systems (CHI EA 2015), pp. 2429–2432. Association for Computing Machinery, New York, NY, USA (2015). https://doi.org/10.1145/2702613.2702653
22. Kimura, R., Nakajima, T.: Opportunities to share collective human hearing. In: Proceedings of the 11th Nordic Conference on Human–Computer Interaction: Shaping Experiences, Shaping Society (NordiCHI 2020), 4 p., October 25–29, 2020, Tallinn, Estonia. ACM, New York, NY, USA (2020). https://doi.org/10.1145/3419249.3421244
23. Kimura, R., Nakajima, T.: Collectively sharing people's visual and auditory capabilities: exploring opportunities and pitfalls. SN Comput. Sci. **1**(5), 1–24 (2020). https://doi.org/10.1007/s42979-020-00313-w
24. Kimura, R., Nakajima, T.: CollectiveEars: sharing collective people's hearing capability, In: Proceedings of the 23rd International Conference on Information Integration and Web-based Applications & Services (iiWAS2021) (2021)
25. Kimura, R., Nakajima, T.: Ambiently presenting multiple perspectives on a human visual perspective. In: Proceedings of the 13th International Symposium on Ambient Intelligence (2021)
26. Kimura, R., Nakajima, T.: Virtualizing human conversation: two case studies. In: Proceedings of the IEEE 10th Global Conference on Consumer Electronics (GCCE) (2021)
27. Kimura, R., Nakajima, T.: Case studies to enhance collectively sharing human hearing: ambient sounds memory and mindful speaker. In: Proceedings of the 10th International Conference on Distributed, Ambient and Pervasive Interactions (DAPI 2022)
28. Koskinen, I., Zimmerman, J., Binder, T., Redström, J., Wensveen, S.: Design Research Through Practice: From the Lab, Field, and Showroom. Morgan Kaufmann (2012)

29. Lim, Y.-K., Stolterman, E., Tenenberg, J.: The anatomy of prototypes: prototypes as filters, prototypes as manifestations of design ideas. ACM Trans. Comput. Hum. Interact. **15**(2), 1–27 (2008). https://doi.org/10.1145/1375761.1375762
30. Lindtner, S., Hertz, G.D., Dourish, P.: Emerging sites of HCI innovation: hackerspaces, hardware startups & incubators. In: Proceedings of the SIGCHI Conference on Human Factors in Computing Systems (CHI 2014), pp. 439–448 (2014). https://doi.org/10.1145/2556288.2557132
31. Löwgren, J.: Annotated portfolios and other forms of intermediate-level knowledge. Interactions **20**(1), 30–34 (2013). https://doi.org/10.1145/2405716.2405725
32. Madan, A., Kumar, S.: Usability evaluation methods: a literature review. Int. J. Eng. Sci. Technol. **4**(2) (2012)
33. Manzini, E., Coad, R.: Design, When Everybody Designs: An Introduction to Design for Social Innovation. The MIT Press (2015). https://doi.org/10.7551/mitpress/9873.001.0001
34. Marita, S., Conny, B., Ruud, B.: Annotated portfolios as a method to analyze interview. In: Proceedings of Design Research Society 2018, pp. 1148–1158 (2018)
35. McCurdy, M., Connors, C., Pyrzak, G., Kanefsky, B., Vera, A.: Breaking the fidelity barrier: an examination of our current characterization of prototypes and an example of a mixed-fidelity success. In: Proceedings of the SIGCHI Conference on Human Factors in Computing Systems (CHI 2006), pp. 1233–1242. Association for Computing Machinery, New York, NY, USA (2006). https://doi.org/10.1145/1124772.1124959
36. Mitrović, I., Golub, M., Šuran, O.: Design Fiction: Eutropia – Introduction to Speculative Design Practice, HDD & DVK UMAS, Zagreb/Split (2015)
37. Nakajima, T., Lehdonvirta, V.: Designing motivation using persuasive ambient mirrors. Pers. Ubiquit. Comput. **17**(1), 107–126 (2013). https://doi.org/10.1007/s00779-011-0469-y
38. Nam, T-J., Lee., W.: Integrating hardware and software: augmented reality based prototyping method for digital products. In: CHI 2003 Extended Abstracts on Human Factors in Computing Systems (CHI EA 2003), pp. 956–957. Association for Computing Machinery, New York, NY, USA (2003). https://doi.org/10.1145/765891.766092
39. Norman, D.: The Design of Everyday Things, Newsprint (2002)
40. Odom, W., Zimmerman, J., Davidoff, S., Forlizzi, J., Dey, A.K., Lee, M.K.: A fieldwork of the future with user enactments. In: Proceedings of the Designing Interactive Systems Conference (DIS 2012), pp. 338–347 (2012). https://doi.org/10.1145/2317956.2318008
41. Orlikowski, W.J., Yates, J., Okamura, K., Fujimoto, M.: Shaping electronic communication: the metastructuring of technology in the context of use. Org. Sci. **6**(4), 423–444 (1995)
42. Orlikowski, W.J., Scott, S.V.: Exploring material-discursive practices. J. Manage. Stud. **52**(5), 697–705 (2015)
43. Pierce, J.: On the presentation and production of design research artifacts in HCI. In: Proceedings of the 2014 Conference on Designing Interactive Systems (DIS 2014), pp.735–744 (2014). https://doi.org/10.1145/2598510.2598525
44. Redström, J.: Making Design Theory. The MIT Press, Cambridge, MA (2017)
45. Stolterman, E., Wiberg, M.: Concept driven interaction design research. Hum. Comput. Interact. **25**(2), 95–118 (2010). https://doi.org/10.1080/07370020903586696
46. Snyder, C.: Paper Prototyping: The Fast and Easy Way to Design and Refine User Interfaces. Morgan Kaufmann, Elsevier Science, San Francisco, CA (2003)
47. Tharp, B.M., Tharp, S.M.: Discursive Design: Critical, Speculative, and Alternative Things. The MIT Press (2019)
48. Zimmerman, J., Forlizzi, J.: Research through design in HCI. In: Olson, J.S., Kellogg, W.A. (eds.) Ways of Knowing in HCI, pp. 167–189. Springer, New York (2014). https://doi.org/10.1007/978-1-4939-0378-8_8

Opening up Smart Learning Cities - Building Knowledge, Interactions and Communities for Lifelong Learning and Urban Belonging

Pen Lister(✉) ⓘD

University of Malta, Msida 2080, MSD, Malta
pen.lister@penworks.net

Abstract. This paper revisits issues arising from prior research carried out by the author examining citizen informal learning through interactions with the real world via augmented reality interfaces triggering place based knowledge. Topics discussed in this paper were not part of the research yet deserve further discussion in that context. Two areas are of particular interest: place based digital knowledge content delivery and user generated content related to place. In other words, how users might freely and easily access knowledge content that relates to features and places they pass through or live in, and how they might digitally interact with their local environment to contribute to a community of memory associated with place [29, 30, 39]. This compiling of the knowledge archive of place, both expert and citizen generated, might be described as the reading and writing of the city, somewhat like [26] or [19], reflecting ideas going back to the Berkeley Community Memory bulletin-boards of the 1970s [7]. Discussion includes the concept of community mapping, briefly examining examples from literature and a prototype, the 'Learner Feedback Map', developed by the author but not used in the final research. The challenges of finding and delivering knowledge content, and of uploading and hosting user-generated content are briefly considered in the context of decentralised networks and the Fediverse.

Keywords: Fediverse · OER · Linked Open Data · Community Mapping · UGC · User-Generated Content

1 Introduction

This paper has been written as a deeper critical reflection on recent research concerning citizen informal learning through interactions with the real world via augmented reality interfaces triggering place based knowledge. Noting issues that were raised during the research deserving further discussion and investigation, two areas of perhaps most significance are discussed, of access to and generation of knowledge related content. These issues were not directly part of the research, but were noted as a consequence of it. In the context of this introduction, it is important to state that the research did not benefit from external funding sources and therefore selected to make use of free smartphone apps and digital platforms that were currently available at the time to support the

N. A. Streitz and S. Konomi (Eds.): HCII 2023, LNCS 14037, pp. 67–85, 2023.
https://doi.org/10.1007/978-3-031-34609-5_5

technological aspects of the activities and interactions being investigated. This meant that the researched learning experiences represented what might be achieved by anyone facilitating such activities in real-world scenarios who had low or no funding. In the view of this author (the researcher) this is important, as it took an approach of authentic research of this kind, of real-world augmented reality activity design and implementation without extra funding or bespoke mobile apps, and the challenges that this approach subsequently highlighted.

A brief summary of the research is provided to facilitate the context of discussion, and to support the reader in understanding what happens when a user accesses or creates knowledge about a location or object in a (usually urban) place. What users think, feel or want to say or do during that process impacts areas of discussion in terms of how expert knowledge might be further explored by users, either on locale or beyond, and of methods for capturing user contributions to place based knowledge in an archive of community memory. This engagement and interaction reflects what is referred to here as the 'reading and writing of the city' that forms the core cultural basis of an urban environment [26].

1.1 Accessing and Creating Knowledge

Discussion is comprised of two related areas: how users access knowledge, either via digitally augmented reality triggering or other geo-coded methods of smarter content delivery, and how users generate knowledge that might be added to community archives, to then potentially (ideally) be maintained as urban collective knowledge memory, e.g. [52]. These two areas are related by means of how knowledge is defined, accessed and delivered, of the ownership of that (digitised) knowledge, and of the intertwined relationship between expert and community generated knowledge. We might describe this relationship as the reading and writing of the smart city, somewhat after [26] or [19].

Practical and technical considerations are part of the debate of this paper, within the two areas of concern. Provision for enabling user generated content (UGC) focuses on community knowledge mapping, an initiative that has seen consistent uptake and implementation for a number of years, further discussed below and later. For more streamlined and effective delivery of knowledge, focus is placed in a number of related debates. Smarter delivery and findability [15, 41]; discourses around quality and purpose of effective metadata and the role of Linked Open Data, e.g. [6, 15, 52], and the potential of the ActivityPub[1] protocol to share knowledge efficiently in a civic federated archive [11, 13, 48].

To further reflect on mechanisms by which users may contribute their own memories, knowledge, experiences and media content, the paper discusses the concept of the user feedback map. Several examples from past initiatives found in the literature are provided that demonstrate how users have contributed to knowledge banks of a local area through creation of local community maps of places, features or events added by user citizens who live or work there (Mapping for Change Community Maps[2], MapLocal[3], Culture

---

[1] https://activitypub.rocks/

[2] https://mappingforchange.org.uk;   e.g.   https://communitymaps.org.uk/project/archway?center=51.5657:-0.1337:14

[3] https://chrisspeed.net/?p=1303

Map Malta[4], and many others[5]). These initiatives have much in common, utilising simple digital functionality (usually a website and a Google or Open Maps feature) that permit anyone with an Internet connection to contribute their own information and content. As part of the authors own research, a 'Learner Feedback Map' was developed as a prototype to show the feasibility of a simple web form user interface with interaction functionality to upload geocoded content for building knowledge maps of user generated contributions viewable to others.

2   Context of Prior Research

The prior research that forms the basis for the topics of debate in this paper concerned citizen informal learning in real-world locations using augmented reality (AR) triggering that provided multimedia content and optional tasks. Two urban locations were used to situate these AR based activities, London UK and Valletta, Malta, each being designed as a 'smart learning journey' comprised of several related locations along a route that could be undertaken as a whole (of walk-able distance) or as stand alone points of interest. Each featured location had an AR trigger using image recognition, which on being triggered offered the user an interface of icons linking to various content choices - videos, images or written content in webpages. Some location trigger points also offered suggested tasks in the form of question prompts, to provide ideas for how to engage in the given location. The HP Reveal free smartphone app (formerly known as Aurasma) was used to facilitate these AR triggers, with the interface being designed and built using the HP Reveal Studio web application. The interface of content choices was very similar for both journey activities, though the journeys themselves had different themes: creative writing and English literature heritage (London), and Maltese democracy (Valletta). Participants were drawn from various undergraduate and postgraduate students cohorts, and took part voluntarily. Figure 1 (left) shows the London UK medieval St Olave's church noticeboard augmented by the icon interface triggers and (right) shows the Valletta Malta Parliament Building entrance with its augmented reality interface being triggered through the HP Reveal camera image recognition.

The project itself was investigating development of pedagogical concepts arising from participant experience using the methodology of phenomenography, which examines the focal awareness and derived meaning for a user [34]. However, other issues were apparent in the transcripts that merit further discussion outside of the phenomenographic research approach, or of any potential pedagogical design considerations. These are the later observations made by the researcher when reflecting on the transcript themes, and relate to technological and digital content related aspects. The two related areas nominated at the beginning of this paper - accessing and creating knowledge content - involve both technological and practical considerations. Key technical problems are effectiveness of metadata and content delivery mechanisms, ownership of data and content, and

---

[4] Now defunct, however available via the Internet Archive Wayback Machine, e.g.: https://web. archive.org/web/20161203012651/https://www.culturemapmalta.com/ or https://web.archive. org/web/20180920013724/https://www.culturemapmalta.com/

[5] Oxford Bibliographies for Community Mapping https://doi.org/10.1093/OBO/978019987 4002-0184 & Cultural Mapping https://doi.org/10.1093/OBO/9780199756841-0249

Fig. 1. (L) London UK St Olave's noticeboard with AR icon interface; (R) Valletta Malta Parliament Building entrance viewed through HP Reveal camera triggering the AR interface

intellectual property concerns. Key practical issues are provision for users to upload and share content, and how preservation of this archive of citizen memory of place might be achieved. To glimpse what citizens experience in terms of accessing and creating knowledge content, we can reflect on what participants in the research said. Table 1 includes interview transcript extracts talking about provided content and making choices about that content. Table 2 includes transcript extracts talking about creating and uploading multimedia content in various contexts.

Table 1. Showing actions and contexts of consuming provided knowledge content

Summary of interest	Quote	Pn
Information provision: useful/ too much; Discussing is useful *Googling* is useful	"… it's nice to be able to use your smart phone … in terms of the information itself … because there was so many links for each kind of sort that we eventually stopped looking at the information… and then kind of just discussing the places ourselves or even Googling things ourselves because we found that was a little bit easier for us to do …"	P1

(continued)

Table 1. (*continued*)

Summary of interest	Quote	Pn
What is memorable about place is the knowledge associated with it	" ... *I think initially you're approaching place but then what kind of seems to stick (is) what author was attributed to that place. So for example ... there is the Charles Dickens right next to the George and Vulture, ... it seems to be the kind of literary figure that resonates after having seen a place...*"	P4
Googling own information may be more important than providing any	" ...*We walk around (and) use the app where you move your phone over it and it gives you information. It's kinda like I can get that information if I just Google it and searched a few things couldn't I?*"	P6
Provided content about place: more real, engaging, relating to creating own content, making content choices	"... *if we look at the monument, a video for example of the great siege, it would've been more interactive, real, you're seeing it, it's relevant... you're not seeing it as a waste of time ...*" "... *you're just going to have bits and pieces there distributed according to where you are ... some videos for you to see and maybe watch them later but at the moment ... you're being engaged into seeing what you have to do, take pictures and do the task at that time ...*"	P7

Table 2. Showing experiences of creating and uploading own content

Summary of interest	Quote	Pn
Contributing content that is more personal, perhaps more original	*I wanted to try and contribute something personal... something bit more individual, for the sake of sharing and learning, I would personally prefer to see ten different poses in front of a statue or ten different corners of the building rather than ten very similar photos of the front face of the building just because its more interesting to look at ...*"	P21

(*continued*)

Table 2. (*continued*)

Summary of interest	Quote	Pn
Problems with uploading video content Interest in the cultural mix of the present day location	*"... I did try to take some videos of like the first one at the gate and there was like a musician playing it was kind of cool like Bob Dylan-esque music, and there was like a group of Chinese tourists and like the big screen like the big gate so it was kind of like lovely mix but I couldn't get my video to upload..."*	P22
Observations about socio-temporality contrasting ideas and habits of the 'exact' location through time	*"... cos there was like, like this video of like a chariot (horse drawn carriage) going by, and then in real life we're taking a video of ... this guy playing guitar, and singing. And ... people walking through, and baby strollers, and stuff, so its just like that picture and like the video that we took are, like what we are really seeing are very different but its ... the same exact place you know, its been there for hundreds of years and I love that. ..."*	P23

These short excerpt examples from participant transcripts provide various perspectives about interactions with content - amount and choice; ability to 'Google' search; evocation of deeper reflections about the socio-temporality of the city; evocation of cultural knowledge related to place forming deeper place-based memory attribution; situated content being 'real' and adding engagement value, and so on. These pose the issues that are the basis for the discussion in this paper.

3　Reading and Writing the City

Reading and writing the city is a way of describing the process by which citizens read and contribute knowledge content related to urban places. For example, reading expert science, literature, art or cultural heritage, and then contributing to a community archive of citizen memoir and lived experience about those places (to also be able to read what others say).

Discussion here is scoped in terms of UGC that includes casual social media comments and content sharing to more complex creative work, for example photography, street art or situated creative writing such as poetry or story telling via digital means (e.g. ambient literature, [49]). UGC is considered as contributions to community content archives that build the city as digital/real-world memory in parallel to the expert knowledge attached digitally to place by geocoding and accessed via smart technologies. The methods by which expert knowledge content might be provided or sourced (discovered) by users, and how they might add to their community archive are part of considerations. Discussion is positioned in the context of the open, interactive city [38], and a "frictionless learning environment ... (of) ... space, time, resources and community interaction" for individual or group learning needs [40]. This means open data, the open knowledge commons, and the increasing relevance of this being hosted on open distributed networks, sometimes referred to as the Fediverse[6].

3.1 Finding and Delivering Expert Knowledge

Considerable research exists relating to methods by which information can be delivered in smarter ways, e.g. [15, 53]. I have previously argued that the knowledge commons[7] might make use of simple metadata properties from the Open Graph[8] [35], with perhaps only one or two additional useful pedagogical properties being added to those already existing, similar to [1]. This topic can be contentious amongst researchers, with different groups researching different methods, chief among these and potentially most popular with educators are the Open Educational Resources Schema[9], based on Google Schema[10] or the Learning Resource Metadata Initiative[11], based on the Dublin Core[12] metadata system. The key challenge with these or other systems are that they are only partially interoperable, and are often not actually used by those who publish knowledge content [44]. This remains an on-going issue for those who aim to connect the Internet of Things (IoT) and place to the connected knowledge seeker, with no end in sight. Hillerbrand [20] summarises this with: "(t)hese wild debates occur primarily within the technical community. The result is an echo-chamber debate that bears little connection to the nontechnical problems faced by businesses, especially consumer-facing businesses" (2016, p. 214). Replace 'businesses' and 'consumer facing business' with 'educators and 'citizen-facing educators' or similar, and the issue is the same.

More and Better Metadata. Current work highlighted here focuses on increasing interest in the literature on metadata for open knowledge and open educational resources, as well as noting an increase in training academic or information science staff to understand and implement metadata, e.g. [27]. Practical examples are seen in staff portal support pages at Macquarie University, Australia[13], or Imperial College, London, UK[14], showing the need to add good search and social metadata, using Dublin Core, Open Graph or Twitter Cards. This would have been highly unusual even only a few years ago. The conversation amongst practitioners themselves therefore (not just technologists) has turned

---

[6] https://axbom.com/fediverse/

[7] Knowledge Commons definition: https://en.wikipedia.org/wiki/Knowledge_commons

[8] The Open Graph protocol https://ogp.me

[9] Open Educational Resources Schema http://oerschema.org/docs/

[10] Schema.org http://schema.org/docs/about.html

[11] LRMI https://www.dublincore.org/specifications/lrmi/lrmi_1/

[12] Dublin Core https://www.dublincore.org/

[13] https://staff.mq.edu.au/support/marketing-and-communications/website-guides-and-resources/squiz-newsletter/news/news/how-to-write-good-metadata

[14] https://www.imperial.ac.uk/staff/tools-and-reference/web-guide/t4-site-manager/content-types/social-metadata/

toward metadata, perhaps regarded as the best solution for content management and find-ability [17, 27, 46]. Contexts range between cultural heritage, tourism, open educational resources and others, with varying approaches to utilising smarter technologies and IoT infrastructure for better providing knowledge content to smartphone or desktop, just-in-time queries [21, 27, 51]. How we resolve the issue of a more fluid and standardised connectivity between knowledge, experts and citizens remains a significant challenge [37, 48].

Multiple issues arise in the searching and retrieving of content, both in access and selection choices and in the connected relationships of searchable databases, or the possibility of search serendipity [16, 31]. In the case of the urban real-world just-in-time Google searching described by P1 (Table 1), serendipity may be relevant when P1 says it was 'easier' to 'just Google things' than go through the provided content choices. Perhaps the act of discovering content is as much part of interaction and engagement reward as the quality of the content itself. Not defining search results or provided content too rigidly might foster new ideas, though this can also be a problem of too little information to make informed choices. For example, Google Lens[15] smart search results remain simplistic and lack means by which a user can determine what is relevant to them at that time. As I have argued elsewhere [33, 35], perhaps a more streamlined connectivity to Google Lens via configurable (ideally open) API[16], with refined displays of results may be the way to integrate both expert or user-generated geospatially related knowledge in any connected urban environment.

The Role(s) of UGC in Metadata. User generated content can form a valuable and engaging aspect of cultural knowledge and experience in public spaces [42], and additionally UGC content or metadata may be used to establish further information about user-participant experience of events or places [14, 18]. While UGC offers usefulness for other users and for civic event organisers or similar, some potential problems arise when UGC forms part of re-usable knowledge repositories. Issues such as copyrighted content that may form all or part of a UGC upload [28] or maintaining the integrity of UGC within a more formal information management system delivery [23] are two examples.

4   Community Archives

If we are to foster inclusive smart cities that are truly built around the people who live in them (past, present and future) then we must consider how to effectively capture the meaning and lived experience of those lives. Citizen experiences may be formed as part of interactions with expert knowledge, or consist of more informal experiences of everyday life, and together they form an archive separate from any expert knowledge, arguably distinct from any social media platform or proprietary technological implementation (and subsequent ownership by private enterprise). These are the urban archives of citizens, the memory of the city [2, 19, 36, 47] and need to be preserved for posterity, as the city is the physical embodiment of the history of the people who live in it ([9] in [26]). Two

---

[15] https://lens.google/
[16] https://en.wikipedia.org/wiki/API

issues are therefore pertinent: how users upload to the civic archive, and who owns the archive and the data within it. These issues are discussed in following sections.

4.1 Community Mapping

Community mapping is interpreted here as the ability and affordance for communities to map points of interest in their local area and add textual or rich media content for others to find. This can be for a wide range of purposes, for example events, facilities, work opportunities, arts and creativity, conservation or urban planning feedback could all be part of a mapped network of citizen activity and daily life. Cultural mapping is defined in Oxford Bibliographies [12] as:

> *"Cultural mapping ... aims to make visible the ways local stories, practices, rela-tionships, memories, and rituals constitute places as meaningful locations ... cultural mapping has generally evolved along two main branches: The first begins with cultural assets, seeking to identify and document tangible and intangible assets of a place to ultimately develop a cultural resource or asset mapping. The second branch begins with a culturally sensitive humanistic approach, seeking to articulate a "sense of place," people-place meanings, and distinctive elements..."*

Community mapping merits it's own page in the Oxford Bibliographies record [43], and offers the following definition:

> *"Community mapping is best characterized as a collaborative mapping exercise, in which local voices are articulated, as against standardized modes of mapping, which have historically frequently reflected more top-down or expert forms of knowledge. As such it is in theory participatory, inclusive, and appropriate to local needs, interests, and goals."*

Community maps can sometimes be more overtly political, known as 'counter-mapping' (e.g. [10]), where local communities may challenge an 'official' map of an area by creating their own alternative version for political or citizen activism purposes. I would suggest that the difference between community and counter-mapping can be a moot point, depending on the purpose of any community mapping project. Community or cultural mapping has been a popular method by which citizens are empowered to create a record of their own locality, and has 'a long trajectory' [43], with plentiful literature documenting initiatives of this kind. Next, three examples of community mapping are highlighted for purposes of bringing to life what community mapping is and why it might be used within contexts similar to the research informing this paper.

MapLocal (Speed, 2013) was an Android smartphone app developed as part of a research project 'Localism and Connected Community Planning', to 'unlock the creativity of communities by gathering materials to inform neighbourhood planning'. While a MapLocal webpage exists[17], as well as the original project guide [25] and academic publication [24], the content and the app are defunct, and no longer able to be seen or contribute to further initiatives or knowledge banks in the area. The University College

---

[17] See footnote 3.

London Mapping For Change[18] project worked with "groups and organisations who want to understand, improve and produce information about the places that matter to them" (from their website), with UK based initiatives mainly in the London area. Their Community Maps are grouped into themes of Sustainability, Health and Wellbeing, People and Society and Planning and Urban Design, with various local mapping projects listed in each. Most projects appear to be seven or eight years old, and it is difficult to establish whether they are still used, though maps are intact and fully interactive. The Culture Map Malta project was somewhat similar to Mapping for Change, though was part of the Valletta European City of Culture 2018 events and activities and therefore had a different purpose. With an emphasis on civic heritage, it documented historic and community places of interest in the Valletta and beyond in Malta. Using similar web-based technology to Mapping for Change, citizens were invited to add their contributions so that visitors to the city might find places of interest when they came for a holiday or as part of a cultural event. Sadly this project is now completely defunct, and can only be found via the Internet Wayback machine[19]. All three examples demonstrate the value and usefulness of community mapping and the range of purposes for which it can be adapted, as well as the unfortunate fact that none of the knowledge content survives either at all or in any usable format. Arguably, these projects would benefit from being included in established civic digital archives and retained for posterity as records of community, content and life being lived at that time in those places.

The Learner Feedback Map, a practical example of a community user-feedback map developed by the author is described in the following section, and highlights the challenges and reasons for subsequent abandonment of this tool as part of the technological solutions used in the research informing this paper.

4.2 The 'Learner Feedback Map'

The practical example of a user-learner feedback map described in this section was developed by the author as a simple and workable solution to the issue of how participant learners might be able to upload comments, photos or videos pinned to a specific location by using an online form. This would have solved the issues that P22 describes, provided in transcript excerpt Table 2.

Technology used was a combination of 'off-the-shelf' readily available apps and services, additionally utilising open source JavaScript libraries, Google Sheets scripts and free web services. These are listed in Table 3 with short commentary about each.

A learner feedback map was created for both smart learning journey activities being investigated and it worked very well in testing scenarios, with the maps displaying user feedback in an accurate, appealing and interactive way. Maps were demonstrated to other academics, some asking which app I had used to make it as they wished to make one too. I displayed the code and the technology chain listed in Table 3, and explained that there was no single 'app', there was only web developer technology and ad-hoc solutions. Indeed, I had tested other apps that might achieve what was needed,

---

[18] https://mappingforchange.org.uk/

[19] Culture Map Malta in 2018 https://web.archive.org/web/20180614133520https://www.cultur emapmalta.com/

Table 3. Technologies used to build the Learner Feedback Map

Technology	Short Description	Further comments
Jotform	Free online form service that included location finder	*Jotform[20] offered functions that at the time were not available elsewhere: upload video, audio, record video, GPS location co-ords submission. Easy to implement, choice of internal hosting or exporting data submissions*
Google Sheets	Using Google drive hosted data from Jotform responses	*University of Malta Google Drive was a more secure option to host data (research ethics/privacy); also running Google sheet scripts to configure co-ords data output*
Zapier	A connectivity actions service similar to 'If This Then That'	*Zapier[21] is a versatile connective functions platform, connecting one online service with another, with particular actions executed on specified event. Used to add Jotform submissions to Gsheet rows. Also used to publish to social media (Facebook or Twitter) when form events executed*
Sheetsee.js	A JavaScript library allowing Gsheets information to be visualised on a map	*Sheetsee was an Open Source JavaScript library authored by Jessica Lord[22] that visualises data from Google Sheets into html tables, diagrams or maps. Functioning in updated version until 2021, defunct as of 2022 due to Tabletop.js dependency no longer supported by Google. Needs geo-coordinates delivered in specific way, connects to Google Sheets via G-sheet key*
JSON/CSS	Code that permits visual styling of data	*JSON/CSS configuration permits design flexibility for displaying data cards on map pins in webpages. I displayed journey name, text comments and uploaded image in each map pin card. Username was not displayed*
OpenStreetMap	Mapping	*OpenStreetMap[23] is open source mapping that can be customised using tiles. Sheetsee.js had its own tile set but this could be configured if further desired*
WordPress website	Webpage to host & display the interactive maps	*The final link in the chain was displaying the Learner Feedback Map, I used a self-hosted WordPress website at smartlearning.netfarms.eu[24] to do this*

---

[20] https://www.jotform.com/

[21] https://zapier.com/

[22] jlord Github https://github.com/jlord

[23] https://www.openstreetmap.org/

[24] http://smartlearning.netfarms.eu/scl-learner-feedback-map/ (archived).

especially alert apps (ThunderMaps[25], which would have been costly for multiple user accounts) or older location-based learning apps (7Scenes[26], which was rather limited visually, though had excellent journey planner designs). These or other apps were not suitable for what I needed, which was to permit participants of the researched smart learning journey activities a way to easily upload their own contributions to the journeys themselves, attached to a geocoded pin. These could then create activity feedback maps of user experience to be accessed by others and developed over time. Figure 2 (left) shows the Malta Learner Feedback Map, with an example of a possible tourism training activity and photo of the Auberge de Castille, Office of the Prime Minister, and (right) shows the London Learner Feedback Map, with comments about the Literary London journey activity and including a screen capture of the HP Reveal activity channel.

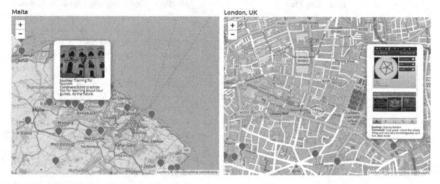

Fig. 2. (L) the Malta Learner Feedback Map, with example of tourism training activity; (R) the London Learner Feedback Map, showing the Literary London journey activity with screen capture of HP Reveal activity channel

I took the decision to not use the feedback maps in the live research because of script conflict with other apps, and the reliability of the technologies due to multiple dependencies and related risk. The form worked well in a stand-alone capacity but when embedded in the HP Reveal app browser window the location submission would not work, encountering JavaScript conflicts. This was frustrating, as otherwise it would have worked nicely. I could have shared the form via other means, but felt I was overloading participants with too many apps. Soon after, the scripts used to visualise the data into maps became obsolete (both Sheetsee.js configuration and then the Tabletop.js library itself). The data from tests is intact, but not publicly viewable. The risks of using proprietary apps or script libraries are commonplace, as these might (quickly, or unpredictably) become dysfunctional or obsolete. This has happened to ThunderMaps, 7Scenes and HP Reveal itself, as well as to the Edmodo mobile learning app [22] that was also used in the project. This highlights in stark practical terms the challenges for low or no cost smart city activities, where citizens themselves are creating engaging initiatives using the technology they find around them, only for that technology to break or suddenly be withdrawn, and all UGC is lost.

---

[25] https://web.archive.org/web/20160125154905/https://learn.thundermaps.com/
[26] https://web.archive.org/web/20160311151804/http://7scenes.com/

5 The Decentralised Future of the Knowledge Web

Within the scope of discussion in this paper, there are two 'halves' to the problem of hosting and delivery of digital knowledge content to users as and when they require it in urban connected environments. Expert knowledge has a range of problems perhaps mainly relating to intellectual property licensing and subsequent ease of access, reuse and sharing by the public. User knowledge content has its own problems relating to uploading, hosting and subsequent access and delivery. The debate in this section refers both to the digital infrastructure of efficient knowledge content delivery (expert or UGC), and to the ownership of the servers and apps in which that data sits, the latter issue being perhaps more significant than is initially apparent.

Increasingly, debate in academic circles and elsewhere within digital development communities has turned towards the future of Internet platforms and services, particularly in light of the risks of proprietary ownership of data [32, 48] as well as the extractive nature of 'informational capitalism' [48]. This debate is complex and this paper can only provide some overview of the possible solutions being discussed that may support free access to expert knowledge delivery and how to potentially capture and store UGC in publicly owned civic archives. Current debates have progressed from the Internet of Things Linked Open Data (LOD)/Linked Open Services concepts [15] towards divergent ideas that encompass LOD, interoperable metadata and embracing the promise of decentralised (federated) networks. This challenges the centralised dependency on (usually) private monopoly platforms, e.g. [48, 50] and the walled gardens of non-reliable, non-portable content and communication they create [4, 32]. Conversely, the decentralised server model of microblogging communication app Mastodon, and the ActivityPub protocol demonstrate potential for a federated universe of agnostic data sharing and notifications across apps, platforms and servers. This ad-hoc connected collection of servers and users of apps that communicate is generally known as 'the Fediverse[27]'. In a Mastodon[28] post, Idehen[29] (2023) provides a succinct and easy to understand explanation: "The Fediverse is a Federation of loosely coupled systems that perform CRUD[30] operations (ActivityStreams[31]) using a common protocol (ActivityPub[32])".

So, why is the Fediverse important to our discussion about smarter (more efficient, better) delivery and creation of knowledge content in the smart learning city? For user citizens of the smart learning city, this essentially means that provision of open content from experts residing in multiple source databases (e.g. Open Access published work, preprints or open educational resources) can then be shared and subsequently

---

[27] https://en.wikipedia.org/wiki/Fediverse

[28] https://joinmastodon.org/

[29] @kidahen@mastodon.social (thread: https://mastodon.social/@kidehen/109684267932110 804).

[30] CRUD is 'Create, read, update and delete'; https://en.wikipedia.org/wiki/Create,_read,_upd ate_and_delete

[31] https://en.wikipedia.org/wiki/Activity_Streams_(format).

[32] ActivityPub / Social Working Group https://www.w3.org/TR/activitypub/

backtracked[33] for where it is shared to, or accessed in an open landscape of apps and communities. These ActivityStream operations and ActivityPub protocols together can 'talk' with any federated server and user on it using any application that adopts the protocol. Two things are therefore accomplished, an open ownership culture, and a common communication method. Saunders [48] outlines a conceptual model envisaging a peer-to-peer led, sharing, decentralised network for open science, that we should design multiple protocols "with extensibility in mind" that are interoperable and added to as they become re-used and adapted. Going on to discuss instances (servers) within the federated universe that "… are hosted independently and can choose to federate with other instances to enable communication between them" (2022, p. 94). Further suggesting we "decouple interfaces from the underlying data so that we have a continuous communication (and) different interfaces are just views on the data" (p. 95) fits well with the concept of multiple ad-hoc low or no cost apps and 'smart enough' [3] functionality, e.g. geocode + image triggering, working with open protocols to see the same data through different interfaces that could be envisaged as a future of the smart enough smart learning city. Linked Data Notifications (LDN) [5] for knowledge availability or other information may be significant in delivery within smart urban (learning) content findability and access. Platform interoperable content sharing and semantic web techniques of pingback (see related prior mention of trackback) are configured into the LDN protocol, to support decentralisation, that is, "data and applications that are loosely coupled, and users are empowered to choose where their data is stored or held" [5, p. 539]. Amongst other technical specification discussion, Restful API[34] is acknowledged for its suitability to persistent notification support, resource organisation, discovery and description, and for 'CRUD' (create, read, update, and delete) operations (p. 541), somewhat as indicated earlier in [15].

Related intellectual property discussion in Saunders [48] regarding the problematic walled gardens of academic publishing models certainly imply that for expert knowledge to be openly accessible and easily deliverable on demand means it has to be open knowledge, open data, open access or open educational resources. If protocols were able to find relevantly tagged content from these sources there would be few other barriers to delivering it. Still relevant concerns about UGC and remixed copyrighted works [28] require intelligent metadata analysis, e.g. [17] to assist in moderating any copyright infringement from UGC remixed and shared works. This may indeed also be somewhat part of the related concerns for the role of the user and UGC to contribute to cultural archives, where studies such as the European project SPICE [8] researched methodologies for "producing, collecting, interpreting, and archiving people's responses to cultural objects, with the aim of favouring the emergence of multiple, sometimes conflicting viewpoints, and motivating the users and memory institutions to reflect upon them". This perhaps highlights not only the roles for user experience and user contribution to archived 'memory' content, but also perhaps the roles of those who moderate and curate such content [23]. It is clear from cursory examination of Facebook social media groups such as British

---

[33] I use this expression as it harks back to the common method that bloggers used to be notified of who was sharing their posts, where and in what context. (WordPress still offers this feature in their post admin interface).

[34] https://restfulapi.net/

Social History, Vintage News or (many) others that citizen memories and experience of place are not always associated with specific heritage or cultural features, but rather may be associated with places that seem quite arbitrary and indistinct, such as local bus stations, shops or office buildings. This is evident from multiple posts in those groups. Surely this citizen memory of place deserves some preserving for posterity beyond the 'memory institutions' referred to in [8] and might be better served to be held in publicly owned (federated) servers, that could be 'loosely connected' with any number of institutions and applications through open protocols such as ActivityPub, and Linked Data Notifications via open APIs.

The Risks of Proprietary Service and Repository Ownership. When proprietary platforms, apps and technologies are used and content is uploaded to those databases, the content and personal data of those author users (expert or citizen) is then owned by the private company. Proprietary ownership of knowledge, whether expert or user generated, becomes a disconnected set of walled gardens, where data (knowledge content) cannot be accessed unless a dedicated proprietary app or service is used. The knowledge content is therefore corralled into private collections, and risks not being accessible, personal data being utilised (or sold) for other non-agreed purposes, or content may be lost altogether due to private companies being sold, liquidating or otherwise closed down. As noted in the prior examples of community mapping and the specific case of the learner feedback map, if the technologies being utilised are withdrawn, the content itself does not usually survive.

6 Limitations of This Paper and Scope for Further Research

Discussion in this paper has endeavoured to provide a brief outline of some of the challenges and possible solutions for a truly open smart learning city - the frictionless environments of casual learning and cultural interactions described in [40]. This author has offered a layperson's interpretation of some of the technological issues at hand, placed in a context of how real people interact with their digitally connected world as either citizen users or facilitators of activities supporting urban culture and daily life. The scope of this paper invites further research into reading and writing the smart enough [3] city, perhaps using a variety of design approaches and participant users. Focus might be on smart digitally enhanced creative activities using ad-hoc apps and technological solutions to *discover, read and write the belonging of the city*. At time of writing, potential concepts and approaches perhaps based in multiple cities, countries and universities are being further investigated.

7 Conclusions

The accrued knowledge of the smart city, both derived from sciences or humanities experts as well as citizen communities has over time become a challenge for how to manage it, own it, maintain it and offer equitable access to it. But concepts of smart cities have become much more people orientated, and as Boy [3] argues, "(u)rban space is not just a container for social relations, but a product of social relations". How we achieve in practical terms a technologically infused urban connected environment without compromising the privacy and freedom of the individuals who live in it remains to be seen. Certainly, these issues are surfacing as high profile concerns; Tim Berners-Lee recently reiterating this growing problem [45].

The aim of this paper has been to acknowledge the interplay between citizen and place, for both expert knowledge and UGC. This author cannot claim knowledge beyond a general grasp of the technical implications involved, however has offered a layperson's overview of potential issues and possible solutions for an open knowledge web. Data and content needs to be decoupled from platforms and apps, thereby empowering users (expert and citizen) to move between platforms, viewing and sharing the same (open) data sources, and that archived content is owned and maintained in civic federated archives for the benefit of all.

References

1. Badita, F.: Changing the world of Publishing - Creating an Open Graph Standard. Medium (2016, November 28). https://medium.com/@baditaflorin/changing-the-world-of-publishing-creating-a-open-graph-standard-7fd3191038c6
2. Bergum, S.: This city is an archive: squatting history and urban authority. J. Urban Hist. **48**(3), 504–522 (2022). https://doi.org/10.1177/0096144220955165
3. Boy, J.: Smart Enough or Too Smart? Territorial Platforms, Social Reproduction, and the Limits to Digital Circuits of Dispossession. Limits 22, Eighth Workshop on Computing within Limits (2022). https://computingwithinlimits.org/2022/papers/limits22-final-Boy.pdf
4. Capadisli, S.: Linked Research on the Decentralised Web. Doctoral Dissertation. University of Bonn, Germany (2020). https://hdl.handle.net/20.500.11811/8352
5. Capadisli, S., Guy, A., Lange, C., Auer, S., Sambra, A., Berners-Lee, T.: Linked data notifications: a resource-centric communication protocol. In: Blomqvist, E., Maynard, D., Gangemi, A., Hoekstra, R., Hitzler, P., Hartig, O. (eds.) ESWC 2017. LNCS, vol. 10249, pp. 537–553. Springer, Cham (2017). https://doi.org/10.1007/978-3-319-58068-5_33
6. Carpenter, T.: Article Sharing Framework: Facilitating Scholarly Sharing Through Metadata. The Scholarly Kitchen, (2021, May 17). https://scholarlykitchen.sspnet.org/2021/05/17/stm-article-sharing-framework/
7. Carroll, J.M., et al.: The internet of places at community-scale: design scenarios for hyperlocal neighborhood. In: Konomi, S., Roussos, G. (eds.) Enriching Urban Spaces with Ambient Computing, the Internet of Things, and Smart City Design, pp. 1–24. IGI Global (2017). https://doi.org/10.4018/978-1-5225-0827-4.ch001
8. Daga, E., et al.: Integrating citizen experiences in cultural heritage archives: requirements, state of the art, and challenges. Journal on Computing and Cultural Heritage **15**(1), 1–35 (2022). https://doi.org/10.1145/3477599
9. de Certeau, M.: The Practice of Everyday Life. University of California Press (1984)
10. Dinler, M.: Counter-mapping through digital tools as an approach to urban history: investigating the spatial condition of activism. Sustainability **13**(16), 8904 (2021). https://doi.org/10.3390/su13168904
11. Dulong de Rosnay, M., Musiani, F.: Alternatives for the internet: a journey into decentralised network architectures and information commons. TripleC: Communication, Capitalism & Critique **18**(2), 622–629 (2020). https://shs.hal.science/halshs-02917474
12. Duxbury, N., Redaelli, E.: Cultural Mapping. Oxford Bibliographies (2020, August 26). https://doi.org/10.1093/OBO/9780199756841-0249

13. Findlay, C.: Participatory cultures, trust technologies and decentralisation: innovation opportunities for recordkeeping. Archives and Manuscripts **45**(3), 176–190 (2017). https://doi.org/10.1080/01576895.2017.1366864
14. Girardin, F., Blat, J., Calabrese, F., Dal Fiore, F., Ratti, C.: Digital footprinting: uncovering tourists with user-generated content. Pervasive Comput. **7**(4), 36–43 (2008)
15. Gyrard, A., Patel, P., Sheth, A.P., Serrano, M.: Building the web of knowledge with smart IoT applications. IEEE Intell. Syst. **31**(5), 83–88 (2016). https://corescholar.libraries.wright.edu/knoesis/1123
16. Haklay, M.: Beyond Quantification, We Need a Meaningful Smart City. Urban Pamphleteer. University College London, UK (2013). https://www.ucl.ac.uk/urban-lab/sites/urban-lab/files/UrbanPamphleteer1.pdf
17. Hart, L., Bardoli, J.: How automated content tagging improves Findability. Techtarget (2020, October 19). https://techtarget.com/searchcontentmanagement/tip/AI-in-content-management-supports-tagging-search
18. Hauthal, E., Burghardt, D.: Mapping space-related emotions out of user-generated photo metadata considering grammatical issues. Cartogr. J. **53**(1), 78–90 (2016). https://doi.org/10.1179/1743277414Y.0000000094
19. Hetherington, K.: Rhythm and noise: the city, memory and the archive. Sociol. Rev. **61**(1), 17–33 (2013). https://doi.org/10.1111/1467-954X.12051
20. Hillerbrand, E.: Semantic web and business: reaching a tipping point? In: Workman, M. (ed.) Semantic Web, pp. 213–229. Springer, Cham (2016). https://doi.org/10.1007/978-3-319-16658-2_11
21. Hu, X., Ng, J., Xia, S.: User-centered evaluation of metadata schema for non-movable cultural heritage: murals and stone cave temples. J. Am. Soc. Inf. Sci. **69**(12), 1476–1487 (2018). https://doi.org/10.1002/asi.24065
22. IBL News: Edmodo.com Will Shut Down Its Platform and Service on September 22. IBL News (2022, August 24). https://iblnews.org/edmodo-com-will-shut-its-platform-and-service-on-september-22/
23. Jansson, I.-M.: Organization of user-generated information in image collections and impact of rhetorical mechanisms. Knowl. Organ. **44**(7), 515–528 (2017). https://doi.org/10.5771/0943-7444-2017-7-515
24. Jones, P., Layard, A., Lorne, C., Speed, C.: Localism, neighbourhood planning and community control: the MapLocal pilot. In: O'Brien, D., Matthews, P. (eds.) After Urban Regeneration: Communities, Policy and Place, pp. 165–179. Policy Press, Bristol, UK (2015). http://oro.open.ac.uk/69275/1/Maplocal.pdf
25. Jones, P., Layard, A., Speed, C., Lorne, C.: MapLocal Project Guide (2013). https://chrisspeed.net/wp-content/uploads/2013/10/MapLocal-Small.pdf
26. Jordan, S.: Writing the smart city: "relational space" and the concept of "belonging". Writing in Practice: Journal of Creative Writing Research **1**(1) (2015). https://www.nawe.co.uk/DB/wip-editions/articles/writing-the-smart-city-relational-space-and-the-concept-of-belonging.html
27. Keck, H., Heck, T.: Improving tagging literacy to enhance metadata and retrieval for open educational resources. In: Proceedings of the Conference on Learning Information Literacy across the Globe, Frankfurt am Main, Germany (2019). https://doi.org/10.25657/02:17763
28. Kim, H., Breslin, J., Choi, J.H.: Semantic representation for copyright metadata of user-generated content in folksonomies. Online Inf. Rev. **34**(4), 626–641 (2010). https://doi.org/10.1108/14684521011073025
29. Kinsley, S.: Memory programmes: the industrial retention of collective life. Cultural Geographies **22**(1), 155–75 (2015). https://www.jstor.org/stable/26168631
30. Kitchin, R.: The timescape of smart cities. Ann. Am. Assoc. Geogr. **109**(3), 775–790 (2019). https://doi.org/10.1080/24694452.2018.1497475

31. Kop, R.: The unexpected connection: serendipity and human mediation in networked learning. Educ. Technol. Soc. **15**(2), 2–11 (2012). https://www.jstor.org/stable/jeductechsoci.15.2.2
32. Lelešius, G.: Improving Resilience of ActivityPub Services. Undergraduate Dissertation, Computer Science Tripos – Part II, University of Cambridge, UK (2022)
33. Lister, P.: Ways of experiencing technology in a smart learning environment. In: Streitz, N.A., Konomi, S. (eds.) Distributed, Ambient and Pervasive Interactions. Smart Living, Learning, Well-being and Health, Art and Creativity. HCII 2022. LNCS, vol. 13326. Springer, Cham (2022). https://doi.org/10.1007/978-3-031-05431-0_11
34. Lister, P.: The pedagogy of experience complexity for smart learning: considerations for designing urban digital citizen learning activities. Smart Learning Environ. **8**(1), 1–18 (2021). https://doi.org/10.1186/s40561-021-00154-x
35. Lister, P.J.: A smarter knowledge commons for smart learning. Smart Learning Environ. **5**(1), 1–15 (2018). https://doi.org/10.1186/s40561-018-0056-z
36. Lundemo, T.: Mapping the world: les archives de la planète and the mobilization of memory. In: Blom, I., Lundemo, T., Røssaak, E. (eds.) Memory in Motion Archives, Technology, and the Social. Amsterdam University Press (2017). https://doi.org/10.5117/9789462982147
37. Martin, P., Magagna, B., Liao, X., Zhao, Z.: Semantic linking of research infrastructure metadata. In: Zhao, Z., Hellström, M. (eds.) Towards Interoperable Research Infrastructures for Environmental and Earth Sciences. LNCS, vol. 12003, pp. 226–246. Springer, Cham (2020). https://doi.org/10.1007/978-3-030-52829-4_13
38. McKenna, H.: Rethinking learning in the smart city: innovating through involvement, inclusivity, and interactivities with emerging technologies. In: Gil-Garcia, JRamon, Pardo, T.A., Nam, T. (eds.) Smarter as the New Urban Agenda. PAIT, vol. 11, pp. 87–107. Springer, Cham (2016). https://doi.org/10.1007/978-3-319-17620-8_5
39. McKenna, H.P.: Human-smart environment interactions in smart cities: exploring dimensionalities of smartness. Future Internet **12**, 79 (2019). https://doi.org/10.3390/fi12050079
40. McKenna, H.P., Chauncey, S.: Taking learning to the city: an exploration of the frictionless learning environment innovation. In: Proceedings of EDULEARN14 Conference, Barcelona, Spain (2014)
41. Morville, P.: Ambient Findability. O'Reilly Media, USA (2005)
42. Palmer, J.M.: The resonances of public art: thoughts on the notion of co-productive acts and public art. Urban Public Art: Geographies of Co-Production: City & Society **30**(1), 68–88 (2018)
43. Perkins, C.: Community Mapping. Oxford Bibliographies (2018, February 22). https://doi.org/10.1093/OBO/9780199874002-0184
44. Pospelova, P.: Schema markup in university websites. Deleted Agency (2014, June 14). http://www.deleteagency.com/news/schema-markup-in-university-websites
45. Renjifo, D.: Inventor of the world wide web wants us to reclaim our data from tech giants. CNN (2023, January 6). https://edition.cnn.com/2022/12/16/tech/tim-berners-lee-inrupt-spc-intl/index.html
46. Řezník, T., et al.: Improving the documentation and findability of data services and repositories: a review of (meta) data management approaches. Comput. Geosci. **169**, 105194 (2022). https://doi.org/10.1016/j.cageo.2022.105194
47. Roberts, L.: Navigating the 'archive city': digital spatial humanities and archival film practice. Convergence: The International Journal of Research into New Media Technologies **21**(1), 100–115 (2015). https://doi.org/10.1177/1354856514560310
48. Saunders, J.L.: Decentralized Infrastructure for (Neuro) science (2022). arXiv preprint arXiv:2209.07493
49. Spencer, A.: What in the world is ambient literature? The Writing Platform (2017, Aug 10). http://thewritingplatform.com/2017/08/world-ambient-literature/

50. Srnicek, N.: Platform Capitalism. Polity, Malden, MA, USA & Cambridge UK (2017)
51. Tlili, A., et al.: Towards utilising emerging technologies to address the challenges of using open educational resources: a vision of the future. Educ. Technol. Res. Dev. **69**(2), 515–532 (2021). https://doi.org/10.1007/s11423-021-09993-4
52. Van Hooland, S., Méndez Rodríguez, E., Boydens, I.: Between commodification and engagement: on the double-edged impact of user-generated metadata within the cultural heritage sector. Libr. Trends **59**(4), 707–720 (2011). https://doi.org/10.1353/lib.2011.0011
53. Zouaq, A., Jovanović, J., Joksimović, S., Gašević, D.: Linked data for learning analytics: potentials and challenges. In: Lang, C., Siemens, G., Wise, A., Gašević, D. (eds.) Handbook of Learning Analytics, 1st edn., pp. 347–355. Society for Learning Analytics Research (SoLAR) (2017)

Weather Forecasting Limitations
in the Developing World

Jay Lofstead(✉)

Sandia National Laboratories, Albuquerque, NM 87185-1319, USA
gflofst@sandia.gov

Abstract. The first high performance computing (HPC) capability any developing country deploys is weather forecasting. In the developed world, we take for granted widely available, high quality forecast models that give us 48–72 h of excellent quality and up to 10 days of good quality forecasts. These forecasts enable planning to protect life and property. One recent example of the importance of this capability is in Mozambique. Days of torrential rains led to catastrophic flooding and loss of life. Good quality weather forecasting and effective communication could have warned people to either reach higher ground or otherwise evacuate low lying and flood prone areas.

With extensive computational resources, the developed world continuously not only offers models, but also checks forecasts against measurements to find gaps and errors in the models. As these are identified, they are being tweaked continuously improving forecasting models for that country or group that supports the forecasting center.

This persistent need for extensive, high capacity HPC resources to better protect the population is not available to developing countries that lack the resources to even operate a basic forecasting model. For example, on the African continent, the most advanced HPC resource, by far, is the Lengau machine in South Africa installed in 2016. It is now old and far behind the needs of current forecasting models. The rest of Africa has been receiving machines South Africa's CHPC and CSIR have been accepting as donations from the developed world and redeploying them, generally in much smaller pieces, across the continent. Even with these resources, the forecasting models are too complex to complete their calculations to offer timely forecasts for the areas in which these machines are installed.

The recent developments of Machine Learning (ML) models to replace complex physics in systems where humanity either does not understand the physics sufficiently or the physics is too complex to model with current computational resources is extremely promising for rapid solutions on limited hardware. The development of initial weather forecasting models using ML components have been deployed, but these models, like all forecasting codes, are tightly held property of the creating institutions.

Ethically, what obligations does the developed world have to share these potentially slightly less accurate, but vastly more efficient and computationally compact systems with the developing world? This paper explores this topic from many directions seeking to understand the issue more completely.

N. A. Streitz and S. Konomi (Eds.): HCII 2023, LNCS 14037, pp. 86–96, 2023.
https://doi.org/10.1007/978-3-031-34609-5_6

Keywords: ethics · hpc · weather forecasting · developing world · foreign aid

1 Introduction

While it is a common, but unattributable quote in the United States, "if you don't like the weather, just wait a few minutes," it speaks to the relentless change true to weather worldwide. Modern forecasting tools generate varying quality and detailed forecasts continuously worldwide. However, this is really only true in places with sufficient wealth and computing infrastructure to afford to deploy the pervasive data collection and extensive computational power to extrapolate current observations into accurate forecasts. In the developed world, these readily available forecasts are so common as to seem just a part of the fabric of life. Those of us with this luxury take advantage of these forecasts to plan ahead avoiding inclement or dangerous weather and can even defend or evacuate in the face of extreme weather. This luxury is not shared evenly across the world.

With Machine Learning (ML) becoming a pervasive part of everyday life, many believe humanity will have ubiquitous, continually updating, high quality forecasts at hand anywhere in the world. The radically reduced computational requirements for running an ML model compared to direct numerical simulation can potentially change the world. However it is not that simple.

Machine Learning is being deployed in countless different devices and services to craft results using less complex code and using far less computational resources. For example, self-driving cars still have not achieved fully autonomous, safe systems, but the progress is broad and significant [11]. In other areas, such as social media, algorithms decide what to put in each user's news feed to drive engagement and increase advertising revenue. While these are consumer facing or consumer focused deployments, science, medicine, and engineering are also deploying ML. For example, for medicine, progress is still being made improving direct computational modeling [19]. However, those advancements have limitations. For other systems, such as MRI, ML is a promising approach to reconstruct how an image should look by "correcting" noisy or corrupted data [3]. This noise and corruption is a part of the data collection process and best practices dictate using other computationally intensive and potentially less accurate techniques to correct the flaws inherent in the data collection. In this case, training a model on what a brain should look like enables correcting brain imaging to remove the collection errors.

For science applications, the simple statement is that physics knowledge is neither complete nor always computationally viable. For example, some physics phenomena is still not well understood [12]. In other cases, the complexity makes the problem infeasible to solve directly. For example, for perfect weather forecasting, perfect solar models, space weather, and a precise surface description of the earth including the atmosphere layers and ocean layers is needed. The data size of this alone is far beyond the capability of any machine on the planet today. For a climate model with multiple layers of ocean and atmosphere models and a 1 km area per computational point, the data already exceeds 1 PB. Adding in 1000 s s of times more detail and the additional models far exceeds the capabilities of any machines on the planet.

However, using ML to replace some of the physics complexity is leading to promising results using far less complex computations and far faster than direct computation [9]. Jalali describes three approaches for replacing the physics. First, scientists are using a deep neural network to replace a partial differential equations (PDE) solver. In this instance, either a physics specific model is generated based on initial conditions and the formulas involved or a more general PDE solver that would work for any physics. The former is more effective currently, but the latter would ultimately be a powerful tool for many different kinds of physics. The second approach is using Fourier Neural Operators [10]. The general idea is to map from initial conditions to solutions to create a neural network that can approximate solutions for initial conditions it has not experienced yet. The last approach is to use video and let the neural network learn the physics from the video. A great example of this are animated weather forecasts for things like rain or wind. Different video and numeric based models could be developed that each substitute for some complex calculations greatly reducing the forecasting computational complexity. This is not without a downside, unfortunately.

Hill et al. explored how to make effective ML-based forecasting models and discovered some base conditions. To train these models, detailed observational data is required [7]. With sufficient historical data at a fine grained enough resolution, reasonable models can be developed over time. However, even these are not up to the standards an experienced human forecaster can provide [7]. For an area without detailed measurements over a long period of time, even these models are not feasible. The United States has significant resources deployed to collect detailed observational data across the country as well as weather balloons to collect atmospheric data, satellites to collect observations from space, and a long, well documented observational history. Even with this information, generating a model better than a human has proved impossible so far [7].

Unfortunately, having quality models and observational infrastructure reinforces the wealth gaps and competitive advantages for the developed world over the developing world. One of the first HPC capabilities every country wants is weather forecasting given the humanitarian and economic impact of worse or no predictions. Modern hurricane forecasting has improved the window for warnings of imminent landfall by as much as 24 h leaving countries that cannot afford such technology at higher risk for natural disaster impacting both people and the economy. The major impacts of storms on Eastern Africa the last several years has demonstrated the need for better models and communication to get people to safety [1,15,16]

This paper explores some of the ethical considerations related to weather forecasting in the developed and developing world. We posit that a short term investment in increasing local forecasting capabilities globally can both decrease deaths and property damage while also reducing the amount of aid offered for disaster relief.

The rest of the paper is structured as follows. First in Sect. 2 is a more detailed discussion of what is and is not possible with weather forecasting and what is needed to improve the capabilities globally. Second, in Sect. 3 is a discussion of what obligations the developed world may have to the developing world and how that may affect any decisions. Next in Sect. 4 is a discussion of the costs involved, including both up-front data collection as well as computational modeling and compared against foreign aid. Finally a conclusion is offered in Sect. 5.

2   Forecasting

Weather forecasting can have enormous economic and human welfare impacts. Being able to plan for crops, to protect against storm damage, or to evacuate to protect human lives all demand a strong investment in forecasting tools and technology. To that end the American National Oceanographic and Atmospheric Administration (NOAA) has invested in several HPC centers just to refine our knowledge and models used for production forecasting. These systems are in addition to the production forecasting systems used daily. Each of these systems [14] is larger than the largest machine in all of Africa and South America [17], which was installed in 2016. This investment shows the priority this capability achieves for the United States residents. That priority is shared by most of the world, but the investment is far beyond the means of many countries.

A further refinement to weather forecasting is the Nowcast. This is a short term forecast from "now" up to six hours in the future. The advantage to these forecasts is they can be very accurate for storm tracks and local impacts. The challenge is the short time frames makes direct numerical calculation difficult except on the most capable machines.

With many different agencies worldwide offering forecasting services, typically mainly for a region or country, many different models have been developed and each requires their own set of observational data as initial conditions from which to extrapolate the forecast. While forecasts are shown as singular entities, the reality is far more complex. Figure 1 shows an example.

In Fig. 1, each line is labeled with the name of a different forecast model and shows the low pressure system path over five days. For storms like hurricanes, typically this is shown as a cone representing where the storm center is expected to be over time. This complexity shows that each model has biases based on what physics was included as well as the initial data and the model initialization parameters. In some cases, these parameters may include a pseudo-random number seed to offer a less rigidly fixed model. Over a series of runs, this variability can offer a better model in aggregate as it shows many more possible outcomes enabling forming a consensus averaged in some way from all of the forecast model runs. A combination of both numerical averaging tools as well as forecaster experience will generate the final predictions.

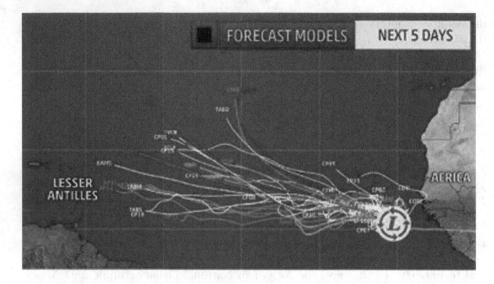

Fig. 1. An example of the "Spaghetti Lines" averaged to form a forecast

As should be expected based on the above information, not all models and not all parts of the world for each model will generate the same quality forecasts. Initial condition observations are a significant consideration. During the COVID-19 shutdown, the United States weather forecasting may have suffered because it lacked the atmospheric data collected by many commercial aircraft [4,8,18]. These planes, already flying for other purposes, also carry instruments to collect atmospheric data that is then used for forecast models. Areas with limited air traffic will necessarily lack this additional data to feed into their forecast models penalizing them further.

The European Centre for Medium-Range Weather Forecasts reports [6] that while the model quality they use continues to improve globally, the quality in the southern hemisphere is significantly behind that of both Europe and Northern Hemisphere forecasting. In this case, they have improved what their model can do for the southern hemisphere, as shown in the report, but it still trails northern hemisphere accuracy over time. With so much of the developing world in the global south, this demonstrates the difficulty in the developed world has in sharing models with the developing world. Even if these models were shared, they would not yield the same quality without adequate additional infrastructure collecting data across the land and through many atmospheric layers at many points.

By having dedicated computational resources to support regular and frequent weather forecasting runs, the developed world has significant economic advantages. In areas that completely or nearly completely lack domestic HPC resources, they have to rely on shared resources. Instead of direct model runs that can take advantage of computational steering through active monitoring (regular, persistent access), these areas, at best, must rely on batch, disconnected, resources. If they are fortunate, they can get computational priority rather than having to wait for a "fair" turn at the resources. While this costs dramatically less in the short term, it also offers significantly less value. Not only can Nowcasting not reliably be done, medium term forecasting may not even run sufficiently fast to have results in a useful time frame. Further, additional computational resources necessary to test model results against observations to help refine and improve models over time will also not be possible. As the developed world's models improve, these would be static.

The combination of the need for Nowcasting to localize storm impact for the next few hours to the longer term planning that 3–10 day forecasts can offer both require a persistent capability to gather observational data regularly and widely, run models essentially continuously to offer up to date forecasts quickly after the next set of observational data can establish a new starting point, and extensive model result/observation comparisons to improve the model over time. This persistent computation need with an ever growing data storage and archiving system requires extensive investment. In areas where basic food security cannot be met by a large percentage of the population, spending on this forecasting enterprise can seem like money spent on less important things.

Overall, weather forecasting requires detailed observational data for model staring conditions, many forecast model runs to generate the most likely outcome, and regular model refinement runs. This computational infrastructure alone is both expensive and high impact for a country. The potential life saving and reduced property loss can greatly reduce the immediate and resulting tragedy from large storms and resulting flooding and other damage.

3   Ethics

Countries in the developed world have long relied on lower safety and environmental standards of the developing world and lower labor costs to make cheaper products. In return, the developed world may offer development assistance in the form of education, infrastructure development, economic investment, or other incentives. For a place like the United States, that means that they have privatized the economic advantages to United States companies while helping to make a richer, hopefully more stable country benefiting the United States government through less need to monitor and thwart a threat to global security from that region. While many of the advantages for each party do materialize, often they do not materialize at the same time nor in proportions according to need. For example, the infrastructure from a manufacturing plant to a port or airport may be improved, but the rest of the city may be left with little to no infrastructure investment. These corridors help the foreign investors, but do not help all of the local people the investment is intended to support. The secondary effect of making things better in one part and the effects ripple out into the rest of the city may or may not happen.

Ethically, it is unclear what the developed world actually owes the local population or region in exchange for the establishment of a relatively good paying and relatively safe employer compared to other options. Some may suggest that by offering workplace safety standards that are the best in the region, but still far below domestic United States or European standards, is a tradeoff most seem willing to make for the short term economic impact. Potential corruption aside, these benefits certainly fall to the few rather than the masses affected by the plant.

However, consider what might be owed to the United States taxpayers that have invested in a region to help both their economic interests as well as the foreign policy interests of the home country. The United is used as an example, but this could just as easily be Europeans or other developed world investor. China would likely fall into this category as well as part of the BRICS countries. In this case, do the investor countries owe these individuals and companies that are taking economic and personal risk any additional protections by offering improved weather forecasting? For example, knowing the likelihood and severity for flooding in a region can affect plant placement decisions affecting costs and security measures needed. Knowing that a storm is likely to be severe that it is safest to send workers home early to move their families to safety rather than risk a little additional work time makes the company more efficient as workers will have less missed work and fewer people will have to quit due to having to take care of their family after a disaster.

From a pure humanitarian perspective, the United States and Europe project an image of protecting humans and the environment at home. Based on this reputation, can they maintain goodwill, and therefore foreign policy priorities, in a region if they do not live up to those standards in that region as well?

Weather forecasting, as described in Sect. 2, can have enormous impact on both the day to day lives of ordinary citizens as well as both the economically and politically elite. Rain and wind do not care a person's societal status. Flooding may be limited to areas where people cannot afford to live in a less flood prone area. Even then, flash flooding at extraordinary times can even hit the seemingly most secure.

Overall, some of the major ethical questions we must face are the following:

1. What do the developed, investor nations owe a region in which the developed country has an interest be it political or economic?
2. How broadly do developed, investor nations need to ensure what is owed is distributed?
3. What do developed investor nations owe a region to protect their ex-pats that have agreed to invest in an area to serve both their and our own interests?

Other questions that particularly relate to the economics of these questions are covered in the Costs section (Sect. 4).

4 Costs

The United Nations Framework Convention on Climate Change (UNFCCC) has been organizing the Conference of the Parties (COP) events annually. The COP-27 meeting recently released their reports that included a survey on the economic impact of severe storms and how much foreign aid helped to cover those costs. For the developing world, the results are startling. First, the total foreign aid for disaster relief [2] amounts to about 3% of the economic impact of the event. This tiny sum demonstrates that significant aid that can truly address the impacts is both expensive and politically unpalatable for donor nations. Instead of the kind of aid that can help the country seriously recover, the aid simply demonstrates the concern, but not the commitment, to what happens.

One of the other outcomes of the COP-27 meeting was a measure of the potential life saving as well as property damaging savings from just 24 h advance warning. The study demonstrates that 24 h notice can cut the ensuring damage by 30% [13]. While this is minimal for most forecasting models, the fact that so many still suffer these significant impacts shows that the investments should be made and that they will have a positive return on investment over time. Avoiding the worst impacts of a single disaster per year is likely enough to fully fund, with a surplus, the entire weather forecasting infrastructure a country may need.

United States foreign aid has been both economic and military. There is a particular motivation for offering different kinds of aid and has been analyzed [5]. This research shows that while military aid has always been understood to be affected by politics, disaster relief, in spite of being advertised as nonpolitical, it also suffers from political considerations. With the average disaster relief budget being a tiny fraction of foreign aid at an average of $151 million from 1964 to 1995, it does not begin to address the potential impact that investing in weather infrastructure to increase political stability in a region would offer. While the investment would not be military, it would align with the United States policy of investing in people rather than governments. These realities affecting disaster relief leave United States interests less secure. The long-term impact nature of weather forecasting investments may be one motivating factor eliminating it from consideration as part of foreign aid expenditures.

The weather forecasting engines the developed world employ offer us significant advantages over those that lack the same capabilities. While the developed world's investment was slow and over time, its continued investment is not a trivial sum. With the number of severe damage storms and loss of life, they can better predict and evacuate all they can to safety saving lives and property. Overall, the economic benefits have proven themselves regularly prompting the continued infrastructure investment.

The costs of deploying high quality forecasting models, particularly if machine learning-based models can reduce the computational costs dramatically–as long as adequate observational data can be collected to create the models–is relatively affordable for the developing world. With our foreign aid money developed nations allocate to help after disasters, they can carve off some to offer seed funding to help countries develop domestic infrastructure. This will both help that region as well as help our own political and economic interests. A country suffering less loss of life and property damage from severe storms can be more stable and develop more opportunities for the local population. The safer investments by domestic companies in a developing world country as measured by weather, economic, and political stability is a strong motivator. The risk is much lower and the return is more certain.

Considerations like sharing satellite data with these countries, assuming our capabilities naturally offer coverage "for free" should be considered an automatic decision. Deploying additional satellites to support developing regions solely may be good economic policy as well.

Overall, a small investment up front to build stronger weather forecasting capabilities both for Nowcasts as well as medium range forecasts is a good investment for everyone in the short term and long term.

5   Conclusion

The initial cost of weather forecasting infrastructure, simply for the computational data centers, the computers themselves, and ongoing operational and maintenance costs, can be high. The cost savings will come once models have been refined and sufficient data collection capabilities both have been deployed as well as have collected years worth of data. The cost of deploying and maintaining instruments across a region as well as adding sensors to whatever aircraft fly in the area can be quite small. With labor costs low and the cost of living for the local populace also being low, this data collection can be done inexpensively. While this reinforces low pay, the benefits to the economy and the populace over time will yield rising stability and pay for everyone. At least that is the hope of the local populace.

The impact for preventing loss of life and serious property damage can be enormous. The benefits of being able to provide Nowcasts using continuous modeling as well as medium range forecasts cannot be understated. Localizing a storm and measuring the particular qualities that will affect things like localized flooding is crucial to saving lives and protecting property.

The ethical issues largely fall into what do developed investor nations owe these regions as an "investor" in them? In this case, investor is in quotes to emphasize that while the investing nation or region gain benefits, the benefits granted to the populace at large may be limited or missing. The amount of wealth generation across a broad group of locals is also likely limited. Seeing the political and economic interests in the area, is it worthwhile to have these interests and not protect them by investing in infrastructure that a company is unlikely to need directly? A company may build a road to a port or a school to take care of workers' children so they can work more, but how much are they willing to spend on something they see little immediate benefit from? Surveys can address land issues and the other benefits may be hard to quantify economically. That leaves the home country with the interests to protect over the long term.

If foreign aid is intended to help those that suffer natural disasters, why not help prevent the disasters in the first place, or at least reduce the severity? The data shows the dramatic cost reduction by simply giving 24 h notice.

Acknowledgements. Sandia National Laboratories is a multimission laboratory managed and operated by National Technology and Engineering Solutions of Sandia, LLC, a wholly owned subsidiary of Honeywell International, Inc., for the U.S. Department of Energy's National Nuclear Security Administration under contract DE-NA0003525.

References

1. Adler, R., et al.: The role of satellite information in forecasting, modeling, and mapping the 2019 mozambique flood. J. Flood Risk Manage. n/a(n/a), e12843 (2020). https://doi.org/10.1111/jfr3.12843. https://onlinelibrary.wiley.com/doi/abs/10.1111/jfr3.12843
2. Becerra, O., Cavallo, E., Noy, I.: Foreign aid in the aftermath of large natural disasters. Rev. Development Econ. **18**(3), 445–460 (2014). https://doi.org/10.1111/rode.12095.https://onlinelibrary.wiley.com/doi/abs/10.1111/rode.12095
3. Bilgic, B., et al.: Highly accelerated multishot EPI through synergistic combination of machine learning and joint reconstruction. CoRR abs/1808.02814 (2018). http://arxiv.org/abs/1808.02814
4. Chen, Y.: Covid-19 pandemic imperils weather forecast. Geophys. Res. Lett. **47**(15), e2020GL088613 (2020). https://doi.org/10.1029/2020GL088613. https://agupubs.onlinelibrary.wiley.com/doi/abs/10.1029/2020GL088613 e2020GL088613 2020GL088613
5. Drury, A.C., Olson, R.S., Van Belle, D.A.: The politics of humanitarian aid: U.s. foreign disaster assistance, 1964–1995. J. Politics **67**(2), 454–473 (2005). https://doi.org/10.1111/j.1468-2508.2005.00324.x
6. Haiden, T., Janousek, M., Vitart, F., Ben-Bouallegue, Z., Ferranti, L., Prates, F.: Evaluation of ecmwf forecasts, including the 2021 upgrade (09/2021 2021). 10.21957/90pgicjk4, https://www.ecmwf.int/node/20142
7. Hill, A.J., Herman, G.R., Schumacher, R.S.: Forecasting severe weather with random forests. Monthly Weather Rev. **148**(5), 2135–2161 (2020). https://doi.org/10.1175/MWR-D-19-0344.1. https://journals.ametsoc.org/view/journals/mwre/148/5/mwr-d-19-0344.1.xml
8. Ingleby, B., et al.: The impact of covid-19 on weather forecasts: a balanced view. Geophys. Res. Lett. **48**(4), e2020GL090699 (2021). https://doi.org/10.1029/2020GL090699. https://agupubs.onlinelibrary.wiley.com/doi/abs/10.1029/2020GL090699, e2020GL090699 2020GL090699
9. Jalali, B., Zhou, Y., Kadambi, A., Roychowdhury, V.: Physics-ai symbiosis. Mach. Learnin. Sci. Technol. **3**(4), 041001 (2022). https://doi.org/10.1088/2632-2153/ac9215
10. Li, Z., et al.: Fourier neural operator for parametric partial differential equations. arXiv preprint arXiv:2010.08895 (2020)
11. Monticello, M.: Ford's bluecruise ousts gm's super cruise as cr's top-rated active driving assistance system (2023). https://www.consumerreports.org/cars/car-safety/active-driving-assistance-systems-review-a2103632203/

12. NewScientist: 10 mysteries physics can't answer.yet (2023). https://www.newscientist.com/round-up/physics-questions/
13. Nitu, R., Stuart, L., Allis, E., Kaya, F., Santamaria, L., Teruggi, G.: Early warnings for all: the un global early warning initiative for the implementation of climate adaptation (2022). https://library.wmo.int/index.php?lvl=notice_display&id=22154#.Y2pDuexByqA
14. NOAA: Hpcc locations and systems. https://www.noaa.gov/organization/information-technology/hpcc-locations-and-systems
15. Petricola, S., Reinmuth, M., Lautenbach, S., Hatfield, C., Zipf, A.: Assessing road criticality and loss of healthcare accessibility during floods: the case of cyclone idai, mozambique 2019. Int. J. Health Geogr. **21**(1), 14 (2022)
16. Ramayanti, S., et al.: Performance comparison of two deep learning models for flood susceptibility map in beira area, mozambique. Egyptian J. Remote Sens. Space Sci. **25**(4), 1025–1036 (2022). https://doi.org/10.1016/j.ejrs.2022.11.003. https://www.sciencedirect.com/science/article/pii/S1110982322000941
17. top500: Lengau. https://www.top500.org/system/178793/
18. Viglione, G., et al.: How covid-19 could ruin weather forecasts and climate records. Nature **580**(7804), 440–441 (2020)
19. West, B.L., et al.: Tetris: a streaming accelerator for physics-limited 3d plane-wave ultrasound imaging. In: 2019 56th ACM/IEEE Design Automation Conference (DAC), pp. 1–6 (2019)

Risk Framework for the Use of AI Services Driven by Citizens Themselves

Takashi Matsumoto[1,2(✉)], Mika Kimura[2], Teruka Sumiya[3,4], and Tomoyo Sasao[1]

[1] The University of Tokyo, 7-3-1 Hongo, Bunkyo-ku, Tokyo, Japan
takashi2.matsumoto@tohmatsu.co.jp
[2] Deloitte Tohmatsu Consulting LLC, 3-2-3 Marunouchi, Chiyoda-ku, Tokyo, Japan
[3] C4IR Japan, World Economic Forum, , 1-12-32 Akasaka, Minato-ku, Tokyo, Japan
[4] Pnika, 4-20-20 Onta, Higashimurayama, Tokyo, Japan

Abstract. As the issues and needs faced by citizens become more diverse and complex, there are high expectations for the utilization of machine learning AI. However, AI with complex logic is difficult for humans to interpret, and there are concerns about various risks such as the impact of environmental changes, fairness, and accountability. In addition, due to the uncertainty of the AI model, it is difficult for the AI model alone to sufficiently cope with the risks, and countermeasures in cooperation with related technologies and non-technologies are necessary. In the development of AI services for citizens' daily lives, AI developers are required to consider countermeasures by encouraging participation of citizens in order to understand various issues and concerns that citizens may have. In addition, the knowledge of various experts is also needed to examine issues related to technology, safety, legal compliance, and ethics. In this study, in the process of considering a new AI service in the living lab, we use the Risk Chain Model, which is a risk analysis framework with citizens and experts to examine whether the risk scenario and risk control for AI service can be sufficiently considered.

Keywords: Human-Centered Artificial Intelligence · AI · Smart City · Citizen · Living Lab · Risk Management

1 Introduction

As people's lifestyles diversify, the issues and needs of citizens become more diverse and complex, and there are high expectations that AI can be used to solve increasingly complex problems. Machine learning AI, which is currently widely applied, has the potential to predict solutions to complex problems with high accuracy by optimizing algorithms using large amounts of training data, which has been difficult with conventional technologies. Machine learning AI is used in many fields. The logic of AI model is difficult for humans to understand and sometimes outputs unexpected results, so it is necessary to pay attention to risks that have not been emphasized by conventional technologies [1, 2]. For example, the risk that the prediction performance of AI model is decreased due to the change in data distribution by environment changes; the risk of making unfair judgments about certain groups; the risk of making significant errors in judgment due to minute information that humans cannot recognize; lack of interpretability of AI decisions, which does not convince stakeholders, etc. are concerns [3, 4]. In fact, there have been cases in which significant economic losses have been incurred as a result of the use of AI. Zillow, a real estate brokerage marketplace in the U.S., was using a service that utilizes AI to make real estate transaction decisions, but while real estate prices skyrocketed due to the pandemic, the AI continued to make real estate transaction decisions based on past transaction data, causing significant losses to the company [5]. On the other hand, risks to human-rights and ethics by AI are also becoming apparent. In the United States, COMPAS, an AI that predicts recidivism rates, became a major issue when it was pointed out that racial judgments had a strong influence on the calculation of recidivism risk [6]. In cases where AI is used to score creditworthiness for citizens, there are concerns about the lack of accountability of AI model [7] and the risks associated with the unauthorized purpose use of calculated credit scores [8]. In addition, AI model itself is fraught with uncertainty, making it difficult for AI model alone to adequately address all risks and requires coordination with measures in related technologies and non-technologies [9].

The development and utilization of AI may affect not only the users of AI, but also various stakeholders, such as the target of AI prediction, workers collaborating with AI, and providers of learning data, etc. Therefore, AI developers should communicate with multi-stakeholders and consider various impacts while developing AI [10]. Therefore, it is expected that development projects should encourage citizen participation when developing AI services that affect the lives of citizens. In recent years, open innovation has been experimented, in which citizens take the initiative in developing technologies and collaborate with various stakeholders to expand the implementation of AI service. In Barcelona, citizens have taken the initiative in building "Guifi.net", a decentralized and managed network infrastructure, and in developing the "Smart Citizen Kit a distributed management network infrastructure [11].

While citizens are expected to participate in AI development projects, there are also issues related to technology, safety, legal compliance, and ethics in the development and utilization of AI, which require the knowledge of various experts [10]. In this study, we examined whether citizens can sufficiently consider various risks related to AI service with experts by using the Risk Chain Model, a risk analysis framework, in the case of citizen-led prototyping AI service. The Risk Chain Model is a framework in which risk scenarios affecting AI service are discussed with various stakeholders, and AI system, service providers, and users cooperate to study risk control [9]. Although case studies have been conducted on various use cases developed by enterprises, no studies have been conducted on use cases developed by citizens. In the workshop for citizen-led use case studies using AI cameras, citizens will be able to develop various risk scenarios affecting various stakeholders with experts by utilizing the Risk Chain Model, a risk analysis framework, at the living lab.

2   Related Works

Norbert organizes the following three challenges for AI technology; impossible and error-prone behavior, robustness, and lack of transparency, traceability, and accountability [12]. While the first two could be solved through technological advances, the last challenge is expected to remain [13]. Privacy considerations are essential for the use of big data in smart cities [14], but in order to enjoy the smartness of technology and develop a city that meets the needs of its citizens, citizens themselves should have the right to control what and how their data is collected and processed It has been suggested that they should have the right to control what data is collected and how it is processed [13]. In Sidewalk in Toronto, Canada, a closed forum for citizens decided how the technology would be used, and the plan was cancelled due to citizen opposition [15]. Without mechanisms for public participation, the crisis of trust will only deepen [16].

The importance of citizen involvement from the stage of city planning has been discussed in various ways [17–20]. On the other hand, the difficulty for citizens to work independently has also been pointed out [18, 21]. It is also believed that the involvement of various stakeholders allows ideas to be discussed from multiple perspectives [22] and reduces decision-making errors [16]. In order to achieve co-creation among stakeholders, it is noted that it is important to involve each stakeholder from the early stages of the project [23, 24].

3   Approach

3.1   Scope

In this study, we focus on a case in which a new AI service is examined by citizens in a workshop conducted by the living lab. In the process of studying AI services related to the daily life of citizens, we utilize the Risk Chain Model, a risk analysis framework, to examine whether it is possible to recognize various risk scenarios and to study technological and non-technological risk control by using the knowledge of both citizens and experts.

3.2   Risk Chain Model

As a risk analysis framework for AI services, we used the Risk Chain Model developed by the Institute for Future Initiatives of the University of Tokyo [9], in which the author of this paper also participates. Many research institutes [25–28] and AI development companies [29–31] have developed various tools and frameworks. However, most of them are intended to be used by developers, and require an understanding of specialized knowledge related to AI in order to use them. In addition, there is little public information on the examples of their use. The Risk Chain Model is a framework to consider risk controls for various risks associated with AI services by linking AI System/Service Provider/User [9]. It is characterized to examine risk controls in collaboration with various stakeholders, not limited to data scientists, by linking technological and non-technological components in a risk chain. Guidebooks and case studies are available so that non-AI developers can also conduct the study. As of February 2023, 12 case studies have been published, including Recruitment AI (Case01), Unstaffed Convenience Store (Case02), Verification of Recidivism Possibility AI (Case06), Driver-less Bus (Case10), etc. [32]. The Risk Chain Model is studied in the following steps.

Consider a Use Case. Before conducting the study, outline the use case of the AI service. At this stage, the values and objectives, AI model, the prediction target, the users, and the usage are clarified. For example, when considering the use case of an AI camera to be used in the city, the information shown in Table 1 should be prepared as an outline of the use case.

Table 1. Use Case Overview (Case: AI camera)

Values and objectives	AI model	Prediction target	User	Usage
• Safety of citizens • Comfortable urban environment • Reduction of security guard workload • Secondary use of data	Real-time human pose estimation	Citizen poses (cowering, violent behavior, possession of weapons, entering a restricted area)	Security guard	Notify the user when the pose of the predicted target is recognized

Risk Assessment. Identify risk scenarios that affect the use and operation of AI services. Risk scenarios are not limited to risks that may hinder business objectives, but also include ethical risks. The risk targets are not limited to AI users and forecasters, but also include operators, workers collaborating with the AI service, learning data providers, and others. Therefore, it is desirable to consider risk scenarios together with various stakeholders. For example, if risk scenarios are considered in the use case of AI cameras, risk scenarios affecting citizens, service providers, security guards, and workers are identified as shown in Table 2.

Risk Control. Risk control is examined using the map of the Risk Chain Model (See. Figure 1). There are three colored areas in the map. The green area is AI system, which includes AI model, data, system infrastructure, and other control functions. The blue area is service provider, which includes code of conduct, service operation, and communication with users. The orange region is user, which includes understanding of AI service, utilization of AI service, and usage environment. Using one map for each risk scenario, identify the relevant components (white boxes placed in each region) and draw a risk chain (red line), considering the order in which the risks are manifested. The risk chain does not necessarily consist of a single line, but may branch or aggregate, and may be a loop structure.

Table 2. Risk Scenario (Case: AI Camera)

Risk Scenarios	Affected Person
1. Some places do not achieve the expected effect	Service provider Citizens, Security guard
2. Data is not utilized	Service provider
3. Malfunction or data leakage due to cyber attacks	Service provider
4. Destruction of cameras	Service provider
5. Missed physical or violent behavior	Citizens
6. Misrecognition of normal behavior	Citizens
7. Recognition errors due to noise	Service provider Security guard
8. Recognition errors due to changes in the city environment	Service provider, Citizens, Security guard
9. Use of data for other purposes	Citizens
10. Invasion of privacy	Citizens
11. Obstruction of the landscape	Citizens, Workers
12. Deterioration of living conditions due to excessive surveillance	Citizens, Workers
13. Falling of cameras	Citizens
14. Deterioration of public safety in areas where cameras are not present	Citizens, Workers
15. Overloading of security guards due to excessive detection	Security guard
16. Missed incidents due to security guards' dependence on AI	Security guard

Risk controls are considered for each element associated in the risk chain. For each risk scenario, multiple technological and non-technological risk controls are associated with each risk scenario, so that a stepwise risk reduction can be considered. Since the contents of the study may be biased by the experience of the participants, it is desirable to conduct a role play including stakeholders who have knowledge in each area of AI System/Service Provider/User. In the use case of the AI camera, when examining the risk chain of the risk scenario "1. Some places do not achieve the expected effect", the risk control is identified as shown in Table 3.

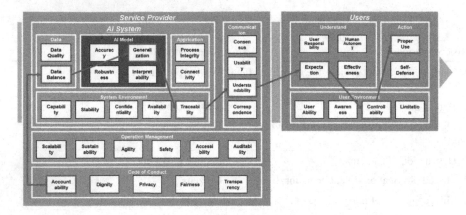

Fig. 1. Risk Chain Model

Table 3. Risk Controls (Risk Scenario: 1. Some places do not achieve the expected effect)

Risk Scenario	Risk Controls (AI System)	Risk Controls (Service Provider)	Risk Controls (Users)
1. Some places do not achieve the expected effect	(3) Ensure the quality of training data (Data Quality) (4) Ensure generalization of AI model for location (Generalization) (5) Recording of AI decision results (Traceability)	(1) Ensure that benefits are not biased by locations (fairness) (2) Clarify expectations for AI service (Accountability) (6) Monitoring AI performance (Auditability) (7) Explanation of expected effects to citizens (Consensus) (11) Improvement of AI model (Sustainability) (12) Development of individual AI models for locations (Capability)	(8) Explanation of the expected effects of AI cameras (Expectation) (9) Preparation of means to provide opinions to the management (Controllability) (10) Citizens can submit their opinions to the operator (Proper-Use)

3.3 Living Lab - Urban Design Studio for Everyone of Urban Design Center Kashiwa-No-Ha (UDCK)

Urban Design Center Kashiwa-no-ha (UDCK), based in Kashiwa City, Chiba Prefecture, Japan, operates a living lab called "Urban Design Studio for everyone" [33]. Based on this living lab, we conducted a workshop to propose three AI services using AI cameras by citizens for the purpose of solving problems in the city. A group of citizens will discuss a use case. Prototyping and user surveys were conducted to the extent technically feasible to improve the feasibility of the use case, and the use case was finally presented in a public forum including online distribution.

3.4 Method of This Project

The Risk Chain Model was utilized in the prototyping of each use case conducted in the living lab workshop. The results of each use case were qualitatively evaluated in terms of "Various risk scenarios" and "Technical and non-technical risk control".

Various Risk Scenarios. For each use case, risk assessment (3.2) was conducted to qualitatively evaluate the risk scenarios including safety, economic efficiency, human rights (fairness and privacy), etc. Comprehensiveness of risk scenarios (1) and Diversity of stakeholders exposed to risk (2) were qualitatively evaluated. In addition, we evaluated the existence of risk scenarios recognized through the knowledge of citizens or experts (3) who participated in the discussion.

Technical and Non-technical Risk Control. The risk controls were identified in each use case using a risk chain (3.2). We evaluated whether risk control is considered in each domain of AI System (4)/Service Provider (5)/Users (6) without relying on a single technological element. In addition, we evaluated the existence of risk control which does not exist in the existing case and is considered by the citizens (7).

4 Experiment

4.1 Workshop

The workshop was conducted from May to September 2022 (Table 4) at UDCK.

Lecture (May 14 2022 to Jun 04 2022). Before examining use cases, a three-day lecture was held for workshop participants. The participants examined the problems of the city (Day1) and the expectations of the AI camera (Day2) using LEGO Serious Play. In Day3, we conducted a study using the Risk Chain Model for AI cameras in order to learn how to use the Risk Chain Model.

Group Work: Use Case Ideation (Jun 04 2022 to Jul 22 2022). After three days of lectures, the participants were organized into groups based on the similarities in the issues and expectations of AI cameras presented by each participant on Day 1 and Day 2. Each group started to consider use cases led by the participants. Three use cases, "Recommendation of walking routes for pets," "Visualization of the excitement of events in the city," and "Signage that collects and visualizes Signage that collects and visualizes the good and bad points of the city" were discussed.

Interim Presentation (Jul 23 2022). The three groups presented the challenges and proposed solutions for the use case. Experts in the field of smart city and technology governance (promoters of initiatives in other local governments, project promoters at the World Economic Forum, consultants, university researchers, Kashiwa City officials, and area management companies) provided feedback on each group's presentation. The feedback included ideas on the problem setting, personas, and realization methods, as well as reference cases. General citizens participated as audience members, and the presentations were streamed on online.

Group Work: Prototyping Use Case (Jul 24 2022 to Sep 16 2022). Each group improved the use case based on the comments made at the interim presentation, and conducted prototyping. The prototypes were created as web applications, etc., and improvements were made based on questionnaires to test users. In this prototyping phase, risk scenario and risk control were examined using the Risk Chain Model.

Final Presentation (Jul 23 2022). The three groups presented the final contents of their use cases. The proposals included the target problem, solution, contents of prototyping (including survey results), important risk scenarios considered in the Risk Chain Model, and risk control (functions to be incorporated into service operation). As with the interim presentations, feedback from experts was provided, and the presentations were streamed online with the participation of the general audience.

Table 4. Workshop Schedule

Date	Activities	Location
May 14 2022	Kick off Lecture Day1: LEGO Serious Play	UDCK
May 28 2022	Lecture Day2: LEGO Serious Play	UDCK
Jun 4 2022	Lecture Day3: How to use Risk Chain Model	UDCK
From Jun 4 2022 to Jul 22 2022	Group work: Use case ideation	Online and UDCK
Jul 23 2022	Interim presentation	UDCK
From Jul 24 2022 to Sep 16 2022	Group work: Prototyping (*)	Online and UDCK
Sep 17 2022	Final Presentation	UDCK

* Conducted analysis using Risk Chain Model

4.2 Use Case

The workshop participants were divided into groups to examine use cases. In the study using the Risk Chain Model, the study is conducted as a role play among AI System/Service Provider/User, which requires at least four participants per use case, including one facilitator. Although the number of use cases has not been strictly considered, we decided to consider multiple use cases. A total of 13 people including citizens, workers, and students of Kashiwa-no-ha participated in the workshop. Therefore, the workshop participants were organized into three groups of at least four persons in each group (Table 5). The workshop management team supported the promotion of each group as needed.

Group A: Recommendation of Walking Routes for Pets. This use case was examined under the theme of making a friendly town where people can live without worrying about rules and manners. To avoid stressful encounters between pet owners who walk their dogs in the Kashiwa-no-ha area and citizens who are not good with dogs, AI service estimated comfortable dog walking routes for both citizens based on information obtained by AI cameras, and displayed on a smartphone application, which provides a recommendation of walking routes for pet owners. The AI camera acquires data on location, time, temperature, humidity, surface temperature, brightness, and human flow, and estimates appropriate walking courses and times.

Group B: Visualization of the Excitement of Events in the City. This use case was examined under the theme of enabling citizens to feel the excitement of the city by using AI cameras installed in Kashiwa-no-ha area to recognize the emotions of people gathering in the area and displaying icons and event information on a map of Kashiwa-no-ha area on the Internet. AI cameras at each location recognize people, strollers, bicycles, etc., and analyze the emotions of the people based on their facial expressions, etc., to express the fun of each location (many people in high spirits, parents and children with children gathered, active exercise, etc.).

Group C: Signage that Collects and Visualizes the Good and Bad Points of the City. This use case was examined with the theme of enabling citizens to recognize the good and bad points of the city and to work together to improve the city. AI classification model classified into the positive information (e.g., seasonal flowers have bloomed) and negative information (e.g., roads and facilities are broken) collected in the city recognized by AI cameras installed in the Kashiwa-no-ha area recognize and posted by citizens that submit photos and free text via smartphones, etc. and visualized on signage and websites posted in the city.

4.3 Risk Chain Model in This Workshop

Each group gathered at UDCK to discuss the Risk Chain Model. The research team of the Risk Chain Model at the University of Tokyo, participated in the discussion and gave advice on how to use the model in response to the participants' questions.

The risk assessment was conducted with researchers on AI governance, researchers on smart cities, and personnel from area management companies in each group. Specifically, participants raised risk scenarios on post-it notes, and risk scenarios to be identified were organized by grouping them (See. Figure 2).

When discussing risk control, it is desirable to include participants who have knowledge of AI System/Service Provider/User. However, it is assumed that it may be difficult to cover all the participants with knowledge in some groups, so we created our own 47 cards as candidates for risk control, referring to the case study [32] of the Risk Chain Model published by the University of Tokyo. When conducting the study using the Risk Chain Model, participants at each table are divided into the roles of AI System/Service

Table 5. Group Overview

Group	Theme	Number of people	Use Case	Role of AI camera
A	Making a friendly town where people can live without worrying about rules and manners	4	Recommendation of walking routes for pets	Understanding Dog Behavior in the City
B	Enabling citizens to feel the excitement of the city	5	Visualization of the excitement of events in the city	Emotional analysis through images
C	Enabling citizens to recognize the good and bad points of the city and to work together to improve the city	4	Signage that collects and visualizes the good and bad points of the city	Recognize images corresponding to good and bad points of a city

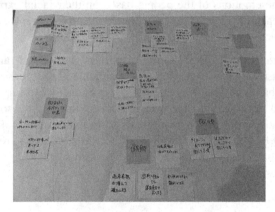

Fig. 2. Risk Assessment

Provider/User and role-play. Participants discussed risk control, referring to the cards as necessary. After that, the risk control cards were placed on the mat (See. Figure 3) on which the map of the Risk Chain Model was outputted, and the risk control of technical and non-technical risks were related by drawing the risk chain (See. Figure 4). When a risk control that did not exist on the prepared cards was considered, we placed it on a post-it and linked it to other risk controls by drawing a risk chain.

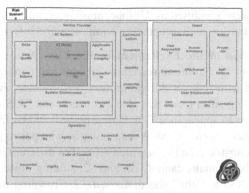

Fig. 3. Risk Chain Model map for the workshop

Fig. 4. Workshop

5 Results

5.1 Risk Scenarios Identified in Use Cases

Finally, for each use case, the risk scenarios listed in Table 6 were recognized. In order to examine the comprehensiveness of risk scenarios, we classified each risk scenario based on its contents. The classification items are based on the Dimensions of Trustworthy AI described in the book "Trustworthy AI" by Beena Ammanath [3]: fair and impartial (Fair), robust and reliable (Robust), respectful of privacy (Privacy), safe and secure (Safe), responsible and accountable (Responsible), and transparent and explainable (Transparent). Risks related to economic loss and satisfaction of citizens are classified as (Responsible).

Group A: Recommendation of Walking Routes for Pets. Five risk scenarios were identified in this group. The participants in this group were pet owners, and the risk "1. Dangerous induction" was raised due to dog allergies, contact with humans (especially with children), and so on. In addition, a researcher of AI Governance who participated in the discussion commented on the need to modernize appropriate walking routes if there are changes in streets and facilities, and "3. Inability to cope with changes in the urban environment" was recognized. The "4. Division of citizens" was discussed as a risk to pet owners and dog-phobic citizens who are fixed from the walking course. Other risks to the operator were identified as "2. Inaccurate information leading users away" and "5. Maintenance burden such as updating equipment and information".

Group B: Visualization of the Excitement in the City. Nine risk scenarios were identified in this group. "1. Failure to recognize citizens and damage the reputation of the event" was raised as a risk for AI recognition performance. Fairness in terms of appearance, location, organizers, etc. was also a concern, and "3. Smiles are not recognized due to differences in appearance", "4. Unfair places", "5. Unfair representation of excitement by organizers" were raised. A data scientist who participated in the discussion commented on a hostile case [4] in which AI makes different judgments based on minute information that humans cannot see, and "2. Adding noise to images to make certain events appear less exciting" was discussed. "7. Crowding into events that limit the number of people" was identified as a risk to event participants. "6. Negative impact on neighborhoods due to excessive crowding", "8. People are forced to participate in the event" and "9. Visualization of citizens' private life in the city" were also identified.

Group C: Signage that Collects and Visualizes the Good and Bad Points of the City. Six risk scenarios were identified in this group. In this case, citizens submit issues, which are then classified by AI and visualized by citizens. Therefore, the risks associated with building a relationship with citizens are "2. Issues are not resolved and citizens' dissatisfaction grows" and "5. Important issues are not recognized due to misclassification of positive/negative". "3. Issues of certain groups are not recognized due to the bias of users" and "4. Issues posted become personal attacks" were identified as risks related to the fairness and uncertainty of AI. "1. Negative impression of the city" and "6. Excessive recognition of issues increases the load on the local government" were also identified as city management.

5.2   Risk Controls Identified in Use Cases

Each group examined the risk control corresponding to the risk scenario using the Risk Chain Model. Table 7 shows the results of selecting the most important functions in the operation of AI service from the identified risk controls.

Group A: Recommendation of Walking Routes for Pets. In the AI System, it is considered to perform "Adjustment of bias of training data (dog breed, etc.)" and "Output of decision basis (number of dogs, breeds, etc.)" so that various breeds can be judged fairly. And "Correction of output results (walking course)" when there is an accident on the walking course recommended by AI. In the Service Provider, a team for "Coordination of event information in town and at facilities" should be organized, and "Consideration of individual models for each location" should be performed for locations where the prediction accuracy is clearly different. For users (citizens), the smartphone application will provide "Registration of pet information (breed, allergies, etc.)" and "Visualization of hazard information (construction, congestion, allergic reaction, etc.) on walking courses" in the smartphone application.

Group B: Visualization of the Excitement in the City. In the AI System to be able to appropriately identify various persons, including those wearing or not wearing masks,

Table 6. Risk Scenario (Use cases)

Gr	Use Case	Risk Scenarios	Affected Person	Classification
A	Recommendation of walking routes for pets	1. Dangerous induction (dog allergy outbreak, contact with humans or other animals in close quarters)	Citizens, Pet	Safe
		2. Inaccurate information leading users away	Service provider	Responsible
		3. Inability to cope with changes in the urban environment	Citizens, Pet	Robust
		4. Division of citizens (pet owners or citizens who do not like dogs)*	Citizens	Fair
		5. Maintenance burden such as updating equipment and information	Service provider	Robust
B	Visualization of the excitement in the city	1. Failure to recognize citizens and damage the reputation of the event	Event Organizers	Robust
		2. Adding noise to images to make certain events appear less exciting*	Event Organizers	Robust
		3. Smiles are not recognized due to differences in appearance	Event participants	Fair
		4. Unpopular places	Citizens	Fair
		5. Unfair representation of excitement by organizers	Event Organizers	Fair
		6. Negative impact on neighborhoods due to excessive crowding	Citizens	Responsible
		7. Crowding into events that limit the number of people	Event participants	Safe

(*continued*)

Table 6. (*continued*)

Gr	Use Case	Risk Scenarios	Affected Person	Classification
		8. People are forced to participate in the event	Citizens	Responsible
		9. Visualization of citizens' private life in the city	Citizens	Privacy
C	Signage that collects and visualizes the good and bad points of the city	1. Negative impression of the city as a whole	Government	Responsible
		2. Issues are not resolved and citizens' dissatisfaction grows	Service providers	Responsible
		3. Issues of certain groups are not recognized due to the bias of users	Citizens	Fair
		4. Issues posted become personal attacks	Citizens	Privacy
		5. Important issues are not recognized due to misclassification of positive/negative	Citizens	Robust
		6. Excessive recognition of issues increases the load on the local government	Service providers	Responsible

* Risk scenarios considered by incorporating the opinions of non-citizens experts

in various event environments, it was considered to have functions such as "Camera noise cancellation", "Sufficient training data (presence/absence of masks, etc.)", and "Ensure generalization performance of AI model" as well as "Detection of crowding.". For the Service Provider, "Privacy and fairness policies" and "Setting a maximum number of dense people per location" were considered in the operation, and "Description of AI camera locations, detection details" was discussed for event organizers and participants. For users (citizens, event organizers), "Web-based publication of event excitement and crowding" and "Complaint window from Neighbors" and "Notification to event organizers and participants" were considered.

Group C: Signage that Collects and Visualizes the Good and Bad Points of the City. In the AI System, the function to perform "Ensure generalization performance of AI model", "Record decision results and posting frequency", and "Output high frequency was considered. In the Service Provider, "Positive/negative and non-biased output expressions" are performed, and "Verification of contributor bias/high frequency keywords/retention issues" in signage are performed. In addition, "Publicity at facilities/events" was considered to reduce the bias of contributors. For users (citizens), "Collection of opinions from citizens" including the design of SNS hashtags was considered necessary to recognize issues that should be prioritized.

Table 7. Service Management Functions

Gr	Use Case	AI System	Service Provider	Users
A	Recommendation of walking routes for pets	- Adjustment of bias of training data (dog breed, etc.) - Output of decision basis (number of dogs, breeds, etc.) - Correction of output results (walking course)	- Coordination of event information in town and at facilities - Monitoring of AI decision results - Consideration of individual models for each location	- Registration of pet information (breed, allergies, etc.)* - Visualization of hazard information (construction, congestion, allergies, etc.) on walking courses
B	Visualization of the excitement in the city	- Camera noise cancellation - Sufficient training data (presence/absence of masks, etc.) - Ensure generalization performance of AI model - Detection of crowding	- Privacy and fairness policies - Setting a maximum number of dense people per location* - Description of AI camera locations, detection details, and expression methods	- Web-based publication of event excitement and crowding - Complaint window from neighbors - Notification to event organizers and participants
C	Signage that collects and visualizes the good and bad points of the city	- Ensure generalization performance of AI model - Record decision results and posting frequency - Output high frequency keywords and stagnant issues	- Positive/negative and non-biased output expressions* Positive/negative and non-biased output expressions - Verification of contributor bias/high frequency keywords/retention issues - Publicity at facilities/events*	- Collection of opinions from citizens (dedicated SNS hashtag)

* Added risk control that does not exist on the cards prepared

Each group identified the necessary risk control functions through the above risk studies, and presented their final proposals for each use case at the final presentation meeting. The proposals included important risk scenarios related to the use case and functions that should be incorporated into the service operation as risk control.

6 Consideration

6.1 Various Risk Scenarios

Based on the risk scenarios identified in each use case, we qualitatively evaluated the comprehensiveness of risk scenarios (1) and diversity of stakeholders exposed to risk (2). In addition, we evaluated the existence of risk scenarios (3) that could be recognized from the viewpoints of both citizens and experts in the discussion.

Comprehensiveness of Risk Scenarios (1). In Group A, two "Robust" risks such as changes in the urban environment, one "Safe" risk related to citizens and pets, one "Responsible" risk that is user-independent, and one "Fair" risk as a division of citizens were identified. In Group B, three risks of "Fair" related to event organizers and citizens, two risks of "Robust" related to the prediction performance of AI, two risks of "Responsible" related to citizens' satisfaction, one risk of "Safe" related to participants was identified, and one "Privacy" risk related to citizens was identified. In Group C, three "Responsible" risks related to the reputation of the city as a whole and its operation, and the operational burden of the letters themselves, one risk each for "Fair" and "Privacy" of citizens, and one "Robust" risk related to the accuracy of the classification by AI were identified.

No risk scenario classified as "Transparent" was identified in all groups. However, referring to the results of the risk control study (Table 7), some of the risk scenarios were related to "Transparent," such as the basis of AI decisions and visualization of information to stakeholders. In Group A, "Output of decision basis (number of dogs, breeds, etc.)" and "Visualization of hazard information (construction, congestion, allergies, etc.) on walking courses" are identified as risk control. In Group B, "Description of AI camera locations, detection details, and expression methods" and "Notification to event organizers and participants" are identified as risk control. In Group C, "Verification of contributor bias/high frequency keywords/retention issues" are identified. It was confirmed that risk scenarios were comprehensively examined in each group (Table 8).

Diversity of Stakeholders Exposed to Risk (2). In Group A, three risks affecting citizens who are users of AI services and their pets are considered. Among them, risks specific to animals (allergies) and risks to citizens who are not pet owners are also considered. Two risks were also identified for the operator of the AI service. In Group B, four risks affecting citizens regardless of whether they participate in the event or not, three risks affecting the organizer of the event, and two risks affecting the participants were identified. In Group C, three risks affecting citizens, two risks affecting AI service operators, and one risk affecting the government were identified. It was confirmed that each group was able to consider risks to various stakeholders.

Risk Scenarios Recognized Through the Knowledge of Citizens or Experts (3). The risk scenarios that could be identified from the perspective specific to citizens were identified. In Group A, "1. Dangerous induction" was raised against the background of many children living in the Kashiwa-no-ha area. "3. Inability to cope with changes in

Table 8. Classification of Risk Scenarios

Gr	Use Case	Fair	Robust	Privacy	Safe	Responsible	Transparent
A	Recommendation of walking routes for pets	1	2		1	1	*
B	Visualization of the excitement in the city	3	2	1	1	2	*
C	Signage that collects and visualizes the good and bad points of the city	1	1	1		3	*

* Considered in risk controls (Table 7)

the urban environment" was also raised as a reason for the boredom of a standardized life. In Group B, the risks affecting the lives of citizens were "6. Negative impact on neighborhoods due to excessive crowding", "8. People are forced to participate in the event", "9. Visualization of citizens' private life in the city. In Group C, "1. Negative impression of the city", "2. Issues are not resolved and citizens' dissatisfaction grows", and "5. Issues are not recognized due to misclassification of positive/negative" were raised.

Risk scenarios identified by the experts' findings were also identified. In Group A, a risk scenario "3. Inability to cope with changes in the urban environment" was identified by an AI governance expert who commented that AI cannot make appropriate predictions unless the data is updated. In Group B, the data scientist who participated in the discussion provided knowledge on the robustness of AI, and identified "2. Adding noise to images to make certain events appear less exciting. It was confirmed that a new risk scenario was identified by the knowledge provided by both citizens and experts.

6.2 Technical and Non-technical Risk Control

Based on the risk control examined using the risk chain in each use case, we qualitatively evaluated whether a risk control that relates AI System (4)/Service Provider (5)/User (6) without relying on a single technological element is considered. We also evaluated whether there exists a risk control (7) considered by citizens, which is not included in the existing risk chain models.

Risk Control of AI System (4). As risk controls common to each group, risk controls related to the collection of training data (Group A "Adjustment of bias of training data (dog breed, etc.)", Group B "Sufficient training data (presence/absence of masks, etc.)") and fairness of AI model (Groups B and C "Ensure generalization performance of AI model") were examined. In addition, information output for the purpose of abnormality monitoring (Group A: "Output of decision basis (number of dogs, breeds, etc.)", Group B: "Detection of crowding", and Group C: "Output high frequency keywords and stagnant issues") were examined. As a risk control specific to each group, Group A examined

"Correction of output results (walking course)" as a response to changes in the urban environment (especially when accidents, construction, or other hazards occur). In Group B, "Camera noise cancellation" was identified to maintain the quality of image information recognized by AI. In Group C, "Record decision results and posting frequency" was also considered to monitor the bias of posted assignments.

Risk Control of Service Provider (5). Monitoring (Group A "Monitoring of AI decision results" and Group C "Verification of contributor bias/high frequency keywords/retention issues") was considered as risk controls common to all groups. In addition, individual measures for each location in the city (Group A "Consideration of individual models for each location" and Group B "Setting a maximum number of dense people per location") were considered. As a risk control specific to each group, Group A identified "Coordination of event information in town and at facilities" as a response to changes in the urban environment. In Group B, it was considered to establish "Privacy and fairness policies" for citizens, event organizers, and participants, and to provide "Description of AI camera locations, detection details, and expression methods" for citizens, event organizers, and participants. In Group C, it was considered that "Positive/negative and non-biased output expressions" for city information displayed on signage and "Publicity at facilities/events" to reduce user bias.

Risk Control of Users (6). As risk controls common to each group, risk controls related to the collection of opinions from citizens (Group B: "Complaint window from neighbors" and Group C: "Collection of opinions from citizens (dedicated SNS hashtag)") were considered as risk controls common to each group. As risk controls specific to each group, in Group A, the "Registration of pet information (breed, allergies, etc.)" and "Visualization of hazard information (construction)" were considered to prevent pets from being led to places where allergies may occur. In Group B, "Web-based publication of event excitement and crowding" and "Notification to event organizers and participants" were considered to manage the crowding situation at event sites. In each group, the Risk Chain Model was used.

In each group, it was confirmed that the risk control in each of AI System/Service Provider/User can be sufficiently studied by using the Risk Chain Model.

Risk Control Added by Citizens (7). In this study of risk control using the Risk Chain Model, we created 47 cards as candidates of risk control by referring to the case study of the Risk Chain Model published by the University of Tokyo [32], for the purpose of supplementing our expertise. In the actual study, risk controls that did not exist in the risk control cards were examined by citizens. In Group A, "Registration of pet information (breed, allergies, etc.)" in the user domain, "Setting a maximum number of dense people per location" in Group B, and "Positive/negative and non-biased output expressions" in Group C in the service provider domain. In all groups, it was confirmed that there existed risk controls that were not included in the existing risk chain model studies, but were newly considered by the citizens.

6.3 Results

The results of this study confirm that "various risk scenarios" and "technical and non-technical risk control" can be considered by using the Risk Chain Model, which is a risk analysis framework, in cooperation with citizens and experts. The stakeholders affected by the utilization of AI are wide-ranging, and it is difficult to determine the extent to which they should be involved in the process. In this study, the target population was the citizens who applied for the living lab. Citizens who participate in the living lab often have high literacy and motivation, so a method to collect the opinions of the silent majority is required. In addition, in the study of risk control, it is necessary to secure the human and resource resources needed to realize the service, and if the costs incurred by the service are not controlled within an appropriate budget range, it will be difficult to sustain the AI service.

7 Conclusion

In the process of prototyping a new AI service in the living lab workshop, the risk was comprehensively identified by the collaboration between citizens and experts using a risk analysis framework. The risk control measures were reflected in the AI service proposals from the citizens. It is expected that the number of cases like Barcelona, where citizens take the initiative in technology implementation, will increase in the future. We expect that various technologies including AI will be socially implemented as trusted services by considering sufficient risk control by multi-stakeholders as in this study.

References

1. OECD: OECD Multilingual Summaries Artificial Intelligence in Society, June 11 2019
2. Jobin, A., Ienca, M., Vayena, E.: The global landscape of AI ethics guidelines. Nat. Mach. Intell. **1**, 389–399 (2019)
3. Ammanath, B.: Trustworthy AI: A Business Guide for Navigating Trust and Ethics in AI, 1st edn. Wiley, USA (2022)
4. Goodfellow, I.J., Shlens, J., Szegedy, C.: Explaining and Harnessing Adversarial Examples, 3rd version (2015). https://arxiv.org/abs/1412.6572, last accessed February 10 2023
5. Datta, A.: The $500mm+ Debacle at Zillow Offers – What Went Wrong with the AI Models?. insideBIGDATA, December 19 2022. https://insidebigdata.com/2021/12/13/the-500mm-deb acle-at-zillow-offers-what-went-wrong-with-the-ai-models/, last accessed February 10 2023
6. ProPUBLICA Homepage. https://www.propublica.org/article/machine-bias-risk-assess ments-in-criminal-sentencing, last accessed February 10 2023
7. Kiviat, B.: The moral limits of predictive practices: the case of credit-based insurance scores. Am. Sociol. Rev. **84**(6), 1134–1158 (2019)
8. epic.org Homepage. https://epic.org/epic-files-complaint-with-ftc-about-airbnbs-secret-tru stworthiness-scores/, last accessed February 10 2023
9. Matsumoto, T., Ema, A.: RCModel, a Risk Chain Model for Risk Reduction in AI Service. The University of Tokyo (2020). https://ifi.u-tokyo.ac.jp/en/news/4815/, last accessed February 10 2023
10. Ema, A., et al.: Future Relations between Humans and Artificial Intelligence: A Stakeholder Opinion Survey in Japan. IEEE (2016). https://ieeexplore.ieee.org/document/7790979, last accessed February 10 2023
11. Capdevila, I., Zarlenga, M.I.: Smart city or smart citizens? The Barcelona case. J. Strateg. Manag. **8**(3), 266–282 (2015)

12. Streitz, N.: Beyond 'smart-only' cities: redefining the 'smart-everything' paradigm. J. Ambient. Intell. Humaniz. Comput. **10**(2), 791–812 (2019)
13. Streitz, N.A., Riedmann-Streitz, C.: Rethinking 'smart' islands: toward humane, self-aware, and cooperative hybrid islands. Interactions **29**(3), 54–60 (2022)
14. Lim, C., Kim, K.J., Maglio, P.P.: Smart cities with big data: reference models, challenges, and considerations. Cities **82**, 86–99 (2018)
15. Goodman, E.P., Powles, J.: Urbanism under google: lessons from sidewalk Toronto. Fordham L. Rev **88**, 457 (2019)
16. Fiorino, D.J.: Citizen participation and environmental risk: a survey of institutional mechanisms. Sci. Technol. Human Values **15**(2), 226–243 (1990)
17. Arnstein, S.R.: A ladder of citizen participation. J. Am. Inst. Plann. **35**(4), 216–224 (1969)
18. Cardullo, P., Kitchin, R.: Being a 'citizen' in the smart city: up and down the scaffold of smart citizen participation in Dublin, Ireland. Geo Journal **84**(1), 1–13 (2019). https://doi.org/10.1007/s10708-018-9845-8
19. Goodman, N., Zwick, A., Spicer, Z., Carlsen, N.: Public engagement in smart city development: lessons from communities in Canada's smart city challenge. The Canadian Geographer/Le Géographe canadien **64**(3), 416–432 (2020)
20. de Hoop, E., Moss, T., Smith, A., Löffler, E.: Knowing and governing smart cities: Four cases of citizen engagement with digital urbanism. Urban Governance **1**(2), 61–71 (2021)
21. IEEE/ACM 41st International Conference on Software Engineering 2019, pp. 41–50. IEEE (2019)
22. Salvia, G., Morello, E.: Sharing cities and citizens sharing: perceptions and practices in Milan. Cities **98**, 102592 (2020)
23. Kalinauskaite, I., Brankaert, R., Lu, Y., Bekker, T., Brombacher, A., Vos, S.: Facing societal challenges in living labs: towards a conceptual framework to facilitate transdisciplinary collaborations. Sustainability **13**(2), 614 (2021)
24. Mahmoud, I., Morello, E.: Co-creation pathway for urban nature-based solutions: testing a shared-governance approach in three cities and nine action labs. In: Smart and Sustainable Planning for Cities and Regions: Results of SSPCR 2019—Open Access Contributions, 3, pp. 259–276. Springer International Publishing (2021). https://doi.org/10.1007/978-3-030-57764-3_17
25. AI Risk Management Framework Second Draft, pp. 10–16, NIST, USA, August 18, 2022. https://www.nist.gov/system/files/documents/2022/08/18/AI_RMF_2nd_draft.pdf, last accessed February 10 2023
26. Machine Learning Quality Management Guideline 2nd Edition, AIST, Japan, May 16 2022. https://www.digiarc.aist.go.jp/en/publication/aiqm/aiqm-guideline-en-2.1.1.0057-e26-signed.pdf, last accessed February 10 2023
27. Model AI Governance Framework second edition, IMDA and PDPC, Singapore, January 21 2020. http://go.gov.sg/ai-gov-mf-2, last accessed February 10 2023
28. Ethics, Transparency and Accountability Framework for Automated Decision-Making, Central Digital and Data Office, Cabinet Office, and Office for Artificial Intelligence, UK, May 13 2021. https://www.gov.uk/government/publications/ethics-transparency-and-accountability-framework-for-automated-decision-making, last accessed February 10 2023
29. Google: Responsible AI practices,. https://ai.google/responsibilities/responsible-ai-practices/, last accessed February 10 2023
30. Microsoft: Microsoft Responsible AI Standard, v2, June 2022. https://blogs.microsoft.com/wp-content/uploads/prod/sites/5/2022/06/Microsoft-Responsible-AI-Standard-v2-General-Requirements-3.pdf, last accessed February 10 2023
31. AI Ethics Impact Assessment White Paper, Casebook, and Practice Guide, Fujitsu, February 21 2021. https://www.fujitsu.com/global/about/research/technology/aiethics/, last accessed February 10 2023

32. AI Service and Risk Coordination Study Group. The University of Tokyo. https://ifi.u-tokyo.ac.jp/en/projects/ai-service-and-risk-coordination, last accessed February 10 2023
33. Urban Design Center Kashiwa-no-ha (UDCK). https://www.udck.jp/, last accessed February 10 2023

The Nurturing of Theory for Smart Environments and Spaces: The Case of Ambient Theory for Smart Cities

H. P. McKenna[✉]

AmbientEase, Victoria, BC V8V 4Y9, Canada

Abstract. Motivated by the need to continue developing the theoretical foundations for smart cities, together with the underexploiting of theory, the purpose
of this paper is to explore ways of nurturing theory for smart environments and
spaces using ambient theory for smart cities as a case example. A review of the
research literature for smart environments is provided followed by a review of the
literature pertaining to the nurturing of theory. Informed by the literature reviews,
a conceptual framework for theory nurturing in smart environments is formulated
and then operationalized for use in this paper using an exploratory case study approach combined with an explanatory correlational design. Variables relevant to the
nurturing of theory in smart environments are identified, assessed, and correlated
in the exploration of patterns and relationships. Findings also emerge pertaining
to theory nurturing through online conference discussions and activities such as
polling. Limitations and mitigations of this paper are identified while future directions emerge as opportunities and challenges going forward, opening the way for
potentially interesting and rich discussions for urban researchers, practitioners,
and planners.

Keywords: Adaptability · Algorithm-Assisted Theorizing · Awareness ·
Contexts · Discovery · Dynamic · Emergent · Meaningful Action ·
Meaningfulness · Online Conference Polling · Special Properties of Theory ·
Theory Building · Theory Development · Urban Design

1 Introduction

This paper is motivated by the need for developing a stronger theoretical foundation for
the smart cities' domain, for smart environments and spaces (Batty, 2013; Roy, 2009) [1,
2], and for urban spaces more generally (Brenner, 2019) [3]. While various theories have
been advanced in support of increasing the understanding of smart cities (Batty, 2020;
Harrison and Abbott Donnelly, 2011) [4, 5], ambient theory for smart cities has been
proposed as a theory intended for "involving people more meaningfully and taking their
needs into consideration" (McKenna, 2021) [6], in support of "designs, developments,
and implementations of smart environments." As such, the purpose of this work is to
explore ways of nurturing a theory for smart environments and spaces using the case of
ambient theory for smart cities.

N. A. Streitz and S. Konomi (Eds.): HCII 2023, LNCS 14037, pp. 118–130, 2023.
https://doi.org/10.1007/978-3-031-34609-5_8

In terms of approach, this paper provides a review of the research literature focusing on the use of theory in smart cities and environments. The theory research literature is also reviewed to provide guidance on ways to nurture a theory (Higgins, 2004) [7] and to learn more about the definition, purpose, and value of the notion of theory nurturing. Based on the literature reviews, a conceptual framework for theory nurturing is formulated to guide the case study exploration in this paper which is combined with an explanatory correlational design. The conceptual framework is also intended to serve as a model for research and practice in support of theory use going forward using the example of ambient theory for smart cities.

Objectives. The primary objectives of this paper are to a) explore theory for smart environments; b) explore the notion of nurturing a theory; and c) formulate and operationalize for use in this paper a conceptual framework for theory nurturing in smart environments using the example of ambient theory for smart cities.

2 Background

In support of the notion of nurturing a theory, it is worth noting the claim by Nardi (2021) [8] that "many existing theories are underexploited" giving rise to the question of how theories such as ambient theory for smart cities might be nourished and put-to-use, as in, "appropriating theory". Nardi and Redmiles (2002) [9] point to the importance of the role played by theory "to promote dialog, create community, and illume the world" giving rise to the question of how such purposes for theory might be accomplished in the context of smart environments in relation to theories such as ambient theory for smart cities.

2.1 Definitions

Definitions, drawing mostly on the research and practice literature, are provided for key terms used in this paper.

Ambient. McCullough [10] describes the ambient in relation to the environment as "that which surrounds but does not distract" and notably as "an awareness of continuum and continuum of awareness."

Nurture. Merriam-Webster Dictionary [11] defines nurture as to "care for."

Smart Environment. Building on a definition by Das and Cook (2006) [12] that moves beyond comfort for inhabitants, Reig, Fong, Forlizzi, and Steinfeld (2022) [13] provide a definition of smart environment as "a small world in which agents and devices work continuously and collaboratively toward shared and/or complementary goals."

2.2 Paper Overview

What follows is this paper is the development of a theoretical perspective for the nurturing of theory in relation to smart environments, formulation of a conceptual framework for theory nurturing in smart environments, a description of the methodology used for the exploration in this paper, the presentation of findings, a discussion of findings, and the conclusion including limitations and future directions.

3   Theoretical Perspective

A review of the research literature is provided for the use of theory pertaining to smart cities, environments, and spaces followed by a review of the theory literature pertaining to theory nurturing.

3.1   Use of Theory for Smart Cities, Environments, and Spaces

Gračanin, Lasisi, Azab, and Eltoweissy (2019) [14] seek to complement the focus on technology in smart built environments (SBEs) by proposing the addition of "human aspects" including "empathy, privacy, and ethics" (EPE) using a game theoretic model. McKenna (2021) [6] proposes ambient theory for smart cities in response to the need for improving understandings of the smart city concept as well as the ambient dimension of contemporary urban life (Nakashima, Aghajan, and Augusto, 2010) [15], with awareness and meaningful action as key components. Augusto (2022) [16] advances a theory of contexts for intelligent environments (IEs) "to express simply and clearly how preferences and expectations of the various users can be taken into consideration and the performance of the system can be linked to overall satisfaction" since, it is argued, the notion of context requires "a deeper and more careful understanding to create more effective context-aware systems." Streitz (2019) [17] advances theoretical foundations for the design of future cities in the form of the Citizen Cooperative City Contract (CCCC) in support of a human-centered design approach that transforms the smart cities notion to Humane, Sociable and Cooperative Hybrid Cities. The CCCC is further articulated by Streitz (2021) [18] in support of "appropriate, livable, sustainable, and resilient spaces." Streitz and Riedmann-Streitz (2022) [19] extend the CCCC to humane, self-aware and cooperative hybrid islands and the formation of Islanders Cooperative Island Contract (ICIC) while Streitz, Riedmann-Streitz, and Quintal (2022) [20] extend the ICIC to islands for innovation and research, incorporating nudge theory that serves to change the "choice architecture" for everyone involved. Reig et al. (2022) [13] identify five types of smart environments based on a review of the literature enabling the deriving of five lenses (with variations) "for discussion and research" as: how an environment comes to be smart (designed, emergent), focus and goals (system focused, people focused), adaptability (static, evolving), necessity of intelligence (essential, supplemental), and handling of attention (directed, ambient). Reig et al. [13] describe attention as "directed" or "ambient" in smart environments where, in the latter case, "users of the environment" are "issuing a command to turn on the lights 'into the ether'", as in, the ambient. It is also worth noting that Reig et al. [13] caution "[r]esearchers and designers of smart environments" to "make concerted efforts to anticipate the possible negative outcomes of the interfaces and interactions—and, more broadly, the experiences— that they are creating and promoting."

Table 1 provides a summary of the literature for theoretical perspectives on smart environments by author and year, over the time period of 2006 to 2022.

In summary, key theoretical perspectives on theory use in smart cities, environments, and spaces emerging from this review of the research literature, include but are not limited to, smart environments for inhabitant comfort; ambient dimensions of contemporary urban life; human aspects in smart built environments (SBEs); humane, sociable and

Table 1. Examples of theory use in smart environments in the literature.

Author	Year	Theoretical Perspectives in Smart Environments
Das & Cook	2006	Defining smart environments for inhabitant comfort
Nakashima et al	2010	Ambient dimensions of contemporary urban life
Gračanin	2019	Empathy, privacy & ethics in SBEs & game theory
Streitz	2019	Humane, sociable & cooperative hybrid city; CCCC
McKenna	2021	Awareness; Action; Ambient Theory for Smart Cities
Streitz	2021	Citizen + Cooperative City Contract (CCCC)
Augusto	2022	A theory of contexts for intelligent environments (IEs)
Reig et al	2022	Lenses for five types of smart environments
Streitz & Ridemann-Streitz	2022	CCCC, Islanders + Cooperative Island Contract (ICIC)
Streitz et al	2022	Humane, self-aware & cooperative hybrid islands

cooperative hybrid city; awareness and meaningful action through ambient theory for smart cities; theory of contexts for intelligent environments (IEs); smart environment lenses; citizen + cooperative city contract (CCCC); extending or expanding CCCC to islanders + cooperative island contract (ICIC); and humane, self-aware and cooperative hybrid islands.

3.2 Nurturing a Theory

Higgins (2004) [7] describes ways in which to nourish a theory, such as, using a theory to "promote discovery" while also suggesting that "[w]hen new data demonstrate that there are some problems with the theory" being used, "then intervene to help the theory change and develop in ways to meet its full potential." Pushing the boundaries or "envelope" of the theory is also encouraged by Higgins (2004) [7], as a way to "explore the full scope" of the theory and "its special implications" and the importance of enabling a theory to make contact with the world is highlighted. From a management perspective, Eisenhardt and Graebner (2007) [21] describe the building of theory using one or more case studies, identifying challenges and opportunities. Corley and Gioia (2011) [22] organize the theory building literature into the two categories of originality and utility, where the former presents as revelatory or incremental and the latter presents as practically useful or scientifically useful. In support of adaptiveness, Corley and Gioia (2011) [22] call for more "scope" and "an orientation toward 'prescience' as a way of achieving scope" as in "the process of discerning or anticipating what we need to know." In providing guidance on teaching theory and theory building, Byron and Thatcher (2016) [23] identify a series of questions, one of which is "whether we should care about theory" and in response, argue that it is important to "understand that theories are the mechanisms that help us explain why some part of the world works the way that it does" while acknowledging the value of theory for guiding research question development and making sense of findings.

Gregor (2017) [24] describes the theory contribution canvas, formulated as a tool to assist researchers in identifying the nature of their contribution, whether to theory building, testing, qualifying or the expanding of a theory. Shepherd and Suddaby (2017) [25] provide a systematic review of the theory building literature in the management domain, identifying the need for integration while proposing the notion of pragmatic empirical theorizing to encourage theorizing from quantitative findings. The notion of care associated with nurturing (Merriam-Webster Dictionary, 2022) [11] is suggestive when considering the work of Fors and Lennerfors (2019) [26] who advance the individual-care nexus theory in the context of sustainable entrepreneurship, urging the use of "a vocabulary of care" and the development of "caring practices" all of which could be relevant to smart spaces in the public realm. Shrestha, He, Puranam, and von Krogh (2020) [27] explore the value of machine learning (ML) techniques such as "algorithm supported induction" for theory building from data involving pattern detection while pointing to the potential going forward for interpretable AI (artificial intelligence) in algorithm-assisted theorizing. Augusto (2022) [16] delves deeper into understandings of context, seeking to extend and rethink context-awareness in smart environments in formulation of a theory of contexts for intelligent environments (CIEn). Streitz and Ridemann-Streitz (2022) [19] employ the use of nudge theory in combination with Islanders + Cooperative Island Contract (ICIC) while furthering the scope of the theoretical framework for citizen + cooperative city contract (CCCC) to extend to Islanders + Cooperative Island Contract (ICIC).

Table 2 provides a summary of the literature for discussions and examples of theory nurturing by author and year, over the time period of 2004 to 2022.

Table 2. Discussions and Examples of Theory Nurturing in the Literature.

Author	Year	Theory Nurturing
Higgins	2004	Contact; Discovery; Identify problems; Push boundaries
Eisenhardt & Graebner	2007	Building theory from one or more cases
Corley & Gioia	2011	Originality & utility (support of 'scope' & 'prescience')
Byron & Thatcher	2016	Caring about theories as mechanisms for understanding
Gregor	2017	Theory building, testing, qualifying, or expanding
Shepherd & Suddaby	2017	Pragmatic empirical theorizing
Fors & Lennerfors	2019	Individual-care nexus theory; Caring practices
Shrestha et al	2020	Algorithm supported induction for theory building
Augusto	2022	Theory of contexts for intelligent environments (CIEn)
Streitz & Ridemann-Streitz	2022	Extending frameworks, CCCC to ICIC

In summary, key elements of theory nurturing emerge from this review of the research literature, including but not limited to discovery, problem identification, pushing boundaries, making contact with the world, and extending or expanding the theory.

3.3 Conceptualizing Theory Nurturing in Smart Environments

Informed by the literature reviews in Sects. 3.1 and 3.2, a conceptual framework for theory nurturing in smart environments is presented in Fig. 1 using the example of ambient theory for smart cities. Ambient theory for smart cities (ATSC) is characterized by components such as awareness, people and technology interactions, smart environments that are adaptive, dynamic, emergent, interactive, and pervasive in support of meaningful action for planning, designing, and creating [6].

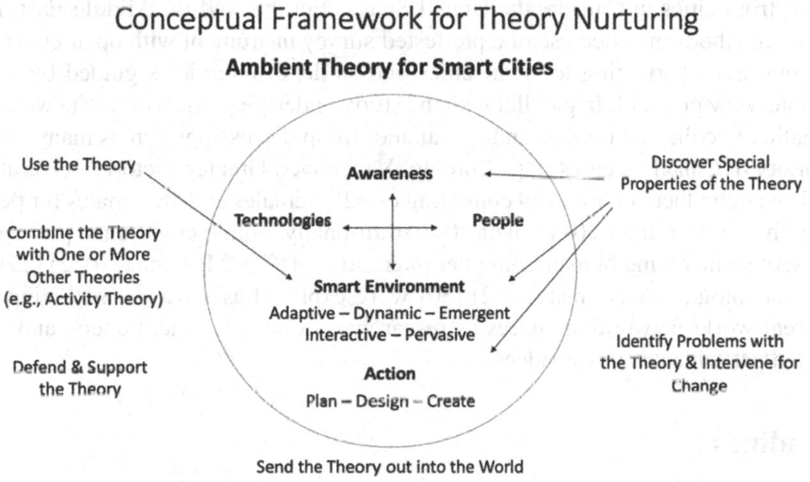

Conceptual Framework for Theory Nurturing

Ambient Theory for Smart Cities

Use the Theory

Combine the Theory with One or More Other Theories (e.g., Activity Theory)

Defend & Support the Theory

Awareness

Technologies ↔ People

Smart Environment
Adaptive – Dynamic – Emergent
Interactive – Pervasive

Action
Plan – Design – Create

Discover Special Properties of the Theory

Identify Problems with the Theory & Intervene for Change

Send the Theory out into the World

Fig. 1. Conceptual framework for theory nurturing in smart environments.

ATSC is said to be "intended for use in smart environments" and "where awareness and sensing are present" with "technologies supporting enhanced awareness and spaces accommodating more aware people and their multisensorial capabilities" (McKenna, 2021) [6] and as such, is amenable to many types of nurturing in the form of adaptability for use in smart environments; discovery of special properties such as awareness, interactivity, and meaningful action; potential to be combined with other theories such as activity theory; defense and support of the theory in that it is said to be "opening spaces for dialogue" [6]; identification of problems with the theory and the potential to intervene for change; and enabling the theory to make contact with the world.

4 Methodology

The research design for this paper uses an exploratory case study approach, recommended for the investigation of contemporary phenomena (Yin, 2017) [28] – in this case, pertaining to smart environments and the ambient – combined with an explanatory correlational design, since case studies "have been needed to examine the underlying processes that might explain a correlation" (Yin, 2017) [28]. The example of ambient theory for smart cities (ATSC) is used in this paper in the exploration of learning whether and how a theory is being nurtured. As such, the *information* variable is explored as a proxy for *awareness* in smart environments, a key element of the ATSC proposition. The *meaningfulness* variable is also explored as a key element of the ATSC proposition in support of people and their potential for action. Additionally, insight is sought into ATSC in terms of aspects that might be missing, in order to improve the theory and to improve the uptake of the theory for city planning and design in urban environments.

Using an online space, people were invited to sign up for the study and demographic data were gathered during this process including age range, gender, location, and self-categorization (e.g., educator, student, community member, etc.). Study participants emerged from cities in Canada, the United States, Europe, and the Middle East. Data collection methods included use of a pre-tested survey instrument with open-ended and closed questions pertaining to smart cities and in-depth interviews guided by a pre-tested interview protocol. In parallel with the study underlying this work, data were also systematically collected through individual and group discussions across many sectors in a variety of Canadian cities (e.g., Toronto, Vancouver, Greater Victoria). Overall, an analysis was conducted for n = 79 consisting of 42% females and 58% males for people ranging in age from their 20s to their 70s. Additionally, online conference poll spaces across sectors involving human-computer interaction (HCI) (McKenna, 2022) [29] and future technologies (McKenna, 2022) [30] were explored as a way of gathering data in the real world networking spaces of researchers, students, practitioners, and other interested participants and attendees.

5 Findings

Findings for the nurturing of ambient theory for smart cities are presented in this section where Sect. 5.1 focuses on survey, interview, and group and individual discussion findings while Sect. 5.2 focuses on online conference polling and other feedback related to paper presentations.

5.1 Case Study and Explanatory Correlational Findings

When asked to assess the extent to which elements such as *meaningfulness* contribute to increased value for data in smart cities, as shown in Table 3, on a Likert type scale where 1 = Not at all and 7 = Absolutely, 75% of survey participants responded toward the upper end of the scale at position 6 (Sure) and 25% responded at the upper end position of 7. When asked to assess the extent to which factors such as *information* contribute to the making of smart cities, 25% of survey participants responded at position 5 (Sort of), 25% at position 6 (Sure) and 50% at position 7.

Using the Real Statistics add in for Microsoft Excel (Zaiontz, 2023) [31], a Spearman correlation coefficient for ordinal data of .54 emerges and, according to Creswell (2018) [32], correlations in the .35 to .65 range "are useful for limited prediction."

Qualitatively, when asked to identify "other elements that contribute to your idea of a smart city?", a public administration executive responded with "learning capabilities" and "culture" while an educator responded with "appropriating the concept" along with

Table 3. Correlation between assessments of meaningfulness and information.

Variables	Assessments	Correlation
Meaningfulness	6 (75%); 7 (25%)	.54
Information	5 (25%); 6 (25%); 7 (50%)	

"implementing those technologies that would have the highest impact in solving current problems the city has." Another educator identified the importance of people and "the integration of the human entity in its surroundings for discovery, sociability and connectedness."

5.2 Online Conference Poll and Discussion Findings

Online conferences provided opportunities for real world explorations through platforms such as Whova, with networking and interaction features including messaging, discussion, and polling. For example, during a Future Technologies Conference (FTC 2021), polling was conducted pertaining to 'the ambient' in relation to a paper presented on ambient theory for smart cities (McKenna, 2022) [30]. Additionally, during an HCII 2022 conference, polling was conducted pertaining to ambient theory in smart cities in relation to a paper presentation (McKenna, 2022) [29].

During the FTC2021 conference, two polls were conducted with the questions, options, and responses shown in Tables 4 and 5.

Table 4. FTC2021 poll 1 pertaining to 'the ambient'.

Options	Responses (n = 21)
a) People	19%
b) Technology	5%
c) People interacting with technologies	76%

Poll 1 (FTC2021): What contributes to 'the ambient' in your city?

In response to poll 1 (Table 4), from a total of 21 responses, 19% of respondents selected a) People; 5% selected b) Technology; and 76% selected c) People interacting with technologies.

In response to poll 2 (Table 5), from a total of 16 responses, 44% of respondents selected a) Cultural events; 19% selected b) Economy; 31% selected the Urban mobility option; and 6% selected Other.

During the HCII2022 conference, one poll was conducted with the question, options, and responses shown in Table 6 where five checkbox options are included, meaning that more than one item could be selected.

In response to this poll (Table 6), from a total of 93 responses, 23% of respondents selected a); 20% selected b); 46% selected c); 32% selected d); and 4% selected e).

Table 5. FTC2021 poll 2 pertaining to 'the ambient' as 'heightened awareness'.

Options	Responses (n = 16)
a) Cultural events	44%
b) Economy (e.g., smart products, recommending of products, etc.)	19%
c) Urban mobility options	31%
d) Other	6%

Poll 2 (FTC2021): Where do you notice 'the ambient', as in, 'heightened awareness' in your city?

Table 6. HCII2022 poll on the usability of ambient theory for smart cities.

Options	Responses (n = 93)
a) ASTC could guide urban researchers	23%
b) ASTC could guide urban practitioners	20%
c) ASTC could help us think differently about urban design	46%
d) I have no idea	32%
e) Other	4%

Poll 1 (HCII2022): How would ambient theory for smart cities (ATSC) be usable in your city?

Additionally, when entering the session on urban life and smart cities, participants were asked to respond to the question: *Why do smart cities matter?* Responses included comments such as "They are an opportunity to rethink the city"; "to lower levels of automobile traffic"; and "promote better, more healthy and environmentally friendly spaces." It was noted that whether such opportunities are taken in smart cities "is dependent on how well IoT folks approach their designs" where IoT refers to the Internet of Things. In response to the paper presentation on ambient theory for smart cities (McKenna, 2022) [29], a conference participant commented that "when you see a theory like this it does promote quite inventive thinking in other directions" adding that "the attributes of usability in this ambient theoretical scoping actually is a very, very interesting way of thinking about usability factors in these contexts."

6 Discussion

Findings pertaining to the nurturing of theory using ambient theory for smart cities as an example are discussed in this section in relation to the types of theory nurturing shown in Fig. 1, including – defend and support; discovery of special properties; make contact with the world; identifying problems with the theory; and theory use and uptake.

Defend and Support. Two variables are identified and explored in this paper for use with ambient theory for smart cities (ATSC), namely *information* as a proxy for awareness and *meaningfulness* as a proxy for action. Based on survey assessments of the variables, a Spearman correlation for ordinal data of .54 emerges with "limited prediction" (Creswell, 2018) [32] potential. The variables explored in this paper serve to complement the series of variables for working with ATSC found in other publications on the theory [6, 29, 30, 33] and as such, could be said to further defend and support use of ATSC.

Discovery of Special Properties. Findings in conference spaces indicate that the 'special properties' (said to be important for theory nurturing) of ambient theory for smart cities are being discovered in terms of an online conference polling conducted during the HCII2022 conference (Table 6) where 46% of respondents indicated that ambient theory for smart cities "could help us think differently about urban design." It is also important to note that 4% of respondents selected the "other" category indicating the need for further probing to discover what "other" ways that ATSC "would be usable" in the city. To the extent that ambient theory for smart cities is found to promote discovery, nurturing of the theory would seem to be occurring.

Make Contact with the World. It could be said that the nurturing of ambient theory for smart cities is occurring in terms of enabling the theory to make contact with the world through conference presentations, discussions, and polling (McKenna, 2022) [29, 30] and also through other publications (McKenna, 2023) [33]. Indeed, among the approaches to the exploration of theory in this paper, such as that of using an online interactive conference networking space, possibly provided the theory with a 'chance to push the envelope' [7] in the minds of those responding to the conference poll enabling researchers to learn more about the 'full scope of its special implications' [7] in terms of adaptive and dynamic potentials while opening possibilities to stimulate interesting discussions, debates, and interpretations going forward.

Problems with the Theory. It is worth noting that 32% of conference poll respondents (Table 6) indicated they had "no idea how ambient theory for smart cities would be usable in their city" and this is understandable given the newness and early-stage development of the theory (McKenna, 2021) [6]. This level of response (32%) is also suggestive of the understandable lack of awareness of the theory and the extent of nurturing still to be done in assisting people to learn more about the theory as well as how to engage with the discovery of potentials for the theory.

This paper also seeks to push the boundaries of ATSC to extend more generally to smart environments and to smart spaces in accommodating aspects that might seem to be missing, in order to improve the uptake for city planning and design of urban environments.

Theory Use and Uptake. That 68% of respondents to the HCII2022 conference poll (Table 6) seem to be aware of ambient theory for smart cities (ATSC) suggests a possibly significant consideration and potential for uptake of the theory. That FTC2021 conference poll respondents (Table 4 and Table 5) seem to be aware of 'the ambient' particularly in relation to people interacting with technologies (Table 4) at 76% and to cultural events (Table 5) at 44% suggests good potential for the uptake of a theory pertaining to the ambient such as ambient theory for smart cities (ATSC).

It should be noted that participation in online conference polling and other activities was perhaps motivated in part as a way of garnering leaderboard points, yet participants did choose to respond to the poll on ATSC (Table 6), among many other polls to choose from.

7 Conclusion

In conclusion, this paper explores approaches to the nurturing of theory for smart environments using the example of ambient theory for smart cities and as such, is significant in several ways. Firstly, a contemporary, real-world theory in the evolving domain of smart cities is being nurtured, and as it were, 'allowed to develop through contact with the world' to use the words of Higgins [7]. Secondly, through nurturing of the theory, ambient theory for smart cities is being generative possibly of what Higgins [7] would refer to as 'new ideas and new discoveries' (e.g., pertaining to urban design) while contributing to ongoing understandings of smart cities and smart environments and associated potentials. And finally, with the understanding that theories are by nature, dynamic, evolving, and adaptive, this paper seeks to contribute a welcoming dimension to the theoretical environment for the rapidly evolving, complex, and challenging domains of smart cities, smart environments, and smart spaces, in order for theories such as ambient theory for smart cities to grow, evolve, and flourish. Among the limitations of this paper is the use of proxies for the variables explored and this may be mitigated going forward, by the use of other, more direct variables. Indeed, limitations of this work serve to inform research and practice opportunities and challenges going forward. As such, this paper encourages uptake and ongoing use of theories for smart cities, regions, and environments through exploration, testing, further validation, discussion, extension, and interpretation whether focusing on ambient theory for smart cities, activity theory, or other theories relevant to smart environments and spaces.

References

1. Batty, M.: Big data, smart cities and city planning. Dialog. Hum. Geogr. **3**(3), 274–279 (2013). https://doi.org/10.1177/2043820613513390
2. Roy, A.: The 21st century metropolis: new geographies of theory. Reg. Stud. **43**(6), 819–830 (2009). https://doi.org/10.1080/00343400701809665
3. Brenner, N.: New Urban Spaces: Urban Theory and the Scale Question. Oxford University Press, New York (2019)
4. Batty, M.: Defining smart cities: high and low frequency cities, big data and urban theory. In: Willis, K.S., Aurigi, A. (eds.) The Routledge Companion to Smart Cities, pp. 51–60. Routledge (2020). https://doi.org/10.4324/9781315178387-5
5. Harrison, C., Abbott Donnelly, I.: A theory of smart cities. In: Proceedings of the 55th Annual Meeting of the ISSS. International Society for Systems Sciences, pp. 521–535. ISSS, UK (2011)
6. McKenna, H.P.: The importance of theory for understanding smart cities: Making a case for ambient theory. In: Streitz, N., Konomi, S. (eds.) HCII 2021. LNCS, vol. 12782, pp. 41–54. Springer, Cham (2021). https://doi.org/10.1007/978-3-030-77015-0_4
7. Higgins, E.T.: Making a theory useful: lessons handed down. Pers. Soc. Psychol. Rev. **8**(2), 138–145 (2004)

8. Nardi, B.: Appropriating theory. In: Sonnenwald, D.H. (ed.) Theory Development in the Information Sciences, pp. 204–221. University of Texas Press (2021). https://doi.org/10.7560/308240-014

9. Nardi, B., Redmiles, D. (eds.): Activity theory and the practice of design. J. Comput.-Support. Coop. Work, **11**(1–2) (2002)

10. McCullough, M.: Ambient Commons: Attention in the Age of Embodied Information. The MIT Press, Cambridge (2013). https://doi.org/10.7551/mitpress/8947.001.0001

11. Merriam-Webster Dictionary: Nurture (2022). https://www.merriam-webster.com/dictionary/nurture. Accessed 27 Dec 2022

12. Das, S.K., Cook, J.: Designing and modeling smart environments. In: Proceedings of IEEE International Symposium World Wireless, Mobile Multimedia Networking, pp. 490–494 (2006)

13. Reig, S., Fong, T., Forlizzi, J., Steinfeld, A.: Theory and design considerations for the user experience of smart environments. IEEE Trans. Human-Mach. Syst. **52**(3), 522–535 (2022). https://doi.org/10.1109/THMS.2022.3142112

14. Gračanin, D., Lasisi, R.O., Azab, M., Eltoweissy, M.: Next generation smart built environments: the fusion of empathy, privacy and ethics. In: First IEEE International Conference on Trust, Privacy and Security in Intelligent Systems and Applications (TPS-ISA), pp. 260–267 (2019). https://doi.org/10.1109/TPS-ISA48467.2019.00041

15. Nakashima, H., Aghajan, H., Augusto, J.C. (eds.): Handbook of Ambient Intelligence and Smart Environments. Springer, New York (2010). https://doi.org/10.1007/978-0-387-93808-0

16. Augusto, J.C.: Contexts and context-awareness revisited from an intelligent environments perspective. Appl. Artif. Intell. **36**(1), 2008644 (2022). https://doi.org/10.1080/08839514.2021.2008644

17. Streitz, N.: Beyond 'smart-only' cities: redefining the 'smart-everything' paradigm. J. Ambient. Intell. Humaniz. Comput. **10**(2), 791–812 (2018). https://doi.org/10.1007/s12652-018-0824-1

18. Streitz, N.A.: From smart-only cities towards humane and cooperative hybrid cities. Technology | Architecture + Design (Special Issue on Intelligence) **5**(2) 127–133 (2021). https://doi.org/10.1080/24751448.2021.1967050

19. Streitz, N.A., Riedmann-Streitz, C.: Rethinking 'smart' islands towards humane, self-aware, and cooperative hybrid islands. Interactions **29**(3), 54–60 (2022). https://doi.org/10.1145/3527200

20. Streitz, N.A., Riedmann-Streitz, C., Quintal, L.: From 'smart-only' island towards lighthouse of research and innovation. In: Streitz, N.A., Konomi, S. (eds.) Distributed, Ambient and Pervasive Interactions. Smart Environments, Ecosystems, and Cities. Lecture Notes in Computer Science, vol. 13325, pp. 105–126. Springer, Cham (2022). https://doi.org/10.1007/978-3-031-05463-1_8

21. Eisenhardt, K.M., Graebner, M.E.: Theory building from cases: opportunities and challenges. Acad. Manag. J. **50**(1), 25–32 (2007). https://doi.org/10.5465/amj.2007.24160888

22. Corley, K.G., Gioia, D.A.: Building theory about theory building: what constitutes a theoretical contribution? Acad. Manag. Rev. **36**(1), 12–32 (2011). https://doi.org/10.5465/AMR.2011.55662499

23. Byron, K., Thatcher, S.M.B.: Editors' comments: What I know now that I wish I knew then—teaching theory and theory building. Acad. Manag. Rev. **41**(1), 1–8 (2016)

24. Gregor, S.: On theory. In: The Routledge Companion to Management Information Systems. 1st Ed. pp. 57–72. Routledge, London (2017)

25. Shepherd, D.A., Suddaby, R.: Theory building: a review and integration. J. Manag. **43**(1), 59–86 (2017). https://doi.org/10.1177/0149206316647102

26. Fors, P., Lennerfors, T.T.: The individual-care nexus: a theory of entrepreneurial care for sustainable entrepreneurship. Sustainability **11**(18), 4904 (2019). https://doi.org/10.3390/su11184904
27. Shrestha, Y.R., He, V.F., Puranam, P., von Krogh, G.: Algorithm supported induction for building theory: how can we use prediction models to theorize? Organ. Sci. **32**(3), 856–880 (2020). https://doi.org/10.1287/orsc.2020.1382
28. Yin, R.K.: Case Study Research: Design and Methods, 6th edn. Sage, Thousand Oaks (2017)
29. McKenna, H.P.: Exploring the usefulness and usability of ambient theory for smart cities. In: Streitz, Norbert A., Konomi, Shin'ichi (eds.) Distributed, Ambient and Pervasive Interactions. Smart Environments, Ecosystems, and Cities. Lecture Notes in Computer Science, vol. 13325, pp. 169–180. Springer, Cham (2022). https://doi.org/10.1007/978-3-031-05463-1_12
30. McKenna, H.P.: Is ambient theory for smart cities even a theory? An affirmative assessment. In: Arai, K. (ed.) FTC 2021. LNNS, vol. 359, pp. 550–558. Springer, Cham (2022). https://doi.org/10.1007/978-3-030-89880-9_41
31. Zaiontz, C.: Real statistics using excel (2023). www.real-statistics.com
32. Creswell, J.W.: Educational Research: Planning, Conducting, and Evaluating Quantitative and Qualitative Research, 6th edn. Pearson, Boston (2018)
33. McKenna, H.P.: Urban Life and the Ambient in Smart Cities, Learning Cities, and Future Cities. IGI Global, Hershey (2023). https://doi.org/10.4018/978-1-6684-4096-4

Future Living Lab/Design Research Project to Explore Local Values for Infrastructure Services with the Participation of Residents

Takashi Shirasawa[✉]

Hitachi, Ltd. Research & Development Group, 1-280, Higashi-Koigakubo, Kokubunji 185-8601, Tokyo, Japan
Takashi.shirasawa.sf@hitachi.com

Abstract. The structural decline in Japan's population has led to improved convenience so that everyone is able to live on one's own. The result, however, has been a weakening of mutually supportive communication. These shifts in social structure provide people with opportunities to fundamentally reconsider the existing social infrastructure services and the way residents relate to infrastructure. In this research, the future infrastructure service that should be developed is "infrastructure service with the participation of residents, in which residents build their own flexible infrastructure service suitable for the size of their community," and the necessary activities for building such a service are summarized in four categories. In addition, the especially important "Value Exploration," which explores values that should be cherished in the community with anticipation of future changes in the community, and "Community Creation," which creates the driving force for such activities, are reported with case studies of their activities. Through the reflection on the case studies of activities, it was possible to confirm the importance of "value exploration" and to discover a new role that social infrastructure services should carry in the future, which is the role of "engagement" to encourage people to change their own ways of living. The challenges for further research are to build a system based on the values explored and to embed it in the community, and to achieve this, the four activities must be connected and the process needs to be cycled.

Keywords: Living Lab · Design Research · Infrastructure Service · Engagement

1 Introduction

Japan is a country with unprecedented challenges that is suffering from a structural population decline. While the declining birthrate and aging population demand convenient services to compensate for the shortage of labor, the increasing sophisticated services, especially in urban areas, have made it possible for a single person to complete many activities of daily life. This improved convenience has led to a decline in local community participation and a weakening of mutually supportive communities. Furthermore, in rural areas, it is difficult to maintain large conventional infrastructure services due to a decrease in the number of users and lack of financial resources. As a result, the local transportation is disappearing, such as the number of discontinued bus routes expanding each year. [1].

In the shift from urban concentration to rural decentralization of lifestyles, it is necessary for Japan's infrastructure services to transition from existing forms of large, uniform services provided to everyone to more flexible forms that adapt to the size of the community and the way people live. As a measure embodying this flexible infrastructure service, the Japanese government is promoting "The Vision for a Digital Garden City Nation" [2] to create a mechanism to implement solutions to social issues utilizing digital technology and local asset.

In contrast, experiments of local services using digital technology are often focused on the functional verification of the technology, or the experiment itself becomes the goal, therefore, the services considered are not established as local services. Hill [3] of the Swedish Innovation Agency provides a perspective on the role of local infrastructure services as a means, not an object, to make a society of people happy, and that broader societal benefits need to be considered. Therefore, it is important that not only the companies and governments that conduct the experiments, but also the residents who are engaged in the experiments, be involved in the infrastructure as their own. For example, Oakland, California, has begun a practice such as Tactical Transit [4] in which the local residents, as well as local government and companies, are involved as users in the process of studying the best bus routes for their community and taking ownership of the city's transportation system. The infrastructure service that we aim to build is a new, small, flexible form that utilizes digital technology and suits the size and needs of the local community, furthermore, the operation of the service is a participatory infrastructure service in which local residents are involved on their own terms. However, the current infrastructure services are uniform regardless of the size of the community and are inflexible, following existing rules. Furthermore, the attitude of users toward these infrastructure services is that these services are a matter for the government, not for the users themselves, and are not even of concern about infrastructure service itself.

In order to build ideal infrastructure services from the current situation, it is necessary to revise the preconceived notions about the role of infrastructure services that have been imprinted on many residents, such as that infrastructure services are government-led, and that residents and businesses cannot be involved also that these services cannot be easily modified or improved. And while individuals and NPOs are widely active in response to the current infrastructure services, they are working individually and thus do not engage in major activities to build well-established infrastructure services. Therefore, it is necessary to unite these activities under a common goal and create a driving force for ongoing activities. We believe that the best approach to involve various stakeholders and to transform people's mindsets and manners is to create open innovation [5] that transcends the boundaries of industries, rather than one company.

Infrastructure services described in this paper refer to "facilities and services that are considered public infrastructures and mechanisms that support society and our daily lives, and are indispensable to our daily lives, such as electricity, gas, water, roads, railroads, and other transportation facilities, and telecommunication services such as telephone and Internet" [6].

2 A Practical Approach to Building Infrastructure Services with Participation of Residents

2.1 The User-Driven Open Innovation Method: Living Lab

In considering a mechanism for social infrastructure services in which citizens are the main users and diverse stakeholders are involved in providing value, we referred to living lab, a user-driven open innovation method. Living labs that has the background of "Open Innovation 2.0" a European policy that aims for smart and sustainable value creation by a diverse range of stakeholders, are co-creation activities involving users and residents, and although living labs originated in the U.S., it is reported that they have been active in Europe since around 2000 [7]. Living labs have not attracted much attention in Japan, where many companies are reluctant to collaborate with other companies [8]. However, the SDGs set in 2015 have triggered the government and many companies in Japan to start facing social issues, accelerating various activities toward a sustainable society. Social issues are complicated by a variety of factors, and the technology and solution requirements for solving them are uncertain, so they cannot be handled by a single company or government alone. Furthermore, since social issues are closely related to peoples' daily lives, such as childcare support, the elderly, and poverty issues, it is necessary to grasp the issues from the perspective of people living in the society, and to verify and evaluate solutions to these issues. As a result, the activities of living labs, in which governments and companies work with citizens to implement innovations, have become the focus of much attention in Japan.

2.2 Explore New Meanings in Practice

Kimura, whose topic was "The Possibility of Living Labs and Structural Challenges in Japan" [9] described the following patterns of different aims and approaches in conducting activities in living labs. Pattern 1 is a "living lab where connections are made" where people who have never collaborated before coming together and begin to create activities with involvement. Pattern 2 is a "problem-solving living lab" that addresses urgent issues based on facts of daily life. Pattern 3 is a "living lab that creates new meanings" which aims to solve social issues through the creation of new meanings, specifically new visions, and values for daily life. Kimura also notes that patterns 2 and 3 are projects that are undertaken with specific aims, but that this difference is often not recognized. We believe that "developing relationships" is an essential activity for the diverse stakeholders of infrastructure services to work together to promote activities in the community and summarize the pattern of living labs into the following two categories.

Pattern A "Creating new meanings + developing relationships" is activities that aim to solve social issues through the discovery of new visions and values for daily life involving a variety of stakeholders.

Pattern B "Problem solving + developing relationships" is activities to solve urgent issues with diverse stakeholders involved in the field and the issues to be addressed, based on the facts on the field of daily life.

While both patterns are necessary activities to consider for infrastructure services, the challenge for us is to transition from the existing relationship between people and infrastructure services to a new relationship that is adapted to a changing society. This means discovering new meaning in the relationship between people and infrastructure services, and focusing on the process of Pattern A. And workshops and dialogues are being held around the world, including in Japan, to create a new meaning for Pattern A. The concept is being put together as a vision for the future, but there can still be a great distance between the meaning discovered and our own lives.

The SPACE10 [10], established by IKEA, the world's largest furniture retailer, portrays the theme as a concept for tomorrow, not for today's business, such as the food crisis, climate change, and housing shortages. And to deepen understanding of the concept, prototypes that allow visitors to experience the concept are exhibited in the lab space. This approach represents one direction to shorten the distance between people and infrastructure services, and we believe that, as with Pattern B, it is important to have a practical, field-based, proof-of-concept perspective for activities that create new meanings.

2.3   Embedding Services in Society

Even if a new meaning is discovered and a service that embodies that meaning is created, it cannot function as an infrastructure service unless it is accepted and permeated by society. For example, the issue of contact verification applications introduced in Japan as a countermeasure against infectious diseases related to COVID-19 has not been sufficiently widespread. The application had the simulation that "to reduce the cumulative number of infections by half, about half of the population needs to use the application," but the application was not effective due to insufficient social acceptance, with only about 40 million cases (about 30% of the population) even after two years since its release [11]. As described above, even though digital services can solve social issues directly related to our daily lives, they will become unused services if they do not successfully penetrate social acceptability. This consideration of social acceptability is an important perspective for establishing infrastructure services in society.

2.4   Four Activities to Create Infrastructure Services with the Participation of Residents

Based on the above perspectives, the following four activities (see Fig. 1) are necessary when considering the creation of infrastructure services with the participation of residents for future society, which is our goal.

1. Value Exploration: Activities to find new roles and requirements for infrastructure service responsibilities.
2. System Construction: Activities to embody the values found in the "Value Exploration" into services that are useful in the real world, and to build a "system" that defines the roles and responsibilities of the people involved so that it can function within the community.
3. Embedding Into Society: Activities to develop an operational system for involving people and checking their adaptation status to enhance the social acceptability of the new system created in the "System Construction".

4. Community Creation: Activities to make members and create touchpoints with society to gain driving force for the above three activities.

Value Exploration

Activities to find new roles and requirements for infrastructure service responsibilities.

System Construction

Activities to embody the values into services that are useful in the real world, and to build a "system" can function within the community.

Embedding Into Society

Activities to develop an operational system and to enhance the social acceptability of the new system

Community Creation

Activities to make members and create touchpoints with society in order to gain driving force for the above three activities.

Fig. 1. Four activities to create infrastructure services with the participation of residents

2.4.1 Value Exploration

This corresponds to Pattern A. "Creating new meanings + developing relationships" of living lab activities, which can be rephrased as activities to create new meanings together with local residents while capturing future changes in the community. Therefore, in considering the process of this activity, we referred to the cycle of the "search," "experiment," and "evaluation" processes described in "WISE PLACE LIVING LABS Making Futures Together," [12] a guideline for living lab practice published by Future Center Alliance Japan (FCAJ), a general incorporated association that conducts research, promotion, and practice related to innovation creation places. While the process presented by FCAJ covers the activities of the entire living lab that produces the service, we propose to apply this process cycle in the "Value Exploration" activities. As indicated in 2.2, a prototype that enables people to experience new meanings found through dialogue in the community will be created and experimented with in the community. Then, the new meaning is evaluated through observation of the experiment and interviews with residents. This process should be repeated to clarify the new meaning.

2.4.2 System Construction

Pattern B. "Problem solving + developing relationships" is an activity that is conducted in many living labs. The case in reference is an activity considered by the Tama-pura Living Lab. It was an experiment to solve the apparent problem of revitalizing a declining local community by implementing a new meaning of "mutual aid" among residents in the community with a "system" called a local currency that could be used continuously and was useful [13]. Here, it is important to evaluate whether a "system" can be developed and continuously operated that residents can use and recognize its effectiveness, and to consider what roles should be assigned for its operation.

2.4.3 Embedding Into Society

As mentioned in Sect. 2.3, no matter how advanced a service is built through digital technology, if its acceptability does not spread throughout society, the service cannot become established in the community and will end up as a PoC. Therefore, these activities should again return to the user's perspective and identify potential future risks that may arise through service use, such as usability, data handling, and the impact of service use on others. Furthermore, it is necessary to identify risks in terms of acceptability and ethics for various users in society, such as those who are interested in, opposed to, or indifferent to the target service. Then, we intend to develop an environment and operational structure in which residents can use the system to provide value while responding to the extracted risks through practice.

2.4.4 Community Creation

In the living lab pattern, this corresponds to "developing relationships" utilizing a place, but it does not envision activities that are tied to a real place and constitute a solid organization, as is the case with general living lab activities. The reason is that the set of activities from "Value Exploration" to "Embedding Into Society", which begin with finding new meanings, aim to assemble new meanings while collaborating with various individuals, groups, and organizations that are working to face future local issues. However, the activities of these individuals, groups, and organizations do not have a large impact on society and the community, and they do not have the strength to sustain themselves. Therefore, it is important to create a mechanism to create horizontal cooperation under the common theme of confronting future local issues, and to lead to the driving force to sustain these activities.

2.5 Future Living Lab Activities Focused on the Creation of New Meanings and Community Creation

To develop a completely new type of infrastructure service with the participation of residents, we have focused their efforts on the initial process of "Value Exploration" and "Community Creation" to sustain it. And we named it "Future Living Lab" because its activities are future-oriented and based on the living lab. The following is a description of the "Value Exploration" and "Community Creation" that took place in the two areas.

3   Case Studies

3.1   Case1: Value Exploration "Bring and Eat. My Vegetables"

Active period: from 1st Aug. 2018 to 31st Mar 2019.

Experimental period: from 24th Nov. And 16th Dec. 2018.

This is the first Future Living Lab activity conducted in Kokubunji City, a suburb of Tokyo where our research institute is located (see Fig. 2). Through community designers who are well versed in local conditions and have extensive local contacts, we were able to engage in dialogue with various local stakeholders, including farmers who produce local

Fig. 2. Kokubunji and Tama Area Location

vegetables in the Kokubunji area, NPOs that deliver local vegetables to local restaurants, and restaurants that actively use local vegetables.

What became clear from the dialogue was the existence of a gap in how people define the meaning of locally produced vegetables for local consumption. While farmers, NPOs that support the delivery of local vegetables, and local restaurants envisioned a worldview of creating a culture of coexistence between agriculture and residential areas in urban and suburban areas for future through local production for local consumption, local residents had only an image of being able to obtain cheap, fresh brand-name vegetables.

We focused on this gap in the perception of the meaning of local production for local consumption and planned an experiment to create an opportunity for local residents to understand through experience the new meaning of a culture of agricultural and residential coexistence as envisioned by farmers and NPOs.

The experiment would take advantage of an annual community event that was expected to have many participants. Local residents would purchase locally grown vegetables from farmers and bring them to restaurants themselves. Then, local residents can have the vegetables they bring to the restaurants cooked and eaten. This system allows participating residents to experience a part of the closed circle of local production for local consumption within the community, from production to delivery, processing, and consumption. We created a prototype of this system concept and a web application to support the system, which allows participants to make reservations at restaurants that would cook the vegetables they have purchased (see Fig. 3). The involvement of local residents in this series of circles created new relationships among stakeholders who had never before crossed over through vegetables.

Participants in the event commented that "it is interesting to be able to feel the presence of farmers closer to home" and "I would be happy if I could use this system on a daily basis." By creating a connection between residents and producers, we were able to confirm a change in the residents' awareness of urban agriculture. Through direct communication with local residents, participating farmers also commented that "the creation of connections among farmers, restaurants, and residents helps motivate farmers," confirming that the connections among people within a community can led to the strength of local activities.

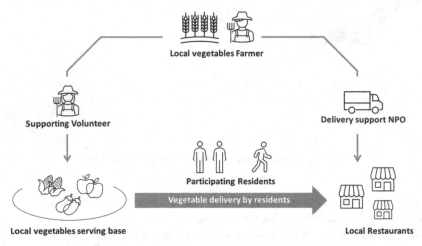

Fig. 3. Local Production for Local Consumption Circulation System

3.2   Case2: Community Creation "TAMA Future Co-creation Conferences"

Active period: since 1st Apr. 2019.

While the 3–1 project was meaningful in sharing new meanings found in the community with the public through experimentation, it was strongly characterized as a one-off event and could not be made into an ongoing activity that is rooted in daily life. Therefore, the community designer and we began to explore the formation of a community that would create opportunities and places to continue relationships with local stakeholders who empathized with such a new meaning of exploration. The community designer was positive that large companies, such as the organization to which we belong, are interested in community co-creation. In contrast, he advised that when such activities expand and cover a wider value chain, there is a possibility that organizations and small and medium-sized enterprises (SMEs) that are part of the value chain could be exploited. Therefore, rather than having one organization take the lead, we envisioned a community that emphasizes the perspective of exposing their activities to the community and engaging in dialogue on the theme of the community's future.

We have started an experimental collaborative media project called "Tama Future Co-creation Conference "[14] to create opportunities for future-oriented collaboration among companies, local governments, academic institutions, and startups based in the Tama area, which also includes Kokubunji city.

This activity is a community that creates collaborative creation projects by conducting three main processes (see Fig. 4) and communicating a series of activities via web media. The first process is "Dialogue," an in-depth dialogue with organizations and companies involved in community activities in the Tama area to find out what kind of future changes they see in the community through their activities. By starting with this activity, the organizations and businesses that are implementing the practice can get hints and ideas for capturing new meanings through dialogue. The next process is a "monologue," an activity in which local organizations and businesses interviewed in the "dialogue" are asked to capture changes in the community and discuss within their organization or business members what new meaning they are trying to find. This activity once again facilitates confirmation of what they are trying to capture through their experiment. Finally, a "meet-up" is an activity in which local players who share the new meaning discussed in the "monologue" are invited to participate, and the assembled players and companies discuss how to incorporate this new meaning into their services. This step requires clear objectives and intentions for the activity, as it is the place to actually have serious discussions with local players. The first two activities allow the participants to take the time to reflect on their own activities, allowing for lively discussions with local players who are not involved at all.

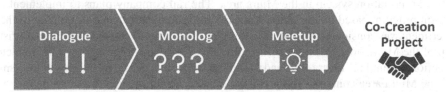

Fig. 4. Three Main Processes in "Tama Future Co-creation Conference"

In a general living lab, a place is created where physical gatherings can take place, stakeholders related to the theme of the living lab gather, and an operational structure is established with clearly defined roles, but we decided not to take this form. This is because our goal is not to solve the actual local problems, but to search for new meanings for the future that have not yet been clarified, and therefore it would be difficult to have a discussion with a large group from the beginning, and we believed that a form that is easy to discuss and flexible in size would be more suitable. This approach has allowed us to maintain relationships with various local players and create new meanings from the dialogue we have had with them over time, although the implementation of collaborative projects has not yet been numerous.

3.3   Case3: Value Exploration "MAP Of the Miura Coast Made by Everyone"

Active period: from 1st Apr. 2021 to 31st Dec. 2021.

Experimental period: from 11th Sept. And 30th Sept. 2021.

The project was conducted in the Miura area of Kanagawa Prefecture, a suburb of Tokyo where our research institute was located (see Fig. 5). The characteristics of the area are that the population is declining faster than the national average, so it is necessary to consider new infrastructure services suited to the area. And while there are many activities to revitalize the area, there is a sense of stagnation in the entire area, which is a problem in this area. [15].

Fig. 5. Miura Kaigan and Miura Area Location

This project was conducted in cooperation with a rail company that serves as the main transportation system in the Miura area. The rail company plans to implement a tourism program based on the Miura Kaigan Station in the area, and the content of the experiment was considered in relation to this plan. The experiment was to create a tourist map of the Miura area by asking visitors and local residents to write down the hidden attractions around the Miura area, and to explore the resources and new forms of tourism that the Miura area contains. The prototype created for this project was a white map 9 m wide and 2.4 m high that was installed in front of Miura Kaigan Station for 20 days, and residents and visitors were asked to write their "favorite way to spend time in Miura area" on stickers and attach them to the map (see Fig. 6).

Fig. 6. The prototype "Map of The Miura Coast Made By Everyone"

We also prepared three different participation methods with different levels of stress to avoid low participation, but in fact, participation was stable throughout the period with more than 500 participants, far exceeding our expectations (see Fig. 7). Of particular interest was the content of the stickers. About the same number of general informational items were attached to the stickers with their own thoughts and stories, which are usually difficult to express out loud (see Fig. 8). And due to the characteristics of the area as a tourist destination, we initially expected that the number of writings from people outside the area would be considerably larger than those from residents within the area. However, the numbers of stickers were almost equal, indicating the strength of the interest and affection of the residents for the area.

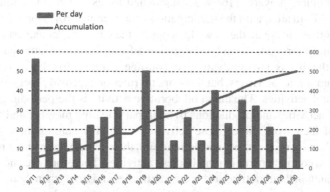

Fig. 7. Changes in the daily and cumulative number of stickers pasted during the project

Fig. 8. Positive Thoughts on the local community visualized

We also received feedback from a local resident who said, "This is the first time I've learned that there are so many people who love this area."

Although it is not possible to measure how much thought was put into each sticker by the people who participated in this project, the fact that they empathized with the positive content about community-based facilities and places, such as elementary schools, led the participants to interpret that there were many people in the area who felt the same way, and to add their own thoughts to the stickers. In fact, it is believed that the presence and traces of "affection and commitment to the area" created a chain of empathy that resulted in more than 500 stickers being placed on the map. Initially, this was an experiment to explore new forms of tourism utilizing local tourism resources together with rail company. However, the active participation of not only visitors but also local residents unexpectedly expressed their affection and commitment to the area. This exposure not only gave us a new opportunity to learn that there are people who feel the same way about the local area, but also to find a new meaning as civic pride, rather than tourism, in the resources that the area contains. We believe that this new meaning cannot be assumed in advance but can only be discovered from the local context through practices.

3.4 Case 4: Community Creation "Koyart"

Active period: since 1st Aug. 2018.

This community, "koyart" [16] was established by us and a community designer working in the Miura area, with the participation of university professors of architecture and companies that can create their own huts, under the theme of "considering the future of the community through art and the creation of huts". The unique feature of this community is that it sets a major theme to encourage members to take a more proactive approach to community activities, but there are no rules or approval processes regarding the approach and activities. The only collaborative activity is the periodic gathering of actual cases of activities and productions by each participating member and their public presentation of their work. Since these activities are highly autonomous, with a high degree of freedom for each activity and community, there was concern about maintaining the motivation to continue participating in these activities. Therefore, we encouraged the members to maintain their motivation for their activities and strengthen their engagement in the community by regularly promoting the activities in well-known media and art events as well as exhibiting them in museums, which are attractive to members. In addition, because of the theme of "considering the future from the community" and the fact that university and high school students from the Miura area were the core members, it was easy to obtain support from local residents and to attract attention within the local community when expanding individual activities in the community, and these factors encouraged the driving force of this community. Although each of the student works was small, the exhibition had a powerful impact by bringing together works of rich individuality that expressed the students' feelings toward the local community (see Fig. 9).

Fig. 9. Exhibition at the Yokosuka Museum of Art

As a result, the Yokosuka Museum of Art has become a regular exhibition, and local universities have incorporated this initiative into their educational curriculum. The rail company that conducted the experiment with us in 3.3 also recognized the potential for new tourism in the message that this community was delivering and promoted collaboration with us.

For activities that are not aimed at solving a particular technology or local issue, but rather at discovering new meanings from the context through local practices, we believe that a form of community that freely expresses activities and ideas from unique perspectives and unites these activities to create a significant impact, such as the activities of this community, is appropriate.

4 Conclusion

4.1 "Engagement" is a Key Factor of New Infrastructure Services

By separating out the "Value Exploration" and "Community Creation" activities from the four activities required to create infrastructure services with the participation of residents, we were able to discover a new meaning of what the role of new infrastructure services is. That is, through infrastructure services, relationships are created between people and between people and communities, creating "engagement" that not only improves the convenience of one's life, but also allows one to change oneself.

This concept of "engagement" is based on Nakajima's idea of "engagement" as a specialist in Eastern philosophy. In describing the image of human beings in the future society, Nakajima says that even if consumption shifts from goods to services, the concept of "ownership" is at the root of people who consume, and the excellent services that symbolize "*koto*" consumption are merely a variant of ownership. And services that place value on possession expand what one can do but cannot change oneself. He mentions that in order to build a prosperous society, we should value "engagement," which is not reduced to possession, but transforms oneself. [17] By adding this "engagement" function to infrastructure services, it is possible to create a cycle in which people and people, people and communities, and people and infrastructure services transform each other in order to build a society of well-being.

The following is a summary of the four functions that we have found through our activities to create "engagement" with the new infrastructure services.

1. Expressing positive feelings about the local community
   This function confirms the presence of other residents and their feelings about the community. And by sharing a positive sense of community, it encourages action toward engagement. It also provides an opportunity for new visitors to become engaged in the community.
2. Creating an open environment where everyone can take on new challenges.
   Create an environment where individuals with an interest in the community can easily try something if they want to. As small challenges are expressed in the community, it creates an opportunity to connect with people around to support them and exchange words directly with them.
3. Connecting each activity to create new activities
   Create new services by connecting multiple activities. In addition, it simplifies complicated mechanisms such as money transfers and contracts that arise when connecting activities.
4. Uniting the activities of residents to deliver the thoughts of the community outside of the community
   Provide opportunities for local residents to communicate about their community to the outside community. Feedback from outside the community helps the residents themselves to learn about aspects of the community that they had not noticed before. This activity generates a driving force for community activities.

We believe that these functions (see Fig. 10) will be important perspectives when considering new infrastructure services, not only focusing on functionality, but also on how to bring about changes in the relationships between people and between people and communities.

1. Expressing positive feelings about the local community
2. Creating an open environment where everyone can take on new challenges
3. Connecting each activity to create new activities
4. Uniting the activities of residents to deliver the thoughts of the community outside

Fig. 10. Four functions to create "engagement" with the new infrastructure services

4.2 " Value Exploration " is Important for New Infrastructure Service

Looking back over the past three years of practice, including cases not included in this paper, we found that the new meanings explored were not found in a planned manner, but through cycle of the process of exploration, experimentation, and evaluation of the culture to be cherished and thoughts about the community that were revealed through dialogue with the local residents. Furthermore, while the current issues are very easy to understand and realize, it is easy to look away from other possibilities, so we believe that the new meaning became easier to recognize because we separated the activities from the activities to consider a useful system of "System Construction".

In Japan in particular, the living lab is challenged with the "System Construction " to develop a useful system and the " Embedding Into Society " to examine how to make the system take root in the community. However, to consider new infrastructure services for the future, the "Value Exploration" which is the study of creating new meanings that we have been conducting, is an extremely important activity.

4.3 Toward the Next Steps

Although we indicated the importance of "Value Exploration," local residents do not recognize the vegetable delivery by residents and the tourist board in front of the train station, which we experimented with, as a necessary new infrastructure service for the community, and local residents want to build a service that is actually useful. Therefore, the next step that we will focus on is to connect the value found in the "Value Exploration" to the "System Construction" and "Embedding Into Society". And we believe that the connected flow is not in one direction, but in both directions (see Fig. 11). For example, the value found in the "Value Exploration" section, "Culture of Agriculture and Residential Coexistence," will be applied in the "System Construction" section to create a more practical mechanism, such as setting up a fan site for local vegetables that connects farmers and delivery support NPO with local residents or using local currency to support local vegetables. If, as a result of the "Embedding Into Society" section, the acceptability of the system is investigated and it is found that there is a possibility of disparities among residents depending on their involvement in the community, it is an important process to return to each activity, such as returning to the "System Construction" section to review the specifications of the system or returning to the "Value Exploration" section to reconsider whether the values found were appropriate for the community and residents' changes. And to achieve this, we believe that collaboration among the various experts involved in each initiative is necessary. For example, in the "System Construction" activity, system developers and engineers are needed to create a system that can be used continuously in the community and that guarantees economic efficiency, as well as a system that enables people to enjoy the value of the system. In addition, in the "Embedding Into Society" activity, we believe that it will be necessary to collaborate with engineers and professional analysts for the analysis and evaluation of the collected data as well, and with social scientists and experts in technology ethics for the verification of acceptability. We would like to encourage collaboration with various specialists.

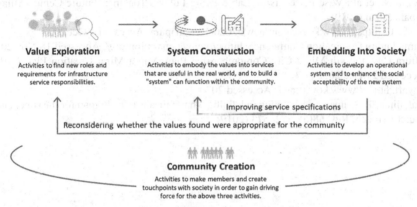

Fig. 11. Follow of four activities to create infrastructure services with the participation of residents

Acknowledgments. I would like to thank Mr. Hiroki Sakai of D-land, Mr. Yohei Takahama of the NPO "Meguru Machi Kokubunji," Mr. Ryo Ishii of PEEKABOO Co., Ltd., Mr. Tadahiro Sasaki of Keikyu Corporation, Mr. Dai Fujiwara of DAIFUJIWARA AND COMPANY, and everyone who supported this research. I am also grateful to created together this research with Maiko Kaneda, Kosuke Matoba, Tasuku Soga, Shoichi Kanzaki, and Moroe Oishi, Toshiomi Moriki, Yutaka Iwaki, Ryouta Niizeki, Shinnosuke Tanaka, members of Vision Design team in Hitachi's R&D group and especially many thanks go to Yoshitaka Shibata for comments and suggestions.

References

1. Ministry of Land, Infrastructure, Transport and Tourism. https://www.mlit.go.jp/policy/shingikai/content/001311082.pdf. Accessed 9 Sept 2019
2. Digital Agency: the vision for a digital garden city nation". https://www.digital.go.jp/policies/digital_garden_city_nation/. Accessed 6 Feb 2023
3. Hill, D., et al.: Designing Missions, p. 33. Vinnova, Sweden (2022)

4. Transit Center. https://transitcenter.org/why-tactical-transit-is-the-next-big-thing/. Accessed 19 Dec 2016
5. Chesbrough, W.H.: Open Innovation: The New Imperative for Creating and Profiting from Technology. Harvard Business School Publishing, Harvard (2003)
6. Hitachi, Ltd. Research & Development Group. https://www.hitachi.com/rd/glossary/s/social_infrastructure.html. Accessed 2023
7. New Energy and Industrial Technology Development Organization: Open Innovation White paper 2nd edn. Research Institute of Economy, Trade and Industry, Japan (2018)
8. studio-L, Living Lab Introduction Guidebook, pp.2–3. Ministry of Economy, Trade and Industry, Japan (2020)
9. Kimura, A.: The Possibility of Living Labs and Structural Challenges in Japan, pp 81–97. Research and Legislative Reference Bureau Nation Diet Library, Japan (2021)
10. SPACE10. https://space10.com/. Accessed 2023
11. Ministry of Health, Labour and Welfare. https://www.mhlw.go.jp/stf/seisakunitsuite/bunya/cocoa_00138.html. Accessed 17 Nov 2022
12. Kono, N., et al.: Wise Place Living Lab Making Futures Together. Future Center Alliance Japan, Japan (2019)
13. KAYAC. https://www.kayac.com/news/2020/10/tamapura. Accessed 1 Oct 2020
14. Tama Future Co-creation Conference. https://www.tama-mirai.org/. Accessed 18 Nov 2022
15. Miura City, the 4th Miura City Comprehensive Plan, Miura Mirai Creation Plan (2017). Accessed 22 Dec 2022
16. koyart. https://www.koyart.net/. Accessed 2020
17. Nakajima, T.: Human co-becoming redefining what it means to be human for the super smart society. Hitachi Rev. **68**(5), 572–573 (2019)

AR-Enabled Interface for IoT Water Management Systems in Smart Cities

Vasileios Sidiropoulos[1]($\boxtimes$), Athanasios Sidiropoulos[2], Dimitrios Bechtsis[1], and Fotis Stergiopoulos[1]

[1] Department of Industrial Engineering and Management, School of Engineering, International Hellenic University, 57001 Thermi, Thessaloniki, Greece
billsidiropoulos27@gmail.com
[2] Department of Mechanical Engineering, Division of Industrial Management, Polytechnical School, Aristotle University of Thessaloniki, 54124 Thessaloniki, Greece

Abstract. AR technologies could provide effective and efficient solutions in challenging domains, such as Smart Cities and promote human-city interactions. Smart Cities have a complex structure with constant and real-time information exchange. In this context, the design and development of sophisticated software tools with a human-centric approach is a necessity. The Internet of Things is the cornerstone of Smart Cities and provides ubiquitous connectivity and real-time data exchange. To this end, IoT is an enabler of AR Human Computer Interactions. Critical Smart City infrastructures, such as water management systems, are of great importance as they can raise awareness among the public about environmental and social issues.

This paper demonstrates a novel system architecture that enables citizens and practitioners to interface with IoT water management systems in the Smart City context. In order to demonstrate the architecture's capabilities, a pilot system was developed. The pilot system showcases a water quality monitoring system and an AR application, featuring two types of users, citizens and administrators. The AR application provides different functionalities based on the user type. Citizens are able to get critical information regarding water quality, while administrators are also provided with insights about the hardware and the IoT infrastructure.

The proposed system aims to establish an easy-to-use infrastructure that engages citizens and practitioners in the Smart City ecosystem, with the use of innovative state-of-the-art immersive technologies. The utilization of AR as an HCI interface between end-users and IoT systems can accelerate the adoption of AR applications in the Smart City context.

Keywords: Augmented Reality · Mixed Reality · IoT · Smart City · Water quality

1 Introduction

Augmented Reality (AR) is an innovative technology that transforms the way people interact with their surroundings. It involves the overlay of digital information on the physical environment, enhancing user's perception of the real world with added value

© The Author(s), under exclusive license to Springer Nature Switzerland AG 2023
N. A. Streitz and S. Konomi (Eds.): HCII 2023, LNCS 14037, pp. 147–155, 2023.
https://doi.org/10.1007/978-3-031-34609-5_10

content. AR provides promising applications in the realm of Smart Cities, where it can be used to improve the quality of life for citizens and increase operations efficiency [1, 2].

Smart Cities have a complex structure and are considered as a system of systems with constant and real-time information exchange. In this dynamic environment, citizens have the need to interact and exchange information using user-friendly and accessible means. In this context, the design and development of sophisticated software tools with a human-centric approach is a necessity [3]. The Internet of Things (IoT), as the cornerstone of Smart Cities, provides ubiquitous connectivity and real-time data exchange with established protocols. Thus, IoT can act as an enabler for the integration of AR applications in the Smart City context [4]. The combination of AR and IoT can create meaningful experiences in the urban realm [5].

AR technology provides added value services in human-computer and human-to-human interactions. Studies regarding AR applications indicate a high adoption rate from users and showcase the AR advantages in usability and effectiveness over web-based and mobile applications [6]. Moreover, the usability of AR applications is not limited to specific target groups indicatively young or experienced users, which designates AR as the optimal interaction means for a broad area of use cases [7].

Smart Cities improve citizens' quality of life by monitoring and controlling critical indicators, such as water quality [1]. Water quality is a critical issue in urban environments, and data streams should be collected and analyzed in real-time. IoT systems are advancing, and water quality monitoring is gaining the attention of many researchers [8, 9]. By integrating AR technologies and IoT systems, city officials and maintenance workers can access visual representations of water quality data in the field, allowing them to quickly identify and address any issues that may arise [10].

The use of AR in water quality monitoring has also the potential to significantly improve the efficiency of these systems. AR can visualize data more intuitively and interactively, making it easier for city officials and maintenance workers to understand and respond to changes in water quality. Additionally, AR provides user-friendly on-site operation support while enabling seamless remote assistance from experts [11].

Nonetheless, in order to harness the full potential of AR technology, a holistic approach to develop robust AR HCIs for configuring IoT devices' and handling data streams is needed [12]. To this end, this paper proposes a novel system architecture that enables citizens and administrators to interface with IoT water management systems in the Smart City context. The system automatically connects to the underlying IoT infrastructure and establishes connections via IoT protocols such as Message Queuing Telemetry Transport (MQTT) and Long Range Wide Area Network (LoRaWAN). The AR application enables on-site operations, including real-time data monitoring, system monitoring and IoT device configuration. In order to evaluate the system, as the literature proposes [13], the research team developed a pilot system. The pilot system utilizes the proposed architecture and unveils its potential.

2   Architecture Overview

The proposed architecture consists of three layers, namely the communication/data layer, the hardware layer and the application layer. The communication/data layer holds the IoT Gateways and MQTT Servers as well as the Data Sources that constitute the IoT system. The hardware layer includes the microcontroller, the sensors and the equipment for the IoT infrastructure. Lastly, the application Layer entails the AR application of the proposed architecture (Fig. 1).

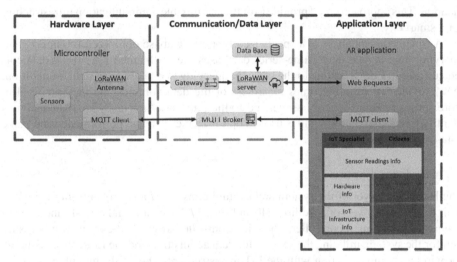

Fig. 1. Proposed system architecture

2.1   Communication/Data Layer

LoRaWAN and MQTT are two well-known IoT communication protocols. LoRaWAN is a communication protocol designed for low-power and long-range communication of IoT devices. It operates in the sub-gigahertz frequency bands, providing coverage over long distances and penetrating through building walls making it suitable for use in urban areas. LoRaWAN utilizes a star-of-stars topology in which gateways connected to the internet relay messages between the end devices and a central network server. LoRaWAN is used in Smart Cities due to its ability to support large amounts of connected devices with low-bandwidth requirements and its high scalability factor. LoRaWAN has demonstrated reliable performance in smart city applications such as waste management, environmental monitoring, and transportation [14, 15].

MQTT is a publish-subscribe lightweight messaging protocol. It is designed to be used on top of TCP/IP and has a small footprint, making it well-suited for resource-constrained devices and low-bandwidth networks. MQTT is often used in smart cities due to its ability to handle high numbers of connected devices and its efficient use of bandwidth [16].

Both LoRaWAN and MQTT are suitable communication protocols in smart cities due to their ability to support a large number of connected devices and their bandwidth management efficiency. However, they have some notable differences. LoRaWAN utilizes a spread spectrum modulation technique in the sub-gigahertz frequency bands, which allows for long-range communication and strong penetration through obstacles. In contrast, MQTT is based on TCP/IP and has a smaller footprint, making it well-suited for resource-constrained devices. As it is evident, both LoRaWAN and MQTT could be used in smart city. LoRaWAN could be used for long-range communication and MQTT could be utilized for resource-constrained devices or for direct device-to-device communication. This approach could provide a robust and flexible communication infrastructure for a smart city.

A time-series database is a specialized type of database optimized for storing and querying time-tagged data. Time-series databases are well-suited for storing data collected from IoT devices, due to the efficient querying and analysis of data. In addition, they provide fast response times regardless of the data volumes and they are used to store sensor readings, energy usage, and traffic patterns. As a last step, data analytics identify trends and patterns and is used to optimize the systems' performance and make data-driven decisions.

2.2 Hardware Layer

The Hardware Layer of the system architecture consists of a microcontroller equipped with water-quality sensors. Additionally, a LoRaWAN antenna and a Wi-Fi module are connected to the microcontroller. The microcontroller serves as the primary processing unit for the system, utilizing the sensors for data acquisition and the LoRaWAN antenna for wireless communication with the IoT infrastructure. The Wi-Fi module allows for the establishment of a secure MQTT connection, enabling efficient data transfer, for on-site operations.

2.3 Application Layer

At the application layer an AR mobile application has been developed using the Unity game engine. Unity's ability to simulate real-world environments, along with scripting capabilities and cross-platform support make it a powerful and widely-used tool for researchers [17]. The application's functionalities are divided into two sub-categories, the AR utilities and the IoT interconnections. Additionally, the application categorizes users into two types, citizens and administrators. The provided functionalities differ based on the user type.

AR Utilities. For the AR utilities' development, the research team utilized the Vuforia SDK. The Vuforia SDK provides a powerful and versatile set of tools for creating AR applications that include image recognition and tracking which was used in this research. An image target was used for the initiation of the AR experience. As the application recognizes an image target, 3D objects and graphs regarding the hardware and the sensor readings are presented at the AR layer.

IoT Interconnection. The AR application automatically establishes a connection to the IoT infrastructure. Once identified, the image target initiates the AR experience. The image target contains the unique ID of each hardware device, which is necessary to retrieve the corresponding data from the database or to connect to the MQTT server. In addition to the image target, the application uses location data from the mobile phone to determine if the user is on-site and near the device. In that case, both MQTT and LoRaWAN connections are possible. The MQTT protocol provides a direct connection between the AR application and the microcontroller, enabling real-time data exchange. On the other hand, the LoRaWAN infrastructure provides access to the database that holds historical data.

3 Pilot System

The research team developed a pilot system in order to demonstrate the applicability of the proposed architecture. The pilot system follows the proposed system architecture and the three layers were implemented from the ground up. As mentioned above, in each mode, the application is able to connect to the IoT infrastructure with either MQTT or LoRaWAN protocols. Each protocol provides specific information to the application.

Communication

The pilot system utilizes the LoRaWAN protocol through the LoRaWAN antenna on the microcontroller, for the communication layer. LoRaWAN gateways were already available near the pilot system's installation point. For the MQTT connection, the local network was utilized. Lastly, a local time series data base was implemented in order to store the data.

Hardware

Regarding the hardware, an esp32 microcontroller and four water quality sensors namely pH, electric conductivity, ORP and temperature, were used. The microcontroller provides built-in Wi-Fi connection capabilities which are used for the MQTT protocol implementation. In addition to the sensors a LoRaWAN antenna module, the RN2483A, was connected to the microcontroller to connect to the Lora Gateway.

Application

The Augmented Reality (AR) application utilizes a user-friendly interface with self-explanatory features for user navigation. There are two modes in the application namely, citizens' mode and administrators' mode. Users can switch between modes in order to get access to different features. It is worth noting that in the pilot system, the application does not provide user profiles and allows mode switching without verification. In order to initiate the AR experience from the mobile device, the user identifies the image target of the water monitoring device. Once the image target is recognized, the application links the image target with the corresponding ID. At this stage, the application connects to the underlying LoRaWAN server and retrieves the stored location of the hardware device. The application then compares the GPS location of the mobile device to the stored location to determine if the user is near the device. If the user is on-site, the AR application will automatically connect to the MQTT server, which is hosted on the hardware device.

The citizen's mode provides access to the sensor readings. Citizens are able to see the real-time value of each critical water quality metric. In addition, a graph that shows past readings can be displayed (Fig. 2).

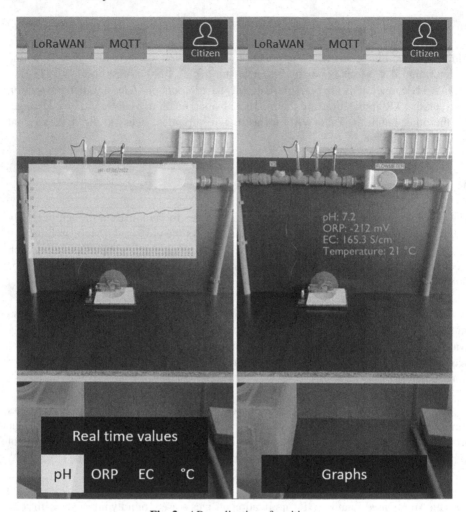

Fig. 2. AR applications for citizens

In contrast, the mode for administrators includes additional functionality for device configuration and information pertaining to the Internet of Things (IoT) infrastructure. The "Device Configuration" tab provides information about the hardware and allows for modification of sensor reading intervals and data transmission intervals while the "IoT Information" tab provides information about the IoT infrastructure (Fig. 3).

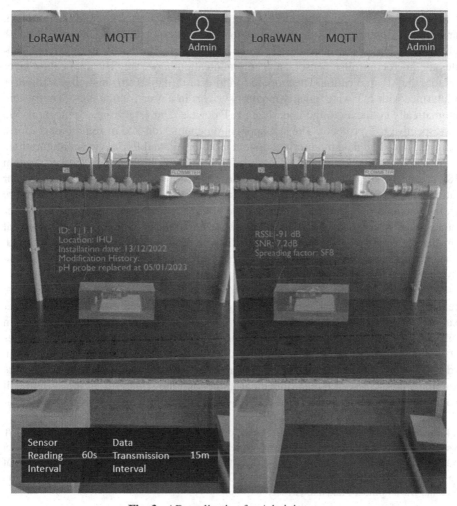

Fig. 3. AR application for Administrators

4 Conclusion

This paper has proposed a novel system architecture for an AR-enabled interface for IoT water management systems in Smart Cities. The proposed architecture utilizes the strengths of both AR and IoT technologies to improve the quality of life for citizens and increase the efficiency of city operations. Moreover, the system is designed with a human-centric approach, which is crucial in Smart Cities, making the system user-friendly and intuitive. This is an important aspect of the proposed architecture as it allows citizens to have access to information about the water quality in a convenient way and allows administrators to access the information about the hardware and the IoT infrastructure in a more efficient way.

The proposed system architecture is composed of three layers: communication/data, hardware and application. The communication/data layer includes IoT Gateways, MQTT Servers, and Databases that constitute the IoT system. The hardware layer incorporates the microcontroller, sensors, and communication hardware. The application layer includes the AR application. The proposed architecture enables citizens and practitioners to interface with IoT water quality monitor systems in a user-friendly way. The system automatically connects to the underlying IoT devices and establishes connections via the respective IoT protocol. The AR application enables on-site or remote operations, including real-time data monitoring, system monitoring, and IoT device configuration.

According to the literature, AR is a useful technology in the Smart City ecosystem [18], nonetheless, a system architecture for the integration of AR and IoT technologies for water management systems in Smart Cities is missing. The proposed system architecture has the potential to significantly improve the efficiency and effectiveness of IoT water management systems in Smart Cities. Lastly, the architecture can be used as a blueprint for other Smart City applications and will pave the way for future research in this field. It has the potential to improve the transparency of Smart Cities and enable citizens to have a more active role in the management of their city's resources.

With that being said, the system architecture is in a preliminary phase and there are some key technological limitations as well as some research gaps that need further examination from the research community. First of all, safety and privacy issues are not in consideration at the current stage. If the system would be used in Smart Cities both issues should be solved prior to wide adoption. Additionally, the pilot system was created in order to evaluate the system, but in the current stage, only the technical limitations were examined. Future research regarding the usability and the scalability of the system will provide insight into the potential of the proposed architecture, in real-world scenarios.

Acknowledgement. This research was carried out as part of the project "iWet: Intelligent IoT System for Quantitative and Qualitative Measurements for water distribution networks" (Project code: KMP6-0072250) under the framework of the Action "Investment Plans of Innovation" of the Operational Program "Central Macedonia 2014 - 2020", that is co-funded by the European Regional Development Fund and Greece.

References

1. Salah-ddine, K., Badouch, A., Mustapha, K., Karimi, K.: Augmented reality services implemented within smart cities, based on an internet of things infrastructure, concepts and challenges: an overview. 7 (2018)
2. Bohloul, M.: Smart cities: a survey on new developments, trends, and opportunities. J. Ind. Integr. Manag. **05**, 311–326 (2020). https://doi.org/10.1142/S2424862220500128
3. Tsampoulatidis, I., Komninos, N., Syrmos, E., Bechtsis, D.: Universality and interoperability across smart city ecosystems. In: Streitz, N.A., Konomi, S. (eds.) Distributed, Ambient and Pervasive Interactions. Smart Environments, Ecosystems, and Cities. Lecture Notes in Computer Science, vol. 13325, pp. 218–230. Springer, Cham (2022). https://doi.org/10.1007/978-3-031-05463-1_16

4. Shinde, G.R., Dhotre, P.S., Mahalle, P.N., Dey, N.: Augmented Reality and IoT. In: Shinde, G.R., Dhotre, P.S., Mahalle, P.N., Dey, N. (eds.) Internet of Things Integrated Augmented Reality. Springer Briefs in Applied Sciences and Technology, pp. 55–71. Springer, Heidelberg (2021). https://doi.org/10.1007/978-981-15-6374-4_4

5. Sanaeipoor, S., Emami, K.H.: Smart city: exploring the role of augmented reality in placemaking. In: 2020 4th International Conference on Smart City, Internet of Things and Applications (SCIOT) [Preprint] (2020). https://doi.org/10.1109/sciot50840.2020.9250204

6. Yagol, P., et al.: New trends in using augmented reality apps for smart city contexts. ISPRS Int. J. Geo-Inf. **7**(12), 478 (2018). https://doi.org/10.3390/ijgi7120478

7. Pokric, B., et al.: Engaging citizen communities in smart cities using IOT, serious gaming and fast markerless augmented reality. In: 2015 International Conference on Recent Advances in Internet of Things (RIoT) [Preprint] (2015). https://doi.org/10.1109/riot.2015.7104905

8. Syrmos, E., et al.: An intelligent modular water monitoring IOT system for real-time quantitative and qualitative measurements. Sustainability **15**(3), 2127 (2023). https://doi.org/10.3390/su15032127

9. Deploying full water metering at the household/final user level (no date). https://greenbestpractice.jrc.ec.europa.eu/print/pdf/node/586. 6 Feb 2023

10. Davis, K., Smith, J.E.: City probe finds 'human error' responsible for spiking hundreds of water bills, Tribune. San Diego Union-Tribune (2018). https://www.sandiegouniontribune.com/news/environment/sd-me-water-bills-20180208-story.html. Accessed 6 Feb 2023

11. Palmarini, R., et al.: A systematic review of augmented reality applications in maintenance. Robot. Comput.-Integr. Manuf. **49**, 215–228 (2018). https://doi.org/10.1016/j.rcim.2017.06.002

12. Jo, D., Kim, G.J.: AR enabled IOT for a smart and interactive environment: a survey and future directions. Sensors **19**(19), 4330–4347 (2019). https://doi.org/10.3390/s19194330

13. Kaji, S., Kolivand, H., Madani, R., Salehinia, M., Shafaie, M.: Augmented reality in smart cities: a multimedia approach (2018). http://researchonline.ljmu.ac.uk/

14. Augustin, A., et al.: A study of lora: long range & low power networks for the internet of things. Sensors **16**(9), 1466 (2016). https://doi.org/10.3390/s16091466

15. Georgiou, O., Raza, U.: Low power wide area network analysis: can lora scale? IEEE Wirel. Commun. Lett. **6**(2), 162–165 (2017). https://doi.org/10.1109/lwc.2016.2647247

16. Rubí, J.N., Gondim, P.R.: IOT-based platform for environment data sharing in smart cities. Int. J. Commun. Syst. **34**(2), e4515 (2020). https://doi.org/10.1002/dac.4515

17. Lambrecht, J., et al.: Towards commissioning, resilience and added value of augmented reality in robotics: overcoming technical obstacles to industrial applicability. Robot. Comput.-Integr. Manuf. **71**, 102178 (2021). https://doi.org/10.1016/j.rcim.2021.102178

18. Fernandez, F., et al.: The augmented space of a smart city. In: 2020 International Conference on Systems, Signals and Image Processing (IWSSIP) [Preprint] (2020). https://doi.org/10.1109/iwssip48289.2020.9145247

An IoT Framework for Heterogeneous Multi-layered Access in Smart Cities

Evangelos Syrmos[1](✉) , Dimitrios Bechtsis[1] , Ioannis Tsampoulatidis[2,3] ,
and Nicos Komninos[3]

[1] Department of Industrial Engineering and Management, School of Engineering,
International Hellenic University, Thessaloniki, Greece
syrmevag@iem.ihu.gr
[2] Infalia PC, Thessaloniki, Greece
[3] URENIO Research, Faculty of Engineering, Aristotle University of Thessaloniki,
Thessaloniki, Greece

Abstract. The proliferation of the Internet of Things has been instrumental in the digitalization of smart cities, where various technologies are leveraged to enable data utilization. However, achieving interoperability among diverse technologies remains a challenge due to heterogeneity. In this regard, ontologies have been proposed as a standalone solution that semantically enriches IoT data. Nevertheless, ontologies are still underutilized due to several limitations as systems become more complex. In order to overcome these limitations and provide a single point-of-access for all smart city layers, this paper presents a theoretical IoT framework that minimizes the requirement of interdisciplinary knowledge to operate IoT platforms, while utilizing existing ontologies in a complementary manner to build a high-level ontology schema. The framework is comprised of five fundamental axes/pylons that enable frictionless usage and configuration in order to extract data from all employed smart city layers via an adapter. This can be beneficial for smart cities such that legacy or under-utilized IoT platforms can be integrated with the framework and provide additional information reducing the costs. External operators, applications and platforms can configure the axes in order to extract data regarding their needs and make better decision making.

Keywords: IoT · Framework · Smart Cities · Ontologies · Interoperability

1 Introduction

IoT is becoming the core technology for enabling message broadcasting and inner communication between all smart city ecosystems. Therefore, smart cities (SC) consist of a plethora of sub-ecosystems (domains) that handle specific needs, however, integrating diverse technologies in order to achieve interoperability is challenging [1]. Initiatives that foster interoperability and decrease heterogeneity have been at the forefront of the research community [2]. Interoperability is a challenging facet across diverse SC ecosystems that utilize different technologies to generate, transform, broadcast and store data [3].

© The Author(s), under exclusive license to Springer Nature Switzerland AG 2023
N. A. Streitz and S. Konomi (Eds.): HCII 2023, LNCS 14037, pp. 156–171, 2023.
https://doi.org/10.1007/978-3-031-34609-5_11

The maturity of ontologies enabled the categorisation of objects and and their surrounding environments in hierarchical trees by highlighting specific descriptions and functionalities. Ontologies have been proposed in frameworks that strive for interoperability [4]. From the IoT perspective, however, ontologies have been utilized as a classification and semantic enrichment tool on data streams [5]. Ontologies such as Sensors, Observation, Sample, and Actuator (SOSA), and Semantic Sensor Network (SSN) are used for providing additional meta-information regarding IoT sensors [6], however, Gonzalez-Gil state that although ontologies are beneficial, limitations must be considered thoroughly [7]. When scaling is required, the complexity of integrating ontologies significantly increases, due to the lack of automated relationship mechanisms, while the lack of a single framework that tackles the fragmentation and heterogeneity leads to a high maintenance cost of IoT systems. Interoperability between different ontologies is also a requirement even in a single domain as different definitions for the same characteristics may exist. Moreover, semantic heterogeneity could hinder the adoption since the representation of ontologies can be different while the usage from IoT stakeholders can lead to semantic ambiguity [8, 9]. Performance is also considered a limitation in ontology adoption, especially in real-time and resource-constraint devices. In order to strengthen the operational capacity of SC stakeholders, heterogeneous IoT devices with diverse specifications and features should have as a basis a common understanding of the context of their shared data. To this end, the proposed IoT framework addresses heterogeneity in the IoT ecosystem by introducing 5 pillars as common scales of measurement while proposing an ontology that leverages two axes for a double alignment approach. The framework proposes a junction of two solutions in order to reduce heterogeneity and improve interoperability. A four-stage ontology integration and a central-hub acting as a domain-neutral ontology are proposed for utilizing existing domain-specific ontologies whilst introducing a hierarchical observation for seamless discovery.

Proprietary IoT platforms and/or applications that interface with the IoT devices have been developed to provide easy access to city officials. However, integrating IoT platforms from various domains and SC ecosystems in a single point-of-access is challenging due to the demand of high technical literacy [10]. The proposed IoT framework presents the fundamental axes that enable operators to interact and retrieve information across all SC ecosystems. This abstraction from domain-specific IoT platforms reduces the necessity for city operators to possess direct access and familiarity with each constituent system in each SC sub-ecosystem. In order to facilitate the extraction of relevant information abstraction can ultimately improve decision-making. Existing platforms can integrate with the framework via the adapter layer while legacy applications can be retrofitted. This approach reduces the technical debt from underutilized platforms due to a lack of specialized personnel. The point of the matter is that the proposed framework minimized the requirement of interdisciplinary knowledge to operate IoT platforms since the adaptation of data to the presented framework is handled by domain experts.

The remainder of the paper is structured as follows: The fundamental axes/pylons of the theoretical IoT framework are presented in Sect. 2. Section 3 highlights the impact of the framework on SC layers. In Sect. 4, a detailed analysis of the data alignment from diverse urban datasets and ontologies is presented. Section 5 provides a use case scenario that leverages the theoretical framework. Finally, Sect. 6 concludes the paper.

2 Fundamental Axes

It is evident that IoT device integration and deployment in SCs is increasing at a rapid pace, which imposes several challenges. Smart sensors and actuators that enable real-time sensing capabilities significantly differ inside a specific SC layer. Therefore, device interfacing for data extraction demands specialized knowledge and in-depth domain understanding. For instance, a smart water metering solution integrated into the infrastructure layer that measures real-time water consumption demands different interfaces compared to a smart sensor that monitors traffic congestion on a highway [11–13]. Ontologies can provide the necessary object descriptors for capturing functionality traits and features. However, ontologies lack scalability when a high-level observation of multi-layered data aggregation is required, due to the fact that every ontology has different descriptors for a single object. Post-correlation and mapping of aggregated data requires an interdisciplinary approach to develop a high-level ontology schema. Moreover, this approach hinders scalability when new objects and smart city layers are included.

To this end, a theoretical framework is presented, addressing the scalability concerns by having five fundamental axes as context descriptors for the IoT devices. This design facilitates seamless interaction with all SC layers by using each axis as a configurable option that enables frictionless data aggregation across the smart city ecosystem. The framework presents the following axes:

1. Temporal
2. Spatial
3. Variation
4. Intensity
5. Edge capabilities

As shown in Fig. 1 the framework's architecture addresses scalability and data handling activities in the SC layers by proposing a five-axes framework, a meta-ontology along with an adapter layer. The framework itself is responsible for receiving incoming requests from external applications and modifying the requests based on the five available axes. Thereafter, according to the five provided axes, a final query is created that is passed through a meta-ontology and the adapter layer before accessing each SC layer separately.

The auditability provided by the framework is considered a key enabler in interfacing with the system across multiple smart city layers without requiring background knowledge of the underlying applications. However, for enhanced applicability and reliability, the meta-ontology adapter is responsible for interfacing with every layer. Providing specific axes as interface configurators facilitates the abstract representation of the interconnected sub-systems of each SC ecosystem.

External applications request data in order to identify useful information patterns. The adapter is responsible for interfacing with individual systems in every SC layer. Existing systems developed by domain experts are required to expose connectivity solutions that interface with the adapter. Which expedites the development processes and removes interdisciplinary overhead. The meta-ontology aggregates information from multiple ontologies that are included at every SC layer and propagates datastreams to

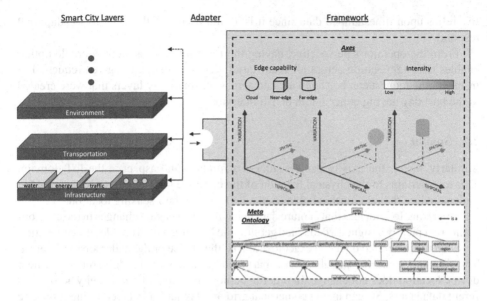

Fig. 1. High-level architecture and fundamental axes/pylon of the framework

the framework. Finally, the five axes are able to finetune multiple data streams using the axis boundaries.

A variety of configurations can be effectively established by the incoming queries. For instance, the request can be translated into a variety of configurations that adjust accordingly to every axis as presented in Fig. 1.

Having five axes to configure provides all the necessary means of extracting data across all involved smart city layers while combining information across multiple axes can enable further feature extraction and shed light on unknown areas. A theoretical description of each axis/pylon is presented along with a query example for better comprehension.

2.1 Temporal

The temporal axis, has a crucial role in the proposed theoretical framework. Time is a fundamental aspect during the generation and processing of information by IoT devices as data streams are constantly being generated. Specifically, the ability to capture and annotate data on the fly is essential for effectively understanding and utilizing them for further operations.

To facilitate this, datastreams are timestamped by the devices themselves which enable the comprehension of the fluctuation of data. Data sampling rates are also critical for estimating specific characteristics. The correlation of the timestamps, the sampling rates and the measured values with the data streams contributes to identifying patterns, trends and anomalies that would not be apparent without considering the temporal aspect of the data.

Furthermore, this axis also enables the development of time-sensitive decision-making, such that the system is able to react to the changing environment in real-time.

IoT relies upon timestamped data since it is a vital aspect of the systems to adapt and respond.

From the operator's perspective, having the temporal axis as a configurable option enables data aggregation across all smart city layers that match the given request. For instance, the request can be "fetch all data across all smart city layers that were created in the past day having either 1-min or 1-h intervals".

2.2 Spatial

Similarly, the spatial axis is also considered a fundamental aspect in the IoT domain. This axis pertains to the physical location of the employed IoT devices and is crucial in understanding the relationship between the devices and their sensing location.

Operating IoT devices that capture data in the field by sensing changes in the environment are typically assigned a dedicated geographic location which enables the correlation between the generated data, the exact location of the device or the wider area of interest. The significance of the spatial aspect is particularly pronounced in IoT solutions where device location does not change. In order to achieve locational homogeneity across different data layers, SC can use a geometrical grid as a layout for data recording reference where grid cells can act as spatial entities. This common spatial reference approach can ultimately reduce spatial fragmentation.

In these cases, IoT management platforms running on the cloud are responsible for registering device information including the. Furthermore, these platforms annotate incoming information based on the broadcasted device ID and their registered location before data are being stored in the database. On the other hand, devices that change their location constantly are equipped with specialized hardware (such as GPS antennas) that track the geographic location and annotate data before transmission.

Operators can request information based on certain criteria e.g., fetch all data across all smart city layers that are located in a specific area between latitude-A, longitude-A and latitude-B, longitude-B, this query will return all devices that are within the specified area, while the framework could aggregate the measurements and compute the mean value for this area.

2.3 Variation-Fluctuation

Having the ability to configure the aggregated data based on sensor variations is critical for enabling domain experts to evaluate each aspect. This axis presents the ability to map data fluctuations across all involved smart city layers. Hence, bridging the information about the dynamic nature of IoT systems that monitor the environment. For instance, a deployed temperature sensor monitors the ever-changing value throughout the day. Values such as temperature, and humidity have low fluctuations while a traffic sensor that monitors the pedestrian or vehicle flows can be categorized as a high variation device. Therefore, this axis can be considered complementary since high-fluctuating devices can leverage the ability of the system to detect critical events or anomalies.

2.4 Intensity

Intensity is another aspect of configuring the query based on the amount of generated data across all smart city layers. Specifically, intensity is directly related to the temporal axis/pylon, however, the frequency of data generation is promoted by employing intensity as an axis/pylon. For instance, operators might request data with a frequency of 5ms without hard-lined boundaries on time, thus forcing the theoretical framework to request data that have the ability to transmit and sample data at a such high rate. Similarly, combining intensity with spatial axis can ultimately provide direct insight into generated data in a given geographic location. The requested location can also be identified as a high or low-intensity area that is being monitored. Smart cities can benefit from this axis by identifying the IoT readiness of the smart city. Intensity and IoT-readiness are intertwined due to the fact that high intensity can be achieved purely on high digitalization and IoT adoption. Enforcing digitalization across all districts in smart cities will indisputably lead to a highly digitalized city that operates with minimal human intervention. Smart cities fed with high frequency and variety of data across all layers facilitate proactive behaviours, while underdeveloped areas can be strengthened to enable digital transformation.

2.5 Edge Capability

With the rising adoption of edge computing in the IoT landscape, we opted to include edge computing in the proposed theoretical framework.

Far-edge is the least compute capable category by all means, due to the fact that constrained devices are included. These devices lack computing resources and processing power required to perform intensive operations. In most cases, these devices are used for integrating multiple sensors that require external computing units to monitor the environment. For instance, LoRaWAN end nodes which are required to operate on batteries for multiple years are not able to perform on-site computation on the aggregated data.

On the other hand, the near-edge is considered a more capable category for performing highly optimized algorithms and machine learning techniques. Gateways and hubs consolidate the edge layer since these devices are required to accommodate multiple transmitting devices on multiple channels at the same time. Of importance to understand in this regard is that these devices are able to process incoming data by multiple devices in real-time, and perform data-cleaning, formatting and filtering with intelligent algorithms or even with machine learning models. However, deploying machine learning models on such devices requires decreasing the overall size of the model while sacrificing the accuracy in order to be utilized by the device.

The last category is the cloud, which is mostly directed to the platforms and/or applications that act as data aggregators. These have the ability to perform heavy workloads and intensive operations on all data without affecting accuracy and performance. Most of the time these are located on servers with highly capable hardware.

Concluding, this axis/pylon has been introduced mainly for providing operators with the flexibility to query information about the employed devices accordingly. For instance, operators can request for all information across all smart city layers that have far-edge computing capabilities. This will return all device values that meet the specified criteria.

3 Axes' Impact on Smart City Layers

The proposed framework presents several key benefits to SCs by improving the overall efficiency and effectiveness of process management activities. The five fundamental axes foster the datastream alignment that decreases the fragmentation and heterogeneity aspect. Moreover, it enables the use of datastreams based on specific scales of measurement in a homogenized format. Specifically, the framework provides a single point of access to multiple platforms that have been developed and underutilized. This streamlines the data extraction process which ultimately reduces the friction between data aggregation from different sources across all SC layers. This not only reduces the personnel requirements but also enables non-specialized operators to access data from multiple city ecosystems, align them on a single context vertical that supports the decision-making process. Urban planners can make forecasts and better decisions on resource management, while real-time event handling can greatly be improved.

Another highly influential aspect of the framework is that data extraction across all city layers provides urban planners with a holistic view of the city, allowing them to make informed decisions and implement effective strategies. Moreover, data correlations, patterns and forecasts can be observed across different city ecosystems which by design is difficult to achieve due to high complexity.

The framework also contains a top-level ontology that is embedded in a central hub in order to leverage two of the fundamental axes as alignment planes. The use of a top-level hierarchical domain-neutral ontology can be easily adopted by completely different cities. Due to the fact that a spatial and temporal alignment acts as the driving verticals that facilitate the representation of data across multiple data layers on a common reference entity.

The provided flexibility to configure the data extraction process according to specific requirements is possible via the given axes. It is crucial to ensure that the framework is tailored to meet the needs of each city, maximizing its overall effectiveness. Consequently, urban planners can select the data streams and the accuracy levels within the framework (positioning the data stream within the five axes) to improve the overall effectiveness.

Another key impact of the framework is that it enables the connectivity, and integration of individual applications, reducing the overall complexity and fragmentation of existing platforms. Underutilized applications can also be retrofitted into the framework which can increase the Return on Investment (ROI) and increase frameworks' reach on uncharted areas.

4 Data Alignment Across Urban Datasets and Ontologies

4.1 Pooling of Urban Datasets: Fragmented and Siloed Information

Following the multi-level observation and data collection we described in the previous sections, a pool of datasets that depict a city or its ecosystems is created. This data pool is fragmented and heterogeneous. Heterogeneity is due to different sources of data, different organization principles, scales of measurement, and many other features specific to each data source used. Consequently, it becomes particularly difficult to get a comprehensive view of the available data assets, reconcile them, and get meaning about the realities of the city these data capture and represent. There are two types of fragmentation and heterogeneity in a dataset created from the juxtaposition of multiple data sources, layers of observation, and recording systems.

First, there is a spatial or temporal fragmentation of the data as they are recorded along different spatial entities or different time periods. For instance, building-related data can be recorded using the "building" as a spatial entity of reference; land use data can be recorded using the "building block" as a spatial entity of reference, and infrastructures can be recorded using the "city grid" as a spatial entity of reference. The dimensions and location of these spatial entities differ substantially (Fig. 2). However, we need to achieve locational homogeneity of data by using common spatial entities of reference across different data layers. We may use the city grid and aggregate buildings, land uses, activities, and other data at this spatial level. Or we may plot a geometrical grid over a city and use the grid cells as spatial entities of reference for data recording. No need to say that locational homogeneity is important if we wish to represent the realities of a city in a comprehensive way. The same fragmentation applies to temporal data if the recording of different categories of data took place in different time periods.

Fig. 2. Spatial units at the level of the building (red), building block (green), and city grid (blue)

Second, there is semantic heterogeneity as data capture and represent different aspects of the urban reality along different taxonomies. Whatever the spatial entity of reference, data recording concerns data related to (a) the landscape and physical environment of cities, such as buildings, constructions, infrastructures, and natural ecosystems, (b) the social characteristics of cities, such as land uses, activities, events, communities and groups, crime, etc. (c) the digital infrastructure of cities, broadband networks, sensors, IoT, websites and social media, and (d) the population, age groups, employment, income and wealth, and many other characteristics [14]. Each category of data is described by a taxonomy or ontology, which is a description of data structure with classes, properties, relationships, and axioms. Taxonomies offer the basis to ensure both data consistency and understanding of the underlying data model. For instance,

- buildings can be described with the Building Topology Ontology, a minimal OWL DL ontology, having as classes those of building, element, interface, site, space, storey, and zone [15]
- conditions of the environment can be described with the Web of Things (WoT) ontology [16], or the Thing Description (TD) Ontology [17]
- land uses can be described with the Land Use Ontology that captures types of land use and cover over time [18],
- activities can be described with the NACE Rev. 2 standard classification of economic activities [19],
- risks and city threats can be described by using a risk ontology [20].

Semantic alignment and content correlation are important because they give meaning to data. A bus station in the freezing north is not the same as a bus station in the Mediterranean; a school in a high-crime area is not the same as a school in a zero-crime village. Present knowledge changes past knowledge, offering new interpretations of past events. Correlations give new meaning, which is lost when data is fragmented and heterogeneous. However, the integration of content in datasets created along different ontologies is more challenging than their spatial integration.

4.2 Methods to Align Heterogeneous Datasets

Integrating data from heterogeneous sources and making queries is an important topic in database design, multi-disciplinary engineering, semantic web applications, and elsewhere, having as an objective to provide comprehensive access to heterogeneous data sources. Some methods use ontologies and RDF schemas to represent content from heterogeneous sources.

Osman, Yahia, and Diallo address the heterogeneity problem through the integration of existing ontologies to build a new more coherent one [21]. They offer an overview of the literature with the most relevant works in the field, key definitions of ontology integration, integration principles, consequences, and techniques. Ontology integration can be split into repairing, matching, and merging steps, each one preparing the terrain for the next step. The key process is ontology matching, also referred to as ontology alignment, which consists in establishing semantic correspondences between the entities of different ontologies, mainly matching classes and properties of different ontologies. Ontology alignment is the outcome of this matching process. Following the authors, the ontology integration workflow is developed in four phases: (a) pre-processing, to analyse input ontologies and improve their quality in order to reduce the matching effort, (b) matching, which identifies correspondences between the input ontologies and pairs of equivalent entities across the ontologies under consideration, (c) merging with inputs from all entities into a new integrated ontology, and (d) post-processing, to assess, repair and refine the resulting new ontology. Throughout this paper, they provide exhaustive matching, alignment, and correspondence types, as well as types of ontology merging and ontology integration.

A similar review can be found in the paper of Ekaputra et al. on ontology-based data integration in multi-disciplinary engineering environments [22]. They report on 23 applications from both the semantic web and system engineering and identify authors and methods, integration variants, key problems, strengths, and limitations of the different integration approaches.

Wang et al. present a different approach based on a mediator-wrapper architecture that includes four layers: (1) an application layer to communicate with users; (2) a mediating layer to perform data integration; (3) a wrapper layer which contains wrappers for data sources; and (4) a source layer giving access to heterogeneous data sources [23]. The core component in the proposed solutions to solve the heterogeneity problem is a relational schema based on an entity-relationship diagram (ERD), which interconnects tables of a relational database over an ontology and RDF associations (Fig. 3).

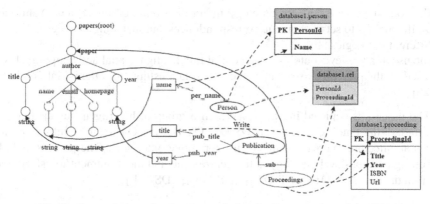

Fig. 3. Semantic mapping between relational schemas and ontology [21]

An earlier paper by Dou and LePendu, discussed ontology-based integration for relational databases [24]. For them "a merged ontology is the ontology equivalent of a global view over local schemas. It consists of common elements from a source ontology and a target ontology but also defines the semantic mappings between them as bridging axioms. A merged ontology allows all the relevant symbols in a domain to interact so that facts can be translated from one ontology to another using inference over the bridging axioms". They argue that defining semantic relationships between concepts is too subtle for full automation and human interaction is needed. Thus, they define the bridging axioms manually, based on the understanding of semantic relationships between the local schemas.

Elmhadhbi, Karray, and Archimède show a different path in which semantic interoperability across different systems and information sources can be achieved by aligning to upper-level ontologies to come up with a shared vocabulary and understanding [25]. They present a use case in which the Basic Formal Ontology (BFO), an upper-level ontology, and the Common Core Ontology (CCO), a mid-level ontology, are combined to define a new ontology for firefighters composed of 429 classes and 246 relations. The upper-level ontology helped to improve data quality, to reduce development time and especially facilitate information integration, avoid inconsistencies and achieve both syntactic interoperability to exchange information and semantic interoperability to ensure that information exchanges make sense under a common understanding.

The above literature briefly presented shows that merging ontologies is a largely manual and time-consuming process. It contains aspects that are equivalent to building a new ontology from scratch, using classes, instances, object properties, annotations, data properties, and axioms of the heterogeneous datasets under consideration. Eventually, depending on the number of ontology entities to be integrated, building a new ontology might be less time-consuming and more coherent.

4.3 Integration and Alignment of Fragmented Urban Datasets

The path we propose to integrate heterogeneous datasets for a city organized by a group of different ontologies combines two approaches:

- The four-stage workflow for ontology integration outlined by Osman, Yahia, and Diallo enables to set of semantic correspondences and matching between entities of different ontologies [19],
- The use of a top-level ontology as a central hub to align spatial and temporal classes based on the presented axes and create new relationships from the initial ontologies [26].

The process is depicted in Fig. 4 in which a group of heterogeneous datasets and their underlying ontologies (DS-O1, DS-O2, DS-O3, DS-O4) evolves into a hub and spokes architecture to create a suite of interoperable ontologies. The process includes the setting of a top-level ontology at the central hub and the alignment/transformation of initial datasets (DS-O1$_{TR}$, DS-O2 $_{TR}$, DS-O3 $_{TR}$, DS-O4 $_{TR}$).

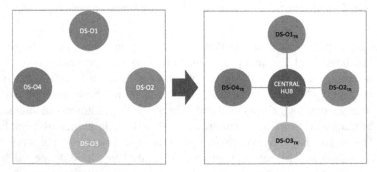

Fig. 4. Integration and alignment of heterogeneous datasets and ontologies

Three objectives guide this double alignment process: (a) the need to create a new hierarchy over all data classes included in the initial datasets, (b) the need to align the spatial and temporal classes across different ontologies, and (c) the need to introduce new properties connecting instances across the ontologies used, thus creating new meaning at the intersection of initial ontologies.

The Central Hub. A domain-neutral ontology is developed in the central hub to connect with domain-specific ontologies and support retrieval and discovery throughout the datasets. ISO/IEC 21838–1:2021 specifies the requirements for a top-level hub ontology, defining the relations between top-level ontology and domain ontologies and the role of a top-level ontology in definitions and axioms of domain-specific ontologies [27]. As a top-level ontology at the central hub, we propose the BFO-ISO, an ontology evolved from the Basic Formal Ontology (BFO) and defined as top-level ontology by ISO 21838–2 [28]. BFO is widely used to facilitate interoperability across multiple engineering-related ontologies; is a realist formal ontology representing high-level universal types of things; does not contain any domain-specific knowledge [29, 30]. We have used BFO to develop the SC ontology and provide a better understanding and description of the smart/intelligent city landscape, identify main components and processes, and clarify core entities related to the integration of physical, social, and digital dimensions of a city [31].

The class hierarchy of BFO-ISO: ISO 21838–2 includes a limited number of entities. It starts with the dichotomy between *continuants* (material or immaterial entities that continue to exist through time while maintaining their identity) and *occurrents* (procedures that unfold over a time period); adopts the dichotomy between *independent* and *dependent* entities (depending on the existence of other entities, such as quality, role, function); defines as *specifically dependent continuants* those that cannot migrate from one bearer to another; classifies *immaterial* entities in *sites, fiat boundary continuants*, and *spatial regions*, which are particularly important distinctions in geography and city planning; classifies *occurrent* entities in *processes, temporal regions, spatiotemporal regions;* and uses, as all ontologies, the distinction between *instances* (individuals, particulars) and *universals* (generals, types) (Fig. 5) [32].

The top-level ontology at the central hub created with BFO-ISO should contain all classes allowing the alignment of initial ontologies. The spatial regions and temporal regions should be defined in ways to allow matching with the spatial and temporal classes of initial ontologies, enabling spatial and temporal synchronization of data. New object and data properties should be defined at the level of the central hub across the initial ontologies.

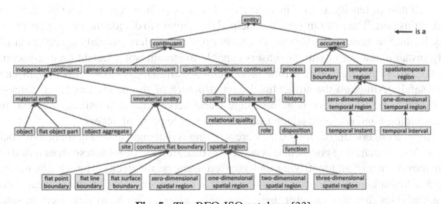

Fig. 5. The BFO-ISO ontology [33]

Transformations of Initial Datasets. Three types of transformations are needed to make city datasets semantically interoperable, semantic alignment, spatial alignment, and temporal alignment.

Semantic alignment is required if the same thing is denoted by different terms in different datasets, e.g., "innovation area" and "innovation zone" or "industrial district" and "industrial area", or "yard" and "outdoor area". In owl, "owl:equivalentClass" provides class equivalence, allowing a class description to have the same class extension as another class description, meaning that two classes are alternate names, are equivalent definitions of the same thing, or have the same set of instances.

Spatial alignment is required if data is recorded at different spatial entities, as shown in Fig. 2, at the building, building block, and city grid levels. If so, there is a need to introduce new spatial classes (fiat boundary or spatial region) that are common across datasets. Cities are full of physical boundaries and fiat boundaries that define land properties, administrative regions, postal districts, urban communities, and other human-induced demarcations. Data records follow these demarcations and to achieve data interoperability, there is a need to transform the initial datasets to new spatial categories common across datasets.

Temporal alignment is also required if data is recorded in different time periods. Introduction of common temporal entities with properties such as "hasBeginning" and "hasEnd", and therefore common temporal intervals across datasets is a way to align datasets (see also, Time Ontology in OWL) [34]. There is also a need to transform the initial datasets to match the common temporal entities across datasets.

5   Use Case

An indicative use case scenario to highlight the potential use of the proposed framework in a SC which adopts all five axes is presented below;

Harbor authorities, recently included their legacy system, controlling the installed sensors network in the wider harbor area, into the proposed framework adapter. A cruise ship approaches the coastal city and the captain asks for available live sensors data (temporal axis) from the area around the port (spatial axis). Among various sensors streamed to the ship, the captain focuses on data coming from sensors measuring water height every 20 min (intensity axis). The selected interval is sufficient as the tide is relatively mild in this port. The extra information helped the captain to decide the most appropriate quay leading to faster debarkation. The harbor authorities have already agreed to gradually install a new set of similar sensors capable to stream water height on one-second interval, providing near-to real-time measurements allowing bigger ships to approach more safely. Although the streamlined data structure of the newly employed sensors is different, the framework is able to ingest and serve data in a unified way via the meta-ontology and enclosed adapter layer in the single point of access.

The passengers, during their trip, were wearing wristbands allowing them to unlock their cabins, purchasing goods, and benefiting cruise ship to optimize resources based on their movements (e.g., identifying understaffed areas on the deck). The wristbands are broadcasting a unique identifier but some elderly passengers also consent to wear more advanced ones that also monitor their medical condition (i.e., heart rate, oxygen saturation in the blood) and broadcast in real-time. These wristbands are compatible to the proposed framework and they are broadcasting anonymous data in hotspots around the city. In case of an unusual peak of heart pulse (variation-fluctuation axis) in one passenger's wristband, while navigating through the city, has triggered an alarm. Local health centers are constantly fetching anonymized health-related information about citizens via the framework adapter in a given area.

At a higher level, the local authorities are able to collect big data from the sensors around the city in a dedicated cloud-based application (edge capabilities axis) and process historical data, including cruise ship visits. Combining different sensor data (weather, traffic, pollution, electricity consumption, etc.) with static information such as rent prices, yearly events (e.g., conferences) they can get useful insights and decide on future policies that could benefit the city and its citizens.

The presented use case has demonstrated the applicability of the proposed framework by introducing interactions with each frameworks' axis. It is important to note that interoperability is achieved by the adapter layer in conjunction with the meta-ontology, the scenario that highlights this possibility is the integration of new water sensors more capable to measure in high frequency with legacy water sensors. Furthermore, the wristband scenario showcases the exploitation of combining multiple framework axis to drive operational efficiency and instantaneous response in case of emergency. Lastly, the local authority's scenario presents an envisaged monitoring setup that aggregates data across a variety of sensors with different edge computing capabilities across multiple smart city ecosystems.

6 Conclusion

In this article, we have introduced an IoT framework that has the capability of offering a comprehensive arrangement for interfacing with smart city IoT platforms and/or applications. The framework is structured around five distinct axes, each of which is focused on specific functionalities. Furthermore, the combination of these axes with different configurations has the potential to significantly enhance the information retrieval process. A top-level neutral ontology is introduced as an integration mechanism of domain-specific ontologies to reduce heterogeneity and establish a multi-axes alignment. Given the usability of each axis, a use case has been presented that highlights the utilizations and applicability in real-world scenarios. Finally, the adoption of the proposed framework by contemporary smart cities can support the transition to the meta-information era where big data demands efficient data management across a variety of data sources.

Acknowledgements. This research was carried out as part of the project "iWet: Intelligent IoT System for Quantitative and Qualitative Measurements for Water Distribution Networks" (Project Code: KMP6-0072250) under the framework of the Action "Investment Plans of Innovation" of the Operational Program "Central Macedonia 2014 2020" that is co-funded by the European Regional Development Fund and Greece.

References

1. Tsampoulatidis, I., Komninos, N., Syrmos, E., Bechtsis, D.: Universality and interoperability across smart city ecosystems. In: Streitz, N.A., Konomi, S. (eds.) Distributed, Ambient and Pervasive Interactions Smart Environments, Ecosystems, and Cities. Lecture Notes in Computer Science, vol. 13325, pp. 218–230. Springer, Heidelberg (2020)
2. Silva, B.N., Khan, M., Han, K.: Towards sustainable smart cities: a review of trends, architectures, components, and open challenges in smart cities. Sustain. Cities Soc. **38**, 697–713 (2018). https://doi.org/10.1016/j.scs.2018.01.053
3. Tang, S., Shelden, D.R., Eastman, C.M., Pishdad-Bozorgi, P., Gao, X.: A review of building information modeling (BIM) and the internet of things (IoT) devices integration: Present status and future trends. Autom. Constr. **101**, 127–139 (2019). https://doi.org/10.1016/j.aut con.2019.01.020
4. Costin, A., Eastman, C.: Need for interoperability to enable seamless information exchanges in smart and sustainable urban systems. J. Comput. Civ. Eng. **33**(3), 04019008 (2019). https://doi.org/10.1061/(asce)cp.1943-5487.0000824
5. Hassani, A., et al.: INFORM: a tool for classification and semantic annotation of IoT datastreams. In: 2021 IEEE 7th World Forum on Internet of Things (WF-IoT) (2021). https://doi.org/10.1109/wf-iot51360.2021.9594994
6. Haller, A., Janowicz, K., Cox, S., Le Phuoc, D., Taylor, K., Lefrançois, M.: Semantic Sensor Network Ontology (n.d.). https://www.w3.org/TR/vocab-ssn/. Accessed 20 Jan 2023
7. Gonzalez-Gil, P., Martinez, J.A., Skarmeta, A.F.: Lightweight data-security ontology for IoT. Sensors **20**(3), 801 (2020). https://doi.org/10.3390/s20030801
8. Ganzha, M., Paprzycki, M., Pawłowski, W., Szmeja, P., Wasielewska, K.: Semantic interoperability in the Internet of Things: an overview from the INTER-IoT perspective. J. Netw. Comput. Appl. **81**, 111–124 (2017). https://doi.org/10.1016/j.jnca.2016.08.007
9. Agarwal, R., et al.: Unified IoT ontology to enable interoperability and federation of testbeds. In: 2016 IEEE 3rd World Forum on Internet of Things (WF-IoT) (2016). https://doi.org/10.1109/wf-iot.2016.7845470
10. de Matos, E., et al.: Context information sharing for the Internet of Things: a survey. Comput. Netw. **166**, 106988 (2020). https://doi.org/10.1016/j.comnet.2019.106988
11. Syrmos, E., et al.: An intelligent modular water monitoring IoT system for real-time quantitative and qualitative measurements. Sustainability **15**(3), 2127 (2023). https://doi.org/10.3390/su15032127
12. Chong, H.F., Ng, D.: Development of IoT device for traffic management system. In: 2016 IEEE Student Conference on Research and Development (SCOReD) (2016). https://doi.org/10.1109/SCORED.2016.7810059
13. Avatefipour, O., Sadry, F.: Traffic management system using IoT technology - a comparative review. In: 2018 IEEE International Conference on Electro/Information Technology (EIT) (2018). https://doi.org/10.1109/eit.2018.8500246
14. Komninos, N., Bratsas, C., Kakderi, C., Tsarchopoulos, P.: Smart city ontologies: improving the effectiveness of smart city applications. J. Smart Cities **1**(1) (2016). https://doi.org/10.18063/jsc.2015.01.001
15. Rasmussen, M.H., Pauwels, P., Lefrançois, M., Schneider, G.F.: Building topology ontology (2021). https://w3c-lbd-cg.github.io/bot/, Accessed 20 Jan 2023
16. Kaebisch, S., McCool, M., Korkan, E., Kamiya, T., Charpenay, V., Kovatsch, M.: Web of Things (WoT) Thing Description 1.1 (2021). https://www.w3.org/TR/wot-thing-description/. Accessed 20 Jan 2023
17. Charpenay, V., Lefrançois, M., Villalón, M.P., Käbisch, S.: Thing Description (TD) Ontology (n.d.). https://www.w3.org/2019/wot/td. Accessed 21 Jan 2023

18. Katsumi, M.: Land use ontology (2023). https://enterpriseintegrationlab.github.io/icity/Lan dUse/doc/index-en.html. Accessed 23 Jan 2023
19. European Commission: Statistical classification of economic activities in the European Community NACE Rev. 2 (2006). https://ec.europa.eu/eurostat/documents/3859598/5902521/KS-RA-07-015-EN.PDF. Accessed 24 Jan 2023
20. Risk Data Ontology - Open Risk Manual (2023). https://www.openriskmanual.org/wiki/ Risk_Data_Ontology
21. Osman, I., Ben Yahia, S., Diallo, G.: Ontology integration: approaches and challenging issues. Information Fusion **71**, 38–63 (2021). https://doi.org/10.1016/j.inffus.2021.01.007
22. Ekaputra, F.J., Sabou, M., Serral, E., Kiesling, E., Biffl, S.: Ontology-based data integration in multi-disciplinary engineering environments: a review. Open J. Inf. Syst. **4**, 1–26 (2017)
23. Wang, J., Lu, J., Zhang, Y., Miao, Z., Zhou, B.: Integrating heterogeneous data source using ontology. J. Softw. **4**(8), 843–850 (2009). https://doi.org/10.4304/jsw.4.8.843-850
24. Dou, D., LePendu, P.: Ontology-based integration for relational databases. In: Proceedings of the 2006 ACM Symposium on Applied Computing (2006). https://doi.org/10.1145/1141277. 1141387
25. Popplewell, K., Thoben, K.-D., Knothe, T., Poler, R. (eds.): Enterprise Interoperability VIII. PIC, vol. 9. Springer, Cham (2019). https://doi.org/10.1007/978-3-030-13693-2
26. Ruttenberg, A., Smith, B.: JOWO-2019-Tutorial-BFO-ISO.pptx | Powered by Box (2019). https://buffalo.box.com/v/BFO-ISO-JOWO. Accessed 23 Jan 2023
27. ISO/IEC (2021). ISO/IEC 21838-1:2021. https://www.iso.org/standard/71954.html. Accessed 26 Jan 2023
28. ISO/IEC (2021b). ISO/IEC 21838-2:2021. https://www.iso.org/standard/74572.html. Accessed 26 Jan 2023
29. Smith, B., Ceusters, W.: Ontological realism: a methodology for coordinated evolution of scientific ontologies. Appl. Ontol. **5**(3–4), 139–188 (2010). https://doi.org/10.3233/AO-2010-0079
30. Hagedorn, T.J., Smith, B., Krishnamurty, S., Grosse, I.: Interoperability of disparate engineering domain ontologies using basic formal ontology. J. Eng. Des. **30**(10–12), 625–654 (2019). https://doi.org/10.1080/09544828.2019.1630805
31. Komninos, N., Panori, A., Kakderi, C.: The smart city ontology 2.0: assessing the components and interdependencies of city smartness (2021). www.preprints.org. https://doi.org/10.20944/ preprints202108.0101.v1
32. Smith, B.: On classifying material entities in basic formal ontology. In: Interdisciplinary Ontology: Proceedings of the Third Interdisciplinary Ontology Meeting, pp. 1–13. Keio University Press (2012)
33. ISO/IEC (2023). ISO/IEC 21838-2:2021. https://www.iso.org/obp/ui/#iso:std:iso-iec:21838:-2:ed-1:v1:en. Accessed 26 Jan 2023
34. Cox, S., Little, C.: Time ontology in OWL (2022). https://www.w3.org/TR/owl-time/. Accessed 26 Jan 2023

Applications of Bioacoustics Human Interface System for Wildlife Conservation in Nepal

Leo Uesaka[1]([✉])[iD], Ambika Prasad Khatiwada[2], Daisuké Shimotoku[1][iD],
Laxmi Kumar Parajuli[1][iD], Manish Raj Pandey[2], and Hill Hiroki Kobayashi[1][iD]

[1] Information Technology Center, The University of Tokyo, 6-2-3 Kashiwanoha,
Kashiwa-shi, Chiba 277-0882, Japan
{leo.u,shimotoku,parajuli,kobayashi}@ds.itc.u-tokyo.ac.jp
[2] The National Trust for Nature Conservation (NTNC), Khumaltar, Lalitpur, Nepal

Abstract. Bioacoustics mediated passive and non-invasive monitoring of soundscape ecology has attracted increasing interest for *in situ* wildlife conservation. The popularity of bioacoustics tools is mainly attributable to their low storage volume, ease of transmission, and the possibility of performing data analysis in a retrospective manner. In achieving high-technology-assisted wildlife conservation, one obvious caveat for installing high-end bioacoustics tools in rural communities is the lack of skilled manpower with concurrent educational and training backgrounds in ecology and Information and Communications Technology (ICT) domains. With a motivation to explore the potential of bioacoustics for ecological research, the University of Tokyo (UT) and the National Trust for Nature Conservation (NTNC) are currently in a pilot phase to understand the usability of bioacoustics technology for wildlife conservation in Nepal. This perspective paper discusses the potential and limitations of bioacoustics studies for nature conservation, particularly in the Nepalese context.

Keywords: Bioacoustics · Human Computer Biosphere Interaction · Nature Conservation · Human Computation

1 Introduction

1.1 Introduction of Bioacoustics

Computer technology is crucial to biodiversity conservation. Human-Computer Biosphere Interaction (HCBI), a relatively new academic discipline, studies the interaction between humans and ecosystems through computer-based technology. Bioacoustics, also known as eco-acoustics, is one of the usual methods in HCBI that can be used to document the spatial and temporal variation of animal sounds. It is a cost-effective and non-invasive technology for nature conservation research. Bioacoustics has advanced primarily due to the recent advances in analytical approaches and the development of the digital audio technologies that allow us to record a tremendous amount of audio data for a prolonged period [12,14]. The popularity of bioacoustics tools is attributable to their traceability, low bandwidth, and non-invasive analysis. Compared to the conventional visual census approach, we can quickly revisit the recorded sound as long as the data is stored on physical hard disks, USBs, or in a cloud-based data storage system. Further, audio data is easily transmitted through the network as it occupies a lower server capacity than other methods, such as video streaming. Bioacoustics studies are also cost-effective; anyone with limited resources can record animal sounds. As various animals use acoustic communication, including mammals, birds, amphibians, fish, and insects [9,13], a broad range of species can be sampled by bioacoustics.

While installing and maintaining a bioacoustics human interface system is relatively easy for a skilled person, this is not always the case for ecologists in rural areas who may need to become more familiar with Information and Communications Technology (ICT) devices. In addition to the technical factors that delay the installation of high technology-assisted conservation, we also need to consider the social circumstances around several protected areas. Nature conservation can only be achieved to a satisfactory level with the cooperation of local citizens. Local attitudes towards novel technologies are an essential determinant of the conservation process. Thus, the utilization of bioacoustics technology for research and conservation purposes should be carefully evaluated both from the technical and social aspects.

1.2 Our Previous Studies Using Bioacoustics

Soundscape research, in general, has mainly focused on green areas within cities, such as urban parks [6,15]. There needs to be more research on continuous soundscapes in outdoor environments as well. The lack of infrastructure, such as networks and power supplies, makes it difficult to use computers in the natural outdoors. This section introduces our soundscape research studies in outdoor environments that lack network access and commercial electrical power sources.

Soundscape Studies in Iriomote Island. Iriomote island, located at the southernmost tip of Japan, is home to the Iriomote wildcat - an endemic species with an estimated population of only about 100 animals. The Iriomote wildcat needs protection because the increased number of tourists has threatened its habitat in recent years. Kobayashi et al. [5] initiated a project to live stream the sound of wild cats by installing microphones in their habitat. They also succeeded in garnering public attention toward its conservation.

Cyberforest Project. In 1998, Saito et al. installed a video camera in the Chichibu Experimental Forest of the University of Tokyo to archive long-term changes in the natural environment. In collaboration with Kobayashi et al., ICT was utilized to transmit data to a server in the university via satellite communication, using a web camera and a microphone connected to an IP encoder. This landscape camera data has been used for educational and research purposes [10]. The project, which initially started with a single observational facility, now hosts more than five observational facilities across Japan. The observation site on Funakoshi Oshima (on the Pacific coast of Iwate Prefecture, Japan) is on an uninhabited island.

Research in Namie, Fukushima. International Atomic Energy Agency (IAEA) recommends long-term ecosystem monitoring in areas impacted by nuclear disasters. However, researchers' health will be at risk if they work within a high-radiation area for a prolonged period. Therefore, it is necessary to use ICT devices that remotely permit continuous biodiversity monitoring. With this motivation, Kobayashi et al. installed a bioacoustics setup in Namie, Fukushima. Namie city was severely affected by the Great East Japan Earthquake, Tsunami, and nuclear radiation in March 2011. This project started with a year of literature search (2011), followed by governmental approval (2012–2014) and fundraising from the stakeholders (local citizens and governmental authorities). It took five years to coordinate with local stakeholders such as landowners. Even though the exclusion zone is an uninhabited space, locals were not very receptive with the idea of conducting academic research there. Of course, this feeling is understandable as the locals have houses and properties and have spent several decades in the disaster-hit area. Therefore, before venturing into the research project, Kobayashi et al. visited several residents and tried to convince them about the necessity of radioecology research. In some cases, Kobayashi's plans were understood in a single visit, while it required multiple visits in case of some residents. The installation of a transmitter station with satellite Internet was achieved in 2015. Finally, based on official preparations and approvals, a local electric company agreed to sign a service contract with Kobayashi et al. in 2016 after an intensive feasibility survey of all the transmission facilities at the location. The final construction was completed at the end of March 2016.

The images and sounds recorded by the system are stored on a server at the University of Tokyo. These data have been partially analyzed by machine learning. For example, we reported that the time spent by warblers singing around the high-radiation area might differ from that of warblers found in other locations [4]. In addition to the real-time streaming of sound through the Internet (Fig. 1), several exhibitions have also been made by Kobayashi et al. so that people worldwide continue to remember the level of destruction caused by the March 2011 disaster.

1.3   Bioacoustics in Nepal

Nepal has a unique topography spanning an altitudinal difference of nearly 8800 m. Nepal occupies only 0.1% of the global area but harbors almost 3% of the world's biodiversity. Therefore, it is an excellent place for ecological research. Nepal is also known as one of the successful countries in regards to biodiversity conservation. For example, the global commitment to doubling the tiger population in 2022 was fulfilled. However, investment is significant mainly because

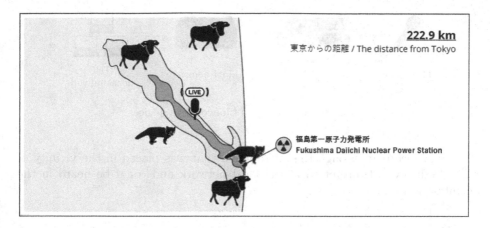

Fig. 1. Screenshot of radioactivelivesoundscape.net (website for real-time distribution of sound from Fukushima).

active monitoring is practiced in Nepal. Several conservation-related supports also come from international donor agencies. This may not be sustainable for long-term conservation efforts in Nepal. To be self-sustaining, it will be necessary to adopt cost-effective methods that permit uninterrupted passive monitoring of wild animals. Bioacoustics tools could be one of the best options in the case of Nepal.

Bioacoustics research in Nepal seems to be mainly applied in the case of birds. For example, simple tape recordings of avian sounds were conducted, and new species were identified [8]. Bioacoustics data has also been analyzed by machine learning to distinguish between the calls of two species in the mountains of Nepal [16]. Furthermore, Beeck et al. [1] used an acoustics camera to study low-frequency nasal call emissions in elephants in Chitwan (https://www.gfaitech.com/applications/bioacoustics). These studies show the potential of bioacoustics studies for wildlife research in Nepal.

2   Simple Bioacoustics Set-Up

Here we provide a simple description of the experimental setup of the bioacoustics tool that was used for the pilot experiment in Nepal (Fig. 2). A microphone (Dynamic Microphone SM63, SHURE, Niles, IL, USA), amplifier (302USBX-ENYX, Behringer, Willich, Germany), and the Instreamer (BARIX, Zürich, Switzerland) were briefly placed right next to the NTNC's office which is adjacent to the Chitwan National Park. The microphone signal is connected to an amplifier for an amplified input to the Barix instreamer. Barix instreamer is an encoder to transmit the microphone signal via IP network to the local network in NTNC's office. At this time, the encoding format is MP3.

Microphone   Amplifier   Instreamer   NTNC's
                                                     local network

Fig. 2. General setup of bioacoustics devices

Sound recorded through the microphone that was placed in the vicinity of NTNC office was transmitted to the local network and could be heard in the neighboring room.

3   Discussion

3.1   Feasibility and Challenges of Bioacoustics Research in Nepal

In Nepal, various plans and policies are in place to facilitate sustainable economic growth and biodiversity conservation through high technology. 15th National Periodic Plan, National Agroforestry Policy 2019, Forestry Sector Strategy (2016–2025), and Nature Conservation National Strategic Framework for Sustainable Development (2015–2030) envisage the use of high technology for sustainable biodiversity conservation in Nepal.

The detection range of the microphone piloted in the NTNC office in Chitwan was about 20–30 m for usual human conversation. However, bird song had somewhat longer range. Short sound range constrains the number of wild animals and birds that could be sampled. When embarking on a full-fledged research project, it will be necessary to perform several optimization steps to increase the detection range. At the same time, care should be taken not to make the sound range very long such that the human conversation from park offices and human settlements can be heard. The microphone should be placed in the middle of the forest so that it is reasonably far away from the park office or human settlements. Similarly, a clear notice must be placed at the microphone installation site warning that the conversation may be captured if humans speak within the detection range.

As this pilot test lasted for only a couple of hours, no housing facilities were built. However, if NTNC is to adopt this technology for a long-term research, a housing facility should be constructed to protect bioacoustics devices from damage due to rainfall, heat, moisture, and animal attack. However, the trade-off is that the detection range to sample sound decreases when the bioacoustics devices are maintained at the housing facility.

Internet access could be a concern if the installation site is far from the NTNC office. It may be somewhat challenging to get Internet access in the middle of the forest (Fig. 3). Installation of optical fibers at such locations and/or continuous Internet access through cellular phones could be an alternative. Internet access may only be necessary when we want to perform live streaming of animal sounds.

If live streaming is not desired, it is possible to store the sound on physical hard disks. Audio data consumes much less physical space than visual data, so several terabytes (TB) of the hard disk could be enough to record several weeks of data from a given location.

Fig. 3. (Left) Landscape in Chitwan National Park. (Right) Warning board for the tiger zone in the park.

NTNC is primarily interested in applying high-technology bioacoustics tools for the animal census. Using deep learning, theoretically, it is possible to estimate the species abundance at a particular landscape with rather high accuracy [11]. However, counting the number of animals or birds within the same species will be challenging. The degree of intra-species vocal individuality may differ depending on the species. Nevertheless, to start with, it may be better to try bioacoustics to count the abundance of sparsely distributed animals, such as the snow leopards, as they have an extensive home range in the mountains, and clear territorial segregation exists between individuals. The estimation obtained by bioacoustics tools could be correlated with other methods, such as scat DNA analysis and camera traps.

So far, most bioacoustics data has been sampled over a relatively limited time frame. However, some recent research provides a continuous live stream of sound-scape from the natural environment. As described earlier, our work in Fukushima (Radioactive Live Soundscape Project, https://radioactivelivesoundscape.net) can be an excellent leading example. Similarly, live soundscape streaming from Sapsucker Woods Sanctuary by The K. Lisa Yang Center for Conservation Bioacoustics at the Cornell Lab of Ornithology is another excellent example. Uninterrupted electricity and Internet supply will be required for live streaming, which could be one of the bottlenecks for achieving live streaming from the bioacoustics system in Nepal. Hosting a server and reliably maintaining it 24/7 could be very costly as dedicated round-the-clock manpower is necessary. The annual cost for continuous operation of servers could go up to several thousand US dollars. To start with, in Nepal's case, at present, it will be first necessary to increase human capacity and awareness regarding the bioacoustics system through regular work-shops and training. Once the essential physical infrastructure and human capac-ity are developed, bioacoustics devices could gradually be installed in Nepal for biodiversity conservation and research purposes. Before installation, obtaining the required permission from the authorities in the national parks will also be necessary. Further, the proper installation site should be carefully chosen as the surrounding inadvertent noise may mask the desired sounds.

Similarly, storing and interpreting several terabytes of data could also be challenging. How to analyse the sound could be an issue. NTNC does not have a machine learning expert to analyse the sound. The establishment of a dedi-cated bioacoustics unit as part of the Department of Species Conservation and Research in NTNC to support the application of bioacoustics technology could be one of the ways. Recruiting engineering and computer scientists trained in Artificial Intelligence (AI) could be a way forward. It is also necessary to take the initiative by the University of Tokyo to train a couple of researchers in NTNC regarding the operation and maintenance of bioacoustics. Establishing a dedi-cated server and having round-the-clock personnel to ensure the server's smooth operation could be necessary for live streaming.

3.2   Perception Regarding Bioacoustics Devices by Researchers and Conservation Officers in Nepal

The bioacoustics device's successful pilot testing and compatibility with Nepal's electricity and Internet facility raised curiosity for its further use and implication for biodiversity research and conservation. When piloting the device in Chitwan, its potential for biodiversity research in Nepal was discussed among available wildlife biologists and researchers from NTNC and the University of Tokyo. The discussion identified several avenues for wildlife monitoring, assessment, and con-servation. If bioacoustics devices can be used appropriately in Nepal, it may decrease the human labor and financial resources needed for wildlife monitoring. For example, the Government of Nepal invests significant resources in monitoring tigers, rhinos, and elephants. Bioacoustics can be used to monitor these species and also reduce human-wildlife conflict. For large mammals, the device can be placed on the edge of farmland or forest area to record the sound of a particular species when it approaches farmland or settlement. We can also set up an early warning system so that the farmers, villagers, and wildlife conservation authori-ties can be well notified in advance to intervene with appropriate approaches to minimize the human wildlife conflict.

In Nepal, bioacoustics could be particularly useful for sampling reptiles, amphibians (for example, frogs), or birds sound in protected areas, including national parks and wildlife reserves in Nepal. It may also be tested in the central zoo in Nepal, which NTNC manages. It will be interesting to see how the ani-mals communicate at night. The central zoo attracts many visitors, particularly from educational institutions in Nepal. The recorded sounds and videos could be shown to students for educational purposes. During the discussion between NTNC and the University of Tokyo, it was suggested that before full-fledged implementation of bioacoustics technology, it would be better to perform pilot studies in different ecological settings in Nepal so that we can be more certain about the relevance of bioacoustics in relation to diurnal, seasonal, and other climatic variations. Even the bioacoustics setup could be deployed in each location for a few weeks at a specified time. However, extensive pilot testing in multiple locations requires considerable time and financial resources. Such extensive pilot testing may only be justifiable when NTNC performs a full-fledged bioacoustics study in the future.

Bioacoustics can also be linked to Environmental Services Payment (ESP). The sound and video of endangered and critically endangered species from the wild can be listened to and heard from urban areas elsewhere in the world. For example, the sound of tiger roars, elephant rumbles, and herpetofauna calls can be heard in real-time. End users can get access to this sound on a subscription basis. Significantly, NTNC can generate funding for species conservation through this sort of mechanism. This would make conservation project more sustainable and create a long-term impact on species conservation in developing countries.

However, as mentioned earlier, there are some limitations of this device from an ethical perspective. How can we entrust human privacy when we use this device in the vicinity of human settlements? The device will likely detect sound from a distance. Using it for the worthy cause of wildlife research and conservation might negatively affect human privacy. Therefore, it is recommended to have proper permission from the government of Nepal, considering human privacy issues before its implementation.

3.3 Need for Connecting Bioacoustics to Human Interface

The interaction between animals and computer technology has not really entered the mainstream of computer science, as rightly argued by Mancini [7]. In fact, Mancini can be credited with her pioneering efforts to explore animal-computer interaction, including the organization of conferences. The researchers in the animal-computer interaction domain believe that it is not really the lack of the technology that has hindered this research field. Rather, the lack of an interface that can facilitate human interaction with remote animals can be a missing element for further advancement of animal-computer interaction domain.

The continuity of bioacoustics can only be ensured if the researchers work in harmony with the locals, and the locals are also included as essential stakeholders of the technology. For this reason, the HCBI discipline envisages the need for a human interface system to complete a research task with minimal resources. The Internet and cloud sensing development has provided opportunities for common people to engage as citizen scientists [2]. The vast amount of data uploaded by ordinary citizens can be one of the ideal tools for experts to increase the horizon of data collection. Conservation officers can make use of these data for biodiversity conservation. However, we should be aware that sole reliance on citizen science may not always yield a positive result. The continuity problem seems to be a significant problem when working with citizen scientists [3]. Citizen scientists are purely involved on a voluntary basis, mostly in pursuit of their hobbies. Thus, researchers should also develop alternative plans to sample data when data collection through citizen scientists does not go as planned.

3.4 Summary

Bioacoustics tools are receiving increasing attraction from researchers. Even in natural outdoors, where power and network supplies are limited, Kobayashi et al. initiated a project to bio-acoustically detect Iriomote wildcats, an endemic and endangered species, by installing microphones in their habitat in Japan and are successful in garnering public attention towards its conservation. This successful project must be up-scaled in developing countries like Nepal to conserve and manage endangered species like pangolins, tigers, and other vital species. The bioacoustics tool is successfully piloted against its compatibility with Nepal's available electricity and Internet facility. The next step can be to use this instrument for biodiversity research and assessment, species monitoring and management, and law enforcement to control poaching and mitigation of illegal wildlife trafficking. However, it is recommended to address human privacy issues when using it for soundscape-related research with proper approval from the governmental agencies.

Acknowledgements. This study is supported by the Coordination Funds for Promoting Aerospace Utilization grants (2021–2023) from the Ministry of Education, Culture, Sports, Science, and Technology (MEXT) and FOREST program (JPMJFR211B) from Japan Science and Technology Agency (JST).

References

1. Beeck, V.C., Heilmann, G., Kerscher, M., Stoeger, A.S.: Sound visualization demonstrates velopharyngeal coupling and complex spectral variability in asian elephants. Animals (Basel) **12**(16) (2022)
2. Dickinson, J.L., Bonney, R.E. (eds.): Citizen Science: Public Participation in Environmental Research. Cornell University Press, Ithaca (2015). https://doi.org/10.7591/9780801463952
3. Keita, F., Yoshio, M., Akira, Y., Nao, K., Kumiko, T., Takeshi, O.: Mammal assemblages recorded by camera traps inside and outside the evacuation zone of the fukushima daiichi nuclear power plant accident. Ecol. Res. **31**(4), 493 (2016)
4. Kobayashi, H.H., et al.: A real-time streaming and detection system for bio-acoustic ecological studies after the fukushima accident. In: Joly, A., Vrochidis, S., Karatzas, K., Karppinen, A., Bonnet, P. (eds.) Multimedia Tools and Applications for Environmental & Biodiversity Informatics. MSA, pp. 53–66. Springer, Cham (2018). https://doi.org/10.1007/978-3-319-76445-0_4
5. Kobayashi, H.H., Matsushima, J.: Basic research in Human-Computer-Biosphere interaction. Buildings **4**(4), 635–660 (2014)
6. Liu, J., Kang, J., Behm, H., Luo, T.: Effects of landscape on soundscape perception: soundwalks in city parks. Landsc. Urban Plan. **123**, 30–40 (2014)
7. Mancini, C.: Animal-computer interaction: a manifesto. Interactions **18**(4), 69–73 (2011)

8. Martens, J.: Vocalizations and the discovery of a cryptic species in the timaliid genus pnoepyga in nepal. Bioacoustics J. **4**(1), 65 (1992)
9. Mellinger, D.K., Stafford, K.M., Moore, S.E., Dziak, R.P., Matsumoto, H.: An overview of fixed passive acoustic observation methods for cetaceans. Oceanography **20**(4), 36–45 (2007)
10. Saito, K., et al.: Utilizing the cyberforest live sound system with social media to remotely conduct woodland bird censuses in central japan. Ambio **44**(4), 572–583 (2015)
11. Sethi, S.S., et al.: Soundscapes predict species occurrence in tropical forests. Oikos 2022(3) (2022)
12. Snaddon, J., Petrokofsky, G., Jepson, P., Willis, K.J.: Biodiversity technologies: tools as change agents. Biol. Lett. **9**(1), 20121029 (2013)
13. Sugai, L.S.M., Silva, T.S.F., Ribeiro, J.W., Llusia, D.: Terrestrial passive acoustic monitoring: review and perspectives. Bioscience **69**(1), 15–25 (2018)
14. Villanueva-Rivera, L.J., Pijanowski, B.C., Doucette, J., Pekin, B.: A primer of acoustic analysis for landscape ecologists. Landsc. Ecol. **26**(9), 1233–1246 (2011)
15. Zhang, M., Kang, J.: Towards the evaluation, description, and creation of soundscapes in urban open spaces. Environ. Plann. B. Plann. Des. **34**(1), 68–86 (2007)
16. Zhong, M., et al.: Bioacoustics and machine learning for automated avian species monitoring in global biodiversity hotspots. J. Acoust. Soc. Am. **148**(4), 2442 (2020)

How Citizens Participation Begin and Continue in Developing Smart Cities

Mika Yasuoka[✉] [iD]

Roskilde University, Roskilde, Denmark
mikaj@ruc.dk

Abstract. "Smart Cities" where utilize city data and ICT technology to improve urban living, have attracted attention in the world. Externalized characteristics of smart cities around the world are diverse, while smart cities in Nordic countries are often introduced as future city design with citizen participation. However, how exactly citizens participation begins and continues smart city projects has not fully been explored, yet. In this paper, we analyzed Danish smart cities from the three axes of the *subject* of action, the applied *technologies*, and the *instruments* for realization, and derived three potential devices that bring citizens' autonomous participation. The investigation identifies constant citizens' participation rooted in society as a mechanism, which is enabled with joint citizens decision-making by accessing to resources and commending ways of collaborating. The finding of this paper contributes to the participatory researchers on smart cities, who values citizens' autonomous participation in design.

Keywords: Participatory Design · Smart Cities · Co-cCeation · Citizens' Participation · Participation in Design · Autonomy

1 Introduction

In our highly digitized modern world, we have witnessed that the city planning and urban development have incorporated with city informatics and digitalization in every corner of our everyday life [1, 2]. Some are called "smart cities", which have characteristics with social infrastructure using (advanced) technologies such as everyday transaction data, sensors, IoT, and AI [3, 4]. The modern cities efficiently and effectively builds, operates, and utilizes living and industrial infrastructure, and services, improves the citizens' quality of life with the help of ICT technologies, and aims for continuous economic development [5–8].

However, currently, the definition of smart cities are varied and often discussed from different angles [3, 9]. While many cities with utilizing varieties of data generated in cities, and many ICT initiatives have been recognized as smart city projects, the perceived characteristics are very different from project to project. Some are characterized as technology driven projects with emphasis on high-tech implementation in cities [10–12], while others are driven by human-centered approach with emphasis on social capitals and citizens participation [13–15]. Some smart cities are led by mega IT companies [16,

N. A. Streitz and S. Konomi (Eds.): HCII 2023, LNCS 14037, pp. 182–192, 2023.
https://doi.org/10.1007/978-3-031-34609-5_13

17], while other cities are conducted as strategic national initiatives [18, 19]. Among such a wide variety of cases, smart cities in Nordics are uniquely characterized with its co-creation and citizens' participation [20]. Based on the well-known world leading Nordic digital infrastructure [21, 22], quite a few articles introduce Nordic smart cities as places formed by citizens through multiple types of collaboration with the public, the industries, and the academic researchers [20, 23].

Despite the seemingly collective agreement and understanding that such smart cities in Nordic countries are co-created with citizens, what exactly it is to participate in participatory design (PD) has not fully been explored in general [24], even considering projects on smart cities. We have little knowledge how smart city design involving citizens can be conducted, and why citizens' activities and commitment could continue and sustain in city sphere. Although a phrase, "Cities created by citizens" sounds very attractive, PD research has experienced that it is not an easy task to encourage citizens' participation, achieve commitments and co-creation [25, 26].

Based on this awareness of the potential challenge of citizen participation in smart city projects, the authors conducted a survey based project on Nordic Smart Cities (here after, *Norsities*) [5], in which 100 Nordic smart city projects were collected and analyzed from the citizens participation perspectives. This paper focuses especially Danish cases among all Nordic regions as authors involved some of the projects.

The rest of the paper is formulated as follows. The survey method and three Danish smart city cases as examples are introduced in Sect. 2 and 3. Then, Sect. 4 discusses findings, the three socially embedded factors as a part of a mechanism that enables citizens participation in design in Danish smart cities. Lastly, the paper summarizes the work and concludes.

2 Data Collection Method

The research question of the *Norsities* project is how do citizens participation begin and continue in smart city projects? Based on the *Norsities* project, which collected 100 Nordic smart city cases, this paper focus on Danish smart city cases.

2.1 Data Collection

The targeted 100 smart city cases were collected from December 2020 to August 2021 mainly based on the desktop search due to Covid-19 pandemic influence. The collected data varies from official documents and reports to in-depth interviews [27]. The overview of the collected data is as shown in Table 1.

The *Norsities* extracted smart city projects of five Nordic countries (Denmark, Finland, Iceland, Norway, and Sweden) through open and accessible materials (public and private reports and web search) and interviews with experts. The collected smart city projects were listed, and related project materials were recollected by accessing each project site and contacting project owners. In addition, when possible, online or face-to-face interviews were conducted with key persons of the selected projects.

The collected smart city projects were 30 Danish, 28 Finish, 6 Icelandic, 26 Norwegian and 23 Swedish projects. Note that the total number exceeds 100 cases since there are a couple of cross-country projects.

Table 1. The overview of the collected data.

Data Style	#	Main sources
Reports by public organizations	34	EU, Nordforsk, Each government
Reports by private organizations	23	Private research institutions, Private organizations
Web Search	124	Project websites
Interviews	12	Practitioners, Researchers, Project managers

3 Method

Based on the collected data including reports, websites and interview data, characteristics of each smart city were extracted, and analyzed with KJ Method [28]. In the process, the three predefined axes of the *subject* of action, the applied *technologies*, and the *instruments* for realization were used as a preliminary analysis framework. The *subjects* of action are entities, which initiate, promote, and maintain the smart city project, and it is roughly divided into three categories: the public, the industry, and the citizens. The applied *technologies* specify the central concern or challenge of the smart city project, including the degree of utilization of technology. For example, in Nordic smart city projects, technology is not always emphasized or mentioned as a main agenda even if they call themselves as smart cities. Some projects might emphasize its environmental consideration or co-creation aspects realized with ICT means, rather than explain as technology-driven ICT projects. Lastly, the *instruments* for realization aim to identify keys for achieving the project goals. For example, this concerns ecosystem or mechanism to support the smart city project, and its key stakeholder participation.

4 Cases

Among the 100 Nordic smart city projects, 30 cases are danish. Among them, the authors selected three cases as examples, which will be elaborated further from citizens' participation perspective. The three exemplified Danish cases were selected intentionally with different *subjects* of action: the public, the industry, and the citizen-initiated smart city projects for better comparison. The overview of each case is shown in Table 2.

Table 2. The three examples from Danish smart city projects.

Cases	Subject	Instrument
Roskilde Festival	Citizen	PD, ICT and technogy implementation
Refshaleøen –city development site	Industry	PD, Community building
DOKK1 – public library	Public	PD, Innovation through making (fablab)

Below, we introduce the outline of the three cases with the emphasis on citizens' participation aspects of the projects.

4.1 The Roskilde Festival as Smart City Living Lab

The Roskilde Festival is chosen since citizen as the main subjects of action. The city functions are designed through stakeholder participation, and accelerator of smart city design is its ICT and technological implementation applied to dwellers of this temporary city by citizens themselves. The Roskilde Festival is a globally known as an annual outdoor music and art festival, initiated in 1972 [29, 30]. The festival made the city of Roskilde known to music fans around the world. With the slogan "Music, Art, Activism, Camps and Freedom", 130,000 people gather every year at the festival, where many participants stay together as outdoor campers around the event venue for more than eight days. Some people even settle there for a month. To some extent, it means that a new city of Roskilde Festival with 130,000 population suddenly emerge in vast green area with a time limit. The festival is not only a music, but also performance and talk festival held as paradelle events. At the festival, new technologies and services are tested, ranging widely from new digital currency, sustainable houses, high-tech toilet system to sustainable electricity grid. This infers that the festival provides a stage for living lab [31–33] of digital solutions to temporary residents for a short period, often in collaboration with local universities, technology companies, and high tech startups.

The Roskilde Festival is characterized and known as citizens festival [29, 30] as organized by a legal entity, non-profit organization (NPO, *forening* in Danish. See 5.3) and operated by more than 30,000 volunteers. In monthly meetings, new project ideas at the festival are proposed and examined by the *forening* members, and an annual program is defined through a democratic decision-making process. The participants of the Roskilde Festival are diverse, ranging from citizens, local governments, local industries, global companies, and educational institutions to music fans. All contribute to the Roskilde Festival as an opportunity for participating city design, which occasionally influence longitudinal regional development such as community formulation and local industrial growth.

4.2 Refshaleøen, City Development Site

Refshaleøen is an industry led smart city project, where new citizens, new project and new businesses participate to form a city with social as well as business activities, and where new citizen community is formulated with the help of the industry. Refshaleøen is a vast area (525.000 km2) situated in the center of Danish capital, Copenhagen, previously used as shipyard and factory site. Although Refshaleøen is in the middle of the urban revitalization program, the site has already attracted attention of various innovators as future city. The unique aspect of Refshaleøen resides in its potential charm of the unshaped city of the future, which attracts artists, entrepreneurs, and students. Due to its chaotic and open-ended city characteristics, Refshaleøen generates new standards for urban development where new form of urban community has been integrated and where several solutions for urban problems have been tested.

The city development corporation, *Refshaleøens Ejendomsselskab A/S* (hereafter, R.F.A/S) is responsible for Refshaleøen area development and management, and currently the company organizes rental service of the area in cooperation with the local municipality. R.F.A/S, however, do not promote detailed development plan of the area.

Moreover, R.F.A/S limits their role only to manage, lend out the renovated buildings and district, support proposed cultural and industrial projects, and support establishing local community by building bridging residents, start-ups, and entrepreneurs. On the other hand, residents in the district and local project stakeholders play a central role to design the future city. The future city, Refshaleøen is gradually shaped by the residents and projects stakeholders including entrepreneurs who run business (such as restaurants and cafes, music and art festivals, outdoor sports facilities, and container houses for students) at site. For example, container house established by a collective citizens' NPO, *forening* has developed comfortable and affordable sustainable container houses with in-depth consideration of lighting, heading and sower system with the help of IoT technologies, sensors, and advanced materials. Such bottom-up activities of residents, artists and entrepreneurs form a central position of the regional revitalization program at Refshaleøen. The Refshaleøen's smart city solution is tested somewhat chaotic way rather than a planned process, by the hands of citizens with diversity.

4.3 DOKK1, the Public Library as a Hub of Smart City

DOKK1 is public-led smart city project, where citizens and industries utilize a library space to make their city life better as a hub of Aarhus smart city. DOKK1 is the central public library of Aarhus, the second largest city in Denmark, established in 2015. DOKK1 offers not only books to lent, but also provide spaces where digital fabrication and tinkering workshops are offered, VR and games are experienced, and new possibilities of healthcare robots are investigated and discussed through exhibition and workshops. It is a place where citizens at all ages can gather, experience and test advanced technologies and digital solutions for future as a part of their daily life.

The future library, DOKK1, was designed through 13 years' dialogues with various citizens such as children and adults, men and women, immigrants, the disabilities as well as experts on different domains. This dialogue before the construction, made it possible to draw a "new library" from citizens perspectives through workshops and public hearings organized by the city of Aarhus and local design companies.

Nowadays, various citizens' NPOs, *forenings,* organize cultural as well as business events, exhibitions, and services are provided, ranging from health consultation to homework support. Local *forenings* with residents' members organize and commit to the event planning and operation, in collaboration with the library, industries, universities and other *forenings*. DOKK1 functions as a city activity hub, where residents gather and share future city vision by utilizing physical library space and co-design by organizing and participating in various activities.

5   Analysis

5.1   A Mechanism that Enables Citizens Participation

The three Danish smart city cases show that the various actors in city gather, form a community, initiative urban development activities in a broad sense in tangible and intangible ways. Even when projects are initiated by public (DOKK1) and industry

(Refshaleøen), there are always citizens who are actively participate. Then, the question is that why it is possible for citizens, in Danish smart city projects, to be actively involved in designing smart cities? Our preliminary analysis externalized a few devices which are potentially key enablers especially when citizens actively participate in designing smart cities. They achieve joint citizens decision making by accessing the resources and commending particular ways of collaborating which are rooted in Danish society potentially as a part of participation mechanism. We especially focus on three devices in this paper: *fund, organization,* and *process.*

5.2 Fund, a Way to Access Resources

Fund opportunity is widely practiced as a easy way to access financial resources. In Denmark, citizens might contribute intangible resources such as time and knowledge as volunteers when they are involved in smart city activities. However, operation costs are hardly paid by volunteers, but covered by external funds so that financial base hardly hit citizens' own pockets. This implies that those who want to run small initiatives and activities in Danish cities have a way to get financial supports relatively easily.

Majority funds offered to such citizens' activities are provided by the central or local government (for example, the Agency for Culture and Palace for cultural and societal programs) and by the private fund organizations (for example, Novo Nordisk fund and Carlsberg foundation). The project duration and domains are often determined by fund providers, and previously many ranges of social projects such as culture, art, and sports have been financially supported. Recent years, funds opportunities for sustainable development, environment, promotion of diversity, and technology and innovation projects have drastically increased [34].

At Roskilde festivals, many Danish citizens' NPOs, *forenings*, and startups acquire such external funds to plan and implement their technologies on site. Moreover, a fund organization, *the Fund Roskilde Festival*, was established under the festival group, which every year provides financial supports to multiple *forenings* on selected theme. Similarly, many events and start-ups projects at Refshaleøen and DOKK1 have been supported by fund money.

5.3 Forening, a Way of Collaborating

The second key is Danish NPO organization, *forening*. *Forening* is a part of the Danish social system that supports citizens with a purpose to act on their purpose in an organized manner. Forening is a publicly recognized legal entity and used for all types of social activities, from local soccer clubs, music classes, cultural organizations, political organizations, religious organizations, to associations with cancer patients. Other specialized organizations such as cultural festivals and scientific event can often be *forenings*. We use a word, *forening*, instead of translated version, NPO, as *forening* is unique Danish social entity, to the extent of the authors' knowledge, and the concept of forening covers wider range than ordinary functions of NPO.

Forening can provide a useful framework when citizens want to do something with someone with purpose. The benefits of creating a publicly recognized activity group are enormous. For example, Danish forenings can use public facilities such as schools, sports facilities and library's meeting rooms free of charge, and access to abundant funds opportunities. Alternatively, there are also constraints, include minimal number of committed members, a requirement of accepting new members, transparency assurance in management decision-making by holding open regular meetings. In meetings, usually forening use *dagsorden* (discussed below) and keep organized documentations, open and accessible.

In Denmark, using the forening device, many citizens take actions immediately, when they urge to stand up. They obtain funds relatively easily and carry out small-scale projects as a first step. Last couple of years, young people aged 16–29 have established political and cultural forenings on environmental issues [34], which indicate, in Denmark, social issues quickly become visible social movement. Because of this device, citizens can participate smart city activities with high mobility.

Roskilde Festival, Refshaleøen Residence Community, and Refshaleøens container house, *the CPH Village,* were established as forenings. Such forenings sometimes evolve to business entities by being recognized of its business potentials.

5.4 Dagsorden, Joint Citizens' Decision Making

In any meetings at *forenings*, citizens use *dagsorden*, which can be translated "agenda" in English. At first glance it is just a list of "agenda" of today's meeting, however there are further tacit meanings.

Dagsorden is not considered anything special in Danish society and is incorporated into daily life from pupils' class meetings to corporate monthly conference. *Dagsorden* is an indispensable device for everyday meetings, which is usually distributed to the meeting participants in advance as a list form with some reference material attached. The unique characteristics resides not in the content but in the composition of the agenda. In a typical *dagsorden*, a meeting is to begin with choosing a chairman and a secretary and checking the list of agenda of the day whether there are any excess or deficiency. Moreover, additional items or comments are welcomed. In industrial settings, there might be a fixed person who serves as a chairman or secretary. However, typical forening meetings begin with the election of a chairman and a secretary and collectively checking validity of agenda before discussion begins.

Dagsorden is a device which explicitly present all participants at meetings are equal. No single authority exists, or no selected group of people run meetings, or make decisions. The meeting records are open to the public so that anyone who are interested in or doubt about the decisions or results of the meeting can access to the relevant data. The chairman and secretary are randomly selected at each meeting, and due to its transparency, it is difficult to maliciously change agenda, or fake records.

6   Discussion

We have looked at a series of projects to better understand how citizens participation begin and continue in developing smart cities from co-creation perspectives. PD looks at a design practice from the idea of autonomy, self-realization and empowerment, while what exactly it means to participate on smart cities development has not fully been explored [24]. In the context of city planning and city revitalization of smart cities, it is not always necessarily designers who involves citizens to design our future cities. Here, there are some smart city projects initiated PD researchers. However, many Danish smart cities we have investigated, have been initiated by diverse subjects of action, often involving citizens. We see some aspects of PD such as autonomy, self-realization, and empowerment in the smart city projects. Then, what shapes the possibilities of citizen participation?

From the investigations of three Danish smart city projects, we want to discuss two aspects: strategic stages for autonomous, self-realization and empowerment, and autonomous participation mechanisms.

6.1 Strategic Stages

The strategic stage could afford citizens' tangible and intangible activities and participation in the smart city initiatives. By creating an accessible and visible place and space for participation, activities in smart cities are spawn among citizens who are aware of urban challenges and potential solution ideas.

Among our three cases, first, the Roskilde Festival, by providing a stage as a temporary 'Roskilde Festival City' afford anyone who has new and innovative ideas challenges for future city. Secondly, Refshaleøen as a chaotic industry-driven vast and blank district, succeed to transmit a message that any wild ideas for regional revitalization and re-construction of urban community are welcomed. DOKK1 is an organic public-driven place that guarantees anyone of all ages can freely access and utilize the places at their disposal.

The importance of staging for innovation has been discussed widely. Opland [35] pointed out the importance of preparing arena such as Hackathon. Although his argument was discussed in the context of employee driven digital innovation (EDDI), which is another context than citizen participation, his research indicates strategic stage invite participation.

6.2 Autonomous Participation Mechanism

Together with the strategic stages, there is also a strategic mechanism for autonomous participation, which formulate a foundation of citizens participation in Danish smart city initiatives. The mechanism makes it easier to foster citizens autonomy in participation together with motivation, commitment, and empower bottom-up activities, and support sustainable smart city initiatives. Bratteteig [24] articulated decision making in design is necessary in participation in PD, thus to share power with users is necessary. In our cases, citizens utilize *fund*, *forening* and *dagsorden*, which became devices to practice power of decision making in smart city design. They play as a strong presence of principles in PD "to share power with users [citizens] and to respect 'people's [citizens'] expertise and their rights to represent their own activities to others' [36].

Activities within a frame of *forening*, citizens participation is officially supported and socially recognized, which accelerate by obtaining *fund* and opportunities to utilize public free facilities such as schools, sports facilities, and libraries' meeting rooms. In return, the *forenings* are required to keep transparency with open management and regular open meetings conducted based on the formal meeting procedure, *dagsorden*. In this way, the principle of democracy is unconsciously selected, and autonomous participation and co-creation among the diverse citizens are promoted.

7 Conclusion

In response to the question of how Danish citizen participation in smart city projects begin and continue, this paper examines three unique devices of easy to access *fund*, *forening* organization, and decision-making process with *dagsorden* from 30 Danish smart city projects. To promote revitalization of the city and community, "empower citizens" "involve citizens" and "citizens participation" for designing and building smart cities are attractive and comfortable phrases to our ears. However, few citizens could feel ownership or commitment in many smart city projects. Some projects which seem to achieve citizens or end-user participation could easily fade out when resources run out [26, 37]. The main interest of this paper resides in its autonomous, self-motivated participation in design, so that it focuses on mechanisms that make it possible for Danish smart city projects to realized citizens participation before the PD designers' interventions.

The analysis of Danish smart city cases suggests that the unique mechanism is potentially in place to keep individual citizen's motivation and incentives alive through devices where ordinary citizen wish to take actions to make their city more livable. In Denmark, smart city projects can be initiated by any kind of actors such as public initiatives, industrial strategy, and citizens activities. However, with the help of unique mechanisms to promote participation, Danish citizens achieve joint citizens decision making by accessing the resources and unique collaboration process, where citizens are to be involved every corner of smart city initiatives.

The subject of this analysis is limited to the Danish smart city cases, which might not scale to other socio-technical settings. However, the perspective of this paper indicate there could be a certain mechanism with concrete devices to make citizens participation work in smart city contexts. Our work also contributes to provide the fruitful implications for promoting participation in the development of smart cities in other regions.

References

1. Yasuoka, M., Ishida, T., Aurigi, A.: The advancement of world digital cities. In: Nakashima, H., Aghajan, H., Augusto, J.C. (eds.) Handbook of Ambient Intelligence and Smart Environments, pp. 939–958. Springer US, Boston, MA (2010). https://doi.org/10.1007/978-0-387-93808-0_35
2. Ishida, T.: Digital City Kyoto: Social Information Infrastructure for Everyday Life (2000)
3. Dameri, R.P., Cocchia, A.: Smart city and digital city : twenty years of terminology evolution. X Conference of the Italian Chapter AIS, ITAIS 2013, pp. 1–8 (2013)
4. Cocchia, A.: Smart and digital city: a systematic literature review. In: Dameri, R.P., Rosenthal-Sabroux, C. (eds.) Smart City. PI, pp. 13–43. Springer, Cham (2014). https://doi.org/10.1007/978-3-319-06160-3_2
5. Yasuoka, M., Nielsen, J.: Nordic Smart Cities. Gakugei Publishing, Kyoto (2022)
6. Albino, V., Berardi, U., Dangelico, R.M.: Smart cities: definitions, dimensions, performance, and initiatives. J. Urban Technol. (2015). https://doi.org/10.1080/10630732.2014.942092

7. Nam, T., Pardo, T.A.: Conceptualizing smart city with dimensions of technology, people, and institutions. In: ACM International Conference on Proceeding Series, pp. 282–291 (2011). https://doi.org/10.1145/2037556.2037602

8. Aurigi, A., Willis, K., Melgaco, L.: From 'Digital' to 'Smart': upgrading the city. In: ACM International Conference Proceeding Series (2016). https://doi.org/10.1145/2946803.2946813

9. Paola, D.R., Rosenthal-Sabroux, C.: Smart City: How to Create Public and Economic Value with High Technology in Urban Space, 1st edn. Springer, Heidelberg (2014). https://doi.org/10.1007/978-3-319-06160-3

10. Hao, L., Lei, X., Yan, Z., ChnLi, Y.: The application and implementation research of smart city in China. In: 2012 International Conference on System Science and Engineering (ICSSE) (2012)

11. Anthopoulos, L., Fitsilis, P.: From digital to ubiquitous cities: defining a common architecture for urban development. In: Proceedings of 2010 6th International Conference on Intelligent Environment IE 2010, no. June, pp. 301–306 (2010). https://doi.org/10.1109/IE.2010.61

12. Rathore, M.M., Paul, A., Hong, W.H., Seo, H.C., Awan, I., Saeed, S.: Exploiting IoT and big data analytics: defining smart digital city using real-time urban data. Sustain. Cities Soc. **40**, 600–610 (2018). https://doi.org/10.1016/j.scs.2017.12.022

13. Ballas, D.: What makes a 'happy city'? Cities **32**, S39–S50 (2013). https://doi.org/10.1016/j.cities.2013.04.009

14. Al-Nasrawi, S., El-Zaart, A., Adams, C.: The anatomy of smartness of smart sustainable cities: an inclusive approach. In: 2017 International Conference on Computer and Applications, ICCA 2017 (2017) https://doi.org/10.1109/COMAPP.2017.8079774

15. Saunders, T., Baeck, P.: Rethinking smart cities from the ground up. Nesta Innov. Charity Organ. **1**(6), 4–6, (2015). https://media.nesta.org.uk/documents/rethinking_smart_cities_from_the_ground_up_2015.pdf%0Awww.nesta.org.uk. Accessed 1 Feb 2023

16. Marshall, A.: Alphabet's sidewalk labs scraps its ambitious toronto project. Wired (2020). https://www.wired.com/story/alphabets-sidewalk-labs-scraps-ambitious-toronto-project/. Accessed 1 Feb 2023

17. Artyushina, A.: Is civic data governance the key to democratic smart cities? The role of the urban data trust in Sidewalk Toronto. Telemat. Informatics **55**, 101456 (2020). https://doi.org/10.1016/j.tele.2020.101456

18. Su, K., Li, J., Fu, H.: Mart city and the applications. In: Proceedings of 2011 International Conference on Electronics, Communications and Control, ICECC 2011 (2011). https://doi.org/10.1109/ICECC.2011.6066743

19. Shin, H.B.: Unequal cities of spectacle and mega-events in China. City Anal. Urban Chang. Theory Action **16**(6), 728–744 (2012)

20. Doody, L., Walt, N., Dimireva, I., Nørskov, A.: Growing smart cities in Denmark - digital technology for urban improvement and national prosperity (2016). http://um.dk/da/nyheder-fra-udenrigsministeriet/newsdisplaypage//~/media/UM/MarkedsinformationPublications/Growing_Smart_Cities_in_Denmark.pdf. Accessed 1 Feb 2023

21. European Commission: Digital Economy and Society Index 2021 : overall progress in digital transition but need for new EU-wide efforts Main findings of the 2021 DESI in the four areas (2021). https://ec.europa.eu/commission/presscorner/detail/en/ip_21_5481. Accessed 1 Feb 2023

22. United Nations: E-Government Survey 2020 (2020). https://publicadministration.un.org/egovkb/en-us/Reports/UN-E-Government-Survey-2020. Accessed 1 Feb 2023

23. Helsinki, D.: People First: A Vision for the Global Urban Age Lessons from Nordic Smart Cities (2020)

24. Bratteteig, T., Wagner, I.: Unpacking the notion of participation in participatory design. Comput. Support. Coop. Work (CSCW) **25**(6), 425–475 (2016). https://doi.org/10.1007/s10606-016-9259-4
25. Bratteteig, T.: Design research in informatics. Design **19**, 65–74 (2004)
26. Bratteteig, T., Wagner, I.: Disentangling Participation. Springer, Heidelberg (2014). https://doi.org/10.1007/978-3-319-06163-4
27. M. N. C., Yeo, L.J., Legard, A., Keegan, R., Ward, J.K.: Chapter 7: In-depth Interviews. Qual. Res. Pract. Guid. Soc. Sci. Students Res. (2014)
28. Scupin, R.: The KJ method: a technique for analyzing data derived from Japanese ethnology. Hum. Organ. **56**, 233–237 (1997). https://doi.org/10.17730/humo.56.2.x335923511444655
29. Hjortkær, A., Mellergaard, O.D., Temiz, S.D.: Roskilde Festival Guide (2019)
30. Bilde, C., Olesen, T.L., Hjortkær, A.: Årsskrift 2019 (2020)
31. Følstad, A.: Living Labs for innovation and development of information and communication technology: a literature review. Electron. J. Virtual Organ. Networks **10**(August), 99–131 (2008)
32. Kareborn, B.B., Stahlbrost, A.: Living lab: an open and citizen-centric approach for innovation. Int. J. Inno. Reg. Dev. **1**(4), 356 (2009). https://doi.org/10.1504/IJIRD.2009.022727
33. Yasuoka, M., Akasaka, F., Kimura, A., Ihara, M.: Living labs as a methodology for service design - an analysis based on cases and discussions from a systems approach viewpoint. In: Proceedings of International Design Conference, DESIGN, vol. 1, no. 2012, pp. 127–136 (2018). https://doi.org/10.21278/idc.2018.0350
34. Center for Frivilligt Socialt arbejde.: Nye tal om danskernes frivillige engagement (2019)
35. Opland, L.E.: Is motivation always the key ? – Antecedents of employee-driven digital innovation. In Proceedings of HICSS 2023, pp. 4818–4827 (2023)
36. Robertson, T., Wagner, I.: Ethics: engagement representation and politic-in-action. In: Routledge International Handbook of Participatory Design, pp. 64–85. Routledge, London (2012)
37. Bratteteig, T., Wagner, I.: What is a participatory design result? In: International Conference on Proceeding Series, vol. 1, pp. 141–150. ACM (2016). https://doi.org/10.1145/2940299.2940316

Application of Digital Media Technology in the Display Design of Construction Sand Table Model

Mu Zhang[1][✉] and Jinghao Zhao[2]

[1] Shandong University of Art & Design, NO. 02, Nineteen Floor, Unit 1, Building 5, NO. 187, Jingliu Road, Huaiyin, Jinan, China
153962234@qq.com

[2] Shandong Jianzhu University, NO. 02, Nineteen Floor, Unit 1, Building 5, NO.187, Jingliu Road, Huaiyin, Jinan, China

Abstract. The display form of the construction model has been greatly changed along with the rapid development of digital media technology. The traditional construction model is to scale the 3D model evenly with the equal-scale restore technology, and then it is processed with acrylic, resin and other materials according to the scaling size. The shortages are long production cycles, excessively high processing fees and inconvenient transportation and assembling. Nowadays, we apply digital media technology to the production of construction models to make them "alive". The sound, light and electricity are integrated into the display design of the construction model through LED display, sensor interaction, 3D printing and other technical methods. It would not only reduce the production cost and cycle of the construction model but also enhances its visual effect. Participation in the interactive function of the model could enable audiences to know about the internal structure and features of the buildings during the interaction process.

Keywords: Digital Media Technology · Architectural Model · Display Design · Interaction Design

1 Development History and Functions of the Construction Model

Traditional construction sand table models would display the external appearance of the building and its surrounding environment in the form of proportional scaling, which has a unique display function that cannot be replaced by a plane map. It displays a microform of solid in three-dimensional space to people through intuitive and overall visual feeling. It is an entity transformation of an architect's design thinking to make the users intuitively understand the design concept and concept of architecture. Such an ancient and innovative display form of sand table model has gained higher and higher attention from all industries.

1.1 Development History of the Domestic Construction Sand Table Models

The oldest construction sand table was mainly applied to military operations, which was made by craftsmen with sand and gravel according to the topographic features at a certain scale. In ancient times, the function of the construction sand table model was mainly shown in studying the terrain, enemy intelligence and operational plans, organizing and coordinating actions and implementing training. There had been a record of the use of sand tables in China during the Eastern Han Dynasty. According to Hou Han Shu. Biography of Ma Yuan, in 32 AD, Emperor Guangwu of the Han Dynasty attacked Weixiao in Longxi and called the famous general Ma Yuan to discuss the strategy of marching [1]. Ma Yuan was very familiar with the geographic conditions of the Longxi area, and he made a model similar to the actual geography with rice to have a specific analysis of tactics. That is the earliest record of the use of the sand tables in our country.

1.2 Development History of the Foreign Construction Sand Table Models

The earliest record of western countries using the sand table could be traced back to the 19th and 20th centuries. In 1811, Von Leswitz, Prussia, made an exquisite battlefield sand table model with clay and glue [2]. He marked all the roads, bridges, rivers, villages and woods with color coating and created troops and weapons with porcelain blocks. The entire sand table was displayed within Potsdam Palace for the military commanders to have the military deduction. Later, the son of Leswitz showed the topographic features with a sand table and map, and he even demonstrated the mountains, water bodies, roads and so on in the model for showing the topographic data and making people know about the macro-objects from a micro perspective. He showed the distribution of troops and weapons with a timer to have military deduction according to the actual combat mode.

1.3 Functions of Construction Sand Table Mode

After the First World War, the construction sand table model had been applied to transportation, water conservancy, electricity, land and resources, tourism, and other public construction industries. The sand table model was also used for economic development planning and large-scale engineering construction, and the intuitive image was popular with plan decision-makers and engineering technicians. When the modernist architectural arts were more and more popular in the world, the role of the construction sand table model became more and more important in the process of construction design. It would not only help architecture designers reflect on their own designs to better display the creative idea of the designers. Hence, it has been used till now (Fig. 1).

Now, the construction sand table model has been emerging rapidly as a supporting industry of the real estate industry along with the quick development of the real estate industry, and it has been a necessary display method for the sales center. It could highly boost the sales speed of commercial buildings. In the development progress of contemporary architecture, the construction sand table model has an unprecedented development in the production process, production materials or display technology. There is a better display effect, more comprehensive information and highlighted construction features.

Fig. 1. Model

Fig. 2. Model

The construction model would be gradually widely used in life due to the development of scientific technology and the market demand in the future (Fig. 2).

Most of the construction sand table models in the early period were made of ordinary soil, wood and so on. Along with the ceaseless development of materials science, most of the current construction models were made of alloy, plastic and other materials. The development of materials is closely related to the production of the sand table model since the degree of reality restoration is getting higher and higher, and the visual effect is getting better and better (Fig. 3).

The production process of the sand table is also another important factor for the effect of the construction model. In the early period, the models were made of artificial

Fig. 3. Model

sculpture or lathe processing, so there should be several months, even longer times, for the production cycle of a large-scale construction model. The whole process would consume vast manpower, materials and capital. The low production efficiency and restoration degree would be the dominant factor for the development of the sand table development. Along with the development of scientific technology, the sand table processing equipment would be more and more intelligent and accurate, and the manufacturing accuracy of model and production efficiency would be higher and higher. Especially, the maturing 3D printing technology makes a batch production of models possible. 3D printing technology only needs a computer and a 3D printer to produce a set of complete models within a short time (Fig. 4).

The display of modern construction sand table models could not live without digital technology and electronic equipment, and its display method has a closer and closer relationship with technology. With the help of scientific technology, a brand-new display method could deepen people's understanding of the buildings, which is a feature to be presented by the modern construction model. In the future, the construction sand table models would be more and more intelligent, digital and user-friendly. For the sustainable development of the construction sand table model, the model manufacturing industry must keep innovating to study new technology and explore new thinking.

Fig. 4. 3D printing

2 Display the Form and Technology of the Construction Sand Table Model

Traditional construction sand tables were mainly for display due to the limitation of materials and technology. Later, the sand table models are installed with acoustic, optical, electrical and mechanical transmission systems for the continuous improvement of mechatronics. For example, the lights, street lights and ambient lights within the construction model could be lighted. The sound of traffic, the noise of the city and the sound of the weather environment could be displayed through the speaker. On the sand table, the model cars could "run", the mechanical garage model could have automatic lifting and the Ferris wheel in the park could rotate. Though these technologies could make the display of the construction sand table models diverse and modernized, they still belong to the traditional display method without the essential breakthrough (Fig. 5).

2.1 Display Forms of Construction Sand Table Model

The development speed of urbanization has exceeded any period for the rapid development of the global economy and culture. There are daily increasing material and cultural needs, so the traditional construction sand table model applied in real estate, urban planning and other industries would neither fully restore the original buildings and the surrounding topographic features nor enable audiences to have a further understanding of the development, history and future of the objects; thus, it could not meet the demand of multi-angle display function [1]. On the other hand, computer graphics, simulation, artificial intelligence and other high-tech industries have been in the market for the ceaseless development of science and technology. Making up the weakness of

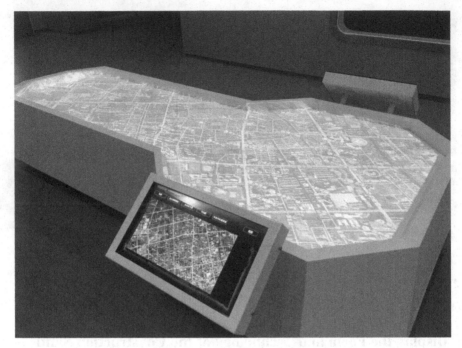

Fig. 5. Multimedia sand table

traditional sand tables with advanced scientific technology for making advanced digital sand tables has been a demand in the market.

The digital sand table is to facilitate audiences to know about the information of the display object with immersive experience through realistic 3D images and real-time interaction, computer generation technology, an advanced display, interaction, recognition and other technologies based on the traditional sand table, so as to reach a comprehensive, multi-angle and profound display purpose. It could not only dimensionally present all attributes of the displayed target object but also interact with the audiences during the process, which is the biggest feature and strength of the digital sand table. For example, in the field of urban-rural planning, the digital sand table could display the development history of the city and present the urban appearance before planning in the monitor through multi-media imaging technology so as to reach the realistic reproduction effect, which could not be made by the traditional sand table. Secondly, the digital sand table could display the construction process of the buildings and the surrounding environment, which would show the past, present and future of the real scene to audiences in the form of virtual animation. Thirdly, a digital construction sand table could display the functional structure and design layout of the target object to audiences through videos, images or 3D animation, such as the functional zoning of office floors, the internal structure of the exhibition center, functional design of building parking area, design of biological circulation system for environment and so on (Fig. 6).

Fig. 6. Multimedia sand table

2.2 Technical Application of Digital Construction Sand Table Model

By far, the display technology applied to the digital sand tables could be divided into presentation and interaction. In view of the presentation technology, designers could deliver the information of the target object to audiences through the screen splicing of LED and LCD. Most of the structures are combined with the screen and real sand table. During their visit to the real sand table, audiences could know about the relevant information about the display object by displaying videos on the screen behind them. Or the real sand table model could be installed on the screen so as to present the surrounding environment, functional area structure and seasonal changes of buildings through the dynamic images on the screen. The interactive technology of digital construction sand tables is mainly virtual reality (VR), augmented reality (AR) and sensors these three types. The technology of virtual reality would require visitors to wear head display equipment to visit the digital sand table in the virtual three-dimensional scenes in the computer through the handle or data glove. The technology of augmented reality means that the real image of a real sand table is collected by a camera and then users would have interaction with the virtual information on the screen through interactive software. The interaction and identification of the sensor means installing the sensor in the display space or the real sand table, and then the computer could trace the visitor's position information, gesture information, action information and expression information through the sensor so that the visitors could have interaction with the virtual information on the digital sand table or the screen through gestures or facial expressions or body movements (Fig. 7).

Fig. 7. AR augmented reality

3 Analysis of the Digital Sand Table Project of Qingdao SCODA Pearl International Expo Center

The digital sand table project in the Qingdao SCODA Pearl International Expo is a core component in the Fifth China International Import Expo -Shandong Exhibition Area. This project was exhibited at China International Import Expo (Shanghai) on November 4, 2022. The digital sand table made the building model of Qingdao SCODA Pearl International Expo Center as a main body to achieve the interaction between visitors and the sand table through a tablet computer and the two groups of LED display systems. The entire system would enable the audiences to know about the functions and surrounding environment of Qingdao SCODA Pearl International Expo and the development progress of the SCODA Demonstration Area through display technology and interactive technology.

3.1 Profile of the Qingdao SCODA Pearl International Expo Center

Qingdao SCODA Pearl International Expo Center is located in the core area of the SCODA Demonstration Area, the north band of Ruyi Lake. The building area of the project is about 168,880 square meters. It is designed by the honorary president and chief architect of China Architecture Design & Research Group, Academician Cui Kai. The design concept means "brilliance from pearl and wonderful sea", which complies with a natural pattern of grand nature. The whole project is adopted with a circular layout symbolizing "harmony" to connect the building group together through a wavy white roof of seven sets of centripetal shells, so as to shape a core image of "sea", "flower", "pearl" and "shell". The overall design is fully integrated with "the features of Shanghai", Qingdao's coastal characteristics and Shandong's cultural heritage as well as the time image of China, openness and inclusiveness. The building roof rises gracefully, and the comprehensive hall seems to be a glossy "gem", which implies the cultural abundance, diversification and inclusiveness of the countries of the SCO and the prosperity of trade between countries of the SCO. The entire construction image looks like a flapping eagle welcoming the guests from all directions on the north bank of Jiaozhou Bay.

Qingdao SCODA Pearl International Expo Center makes the "conference, exhibition, business, tourism and culture" a business characteristic, devoting itself to building up a comprehensive new space for the interactive integration of multiple commercial formats and one-stop cultural experience among countries of the SCO. The Expo Center is composed of seven venues, including venue A, venue B, venue C, venue D, venue E, venue F and venue G. venue A is the business service area; and venues B, C, D and E are the SCO's cultural elements display area, so as to provide cultural exhibition, trade exhibition and roadshow exchange scenes and carrier space for the countries of the SCO. Venues F and G are the multiple comprehensive function centers (Fig. 8).

Fig. 8. Qingdao SCODA Pearl International Expo Center

3.2 Design Concept of Digital Sand Table

We had a research analysis on the shape, function and surrounding environment of the building in the previous period to have observation research on the display environment and display purpose. Through the research, we found that the construction structure of the Expo Center was relatively simple. The shape element originated from the concept of a gem with a round shape as a whole, which could be divided into 8 parts. The surrounding environment was divided into a green belt, lake beach and water pool by a geometric shape. The overall building was white and the surrounding was mainly blue and green. Due to the short design and production cycle, the traditional techniques could not meet the demand of processing time, so we adopted a production method of 3D printing for the model of the main body of the building. 4 3D printers worked together to finish the production task of the model of the main body of the building within one week (Fig. 9).

Fig. 9. Qingdao SCODA Pearl International Expo Center

The exhibition's purpose was to enable audiences to know about the establishment and development history of the SCODA Demonstration Area and the construction process and zone functions of Qingdao SCODA Pearl International Expo Center through the digital table sand model. Through research, we decided to adopt the three-screen linkage mode in the hardware systems, tablet computer, LED at the bottom of the sand table and arc-shaped LED large screen. We designed two display systems and one interactive system to achieve the display effect. Firstly, we designed an arc-shaped LED splicing screen display wall with a height of 2.5 m and a total length of 12.55 m. The display wall mainly bore two contents: 1. Displaying the advertising video of Qingdao China-SCO Local Economic And Trade Cooperation Demonstration Area. The video introduced the establishment, development and future prospect of the SCODA Demonstration Area with several chapters, and there would be a specific introduction to the origin of Qingdao SCODA Pearl International Expo Center. 2. The linkage with the digital sand table of SCODA Pearl. Visitors could have interaction through tablet computers and software, and the functional zoning, geographical location, construction process and relevant pictures and image data of the Expo Center are displayed on the arc-shaped display wall; then there was an interactive introduction with several chapters (Fig. 10).

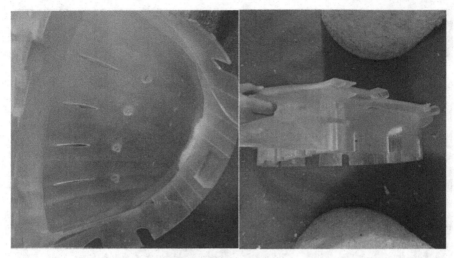

Fig. 10. 3D printing

Secondly, the main body of the digital sand table was against the arc-shaped display wall, and it was combined with the LED at the bottom and the construction model with 3D printing. The overall sand table was adopted with a circular design structure with a diameter of 3.5 m. The display area of the LED screen at the bottom was a diameter of 2.9 m. The main body of the construction model was n a diameter of 2 m. The construction model of the SCODA Pearl was made of 3D printing translucent materials, and the LED at the bottom showed the surrounding environment landscape of SCODA Pearl through the two-dimensional animation, including seasonal changes, dynamic effects of marine background, and changes in the ecological environment, etc. The LED at the bottom worked with a tablet computer to have the zone selection and function introduction of the internal venue of the SCODA Pearl. The overall sand table needed an arc-shaped screen to present the introduction of the zone function and relevant video data of the SCODA Pearl (FIg. 11).

Thirdly, the interactive function of the digital sand table was achieved by the external tablet. We designed a set of functional introduction systems with UNITY3D so that visitors could browse the videos of the Expo Center by clicking the monitor to listen to the introduction of all venues and know about the construction process of the Center. When users operated the tablet computer, the LED at the bottom would show the zone position of each venue. When the light of the LED at the bottom was on, the upper semi-transparent model would reflect the corresponding color, and different color represented a unique zone. The LED at the bottom would have an image linkage with the LED display wall. When the display wall played the introduction of the Expo Center, the LED at the bottom would show the dynamic effect of the sea waves. When the software was operated on the tablet computer, the arc-shaped display wall would play the location animation of the Qingdao SCODA Pearl International Expo. Through the functions mentioned above, I achieved the three-screen interactive system between visitors and the digital sand table (Fig. 12).

Fig. 11. 3D printing model

It took one month for the design and construction of the Fifth China International Import Expo -Shandong Exhibition Area spent. It took 25 days for the scheme design, production in the post period, software production, and animation production of the digital sand table. It spent 5 days assembling and building of digital sand table. There were 3 days for the system debugging, testing and revision. The digital table sand of Qingdao SCODA Pearl International Expo Center was located at the center of the Shandong Exhibition Area. It was the core content of the entire exhibition area and the important component. This project presented visitors with the construction process of the SCODA Demonstration Area and the facilities and functions in the Qingdao SCODA Pearl International Expo Center (Figs. 13 and 14).

Fig. 12. 3D printing model

Fig. 13. Construction site

Fig. 14. Final effect

4   Conclusion

Qingdao SCODA Pearl International Expo Center is an attempt for the large exhibition centers to make sand table model designs with digital media technology. Through the project, we have accumulated abundant experience and proved that the digital media technology would not only improve the visual effect of the construction sand table model but also develop its functions to enhance the publicity of the demonstration target. The traditional construction sand table model would have human-machine interaction with the support of digital media technology, which would greatly enhance the audiences' participation in the projects. The visitors would have a better understanding of the background and materials of the project in an immersive experience with an easier reception of the information delivered by the designers. This attempt is a good explanation for the role and significance of digital media technology in the field of traditional construction sand tables under the background of new technology, which accumulates valuable experience for the project of digital sand table project in the future.

References

1. Jianfeng, H.: Research on Special Effect Technology of Digital Sand Table System. North China University of Technology (2013)
2. Tao, Y.: Investigation on the current situation of construction sand table production and marketing. Shanxi Architec. **43**(09), 223–224 (2017)

Media, Art and Culture in Intelligent Environments

A Clothing-Type Wearable Device that Promotes a Sense of Unity for Viewers of Online Live Performances

Yukari Anbo[1]([✉])[iD], Ryota Matsui[1,2][iD], Yutaka Yanagisawa[2],
Yoshinari Takegawa[1][iD], and Keiji Hirata[1][iD]

[1] Future University Hakodate, Hakodate, Hokkaido, Japan
g2122003@fun.ac.jp
[2] MPLUSPLUS Co., Ltd., Shinagawa, Tokyo, Japan
http://www.mplpl.com/

Abstract. In this research, we developed a clothing-type wearable device called ONE Parka, which promotes an increase in the sense of unity in online live performances. In recent years, demand for live entertainment has been increasing. Nevertheless, it has become clear that, due to factors such as the difficulty of establishing shared sensory communication between performers and viewers in events held online, the degree of satisfaction towards such events is low. Accordingly, our research group conjectured that the direct cause of this low level of satisfaction is that viewers do not feel a sense of unity with performers. In this research, by promoting a sense of unity, we aim to increase the degree of satisfaction towards online live performance. Firstly, we defined the components that form the term 'sense of unity', then investigated appropriate approaches in the proposal of a device. We focused on one possible approach, 'recognition of excitement', and developed the prototype of ONE Parka, which is capable of providing feedback by heart rate and vibration. In an evaluative experiment, we had eleven subjects watch a music video while wearing the prototype and then answer a questionnaire. As a result, it became evident that vibration is effective in recognition of excitement.

Keywords: sense of unity · online performance · wearable device

1 Background

In recent years, demand for live entertainment has been increasing. A survey by the PIA Research Institute [4] has shown that the market scale of live entertainment (estimated total ticket sales of live music /performance events) had been increasing each year, but saw an 82.4% decrease in 2020, compared to the previous year. One major reason for this was the cancellation or postponement of most events due to the novel corona virus. The holding of live music performances online has been popularized as an effect of this, but the corresponding

Supported by organization x.

degree of satisfaction is low [3]. According to the same survey, in response to a question asking what viewers were most dissatisfied with when watching live music transmission, answers included "The atmosphere doesn't make you want to do call and response or all sing together"; "It's no different to watching a video like a music program or DVD"; "Sometimes a bad connection means that the video cuts out partway through or the sound stops, or the video and sound don't match up"; and "It's difficult to concentrate". Therefore, our research group focused on the sense of unity in live music performance. The aim of our research is to increase the level of satisfaction felt by viewers of online live performances, by promoting a sense of unity. In the proposed system, we are aiming to design and implement a device targeted at viewers, which enables them to attain a sense of unity with other viewers or with performers.

As 'sense of unity' is a vague term, it can become a subjective expression. Therefore, in this research we defined 'sense of unity' as being made up of the following four components: 'the accordance of one's behavior with the behavior of those around one', 'the sharing of time with other viewers and performers', 'recognition of excitement', 'sense of immersion'. In this research, we particularly focus on two components, 'recognition of excitement' and 'sense of immersion', and propose ONE Parka, a clothing-type wearable device that fulfils these two components through a vibration-based approach.

In this paper, we discuss the proof-of-concept of ONE Parka. This device uses vibration transmission speakers to feed back excitement as vibrations. By conducting a verification experiment using the prototype of ONE Parka, we investigate whether the proposed approach is valid as a means of promoting a sense of unity, as well as recognition of excitement.

2   Previous Cases

2.1   Research on Music and Vibration

Regarding research up to now, there are several cases of devices that directly transmit the vibrations of music. These include a necklace-shaped device called Hapbeat [6], which directly conveys sound vibrations to the wearer's body, to allow the wearer to experience a sense of presence as if at a live music venue. There is also SOUND HUG [8], which is a balloon-like music device that enables the user to enjoy music by sight and touch through lights and vibration. From these cases, we are able to confirm that vibration has the effect of promoting the audio-visual experience of music. Thus, in our research we formed the hypothesis that, by expressing the excitement of other viewers with the vibration of the music, we can promote the recognition of excitement.

2.2   Method of Measuring Excitement

Regarding a method for measuring viewers' excitement, there are various preceding cases. In their research, Mitsuki et al. [7] verified the extent to which it is

Table 1. Survey on Sense of Unity

No	Question	Answer format
1	Have you ever obtained a sense of unity at a live music performance?	Yes/No
2	At what sort of moment did you feel it?	Multiple choice
3	Have you ever experienced a sense of unity in an online live music performance?	Yes/No
4	If you answered 'yes' to Question 3, at what kind of moment did you feel it?	Free comment
5	From who/what do you think you can obtain a sense of unity?	Multiple choice

possible to estimate viewers' excitement and emotion when watching music performance, from brainwaves and electrodermal activity. As a result, they found that it was possible to analyze interest and emotion by using an electroencephalograph and electrodermal activity sensor.

Further research by Watanabe et al. [5], considered an attempt to use a simple tactile device to enable sighted people to share with visually impaired people the excitement of watching sports. The tactile device comprises two balls connected by a tube. Each ball is gripped by a different person. Squeezing one of the balls hard and sending air to the other ball produces a vivid sensation, sharing excitement in a hands-on manner. In verification, happiness and energetic feelings, nervousness, and excitement were all successfully shared through the varied speed and strength with which the ball was squeezed.

From these kinds of cases, it can be seen that there are various methods for estimating excitement. In our research, referring to the previous cases, we conduct estimation of excitement according to indices from biological information such as heart rate, and expression of excitement by viewers, using sliders or tactile devices.

3 Preceding Survey

In this research, we conducted a survey to investigate the sort of conditions in which a sense of unity emerges and can be obtained. The investigation comprised a survey on people's impressions regarding sense of unity and a survey on 'recognition of excitement', which is one of the components that form a sense of unity. The surveys, conducted using Google Forms, was taken by 379 randomly selected males and females, from people in their teens to people in their sixties. Among these, 278 people responded about sense of unity, while 101 people responded about recognition of excitement.

3.1 Regarding Sense of Unity

The question items in the survey on sense of unity are presented in Table 1.

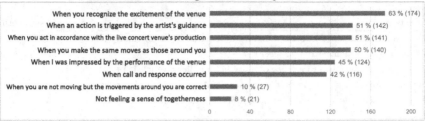

Fig. 1. Question 2 Choices and Answers

Results The answer results for Question 2 in Table 1 are presented in Figure 1. Regarding Question 1, 82% of respondents answered 'Yes'. Regarding Question 2, the most selected item, at 63%, was 'When I sensed excitement in the venue'. Question 3 was answered by the 142 people among the respondents who had experience of participating in an online live music performance. The result was that 32% answered 'Yes'. As a result of asking respondents who replied 'Yes' to Question 3 to then answer Question 4, we received answers relating to recognition of excitement via the comment function, such as "When the comment posting was really speeding up", "When everyone shouts out together in the chat" and "When a comment I posted was momentarily displayed in the venue". We also received answers about reasons involving the performer, such as "When the performer called out to the audience" and "When I heard the artist read out a message to the fans". Concerning Question 5, the most popular item, selected by 82% of people, was 'All the people around you'. Also, the items 'The arrangement of the venue' and 'The performer(s)' were selected by over half of the respondents.

Considerations While 82% of respondents replied that they had obtained a sense of unity in Question 1, only 32% gave the same response to Question 3. From this difference, it can be confirmed that obtaining a sense of unity in an online live performance is difficult. Concerning Question 2, from the fact that many people selected the item 'When I felt excitement in the venue', it can be conjectured that recognition of excitement is valid as a component of feeling a sense of unity. In the free comment section of Question 4, it was confirmed that, even in online live performances participants still obtain a sense of unity by recognizing a state of excitement in other viewers, via the chat function, for example. From this, it can be conjectured that the point made in this research, i.e., that recognition of excitement promotes a sense of unity, is valid in online live performance as well. From Question 5, it is considered that factors arising from the performer(s) and other participants, and factors arising from conditions such as a feeling of immersion, are necessary to feel a sense of unity.

Table 2. Survey on Excitement

No	Question	Answer format
1	Have you ever felt excitement around you at a live music performance?	Yes/No
2	Regarding Question 1, whose excitement did you feel?	Multiple choice
3	Regarding Question 1, in what way did you recognize excitement around you?	Multiple selection
4	When you recognized excitement, did you feel a sense of unity with those around you?	Single selection
5	Do you feel that you want to share your excitement?	Yes/No
6	Regarding Question 5, with whom do you want to share your excitement?	Multiple selection
7	Do you feel that you want to share in other people's excitement?	Yes/No
8	Regarding Question 7, whose excitement do you want to share in?	Multiple selection
9	Do you feel that recognizing excitement affects sense of unity?	1: I feel it does not affect it
		- 7: I feel it does affect it

3.2 Regarding Excitement

The question items in the survey about excitement are presented in Table 2.

Results The answer results for Question 3 in Table 2 are presented in Figure 2. Regarding Question 1, all respondents answered 'Yes'. Regarding Question 2, 69% of respondents selected 'All the audience in the venue participating in the same concert'. Regarding Question, 76% of respondents selected 'Loudness of voices', 75% selected 'Heated atmosphere', and 70% selected 'Behavior such as gestures and hand motions'. Only 38% of respondents, under half, selected 'Vibrations'. In regard to Question 4, 62% answered 'Yes', while 29% answered 'If I have to say one way or the other, then yes'. Regarding Question 5, 84% answered 'Yes' and 16% answered 'No'. In Question 6, the most popular item, selected by 66% of people, was 'Acquaintances who are participating with me'. In addition, the items 'All the audience participating in the same concert' and 'The artist' were also selected by over half the respondents, at 58% and 52% respectively. In response to Question 7, 87% answered 'Yes' and 13% answered 'No'. Regarding Question 8, the most popular item, selected by 64% of people, was 'The artist', but the items 'All the audience participating in the same concert' and 'Acquaintances who are participating with me' were also selected by over half the respondents, at 61% and 52% respectively. Regarding Question 9, 34% of all answers were [6], and 43% were [7], resulting in an average value of 6.

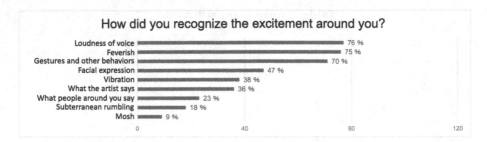

Fig. 2. Question 3 Results

Considerations. From the results of Question 1, it was established that all the respondents who had attended a live performance had recognized excitement. Combining the results for Question 4 and Question 9, it can be seen that 91% of respondents actually felt a sense of unity at the time they recognized excitement, confirming that there is a connection between excitement and sense of unity. From the results of Question 2 and Question 3, it can be understood that participants of on-site performances do not recognize excitement around them from the facial expressions and speech of people nearby so much as they recognize the excitement of an unspecified large number of people, from 'loudness of voices', 'heated atmosphere', 'behavior such as gestures and hand motions', and so on.

'Vibrations', which are treated in this research, was only selected by 38% of respondents, a rather low result, leading us to surmise that vibrations mostly do not have a direct connection to recognition of excitement. Accordingly, when conducting our experiment, we will suggest a relationship between the fluctuation of vibrations and viewers' excitement to subjects beforehand, to make subjects aware that vibrations directly express the excitement of remote viewers. From the results of Question 5 and Question 7, it was confirmed that most people feel positively about sharing excitement. Regarding Question 6 and Question 8, the order of preference for whom respondents wanted to share their own excitement with was 'Acquaintances who are participating with me', 'All the audience participating in the same concert', 'Artist', whereas, in contrast, the order of preference for whose excitement respondents wanted to share in was 'Artist', 'All the audience participating in the same concert', 'Acquaintances who are participating with me'. This shows that there is a difference in who someone wants to share their own excitement with and whose excitement someone wants to share in. In our experiment this time, as a subject for estimation of excitement, we adopt the item that was second most popular in both Question 6 and Question 8: 'All the audience participating in the same concert'.

In response to the question 'Have you ever felt excitement around you at a live music performance?', all the respondents answered 'Yes'. In response to the question 'When you recognized excitement, did you feel a sense of unity with those around you?', 62.4% answered 'Yes', while 28.7% answered 'If I have to say one way or the other, then, yes', confirming that there is a connection between excitement and sense of unity. In addition, in answer to the question 'Do you feel that you want to share in other people's excitement?', 87.1% answered 'Yes' and 12.9% answered 'No'. From this, it was confirmed that recognition of excitement is effective in increasing the sense of unity, and that most people feel positively regarding sharing of excitement.

4   ONE Parka

From the above previous cases and preceding survey, it became clear that vibration promotes viewing experience, that recognition of excitement can promote a sense of unity, that the majority of people feel positively about sharing excitement, and that, at live performances, almost all people recognize excitement in various forms. Stepping off from these results, in this research we proposed, and developed a prototype of, 'ONE Parka', a device that estimates excitement and makes it recognizable through fluctuation of vibration. With reference to prior work such as LIVE JACKET, developed by Ochiai et al. [8], and The Sound Shirt, developed by CUTECIRCUIT [1], the proposed device, ONE Parka, utilizes a clothing-type wearable device that can more effectively convey vibrations by stimulating sense of touch. ONE Parka is targeted at viewers participating in online live performances. The proposed device uses the vibrations of music to express the excitement of remote viewers, to make a target person watching an online live performance recognize the excitement of the remote viewers. Through this, we aim to promote a sense of unity, which is difficult to feel in an online environment, to improve viewers' degree of satisfaction towards online live performance.

4.1   Requirements

The requirements when developing ONE Parka are listed below.

1. The system can express excitement: it makes the user promote their own sense of unity by recognizing the excitement of other viewers. For this reason, it is necessary to feed back viewers' excitement to the user.
2. The system can estimate excitement: it is necessary to estimate the excitement of viewers of an online live performance in real time.
3. The system has durability: if a wearable device is fragile, some of the parts may get broken when the device is being put on or taken off, which potentially has a significant effect on how it feels to use the device.
4. The system does not impede viewing: if the device is detrimental to viewing, the user's satisfaction level may decrease. For this reason, it is necessary to design the device so that it can be used while concentrating on the viewing screen.

4.2   Consideration of a Means of Expressing Excitement

As means of expressing excitement, there are a display, VR, sound effects, lights and vibrations. We explain below whether or not each of these means fulfils our requirements.

Display

As an expression method on a display, we can consider presenting the appearance of excited people, presenting excitement with numbers (figures) or text, or expressing excitement with audio-visual effects. In expression on a display, information can be easily absorbed visually, making it easy to recognize excitement. On the other hand, if components other than the performance are incorporated into the screen the user is looking at, it may impede viewing and thus does not fulfil requirement 4.

VR

As expression methods using VR, we can consider using video images to produce a sense of presence, and, as with the aforementioned display, presenting the appearance of excited people, presenting excitement with numbers (figures) or text, or expressing excitement with audio-visual effects. In expression with VR, information can be easily absorbed visually, making it easy to recognize excitement. In addition, it produces a sense of presence, enabling the user to feel as though they are really in the venue. However, in the case of viewing for a long time, as in a live performance, the user may grow tired and find it difficult to concentrate on viewing. In this case, VR does not meet requirement 4.

Sound Effects

If sounds are heard when listening to music, it is difficult to determine whether a sound is a sound effect or the sound of the music, thus, requirement 1 is not fulfilled. At the same time, when listening to music, sound effects render the music difficult to hear, thus, requirement 4 is not fulfilled.

Lights

As a previous case, there is a portable stage production device that links with online live performances, live video image, music videos, and so on [9]. In the method of expression by lights, it is possible to express excitement with a visual approach. However, when viewing a live performance, lights that are not part of the performance production may impede viewing, thus, requirement 4 is not fulfilled.

Vibration

In expression by vibration, the conditions of excitement are expressed by fluctuation of the vibrations. Vibration is a method of expression by sense of touch and therefore does not incur either visual or aural impediment to viewing. Vibration may impede viewing if it is too strong, but this problem can be solved by adjusting the vibration.

In consideration of these reasons, in this research we adopt an expression method by vibration, which fulfils all four requirements.

4.3   Consideration of a Means of Estimating Excitement

As indices for a means of estimating excitement, we can consider various kinds of information, as introduced in the previous cases we cited, such as brain waves, emotions, heart rate and perspiration. At present, because it difficult to determine which means is best through objective values, we do not decide on a means. Accordingly, detailed consideration is still necessary regarding the estimation method of excitement.

Fig. 3. Workflow

4.4   Workflow

As shown in Figure 3, based on the aforementioned excitement estimation method, ONE Parka quantifies the excitement of remote viewers (hereafter referred to as excitement level) in real time, and uploads the excitement levels to a server. On the server, the excitement levels are aggregated, then the average excitement level is calculated and converted to a certain intensity of vibration. The server sends the vibrational intensity to the client (the microcontroller built into ONE Parka). According to the received vibrational intensity, the microcontroller controls ONE Parka's built-in vibration transmission speakers.

4.5   Prototype

In the prototype, six small vibration transmission speakers weighing approximately 35g each, developed by TafuOn, were installed in the hooded sweatshirt (hoody/Parka), with four speakers on the back section and two speakers on the sleeves. The vibration of music was controlled by directly connecting the speakers to a Lepai LP-2020A+ digital amp, produced by Bukang Technology. Regarding the places to which speakers were attached, we chose the back and sleeves because we place importance on the ease of putting the device on, which

Fig. 4. Developed Prototype (turned inside-out)

is why we adopted a hoody as the type of clothing for our device. To prevent the vibration transmission speakers from becoming detached when the wearer puts on the hoody, we attached the speakers to the underside of the material of the hoody we used and covered them with mesh, through which they come into contact with the wearer. In an experiment using the developed prototype, we verified whether it is possible to promote recognition of excitement, through vibration (Fig. 4).

5   Evaluative Experiment

5.1   Experiment Method

To verify the usefulness of the implemented prototype, an evaluative experiment was conducted, based on evaluation indices such as excitement and sense of immersion. The subjects are 11 undergraduate and postgraduate university students, of whom 5 were female and 6 male. In the prototype used this time, we have not implemented a function to measure heart rate. For this reason, in the verification experiment, referring to the prior work of Farbood [2], we had remote viewers express the timing of excitement in real time by operating a dial. We told the subjects that the heart rate of audience members viewing the same video in a remote location was being detected and fed back as vibration. Prior to the experiment we conducted a survey to find out what artist the subjects liked, and used video of two tracks by the relevant artist in the experiment. Each subject put on the prototype and, after the details of the experiment were explained, the experiment was conducted. In this experiment, evaluation was carried out according to the following three conditions.

Condition 1: No vibration
- No presentation of vibrations
- Subjects are instructed that there are remote viewers watching the same video with the same dynamics

Table 3. Question item

No	Question	Answer format
1	To what extent were you able to feel a sense of unity?	1: To no extent - 7: To a significant extent
2	To what extent were you able to feel the existence of others?	1: To no extent - 7: To a significant extent
3	To what extent were you able to feel the excitement of others?	1: To no extent - 7: To a significant extent
4	To what extent were you able to feel a sense of immersion?	1: To no extent - 7: To a significant extent
5	Regarding the acoustics, to what extent did you feel a difference compared to an on-site live performance?	1: I felt there was no difference - 7: I felt there was a significant difference
6	To what extent were you able to relax and listen to the music?	1: To no extent - 7: To a significant extent

Condition 2: Emphasis of musical rhythm by presentation of vibrations
- Presentation of vibrations
- No alteration of the output of vibrations
- Subjects are instructed that there are remote viewers watching the same video with the same dynamics

Condition 3: Emphasis of the excitement of surrounding viewers, by presentation of vibrations
- Presentation of vibrations
- Alteration of intensity of vibrational output according to excitement level
- Subjects are instructed that there are remote viewers watching the same video with the same dynamics
- Subjects are instructed that the excitement levels of the above remote viewers are reflected in the intensity of the vibrations

To avoid differences due to ordering effects, the above three evaluative experiments were conducted randomly. After the end of each experiment, subjects answered the questionnaire that uses a seven-level Likert scale (Table 3), then answered a questionnaire about their overall thoughts and impressions (Table 4). Regarding Table 4), points of view relating to the viewing experience were subdivided and for each point of view subjects chose the option, from among the three choices, that had left the strongest impression (Fig. 5).

5.2 Results

Each questionnaire result is presented in Figure 6. For each question, the figure presents the evaluation results in each condition.

Question 1

The results concerning the extent to which subjects felt a sense of unity are presented in the top left of Figure 6. The average value was highest for condition

Fig. 5. Scene of the Experiment

3, followed by condition 2, then condition 1. When the Wilcoxon rank-sum test was applied to these results, no significant difference was recognized between condition 1 and condition 2($Z = 1.45, p > .05$), whereas a significant difference was recognized between condition 1 and condition 3 ($Z = 3.07, p < .01$), and condition 2 and condition 3 ($Z = 2.13, .01 < p < .05$).

Question 2

The results concerning the extent to which subjects felt the presence of other people are presented in the upper middle of Figure 6. The average value was highest for condition 3 and lowest for condition 1. When the Wilcoxon rank-sum test was applied, no significant difference was recognized between condition 1 and condition 2($Z = 1.37, p > .05$), whereas a significant difference was recognized between condition 1 and condition 3 ($Z = 2.80, p < .01$), and condition 2 and condition 3 ($Z = 2.27, .01 < p < .05$).

Question 3

The results concerning the extent to which subjects felt the excitement of other people are presented in the top right of Figure 6. There was a large difference between the average values of condition 3, which had the highest value, and condition 1, which had the lowest value. When the Wilcoxon rank-sum test was applied, a significant difference was recognized between condition 1 and condition 2($Z = 2.25, .01 < p < .05$), condition 1 and condition 3 ($Z = 3.73, p < .01$), and condition 2 and condition 3 ($Z = 2.44, .01 < p < .05$).

Question 4

The results concerning the extent to which subjects felt a sense of immersion are presented in the bottom left of Figure 6. The average value was highest for condition 2, but there was not a vast difference between conditions 2 and 3. When the Wilcoxon rank-sum test was applied, a significant difference was recognized between both condition 1 and condition 2($Z = 2.54, .01 < p < .05$) and condition

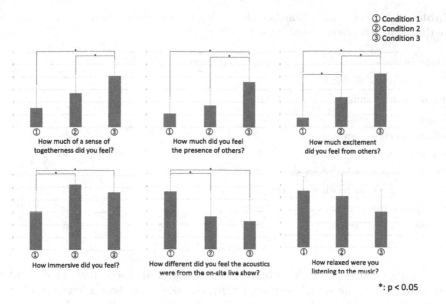

Fig. 6. Questionnaire Results

1 and condition 3 ($Z = 2.15, .01 < p < .05$), whereas no significant difference was recognized between condition 2 and condition 3 ($Z = 1.01, p > .05$).

Question 5

The results concerning the extent to which subjects felt a difference to on-site live performances, regarding acoustics, are presented in the lower middle of Figure 6. The average value was highest for condition 1; there was not a great difference between the average values of conditions 2 and 3. When the Wilcoxon rank-sum test was applied, a significant difference was recognized between both condition 1 and condition 2 ($Z = 2.07, .01 < p < .05$) and condition 1 and condition 3 ($Z = 2.61, p < .01$), whereas no significant difference was recognized between condition 2 and condition 3 ($Z = 0.27, p > .05$).

Question 6

The results concerning the extent to which subjects were able to relax and listen to the music are presented in the bottom right of Figure 6. The average value was highest for condition 2, though there was not a great difference between the average values of conditions 2 and 3. When the Wilcoxon rank-sum test was applied, no significant difference was recognized between condition 1 and condition 2 ($Z = 0.18, p > .05$), condition 1 and condition 3 ($Z = 1.75, p > .05$), and condition 2 and condition 3 ($Z = 1.18, p > .05$).

Impressions After the Experiment

The impressions after the experiment are presented in Table 4. In the items concerning enjoyment, i.e., 'enjoyability of viewing', 'enjoyment of song 1' and 'enjoyment of song 2', there were no subjects who selected 'without vibration'.

Table 4. Answer results (number of people) for the instruction "Please select the method that left the strongest impression"

Point of view	Without vibration	With vibration	Both the same
Enjoyability of viewing	0	9	2
Enjoyment of song 1	0	10	1
Enjoyment of song 2	0	9	2
Disturbance to viewing	2	3	6
Discomfort	1	2	8
Sense of unity with the artist	0	8	3
Sense of unity with other viewers	1	7	3
One's own excitement	0	9	2
Other viewers' excitement	0	6	5

In the items concerning disturbance to viewing, and discomfort, most subjects answered 'both the same', although 'without vibration' had a lower result than 'with vibration'. In the items about sense of unity, over half the subjects selected 'with vibration'. In the items concerning excitement, the majority of subjects felt their own excitement most strongly in the case of 'with vibration'.

6   Considerations

Regarding the extent to which subjects felt the excitement of other people, we consider that an approach using vibration is effective in the recognition of excitement. Also, from the fact that a significant difference was recognized between condition 3 and condition 2, it was confirmed that excitement can be recognized from the intensity of the vibration. Furthermore, regarding sense of unity, the fact that condition 3 had a higher average value than the other two conditions demonstrates that recognition of excitement from vibrational intensity can influence the promotion of a sense of unity.

Concerning the extent to which subjects felt a sense of immersion, from the fact that conditions 2 and 3 each had a higher average value than condition 1, it was implied that vibration promotes a sense of immersion. However, as the average value of condition 2 is slightly higher than that of condition 3, it is possible that in some cases vibrational intensity is detrimental to sense of immersion. Regarding acoustics, a large difference was observed between condition 1, which has no vibration, and conditions 2 and 3, which include vibration, confirming that vibration has a significant influence as one component for enabling a viewer to experience the same kind of acoustics as at an onsite performance. From the fact that there was no significant difference regarding the extent to which subjects were able to relax when listening the music, and from the results for 'disturbance to viewing' and 'discomfort' in the survey on post-experiment impressions, it was confirmed that vibration itself and the intensity of the vibration mostly do not impede viewing. On the contrary, from the items relating to enjoyment in the survey on impressions, it was conjectured that the viewing experience of music accompanied by vibration is effective in increasing viewers' satisfaction levels.

7   Future Prospects

With the prototype we developed this time, we verified whether recognition of excitement by vibration is valid, and were able to confirm the usefulness of this approach. As a future task, we will consider more effective approaches using vibration. Firstly, we will verify how the effect of using the device varies according to the location of the vibration transmission speakers, which were attached only to the back and arms this time, in order to decide more appropriate points to which to attach speakers. Next, we will implement the heart rate measurement system that was not implemented this time, and analyze changes in subjects' heart rates. Following on from this, we will verify the differences of the music-listening experience depending on melody, genre, musical dynamic and loudness. At present, we propose a system that recognizes excitement among viewers, but in future we will also consider a system to promote a sense of unity with the performer(s). Additionally, as it became clear that sense of immersion is also promoted by vibration, we will focus on this aspect and investigate the introduction of VR to produce a sense of presence.

8   Conclusion

In this research, to increase the sense of unity in online live performances, we focused on excitement, which is one component of this, and proposed a system to promote said component. In the experiment, we used the prototype of ONE Parka and verified whether viewing accompanied by vibration is effective in promoting recognition of excitement, when viewing an online live music performance. We had subjects view a music performance under three conditions, each different regarding the usage and intensity of vibration, and rate their impressions. As a result, significant differences were recognized between the three conditions and we obtained the result that vibrational intensity, by changing in accordance with other viewers' excitement, enabled a viewer to recognize excitement.

As future work, we will seek a more effective method to promote 'recognition of excitement' and 'sense of immersion', which are part of the components that make up a sense of unity. More explicitly, we are considering verification of how the wearer's impression changes when the position of vibration changes, verification of how impression changes according to the type of music, and introduction of VR.

References

1. cutecircuit: The sound shirt (2019). http://cutecircuit.com/soundshirt/. Accessed 24 Dec 2021
2. Farbood, M.M.: A Quantitative, Parametric Model of Musical Tension. Ph.D. dissertation, Massachusetts Institute of Technology (2006)
3. Inc.), B., Inc.), L.L.P.: Survey report on attitudes toward live music distribution (2020). https://skiyaki.com/contents/339428. Accessed 26 Oct 2021
4. Institute, P.R.: Live entertainment market in 2019. https://corporate.pia.jp/csr/pia-soken (2020). Accessed 26 Oct 2021
5. J., W., K., A., S., Y., K., K., K, K., A., H.: [sharing the excitement of watching sports using air-transmission tactile communication: a study as a wow ball] kuuki-densousyokkan communication wo riyou sita sport kansen no moriagari kyouyuu : Wow ball tositeno kentou (in Japnanese). Transactions of the Virtual Reality Society of Japan **25**(4), 311–314 (2020)
6. LLC., H.: Haobeat (2019). https://hapbeat.com. Accessed 9 Nov 2021
7. M., M., K., M.: [an attempt to estimate the excitement level of spectators from eeg and skin electrical activity] nouha to hihudenkikatsudou wo motiita kankyaku no moriagari no suitei no kokoromi (in japnanese). In: entertainment computing symposium ronbunsyu. vol. 2021, pp. 370–374. IPSJ Special Interest Group on Entertainment Computing, August 2021
8. Ochiai, Y., GO, T.B.C. Inc, H.: Live jacket (2017). https://www.hakuhodo.co.jp/news/info/38600/. Accessed 24 Dec 2021
9. Y., Y., K., O., K., U., R., I., T., Y., M., F.: [immersive online live system: Led lighting control system that enables synchronized production with live streaming video] immersive online live system: Live haishindouga ni douki sita ensyutu ga kanou na led tentouseigyo system(in japnanese). IPSJ SIG Digital Contents Creation 2021-DCC-28 2021-DCC-28(2), 1–5 (2021)

Research on the Integration of Stage Performance and Virtual Technology in the Digital Media Art Environment

Wei Feng(✉), Lei Xu, and Wei Li

Shandong College of Tourism and Hospitality, 3556, East Jingshi Road, Jinan, Shandong, China
13964076217@163.com

Abstract. Virtual technology provides new ideas for stage art creation, as well as new means for stage performance, and endows stage performance art with new artistic life. Virtual technology has become an important auxiliary means in stage performance and art creation.

Keywords: Stage performance · virtual technology · immersive space · viewing and performing relationship

1 Introduction

With the improvement of people's art appreciation ability and the psychology of pursuing new things, new requirements are put forward for the form of stage performance art. The integration of virtual technology and stage performance in line with the trend has become an imperative reform measure of performance art. Virtual technology improves the effect of stage art design, endows stage with diversified forms of expression, enhances the interaction between performers and audience, reshapes the relationship between watching and performing, and adds more possibilities to stage art.

2 Stage Performance

Stage performance refers to the skill of performing in the space of the stage, which is one of many forms of performance. Performers usually take the theater or theater as the place to provide corresponding performances for the audience [1]. The stage performance uses the actors' body movements, dialogues, singing and dancing and other character modeling methods to deduce the stage programs with stories and bring the audience into the special mood of the plot. There are many factors affecting stage performance, among which the three most important factors are stage design, actors and audience.

N. A. Streitz and S. Konomi (Eds.): HCII 2023, LNCS 14037, pp. 225–237, 2023.
https://doi.org/10.1007/978-3-031-34609-5_16

2.1 Stage Design

Stage design is also called stage art design. It is a stage created by integrating the lighting, sound, art, LED screen and other parts of the stage, and combining the elements of architecture, design, aesthetics, lighting, psychology and other aspects. The main function of stage design is to deepen the stage plot, improve the overall effect of the stage, and create an immersive stage atmosphere.

The factors that make stage performance possible are the excellent skills of actors, and also the elaborate stage. Stage design needs strong artistry and technicality. It is an accessory of actors' performance. A luxurious stage will be covered up by the stage atmosphere even when the actors' performance is defective. Therefore, stage construction also becomes an indispensable part of stage performance. A good scene can not only give the actors a trusted performance space and set off their emotions, but also bring the audience unexpected visual experience and artistic enjoyment through creative design, which resonates and is unforgettable for a long time.

The stage design is divided into two types. One is a physical stage dominated by lighting, stage space, physical background and sound. This stage design is limited by the stage height, size, safety, beauty, capital and other factors, thus restricting the imagination of stage designers; The other is the virtual stage built by using AR, VR, XR, holographic projection and other technologies. This kind of stage does not need to consider the factors of the real stage. The stage designer can freely use his imagination to expand the stage space and design a magnificent dream stage. The virtual stage is the product of the development of digital media art to a certain stage. It not only has the same functions as the physical stage, but also has the value of reuse. It can avoid the material loss caused by the one-time physical stage, and can replace the physical stage.

2.2 Actors

With the advent of the digital era, more and more technological elements have been incorporated into the design of stage performances, and the stage forms have become dazzling. However, actors are still the core elements of stage performances. The actor is like a bridge, connecting the stage and the audience. Both dancers and theatrical actors should devote themselves to the role of the stage, highlight and reflect the appeal of the performance art, bring the audience's emotions into the performance, display the stage image lifelike in front of the audience, and reflect the charm of the stage art.

Stage performance requires certain performance skills. Good actors know how to use performance skills to mobilize the emotions of the audience and close the distance with the audience. However, skill is only a way to help actors improve the performance effect. As an actor, skill alone is not enough. Only with excellent professional quality, solid basic skills and accumulated stage experience can we create a rich, full and infectious image, better reflect the charm of stage performance, and gain more audience recognition.

2.3 Visitors

In fact, both the audience and the actors can be seen as the core of the stage performance, but they play different roles. The actor breathes life into the performance, and the audience receives the artistic emotions brought by the performance, and both parties interact with each other. The audience's influence on the stage performance can be described from two aspects, one is the impact of audience feedback on the actor's performance on the spot, and the other is the impact of audience feedback on the audience's individual.

The audience's influence on the actor's performance can be roughly divided into two aspects: positive and negative. During the performance, the applause and cheers from the audience will stimulate the performance of the actors. The stronger the audience's response, the more engaged the actors are in the performance, and the better the performance effect; On the contrary, the audience's departure will have a negative impact on the actor's psychology, which will distract the actor and affect the performance effect.

The influence of individual audience refers to the influence of the spontaneous feedback behavior of the audience on the stage performance effect on other individual audience when watching the performance. This kind of influence has many forms of expression, which is mainly reflected in the audience's reception of other audiences' praise, complaints and other critical words or body actions on the performance, causing resonance, and thus driving themselves to make tendentious feedback similar to others' behavior.

With the improvement of the aesthetic ability of mass art, the modern innovative performance art forms focus more on the audience, focus on interactive experience, highlight the main feelings of the audience, and provide more possibilities for personalized experience.

3 Virtual Technology

3.1 Overview of Virtual Technology

Virtual technology is the general name of VR (virtual reality technology), AR (augmented reality technology), XR (extended reality technology) and MR (hybrid reality technology). It is the combination of virtual and reality. It is a computer simulation system that can create and experience a virtual world. It uses a computer to generate a simulation environment in which users can obtain immersive experience and produce strong visual impact [2].

3.2 Application Scope of Virtual Technology

The application of virtual technology has been integrated into many industries, such as entertainment industry, medical industry, culture and tourism industry, real estate industry, automobile manufacturing industry, aerospace manufacturing industry, education industry, social communication, e-commerce and so on, such as digital display services in industrial manufacturing based on virtual reality and augmented reality technology, and surgical simulators in medical industry based on virtual reality and simulation technology, Virtual museums, art galleries and other art venues based on virtual reality technology and network technology, and immersive variety shows based on augmented reality technology and holographic projection technology. It can be seen that the deepening cooperation between virtual technology and various industries is the trend of development.

4 Integration of Virtual Technology and Stage Performance

At the initial stage of the application of virtual technology, it is only used in simple scene display, and its application scope is not extensive. After many years of technological iteration, virtual technology provides new ideas for stage art creation, and also provides new means for stage performance, giving stage performance art new artistic life. Virtual technology has become an important auxiliary means in stage performance and art creation. Because of the immersion and interactivity of virtual technology itself, the virtual reality picture finally presented to the audience is also more amazing than the traditional stage. The application and practice of virtual technology in stage performance is more responsive to the aesthetic needs of contemporary audiences, and is of great significance to the development of stage art.

4.1 Virtual Stage

The traditional physical stage performance is limited by the performance venue. The creator needs to consider the size of the stage space, which limits the more magnificent scene display. The situational stage created by virtual technology breaks the limits of space and time, extends the space and time of the stage infinitely, presents the content that cannot be presented in the real world to the audience through virtual technology, endows the stage with more diversified forms of expression and greater imagination space, perfectly reflects the situational nature of the stage, and makes the whole stage performance art appear unprecedented, A shocking audio-visual experience. In recent years, with the improvement of public aesthetic needs and the development of computer technology, there have been many examples of virtual technology applied to stage performances. Among them, the representative performance is the dance "Tang Dynasty" of Zhengzhou Song and Dance Theater (As shown in Fig. 1), which has complete dance performance and stage presentation effect, mature application of virtual technology, good audience experience, and effective dissemination of traditional culture to the public aesthetic. It is the perfect combination of traditional culture and modern technology, realizing cultural inheritance and innovation, providing new ideas for future stage performance, and has important reference significance for stage performance.

Ar + vr.

Fig. 1. Tang Dynasty (Source:Tencent)

"Tang Dynasty" (see Fig. 1) is a dance work of Zhengzhou Song and Dance Theatre. The work tells about an interesting event that took place on the way to the banquet performance by a group of plump musical skills during a banquet held by Li Zhi and Wu Zetian in Luoyang Shangyang Palace more than 1300 years ago. Inspired by the Tang Dynasty musical and dance figurines unearthed from the tomb of Zhang Sheng in Anyang, Henan Province in 1959, a group of thirteen figurines, including eight musical figurines and five dance figurines, are currently in the Henan Museum. After the second creation of the Henan Spring Festival Gala program, the Tang Palace Banquet integrates 5G and AR technology, combines the virtual scene with the real stage, and presents a visual feast of the history of science and technology dialogue.

The technical team of "Tang Dynasty" uses VR lighting technology to carry out overall intelligent control for the lighting requirements of different virtual scenes, one-click scene call, and also uses virtual reality technology to display the lighting effects in various modes in advance to maximize the reality of the scene [3]. From the picture of a beautiful woman with a hairpin flower to the splash-ink landscape painting, and finally to the magnificent palace, each scene is seamlessly linked into a complete story, and the giant female owl statue, the map of the Ming Emperor's luck in Shu, the lotus and crane square pot, the Jiahu bone flute, the picture of a beautiful woman with a hairpin flower, the map of riding preparation, the ramming practice picture, the map of thousands of miles of rivers and mountains, and other national treasures in the museum are interspersed in the scene to find the essence of Chinese culture in the ancient relics. The cultural relics in the museum are endowed with spirituality by AR technology. They interact with dancers on the stage and slowly tell the story behind the cultural relics in the dance. With the development of the plot, the scene also changes. The dance and the virtual scene are perfectly combined. The dancer seems to be a historical figure, leading the audience to swim through the historical picture and appreciate the style of the Tang Dynasty. However, the dancers present will not have the experience of the audience. The actors only integrate the virtual content through their walking, expression, dance movements, and what the audience sees is the feeling of combining the virtual and the real. The five-minute dance allows the audience to realize the journey through the Tang Dynasty.

The fusion of virtual technology and dance led to the Tang Palace Banquet, which became famous and was selected as one of the top ten national IP addresses in 2021. This dance combines all elements popular with the public, interprets the traditional Chinese culture, displays the rich local culture of Henan, integrates modern technology, and has a profound sense of history. Virtual technology makes the dance more narrative, reduces the threshold of appreciating the dance, and lets the audience not have to try their best to understand the artistic conception conveyed by the dance, but just stay in it and watch it quietly. The ingenious idea of moving cultural relics from the museum to the stage in "Tang Dynasty" has led more people into the museum, set off an upsurge of visiting the museum, and further promoted the development of local tourism.

LED Screen + AR.

Fig. 2. "Star Dream" (Source: Netease)

In the stage design of the 2022 Spring Festival Gala, a 720-degree arc screen is created with LED screens. The dome screen integrates the auditorium and the rostrum. The dome screen and the ground screen echo each other, forming a highly scalable three-dimensional performance stage. With the help of virtual technology, AR projection, bare-eye 3D and other new technologies, it creates an immersive space of virtual and real interaction, with strong visual impact and shocking effect. The ground screen and dome screen produce different visual effects according to the change of the program by writing special programs. "Star Dream"(see Fig. 2) is one of the most representative innovative programs. The 720-degree arc screen is transformed into a vast universe. The satellite and space shuttle of "air phase" are slowly circled in the universe by using AR projection technology. The virtual astronauts walk in the space. The children's dancers hold two meters of white feathers and run on the ground. They interact with the virtual giant feathers on the dome, combining virtual and real, The dreamy panorama shows the Chinese people's space dream. Within two hours of the broadcast of this program, major media scrambled to report that the reading volume of microblog exceeded tens of millions, causing a network boom.

Virtual technology represented by VR, AR, MR and XR is subtly changing the design form of stage performance, opening up artistic imagination space for literary and artistic creators, bringing more colorful and beautiful program effects, and also driving the huge transformation of modern stage display form from single to multiple, and providing new ideas for the rejuvenation of traditional culture in the form of stage performance.

4.2 Virtual Idol

Virtual idol is a virtual character created under the joint support of holographic projection technology (a kind of virtual technology), voice synthesis technology, deep learning, brain-like science, biotechnology and other technologies. It has human appearance and behavior, and can be performed in real or virtual stage environment, interact with real actors and stage, so as to provide new experience for the audience. The video platform emerging from the global epidemic in 2020 has become an opportunity for the display and operation of virtual idols. 2021 is known as the year when the development of virtual idols enters the fast lane.

Fig. 3. Luo Tianyi and Wang Peiyu in CCTV (Source: Sina)

Luo Tianyi, a female virtual singer in mainland China, is affiliated to Shanghai Henian Information Technology Co., Ltd., whose name is taken from the beautiful meaning of traditional Chinese culture. Dressed in traditional Chinese clothing, she has the sweet shape of a beautiful girl, beautiful voice and beautiful dancing, and is loved by the young generation. In 2017, Luo Tianyi held the first personal holographic concert at the Mercedes-Benz Cultural Center in Shanghai. The SVIP ticket with a price of 1280 yuan was sold out within three minutes after it was put on the shelf. The attendance rate of the venue for 10000 people reached 80%. Millions of viewers watched the concert through the ACFUN live broadcast platform. The concert not only introduced high-quality dance production team, but also used real-time motion capture system, AR live broadcast system and holographic projection technology, which became the biggest selling points of the concert.

In 2018, Luo Tianyi and Wang Peiyu, a famous Peking opera singer, co-sang "Hope for a Long Life" in CCTV's "Classic Chanting and Spreading" program(see Fig. 3). The fancy Peking Opera, which combines Beijing Opera with electric music, creates a sense of future music, organically combines traditional Chinese culture and trendy culture, and explores a new way to promote traditional Chinese culture, so that people can see traditional Chinese culture from a new perspective and feel the vitality and charm of traditional culture, Arouse young people's love and interest in Chinese traditional culture and Chinese opera art. In 2021, Luo Tianyi participated in the CCTV Spring Festival Gala and performed the song and dance "Listen to Me" with Wang Yuan and Sister Moon. In February 2022, Luo Tianyi was invited to participate in the opening ceremony of the Beijing Winter Olympics and sang the Winter Olympics song "Time to shine", becoming the first Chinese virtual singer to appear on the Olympic stage.

By virtue of his unique style, Luo Tian became a popular virtual singer. He frequently appeared at major domestic parties, adding the interest and sense of technology of stage performances, allowing more companies to see the market value of virtual actors, and successively developed many virtual idols. A-SOUL is a virtual idol team created by Lehua Entertainment at the end of 2020. In December 2021, A-SOUL will participate in the online evening party of "Fantastic Night with Music", and sing the song "Chek Ling" in cooperation with singer Zhu Jingxi. In November 2022, A-SOUL will hold a VR concert of "Wonderful Universe". A-SOUL is different from Luo Tianyi. It uses real-time motion capture technology. Real people wear motion capture clothing, track and capture the position information fixed on the human body from different angles through multiple high-speed optical cameras, and then output the motion posture to the virtual idol through computer algorithms. The A-SOUL live broadcast on stage is different. It uses real-time online live broadcast. On the one hand, it takes a lot of time to adjust and render scenes, characters and materials, on the other hand, it increases the difficulty of technical implementation, and also increases the risk of performance errors. A-SOUL has won the recognition of the audience and the society by virtue of its exquisite skills. It not only has various forms of cooperation and interaction, but also participates in the exclusive activities of multiple brands.

The virtual idol is not only the technological product of the progress of virtual technology, but also the emerging darling of stage performance, and also the disseminator of traditional Chinese culture in the virtual field. Integrate traditional culture into the emerging technology of virtual idol, let the unique charm of national style blossom and bear fruit in the field of virtual technology, and fully display the special charm of the combination of virtual and traditional.

Fig. 4. .Wangfeng VR Concert (Source: Bilibili)

4.3 3VR Theater

With the continuous maturity of virtual technology, VR theater has emerged as an artistic form of expression. VR theater, also known as virtual reality theater, is an audio-visual experience service. Users can experience a variety of virtual reality content through virtual reality headworn display devices. This device closes people's vision and hearing to the outside world and guides users to create a sense of being in the virtual environment. Its display principle is that the left and right eye screens display the images of the left and right eyes respectively, and the human eye produces a stereoscopic sense in the mind after obtaining this information with differences. VR Theater was not recognized by the public at first. In the past three years, due to the continuous impact of the epidemic, the culture and tourism industry has been greatly impacted, and all offline theater performances have been suspended. VR Theater, as a new form of performance that can avoid gathering risks and improve user experience, takes this opportunity to become the best substitute for offline performances and quickly enter the public's view.

The more mature form of VR theater is VR concert. Famous mainland singers Wang Feng and Zheng Jun held VR concert successively in 2022(see Fig. 4). In addition to bringing users the surreal feeling of being at the concert site, the special effects of the customized VR stage are also impressive. The special effects are very immersive, futuristic and interactive, and have obtained a special effect experience beyond the scene.

With the support of VR devices, viewers can freely switch their views according to their preferences, and obtain the best viewing distance next to the singer. From the scene to the real-time rendering of dance beauty, from the interaction to the virtual native of the senses, from the technology to the panoramic interaction of the play, we constantly explore and integrate the boundaries of virtual reality. Create multiple ultimate visual sensory feast. Full-end connection, breaking the physical constraints of time and space, provides a more comprehensive sense of extreme participation than the scene.

In the process of "zero distance" participation, the interest of stage performance has been significantly enhanced. The audience can more deeply understand and feel the profound meaning conveyed by the performance, and effectively realize the role of mass communication of art and culture. It not only shows the public more possibilities of VR technology in application scenarios, but also realizes the technical possibilities of live broadcasting from VR perspective.

5 The Impact of Virtual Technology on the Relationship Between Watching and Performing

The watching relationship refers to the relationship between the actors and the audience during the stage performance. The audience and the actors are the two ends of the bond relationship. The quality of the relationship between the two affects the success of the whole performance. In the traditional viewing mode, the audience is only independent of the performance as a consumer, and the addition of emerging virtual technology can bring changes to the traditional relationship between watching and performing. On the one hand, virtual technology provides more diversified forms of performance for stage performance, breaking the traditional stage pattern, and integrating the stage area and audience at the physical level; On the other hand, virtual technology promotes the participation of the audience, emphasizes the personalized viewing mode of the audience, solves the limitations of the traditional theater viewing perspective, optimizes the viewing experience, and promotes the interaction between the performer and the audience at the psychological level.

5.1 Stage Pattern

The traditional stage consists of framed stage, extended stage and central stage. The stage provides independent performance space for performers, but also isolates the distance between the audience and actors. Virtual technology breaks the pattern between the stage area and the audience, and the audience becomes a part of the stage. The performer can freely change the stage area, jump back and forth between the stage area and the audience, and even include the audience in the stage performance, so that they are completely immersed in the situation created by the designer. The audience resonates with the performer in a specific situation, forming an emotional and artistic interaction, stimulating various senses in a multi-dimensional way, making them intoxicated, producing a sense of pleasure and happiness in body and mind, and obtaining a new immersive viewing experience.

5.2 Free Perspective

Free view technology is a set of fast, dynamic and static "time condensation" content production system applied in the live broadcast environment. As spectators of stage performances, audiences can only passively receive pictures, and free view technology enables audiences to gain more initiative. This technology supports multi-port viewing mode. The audience can independently and interactively change the view angle and position, freely zoom, pause at any time, freeze frame rotation, slow motion surround and other effects by operating the mobile APP, breaking through the traditional fixed point and passive viewing, and improving the experience comfort. In November 2019, at the International Table Tennis Federation Men's World Cup held in Chengdu, the free view live broadcast system developed by the Huawei Space Video Free View Project Team was successfully applied to the live broadcast of sports events for the first time. In the mobile APP, viewers can not only watch the high-definition game scene, but also see the fleeting and wonderful serving and receiving moments of the world's top players by clicking, rotating and other operations on the mobile screen. This disruptive technology has also given Huawei a good appraisal in the industry. In 2021, in the program "Dance Storm" broadcast by Hunan Satellite TV, the project team formed a rainbow shape with 128 synchronous acquisition cameras, and all the machines tracked and shot the dancers in an all-round three-dimensional way to capture the wonderful moments in the dance. Through the high-speed processing of 128 camera data by the cloud server, the effect of viewing at any time node from a free angle of view can be achieved, and even the effect of viewing distance and lens upgrading can be shortened, Therefore, the audience can see a series of pictures of dancers jumping, soaring, freezing, falling, landing and so on to achieve the enjoyment of free viewing.

In the 2022 Beijing Winter Olympic Games, the free perspective technology once again made the audience feel the charm of snow and ice sports from the perspective of science and technology. In order to let the audience have a 360-degree viewing experience without dead angle, 45 synchronous cameras were used to capture and shoot the scene in an all-round way in a competition, and 30 virtual cameras were set between each two cameras to build a 360-degree free viewing space. The huge video data generated by more than 1000 cameras, after being compressed by the video decoder independently developed by the project team, is transmitted through the network of hundreds of 5G base stations near the Olympic site, which effectively guarantees the transmission speed and efficiency of the free view live picture of the event. This codec is an international compression standard AVS3 coding technology led by Academician Gao Wen of Peking University, which is specially used for efficient encoding and decoding of 8K video. Even if audiences from all over the world are not on the scene, they can independently change the viewing angle and position of the stadium at any time and place through the combination of free view technology on the mobile terminal, so as to achieve personalized experience of different perspectives of the same event, obtain immersive high-quality interactive viewing experience, and share this ice and snow sports feast.

The free perspective technology is not only applied to sports events, but also to more scenes such as stage performances, e-commerce, online teaching, etc. with the increasing demand of the audience for full-view viewing experience. The free perspective technology can be flexibly viewed without going out to get a zero-distance on-site experience, experience more beautiful things in the way of technology, and create an extraordinary immersive audio-visual experience.

5.3 Immersive Viewing Mode

Virtual technology creates a multi-dimensional immersive viewing space for the audience and extends the visual boundary of the audience through a full-wrapped presentation. For example, when watching a cross-language performance, the audience needs to rely on the prompt subtitles on the LED screen to read the general idea of the performance content. At the same time, the audience also needs to focus on the actor's performance. The audience's vision is repeatedly switched between the actor and the LED screen, which disrupts the rhythm of the performance and reduces the sense of artistic appreciation experience. The AR technology projects the information such as dialogue translation subtitles and inter-screen conversion introduction into the actor's performance space, making up for the shortcomings of the language narrative art in the cross-cultural performance.

The immersion brought by virtual technology provides a new way of interaction between the audience and the actors, bringing a new artistic experience to the audience watching the performance, while creating more possibilities for the performance.

6 Conclusion

The wide application of scientific and technological means in art can enable the audience to break through the barriers of time and space, and constantly enrich the viewing content and listening experience. In the future, virtual technology will also enable the production of high-quality cultural content, continue to develop the 5G + 8K + VR scene application mode, covering educational events, cultural tourism, medical research, machinery manufacturing and other fields in an all-round way, to meet the needs of people's intelligent work and life.

Technology empowers and art leads. Virtual technology has penetrated into all fields of people's cultural life. In this context, the stage performance art is also constantly innovating, and with the support of virtual technology, it has brought a lot of new experience to the audience, improved the appreciation and artistic transmission of the work, and at the same time, enabled the audience to better perceive the stage performance content and achieve emotional resonance with the actors. In the future, stage performance forms enabled by virtual technology will appear more in people's lives, bring more new artistic experience to the audience, and also create more high-quality artistic works. (全段引用).

In the process of future development, the integration of science and technology and art is the general trend, and the depth and breadth of the integration of the two will be further improved. A new form of artistic expression that integrates perceptual performance art with rational scientific and technological means is an innovative research in the intersection of science and art.

References

1. Manling, Y.: Research on the integration of stage performance and VR technology in the new form of digital media art. Stage Art Res. **8** (middle), 97–99 (2022)
2. Jin, Z.: VR news and its enlightenment on media integration and transformation. Young Journalists **13**, 51–53 (2016)
3. Wei, H.: Overview of the visual effect guarantee for the stage screen of the 2022 Spring Festival Gala of the General Administration. Mod. TV Technol. **3**, 57–60 (2022)

Dashcam Video Curation for Generating Memorial Movies on Tourism Using Multiple Measures of "Tourist Spot Likeness"

Masaki Kawanaka[1]([✉]), Yuki Matsuda[1,2]([✉]) [iD], Hirohiko Suwa[1,2] [iD], and Keiichi Yasumoto[1,2] [iD]

[1] Nara Institute of Science and Technology, Nara 630-0101, Japan
{kawanaka.masaki.kj1,yukimat,h-suwa,yasumoto}@is.naist.jp
[2] RIKEN Center for Advanced Intelligence Project (AIP), Tokyo 103-0027, Japan

Abstract. Recently, a method for the automatic generation of driving sightseeing memorial route movies has been proposed by performing curation on videos captured by a dashcam. Existing methods curate videos by scoring video frames with a single specific measure, however, it is hard to generate the appropriate memorial route movies due to the differences in important perspectives for different users. To solve this problem, we propose the method that represents "tourist spot likeness" with a combination of common measures derived by procedures used in the field of Affective Engineering and curates dashcam videos based on multiple measures. In this paper, we surveyed these representative words to identify the measures that compose the measure of "tourist spot likeness" and construct a model to estimate the score of each measure using dashcam video data as input. As the results of the experiment by using dashcam videos taken in Okinawa, we have derived six measures for curating the dashcam videos and confirmed the proposed models, which estimate each measure scored with a 7-level Likert scale achieved mean MAE of 0.64 (best: 0.52, worst: 0.73).

Keywords: Affective Engineering · Civic and Urban Computing · Human-Centered Artificial Intelligence · Location-based Services · Smart Tourism · Video Curation · Dashcam

1 Introduction

In recent years, an increasing number of travelers have been posting memorial videos created from photos and videos of their travels on social media. Most of the memorial movie generation support systems, such as RealTimes [10], compile photos of multiple tourist spots. Demand for such systems that automatically create memorial videos is growing because they are easy to use, even for users without video editing skills. However, few services provide memorial movie generation

This study was supported in part by JST PRESTO under Grant No. JPMJPR2039.

support systems focusing on tourist routes, especially while driving. Since the trip between tourist spots constitutes a large percentage of sightseeing, many important scenes exist. It can be considered that the memorial tourist movie generation support system focusing on tourist routes helps to share tourist flow more intuitively than the system curates photos taken at multiple tourist spots. In addition to public transportation such as buses and trains, walking and driving are also considered as ways of tourist transportation. In sightseeing using public transportation such as buses and trains, it is difficult to capture tourist routes, but in the case of cars, it is possible to capture tourist routes using a dashcam. As the performance of dashcams improves, they are not only used as evidence recorders in the event of accidents. Still, they are also utilized in tourism support [9], driving skill improvement systems [12], and on-street parking detection [7].

Katayama *et al.* [6] have developed a video curation algorithm to preserve memorable scenes from a dashcam in a memorial video. The algorithm removes redundant parts, such as irreplaceable road trips, stops at traffic lights, and traffic jams, and extracts memorable scenes that are the highlights of the video. To calculate the importance of the frame, they propose a measure named "Okinawa likeness", which is the scale of how well the video frame matches the impression of Okinawa (a prefecture in Japan). Then, the "Okinawa likeness" of dashcam videos taken during sightseeing tours in Okinawa is collected and measured using crowdsourcing, and a machine learning model is constructed to predict "Okinawa likeness" for memorial video curation. However, ambiguous expressions such as "Okinawa likeness" are perceived differently by different people [8], making it difficult to generate appropriate memorial route movies based on the various "Okinawa likeness" assumed by each user, and also difficult to apply the model to other touristic areas.

This paper aims to improve the quality of curation of memorial route movies by expressing "tourist spot likeness" using a combination of general-purpose measures that are less prone to differences in interpretation among people, instead of measures that are prone to differences in interpretation used in previous studies. To achieve this, it is necessary to clarify what combination of impressions people get from tourist spots can express "tourist spot likeness". In this paper, we use dashcam videos taken in Okinawa prefecture, one of Japan's most touristic southern islands. To derive a measure to be used for curating the memorial route movie, we extract clusters of impression words that compose "tourist spot likeness" and select representative words based on procedures used in the field of Affective Engineering. Then, we use these representative words to identify measures of "tourist spot likeness", and construct a CNN model that estimates scores for each measure using dashcam videos. As a result, we identified six measures necessary for dashcam video curation, and confirmed proposed models, which estimate each measure scored with a 7-level Likert scale achieved mean MAE of 0.64 (best: 0.52, worst: 0.73).

This paper is organized as follows: In Sect. 2, we introduce related studies and summarize the position of this research. Next, in Sect. 3, we describe a memorial video curation method using drive recorder images. In Sect. 4, we describe a method for identifying a measure of "tourist spot likeness" using the results of extracting representative words that compose the measure, and in Sect. 5, we construct and evaluate a CNN model for estimating the score of each measure. Finally, Sect. 6 concludes this paper.

2   Related Research

2.1   Video Curation for Route Guidance

A system that provides route guidance must correctly communicate walking and driving routes. Although maps are a simple route guidance system, some users may have difficulty understanding a route with only a map. Therefore, methods have been proposed to facilitate understanding of routes by utilizing curated videos for route guidance [5]. In these methods, the playback speed is increased for parts that are not necessary for route guidance, such as going straight, and curated videos are played at normal speed for parts that are important for route guidance, such as turning right or left. In a study for walking route guidance [5], the first-person video is used to detect landscape transitions based on histogram differences, and curation is performed using a variable frame rate method. For driving route guidance, we use video from a drive recorder to compute an optical flow based on the LucasKanade algorithm to detect left-right turns and curate videos.

2.2   Video Curation for Memorial Video Creation

In recent years, an increasing number of travelers have been posting memorial videos created from photos and videos of their travels on social media. However, the creation of memorial videos using video editing software is difficult for users who do not have video editing skills. For this reason, systems have been proposed to automatically create memorial videos easily for people without video editing skills [10]. However, memorial videos generated by conventional systems lack scenes during travel, a major element of tourism, and fail to reflect the impressive scenes that occur during travel. Therefore, an automatic curation method for memorial videos of the entire tourist tour, including moving around, has been proposed using dashcam video.

In the method of Katayama et al. [6], dashcam videos of tourist routes are segmented into 3-second segments, and the importance of each segment is estimated to evaluate whether it is necessary as a tourist memorial video, and memorial video curation is performed. As an importance estimation model, three image frames are extracted from each 3-second segment video, and an estimation model of "Okinawa likeness" was constructed using category occupancy calculated by DeepLabv3 [2] trained with CityScapes [3] and BDD100k [14], and landmark information obtained by YOLOv3 [11] as features. Crowdsourcing was used to evaluate the "Okinawa likeness" of the segmented videos, which were then used as the correct labels for the scores. However, since the vague expression "Okinawa likeness" is perceived differently by different people, it may not be possible to generate memorial route movies based on the "Okinawa likeness" assumed by each user.

2.3 Position of This Research

In this study, we aim to improve the quality of memorial video curation by expressing "tourist spot likeness" using a combination of measures that are less likely to cause differences in interpretation among people, instead of a measure that is more likely to cause differences in interpretation, based on the video curation method using the importance score proposed in Sect. 2.2. We extract clusters of impression words that compose "tourist spot likeness" and select representative words based on procedures used in the field of Affective Engineering [13], to derive a measure for use in curating memorial route movies using dashcam videos of tourist tours in Okinawa Prefecture.

In this paper, we use these representative words and factor analysis to identify the measures that compose "tourist spot likeness". Then, we construct a CNN model to estimate the scores of each measure, and evaluate and discuss whether the scores of each measure can be estimated or not.

3 Proposed System

The overview of the proposed method is shown in Fig. 1. First, the dashcam video is split into 3-second segments, and the first, middle, and last frames are extracted. When dividing the dashcam video into segmented videos, we divided the video every 3 s, taking into account the characteristic that most people's visual information enters a stable period in 3 s [1]. Three seconds is the approximate time it takes for an object 50m ahead to frame out from the view of a car traveling at 60km per hour, which is enough time to confirm changes in the scenery outside the car. Next, the estimated scores of each measure are obtained from machine learning models that estimate the measures that compose "tourist spot likeness". Finally, segments are selected based on the score of each measure, and a memorial tourist movie is generated.

The importance score used for selecting a segment is calculated from a combination of several measures, as shown in Fig. 2. In the proposed method, the "tourist spot likeness" is defined as follows, using the measures that compose "tourist spot likeness" and the weight parameter.

$$S = \frac{1}{L} \sum_{l=1}^{L} s_l w_l \ , \tag{1}$$

where S denotes the "tourist spot likeness", L denotes the total number of measures, w denotes the weight parameter of measure that composes "tourist spot likeness". The proposed method can freely change the weight parameter w, and can generate a memorial route movie based on each user's idea of "tourist spot likeness".

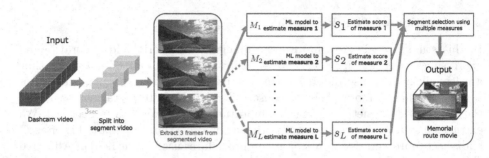

Fig. 1. Overview of proposed method

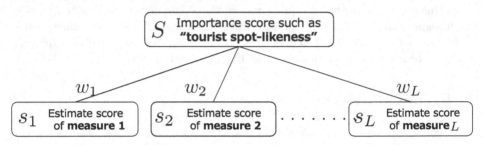

Fig. 2. Measures that compose "tourist spot likeness"

4 Selection of Measures of "tourist Spot Likeness"

To realize the proposed method, it is necessary to clarify what kinds of combination of impressions that people receive from tourist spots can effectively express "tourist spot likeness". This section describes the method to derive "tourist spot likeness" measure.

Hereinafter, we describe the proposed method with an example of dashcam videos taken in Okinawa prefecture, one of Japan's most touristic southern islands.

4.1 Overview of Measure Derivation Method

To derive the measures of "tourist spot likeness" to be used for the curation of memorial route movies, we employ the following procedure inspired by the method in the field of Affective Engineering: (1) Collecting the impression words when watching the dashcam video, (2) Conduct a psychological experiment to calculate the distance in semantic space between impression words, extract clusters of impression words expressing "tourist spot likeness" by hierarchical cluster analysis based on the obtained distance, and select representative words, (3) Using the representative words obtained and factor analysis, a measure of "tourist spot likeness" is derived.

Table 1. Representative words that constitute "tourist spot likeness" for Okinawa prefecture in Japan

Cluster 1	Cluster 2	Cluster 2	Cluster 4	Cluster 5	Cluster 6
radiant (晴れやかな)	comfortable (気持ちいい)	relax (のんびりした)	seaside (海沿いの)	suburban (郊外の)	peaceful (平穏な)
brightly (明るい)	pleasant (心地良い)	loosely (ゆったりとした)	coastal (海岸沿いの)	quiet (閑静な)	composed (落ち着いた)
fresh (清々しい)		calm (穏やかな)	refined (優雅な)	routine (日常の)	silent (静かな)

Cluster 7	Cluster 8	Cluster 9	Cluster 10	Cluster 11	Cluster 12
spacious (開放的な)	warm (暖かい)	dazzling (眩しい)	expressway (高速道路の)	exotic (異国情緒な)	lively (賑やかな)
open (開けた)	animated (生き生きした)	summer (常夏の)	night (夜の)	foreign (異国の)	hot (暑い)
vast (広大な)	tropical (南国な)	new (新しい)	roadside (道路沿いの)	Asian (アジア風の)	

Cluster 13	Cluster 14	Cluster 15	Cluster 16
messy (ごみごみした)	trafficy (渋滞の)	urban (都会の)	dark (暗い)
congestion (渋滞した)	crowded (雑踏の)	downtown (街中の)	narrow (狭い)
stuffy (息苦しい)	cramped (窮屈な)		darkness (暗がりの)

First, we have conducted procedures (1) and (2) using dashcam videos of Okinawa, and the representative words of each cluster obtained by cluster extraction are shown in Table 1.

4.2 Derivation of Measures of "tourist Spot Likeness"

In order to derive a measure of "tourist spot likeness", we used Yahoo! Crowdsourcing[1] to conduct a task in which respondents were asked to rate, on a 7-point scale (1. Strongly agree, 2. agree, 3. Slightly agree, 4. Neither agree nor disagree, 5. Slightly disagree, 6. disagree, 7. Strongly disagree), how they felt about the words shown in Table 1 when watching a dashcam video of Okinawa. The videos used in this experiment were fifty 3-second segment videos generated from dashcam videos taken in Okinawa. In the segment videos, we used dashcam videos of various scenes, as shown in Fig. 3, so that various impression words could be collected. For each video, 10 participants rated how they felt about the three representative words that were presented when they watched the video. If a person did not correctly answer a check question, all of his or her data were discarded.

---

[1] https://crowdsourcing.yahoo.co.jp/.

Fig. 3. Segment video created from drive recorder video taken in Okinawa

A factor analysis using the maximum likelihood method and Promax Rotation was then performed on the means of each evaluation score for each of the 10 videos obtained by crowdsourcing. The number of factors was determined to be 7, based on the criterion that the eigenvalue must be greater than 1. However, as the number of measures increases, the usability of the curation system may decrease because users are required to select which measure is more important when using the system. Therefore, the number of factors in this experiment was set to 6.

The top three absolute values of factor loadings (FL) for representative words showing positive and negative correlations for each factor obtained by factor analysis are shown in Table 2. Here, we define and name the measure of "tourist spot likeness" for each factor. Factor 1 is positively correlated with words that indicate less crowdedness, such as "quiet" and "silent", and negatively correlated with words that indicate more crowdedness, such as "congestion" and "messy", thus Factor 1 is named as "urbanness". Factor 2 has a positive correlation with words that describe the morning and afternoon hours, such as "brightly" and "radiant", and a negative correlation with words that describe the evening hours, such as "darkness" and "night", thus Factor 2 is named as "brightness". Factor 3 is named as "exoticness" because of its strong correlation with words that indicate exoticism, such as "exotic" and "tropical", and Factor 4 is named as "scenicness" because of its strong correlation with words that indicate scenery, such as "seaside" and "coastal". Factor 5 is positively correlated with words that indicate more exhilaration, such as "expressway", and negatively correlated with words that indicate less exhilaration, such as "downtown" and "relax", thus Factor 5 is named as "liveliness". Factor 6 has a positive correlation with words that describe the open view, such as "open" and "vast", and a negative correlation with words that describe the less open view, such as "narrow" and "cramped", thus Factor 6 is named as "openness". The results of the factor analysis indicate that the six measures of "tourist spot likeness" are "urbanness", "brightness", "exoticness", "scenicness", "liveliness", and "openness".

Table 2. Top three absolute magnitudes of factor loadings (FL) for representative words showing positive and negative correlations for each factor, and measure names

	Factor 1	FL	Factor 2	FL	Factor 3	FL
positive correlation	quiet (閑静な)	0.98	brightly (明るい)	0.87	exotic (異国情緒な)	0.91
	silent (静かな)	0.91	radiant (晴れやかな)	0.82	foreign (異国の)	0.88
	relax (のんびりした)	0.87	warm (温かい)	0.51	tropical (南国な)	0.974
negative correlation	congestion (渋滞した)	-0.99	darkness (暗がりの)	-0.97	expressway (高速道路の)	-0.43
	trafficy (渋滞の)	-0.91	dark (暗い)	-0.74	suburban (郊外の)	-0.27
	messy (ごみごみした)	-0.88	night (夜の)	-0.72	congestion (渋滞した)	-0.14
	⇓ "urbanness"		⇓ "brightness"		⇓ "exoticness"	

	Factor 4	FL	Factor 5	FL	Factor 6	FL
positive correlation	seaside (海沿いの)	0.92	expressway (高速道路の)	0.86	open (開けた)	0.47
	coastal (海岸沿いの)	0.91	new (新しい)	0.50	roadside (道路沿いの)	0.43
	vast (広大な)	0.35	dazzling (眩しい)	0.37	vast (広大な)	0.42
negative correlation	routine (日常の)	-0.35	routine (日常の)	-0.42	narrow (狭い)	-0.81
	lively (賑やかな)	-0.24	downtown (街中の)	-0.36	cramped (窮屈な)	-0.29
	narrow (狭い)	-0.16	relax (のんびりした)	-0.33	Asia-like (アジア風の)	-0.26
	⇓ "scenicness"		⇓ "liveliness"		⇓ "openness"	

5 Building of "tourist Spot Likeness" Estimation Model

In this section, we build and evaluate a model to estimate scores using dashcam video data as input for the six measures of "tourist spot likeness" derived in Sect. 4.

5.1 Dataset

In this experiment, we use dashcam videos taken over four days from July 11 to 14, 2020 in Okinawa. When the dashcam video was divided into 3-second segmented videos, 459 videos were generated on the first day, 831 videos on the second day, 1,244 videos on the third day, and 569 videos on the fourth day. In total, 3,103 videos are included in the dataset. We collect the ground-truth labels of how people perceive the measure of "tourist spot likeness" when

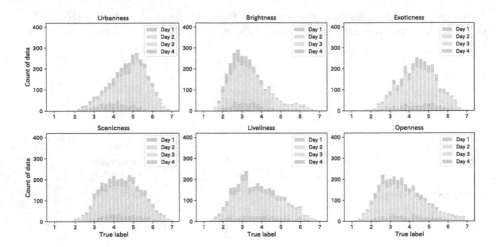

Fig. 4. Relationship between the number of true labels and the number of data in each session

watching the videos, by using Yahoo! Crowdsourcing. Each video is annotated by five people, and the ground-truth label is derived by averaging them. If a person did not correctly answer a dummy question for detecting careless responses, all of their data were discarded and were not included in the following analysis. To inform the meaning of each measure, we provided the following explanations to crowd workers in advance. The "urbanness" measure is closer to 1, the more urban it is, and the closer it is to 7, the more rural it is. The "brightness" measure is closer to 1 for brighter, and closer to 7 for darker. The "exoticness" measure is closer to 1, indicating a sense of exoticism, and closer to 7, indicating a lack of a sense of exoticism. The "scenicness" measure is closer to 1, indicating beautiful scenery, and closer to 7, indicating less beautiful scenery. The "liveliness" measure is closer to 1, indicating exhilaration, and closer to 7, indicating convergence. The "openness" measure is closer to 1, indicating a sense of openness, and closer to 7, indicating a sense of tightness.

5.2   Experimental Conditions

In this experiment, we use ResNet [4], which has been shown to be effective in the field of image recognition, to estimate the scores of the measures that constitute "tourist spot likeness". The model is a trained model of ResNet50 provided by PyTorch. As shown in Fig. 1, the dashcam video is divided into 3-second segment videos, and three images extracted from the 3-segment videos are used as input. The three images used as input are the first, middle, and last frames of the 3-second segment video. When inputting the images into the ResNet, the three images were concatenated in the dimensionality direction where RGB is stored. As output, the number of output classes was changed to 1 to obtain a score for each measure and treated as a regression model. To evaluate generalization

Table 3. Results of the evaluation of six measure score estimation models(MAE)

urbanness	brightness	exoticness	scenicness	liveliness	openness	Mean
0.73	0.52	0.72	0.65	0.59	0.60	0.64

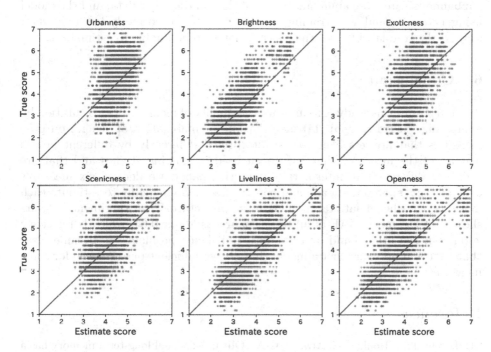

Fig. 5. Relationship between the true values and the estimated results of the six-measure score.

performance, leave-one-day-out cross-validation was conducted with one day's worth of data as the unit. The relationship between the number of true labels and the number of data in each session is shown in Fig. 4. Mean Absolute Error (MAE) was used as the loss function during training, and Stochastic Gradient Descent (SGD) was used as the optimization method with a learning rate of 0.01. The number of mini-batches was 32 and the number of epochs was 20.

5.3 Experimental Results

The results of the MAE evaluation are shown in Table 3, and the results of the estimated measure scores using the ResNet are shown in Fig. 5. Table 3 shows that the mean of MAE for all measures is about 0.64, which indicates that the results are relatively good. Furthermore, Fig. 5 shows that the estimated scores for "brightness", "scenicness", "liveliness", and "openness" increased as the score of the true label increased, indicating that the results captured the trend. On the other hand, for "urbanness" and "exoticness", the estimated scores were concentrated around the center (3–5), indicating that the estimates were not correct. One possible cause of this result is the influence of data bias caused by the division of the test data when conducting the leave-one-day-out cross-validation. As shown in Fig. 4, the data around the true label 6 for "urbanness" are more abundant in Day 3 than in the other data, and the model using Day 1, 2, and 4 as training data is not able to correctly learn the data around the true label 6, and thus is considered to be unable to estimate it.

6 Conclusion

The purpose of this study is to improve the quality of memorial video curation by expressing "tourist spot likeness" using a combination of general-purpose measures that are less likely to be interpreted differently by different people instead of the measures that have been used in existing studies and that are prone to differences in interpretation. In this paper, we derived six measures of "tourist spot likeness" and constructed a CNN model to estimate each measure of dashcam data taken in Okinawa prefecture. The experimental results show that the mean MAE of all the measures is about 0.64, which is relatively good. On the other hand, due to data imbalance problems, it became clear that we could not construct a model that shows sufficient performance for some measures.

References

1. Brady, T.F., Konkle, T., Alvarez, G.A., Oliva, A.: Visual long-term memory has a massive storage capacity for object details. Proc. Natl. Acad. Sci. **105**(38), 14325–14329 (2008). https://doi.org/10.1073/pnas.0803390105
2. Chen, L.C., Papandreou, G., Schroff, F., Adam, H.: Rethinking Atrous convolution for semantic image segmentation, pp. 1–14 (2017). arXiv preprint arXiv:1706.05587
3. Cordts, M., et al.: The cityscapes dataset for semantic urban scene understanding. In: Proceedings of the IEEE Conference on Computer Vision and Pattern Recognition, pp. 3213–3223. CVPR 2016 (2016). https://doi.org/10.1109/CVPR.2016.350
4. He, K., Zhang, X., Ren, S., Sun, J.: Deep Residual Learning for Image Recognition. In: 2016 IEEE Conference on Computer Vision and Pattern Recognition, pp. 770–778. CVPR 2016 (2016). https://doi.org/10.1109/CVPR.2016.90
5. Kanaya, Y., Kawanaka, S., Suwa, H., Arakawa, Y., Yasumoto, K.: Automatic route video summarization based on image analysis for intuitive touristic experience. Sensors Mater. **32**(2), 599–610 (2020). https://doi.org/10.18494/SAM.2020.2616
6. Katayama, Y., Suwa, H., Yasumoto, K.: dash-cum: dashcam video curation for memorial movie generation. In: The 27th Symposium on Information Systems for Society. ISS 2021 (2021). (in Japanese)
7. Matsuda, A., Matsui, T., Matsuda, Y., Suwa, H., Yasumoto, K.: A method for detecting street parking using dashboard camera videos. Sensors Mater. **33**(1), 17–34 (2021). https://doi.org/10.18494/SAM.2021.2998

8. Matsuda, Y.: IoPT: a concept of internet of perception-aware things. In: The 12th International Conference on the Internet of Things, pp. 201–204. IoT 2022 (2022). https://doi.org/10.1145/3567445.3571108

9. Morishita, S., et al.: SakuraSensor: Quasi-realtime cherry-lined roads detection through participatory video sensing by cars. In: Proceedings of the 2015 ACM International Joint Conference on Pervasive and Ubiquitous Computing, pp. 695–705. UbiComp 2015 (2015). https://doi.org/10.1145/2750858.2804273

10. RealNetworks: RealTimes. https://jp.real.com/realtimes/. Accessed 28 Dec 2022

11. Redmon, J., Farhadi, A.: YOLOv3: an incremental improvement, pp. 1–6 (2018). arXiv preprint arXiv:1804.02767

12. Takenaka, K., Bando, T., Nagasaka, S., Taniguchi, T.: Drive video summarization based on double articulation structure of driving behavior. In: Proceedings of the 20th ACM International Conference on Multimedia, pp. 1169–1172. MM 2012 (2012). https://doi.org/10.1145/2393347.2396410

13. Tobitani, K., Matsumoto, T., Tani, Y., Nagata, N.: Modeling the relation between skin attractiveness and physical characteristics. In: Proceedings of the 2018 International Joint Workshop on Multimedia Artworks Analysis and Attractiveness Computing in Multimedia, pp. 30–35. MMArt&ACM 2018 (2018). https://doi.org/10.1145/3209693.3209699

14. Yu, F., et al.: BDD100K: a diverse driving dataset for heterogeneous multitask learning. In: 2020 IEEE/CVF Conference on Computer Vision and Pattern Recognition, pp. 2633–2642. CVPR 2020 (2020)

On the Application and Influence of Interactive Installation in Urban Public Art

JinLiang Tian[✉]

Shandong University of Art & Design, NO. 23 Qianfushandong Road, JiNan, ShanDong, China
164239197@qq.com

Abstract. With the continuous development of the global urbanization, under the background of the digital and informatization society, urban public art has also ushered in new development. In particular, the intervention of interactive art installation has injected new media, communication concepts, and interaction concepts into the public art of contemporary cities. It improves users' experience of urban public art with the help of interaction technology and interaction design, changes people's understanding of traditional public art with new media and new concepts, and affects the development direction of urban public art with new communication concepts. Based on the analysis of interactive art installation's involvement in urban public art, this paper analyzes the application of interactive art installation in urban public art, conducts case analysis, and demonstrates the important role and significance of interactive installation in urban public art. It is hoped that these studies will provide theoretical support for the development of urban public art in the future.

Keywords: Interactive installation · Interactive design · Urban public space

1 The Relationship Between Interactive Art Installation and Urban Public Art

1.1 Installation Art and Urban Public Art

The origin of installation art can be traced back to the work of the artist Marcel Duchamp, who made people realize that ready-made products can also be works of art. Early installation artworks paid special attention to expressing artists' ideas. Under the influence of Dadaism and surrealism, they began to seek meaning, function and influence on space. With the continuous development of installation art, when installation art goes out of art galleries and into social life and urban public space, installation art begins to intervene in the expression of urban public art, which is artwork placed in an open space. This concept came into being with the urbanization process of the United States after World War II, emphasizing the application of works of art in public space. Public art is a comprehensive art form aiming at publicity, and it is a reflection of the contemporary cultural spirit and cultural concept. The concept expression and spatial presentation of installation art are extremely consistent with the expression needs of urban public art. Therefore, in early public art expression, art installation is one of the important performance types.

N. A. Streitz and S. Konomi (Eds.): HCII 2023, LNCS 14037, pp. 250–258, 2023.
https://doi.org/10.1007/978-3-031-34609-5_18

For example, the public artwork "The Knotted Gun" (Fig. 1), presented by Luxembourg to the United Nations Headquarters in 1988, expresses the good wish of abandoning war and yearning for a peaceful life with its intuitive modeling. This installation is placed in the garden of the headquarters of the United Nations, which is a very good place for the expression of public art. This installation of public art still plays an important role today. On April 19th, 2022, the Secretary General of the United Nations Guterres held a press conference in front of this sculpture, calling on Russia and Ukraine, which are at war, to implement a four-day temporary ceasefire on Orthodox Easter, so as to open the humanitarian corridor. The early public art installations mainly focus on sculpture and other physical devices. Their communication mode is similar to traditional easel painting, which focuses on viewing and communication. Although it also emphasizes spiritual and visual communication, the design concept of the works has not highlighted the interactive characteristics. The emergence of interactive device art, on the one hand, is the emergence of new technologies such as computers, which provide technical support for interaction. On the other hand, it is the influence of modern design concepts such as human-computer interaction. In this era, interactive installation works of art are also gradually born.

Fig. 1. The Knotted Gun

1.2 Modern Urban Public Art Needs Interactive Integration

With the continuous development of urbanization, the traditional viewing public artworks can no longer attract public, so many urban public squares and public space artworks are facing the problem of upgrading. How to better attract the public's attention and participation is a problem that needs to be solved in the development of urban public art. The emergence of interactive art installations has better solved this problem. With the development of new concepts and new technologies, especially the continuous development of digital new media technology and interactive design concepts, traditional art installation have also begun to develop in the direction of interaction. This interaction is also manifested in many types, such as mechanical interaction, immersive interaction, experiential interaction, and so on. The so-called mechanical interaction is an interaction that only relies on purely mechanical functions without the assistance of various sensors and other related technologies. This interaction seems to be relatively simple, but if carefully designed, it can still achieve very good artistic effects.

Fig. 2. Cloud Gate

For example, the famous public artwork "Cloud Gate" (Fig. 2) in the Qianxi Park of Chicago, USA, is a purely mechanical interactive work. The appearance of the work is a huge silver bean similar to traditional sculpture. However, the design concept of the work is not only the viewing effect, but also the interactive integration of the audience. The designer presents the mirror effect with high-brightness stainless steel on the surface. The work adopts an open design mode, allowing the audience to enter the interior of the work, participate in the interaction, and integrate into it. The audience can not only watch the reflection effect of various urban skyscrapers, but also feel the image interaction effect similar to the distorting mirror. Even when the audience looks down from the nearby tall building, they can see the gorgeous effect of this device reflecting the sky. Because of this super interactive design, this work has become one of the most popular public artworks in the world. Time described this work as a "tourist magnet" and became a representative work of public art in this city.

Fig. 3. Forest of Life & Future Park

Among the interactive installation, immersive interactive installation is also an important type. The immersive experience work "Forest of Life & Future Park" (Fig. 3) by the new media art group teamLab has made the immersive interactive image experience project popular all over the world. Through the use of digital interactive images in the huge immersive space, the audience can experience the interaction between virtual and real. Through the psychedelic image experience effect, the audience can feel the psychedelic effect of virtual space from hearing, touch, vision and other aspects. This kind of immersive public art experience project has spread to almost every large and medium-sized city, and has become an important type of urban public art. Interactive public installation includes participation and interaction, experience and interaction and other types. There are more and more such cases. For example, the work Cloud designed by Canadian artist Caitlin Brown is a "cloud" shaped installation composed of 6000 light bulbs (Fig. 4). When the work is placed on the square at night in a city, the audience can participate in it and light up any lamp he likes. Every interaction of the audience changes the display effect of the work. The final display effect of this work is not determined by the creator, but by the participation of the audience. With the development of new media technology, artificial intelligence and digital technology, more forms of interaction will emerge. Now, interactive images, virtual reality technology, interactive projection, interactive lighting, etc., have become the most commonly used means of interaction in modern interactive art installation. Interaction is the need of the development of modern urban public art, as well as the trend of its future development.

Fig. 4. Cloud.

1.3   New Demands of Interactive Installation and Urban Public Art

With the development of modern cities, more and more attention has been paid to the function seeking of public space. It is not only the pursuit of urban symbols, but also the exploration of function. In addition to the basic functions of leisure, sports and sightseeing, there are also cultural communication, public communication and humanistic care, etc. Public art is the embodiment of urban cultural spirit. In the past historical period, the design of many public artworks in the city has ignored the importance of audience experience, and many works are passively accepted by the audience. Such works are bound to be difficult to attract the participation of the public, and of course, such works cannot achieve the public value of gathering the masses. The design concept of modern interactive installations emphasizes that the design of the works is not only the works themselves, but also the need to integrate the audience into the works, so that the audience can become an important part of the works and form a complete public artwork together. For example, the French art installation "The Standing Man" (Fig. 5) was first exhibited during the Festival of Lights on Lyon in 2009. It has been exhibited in many public spaces and art festivals. The work uses a life-size human model with a standing posture as the prototype. When the audience embraces the model, the model will light up and change the color of the light, and it can also listen and talk. This installation work not only attracts the audience to participate, but also pays attention to humanistic care and public communication, making the work a window for urban cultural communication. The characteristics and design concepts of interactive installation are in line with the new demands of urban public art development for humanistic care and functional expansion. It is an important development type in the future urban public art.

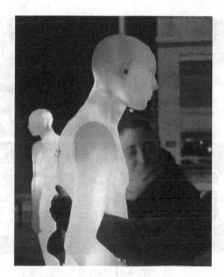

Fig. 5. The Standing Man

2   The Impact of Interactive Installation on Urban Public Art

2.1   Application of Interactive Installation in Urban Public Art

Contemporary urban public art has a wide range of applications. According to the application environment, it can be divided into indoor and outdoor. Outdoor public art can be subdivided into public square, landscape design, outdoor public space, etc. The indoor public domain can be subdivided into public cultural space, public entertainment space, public commercial space, etc. In these fields, we can see the application cases of interactive installation. Its interactive features have been fully utilized and developed in urban public art. For example, the music interactive staircase designed with sound interactive features has been widely used in many shopping malls, subways, museums and other public spaces. These seemingly simple music notes can make people feel a little care in the noisy environment and relieve their tension. There are also intelligent lighting works designed by taking advantage of lighting interaction features, which not only have functionality, but also have environmental protection, good experience and other characteristics. The sound, light and electricity characteristic value of interactive installation has been widely exploited in urban public art. For example, in a small park at the corner of a street, some traditional fitness equipment has been improved by adding counting and imaging effects. Then the sense of experience and participation has been improved. People who exercise can see the number of calories consumed, and children who play seesaw can experience the interactive effect of music and light emitted with exercise. There are more interactive swings, interactive walls, interactive lighting floors, etc. (Fig. 6). These cases fully illustrate that interactive installation have been widely used in various fields of urban public art.

Fig. 6. Figure 6

2.2   The Value of Interactive Installation in Urban Public Art

Interactive art installation are widely used in urban public art, which is determined by their unique value. First of all, its interactive features can attract people's participation more extensively. In public art, such works that can gather popularity are especially needed, since the value of public artworks can only be reflected with the broad participation of the public. Secondly, the application of various new technologies in interactive installation can break through the limitations of three-dimensional space in traditional installation. It can not only use sound, light, electricity and other tools, but also networks, artificial intelligence and other technologies to achieve four-dimensional or even five-dimensional space, and even related experience of virtual space. Moreover, it allows the interactive audience to control, so that they can easily participate in the interaction of the works, and even co-creation. For example, " Pokemon GO " is a game work (Fig. 7). After downloading this app with smartphones, the public can complete the game of catching virtual monsters in the city through the combination of augmented reality technology and real-time maps. This game realizes the combination of virtual space and public art through interactive games. Thirdly, the interactive installation is also a carrier of new media. The new technical means allow multiple media to combine with each other and integrate resources through the connection of digital new media and modern communication technology. With the support of big data, artificial intelligence, blockchain and other technologies, the realization of smart street lights, smart stations and other designs has not only been public artworks, but also achieved the relevant goals of smart cities.

Fig. 7. Figure 7

2.3   Application Significance of Interactive Installation in Urban Public Art

The interactive art installation is a great progress in the development of installation art. Their wide application in the field of urban public art has brought many changes to the development of urban public art. First of all, there is a huge change in the way of experience. From the traditional one-way expression mode dominated by viewing mode to the interactive, immersive and other multi-directional experience modes. For example, the American "Illuminarium Experience Museum" (Fig. 8), It adopts immersive empty design and can experience VR images with naked eyes.This change in the way of experience has also brought the public function of public artworks into better play. Secondly, the appearance of interactive installation makes the audience no longer just a spectator, but a co-participant and creator of the works, and an important part of the works. This design concept not only narrows the distance between the works and the audience, but also causes the audience's attention and self-reflection. This is difficult to complete for traditional public artworks. Thirdly, the interactive art installation is a kind of comprehensive art. They are not only the embodiment of the latest technological achievements, but also the embodiment of new design concepts and new design aesthetics. They have made new improvements in user experience and other aspects. Their application can improve the aesthetic level of the public. Moreover, the advanced design concepts of some works will affect the development of urban public art in the future.

Fig. 8. Illuminarium Experience Museum

Interactive installation has become an important type of expression of modern urban public art. The combination of interactive installation and urban public art is an inevitable result of the development of the times. Interactive installation not only bring new experiences to the audience, gather popularity, and strengthen public communication, but also meet the functional demands of urban cultural communication. Such works have been widely used in urban public art, which reflect their value and has an important impact on the development of urban public art in the future.

References

1. Feng, W.: Research on public art interaction in the context of new technology. J. Nanjing Acad. Arts (Art and Design Edition) (2010)
2. Lili, Z.: Time and Space View of Metro Public Art, Decoration (2011)
3. Feng, W., Weimin, G.: Research on the interactive connotation of digital city public art. Pack. Eng. (2010)
4. Chu, C.: From Site Innovation to Intervention in Social Public Life -- Fifty Years of "Creative Moment" of New York Public Art Institute. Art Watch (2022)

An Analysis of the Origin, Integration and Development of Contemporary Music Composition and Artificial Intelligence and Human-Computer Interaction

Xuanping Wu^(✉)

Department of Composition, Chinese Conservatory of Music, Shanghai, China
meetxuanping@gmail.com

Abstract. 1. Human-computer interaction has become the core concept of artificial intelligence, and the deep integration of music and artificial intelligence makes contemporary music creation including literature, philosophy, aesthetics, and big data research, etc. From the leading, forward-looking, integration, high-end, and anticipation all elaborate that the collaborative innovation and development of music and artificial intelligence will provide fruitful theoretical research results for the new cognition of the new era as well as human innovation and development.

2, until now through various signal capture so that more and more things as a medium to participate in electronic music composition, the way of music composition has become more rich and diversified than ever before. In the new era of artificial intelligence and human-computer interaction in the direction of contemporary music, especially electronic music composition tools like a dark horse, gradually more and more composers to recognize, accept and use in the actual composition.

3. In the field of serious music composition, in order to solve the problems of electronic music in terms of human vacancy and distance in terms of emotional communication with listeners, some composers began to try to combine electronic music with live instrumental music.

4. Entering the second decade of the twenty-first century, the popularity of mobile intelligent terminals, such as smartphones and tablet computers, has brought new developments in human-computer interaction in music composition.

5, artificial intelligence and human-computer interaction in the field of music composition on the application, so with the discipline of computer science development, along the regular and reasonable direction of the rising dimension.

6, music artificial intelligence has been deeply developed.

Keyword: Disciplinary connotations of music composition · Artificial intelligence · Human-computer interaction · Fusion

1 Preface

With the rapid development of computer technology and the gradual popularization of artificial intelligence, information technology has penetrated into all aspects of the culture and art industry chain, and the integration of technology and art will promote the

N. A. Streitz and S. Konomi (Eds.): HCII 2023, LNCS 14037, pp. 259–268, 2023.
https://doi.org/10.1007/978-3-031-34609-5_19

connotative development of artificial intelligence. Human-computer interaction, which involves the intersection of many disciplines such as computer science, behavioral science, design and media research, ultimately achieves the goal of enhancing the user's experience in the process of using a computer. Embedded in the complex material world with information technology as the center, human-computer interaction becomes the core concept of artificial intelligence. The deep integration of music and artificial intelligence in the disciplinary connotation system of music composition makes contemporary music composition include literature, philosophy, aesthetics, and big data research, etc. From the leading, forward-looking, integration, high-end, and anticipation all elaborate that the synergistic innovation development of music and artificial intelligence will have a new impact on the new era of new cognition as well as the development of human innovation by providing fruitful theoretical research results. It not only has a broad development space in the field of technical research, but also has a broad development prospect in technology promotion and market application.

2 Introduction

In recent years, the term Music AI has emerged in the field of music and computing. Music AI is a general and slightly vague concept that can be seen as a direct application of artificial intelligence in the field of music. It includes direct music generation, music content processing, music melody and rhythm analysis, information retrieval MIR (with dozens of applications), and all other music-related applications involving AI such as intelligent music analysis, intelligent music education, score following, intelligent mixing, music robotics, music therapy based on intelligent recommendations, picture and video scoring, and other applications. Music AI is part of Music Technology.

According to Wikipedia the definition of HCI is "Human-computer interaction (HCI) is research in the design and the use of computer technology, which focuses on the interfaces between people (users) and computers " The early medium of HCI was the monitor keyboard. The operator entered commands through the keyboard, and the operating system received the commands, executed them, and responded with the results on the monitor. With the development of computer technology, there are more and more commands and more functions, and human-computer interaction through images has become possible, and people have entered the era of intelligent human-computer interaction.

3 Origin

As early as the early eleventh century, composers found alternative possibilities for musical composition in mathematical logic. Guido d'Arezzo (995–1050), an Italian Benedictine monk and educator of musical practice, pioneered the theory of the six-note scale, which was the earliest model of pitch. By the Baroque period, the control of mathematical logic over music gradually expanded from pitch to rhythm, melody, and vocal counterpoint. This period is represented by polyphonic music, which is the result of the constant change and development of the strict counterpoint of a particular theme, and which provided a logical basis for the later use and development of material in contemporary music and electronic music today.

In the twentieth century, Arnold Schönberg (1874–1951) pioneered and applied the "twelve-tone sequence" system. After nearly a decade of experimentation, Schönberg published his first work composed entirely in the twelve-tone technique, *Suite for Piano Op. 25*, in 1923, completing the construction of a strict technical system for composing twelve-tone music (Fig. 1).

Fig. 1. Arnold Schoenberg (September 13, 1874–July 13, 1951)

WEbern's (1883–1945) "Integral Sequentialism" took mathematical logic to a new level of imaging for musical composition. In his *variations for piano, for* example, the music is completely controlled by a pre-designed sequence of numbers, and in particular, the "Integral Sequentialism" is completely free from the control of the traditional logic of musical development, making mathematical logic the most important influencing factor (Fig. 2).

After World War II, the term "concrete music", originated in France by Pierre Schaeffer in 1948, and his work *Étude aux chemins de* fer for the first time systematically and disciplinarily extended the medium of human-composed music from instruments to tapes, recording devices, and sound machines. In 1954, Stockhausen's work *Studie was the* first time that this real sense of human-computer interaction was published in the form of a score, and human-computer interaction was formally introduced into the field of music composition (FIg. 3).

4   Fusion

Human-computer interaction is the study of people, computer technology and the way they interact with each other. The late 1960s saw the gradual rise of computer music as Moore's Law created affordable music technology, and today more and more things are

Fig. 2. Anton Webern (December 3, 1883–September 15, 1945)

Fig. 3. Karlheinz Stockhausen (August 22, 1928–December 5, 2007)

involved in electronic music creation through various signal capturing mediums, and the ways of music creation have become richer and more diverse than ever before. In this new era, artificial intelligence and human-computer interaction are like a dark horse in the direction of contemporary music, especially in electronic music composition tools, which are gradually recognized, accepted and used by more and more composers in actual composition.

But at the same time, as with other new problems in the humanities and arts, the involvement of artificial intelligence somehow distances the emotions conveyed in music from the actual emotions of the listener. In the current mainstream view, it is still not possible for AI to completely replace human composers. But this does not prevent music AI from developing as a practical, contemporary and richly expandable way of composing electronic music. Artists can now also personalize their work by creating personalized software synthesizers, effects modules and various compositional environments.

After the 1970s, large computer music research institutions were established in various countries, such as IRCAM in Paris, France, and CCRMA at Stanford University, USA, and computer music entered a period of rapid development. With the improvement of computer's ability to analyze music, people's understanding of the nature of sound gradually increased. The French composers, represented by Tristan Murail and Gerard Grisey, created the "Musique spectrale". Grisey's *Partiels are* considered to be the first spectral music works. Since its inception, spectral music has become one of the major genres of contemporary music composition, spanning three generations of composers and a wide range of styles (Fig. 4).

Fig. 4. Gerard Grisey (17 June 1946–11 November 1998)

The emergence of spectral music cannot be separated from the ability of computers to analyze audio. In the field of serious music, software tools such as OpenMusic, an application written as a starting point for the French Institut de recherche et coordination acoustique/musique (IRCAM) spectral composition technique, have been gradually developed. It uses programming logic to systematically generate the elements of music in the form of score fragments or graphic displays. With these materials, the composer can easily, effectively and humanely compose in a spectral, algorithmic or traditional way, based on and referring to them (Fig. 5).

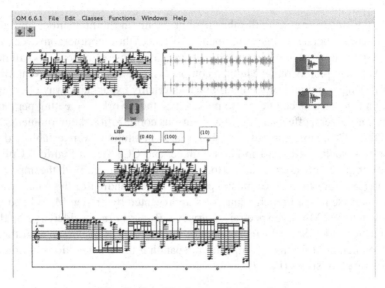

Fig. 5. OpenMusic operation interface

In the field of serious music composition, in order to solve the problems of electronic music in terms of humanistic vacancy and distance in terms of emotional communication with listeners, some composers have started to try to combine electronic music with live instrumental performance. This attempt has been repeatedly employed since the concept of serious electronic music was systematically and theoretically formed, and has become an effective means of bringing the rational, mathematical and logical electronic music closer to the sensual humanistic music.

For example, in Finnish composer Kaija Saariaho's *Verblendungen* for orchestra and computer tape, a live orchestra is synchronized with pre-produced electronic music under the guidance of a conductor. This approach preserves the human touch of the live orchestra and the sensual timbre of the instruments, while adding a new sound to the music that was not previously present, creating a surprisingly new sound and blend of timbres (Fig. 6).

Today, human-computer interaction in electronic music has long evolved from simple human interaction with recording devices to human interaction with computer devices. With the miniaturization and marketization of computers, more and more music production host platforms, such as Logic and Cubase, have started to emerge, which makes electronic music production more and more accessible, and the learning and hardware costs of human-computer interaction to create music are greatly reduced.

At the same time, human-computer interaction has become much closer. From simply people using computers to make sounds, to combining the sounds made using computers with the sounds played by people, to artificial intelligence joining the music production

VERBLENDUNGEN

Kaija Saariaho

Fig. 6. Kaija Saariaho Verblendungen for Orchestra and Computer Tape score example

host platform, massive resources and algorithms can turn music production into a few simple buttons. The Drummer feature in Apple's easy-to-use music production software GarageBand, for example, makes music production at your fingertips with simple operation and intelligent collage of material. These advances have not only promoted the popularity of computer music to replace traditional instrumentation as the main vehicle for popular music, but also brought the field of music creation involving artificial intelligence into the public eye and made it more widely known (FIg. 7).

Fig. 7. The "Drummer" function in GarageBand

5   Development

Entering the second decade of the 21st century, social networking platforms such as Tik-Tok, SnapChat and Instagram gradually realized the importance of modeling, simplifying and reducing the operational difficulty of audio and video editing in their video dissemination process. This is the need to rely on artificial intelligence and human interaction, through big data analysis so that the system can automatically analyze the structure of music, music representation, extraction of sound melody highlights, as music tags, rhythmic melody for short video dissemination greatly reduce operational learning and production time costs.

For example, SpecTNT is a deep interactive learning model designed for music spectrum extraction. Used for batch recognition of music clips in video editing, it can make the effect of intelligent extension more natural, helping creators to extend or shorten the length of music at will to achieve better matching of audio and visual images.

Avia, an AI that takes an input database of existing music and builds a mathematical model around it to create completely original music, goes a step further than the previously mentioned applications and software platforms by taking the computer's ability to process music to Algorithmic Composition, which no longer requires too much human involvement, but only a specific library of tracks to be selected for it. It no longer requires too much human involvement, but simply selects a specific repertoire and learns from it to create new compositions that are similar in style but not just imitations.

Using deep learning techniques, Aiva reads through the text provided by Mozart Aiva has built a mathematical model that reflects its understanding of music. Mathematical model Aiva then uses the models to create completely original compositions. And Aiva can also create personalized tunes based on the type of music entered into the database. For example, if one wants to compose a movie music At the opening of the 2017 NVIDIA GPU Technology Conference, Avia's compositions were used to promote NVIDIA's products and are now at the level of normal commercial commercial music (Fig. 8).

Fig. 8. Avignon symphonic orchestra plays *Symphonic Fantasy in A minor, Op. 24, "I am A.I."* composed by AVIA

6   Outlook

The application of artificial intelligence and human-computer interaction in the field of music composition is thus rising in dimension along with the disciplinary development of computer science in a regular and rational direction. Various intelligent means make the application know more about music and understand it better. The analysis of the content structure of the music itself and the analysis of the chords of the massive music MIDI provide the preconditions for the interactive automatic composing system, which helps the interactive music to create large-scale, high-quality chordal music fragments that are more in line with the public's favorite. This follows the laws of technological development and reflects the important values of human cognition, innovative development and collaborative communication. If the previous generation of AI is called computer intelligence, and arithmetic power, algorithms and data are its hard core, then the new generation of AI is the interactive machine intelligence that has perception, cognition, behavior, learning and growth, and interaction, learning and memory are its hard core. If consciousness, desire, emotion and character are more reflective of human evolution from reptiles to mammals hundreds of millions of years ago, reflected in the brainstem and limbic system, then intelligence is mainly reflected in the unique perception, spatial reasoning and other neocortex that has evolved in the human brain over millions of years.

Looking ahead, music artificial intelligence has been deeply developed. Composition, accompaniment, improvisation, virtual reality, robot conductor, robot performance, robot singing, artificial intelligence in music creation will also appear more new forms of applications will be more popular, with the development of society, and the overall aesthetic improvement of the public, the professional field of creation and the public level barriers or will gradually narrow, and its application will become more and more popular.

References

1. ISMIR 2021 Paper "SpecTNT: a Time-Frequency Transformer for Music Audio"
2. ISMIR 2021 Paper "Semi-supervised Music Tagging Transformer"
3. Kaija Saariaho Verblendungen for Orchestra and Computer Tape

Research on the Application of the Ming Dynasty Clothing Element "ShiDiKe" in Home Fabric Design

Wei Wu[✉]

Ji Nan University, No. 336, Nanxinzhuang West Road, Jinan, Shandong, China
Soa_wuw@ujn.edu.cn

Abstract. The "ShiDiKe" element in clothing prevailed in the Ming Dynasty. This paper takes the Ming Dynasty costume element "ShiDiKe" as the research object, and analyzes the shape, structure, type, and craft of the "ShiDiKe" element from the perspectives of objects, images, and literature. Summarize the elemental characteristics of the Ming Dynasty clothing "ShiDiKe", and discuss its application in modern home fabric design.

Keywords: Costumes of the Ming Dynasty · "ShiDiKe" · Home fabric design · Applied research

1 Introduction

Traditional culture has become the core force for the rapid development of the cultural economy industry, and traditional patterns, as typical of Chinese traditional culture, have extremely high application value. Patterns are attached to the main body of their decoration, which not only has a certain functional basis, but also sometimes has certain symbolic meaning and aesthetic value. The persimmon pedicle pattern [1] is one of the earliest traditional patterns in our country, and its basic shape can be traced back to the Neolithic Age. It can be seen from many literatures and the *Dictionary of Chinese Arts and Crafts*" that there are persimmon pedicle pattern on bronze mirrors from the Spring and Autumn Period to the Han Dynasty, and persimmon pedicle pattern on silk fabrics in the Tang Dynasty, and "**ShiDiKe**"[1] on silk fabrics in the Yuan, Ming and Qing Dynasties. They all have changeable shapes and rich cultural connotations, and have extremely high artistic value. Most of the persimmon pedicle pattern are four-lobed leaves, and the shape of the leaves develops from a simple geometric shape to a complex and realistic shape. The connotation ranges from nature worship to auspicious meaning. The rich shapes and connotations of "ShiDiKe" provide the basis for the wide application of modern design.

---

[1] The evolution of persimmon pattern.

2 Overview of the "Shi Di Ke" in Ming Dynasty Clothing

"Persimmon pedicle pattern" is named for its resemblance to a persimmon pedicle. The basic shape is a cross-shaped structure with a rounded head and tail. It also has other names such as "four-leaf pattern", "square pattern" and "Hou Wen". The "Persimmon pedicle pattern" can be traced back to the Warring States period, and became popular during the Han and Tang dynasties. In the Han Dynasty, it was popular in a large number of hard materials such as bronze mirrors, lacquerware, gold and silverware, and coffin lids in the form of independent patterns. In the Tang Dynasty, it was popular in textiles in the form of continuous squares, and silk such as "Persimmon pedicle silk" was popular. During the Han Dynasty, the shape of "persimmon pedicle pattern" was rich and varied. It deviated from the original "persimmon pedicle" fabric shape and evolved into many exaggerated forms. At the same time, the form of filling other patterns inside the "persimmon pedicle pattern" began to appear, and the prototype of "ShiDiKe" began to appear. The operating position of "persimmon pedicle pattern" in the center of the object is similar to that in Ming Dynasty clothing. Developed to the Song Dynasty, the decorative carriers of "persimmon pedicle pattern" were mainly buildings, porcelain, and textiles, and the application of the original single form of "persimmon pedicle pattern" gradually decreased. In the Yuan Dynasty, "ShiDiKe" were usually decorated around the neckline of clothing, and the four petals were decorated on the chest, back, and shoulders. This form of decoration continued into the Ming and Qing Dynasties. It was the most popular in the Ming Dynasty and became a fixed style in official uniforms. In the Ming Dynasty, "ShiDiKe" evolved rich shapes, structures, and types in terms of shapes, and their symbolic meanings were also extended.

"ShiDiKe" gradually evolved from "persimmon pedicle pattern" in the historical development. It is a suitable pattern with both persimmon stalk-shaped frame and filling patterns, also known as "persimmon pedicle shape". The "ShiDiKe" in the Ming Dynasty is reflected in fabrics, clothing, architecture, porcelain, murals, and picture scrolls, especially in fabrics and clothing, and has formed a high degree of style.

From the Warring States Period to the Ming and Qing Dynasties, during the development process from "persimmon pedicle pattern" to "ShiDiKe", there was a phenomenon of transition from the form of plant pattern and geometric pattern to the complex form of both frame and filling patterns. It shows a path of change from simple to complex, and this complex form reached its peak in the Ming Dynasty and appeared in large numbers in official uniforms. Therefore, we will focus on the "ShiDiKe" in the official uniforms of the Ming Dynasty. The study is carried out from the decorative relationship between the frame structure and the filling pattern in the "ShiDiKe", and the relationship between the persimmon pedicle and the shape of clothing. Because "persimmon" and "thing" have the same pronunciation in chinese, it means everything goes well, everything is safe, and everything is auspicious. Therefore, the persimmon pattern in traditional Chinese auspicious patterns is very popular among people.

In the global context of "cultural awareness" and "localization", hot entries such as "Chinese style", "national trend" and "Hanfu craze" appear frequently. The inheritance and development of traditional culture has become a topic of great concern in the design industry. Cultural and creative industries and fashion industries based on the concept of revival of traditional clothing are gradually emerging in domestic and foreign markets.

Designers take traditional clothing culture as a source of inspiration, and mainly form the redesign of traditional clothing styles, patterns, and colors.

3   The Clothing Element of the Ming Dynasty "ShiDiKe"

In the development and evolution of "persimmon stalk pattern" to "ShiDiKe", it can be seen that the pattern changes in a large span, and the pattern shape changes from simple to complex. In the Ming Dynasty, "ShiDiKe" reached its peak of development and evolved into rich and varied forms. This paper starts from the case study of "ShiDiKe" in Ming Dynasty clothing, and focuses on the analysis of the shape, structure, type, technology and other contents of "ShiDiKe". Based on the in-depth analysis of the pattern of "ShiDiKe", the decorative and aesthetic characteristics of the "ShiDiKe" elements in Ming Dynasty clothing are discussed.

3.1   Shape Change

The basic shape of "persimmon pedicle pattern" is "one point and two bends". From the early development of "persimmon pedicle pattern" to the Ming Dynasty, great changes have taken place in the filling pattern and the shape frame, and the basic shape of "one point and two bends" has been broken. Comparing and studying the appearance of the early "persimmon pedicle pattern" and the "ShiDiKe" before the Ming Dynasty, the changes in the appearance of the "ShiDiKe" in Ming Dynasty clothing mainly include the following three changes:

1) The tip of the four petals gradually becomes rounded. The "persimmon pedicle pattern" in the Han Dynasty has the characteristics of "one tip and two bends". In the Song Dynasty, the four petals gradually disappeared, and the petal shape tended to be smooth. According to the records of *"Creating French Patterns"* [2], the pattern of "ShiDiKe" that has been erased and pointed out frequently appears in architectural

Fig. 1. *Tuan ke Shi Di* (Quoted from the first part of *"Ying Zao Fa Shi"* by Chen Tong)

color paintings (Fig. 1). In the clothing of the Ming Dynasty, there are a large number of "ShiDiKe" with rounded petals without cusps, and "ShiDiKe" with cusps are also more rounded (see Fig. 2).

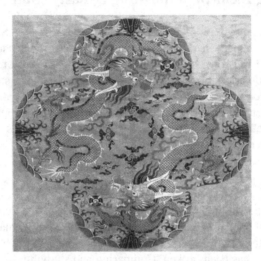

Fig. 2. *Ming Huang Zhi Jin Mang Wen Pao* (quoted from *"Chinese Dragon Robe"* written by Huang Nengfu and Chen Juanjuan)

2) The shape of the valve leaflets has the characteristics of "multi-curvature". The "multi-bend" phenomenon of the shape of the leaflets has appeared in the architectural paintings and fabrics before the Song Dynasty. In the Yuan Dynasty, the popular petal leaf was the "multi-curved" shape of Ruyi head (Fig. 1). Influenced by the shape of "ShiDiKe" in the Yuan Dynasty, the shape of "ShiDiKe" with a wire frame of Ruyi heads was popular in the Ming Dynasty. The petals of the "ShiDiKe" in the blouses with golden yarn and phoenix patterns in the green area of the Confucian Mansion are composed of "four big and one small" Ruyi heads (Fig. 3).

Fig. 3. *Lv Di Jin Sha Feng Wen Duan Shan* (Confucius Museum Collection)

3) The shape of "ShiDiKe" presents three states: closed, semi-closed and boundless. The four sides of the closed "ShiDiKe" are closed and there are no gaps. Most of the openings and closings of the semi-closed "ShiDiKe" shape are near the rotator cuff, and the distance between openings and closings is relatively small. There is no persimmon frame in the shape of the boundless "ShiDiKe", and the filling pattern is in the invisible frame (see Table 1).

Table 1. Legend table of the three shapes of the "ShiDiKe" costume in the Ming Dynasty

appearance	legend	analyze	Product name and source
Closed shape			*Dark green Zhuang Hua Sha Yun Jian Tong Xiu Xi Lan Mang Pao,* Confucius Museum
semi-closed			*Da Hong Se Chou Xiu Guo Jian Qi Lin Luan Feng Wen Nv Pao,* Shandong Museum
borderless			*Dark Brown Zhi Jin Mang Zhuang Hua Sha Dao Pao,* Shandong Museum

3.2 Structural Analysis

The structural feature of the "ShiDiKe" is a combination of a persimmon-shaped frame and a filling pattern. The filled pattern is suitable for the persimmon-shaped frame, and the two parts are harmonious and orderly in combination. The structure of the pattern is the composition and operating position of the formation of the fingerprint.

The appearance structure of "ShiDiKe" is a "cross-shaped" structure, most of the graphic structures are symmetrical, and a few are balanced. According to the classification method of disc-shaped cluster flowers in *History of Ancient Chinese Dyeing and Weaving Patterns*" [3], the symmetrical structure of "ShiDiKe" is divided into central symmetry and axial symmetry, and the balanced structure is called balanced structure. Central symmetry means that one figure can coincide with another figure after rotating 180° around the center point. Axisymmetric means that the graphics are folded in half along a line at the center point, and the graphics on both sides can overlap. A balanced structure means that there is no strict axis of symmetry, and it is usually divided by an S-shaped or swirl-shaped curve at the center point. At present, there are four styles of "ShiDiKe" structures in traditional clothing of the Ming Dynasty: absolute central symmetry, relative central symmetry, relative axis symmetry, and balanced.

1) **Absolute central symmetry**

The centrally symmetrical "ShiDiKe" usually appears on the "persimmon stalk over the shoulder" style. The two main patterns are connected from the chest to the back, from the back to the chest, end to end, and are composed of two parts of the same figure to form a whole. This type of structure is similar to the Taiji diagram, which belongs to the "happy meeting" structure of traditional Chinese patterns. In the red gauze four-beast robes collected by the Confucian Mansion, four unicorns are distributed in the four-petal area of the "ShiDiKe". The direction of the main body is unified in a counterclockwise direction. Two beasts are distributed on both sides of the unicorn. The patterns are filled with different colors, but the overall pattern structure is absolutely symmetrical.

2) **relative central symmetry**

The relatively centrally symmetrical "ShiDiKe" structure refers to the centrally symmetrical structure of the pattern as a whole, but it is not absolutely symmetrical. There are certain deviations in area, volume, direction, distribution position, etc., and this type of structure is called a relative center symmetric structure. Its characteristic is that the pattern is not completely symmetrical, but it feels stable and balanced in the overall vision.

3) **relative axis symmetry**

Axisymmetric structure is "the simplest form in the aesthetic principles of symmetrical form. Because the visual factors on both sides of the symmetrical axis are equal, the graphics are stable, and it is easy to give people a smooth and comfortable visual enjoyment. [4]" The relatively axisymmetric "ShiDiKe" structure refers to the overall axisymmetric structure of the pattern, but it is not absolutely symmetrical, and there are certain deviations in shape, volume, direction, distribution position, etc. In the axisymmetric structure "ShiDiKe" of Ming Dynasty clothing, almost all of them are vertical axis symmetric structures (Table 2).

4) **Balanced**

The balanced structure in "Shi Di Ke" is mostly in the form of a neckline coiling around the main pattern, and there are fewer examples of such patterns than the above three structure examples. This kind of balanced structure often appears in the borderless "persimmon nest", such as the yellow brocade robe with four-clawed dragon pattern and the bright yellow satin robe with golden cloud and dragon pattern in the collection of Jiangxi Museum. The "persimmon nests" in these two cultural relics are both borderless. The pattern distribution is characterized by a main pattern spanning both shoulders and the back, coiling around the neckline for a week, the main pattern is larger in size, majestic and majestic.

Table 2. Structural classification table of "ShiDiKe"

structure			legend	structural analysis	Structural features	product name	source
symmetrical structure	Centrosymmetric	absolute central symmetry			The upper left and lower right parts of the pattern are completely symmetrical in the center	*Ming Huang Di Ke Si Da Ji Hu Lu Guo Jian Long Pao Liao*	Former Collection of Confucian Mansion, Collection of Shandong Museum
		relative central symmetry			The upper left and lower right parts of the pattern are not completely symmetrical in the center, and there are small changes in the direction, details, and position of the pattern, and the overall vision is centrally symmetrical	*Lv Zhi Jin Zhuang Hua Tong Xiu Guo Jian Long Shi Di Duan Li Ling Nv Jia Yi*	Private Collection, He Qisi Collection
balanced structure	Axisymmetric	relative axisymmetric			The left and right parts of the pattern are axisymmetric in the overall vision, and there are small changes in the direction, details, and position of the pattern	*Lv Zhi Jin Zhuang Hua Tong Xiu Guo Jian Long Shi Di Duan Li Ling Nv Jia Yi*	Excavated from Dingling Mausoleum, collected by Ming Tombs Museum
		balanced			There is no strict axis of symmetry, and the decorative area is divided by curves	*Zhi Jin Guo Jian Mang Wen Pao*	Unearthed from the Tomb of King Yixuan in Nanchang, Jiangxi, "Ming Dynasty Court Embroidery" P252

3.3 Type Analysis

The dyeing and weaving patterns of the Ming Dynasty were further enriched and perfected on the basis of the patterns of the Song and Yuan Dynasties. In the Ming Dynasty, "folk culture prospered, and the scope of pattern themes expanded rapidly. Many utensil patterns, natural astronomical patterns, etc. that did not appear in the Song and Yuan

Dynasties or were rarely seen also became popular patterns. [5]" Influenced by the etiquette system at that time, the traditional clothing patterns of the Ming Dynasty formed hierarchical patterns such as twelve chapters, dragons, animals, and complements. The pattern types of the traditional clothing "ShiDiKe" in the Ming Dynasty are mainly composed of two parts: the outer frame border pattern and the inner filling pattern.

1) Outer frame border pattern

The main research objects are closed and semi-closed shapes of "ShiDiKe" in Ming Dynasty clothing. Seawater river cliff patterns, seawater patterns, and ruyitou line frames are the main part of the border decoration patterns, followed by miscellaneous treasure patterns, flower patterns, mountain stone patterns, etc. as auxiliary patterns. The outer frame of "ShiDiKe" is mainly composed of four types of patterns: seawater river cliff pattern, seawater pattern, ruyi head line frame, and auxiliary patterns. According to the combination form of the pattern content, the outer frame and border patterns of "ShiDiKe" have the following combination forms: seawater river cliff pattern, seawater river cliff pattern + auxiliary pattern, seawater river cliff pattern + ruyi head line frame + auxiliary pattern (Fig. 4).

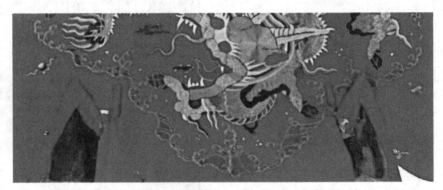

Fig. 4. Sea water pattern + auxiliary pattern(Part of *Da Hong Se Chou Xiu Guo Jian Qi Lin Luan Feng Wen Nv Pao*, Shandong Museum Collection)

2) Patterns inside the "ShiDiKe"

The internal patterns of "ShiDiKe" are mainly main patterns and auxiliary patterns. The main pattern is usually animal pattern, and occasionally there will be a character scene pattern as the main pattern of the scene, and there are many kinds of auxiliary patterns, including small animal patterns, cloud patterns, miscellaneous treasure patterns, flower patterns, character patterns, etc.

3.4 Process Analysis

Weaving, printing and dyeing technology developed to the Ming Dynasty, and various technologies have accumulated rich experience, and the technology has been continuously improved and perfected, among which the flower weaving technology is highly developed. The craftsmanship of "ShiDiKe" is mainly presented in three categories: dyeing, weaving and embroidery.

1) Eyd

The printing and dyeing industry in the Ming Dynasty has become mature in terms of fuel production and dyeing technology. The technique of painting and forming lines was still used in the Ming Dynasty, but it was not used much. The patterns in *Lv Chou Hua Yun Mang Wen Pao* in the old collection of the Confucian Mansion were painted by means of color painting. The color blocks in the gowns are smooth and the details are exquisite (Fig. 5). This method of drawing and painting has the characteristics of "saving labor, low cost, and the exquisite decoration is not inferior to weaving and embroidery. [6]".

Fig. 5. *Lv Chou Hua Yun Mang Wen Pao* (Confucian Collection)

2) Weaving

The weaving industry was developed in the Ming Dynasty, and the manufacturing process of "ShiDiKe" element in the Ming Dynasty clothing mainly included three categories: makeup flower, weaving gold and Kesi silk, among which makeup flower fabric was especially prominent in the Ming Dynasty. Ming Dynasty clothing woven material, are also made of makeup flower technology.

Makeup flowers: "Absorb the weaving technique of weaving Kesi through warp and breaking weft to wind colored wool weft tubes of different colors to make local makeup colors on fabrics such as silk, satin, yarn, cotton and silk, and weave various patterns, which changed the obvious defects of changing colors and color stripes in brocade weaving in the past" [7]. Makeup flower first appeared in the Ming Dynasty *"Tianshui Bergs Record"* [8], applied to all kinds of fabrics, known as makeup satin, makeup flower Luo, makeup flower silk, makeup flower ground, etc., decorative patterns with the color of the faint method, bright colors, coordination. For example, *the Lan Sha Zhi An Hua Zhuang Hua Mang Yi* in the Confucius Museum, the dark yarn makeup on the ground woven "ShiDiKe", the warp between the two flowers are the same, the color weft interwoven, the weaving is fine, and the color is gorgeous (see Fig. 6).

Fig. 6. *The Lan Sha Zhi An Hua Zhuang Hua Mang Yi* (Confucian Collection)

Weaving gold was developed on the basis of the gold weaving craft in the Yuan Dynasty. The gold weaving process is to weave gold threads into the fabric. The gold weaving method includes sheet gold and twisted gold. Sheet gold is also called flat gold, and twisted gold is also called round gold. "Plate gold is to beat gold into gold foil, paste it on thin leather or cotton paper and cut it into gold thread for weaving; twisted gold is to wrap gold sheet on the outside of silk thread and twist it to form gold thread. [9]" In the traditional costumes of the Ming Dynasty, both sheet gold and twisted gold were used. The "ShiDiKe" is woven with gold as a whole, and its weaving details are shown (Fig. 7 and 8). Weaving gold and makeup flowers are also often used in combination. For example, in the collection of the Palace Museum in Beijing, *the Da Hong Luo Di Zhi Jin Zhuang Hua Mang Pao*, the borders of the "ShiDiKe" and the borders of the patterns are outlined with gold threads, and the inside of the gold threads is woven with Zhanghua craftsmanship, making the whole rich and harmonious.

Kesi, that is, the weaving method of "passing the warp and breaking the weft", the longitudinal warp thread runs through the entire width of the fabric, and the horizontal weft thread only interweaves with the warp thread according to the pattern, and does not penetrate the entire width. "Let some small holes and broken marks appear between the pattern and the plain ground, between the color and the color, 'the image of carving in the concept of Chengkong. [10]" Kesi technology was further improved in the Ming Dynasty, and it was mainly used for official clothes. Among the elements of "ShiDiKe"

Fig.7. *Lv Se Zhi Jin Feng Sha Nv Pao* piece of gold wire (Collection of Shandong Museum)

Fig. 8. *Cong Lv Di Zhuang Hua Sha Mang Qun* round gold wire (Collection of Confucius Museum)

is a typical red Kesi ShiDiKe from the late Ming Dynasty with Yunlong and Jinshou characters. It is finely crafted and has various Kesi techniques.

3) embroidery

Embroidery flourished unprecedentedly in the Ming Dynasty. From court embroidery to folk embroidery workshops, embroidery craftsmanship was very popular. Embroidery in the Ming Dynasty created some new embroidery methods, such as sprinkled thread embroidery and large-area nail embroidery in "ShiDiKe". Many elements of

"ShiDiKe" are combined by different stitches to form rich and diverse embroidery texture. In "ShiDiKe", there are embroidery methods such as sprinkled thread embroidery, panjin embroidery, flat gold embroidery, appliqué embroidery, Na embroidery, and velvet paving embroidery, among which sprinkled thread embroidery and panjin embroidery are the most common.

Sprinkling embroidery is the most novel and outstanding embroidery in Ming Dynasty. Sprinkling embroidery was first seen in "Record of Tianshui Icebergs". It is a kind of Jing embroidery, which takes square eye yarn as the ground and embroidered with colorful silk twisting yarn. The embroidery articles are characterized by bright colors and strong contrast. Taking Ming Wanli's bright yellow satin embroidered Golden Dragon flower pattern Jifu robe material as an example, "ShiDiKe" takes sprinkling embroidery as the main embroidery method, integrating a variety of techniques, such as leveling stitch, seed stitch, cross stitch, stitch joint, stitch stitch, net stitch and plain gold embroidery.

Pan gold embroidery, also known as "plain gold embroidery", is made by twisting gold and silver threads in a single or double circular row according to the painting manuscript, and then nailed with various kinds of silk threads. Another method of embroidery is to stitch the outer outline of the pattern with gold threads and leave a space in the middle, which is called "circle gold". For example, the blue compass gold embroidery boa robe in the old collection of Kong Fu is mainly embroidered with plain gold embroidery, nailed thread embroidery and plain embroidery (as shown in Fig. 9). Python head and body are made of plain gold embroidery, python horn, eyebrow hair, dragon ball flame are "circle gold".

Fig. 9. *Lan Luo Jin Xiu Mang Pao* (Quoted from Xu Xiao's *"Research on Ming Dynasty Costumes in the Confucian Mansion Collection"*)

Through the analysis and research of the shape, structure, pattern types and crafts of the "ShiDiKe" in the traditional clothing of the Ming Dynasty, we can see that the clothing styles of the Ming Dynasty are divided into several categories: robes, clothes, shirts, skirts, and trousers. According to the research on the actual objects, the elements of "ShiDiKe" appear concentratedly in the two types of clothing styles, namely robes and clothes. From the point of view of the decorative parts, the "ShiDiKe" is centered on the neckline and distributed in a "cross shape" on the front chest, back and shoulders.

The structure of traditional Chinese clothing is usually a "cross-shaped plane structure", which is a fixed style. For example, the reconstructed structural diagram of the old Confucian blue ground-painted boa garment, the body and the two sleeves are in the shape of a "cross". The decorative part of "ShiDiKe" is in the center of the whole garment, and the four petals face all directions. The length of the two halves of the front chest and the back reaches the waist position, and the length of the two petals of the two sleeves reaches the middle position of the sleeves. The main decorative combinations of "ShiDiKe" in Ming Dynasty clothing can be summarized into three styles: "single persimmon stalks", "persimmon stalks with sleeves", and "persimmon stalks with sleeves and knees". The "single persimmon stalk" style refers to the decoration of a single "ShiDiKe" around the neckline of clothing, and there are few existing verifiable objects. The style of "persimmon stem sleeves" means that on the outside of the "ShiDiKe", a lace pattern from the shoulder to the cuff is decorated on the upper part of the two sleeves. The main pattern of the two sleeves is consistent with the main pattern inside the "ShiDiKe", which is very common. It often appears in both robes and clothing styles, as shown in the figure in the old collection of the Confucian Mansion, the bright red flying fish pattern makeup flower gauze women's gown (Fig. 10). The style of "persimmon stalks with sleeves and knees" is a combination of decorations on the neckline, the top of the sleeves, and the knees. It is common in robes, such as the fragrant-colored hemp flying fish clothing in the old collection of the Confucian Mansion. The content of the patterns on the sleeves and knees echoes the "ShiDiKe". These three types of combined forms were adorned in various shapes of robes and jackets in the Ming Dynasty.

Fig. 10. *Ming Da Hong Se Fei Yu Zhaung Hua Sha Nv Chang Shan* (Shandong Museum Collection)

Ming Dynasty costumes decorated with "ShiDiKe" were usually worn by high-ranking people such as emperors, clans, and powerful officials. Therefore, we can see its majesty and sense of order as a "ritual prestige" from many aspects such as pattern decoration, visual effects, and subject expression. As a complex suitable pattern, "ShiDiKe" embodies the suitable beauty of the pattern. Its suitable form in clothing reflects the suitable order of patterns suitable for clothing, and highlights the beauty of double suitable beauty of patterns. The frame structure and filling pattern of "ShiDiKe" are harmonious and unified, and the fusion of multi-level symbolic meanings such as auspiciousness, harmony between man and nature, center of the universe, stability of the country, and prosperity of descendants reflects the harmonious beauty. The "ShiDiKe" contains a variety of structural forms in the "ten" structure, forming a dynamic aesthetic feeling in the trend and interweaving of the structure. "ShiDiKe" embodies the aesthetic value of harmony and beauty in the aspects of humanities, art and spirit.

4   Lication of the "ShiDiKe" Element in Ming Dynasty Clothing in Home Fabric Design

In recent years, my country's home furnishing industry has developed rapidly. With the economic policy of expanding domestic demand and starting consumption, especially the rapid growth of housing consumption and tourism consumption, the rapid growth of home furnishing consumption has been driven. Home furnishing has become another bright spot of my country's economic growth, and it is extremely dynamic and has great development potential. At present, my country's home fabric design closely follows the international fashion trend and produces many modern and fashionable home fabric products. It is an urgent problem that we need to solve to develop fabric products that are not only contemporary and fashionable but also have Chinese characteristics.

"Home furnishing fabric design" is a relatively independent and systematic project, which not only involves three aspects of fabric design: fabric design, pattern design, product modeling design, but also requires the overall technical strength of the textile industry as technical support. "Home furnishing fabric design" is the ultimate design of fabric products, which integrates the technical level and achievements of all aspects of the textile industry, and is a collection of the technical strength of the textile industry. At present, China's "furniture fabric design" has achieved considerable development in general.

Chinese traditional elements are unique design elements of the Chinese nation. Their broad roots lie in the profound and profound Chinese traditional culture, and they should be inherited and carried forward by designers. These elements have been established in the long historical inheritance, subtly form a certain cultural connotation, and form a regional and cohesive aesthetic phenomenon and aesthetic characteristics. And with the changes of the times, its connotation can be sublimated, and finally become an excellent traditional element that transcends national and national boundaries, time and space and regions. It mainly includes traditional graphic elements such as curly grass pattern, arabesque pattern, twig pattern, blue and white, dragon and phoenix, and text. Contrast harmonious and unified Chinese colors; typical decorative forms such as cheongsam, Chinese tunic suit, mandarin jacket, gown, bellyband, etc. Collars, buttons, knots, slits and other varied details and inlays, rolls, embroidery and other complex decorative techniques; traditional fabrics such as silk, satin and blue calico. If these traditional elements can be reasonably applied to modern home fabrics, it will have a very good market effect and artistic value.

4.1 Application of "ShiDiKe" Modeling Elements

The modeling elements of "ShiDiKe" have the characteristics of simple and simple outline, various internal structures, ingenious and flexible technical methods, and balanced and symmetrical modeling patterns. According to the many characteristics of the "ShiDiKe" modeling elements, it is designed according to its internal and external structure, taking the external shape as the starting point, going deep into the internal structure, and integrating it into the modern home fabric design through direct or indirect methods.

Taking the external shape of "ShiDiKe" as the starting point, it means paying attention to the application of the "meaning" of its external shape when carrying out innovative application of modern home furnishing fabric design. Understand the internal meaning contained in the external shape, and apply it indirectly in the design. Only with a thorough understanding of the "meaning" of "ShiDiKe" can one appreciate the harmonious beauty of rich, balanced and symmetrical shapes it gives people. Because "ShiDiKe" is a typical element in Chinese clothing culture that uses the aesthetic principles of symmetry and balance, it can make people feel a sense of stability and tranquility.

When the home fabric design goes deep into the innovative application of the internal structure of "ShiDiKe", it should pay attention to the use of the "shape" of the internal structure, and directly apply the specific shape of the "ShiDiKe" pattern to modern home fabric design. Among them, "one point and two bends" are the basic structural elements of the shape of "persimmon stalks", and the shape of each "ShiDiKe" has subtle changes. Grasp these subtle changes and apply them to the silhouette, dividing structure lines and decorative lines in the home textile design works to make the home textile works more round and gorgeous, comfortable and pleasant. Only by comprehensively analyzing the "meaning" and "shape" of the external shape and internal structure of "ShiDiKe" can the shape of "ShiDiKe" be truly applied to modern home fabric design (Fig. 11). According to different home furnishing design styles and purposes, the external shape of "ShiDiKe" is unified and coordinated to produce rich modeling features. Combined with the subtle changes in the curve of the "ShiDiKe shape", it is used in the home fabric design to make the overall shape of the home fabric works richer and more beautiful.

4.2 Application of Color Elements of "SHIDIKe"

Color is an important factor that can directly resonate with designers and consumers, so no matter at any time, the use of color is a design element that every designer attaches great importance to. The difference in color style will directly affect the personality and style of home textile products. Use the blue, red, yellow, black, white and other color elements of "ShiDiKe" as the main color for home fabric design, add decorative colors, assist the main decoration of home fabric, and make it bright in tone. Then use the achromatic system of the auxiliary color of the craft to assist the main color and decorative color, and grasp the color ratio for innovative use. By applying the color of "ShiDiKe", the home fabric design has a unique national cultural connotation, and at the same time meets the spiritual needs of consumers (Fig. 12).

Fig. 11. The application of "ShiDiKe" shaped curtains (from Baidu pictures)

Fig. 12. "ShiDiKe" and shape cushion application (from Baidu pictures)

4.3 Application of Pattern Elements of "SHIDIKe"

The auspicious pattern of "ShiDiKe" is very suitable for modern home fabric design. Its pattern is based on nature, pursues the beautiful form of nature, and combines the color elements perfectly blended by nature to create a "ShiDiKe" pattern with extraordinary meaning, which makes people closer to nature. Apply the "ShiDiKe" pattern to modern home fabric design directly or indirectly, that is, directly enlarge or reduce the pattern. Or extract some of the patterns in the pattern and apply them in the home fabric design, which can make people feel friendly and familiar. The indirect application of the "ShiDiKe" pattern is to break up and reorganize the pattern or cut and misplace it to create a new pattern. Or use the law of addition and subtraction to add modern and popular elements to the pattern or reduce the original patterns, take the essence, and design a satisfactory home fabric art work (Fig. 13).

Fig.13. "ShiDiKe" internal pattern door curtain application (from Baidu pictures)

Our country is a country with a profound design culture tradition, and China's traditional elements are a design treasure that has not been well excavated and developed. Wang Shouzhi said that folk customs should return to the mainstream of design. We should integrate traditional elements into it, play the cultural card with Chinese characteristics, and enter the international high-end home furnishing fabric market with designs with Chinese traditional cultural characteristics. Only by truly inheriting the local culture can we strengthen the international competitiveness of my country's home furnishing design and make our country's home furnishing design gradually go to the world.

5 Summary

Most of the traditional clothing relics of the Ming Dynasty are collected by museums, and people cannot touch the "ShiDiKe". The innovative application of "ShiDiKe" in home fabrics not only satisfies people's viewing psychology, but also meets people's needs in daily life. It is an important form of inheriting Chinese traditional culture to apply the traditional clothing element "ShiDiKe" in the Ming Dynasty to home fabric products. The design of "ShiDiKe" home fabric products is based on the traditional clothing element "ShiDiKe" of the Ming Dynasty as the creative element. Extracting the shape of "ShiDiKe", combined with product features and supplemented by modern art composition and current popular aesthetic trends, makes traditional ornamentation shine brightly in modern design applications. The traditional Chinese "ShiDiKe" not only has a strong oriental artistic heritage, but also has an artistic style that is compatible with foreign cultures. The extraction of the decorative elements of "ShiDiKe" and the innovative application in home fabric products can realize the selection and inheritance of the traditional "ShiDiKe" elements, making the "ShiDiKe" elements last forever in traditional patterns.

References

1. [Ming] Song, Y.: Tiangong Kaiwu, vol. 1. Yuelu Publishing House (2002)
2. [Qing] Zhang, T.: Ming Shi Yu Fu Zhi. Zhonghua Book Company, Beijing (1974)
3. [Ming] Wang, Q., Wang, S., (ed.): Sancai Tuhui, vol. 6. Shanhai Ancient Books Publishing House, Shanghai (1988)
4. [Qing] Wu, Y.: Tianshui Bingshan Record. Commercial Press (1937)
5. [Song] Li, J.: Ying Zai Fa Shi Tu Yang. China Building Industry Press (2007). (below): 281
6. Zhao, F.: Zhong Guo Si Chou Tong Shi, p. 11. Suzhou University Press, Suzhou (2005)
7. Zhang, X.: Zhong Guo Gu Dai Ran Zhi Wen Yang Shi. Peking University Press, Beijing (1016)
8. Huang, N., Chen, J., Huang, G.: Fu Shi Zhong Hua - Zhong Hua Fu Shi Qi Qian Nian [M]: Fine Edition. Tsinghua University Press, Beijing (2013)
9. Gao, C.: Zhong Guo Yi Guan Fu Shi Da Ci Dian, vol. 12, p. 484. Shanhai: Shanghai Dictionary Publishing House, (1996)
10. Wu, S.: Zhong Guo Li Dai Fu Zhuang\Ran Zhi\Ci Xiu Ci Dian, vol. 6, p. 337, Jiangsu Fine Arts Publishing House, Nanjing (2011)
11. Weng, W.: A Preliminary Study on the Research and Design of the Traditional Chinese Auspicious Pattern "Dual Bird Pattern", vol. 5, no. 19. China Academy of Art, Zhejiang (2019)
12. Tian, Z., Wu, S., Tian, Q.: History of Chinese Patterns, p. 38. Shandong Fine Arts Publishing House, Jinan (2009)
13. Weng, W.: A Preliminary Study on the Research and Design of the Traditional Chinese Auspicious Pattern "Dual Bird Pattern", vol. 5. China Academy of Art Zhejiang (2019)
14. Xu, X.: Research on Ming Dynasty Clothing in the Old Collection of Confucian Mansion, p. 5. Soochow University, Jiangsu (2018)
15. Jiang, Y.: Research on silk garments woven from persimmon stalks in Ming Dynasty. Chin. Art Res. (12), 4–22
16. Lu, J., Yu, Q.: Clothes of the Ming dynasty—clothing handed down from the Ming dynasty in the Shandong museum. Shandong Art (04), 64–75 (2020)

Analyzing the Design of Online VR Platforms for Accessing Cultural Heritage Resources and Services: Multiple Case Studies in European and American Countries

Ning Zhang[1] , Yizhe Wu[2] , Junyang Li[3](✉) , and Kaijiao Zhang[4](✉)

[1] Institute of Advanced Studies in Humanities and Social Sciences, Beijing Normal University, Zhuhai 519087, China
[2] School of Arts and Communication, Beijing Normal University, Zhuhai 519087, China
[3] School of Information Management, Sun Yat-Sen University, Guangzhou 510006, China
lijy385@mail2.sysu.edu.cn
[4] School of Humanities and Arts, Macau University of Science and Technology, Macau 999078, China

Abstract. To explore the current design of online VR platforms for assessing cultural heritage resources and services, this research selected 20 platforms run by European and American countries as case studies. These cases are analyzed from a user experience perspective with multiple case study methods. It further analyzes the success factors, differences, and causes of the design of these selected VR platforms by following the 5 dimensions proposed by Jesse James Garrett in 2003, they are (1) user needs and product objectives; (2) functional specification and content requirements; (3) interaction design and information architecture; (4) interface design, information design, and navigation design; (5) sensory design. It suggests that the platform design should be planned strategically and systematically, having clear user groups, setting up sustainable cooperation models, providing more diverse interaction experiences for users, developing better functions, and making the platforms easy to use.

Keywords: VR Platform · Cultural Heritage Resource · User Experience · Multiple Case Studies · European and American Countries

1 Introduction

Cultural heritage (CH) is the legacy of history and is divided into tangible and intangible ones, with specific historical, social, technological, economic, and aesthetic values [1]. It is indispensable physical evidence of the development of human society.

Regional and national strategic plans in Europe and the US are issued to promote the conservation and innovative use of cultural heritage resources. For example, *the Creative Europe programme 2021–2027* is the European Commission's flagship programme to support the culture and audiovisual sectors with a budget of € 2.44 billion. The programme's main aims are to: "1) safeguard, develop and promote European cultural and

N. A. Streitz and S. Konomi (Eds.): HCII 2023, LNCS 14037, pp. 287–299, 2023.
https://doi.org/10.1007/978-3-031-34609-5_21

linguistic diversity and heritage; 2) increase the competitiveness and economic potential of the cultural and creative sectors, in particular, the audiovisual sector" [2]. Also, the U.S. Department of the Interior FY released *DOI Strategic Plan - FY 2022–2026* in 2022, in which one of the strategic goals is to "conserve, protect, manage, and restore natural and cultural resources in the face of climate change and other stressors" [3].

CH resources are non-renewable, perishable, and have limited dissemination, making it difficult to reproduce and pass on CH with a single and simple representation method. It can be presented in 2-dimensional (2D) or 3-dimensional (3D) graphics for users to access using digital mediums [4]. Immersive technologies, represented by Virtual Reality (VR), have recently become the mainstream technology for digital reproduction, and interactive and immersive experiences of CH, which is effective in promoting the revitalization and mass dissemination of cultural heritage resources [5].

Apart from CH resources reproduction and preservation, online VR platforms for Cultural Heritage Resources and Services (CHRSs) are typically used for assessing CH resources, applications, training services, business cooperation networks, culture work design, and creation [6]. As a thriving and creative industry, such platforms offer more diverse solutions to promote heritage conservation [7]. Operators, such as government departments, enterprises and research institutions, have explored how to build online VR platforms for CHRSs to provide immersive and interactive educational experiences for the public [8].

The analysis of online VR platforms for CHRSs is of significant value in clarifying the current state of development, problems, and optimization suggestions. Users are the key to measuring the performance of platforms. It is therefore imperative to study the current practices and experiences of developed countries and regions in Europe and the United States from the perspective of users.

2   Literature Review

To fully promote VR-enabled CH conservation and dissemination, there have been a number of practical cases of designing online VR platforms for CHRSs [9]. A typical platform consists of virtual scenes, using multimedia technology, VR hardware, and software to create dynamic simulations of real environments. This allows users to configure exhibit models according to their needs. It is now widely used in site reenactment, museum exhibitions, science and technology education, and other activities [10]. The main platform operators are companies, museums, universities, and government agencies [11].

Users could access the digital-based representations (such as games, animations, 3D models/scenes, and films) of CH artifacts through VR platforms for CHRSs, and also could get information related to industry trends, such as VR-enabled education [12], exhibitions and activities, channels for creating and releasing digital artworks, experiencing, buying VR applications, designing VR product, and customizing solutions for a specific VR application [4, 6].

It is vital to develop and improve VR platforms for CHRSs from user experience. There has been extensive research on this topic, including the virtual exhibition platform [13], the social VR platform for shared VR spaces [14], and the VR novel platform [15].

Normally, these different thematic platforms are evaluated based on the user's experience and interaction performance [16]. In the cultural heritage field, researchers explored the factors that influence users' satisfaction with online cultural heritage collections [17], user interface (UI) design [18], and the technology framework for information system design [19] from the user experience. There is limited research related to the design of online platforms for assessing cultural heritage resources and services. Therefore, this research tends to explore this specific issue.

3   Research Design

3.1   Research Aims and Questions

The main aim of this paper is to analyze the design of online VR platforms for CHRSs in Europe and America. It will also systematically summarize the design experiences, with a view to providing a reference experience for researchers and designers. This paper explores this aim from user experience and sets the main research question, that is:

RQ: what are the current design experiences of online VR platforms for CHRSs in European and American Countries from the user experience?

3.2   Research Methods

A Multiple Case Study Approach. It is wise to use multiple case studies for understanding the phenomenon instead of a single study. This is because the evidence that is generated from multiple case studies is more reliable and stronger [20]. Multi-case studies are characterized by two stages of analysis - intra-case analysis and cross-case analysis. The former is a comprehensive analysis of each case as a whole, while the latter is a unified abstraction and generalization of all cases based on the former. This leads to a more incisive description and a more powerful interpretation [21].

Therefore, this research adopted a multiple case study approach to explore the design of online VR platforms for CHRSs in Europe and America. The first stage is to analyze every single case, and then summarize and conclude the similarities and differences.

Case Collection and Selection Criteria. Researchers searched and selected 20 cases (with 11 cases in Europe and 9 cases in North America) according to the following selection criteria:

The Platform for Accessing Thematic CHR. It could be marine cultural heritage, ceramic heritage, museum collections; or the platform for accessing multiple cultural heritage services, such as training, networking, cultural work design and creation.

Platform Services are Accessible. This is demonstrated by the continuity of the platform's operation, which is openly accessible to users. In addition, the platform is rich in content and has a diverse range of resource types and service channels.

It is Critical that the PLATform's Operators are Authoritative. The researcher usually selects high-quality platforms built by the government, well-known universities, and mainstream enterprises.

Case Description. Based on search engines Google and Bing, 35 online VR platforms for CHRSs in Europe and America were searched. These cases were filtered by selection criteria, resulting in 20 high-quality cases. They fall into two categories: (1) specific platforms for accessing CH resources or services; and (2) general platforms that contain access to CH resources or services. It is shown in Table 1.

Table 1. The selected cases of the online VR platforms for CHRSs in European and American Countries

ID	Platform Title	Description	Operator	Country
1	iMARECULTURE	A specific platform for European maritime CHs	iMARECULTURE	Cyprus
2	IMMENSIVA	A specific platform for artworks and services	Lemongrass Communication	Switzerland
3	VR Art Platform	A specific platform for artworks and services	VR-All-Art AG Company	Switzerland
4	XR4Heritage	A specific platform for cultural attraction heritage and services	Compagnie Les 3 Plumes	Belgium
5	Das Städel Museum	A specific platform for the digital collection, artworks	Das Städel Museum Foundation	Germany
6	Curio	A specific platform for assessing CH resources, applications, and services	Zubr Group	UK
7	DiNAR	A specific platform for museum applications and services	University of York	UK
8	Cornerstone Church of Yuba City	A specific platform for CH application and VRchat application	Cornerstone Community	USA
9	America's Mustang	A specific platform for American mustang services	Mustang Heritage Foundation	USA
10	HTC Vive arts	A general platform for digital artworks and services	HTC VIVE	USA, China
11	Ikonospace	A general platform covering CH services for Web 3D	Ikonospace Company	Germany

(*continued*)

Table 1. (*continued*)

ID	Platform Title	Description	Operator	Country
12	The VR Voyage	A general platform covering resources for museums, art & artifacts, archaeological sites	Forager Education	Canada
13	SideQuest	A general platform covering CH services	SideQuest Group	USA
14	Khora	A general platform covering art, painting, and historical CH services	Khora Group	Denmark
15	Inglobe Technologies	A general platform covering CH resources	Inglobe Technologies Company	Italy
16	Delta	A general platform covering CH resources and services	North Carolina State University	USA
17	Flyover Zone	A general platform covering CH applications and services	Flyover Zone Firm	USA
18	TimeLooper	A general platform covering CH solution services	TimeLooper Firm	USA
19	Zoan	A general platform covering CH services	Zoan Group	Finland
20	HTC Vive port	A general platform covering CH applications	HTC VIVE	USA, China

Analysis Dimensions for the Selected Cases. The design of online VR platforms for CHRSs is a highly comprehensive and systematic project, covering several aspects such as functional plan, resource aggregation and user experience design. The analysis of platform design first requires the determination of reasonable and standardized analysis dimensions. Jesse James Garrett proposed and explained *The 5 Elements of User Experience* in the work entitled *The Elements of User Experience - User-Centered Design for the Web and Beyond* [22]. It divides the experiential elements of product design into five aspects, including the surface (sensory design), skeleton (interface design, information design and navigation design), structure (interaction design and information architecture), scope (functional specification and content requirements), and strategy (user needs and product objectives) as shown in Fig. 1 [22]. This research analyzes the selected 20 cases by following the aforementioned 5 elements and indicators.

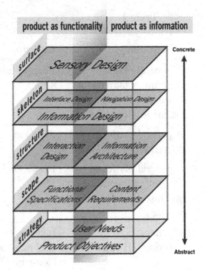

Fig. 1. The 5 elements of user experience proposed by Jesse James Garrett in 2003 [22]

4 Findings

4.1 User Needs and Product Objectives

User Needs. Defining user groups and needs is a prerequisite for the design of online VR platforms for CHRSs. Currently, there are 3 user groups: (1) Most platform users are positioned in a wide range, with no occupational, racial, or age restrictions. Individual applications are restricted by education, professional knowledge, and physical health factors, for example, difficulties in understanding the content or the operational skills in using the equipment. A small number of applications suggest the age of users should be above 6 years old, or above 12 years old. These users are generally enthusiastic about VR cultural heritage experience, VR cultural heritage application design, and publishing; (2) Most platforms also provide services to art training enterprises, VR content developers, and VR equipment suppliers. This cooperation forms a complete upstream and downstream industry chain, providing one-stop services, such as Inglobe Technologies and IMMENSIVA; (3) Most of the platforms are targeted at government agencies, cultural institutions (museums, art galleries, concert halls), educational institutions (schools, universities). They usually focus on establishing online and offline cultural heritage exhibitions, developing VR cultural heritage experience applications, training in related fields, and popularizing cultural heritage knowledge based on VR technology. The representative platforms are TimeLooper.

Product Objectives. The objectives of online VR platforms for CHRSs represent the ultimate purpose and value to be achieved by the platform design. This guides the functional design and content design of the platform.

The current objectives are synthesized from multiple case studies showing as follows: (1) The design of platforms acts as a link to promote cultural exchange between different groups. It builds cultural exchange network relationships and facilitates the interconnection of different user groups to share and create new cultural content. For instance, IMMENSIVA uses a digital CH station as a link to connect users and promote exchange and cooperation between different cultures; (2) The platforms are designed to serve academic research purposes by exploring ways and means of preserving, reconstructing, and disseminating cultural heritage based on VR technology. For example, Delta collaborates with academic research institutions and teaching organizations with the aim of innovating methods for the presentation and dissemination of VR CHRs; (3) The dissemination of CHRs and cultural education for the general public is the core objective of most VR platform designs. For example, DiNAR aims to provide a cutting-edge museum experience for the public based on VR technology. This will enhance the level of understanding and dissemination of museum collections to the general public; (4) The innovative platform design is a service for creative development enterprises to support product innovations and methodological advances in VR cultural heritage applications. HTC Vive Arts, for example, explores the future of VR product design and solution implementation in cultural service organizations, such as virtual museums, art galleries, and libraries; (5) The platforms are designed as channels to promote commercial cooperation in the upstream and downstream industry chains of VR cultural heritage services, creating a more quality experience for consumers. For example, VR Art and XR4Heritage provide solutions to different cultural scenarios, uphold the concept of openness and sharing, and encourage cross-border cooperation.

4.2 Functional Specification and Content Requirements

Functional Specification. There are 3 common functions in the current platform design, including information retrieval, resource display, and resource upload and download, as described below: (1) The information retrieval function is mainly used for online queries, such as browsing the web and finding documents. It can also be used to search directly by entering text. For example, HTC Vive Arts provides a search bar tool in the top right corner of the homepage for searching. SideQuest can support filtering by conditions in the menu bar allowing users to select the exact content of the specific resource they need; (2) The platforms provide users with a variety of information modules to help them fully understand the platform's services. For example, Das Städel Museum, Khora and ikonospace offer modules for information on the building's main body, history, appointment details, digital information on cultural heritage, and examples of excellence. The resource types are usually a combination of graphics, audio, videos, animation, 3D models, and VR sense with interactive functions; (3) The platforms allow users to post content/works for others to learn from and download the resources they need. There are 9 such platforms (out of 20 cases), 6 of which require payment for download, such as the platform Curio, and 3 of which are free to extract, such as the platform SideQuest.

Content Requirements. The contents on the platform focus on three main types of resources, namely museum material collection resources, cultural tourism site resources, and classic artworks.

The specific descriptions are as follows: (1) Museum collections are the most distinctive and representative content on each platform. For example, the cultural content of the Das Städel Museum covers a wide range of museum collections. The current VR museum includes 3D designs of real collections as well as virtual collections. The museum can be designed as a simulation of the original museum or as a purely virtual museum and includes collections from a variety of sources; (2) Cultural tourism sites are also the focus of attention for each platform. Specific objects can be divided into street scenes, landmarks, tombs, engineering, maritime, and other historical sites. iMARECULTURE, for example, focuses on providing resources and services on maritime cultural heritage; (3) The display of artworks is an imperative direction for the platform's content design, which can provide users with rich and intuitive visual information for easy access and experience. For example, Ikonospace's product content covers virtual sculpture, painting, and calligraphy. Platforms have also integrated their own strengths to develop interactive narrative applications. For example, Delta designs history content experiences tailored to students' needs within VR environments to meet the needs of history teaching and cultural science popularization.

4.3 Interaction Design and Information Architecture

Interaction Design. This refers to the way in which the platform responds to the user's information needs. The main channels for supporting user interaction in platform design are dialog boxes, animated icons, and navigation buttons.

The specific description is as follows: (1) The dialog box allows users to interact with the platform by typing in relevant commands, the most common of which are "enter password to log in", "online customer service consultation" and "keyword search" to obtain information. 15 out of 20 platforms cover input interaction. For example, HTC Vive Arts provides the option to enter keywords to find information, contact customer service, and so on [23]; (2) Animated icons allow the user to click on the interaction and have it appeared as a dynamic animation, which enhances interactivity, excites the user, and creates a strong visual impact [24, 25]. Only 4 selected cases (out of 20) covered animated interactions, such as the animated effect that appears when the user hovers over a 3D resource page on XR4Heritage; (3) The navigation button guides and navigates the user's information behavior, such as "click on the button to return to the home page" or "click on the button to give a hint". For example, the platform SideQuest allows users to link to specific areas or participate in platform activities by clicking on the mobility buttons located on the platform interface [26].

Information Architecture. Platform information includes the coordination, planning, design, and arrangement of a particular piece of content. It is normally composed of a repository layer for storing and managing digital information and a service layer for assessing and managing digital information [27].

The specific description is as follows: (1) The platform's repository layer is designed to store and manage digital objects, enabling long-term preservation and access to digital objects [28]. Platforms in this case have created accessible repositories. For example, Ikonospace uses cultural heritage digitized products as storage objects, it regularly updates and maintains the data to facilitate user access to digitized exhibits; (2) The service layer of the platform is designed to be the channel through which users access and manipulate digital objects. This is designed to support access to the content of the cultural heritage repository [28]. Most platforms currently have easy access, such as America's Mustang, which removes IP access restrictions to increase the openness of platform access. Also, Cornerstone Church of Yuba City has content categorization buttons so that users can follow the labels to access the information resources they need.

4.4 Interface Design, Information Design and Navigation Design

The current platform design is well laid out and prioritized. It also makes effective use of global navigation and local navigation design to guide users in their search for information both inside and outside the platform. This is to meet their needs to the greatest extent possible.

This is described in detail as follows: (1) The VR cultural heritage resource platform aims to highlight the nature of the platform's services by considering the platform's own service targets and platform positioning. This needs to be combined with its own platform profile, which needs to be featured in a reasonable position on the platform's homepage. For example, CURIO fully combines its own functional service attributes and logic, placing modules such as cultural heritage management, cultural heritage design, and restoration basis on the homepage. It also places the project introduction, team profile, and online contact in the function column, making the information design layout logical and focused. A small number of platforms have a confusing layout design, such as Delta. This layout has too much information laid out on the page and insufficient explanatory information in graphics and text; (2) Global navigation means that users can search for relevant cultural heritage platform information on the website and also search for keywords on the public domain website to obtain platform information. For example, the platform Delta provides a global navigation function service. There are also many quick navigation designs on the platform homepage, supporting multi-terminal access and an easy information retrieval process [29]; (3) Local navigation refers to the restriction of information accessibility by limiting some of the information to internal site searching. It provides continuous navigation services for only some of the functional modules on the platform. Inglobe Technologies, for instance, treats some information as local navigation and protects the key information of the platform resources [29].

4.5 Sensory Design

The sensory design of a platform is mainly driven by how it looks and how easy it is to use from a user perspective. The details include the following: (1) A platform's aesthetic value refers to its aesthetic design, which reflects the artistic effect of the entire site and also provides a pleasant browsing experience for users. Most platforms have good aesthetic value. With XR4Heritage, the interface colors are predominantly blue, white, and green, providing users with a high-contrast visual experience, and Zoan's overall style follows a virtual cyber style, providing users with a post-modern visual experience. However, some platforms such as Khora set the font color and homepage color to white. This lacks contrast and distinction, making it difficult to attract users to use; (2) Ease of use of a platform is the extent to which it can be accepted or accessed by users. The easier it is to use the platform, the more attractive it will be to users. Currently, most platforms are easy to use. For instance, Flyover Zone provides accessible features and a simple interface design for special groups. VR Art Platform language is popular and simple, reducing user search time. However, there are also some platforms that are not easy to use. For example, the Delta unit layout involves too many elements and involves a lot of proper nouns. This makes it relatively difficult to use.

5 Discussion

5.1 Elements of Success in the Design of Online VR Platforms for CHRSs

The successful design of online VR platforms for CHRSs must have clear design objectives and values, establish common interest aspirations, and define clear service targets. They also should be audience-oriented design, providing tailored and personalized solutions that meet user needs, providing a complete service solution. The resources' content should cover a wide range of scope and be of various types.

User needs can be met by interaction design on platforms. The functional design is complete, and the information architecture is able to clearly define the relationship between the various parts of the platform. It can combine and control various elements, and has a complete interface structure and operating method.

The interface design is logical and effective at highlighting the platform's key points, with a clear layout and neat structure. In addition, the navigation design is easy to navigate, making use of both global navigation and local navigation, which are easy for users to pinpoint target information.

These platform design approaches are high applicability and ease of use for users, compatibility with a variety of resources' forms, extensibility, and decent aesthetic value.

5.2 Differences and Causes of the Design of Online VR Platforms for CHRSs

It is evident that there are significant differences in the design objectives and user groups between various platforms. For example, the IMMENSIVA and the VR Art platform are primarily user- and business-oriented, respectively.

The differences in the design objectives and user groups of the platforms are mainly related to the main operators and their operation modes. These operators currently include enterprises, universities, governments, and cultural institutions. The platforms run by enterprises are commercial in nature, focusing on the promotion of their business and technological development solutions. Those run by universities aim to cultivate students' comprehensive quality and focus on theoretical and technological research. Those run by governments tend to focus on cultural heritage preservation, management, and public education [30].

5.3 Lessons Learned from the Design of Online VR Platforms for CHRSs

The platform design needs to be carefully planned according to organizational aims, so the designer needs to design cultural heritage resource access and service platforms for the public, government, and enterprises respectively. Specifically, the massive data analysis tools of cloud computing can be used to obtain multi-dimensional information such as users' cultural consumption behavior and daily browsing habits to build a portrait of user behavior and recommend resources and services of interest to them. In the long run, it is imperative to actively design a digital resource library of exclusive 3D resources. This can help in enhancing organizational VR content production and supply capabilities, occupying niche markets, shaping organizational IP image, and improving organizational competitive strength [31].

From the practice of platform design in Europe and the United States, business/service cooperation involves multiple parties, such as enterprises and businesses, government and enterprises. They are effective to achieve rapid and healthy development for VR-based heritage platforms. So it is beneficial for operators to actively cooperate with the government, cultural institutions, enterprises, and universities. These organizations should also actively encourage multiparty participation, it will be in win-win situations for improving the efficiency of VR content production, creating platform-specific content products, and maximizing benefits [30, 32].

Platform interaction design needs to provide more diverse interaction experiences such as voice/ graphic interaction. In addition, short videos, serious games, online previews, and other modules can be incorporated into the modules of functional design [33].

In accordance with the platform's characteristics and advantages, the platform design needs to make dynamic adjustments to the page structure, prioritize and highlight the key points, and improve the navigation function to ensure that navigation can be accurately transmitted to each functional module [34].

To improve the ease of use of the platform design, it is necessary to provide users with the option to change the platform's color palette, text size, style, layout, and make the platform's language information popular and easy to understand. It is also vital to provide a variety of browsing formats and create a barrier-free browsing environment.

6 Conclusion

This research explores the design of online VR platforms for CHRSs based on 20 case studies selected from European and American countries. It analyzes and concludes the success factors, differences, and causes of the design of these online VR platforms by following the 5 dimensions proposed by Jesse James Garrett in 2003.

It contributes knowledge about the elements of success, differences, and causes in the design of online VR platforms for CHRS. It further makes 6 suggestions to designers and operators: (1) planning the platform design strategically and systematically; (2) having clear user groups; (3) setting up a sustainable cooperation model involving multiple parties;(4) providing more diverse interaction experiences for users; (5) developing better functions, and (6) making the platforms easy to use.

The key limitation of this research is the limited case studies. This cannot fully reflect the quality of the design of online VR platforms for CHRSs in European and American countries and even the world. To conclude stronger research conclusions in the future, it will be necessary to collect additional case studies.

Funding. This research is funded by the project entitled A Virtual Reality Enabled System Design and Evaluation for the Gamification of Chinese Ancient Books to Promote Chinese Traditional Culture Education Among University Students (Project No.2022GXJK416) approved by the Department of Education of Guangdong Province, China.

References

1. Qiu, Q., Zheng, T., Xiang, Z., Zhang, M.: Visiting intangible cultural heritage tourism sites: From value cognition to attitude and intention. Sustainability **12**(1), 132 (2019)
2. European Commission.: Culture and Creativity: About the Creative Europe Programme. https://culture.ec.europa.eu/creative-europe/about-the-creative-europe-programme. Accessed Jan 2023
3. U.S. Department of the Interior FY.: Office of Planning and Performance Management. https://www.doi.gov/performance/strategic-planning. Accessed 02 Jan 2023
4. Chong, H.T., Lim, C.K., Rafi, A., Tan, K.L., Mokhtar, M.: Comprehensive systematic review on virtual reality for cultural heritage practices: coherent taxonomy and motivations. Multimedia Syst. **28**(3), 711–726 (2022)
5. Zhang, N., Wan, A., Huang, J., Cao, P.: A system design of virtual reality enabled Chinese ancient books for enhancing reading promotion and culture dissemination. In: Streitz, N.A., Konomi, S. (eds) International Conference on Human-Computer Interaction, pp. 217–231. Springer, Cham (2022). https://doi.org/10.1007/978-3-031-05431-0_16
6. Bustillo, A., Alaguero, M., Miguel, I., Saiz, J.M., Iglesias, L.S.: A flexible platform for the creation of 3D semi-immersive environments to teach Cultural Heritage. Dig. Appl. Archaeol. Cult. Heritage **2**(4), 248–259 (2015)
7. Liew, C.L., Goulding, A., Nichol, M.: From shoeboxes to shared spaces: participatory cultural heritage via digital platforms. Inf. Commun. Soc. 1–18(2020)
8. Bakhshi, H., Throsby, D.: New technologies in cultural institutions: theory, evidence and policy implications. Int. J. Cult. Pol. **18**(2), 205–222 (2012)
9. Banfi, F.: The evolution of interactivity, immersion and interoperability in HBIM: Digital model uses, VR and AR for built cultural heritage. ISPRS Int. J. Geo Inf. **10**(10), 1–36 (2021)
10. Wei, S., Li, H.G., Xuedong, X.U.: Research on key technologies of three-dimensional digital reconstruction of cultural heritage in historical and cultural blocks. In: 2021 International Conference on Computer Technology and Media Convergence Design (CTMCD), pp. 222–226. IEEE (2021)
11. Zara, J.: Virtual reality and cultural heritage on the web. In: Proceedings of the7th International Conference on Computer Graphics and Artificial Intelligence, vol. 330, pp.101–112. Limoges, France (2004)
12. Hu, X., Ng, J., Lee, J.H.: VR creation experience in cultural heritage education: a preliminary exploration. Proc. Assoc. Inf. Sci. Technol. **56**(1), 422–426 (2019)
13. Liu, S.: Research on virtual exhibition platform based on user experience. In: 2010 IEEE 11th International Conference on Computer-Aided Industrial Design & Conceptual Design, vol. 1, pp. 711–714. IEEE (2010)
14. Gunkel, S. N., Prins, M., Stokking, H., Niamut, O.: Social VR platform: Building 360-degree shared VR spaces. In Adjunct publication of the 2017 ACM international conference on interactive experiences for tv and online video, pp. 83–84. TVX '17 Adjunct (2017)
15. Mavridou, I., et al.: FACETEQ: a novel platform for measuring emotion in VR. In: Proceedings of the Virtual Reality International Conference-Laval Virtual 2017, pp. 1–3. Core (2017)
16. Anton, D., Kurillo, G., Bajcsy, R.: User experience and interaction performance in 2D/3D telecollaboration. Futur. Gener. Comput. Syst. **82**, 77–88 (2018)

17. Zahidi, Z., Lim, Y.P., Woods, P.C.: Understanding the user experience (UX) factors that influence user satisfaction in digital culture heritage online collections for non-expert users. In: 2014 Science and Information Conference, pp. 57–63. IEEE (2014)
18. Tong, Y., Cui, B., Chen, Y.: Research on UI visual design of intangible cultural heritage digital museum based on user experience. In: 2018 13th International Conference on Computer Science & Education (ICCSE), pp. 1–4. IEEE (2018)
19. Ferretti, U., Quattrini, R., D'Alessio, M.: A comprehensive HBIM to XR framework for museum management and user experience in ducal palace at urbino. Heritage **5**(3), 1551–1571 (2022)
20. Hancock, D.R., Algozzine, B., Lim, J.H.: Doing Case Study Research: A Practical Guide for Beginning Researchers. Teachers College Press, New York City (2021)
21. Wuttke, D.A., Blome, C., Foerstl, K., Henke, M.: Managing the innovation adoption of supply chain finance—empirical evidence from six European case studies. J. Bus. Logist. **34**(2), 148–166 (2013)
22. Hoffmann, H. J.: Jesse James Garrett: The elements of user experience-User-centered design for the Web. I-com **2**(1), 44–44 (2003)
23. Beaudouin-Lafon, M.: Instrumental interaction: an interaction model for designing post-WIMP user interfaces. In: Proceedings of the SIGCHI Conference on Human Factors in Computing Systems, pp. 446–453. CHI (2000)
24. Brajnik, G., Gabrielli, S.: A review of online advertising effects on the user experience. Int. J. Hum.-Comput. Interact. **26**(10), 971–997 (2010)
25. Head, V.: Designing Interface Animation: Improving the User Experience Through Animation. Rosenfeld Media, New York (2016)
26. Kim, Y. S., Kim, M. H., Jin, S. T.: Cognitive characteristics and design creativity: an experimental study. In International Design Engineering Technical Conferences and Computers and Information in Engineering Conference, vol. 4742, pp. 309–317. ASME (2005)
27. Joshi, B.: Patterns of enterprise application architecture: repository, unit of work, lazy load, and service layer. In: Beginning SOLID Principles and Design Patterns for ASP. NET Developers, pp. 309–353. Apress, Berkeley (2016)
28. Phiri, L., Suleman, H.: Managing cultural heritage: information systems architecture. In Cultural Heritage Information Access and Management. Facet Publishing, London (2015)
29. DuBuf, J.H., et al.: The smartvision navigation prototype for blind users. JDCTA: Int. J. Dig. Content Technol. Appl. **5**(5), 351–361 (2011)
30. Davis, E., Heravi, B.: Linked data and cultural heritage: a systematic review of participation, collaboration, and motivation. J. Comput. Cultural Heritage (JOCCH) **14**(2), 1–18 (2021)
31. Ardissono, L., Kuflik, T., Petrelli, D.: Personalization in cultural heritage: the road travelled and the one ahead. User Model. User-Adapted Interact. **22**(1), 73–99 (2012)
32. Kelly, E.J.: Altmetrics and archives. J. Contemporary Archival Stud. **4**(1), 1–21 (2017)
33. Konstantakis, M., Aliprantis, J., Teneketzis, A., Caridakis, G.: Understanding user experience aspects in cultural heritage interaction. In: Proceedings of the 22nd Pan-Hellenic Conference on Informatics, pp. 267–271. PCI 2018 (2018)
34. Marden, J., Li-Madeo, C., Whysel, N., Edelstein, J.: Linked open data for cultural heritage: evolution of an information technology. In: Proceedings of the 31st ACM International Conference on Design of Communication. SIGDOC 2013, pp. 107–112 (2013)

Analysis of the Current Status of the NFT Industry Chain in China

Guangshuai Zhang[✉]

University of Macau Institute of Science and Technology, Taipa Weilong Road, Jiamotang District, Taipa Island, China
zgs1981@qq.com

Abstract. NFT digital artworks have led a new consumption model in the international and China societies. NFT industry is prosperous with diverse forms. With the different network regulatory mechanisms, blockchain functionalities, and policy regulations in international and domestic markets, a distinctive NFT digital collectibles market with Chinese characteristics has emerged. Currently, the digital collectibles market has begun to take shape in the domestic market and is gradually moving towards a standardized and healthy form of the Chinese digital economy, with a focus on intellectual property rights confirmation and the industry chain.

Keywords: NFT · digital economy · blockchain · intellectual property rights confirmation · industry chain

1 Status of NFT

The entire NFT industry chain can be analyzed from several dimensions, including NFT creators, NFT artwork, NFT trading platforms, NFT sales models, and NFT collectors. In the closed loop of China's digital economy, policy and regulations, and unique Chinese culture, the industry chain has formed a distinctive digital economic model.

In China's digital economy environment, the NFT industry chain, based on blockchain technology, has formed a unique digital economic model. From the diversity of NFT creators to the different types of NFT artwork, a variety of digital collection forms have been created. The mainstream NFT exchanges in China have promoted and marketed the market for different types of digital collections, forming relatively standardized primary, secondary, and tertiary market, with market share gradually increasing. At the same time, as platforms have diversified, the sales models for digital collections have become more diverse, responding to the increasing demands of collectors (Figs. 1 and 2).

2 NFT Artist

NFT creators, also known as digital artists, generally appear in two types: individual creators and team creators. Firstly, individual creators often engage in professional and amateur creative hobbies, as well as creating based on certain "celebrity Intellectual

Fig. 1 .

Fig. 2 .

Properties", resulting in individualized creations with a certain style and personal touch. Although the NFT art market is thriving with a large number of diverse works due to the high enthusiasm for creation brought about by the international NFT art craze, there are still limitations on individual creations, such as the sustainability and quality of digital art creation, and the typicality and benchmarking of works are yet to be explored and recognized. Secondly, team creators often consist of companies or teams that specialize in creating artifacts, cultural relics, cultural and creative systems, brands, games and so on. They have a set of more mature industrial design and production standards, with game art assets as the main process. From copywriting design to conceptual design, model production, texture painting, bone binding, baking and rendering, standardized production processes are used, combined with digital technology in fields such as physical and cultural relics, such as 3D scanning and digital splicing, to create a variety of NFT art forms (Fig. 3).

Fig. 3 .

3 ANFT Artwork

The NFT art market has been enriched by the creative efforts of individual artists and teams. Internationally, there are numerous NFT artworks that feature famous intellectual properties that have been transformed or adapted for digital art creation, such as characters from Marvel or anime series. There are also artworks that take the form of CryptoSnoo avatars. Furthermore, collectible moments from news history have been encrypted into NFT collections, as have items from fashion consumption such as music, art, tickets, and photography. These artworks come in various forms including videos, audio, files, games, blind boxes, and portraits, and are increasingly being created for specific consumer groups. For instance, NBA has authorized its IP for programs and stars, and NFT collectible blind boxes have also become an art form. As technology continues to evolve and art forms continue to develop, programmable and generative art have also carved out their own unique market share in the NFT art scene. In the context of China's distinctive digital economy, mainstream NFT art mostly features museum collections, art, and cultural derivatives as the primary encryption objects. The production of encrypted digital art has also flourished in sports, cultural and creative industries, cultural heritage, technology, and tourism sectors (Fig. 4).

4 NFT Digital Artwork and Rights Confirmation Issues

In the context of the development of national digital economy, NFT digital collectibles are facing numerous challenges. While the limited quantity and scarcity of NFTs under blockchain encryption have enhanced their collectible value, they have also led to price

Fig. 4 .

bubbles and exposed many problems in terms of the quality and significance of the works themselves in the early stages of development. Meanwhile, there are also many loopholes in the original asset ownership of physical assets or art objects, such as copyright, secondary development rights, infringement, development of public copyright, and ownership of copyright, which have posed many hidden risks for the ownership of digital art collections. Moreover, digital encryption is a highly energy-consuming process, and the waste of ecological resources it generates is also a significant problem in the production process of NFT art (Fig. 5).

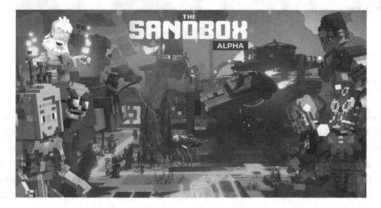

Fig. 5 .

Taking the example of rights confirmation, prior to listing and sale of digital artworks, the domestic market for digital collectibles in China generally confirms the intellectual property rights of digital art collectibles through IP authorization and copyright agreements. Particularly, there are clear agreements and authorization methods for digital copyright, copyright authorization, and secondary development, which enable legitimate operations of copyright. In the NFT digital collectibles market in China, legal supervision will gradually improve, while copyright protection will be addressed from the perspective of decentralization. This is also a characteristic development of blockchain encryption technology in the digital economy in China, and the non-monetization approach will restrain the speculative and virtual currency transactions associated with NFT digital collectibles, ensuring the core position of digital RMB transactions in the economic structure. At the same time, the state is gradually loosening its grip on the digital art trading license and developing a wider range of digital art trading markets, and through laws and regulations, it will suppress speculation and control transactions in the secondary market, ensuring the market stability of digital collectible (Fig. 6).

Fig. 6 .

5 NFT Trading Market Structure

The digital art of asset ownership is traded through NFT exchanges, where the sales of digital art are conducted through various forms such as open, authentication, and invitation. In the international market, where virtual currency is used as trading capital, platforms such as OpenSea provide an open format for digital art to be listed, while art platforms that advocate the notion of "everyone is an artist" attract individual artists and team creators to encrypt and list their works. Other open platforms, such as Rarible, allow artists and artworks to be circulated in the form of copyright fees. SuperRare and NiftyGateway use an authentication system to impose requirements on the products listed on their platforms, further enhancing the qualification standards. Platforms such as Foundation use an invitation-based approach to curate and invite selected works, achieving precision in the selection process (Fig. 7).

Fig. 7 .

In China, virtual currency trading has been proposed as a form of non-currency transaction, and it has been made clear that virtual currency does not have the same legal status as fiat money. Strict limitations have been placed on the illegal public financing of tokens, thereby limiting the commercialization of virtual currency. In addition, "mining" has been classified as an energy-intensive industry, which has established trading rules for NFT digital collections in China. There are three main tiers of NFT trading platforms in China, with AliPay Whale Explorer, Tencent Fantom, Ali Auction, AntChain Fanli, NFT China, and Baidu SuperChain being part of the first tier. They have established their positions in the market, with Ali Auction primarily listing art, sports, and e-sports copyrights as its main encrypted collections; AntChain focuses on cultural and creative industries, crafts, animation, and sports as its primary encrypted collections; and Fantom mainly distributes media and cultural and creative products. NFT China mainly focuses on the listing of art collections. They have formed NFT digital collection sales platforms with unique features. The second tier includes NFT digital collection sales platforms such as Unique Art, GuiCang, Nestle WenGuan, Blue Cat Digital, YouCopyright, and IBOX. The third tier includes more than 20 major NFT digital art sales platforms such as Shuangjing Museum, Cool Tide Play, Cloud Travel, R-space, Rare Digital Collection, Universe Core, Everything Digital Collection, ONE Digital Art, and Vision of Elements. Throughout the domestic digital collection sales platforms, they mainly focus on products such as cultural relics, museums, sports, art, animation, and cultural and creative products. The platform structure is characterized by traditional Internet head companies as the first tier and emerging subdivision fields as the second and third tiers (Fig. 8).

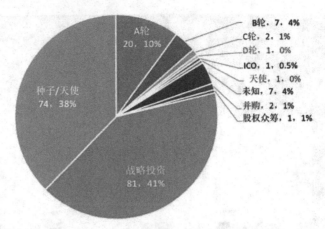

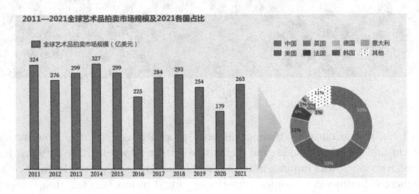

图 4：2017-2023 年中国虚拟偶像核心市场和带动市场规模及预测

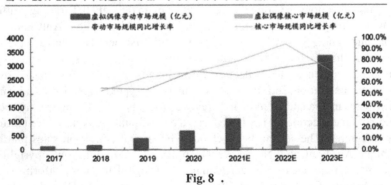

Fig. 8 .

6 Market Analysis of Digital Collections

Under the influence of China's digital economy, industrial economy, cultural market guidance, as well as platforms and collector audiences, the domestic digital collectibles market has formed a relatively stable form of digital collectibles. In terms of popularity, high-heat collections including cultural relics, aerospace, intangible cultural heritage, music, and avatars occupy the market mainstream, while animation, trendy toys, sports, and card collections make up the second tier, and traditional Chinese painting, oil painting, photography, e-sports, and film collections constitute the third tier. From the perspective of collectible forms, Chinese NFT digital collectibles resonate with the national cultural confidence, Chinese regional culture, and other national characteristics, and are developing towards a healthy and positive direction under the guidance of the distinctive Chinese digital economy and cultural industry. With the guidance of the "no coin" mode of NFT digital collectibles operation, the number of single-product releases, market value, and average price of digital collectibles on major platforms have remained relatively stable. In 2021, for example, the number of digital collectibles with a distribution volume greater than one on Whale Vault exceeded 2.6 million, with a total market value of over 51 million yuan and an average selling price of approximately 19.15 yuan. The number of digital collectibles with a distribution volume greater than one on Huan Core was 20,450, including 15,130 priced for sale, 5,326 released for public welfare and other promotional activities, with a total market value of 1.55 million yuan and an average selling price of approximately 102.14 yuan. The number of digital collectibles with a distribution volume greater than one in Unique Art's blind box series was 119,000, with a total market value of 3.56 million yuan and an average selling price of approximately 29.9 yuan. The number of digital collectibles with a distribution volume greater than one on IBOX was about 57,396, with a total market value of approximately 86.67 million yuan and an average selling price of approximately 151.1 yuan. The number of digital collectibles with a distribution volume greater than one on You Copyright was about 59,706, with a total market value of approximately 40.61 million yuan and an average selling price of approximately 68.01 yuan. In 2021, the total distribution volume nationwide was 4.56 million, with a total market value of approximately 150 million yuan and an average selling price of approximately 33.33 yuan. The above data shows that the overall distribution volume and product unit prices are similar to those of traditional arts and crafts collectibles, blind boxes, and other physical products, and are developing in a rational direction. Although there are also special transfer transactions in the secondary market, the overall development is healthy and stable under the constraints of the law, platform, and copyright (Fig. 9).

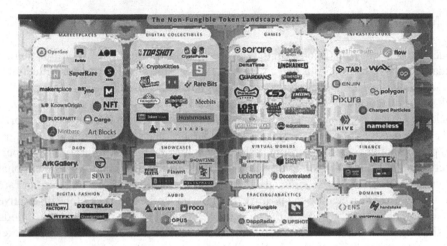

Fig. 9 .

7 NFT Digital Collection Distribution and Marketing Model

The issuance models for NFT digital collectibles in China can be divided into three main categories: the first is the traditional collection model, which has a low issuance volume but high price, and is marketed through gameplay synthesis and popularization. The second is the gifting model, which has a relatively large issuance volume and lower price, and is marketed through special numbering and lottery mechanisms, as well as incentive mechanisms such as collectible synthesis and entry into the original universe. The third is the secondary market model, which generally has a low issuance volume and high unit price, and is marketed through blind box sales, grading empowerment, and mechanisms such as fragment blind boxes and synthesis for the sake of experience (Fig. 10).

Throughout the marketing of the entire product, as the market for collector users becomes more segmented and more high-quality collectibles emerge, marketing channels and sales models are becoming increasingly diverse. Artistic collaborations between artists and top IPs, or the combination of industry cooperation and offline activities, are gradually enriching the industrial forms of NFT digital collectibles, such as the sales model of offline NFT concert tickets empowering online collectibles. At the same time, platform marketing has also diversified from mainstream platforms to various self-media sales models such as Little Red Book(Xiaohongshu), Oasis, Weibo, WeChat public accounts, Zhihu, Douban, and Waiwai (Fig. 11).

Flg. 10 .

With the precipitation of all users, community autonomy has gradually become a new model of community-based marketing. Through innovative user reward mechanisms and bundled sales models for physical and digital collectibles, user accumulation is explored in combination with social fission and fusion, points and invitations. Meanwhile, offline and online public welfare activities and the OpenEdition creative section are co-created and jointly participated in, enhancing interactivity and experiential sensation. The creation and experience of NFT digital collectibles are developing towards a more rich, complete and diverse perspective (Fig. 12).

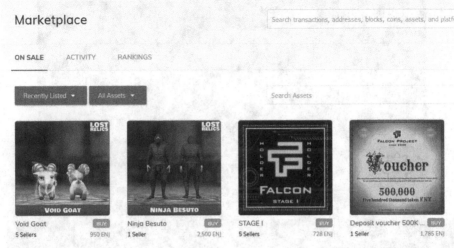

Fig. 11 .

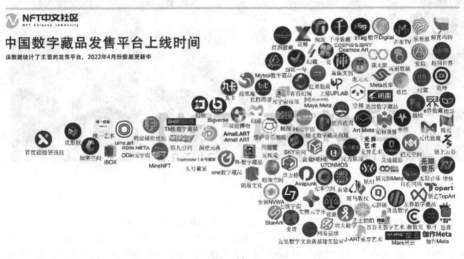

Fig. 12 .

8 Epilogue

In conclusion, the domestic NFT digital art market in China's unique digital economy, under the form of "coinless" transactions, has gradually formed a market for NFT digital art with Chinese cultural characteristics, centered around the digital cultural industry and guided by a unique digital experience on trading platforms for artists, artworks, and collectors. This has resulted in a healthy digital art industry ecosystem, regulated by laws and ownership mechanisms. With the further regulation of NFT digital art in the domestic digital economy, the gradual opening of digital licenses and secondary trading markets, we can expect a safe, stable, and prosperous digital economy with unique characteristics.

Research on Digital Communication of Chinese Traditional Garden

Lili Zhang[✉], XinYu Li, WenJing Yan, Ziqi Yao, and Beile Su

School of Art, Shandong Jianzhu University, No. 1000, Fengming Road, Licheng District, Jinan 250101, Shandong, China
281309090@qq.com

Abstract. Chinese traditional landscape is an important part of Chinese traditional culture, with a long history, diverse forms, rich connotations, fully embodies the wisdom of our working people, left a rich heritage for later generations. However, due to the influence of social changes, technological renewal and other factors, the traditional garden landscape is faced with the survival threat and the development dilemma. The development of digital technology has brought new opportunities for the protection of landscape, and also put forward new requirements for the recording of landscape heritage. In order to promote the better inheritance and development of Chinese traditional landscape in the contemporary economic and social development, it is necessary to carry out the digital protection and inheritance of the traditional landscape, so as to promote the traditional culture to play a greater role in the contemporary society.

Keywords: Chinese traditional landscape · Digital technology · Digital protection and inheritance · Cultural heritage

1 Introduction

The earliest garden form recorded in historical records in China is "garden", dated in the 11th century BC, that is, the late Shang and early Zhou dynasties in the late period of the slave society. After a long and complex and diverse development process, the ancient Chinese garden building art has formed a unique architecture, garden landscape and cultural system. In recent years, the rapid development of digital technology has provided a new way of protecting and inheriting the traditional landscape. Digital images, 3 D models and other data play an important role in the protection of traditional landscape in China. These achievements can provide help for the analysis, protection and research of traditional landscape, and also provide some reference for digital protection schemes, so as to improve the level of replanning and management of traditional landscape.

The 19th International Council on Monuments and Sites (ICOMOS) took "Protection and Interpretation of Cultural Heritage in the Era of Digital empowerment" (protecting and interpreting culturalheritage in the age of digital empowerment) as one of the four core topics of the conference. The digital protection has become an important trend and emerging field of contemporary cultural heritage research and practice. Chinese

N. A. Streitz and S. Konomi (Eds.): HCII 2023, LNCS 14037, pp. 311–321, 2023.
https://doi.org/10.1007/978-3-031-34609-5_23

traditional garden landscape occupies an unshakable position in the world cultural heritage, and it has become the general trend of digital protection and inheritance. Digital technology can provide a complete traditional landscape real, effective and reliable and scientific and reasonable way of protection, but also for the traditional landscape provides a display and promotion of Chinese excellent traditional culture, in the inheritance of ancient Chinese gardening art essence and cultural essence, enhance national identity has played an important role.

2 Overview of Digital Landscape Conservation

2.1 Digital Garden Landscape Protection System

Landscape refers to the beautiful natural environment and recreation area created by using engineering technology and artistic means to transform the terrain, further building mountains, stacking stones, arranging water, planting trees and flowers, building buildings and arranging garden roads. Digital landscape protection refers to the use of computer technology to create electronic files or digital files to express the landscape to support the protection, management and design of the landscape. In 1992, UNESCO used the computer-assisted information management system to digital protect the Angkor Kiln site in Cambodia, successfully opening up a new way of digital protection of the world heritage landscape. With the continuous development of global science and technology, digital technology has also been applied in the design and protection of landscape, and improves the interaction between people and landscape through digital technology. The ever-changing digital technology has brought unprecedented opportunities for the data collection, information storage and presentation of landscape landscape, and has become an important choice for modern landscape design and the protection and inheritance of traditional landscape heritage (Fig. 1).

2.2 The Significance of Digitalization of Traditional Garden Landscape

Traditional garden landscape is a combination of natural landscape and artificial architectural art, which reflects the society, economy, culture and history of a country or region. Digital construction is the embodiment of the scientific and technological development level and comprehensive strength of a country or region, and it is also an indispensable means to protect, inherit and carry forward the landscape heritage. In recent years, digital technology has been continuously applied in the protection of traditional landscape in China, and has become an important means to promote the development of the protection and inheritance of traditional landscape in China. Traditional landscape digital construction compared with the traditional protection technology has irreplaceable advantages, through digital means can put a large number of scattered, repetitive, disorderly, incoherent landscape information integration analysis research, to establish a complete and reliable database system, for landscape heritage protection and inheritance work provide scientific reference basis, also provide data support for urban construction and urban planning.

Fig. 1. The Lion Garden in Suzhou

3 The Present Situation and Existing Problems of Chinese Traditional Garden Landscape

Chinese traditional garden landscape is an important part of Chinese traditional culture. In ancient China, garden was the exclusive of "royal", providing service facilities for rest and entertainment. In modern society, some destructive phenomena: a large number of traditional landscape are facing disappearance and destruction, many famous landscape have been dismantled or transformed, thus losing their original features; many cities lack awareness of traditional culture in planning and construction, and pay insufficient attention to landscape planning and construction, ignoring their protection.

China's traditional garden landscape suffers a great threat, the number of traditional garden landscape decreases, the garden space structure changes greatly, the serious environmental pollution, the ecological deterioration and the lack of traditional garden landscape transformation technology. These situations show that there are some urgent problems to be solved and the lack of countermeasures.

3.1 The Number of Traditional Landscape Landscapes Decreases, and the Spatial Structure of the Landscape Changes

People's requirements for living environment, working environment and leisure and entertainment facilities are getting higher and higher, and there are many traditional garden landscapes that have been unable to meet people's work and life needs. Therefore, a large number of traditional garden landscape has been transformed or even dismantled, for example, Jinan Zhuyuan Garden has been occupied by the organs for a long time, and in the park, the reception room, parking lot, and even the demolition of the hanging gate into a boiler room, the west garden into factories, the original beautiful garden demolition.

There are many reasons for the change of landscape spatial structure, but it can be attributed to the following two points:

1. The influence of the historical background: The historical background is the influence on the development direction and form of the landscape in history, and the relationship between the development direction of the traditional landscape and the development of China's modern society, economy, politics and culture.
2. environmental reasons: now many cities are faced with serious environmental pollution and ecological damage, and the traditional landscape because of its high green area and ornamental value, so more and more government as an important content of environmental protection measures, and for some of the traditional landscape building demolition and renovation.

3.2 The Problem of Environmental Pollution is Becoming Increasingly Serious, and the Ecological Environment is Deteriorating

With the acceleration of urbanization, the traditional landscape is destroyed, and the ecological environment is becoming worse and worse. These include serious water pollution, the decrease of urban water landscape quality, excessive utilization of water resources due to industrial production, population growth, which increase the tension of water resources; air pollution and environmental deterioration; under the influence of industrial construction and road widening, air pollution is decreasing; noise is huge, and many cities have environmental pollution and ecological deterioration in different degrees. These environmental pollution problems not only cause bad effects on the soil and plants in the traditional landscape, but also destroy the ecology.

3.3 Lack of Traditional Garden Landscape Transformation Technology

Traditional landscape has rich cultural connotation and beautiful appearance, but some difficult problems: the original building and the surrounding environment; the original plants need to be preserved or removed; the original building and the surrounding environment. However, modern construction technology and equipment are difficult to meet the requirements of traditional buildings and landscape at the same time. At the same time, because the traditional landscape transformation is often rebuilt after "demolition", there is no complete, detailed, available for future generations to learn from and study and use the data, so there is some difficulty in the restoration.

4 Landscape Application of Digital Technology

4.1 The Collection of the Traditional Garden Landscape Historical Data and the Establishment of the Database

In the protection and inheritance of Chinese traditional landscape, the digital protection and inheritance of traditional landscape is of great significance. It is a long-term and meticulous and continuous work, in this process, the need to constantly accumulate relevant knowledge and experience. In the process of the development of information technology, digital protection and inheritance technology has also been greatly developed, which provides important help for digital technology in the protection and inheritance of traditional landscape culture. With the development of digital technology and the popularization of the Internet, the traditional landscape database can be established, and the digital data resource management platform can be used to realize the management and query of Chinese traditional landscape historical data, cultural heritage and other information data.

At present, the construction of China's traditional landscape resource database is still in the early stage, and the content of the information resource data in the database system is relatively complex, involving many disciplines and many fields. The collection, management and utilization of these resources need to spend a lot of time and energy to complete. Therefore, the establishment of a digital landscape resource database management platform is of great significance for the protection and inheritance of traditional landscape in the future. Through this platform, the most important and valuable content of China's garden culture can be integrated into a platform, so as to provide people with a way to obtain information, learn knowledge and study the traditional garden culture.

4.2 Using 3 D Modeling Technology to Restore the Traditional Garden Landscape

The establishment of the traditional garden landscape model can be selected according to the needs of the design, and the CAD software can be used to make the garden model in the design scheme. Through CAD software, establish 3 d model, can intuitively clear to see the overall layout of the landscape and local details, by scanning, measuring, modeling method of specific data collection of landscape, generate a series of 3 d digital model

Fig. 2. The SU model of the Humble Administrator's Garden

library and the corresponding software program (such as: Photoshop, 3D MAX) or 3 D effect software, etc. These 3 D digital models were then imported into the professional design software for further processing.

In the process of modeling, we need to pay attention to several problems: First, for the traditional landscape, it has a certain regional nature, so we should ensure that each region can be fully utilized. Second, the establishment of a complete three-dimensional model is one of the most effective ways to protect and inherit the traditional landscape, and also one of the most critical and effective ways to realize the virtual reality display system. Third, we need to choose according to different regions and different functions in the modeling process (Figs. 2 and 3).

Fig. 3. The SU model

4.3 Digital 3 D Virtual Scene Display

Using computer virtual reality technology, the traditional landscape information in 3 d environment, in the protection and inheritance of traditional landscape work is of great significance, which not only can make the history of landscape data preserved, also can make people through computer virtual reality technology to achieve more intuitive, more effective viewing experience. Digital garden landscape design model and virtual reality environment can enable people to observe and study the garden landscape more vividly. For the traditional garden landscape and ancient architecture, due to the limitation of the science and technology level at that time, most of its historical data could not be effectively protected and inherited. Therefore, using computer virtual reality and other technologies to virtual display the traditional landscape and ancient buildings has become an effective way to protect and inherit the traditional landscape. First of all, the efficiency of traditional landscape protection and inheritance of traditional landscape is improved by applying computer virtual reality and other technologies, animation and three-dimensional display of traditional landscape, and simulation of ancient buildings. Secondly, after the restoration of the traditional garden landscape and ancient buildings, they can be placed in a simulated environment for display and sightseeing. For example, when a classical Chinese style palace-style ancient building group was built in Beijing Beihai Park, only part of the building components could be repaired due to the limited construction technology. In order to be able to make it back to the original appearance, can use the computer virtual reality technology to establish 3 d environment and simulation operation to implement the repair work, finally installed all components in the ancient buildings installed into the computer running simulation software and animation demonstration program can repair the process of simulation display.

5 The Influence of Digital Technology on Garden Landscape Design

5.1 Promoting Cultural Inheritance and Development

Culture is the soul of a country, and its development degree directly affects the overall strength of the country. Chinese traditional landscape design is also inseparable from the development of culture in the development process of culture. The digital protection and inheritance of Chinese traditional landscape is the effective protection and utilization of China's traditional landscape cultural heritage and China's excellent traditional culture, which contains rich material and spiritual wealth. Therefore, it is necessary to strengthen the digital protection of Chinese traditional garden cultural heritage and Chinese excellent traditional culture, so as to realize its digital protection and inheritance. At present, there are certain limitations in the protection and inheritance of the traditional landscape culture in China, which makes it difficult for the traditional landscape to be well protected and inherited in the future development, which is a major problem in the development of China's traditional landscape culture. And digital technology can combine traditional Chinese landscape design and modern technology, through computer technology, network technology to China's excellent landscape design works to the world, and with the help of modern digital information technology to establish a virtual scene or 3D model, to better show the Chinese excellent landscape works. The integration of digital technology into Chinese traditional garden landscape also has the advantage of strong interaction, so as to realize the combination of Chinese traditional garden landscape culture and modern digital information, and promote the protection and inheritance of Chinese traditional garden landscape.

5.2 Enhance the Operability of the Design

The digital protection and inheritance of landscape can not only promote the promotion of traditional culture, but also effectively enhance the operability of design. At present, the development of traditional landscape design in China is faced with many problems, which are mainly reflected in the following aspects: lack of innovation consciousness, unable to meet the needs of modern society development; insufficient capital investment, the design cost is relatively high; the overall quality of designers needs to be improved. The application of digital technology provides many new ideas, new ideas and new methods for landscape design, so as to enhance the operability and practicability of landscape design and enhance the implementation of landscape design. Digital landscape has high practical value, which can not only provide people with a new, convenient and efficient living environment, but also promote the innovative development of modern landscape, so as to make an important contribution to the construction of the world.

5.3 Promote the Effective Protection and Utilization of Traditional Garden Landscape

Through digital technology can effectively improve the efficiency of garden landscape design, improve its artistry, but also provide the possibility for the development of modern science and technology, and promote the effective protection and utilization of traditional Chinese garden landscape. First of all, in the aspect of architectural space, digital technology can be used to design and plan the building. When planning the building, it can be reasonably designed through computer technology, which can not only get the optimal space effect, but also reduce the construction cost and save the construction time. Secondly, the use of digital technology can make the perfect combination of architectural landscape and landscape, so that China's traditional landscape and modern technology organically combined. Through digital technology, it can not only effectively publicize and display China's traditional culture and the world's history and culture, but also integrate China's history and culture with modernization, science and technology. Digitization has a profound and important impact on the reproduction of traditional landscape in China. Reasonable application of digital technology can improve people's understanding of traditional landscape design, and the protection and inheritance of traditional landscape in China can be better developed. Through the application of digital methods, people can have a deeper understanding of traditional culture. Digital technology can effectively integrate and preserve China's traditional garden landscape, ancient garden architecture and other related information, which can not only effectively protect and use these data, but also provide more data for China's historical and cultural research.

6 Countermeasures and Suggestions Based on the Digital Protection and Inheritance of Traditional Garden Landscape

At the 20th National Congress of the Communist Party of China, General Secretary Xi Jinping stressed the need to inherit the fine traditional Chinese culture and continuously enhance the country's cultural soft power and influence of Chinese culture. Chinese traditional landscape as an important part of our traditional culture, with the help of digital means to achieve more productive protection and inheritance, is promoting cultural self-improvement, casting new brilliant socialist culture, also promote national confidence, reveal national cultural soft power and influence of the Chinese culture of a choice.

Digital technology is an important means to realize the innovation of traditional land-scape. Whether it is creative refining or economic development, it is inseparable from digital technology, which needs digital technology to empower it. Take the Humble Administrator's Garden in Suzhou as an example, because of the huge market demand, the number of people in the park is often thousands of people, and the large flow of people greatly affects the tour experience. If the garden experience hall can be set up, combined with the digital performance, the cultural tourism route design, the tourists can see the digital cultural scene and get the immersive interactive experience, it will inevitably realize the crowd diversion for the "busy" Humble Administrator's Garden, so as to achieve better tour effect. China should speed up the development of tradi-tional landscape digitalization, actively promote the integration of cultural heritage with national characteristics into the "memory of the world", and provide Chinese solutions for promoting the inheritance of human culture and exchanges and mutual learning among civilizations.

7 Conclusion

China's traditional landscape heritage is facing various threats. In the face of the chal-lenges brought by the development of modern technology, inheriting the traditional Chinese garden landscape culture has become the top priority of the current cultural her-itage protection work. After discussing the necessity of the protection and inheritance of Chinese traditional gardens, this paper summarizes the current situation and existing problems of the digital preservation and protection of Chinese traditional gardens, and puts forward some suggestions on the digital protection and inheritance of Chinese tra-ditional landscape. We want to protect the traditional landscape culture for the purpose, in the current technology conditions using digital technology for traditional landscape protection and inheritance to provide technical support, strengthen the utilization of tra-ditional landscape digital resources and its effective integration and utilization, establish the era development demand, with scientific digital protection and inheritance system, for the Chinese traditional landscape provides a can fully display its historical value and cultural connotation of the platform.

References

1. Zhang, P.: The guiding value of digital technology to the transformation of landscape art design. Environ. Eng. **40**(02), 298 (2022)
2. Liu, P., Li, X., Yang, L., et al.: Digital monitoring and early warning mode of traditional village landscape from the perspective of cultural and tourism integration. Econ. Geography **42**(09), 193–200+210 (2022). https://doi.org/10.15957/j.cnki.jjdl.2022.09.022
3. Xiang, W.: Digital tourism—a new model of tourism economic development in China. J. Tourism **37**(04), 10–11 (2022). https://doi.org/10.19765/j.cnki.1002-5006.2022.04.006
4. Zhan, L., Huang, J., Wang, C., et al.: 3D digital presentation of red tourism resources based on landscape gene theory—Take the former residence of Mao Zedong and Yang Kaihui in Qingshuitang as an example. J. Tourism **37**(07), 54–64 (2022). https://doi.org/10.19765/j.cnki.1002-5006.2022.07.010

5. Mo, Q.: Application of digital technology in digital display design of classical garden in China. Environ. Eng. **39**(11), 221 (2021)
6. Lin, C.: Research on the digital protection of Historical Town Landscape (HUL) and the Inheritance of Manchu Traditional Culture—Take Shengjing Imperial City of Shenyang as an example. Heilongjiang Ethnic Cluster **184**(05), 135–139 (2021). https://doi.org/10.16415/j.cnki.23-1021/c.2021.05.014
7. Deng, L.: The construction of red cultural landscape under digital technology. Ind. Build. **51**(07), 266 (2021)
8. Bright Moon. The development of digital space green landscape under new media technology—review of landscape modeling: digital technology for landscape visualization. Environ. Eng. **39**(02), 190 2021
9. Lei, W., Chengcheng, Z.: The artistic performance of digital media art in environmental design—the digital strategy of landscape architecture. Environ. Eng. **39**(05), 250 (2021)
10. Xiaotong, G., Chen, Y., Feng, H.: Digital recording and conservation innovation of cultural landscape heritage. Chin Gardens **36**(11), 84–89 (2020). https://doi.org/10.19775/j.cla.2020.11.0084
11. Tingting, L.: Design of three-dimensional digital reconstruction system of spatial pattern of urban landscape. Modern Electr. Technol. **43**(08), 151–153+157 (2020). https://doi.org/10.16652/j.issn.1004-373x.2020.08.039
12. Luo, M.: Digitization of urban planning and its comprehensive research framework. J. Wuhan Univ. (Eng. Ed.) (03), 26–30 (2003)
13. Song, L., Shuwen, Z.: Digital landscape technology research progress—International Digital Landscape Congress development overview. Chin. Gardens **31**(02), 45–50 (2015)
14. Yao, G., Liu, Z.: Foreign digital protection and inheritance of intangible cultural heritage practice for reference. Southeast Cult. **290**(06):179–185 (2022)

Digital Inheritance of Straw Weaving in Laizhou, Shandong Province

Lili Zhang[✉], WenJing Yan, XinYu Li, Beile Su, and Ziqi Yao

School of Art, Shandong Jianzhu University, No. 1000, Fengming Road, Licheng District, Jinan 250101, Shandong, China
2668085780@qq.com

Abstract. Laizhou grass weaving is a folk handicraft in Shandong Province. Grass weaving has a long history, Laizhou grass weaving with exquisite technology, unique style, strong local characteristics and both appreciation and practical value, won the favor of domestic and foreign merchants, products sold in China and all over the world, shining a unique charm. Grass weaving is the people in the production and life, are closely related to people's life, and then gradually developed into a fine handicraft of function and aesthetics. To some extent, it reflects the living state, national feelings and aesthetic taste of the Chinese people. However, with the development of the society, the ecological environment on which the traditional handicrafts are maintained has undergone great changes, and more and more traditional handicrafts are facing the crisis of inheritance. The development trend of the straw weaving process in Laizhou is not optimistic. In order to adapt to the situation of the new era, the straw weaving process needs to break the old rules and dare to innovate. Laizhou grass-weaving traditional handicraft is an important project in the protection of national intangible cultural heritage, reflecting the crystallization of the wisdom of the working people, and is also an indispensable precious wealth in the field of national handicraft.

Under the background of the rapid development of the society, the protection of traditional folk handicrafts has become an important subject. In recent years, great changes have taken place in various fields with the advent of the digital era, and all kinds of traditional handicrafts are facing great opportunities and challenges. Digital technology has become an important means of communication of traditional process, and at the same time, it can record and save the relevant information of various process more quickly, and timely update relevant information and data. For the innovative design research of Laizhou grass, we should pay full attention to the use of digital technology and closely combine it with modern technology, so as to better promote the protection of Laizhou grass. Based on this, this paper first expounds the current situation of Laizhou grass weaving and the difficulties facing its inheritance as well as the difficulties of digital protection and dissemination, and then explores the application of digital technology in detail, hoping to put forward the efficiency and strategy of improving the protection of intangible cultural heritage of Laizhou grass weaving through digital information equipment.

Keywords: Laizhou grass weaving · Inheritance · Digitalization · intangible cultural heritage

N. A. Streitz and S. Konomi (Eds.): HCII 2023, LNCS 14037, pp. 322–332, 2023.
https://doi.org/10.1007/978-3-031-34609-5_24

1 Introduction

In Shandong grass weaving culture, the most representative is Laizhou grass weaving. According to the records of Laizhou City Annals, more than 1500 years ago, inspired by the braids, used wheat straw to weave wheat straw braids with dragon snake posture. Later generations used such straw braids as straw hats, hence the name "straw hat braids". In the Ming Dynasty, Laizhou grass braid crafts were widely spread in China. By the 1860s, grass braid crafts had attracted the attention of foreign merchants and became one of the first commodities sold overseas in China. But now, due to the new situation of modern market development, a variety of mechanical products and synthetic goods are found in various fields of production, which blocks the development of Laizhou grass weaving process to a certain extent. This situation causes the attention of the government departments and the society, and carry out the protection work from many aspects. Under the development background of the new era, the scientific application of digital technology has played a great role in promoting the protection and dissemination of Laizhou straw weaving. Through the digital application strategy, the cultural ecological environment on which Laizhou grass weaving depends can be improved, so that the inheritance of Laizhou grass weaving will be continuous, and the vitality of the new era will be radiated. So that Shandong hand in the Chinese voice of China on the international stage.

2 The Source Source of Straw Weaving Process

2.1 The Historical Background of Laizhou Grass Weaving

As one of the earliest traditional handicrafts developed by the Chinese people, grass weaving has a long history of development. It is a handicraft made of various herbs as raw materials. The growth area of its raw materials is broad and the production is simple, so the grass weaving handicraft is very common in China. The original straw weaving relics were made by the Hemudu people more than 7,000 years ago. The development of straw weaving technology in Laizhou, Shandong province originated from the folk in the Shahe area more than one thousand years ago. Inspired by the braids, the ancient people made various shapes of straw crafts. With the progress of handicraft technology, the variety of grass weaving are gradually increasing, and the scope of use in life is more and more broad. In the era of reform and opening up, the governments take various measures to encourage the export to expand the export of goods, make the world foreign trade circulation opportunities increase, laizhou straw weaving process firmly seized the opportunity, make weaving handicraft output become the forefront of the grass products, occupies about 70% of the province grass products, formed the largest export folk manual products. In the 21st century, under the influence of modern science and technology and cultural background, the emergence of a large number of mechanical products has caused a certain degree of impact on Laizhou grass weaving crafts. At present, Laizhou grass weaving needs to make innovation, combine with modern technology, keep up with the pace of The Times, and strive to open up a new fertile soil of modern weaving art.

Fig. 1. Schematic diagram of straw weaving raw materials and finished products

2.2 Making Materials for Laizhou Straw Weaving

Laizhou grass weaving handicraft is a kind of grass weaving folk art made of plant stems and leaves. Through different natural conditions and production processes, people can choose a variety of forage for production, so as to produce grass weaving products with different materials, styles, styles, and uses, so it has unique local national characteristics. Among the raw materials used in the compilation process, corn husk and wheat grass are the most commonly cultivated and used weaving materials (Fig. 1).

Corn husk, also known as "corn corn", is an annual grass herb. Straw woven corn skin to choose the middle of the 3 to 6 layers, soft and tough, white and clean color, suitable for weaving. Corn husks were first rubbed by hand, and then there was a hand-pulled spinning wheel, that is, according to the traditional cotton spinning wheel used for spinning and wool. Later, there was an electric spinning wheel, but because the corn skin is short and not easy to connect, the edges are often not smooth, so the quality is not good. Now we mainly pull the spinning wheel by hand.[1]

Wheat grass refers to the stalk of wheat. There are many wheat varieties, mainly wheat, barley, rye and so on. When the wheat is recovered, the straw must be cut first, and then the straw is tied into small bars, and the wheat ears used to weave must be manually rubbed off all the wheat grains above. The machine operation will damage the straw, and then tie it into a large bundle after drying. The final core selection method is to pick the wheat grass into a group according to the thickness, length, color and so on, and then tied into small bars, stored in files. Wheat grass fiber long, strong wear resistance, widely used, so it is generally braided for textile, can also be directly woven. Crops are not only good and cheap, but also important food crops widely cultivated throughout the country.

2.3   The Production Process of Laizhou Straw Weaving

As early as in ancient times, weaving technology has become the main means of Chinese ancestors to produce grass weaving handicrafts. "Compilation" is to use one or a few raw materials, according to the specific rules of coiled, mask to form no clear warp and longitude form. "Weaving" is to establish the scriptures, and then gradually weave latitude formation. The main weaving methods are flat weaving, twisted weaving, weaving, weaving, weaving and so on. Braiding an exquisite grass weaving handicraft, not only need to practice a variety of weaving techniques but also need to pay attention to the grass weaving method, although the grass weaving method is different, but the most basic pinch method is: the thumb pinch the front, the index finger pinch the back. Through constant pressure, pick out different patterns of grass braids (Fig. 2).[2]

---

[1] Qu Ting. Research on straw weaving art in Laizhou, Shandong province [D]. Soochow University, 2009.

[2] Liu Si-fan is there. Study on the Development and change of grass weaving in Laizhou, Shandong Province [D]. Shandong Institute of Arts and Crafts, 2017.

Fig. 2. Grass weaving process display

3   The Status Quo of Laizhou Grass Weaving Inheritance

3.1   The Social Status Quo of Straw Weaving

Shandong Laizhou grass weaving, is our national intangible cultural heritage, is a practical, ornamental and widely spread in the local traditional craft. But due to the development of modern science and technology, the ancient grass weaving technology is gradually lost, the people under the age of 60 engaged in the grass braids has been very few, more are the old people over 70 years old, to relax the way of boredom, and the variety is monotonous, the old artists of the pattern grass braids are very few. Wheat straw, corn skin as the main material of straw weaving crafts less and less, instead of some machine semi-finished products raw materials and other new grass art raw materials. Laizhou grass woven the current trend of development has caused the attention of government departments at all levels, and the grass and other intangible cultural heritage protection and development of propaganda has taken a series of measures, such as application and listed in the second batch of national intangible cultural heritage list, apply for national geographical indication certification trademark, wide apprentice, open courses, etc.

3.2 The Real Dilemma in the Inheritance of Straw Weaving

Laizhou grass weaving handicraft originated from the folk, which is a traditional handicraft skill with national emotion and aesthetic taste, and then gradually developed into an exquisite handicraft with functions and aesthetics. This is the skill that human society develops to a certain stage. However, it is currently influenced by modern technology, consumer market and cultural background. The inheritance and development of Laizhou grass weaving is faced with severe survival difficulties, the decline of the industry, no inheritance and other problems. The protection of the grass weaving process in Laizhou has been imminent, but due to the lack of fixed forms in the process of dissemination, there are few reference materials, and there are many difficulties, which can be understood from the following levels:

The Transmission Medium is Missing
Laizhou straw protection and inheritance need to spread out, let more people know grass, let everyone involved to play a promoting role, but the role of modern media intervention and has not produced strong reaction, in the media operation idea and mechanism factors, most reports are timeliness events, in comprehensive and depth reporting is scarce, which makes laizhou straw production process is not perfect show. Even some media to attract the public's attention, the formalization of the report and the content of the false problems are also more prominent:

There is No Successor to the Inheritors
With the rapid development of economy, the emergence of a large number of urban factories, rural young and middle-aged labor force are pouring into the city, resulting in the gradual decline of rural economy, making the number of rural left-behind old people rise rapidly, the straw weaving process will face the problem of no one to inherit. As the main body of inheritance handicrafts, traditional handicrafts are passed down from generation to generation. The protection of straw weaving technology needs people's strength. However, at present, in order to better survive, more and more young people go to work in big cities and are not willing to spend time studying straw weaving techniques. Laizhou grass weaving technology has a deep historical precipitation, complicated process, learning process is time-consuming and laborious, and the aging phenomenon of craftsmen is more prominent, many precious grass weaving skills are facing the problem of loss, grass weaving craftsmen will face the predicament of lack of successors.

Lack of Innovation in Grass-Weaving Technology
China's social structure system has been constantly improved, people's demand structure has undergone profound changes, and the demand standards are also constantly improving. As a result, some handicrafts are facing the difficulty of transformation and innovation. However, the traditional craftsmen of straw weaving technology are older and have the prejudice of following the old rules in their thinking. They are unwilling to innovate, nor dare not take risks and combine with modern technology. As a result, the current straw weaving crafts cannot break through the old thinking and attract the attention of the public, and the protection and inheritance of Laizhou straw weaving is difficult to maintain. Similarly, due to the influence of geographical location, folk culture and other factors, traditional craftsmen have less external communication, lack of cognition of modern technology, often adhere to the traditional aesthetic concept, do not keep up with the trend of The Times. The old shape of grass weaving crafts is not only difficult to meet the needs of consumers, but also lack of competitive advantages in the market competition, resulting in Laizhou grass weaving crafts from the reality of the public consumption demands, handicrafts will face the dilemma of unsales.

Lack of Brand Awareness
Since the development of traditional handicrafts, there have been many categories, but the business mode of most practitioners have not progressed with the changes of The Times and lack brand awareness. They mistakenly think that brands with several generations are equivalent to their own brands and do not go to the local trademark office for brand registration. Companies without registered trademarks are doomed to do not survive in the fierce market competition. Therefore, only by enhancing brand awareness and conducting brand registration, can the legitimate rights and interests of traditional craft practitioners be protected and effectively prevent the infringement of others. The registered brand is conducive to the better promotion of traditional crafts. Trademark marks will be used in poster brochures and sales products, which facilitates the public to remember and identify, and obtain more development opportunities.

4 Digital Protection and Transmission of Laizhou Grass Weaving

4.1 Digital Application Advantages of Laizhou Straw Weaving

Digital Technology Collection and Storage Advantages
There are many styles of grass weaving handicrafts in Laizhou, but due to the underdeveloped technology, the protection and inheritance of these handicrafts are only limited to the surface of taking photos, written records and book collection. Although it has a certain preservation effect, but in terms of its transmission speed, it is difficult to let more people know about Laizhou straw weaving. With the rapid development of The Times, digital technology has provided new functions and advantages for the protection and dissemination of Laizhou straw weaving process, and improved the quality and efficiency of Laizhou straw weaving transmission on the whole. In the use of new technology, the digital technology is used to process the files and text data of Laizhou straw weaving process, and the data are saved to U disk, CD or disk, effectively avoiding the phenomenon of wet books or insect bites and the loss of data. At the same time, the

Laizhou grass weaving process can also be recorded through digital photography technology, which can improve the integrity of the Laizhou grass weaving process, make the relevant information more orderly, and facilitate the information retrieval. The production process can also be made into animation and released at home and abroad, which not only increases the domestic popularity, but also enables the influence of Laizhou straw editing to spread overseas.[3]

Application of Digital Display and Inheritance Platform
Digital technology not only provides guarantee for the collection and storage of Laizhou straw weaving information, but also provides a new platform for the display and inheritance of Laizhou straw weaving handicraft skills. Specifically, the following two pathways. The first is to carry out a virtual experience platform, using the form of virtual space, so that users experience the process of straw weaving process. The virtual experience platform is similar to a metacom universe, in which highly intelligent artificial intelligence can meet people's interactive needs. People can change the identity they want in the meta-universe, shuttle freely between the real world and the virtual space, and learn the straw weaving process in the "meta-universe". Through an immersive experience, the virtual world is further approached and integrated into the real world. The second is three-dimensional scene modeling. People can use virtual scenes, coordinated display and other animation technologies to show the production process and finished products of Laizhou straw weaving. Use the network and TV to spread laizhou grass weaving, break the limitation of time and space, and let more people see laizhou grass weaving crafts.[4]

4.2 Digital Application Strategy of Laizhou Grass Weaving

Digital Development, the Trend of Inheritance
IP Digital Communication
Laizhou grass weaving is based on the "national intangible cultural heritage", and is integrated into the development trend of China-fashion as much as possible. Combine the traditional grass weaving technology with the modern fashion play, and the core of the tide play lies in the fine workmanship, creative IP, cultural core, and artistic collection. For the grass weaving technology, the creative IP will become the top priority of the combination of "country" and "tide" design. Laizhou straw weaving is subdivided into straw weaving process and grass paste process, and its derivative products also have different characteristics. Grass weaving is mainly ornaments, which can be combined with some fashion technology, but the main elements and technology should highlight grass weaving. For example, the straw weaving scarecrow combined with the spherical joints of BJD doll to realize the straw weaving crafts or other materials that can be freely shaped to make small scenes, but the key or the main body of the picture is reflected by the straw weaving. Grass paste is mainly based on plane and semi-stereo products,

[3] Wu Xueleng. Research on the digital protection of the intangible cultural heritage of traditional handicrafts [J]. Journal of Kaifeng University, 2020,34 (03): 77–79.

[4] Zhou Ling. The Future of the Meta-Universe and Digital Virtual Space: Back to the Study of game Text [J]. Journal of Nanjing University of Posts and Telecommunications (Social Science Edition), 2022,24(05):66–74. https://doi.org/10.14132/j.cnki.nysk. 2022.05.005.

reflecting the natural and simple color of grass weaving process and the characteristics of easy dyeing and strong plasticity. For example, stereo wallpaper, creative refrigerator stickers, etc. Or the grass paste and product image combination, add a certain interest and identification, logo highlight grass weaving technology, in daily life to deepen people's impression.

Carry out e-commerce, live broadcast sales of goods and other modes.
With the development of e-commerce, the traditional offline sales model has been impacted to a certain extent, and online shopping has become the main consumption mode of young people. At present, Internet shopping has developed very mature, and straw handicrafts can be used to carry out online and offline dual sales channels. Online, the popularity and influence of the anchors themselves can be used to sell the goods live online, and with the help of information technology, the products can be presented to consumers in a more intuitive, rich and interesting form. Taobao platform, TikTok platform live selling goods form, currently in the market, this through the host, again by the customer self-help order form, convenient and meet the public demand, grass products can cooperate with live platform to broaden the grass sales channels and sales way, boost the grass industry economic benefits. The majority of Internet users into potential customers, to enhance the social visibility of traditional craft products, to maximize the value of traditional craft products.[5]

Creative and Manual Fusion, Injected into the Era Pattern
In life, our common toys use plush and plastic materials; handicraft ornaments are mostly ceramics, rubber, this phenomenon and materials and processing techniques inseparable. Comfortable hand feel makes plush toys more suitable for close-fitting, low cost and fall resistance is the characteristics of plastic toys, a long cultural tradition, irreplaceable artistic value, as well as rich and mature processing technology so that ceramic materials can steadily stand on the top of handicrafts. And grass woven products do not have a plush comfortable feel, no ceramic thick sense, but it has a natural and simple feeling, light quality and crash resistance quality. Combine straw weaving with splicing toys and doll blind boxes to create novel products (Fig. 3).

Grass Patchwork Toys
Using the characteristics of strong variation of grass weaving materials and strong resistance to fall, we create personalized, diverse and random grass weaving splicing toys, committed to developing the imagination and creativity of people of all ages, and make toys suitable for everyone to play.

Grass Weaving Doll Blind Box
At present, the blind box is popular with its sense of mystery and delicacy, and quickly won the love of teenagers. The brand will be good quality straw braid dolls into blind boxes, into a series of blind boxes packaged sales, will be better than the separate sale of straw handicrafts update. Brands can plan self-made blind box plans. The so-called "homemade" is to purchase good quality from all over the country, classify and make them into blind boxes for sale. Those who provide homemade straw straw products can

---

[5] Li Yue. Application of digitization in the protection and dissemination of intangible Cultural Heritage of traditional handicrafts [J]. Art Mirror, 2021 (24): 62–63.

Fig. 3. Straw toys

get preferential treatment and subsidies. In this form, people of different ages and genders are called on to participate in the production of straw weaving products. This way breaks the labor relationship of "factory——employees" and cultivates and develops a large number of "free straw weaving craftsmen.

5 Conclusion

Social progress promotes the continuous development of various industries. The innovative design research of Laizhou straw weaving should not only keep pace with The Times and develop innovatively, but also maintain its own characteristics from not being replaced by other vulgar cultures. We should pay attention to the use of digital technology to play a role in promoting the protection and dissemination of handicraft intangible cultural heritage, which is also of practical significance for the protection and inheritance of intangible cultural heritage in China. The development of Laizhou grass weaving technology should conform to the trend of The Times, combine with popular elements, and keep up with the pace of The Times. In addition, the Laizhou straw weaving process should be promoted, and more people can know about this traditional handicraft through the digital display and inheritance platform, so as to attract more young people to inherit and develop. It not only provides a new idea for the problem of left-behind elderly, but also provides a new way for the development of traditional straw weaving technology, which has practical significance.

References

1. Wang, N., Wang, X.: The digital inheritance of Chinese traditional Ruo Hengcao weaving. Screen Print, **18**, 6–9 (2022)
2. Wang, Y.: The development path of Laizhou grass weaving under the Internet horizon. Liaoning Silk **03**, 44–45 (2022)
3. Liu Si-fan is there. Study on the Development and change of grass weaving in Laizhou, Shandong Province. Shandong Institute of Arts and Crafts (2017)
4. Ouyang, Q.: Development and application of grass weaving in Laizhou, Shandong Province. Qingdao University (2011)
5. Qu, T.: Research on straw weaving art in Laizhou, Shandong Province. Soochow University (2009)
6. Qu, Y.: The "grass roots" of traditional crafts exist. Shandong University (2009)
7. Li, Y.: Application of digitization in the protection and dissemination of intangible cultural heritage of traditional handicrafts. Art Mirror **24**, 62–63 (2021)
8. Wu, X.: Research on the digital protection of the intangible cultural heritage of traditional handicrafts. J. Kaifeng Univ. **34**(03), 77–79 (2020)
9. Feng, X.: Research on the digital protection and dissemination of traditional crafts. Popular Art **20**, 163–164 (2018)
10. Yang, J.: Research on digital experience and Product Online Marketing of Traditional handicrafts. Yunnan University of the Arts (2017)
11. Zhou, L.: The future of the meta-universe and digital virtual space: back to the study of game text. J. Nanjing Univ. Posts Telecommun. (Soc. Sci. Ed.) **24**(05), 66–74 (2022). https://doi.org/10.14132/j.cnki.nysk.2022.05.005
12. Yu, X.: Live broadcast and "bringing goods": the contemporary inheritance and practice of Yixing Zisha teapot handicraft. Tiangong **13**, 25–27 (2022)
13. Xu, L.: Enlightenment of the creation value of Chinese traditional handicraft. Shandong Art **03**, 13–17 (2022)
14. Zhou, J., Wu, W.: From "creation" to "frontier": the paradigm transformation of handicraft intangible heritage protection. Cult. Art Res. **14**(05), 32–41+112 (2021)

Supporting Health, Learning, Work and Everyday Life

User-Centred Detection of Violent Conversations on Mobile Edge Devices

Amna Anwar$^{(\boxtimes)}$ and Eiman Kanjo

Smart Sensing Lab, Nottingham Trent University, Nottingham, UK
{amna.anwar,eiman.kanjo}@ntu.ac.uk

Abstract. Mobile devices are ubiquitous for users in everyday life, often with individuals throughout their daily routine. The widespread use of mobile devices allows novel technologies to be designed to improve personal security and safety. The research presented in this paper provides additional functionality through pervasive sensors on mobile devices, making use of acoustic recordings and transcriptions to enable violent language detection in near-real time through a user-centred application. The purpose of the application is to provide a tool to improve the safety of individuals who may experience violent conversations. We have developed a mobile application which actively demonstrates applied theoretical practises across both the Tiny Machine Learning and Human-Computer Interaction literature. The application uses the built-in phone speaker and the device's on-board transcription service, providing an improved capability to correctly detect violent language in conversations through user proximity.

Keywords: Violent Language Detection · Mobile Edge Devices · Edge Crime Prevention

1 Introduction

Domestic abuse is a widespread problem; the Crime Survey for England and Wales estimated that 5% of adults 16 years and older had experienced domestic abuse for the year ending March 2022 [13]. The use of technology in crime prevention [10] encourages the use of mobile devices, allowing novel technologies to be designed to improve personal security and safety. Mobile devices are nearly ubiquitous for users in everyday life, often being with individuals throughout their daily routine, including use during work, social, and home activities. The widespread use of mobile phones provides a potential method of detecting incidents in domestic or localised environments. Existing solutions in this area include applications that can track and report problems in specific locations, using methods such as geofencing (e.g., [18]). Crowd-sourced police data has also been investigated, considering how location-based data mapping can be used to improve police reporting and deployment (e.g., [17]). Similar solutions are also used in applications that provide an emergency button to report situations to trusted contacts or law enforcement (e.g., [2]). The research presented in this paper provides additional functionality through pervasive sensors on mobile devices, making use of acoustic recordings and transcriptions to enable violent language detection in near-real time through a user-centred application.

Our investigation also provides a number of design considerations for working with sensitive user-centred data that could be recorded on an end-user device. In particular, the system does not have perfect accuracy and continues to enable self-reporting, which also activates the manual recording function. The mobile application can be activated/deactivated at any point, which can be performed using the in-app interface or through a persistent notification. The notification is displayed at all times to enable the application to run and can also be shown to rapidly activate the recording in the case of an emergency. The activation can also trigger an emergency warning, which could be used to notify a trusted contact or official of a potential situation. Potential concerns regarding the recording of everyday conversations have also been considered; In addition to the persistent notification, which can be toggled at any time, users will have complete control over when the application saves and deletes data. That is, if no issue is detected, the user can immediately delete any sensitive recordings.

The research presented in this paper explores potential design considerations and development choices for the user-centred detection of violent conversations on edge devices. We have developed a mobile application which actively demonstrates applied theoretical practises across both the Tiny Machine Learning and Human-Computer Interaction literature. Our future work will look at measuring these techniques through both quantitative and qualitative studies. We hope to measure the effectiveness of the application in near-real time using real conversations in a lab-based and home environment and also to demonstrate our work to practitioners, who will be asked to provide expert feedback on the designed solution.

2   Background

The fast growth of technology has transformed the way society deals with crimes, from initial research into CCTV cameras (e.g., [20]) and crime mapping (e.g., [27]) approaches to the widespread use of computational data science and machine learning methods (e.g., [21]). Mobile applications have also become more prevalent in the context of technologies for crime prevention; for example, mobile WiFi signals can be used to monitor or track crowds (e.g., [15]) and social media data has been used to detect Twitter violence reports (e.g., [9]). These applications are intended to provide users with a convenient and accessible tool for self-reporting crimes (e.g., [17]), as well as to be notified and gain access to critical information. Crime prevention apps have the potential to greatly improve community safety and allow citizens to play an active role in crime prevention by leveraging the widespread usage of smartphones. The use of mobile technologies has been advanced by the use of the Internet of Things, however, concerns regarding the privacy and legal risks of such devices have been identified [26]. A significant concern related to crime prevention applications is the potential privacy and safety risks to an individual using an application, highlighted by concerns related to smart home technologies [16] and electronic monitoring [22]. Despite this, the potential for mobile applications to be used in domestic environments is clear, should they be implemented correctly [10].

Previous applications have also explored this area [10], as numerous mobile applications have been developed in recent years to facilitate communication of emergency and panic situations to close relatives and policing institutions. For example, Circle of 6 [1] is a mobile app that allows its users to quickly contact a user-defined list of six people and share their current location along with an emergency message. Similarly, there are also apps that have been developed to help prevent crime in various ways to help protect the public. One of such mobile applications is BrightSky [3] (10k+ downloads on Google Play, scores 4.0). BrightSky is a mobile application aimed primarily at victims or potential victims of domestic abuse. There is also a Silent Beacon [2] which is a portable device disguised as a panic button. Once the button is pushed on the app, it triggers it to call 911 while communicating the location and emergency situation with a set of emergency contacts set by the user.

3   Design Considerations

As part of the process of developing the technological solution, considerations related to the design of the application were considered. The purpose of the mobile application was to provide a user-centred process to identify and detect violent language on the device. Ethical concerns related to individual interviews mean that it is necessary to determine, through existing literature and applications, the technical and design considerations that must be made for the application to work effectively. We use user-centred to refer to the application being based around user needs as opposed to any wider data collection task. Therefore, several design considerations were formed through an extensive review of the literature [10] and an identification of existing application design processes.

Self Reporting. Enabling the user to self-report a potential issue was a key design consideration during the development of the application. As with any automated technology, accuracy is not perfect, and therefore users should be allowed to control the recording methods and devices to ensure that reports can be made by the individual user if necessary, at any time, similar to existing applications [2].

Manual Recording. Allowing the user to manually record the audio is also a consideration linked to the previous concept of self-reporting. While existing applications (e.g., [1,2]) consider manual data collection, the main focus of the proposed application is automated data collection; therefore, it is important for designers to consider whether data can be recorded manually and how manually recorded data can be trusted.

Persistent Notification. Notifications are methods of presenting feedback to users; On more modern devices, persistent notifications refer to the continuous display of information or the notification of the capture of background data that occurs. As the edge application requires constant data access, a persistent notification should be shown; in addition, this could provide a useful method of self reporting and manual control to be provided to the user discretely, without using the main application.

Privacy. The nature of domestic violence and abuse means that privacy should be of the highest concern when developing applications for this context. For example, existing work has considered privacy concerns about computer security interventions for survivors of intimate partner violence [14], highlighting the need for correct data handling and reliable local data storage. Despite concerns about the use of technology, the potential of technology that considers privacy has previously been explored [8], and should therefore be critical in the design of future crime prevention applications.

Contact Warnings. Trusted contacts have been implemented in similar applications (e.g., [2]) and are individuals who the user trusts. Depending on the application, trusted contacts can link data to police or security services, close family members, or friends. It is necessary for an application to consider the export of privacy-aware information to trusted contacts without revealing personal or compromising details. Therefore, it is a consideration for application designers to plan and design methods that can effectively share the results of the data while keeping the original files secure.

4 Development

Our research explores a user-centred application to detect violent conversations in real time through a mobile edge device. The purpose of the application is to provide a tool to improve the safety of individuals who may experience violent conversations. The application uses our custom algorithm that is a fusion of text/audio features by making use of four different models [12]. For the text modality, Bidirectional Encoder Representations from Transformers (BERT) [25] and Linguistic Inquiry and Word Count (LIWC) [24] are used to computationally analyse the recorded transcripts. Acoustical audio processing uses a combined deep learning approach, where Mel-frequency cepstral coefficients (MFCC) (e.g., [23]) and a time-domain dense layer (e.g., [19]) are used to process audio for the purposes of classifying violent conversations acoustically. These modalities are then combined into one final output score. Our early results suggest that this fusion of audio and transcribed text analysis is possible, with varying positive accuracy rates depending on the algorithm combination used. The algorithm was then imported using Flutter, with the multi-modal, multi-level algorithm from TensorFlow exported to TensorFlow Lite, which can be run on Android and IOS devices. This enables edge processing to be performed, with all data being stored on the user's device, enabling higher levels of privacy than cloud-based solutions. The algorithm uses the built-in phone speaker and the device's on-board transcription service, providing an improved capability to correctly detect violent language in conversations through user proximity.

4.1 Mobile Development

The mobile application is designed to accompany the previously described TensorFlow Lite algorithm, which has also previously been applied to a Raspberry Pi edge device. The mobile platform provided a novel challenge due to limited processing power and access compared to other formats of edge devices. Despite this, the mobile platform provided the best method to ensure ubiquitous access to devices and the highest probability that the technology is used effectively by at-risk individuals.

The development of the mobile application was completed using Flutter, with Dart used as the main programming language. Flutter was used due to cross-platform compatibility that allowed the application to work on IOS, Android, and web-based devices. Flutter enabled cross-platform development to be performed easily when compared to Java and Swift, additionally the TensorFlow Lite Flutter plugin enabled custom TensorFlow models with multiple inputs to be ran on the edge. Despite this ease of use, Dart did make array manipulation difficult to perform, which was required due to the complex input shapes used by the multi-modal algorithm, with multidimensional arrays being used for most data storage, specifically in the context of the audio modalities. However, most of the data for the input in these modalities was easily accessible through the Flutter APIs, which provided access to the on-device audio, file storage, and notification systems.

The complex nature of the application required several packages to be used during the development process. The main package used was tflite_flutter [4], which enabled the interaction with TensorFlow Lite models using Dart. The application also used the record [6] package, which provided access to recording the audio in 10-second segments, which is required by the TensorFlow model. The application also used the Flutter eventify [5] library, which enabled smoother communication of the outputs to be displayed on the user interface of the application. The matrix2d package [7] was used to perform matrix operations similar to NumPy, which was used for the original algorithm. The key libraries highlighted in this section were used alongside other supporting technologies, which allowed the mobile application to be rapidly prototyped throughout the development process.

The application was therefore developed as a standalone system. The application used audio recording and local storage to record and process the required data. Upon completion of each 10-second recording segment, the TensorFlow Lite algorithm would be activated for use on the recently recorded segment. Upon the matrix operations being complete and the processing completed in the same format as the original algorithm, a resulting value through the form of binary classification is provided, which can be used to detect whether the algorithm determines the segment is violent or not. Using the TensorFlow eventify package [5], it is then possible to provide this data to user interface, which presents that data back to the user. Design considerations in this stage include the storage of the data on the local device, the local edge processing of the complex algorithm, and the potential for close contact or police warnings to be sent during this

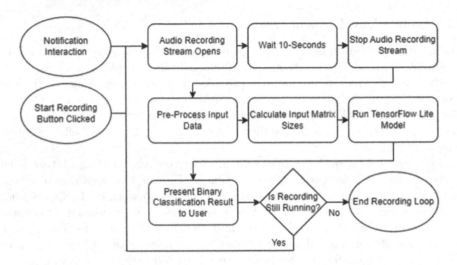

Fig. 1. A diagram presenting the interaction loop of the violent language detection mobile application.

process. The developed application provides an effective method of running the novel multi-modal algorithm on an edge device.

5   Interaction Design

The interaction design of the mobile application is presented in Fig. 1, which provides an overview of how the interaction loop runs. Through this interaction loop, the design considerations of providing the user control and privacy are considered through ensuring that self-reporting and manual recording are included as the main methods for application activation. The application starts recording through a notification interaction, or the start recording button being selected as presented in Fig. 2. This recording button then starts a separate recording loop, which ensures that each 10-second segment is completed before a recording can be completely cancelled. Upon running a recording segment, the screen will display a cancel recording icon as presented in Fig. 3, a notification is displayed, and a animation is played to the user to ensure awareness that the application is active.

As the loop follows the process presented in Fig. 1, information is presented to the user relating to the current application progress, for example, when the recordings are completed or when the algorithm processing is complete. As part of the aim to ensure that the application is as easy to use as possible, information relating to the current status of the application is presented to the user. Figure 4 presents the application view when a potentially violent conversation segment is detected, warning the user, and presenting the associated percentage determined through binary classification. Figure 5 presents the resulting view when the algorithm returns an uncertain result, indicating this through an orange background

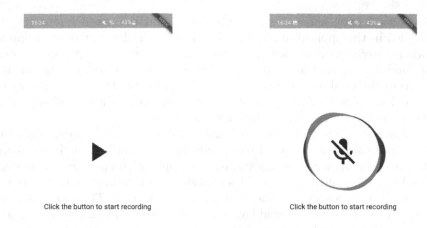

Click the button to start recording   Click the button to start recording

Fig. 2. Application screenshot of the app opening screen.

Fig. 3. Application screenshot during the first recording.

Fig. 4. Application screenshot of display when violent language is potentially detected.

Fig. 5. Application screenshot of display when the algorithm is uncertain if violent language is detected.

and associated text, allowing the possibility for further manual reporting to be included in the application. Finally, Fig. 7 presents the view of the application where no violent conversation is detected as occurring, displaying a green background and relevant associated text. To ensure trust in the system, further details as to the result of the algorithm are also presented to the user through a toast notification at the bottom of the screen, presenting the overall algorithm results and basic descriptions of the background tasks.

The application makes use of two forms of notifications; the previously identified toast notifications are used to provide user feedback through describing results and the current processing status. The application also uses a persistent notification, as presented in Fig. 6. This persistent notification can be selected to be present at all times, or just when the application is open. There are two main purposes of the notification: enabling audio to be recorded in the background on Android devices and allowing the user to toggle the recording at any time through the notification. The notification therefore allows users to know the current status of a recording segment, alongside providing control to enhance user privacy as described in the projects design considerations.

The application presents minimal use of gestures, buttons, and other elements to not overcomplicate the data collection process. This data collection process was identified as needing to be easy to perform to encourage users to turn on/off the device when needed, without fear of selecting the wrong option or clicking

Fig. 6. Application screenshot of the persistent notification that toggles a recording.

Fig. 7. Application screenshot of display when normal conversation is detected.

the wrong button. Figure 2 of the initial view presents the purposefully limited information presented to an existing user who opens the application, meaning that the recording can be started without an overload of information or options. At present, application options can be changed in a case-by-case basis; however, it is hoped that future development will mean that settings are embedded within the application.

6   Safety, Security and Privacy

We designed the violent conversation crime prevention application to prioritise safety and security. The application was designed to protect user privacy through processing all data on the edge, specifically on the end-users device. This enabled all potentially sensitive data to only be accessible through the end-user mobile device, which are often encrypted, however future investigations may need to consider devices which are not always encrypted. User data is collected through the on-device microphone, data is stored on the local device and only used for the purposes of detecting violent conversations. Should data need to be transferred in future iterations, it will be necessary to consider the encryption and secure transfer of the user data. At present, the application does not contain the ability to transfer transcriptions or recordings and therefore only the resulting binary classification could possibly be transferred.

Further consideration needs to be taken to ensure user safety while using the application; this might include an option to hide the application under the name of a different application such as a chat or messaging device. This option would therefore allow the application to share the name, icon, and interface of a different application, with recordings then occurring without the victim opening the named application.

7   Discussion

The application has successfully demonstrated that a novel multi-modal algorithm can be processed in near-real time on an edge device. Furthermore, the contextual application area of violent conversation detection has also been shown to work effectively on a mobile device. The area of mobile devices presents an interesting research scenario, due to the ubiquitous nature of the devices and the accessibility to a user in domestic environments. These domestic environments are expected to be the main area of use for the application; however, there is potential for location-based data to be used in the future to attach extended contextual information to the application (e.g., geofencing, location alerts, Bluetooth sensing) [11]. The application presented positive aspects of running the algorithm on the edge, with the potential for recordings to be more accurate in the future by curating a larger dataset of audio recordings that occur on a similar microphone to one that could be found on a mobile device.

Several potential issues were discovered during the design and development stage of the application. First, the processing power of the mobile device should be considered due to the time required for both audio and text modalities to be detected and converted. It will still be possible for the model to run on less powerful phones, however, the queue system used to manage the order of processing may become backlogged. Potential users and security services should also consider the accuracy of the overall algorithm, despite the high accuracy rate of the contextual situation reported [12]. However, this high accuracy is not perfect, meaning that extra precautions should be taken to ensure user safety while using the application. This also highlights a need for further development using the multi-modal model to occur, encouraging future work to focus on gaining the best possible accuracy alongside the application design giving the user overall control and reporting abilities.

Considerations will need to be made should the application be further developed. In addition to improved accuracy and features, should the application be used by police services for collecting or capturing data, improvements will need to be made as to the storage of data. While existing data is encrypted on the users local storage to ensure privacy, should the tool be used as a method of capturing evidence, changes to the security would need to be made for this. For example, a secure key may need to be generated for access, and a log of deleted recordings and times may need to be kept to ensure that the data collected can be used as evidence in a policing situation.

8   Conclusions and Future Work

The application presented in this article was an effective method of running a novel multi-modal audio-text model on the edge. The work highlights the potential of edge processing for sensitive topics such as domestic violence and crime prevention. Our work considered the design considerations needed for working with sensitive data, while also developing a solution to run a complex machine learning model on the edge. The application could be improved through higher accuracy, which could be through more realistic recordings on devices with similar microphones. We hope that the work presented in this article will be used to encourage future research into technologies, specifically machine learning, for crime prevention on the edge.

Our future work will now focus on fine-tuning the algorithm and the application design considerations. We hope to use the application in lab-based testing scenarios, with the hope of future work that would then test the application in domestic environments. Due to the sensitive nature and subject area of the application, these domestic environments can be simulated with expert interviews to determine the effectiveness of the application. Our overall future work will aim to measure the application in both qualitative and quantitative scenarios, enabling effective results to be reported.

References

1. Circle of 6 (2015). Accessed 12 Oct 2022. https://www.circleof6app.com/
2. Silent Beacon (2019). Accessed 12 Oct 2022. https://silentbeacon.com/
3. Bright Sky (2020). Accessed 14 Oct 2022. https://play.google.com/store/apps/details?id=com.newtonmobile.hestia
4. tflite_flutter: Flutter package (2021). Accessed 31 Jan 2023. https://pub.dev/packages/tflite_flutter
5. Eventify: Flutter package (2022). Accessed 31 Jan 2023. https://pub.dev/packages/eventify
6. Record: Flutter package (2022). Accessed 31 Jan 2023. https://pub.dev/packages/record
7. matrix2d: Flutter package (2023). Accessed 31 Jan 2022. https://pub.dev/packages/matrix2d
8. Al-Alosi, H.: Fighting fire with fire: exploring the potential of technology to help victims combat intimate partner violence. Aggress. Violent. Beh. **52**, 101376 (2020). https://doi.org/10.1016/j.avb.2020.101376
9. Al-Garadi, M.A., et al.: Natural language model for automatic identification of intimate partner violence reports from twitter. Array **15**, 100217 (2022). https://doi.org/10.1016/j.array.2022.100217
10. Anderez, D.O., Kanjo, E., Anwar, A., Johnson, S., Lucy, D.: The rise of technology in crime prevention: opportunities, challenges and practitioners perspectives (2021). https://doi.org/10.48550/ARXIV.2102.04204
11. Anwar, A., Kanjo, E.: Crime prevention on the edge: designing a crime-prevention system by converging multimodal sensing with location-based data. In: Basiri, A., Gartner, G., Huang, H. (eds.) Proceedings of the 16th International Conference on Location Based Services (LBS 2021), pp. 96–100. TUWien, Glasgow, UK (2021). https://doi.org/10.34726/1754
12. Anwar, A., Kanjo, E., Anderez, D.O.: DeepSafety:multi-level audio-text feature extraction and fusion approach for violence detection in conversations (2022). https://doi.org/10.48550/ARXIV.2206.11822
13. Elkin, M.: Domestic abuse in England and wales overview: November 2022 (2022). https://www.ons.gov.uk/peoplepopulationandcommunity/crimeandjustice-/bulletins/domesticabuseinenglandandwalesoverview/november2022
14. Freed, D., Et al.: "Is my phone hacked?" analyzing clinical computer security interventions with survivors of intimate partner violence. Proceed. ACM Human-Comput. Interact. **3**(CSCW), 1–24 (2019). https://doi.org/10.1145/3359304
15. Kanjo, E., Anderez, D.O., Anwar, A., Al Shami, A., Williams, J.: Crowdtracing: overcrowding clustering and detection system for social distancing. In: 2021 IEEE International Smart Cities Conference (ISC2), pp. 1–7 (2021). https://doi.org/10.1109/ISC253183.2021.9562914
16. Lin, H., Bergmann, N.W.: IoT privacy and security challenges for smart home environments. Information **7**(3), 44 (2016)
17. Maghanoy, J.A.W.: Crime mapping report mobile application using GIS. In: 2017 IEEE 2nd International Conference on Signal and Image Processing (ICSIP), pp. 247–251 (2017). https://doi.org/10.1109/SIPROCESS.2017.8124542
18. Maxwell, L., Sanders, A., Skues, J., Wise, L.: A content analysis of personal safety apps: are they keeping us safe or making us more vulnerable? Violence Against Women **26**(2), 233–248 (2020). https://doi.org/10.1177/1077801219832124

19. Pandey, A., Wang, D.: Dense CNN with self-attention for time-domain speech enhancement. IEEE/ACM Trans. Audio Speech Lang. Process. **29**, 1270–1279 (2021). https://doi.org/10.1109/TASLP.2021.3064421

20. Piza, E.L., Welsh, B.C., Farrington, D.P., Thomas, A.L.: CCTV surveillance for crime prevention: a 40-year systematic review with meta-analysis. Criminol. Public Policy **18**(1), 135–159 (2019)

21. Ratnaparkhi, S.T., Tandasi, A., Saraswat, S.: Face detection and recognition for criminal identification system. In: 2021 11th International Conference on Cloud Computing, Data Science & Engineering (Confluence), pp. 773–777. IEEE (2021)

22. Rothstein, L.E.: Privacy or dignity: electronic monitoring in the workplace. NYL Sch. J. Int. Comp. L. **19**, 379 (1999)

23. Sato, N., Obuchi, Y.: Emotion recognition using Mel-frequency cepstral coefficients. Inf. Media Technol. **2**(3), 835–848 (2007). https://doi.org/10.11185/imt.2.835

24. Tausczik, Y.R., Pennebaker, J.W.: The psychological meaning of words: LIWC and computerized text analysis methods. J. Lang. Soc. Psychol. **29**(1), 24–54 (2010). https://doi.org/10.1177/0261927X09351676

25. Tenney, I., Das, D., Pavlick, E.: BERT rediscovers the classical NLP pipeline. CoRR abs/1905.05950 (2019). https://arxiv.org/abs/1905.05950

26. Wachter, S.: Normative challenges of identification in the internet of things: privacy, profiling, discrimination, and the GDPR. Comput. Law Secur. Rev. **34**(3), 436–449 (2018). https://doi.org/10.1016/j.clsr.2018.02.002

27. Zhou, G., Lin, J., Zheng, W.: A web-based geographical information system for crime mapping and decision support. In: 2012 International Conference on Computational Problem-Solving (ICCP), pp. 147–150 (2012). https://doi.org/10.1109/ICCPS.2012.6384228

The Tribrid-Meeting-Setup – Improving Hybrid Meetings Using a Telepresence Robot

Francisco Hernandez(✉) ⓘ, Julia Birke ⓘ, and Angelika C. Bullinger ⓘ

Chair of Ergonomics and Innovation, Chemnitz University of Technology,
Erfenschlager Straße 73, 09125 Chemnitz, Germany
francisco.hernandez@mb.tu-chemnitz.de

Abstract. Hybrid meetings are the standard solution to balance remote and on-site work. They are built around on-site participants, and online and on-demand (offline) participants are at risk of being ignored. This paper set out to determine how hybrid meetings could be more engaging and interactive. As a solution, the Tribrid-Meeting-Setup (TMS) is presented. The TMS allows online participants to have an active role during the meeting by using a Telepresence-Robot (TPR) and give an interactive perspective of the meeting to the on-demand (offline) participants by recording the meeting in a 360° video format. An iterative prototype development approach was implemented for designing the TMS. This article summarizes how to build a TMS, the results of the first test using the TMS, and further recommendations for the TMS.

Keywords: Robots · Avatars and Virtual Human · Remote Work · Hybrid Meetings · Telepresence Robots · Interactive Video Conferencing

1 Introduction

Hybrid meetings result from a constant evolution between working remotely and attending virtual meetings. Hybrid meetings are a proper mixture of remote and onsite employees. Remote employees can join work meetings, workshops, seminars, or conferences via a virtual meeting platform (BigBlueButton, Zoom, Teams, Google Meet, and so on) and interact with the onsite employees when the onsite setup allows it. Hybrid meetings can be a bridge to connect onsite and remote employees, allowing them to interact in the same location. By enabling virtual participation in hybrid meetings, those who would not otherwise be able to attend physically can participate partially or in all of the meetings [1]. The requirement for employees to be physically present at the office can reduce the talent pool available for a company. Mostafa found out that the possibility of working remotely increases the company's attractiveness in the labor market [2].

Meaning that employees whose physical presence is not needed (most of the time) are not bound to the location of the main office. The place of residence of an employee is no longer an issue [3]. In Germany, only one in ten employees wants to return to the office full-time [4]. Hybrid meetings also reduce the amount of physical presence and travel for employees and the carbon footprint [5]. Moreover, hybrid meetings are more cost-effective and easier to organize [6]. There are also many challenges to the correct implementation of hybrid meetings regularly. The internet reliability for the remote employee, the moderation onsite is more challenging, remote employees can be excluded easily, the lack of non-verbal communication, how good the onsite setup is built (number of cameras, microphones, screens, needed), the meeting could take more time as planned, and the increase distractions for all attendees, onsite and online [1, 5, 7].

The article's authors consider it necessary to understand the evolution of remote work (Sect. 2), the adaptation of virtual meetings during the pandemic era (Sect. 3), and the background of hybrid meetings (Sect. 4), to comprehend the potential of the Tribrid-Meeting-Setup (TMS). A prototype of the TMS, which includes a Telepresence-Robot (TPR) and a 360° video camera, was built, and the results of the first prototype testing are presented in this article. Also included in this article are instructions on how to build a TMS, the results of the prototype test, and suggestions for further testing of the TMS.

2   The Evolution of Remote Work

Going to the office and working from there is based on the factory-centralized workplace model from the industrial revolution. A factory must be located near the materials, supplies, means of transportation, and workforce to run efficiently. This work model continues to be valid and used in our current times. Even in business and government organizations that have nothing to do with manufacturing [8]. *We don't think twice about it. In order to work you must go to work. Just like all the other factory workers.*[1]

The concept of "remote work" was initially introduced as Teleworking or Telecommuting by Jack Nilles in 1973 as the use of information technology to replace the commute to and from work. Its main goal was to reduce or eliminate the daily commute from workers of an organization thus reducing in some way the automobile traffic and the consumption of non-renewable energy resources. This was also motivated by the oil crisis from 1973 [9]. The basic idea of this concept was that office workers, such as clerks, accountants, etc., do not necessarily need to be at the office to get their work done [8].

The term remote work can also be found in the literature as working at a distance, teleworking, telecommuting, working from home, mobile work, remote e-working, and work from anywhere. As several European languages such as German, Spanish, Italian or Scandinavian do not have a word for telecommuting, the word teleworking is used. This is why the term telecommuting is more common used in North America, while in Europe the preferred term is Telework [8, 10].

As personal computers continued to miniaturize, increase in performance, and decrease in cost, the concept of "remote work" became a potential alternative to traditional office work for more and more jobs. For this reason, IBM launched an experiment in 1979 in which five employees worked from home. IBM wanted to find out if remote work was possible. Four years later, the number of test subjects had grown to 2,000 remote workers. The concept transformed into a common way of working and quickly

---

[1] Jack Nilles – Making telecommuting happen: a guide for telemanager and telecommuters (1994).

spread. By 1987, the number of remote workers in the U.S. had grown to 1.5 million [11–14].

In 1992, the European Community established the European Community Telework Forum (ECTF) to inform and demonstrate the advantages of teleworking to governments and businesses. By 1998 the number of teleworking or remote working employees had risen to over 4 million - almost 3% of the workforce at that time. [15]. The expansion of the internet also played an essential role in the broader implementation of remote work [10]. In 1999, 6 million Europeans worked from home at least once per week. It was also projected that this number would rise to 16 million by 2005 [16]. n the European Union (27 Countries) 4.5% of employed people worked from home in 2002, whereas in the subsequent years, the number of people working from home varied between 0.1 and 0.9% until it reached 5.4% in 2019. Due to the Covid Pandemic, the number of people working from home rose to a staggering 12% in 2020 and 13.4% in 2021. In Germany there was a variation from 5.4% in 2019 to 13.6% in 2020 to a whopping 17% in 2021. In 2021, Ireland was the country in the European Union with the highest percentage of people working from home with 32%, followed by Luxemburg with 28.1% [17]. The importance that remote work has won in the past decades is also reflected by the amount of research that has been done. From almost no interest or relevance in the '80s and '90s to a constant growth since 2002. In 2020 and 2021 the number of scientific papers related to telework increased significantly [18].

Remote work presents several advantages such as a better work-life balance, reducing costs for the employee and the employer, improving productivity and performance or new job opportunities, just to name a few. But the advantages are directly dependent from the management style and the willingness of the employer and employees to adopt remote work. The creation of clear rules while working remotely are necessary to avoid burn out due to undefined work schedules, work overload, a low degree of autonomy, isolation, not having a defined line between personal and worklife, as well as ergonomic problems due to extended hours in front of the computer [10]. Remote Work is the future of work, and has to be adapted constantly.

3   Virtual Meetings During the Pandemic Era

After two years of the SARS-CoV-2 pandemic, the way we work has been reshaped [19]. We got used to working remotely and to the burden associated with virtual meetings. For example, the technical issues, the amount of online meetings per day, the difficulty to read nonverbal clues, collaborating and interacting with work colleagues, the difficulty to focus, not being able to unplug from work, the loneliness, staying motivated, and the distractions that come with working from home, are some of the reasons that make working remotely challenging [20, 21].

When the conditions made it possible and taking all the necessary precautions (testing, social distancing, wearing a mask, etc.) we could meet with work colleagues at the office, and if you were lucky enough you could go and visit a client or even go to a conference outside of town. Nowadays, virtual meetings have become part of our work routine. On average, we attend nine virtual meetings per month. The average duration of a virtual meeting with three to six participants is about an hour. Virtual meetings with 20+ participants could often last in average more than 70 min [22].

Virtual meetings have several numbers of advantages. For example, participants from remote locations can participate more willingly in virtual conferences, which improves the quality and diversity of the meeting [23]. Online meetings increase employees' productivity and availability, and reduce costs for the employer [14]. But, as mention before online meetings are hard to follow and are not as exciting, captivating, and engagingly as in person meetings [24]. The most significant issues with virtual meetings are:

1. The lack of nonverbal (body language) communication.
2. The mirror anxiety triggered by self-video during the virtual meeting.
3. Being physically trapped due to the limited field of view of the camera.
4. The hyper gaze. The hyper gaze is a perceptual experience of constantly seeing people's eyes. Unlike in-person meetings, where the speaker tends to draw all participants' attention, everyone can see each other directly during virtual meetings.

These four factors contribute to experiencing zoom fatigue [25–28]. During virtual meetings, small talk before or after a meeting is almost nonexistent [29]. Even though all the hardships of virtual meetings, only a small portion of employees want to return to the office full time. In Germany, only 14% of the employees want to return to the office full-time [4]. Also, 76% of employees would like to be able to work from anywhere, and 93% would like to work whenever they want [30]. Virtual meetings are here to stay, and hybrid meetings are the obvious solution. The challenge is how to implement them sustainably.

4   The Background of Hybrid Meetings

Remote working and attending online meetings are the new standard that presents unique challenges for employers and employees. Both need to adapt and find common ground in which their necessities and wishes are fulfilled. The employer wants that remote employees be present for onsite meetings, and remote employees don't want to forfeit the freedom that remote work gives them.

Hybrid meetings are the apparent solution. In theory, hybrid meetings are the perfect mixture of onsite and online meetings. It is a flexible format for the participants, in which one part is online, and the other is present onsite. The online participants don't have to deal with the hustle of traveling, which in some cases can be time-consuming (e.g., planning, booking, the application for a visa, and time zone changes). Hybrid meetings also allow companies to expand their talent pool because the work is not bound to one location [1, 2]. Another advantage of hybrid meetings is the reduction of the employees' carbon footprint, and they are more cost-effective and easier to organize than regular meetings [5, 6].

Vellante (2022) predicts that hybrid work environments will become permanent in the near future. Also that by the end of 2022 29% of the workforce in the United States will work full time remotely, 34% on a hybrid setup and 34% will be full time at the office [31]. Also, a study made by Inavero in 2019 projects that by 2028 3 of every 4 teams in an organization will have remote workers [32]. This is why a new way of attending hybrid meetings is necessary. Hybrid meetings also allow companies to expand their talent pool because the work is not bound to one location [2, 3] (Fig. 1).

Fig. 1. Example of a Hybrid meeting at the chair for ergonomics and innovation at the Chemnitz University of Technology.

Rehak et al. (2020) suggest building a bridge between online and present participants by creating networking environments for both parties, before (matchmaking), during (virtual chats, shared polling, and a dedicated Emcee to connect both audiences), and after (post-event resources) the meeting [33]. McElnay (2021) make the case for a solution to hybrid meetings [34]. He called them "tribrid" meetings. Tribrid means to have participants onsite, online, and on-demand (offline). This way, the event is available for even more people.

The implementation of hybrid meetings presents several challenges, for example, the need for a stable internet connection, a practical setup, and an engaging onsite moderator. The main problem of hybrid meetings is their being built around onsite meetings and the risk of ignoring virtual participants. Also, one of the biggest challenges of online meetings is keeping the virtual participants focused even more when the presentation is not captivating enough or takes a long time. Another disadvantage of hybrid meetings is the lack of interaction between onsite and online participants [1, 5, 7, 35].

After analyzing the challenges and opportunities presented by remote work, virtual and hybrid meetings, the authors drafted the research question of this paper.

RQ. How could hybrid meetings be built to be more engaging and interactive?

The following section - Designing the Tribrid-Meeting-Setup (TMS) - describes the requirements for the TMS, how it was built, and the components needed. A summary of the main findings is provided in Sect. 6.

5 Designing the Tribrid-Meeting-Setup (TMS)

Based on the proposed solutions from Rehak and McElnay, and our own experiences during hybrid meetings at the Chair for Ergonomics and Innovation at the Chemnitz University of Technology, the Tribrid-Meeting-Setup (TMS), including a Telepresence-Robot (TPR) and a 360° video camera was designed. A TPR is a video conference system with remote movement capabilities [36] that has the potential to make the Tribrid-Setup more interactive, captivating, and enjoyable. The TPR is an innovative communication tool that hasn't been used in this setup [37]. The 360° video recording of the meeting provides a more interactive perspective of the meeting for the on-demand (offline) participants.

Section 5.1 briefly explains what a TPR is and why it was selected to be implemented for the TMS. Section 5.2 explain how the TMS was built, the requirements for the participants, and the components needed for the first TMS prototype.

5.1 What is a Telepresence Robot?

There are two components to a TPR system: the physical robot (sensors, actuators, and a screen) and the software (user interface to control and drive the robot). The most remarkable feature of a TPR is the virtual presence of the remote user on the device which merges the real and digital worlds. The TPR remote user or driver can move the robot freely (if possible) in its environment, and interact with other people. Currently, the use of a TPR is intended for indoor use only [36–41] (Fig. 2).

Fig. 2. Telepresence-Robot in the Experimental and Digital Factory (EDF) at Chemnitz University of Technology (1. microphone and cameras, 2. sensors, and 3. self-balancing system).

The concept of telepresence was coined by Marvin Minsky in 1980. According to him, work could be done from home, thus reducing time and energy costs and eliminating possible chemical and physical hazards [42]. *One person could do different jobs in different places*[2]. The first functional prototype was developed by Paulos and Canny in 1998 [43]. This prototype led to the development of the telepresence robots currently available on the market [38, 44].

TPRs are currently used for virtual mobility in the office, medical and nursing staff support, teaching, and research. A few examples of its use in office environments include attending conferences and meeting with colleagues in different locations and saving time and travel [45, 46]. To facilitate communication between isolated patients or residents of nursing homes, a TPR is employed for virtual doctor consultations, nursing and elderly

---

[2] Marvin Minsky – Telepresence. OMNI Magazine (1980).

care [40, 41, 47–49]. As a teaching tool, it is used to connect students and teachers from different locations as well as sick students. The TPR offers people with limited mobility the opportunity to be present at other sites with less effort [50, 51]. Due to adaptability and easy implementation (including learning how to use it) of TPRs, they are a perfect addition to Hybrid Meetings.

5.2 How was the Tribrid-Meeting-Setup Design?

For the development of the TMS, the authors choose an iterative prototype development approach (1. Requirements, 2. Components, 3. Implementation scenario, 4. Testing, and 5. Results) based on the engineering method from Waechter (2019) [52] and design science research of Hevner et al. (2010) [53]. This paper presents the first iteration of the TMS prototype and encourages further testing by other researchers. The authors plan to further test the TMS in internal meetings and in several research projects.

Requirements for the Participants. An expert workshop took place to determine the requirements, types, and tasks of the participants in a TMS.

There are six types of participants in the TMS.

1. Online participants are the participants attending the meeting via a video conferencing software. A minimum number of six online participants was set for the first test. The are no special requirements for the online participants.
2. Onsite participants are the participants attending the meeting onsite. The are no special requirements for the onsite participants.
3. TPR-Remote-Users, are the participants controlling the TPR. The TPR-Remote-Users should have experience using a TPR. This way, extra training or explanation of the functionalities and limitations of a TPR would not be necessary.
4. The moderator (onsite), should have experience using a TPR in case technical problems with the TPR arise. The moderator should also know the TPR technical limitations of the TPR, such as the TPR drivable areas, the battery duration, the necessary lighting conditions, etc. The moderator needs to know the goals and the agenda of the meeting and the role of each participant to clarify the setup for all participants. The moderator is also in charge of starting and stopping the 360° video recording. The moderator should encourage the participation of all attendees during the open discussion and oversee that the conversation stays on track,
5. The presenter (onsite) is the person giving the presentation. The presenter should be onsite and answer all participants questions (onsite or online). The presenter should also know the technical limitation of a TPR and the TMS.
6. On-demand (offline) participants, persons interested in the content and results of the meeting but couldn't attend the live session. The are no special requirements for the on-demand (offline) participants.

Due to covid restrictions, the role of moderator and presenter was taken by the same person during the first test. In future tests, these roles should be separated. There were also no onsite participants apart from the presenter/moderator. The requirements and feedback of onsite participants should be defined and gathered in future testing of the TMS prototype.

Components for the TMS. An expert workshop defined the necessary components of a TMS to enable interaction between all participants. It was concluded that:

1. Two cameras are needed to focus on the presenter/moderator and the onsite participants (TPR-Remote-Users).
2. Two screens are needed, one facing the moderator/presenter and the other the TPR-Remote-Users. The goal is that the onsite participants can see the online participants.
3. The web cameras should have at least a resolution of 1280×720 pixels/720p (HD) to ensure a good video quality for the online participants.
4. The speakers should be suited to the room where the TMS will be built.
5. The microphone should be able to capture the voice of all onsite participants (presenter/moderator and the TPR-Remote-Users).
6. The video conference software should be configured to enable the feedback of the cameras during the meeting.
7. The 360° video recording must be in high resolution. This way, the on-demand (offline) participants could see and read the details of the presentation.

The TMS consisted of the following:

- 2 × webcams (1 Renkforce Full HD 1080P and 1 Logitech Rally),
- (Camera 1 focuses on the presenter, Camera 2 focus on the TPRs),
- 2 × 55in screens with integrated desktops,
- (one facing the presenter, the other the TPR),
- 1 × Omnidirectional Microphone (Logitech Rally),
- 2 × Speakers (Logitech Rally),
- 1 × Presentation Laptop,
- 1 × Video Beamer,
- 1 × 360° camera (GoPro MAX),
- 3 × Telepresence Robots (Model Double 3 from Double Robotics) (Fig. 3).

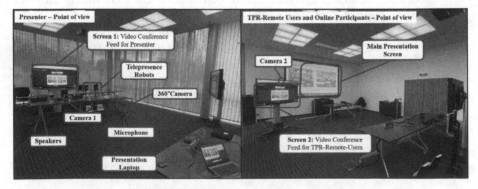

Fig. 3. Components of the Tribrid-Setup

Screen 1 provided video feedback for the presenter, allowing him to communicate directly with the online participants. Even though the TPRs can move freely in the room, during and after the meeting, screen 2 provided video feedback of the online participants to the TPR-Remote-Users and enabled interaction between them. Due to the novelty of the setup, screen 2 was also used as a viewing backup of the presentation for the TPR-Remote-Users. The lighting conditions of the room were not modified. Access to the online meeting for the TPR-Remote-Users was purposely not provided, to reduce distractions and increase the active presence of the TPR-Remote-Users in the room. Camera 1 focuses on the presenter, and camera 2 focuses on the TPR-Remote-Users. The cameras were positioned in this matter, so that the online participants and the TPR Remote users could know who was talking.

For the on-demand (offline) participants to have a more interactive experience and a better view of everything happening during the meeting, the 360° Camera was positioned in the middle of the room to optimize the point of view and avoid editing the 360° video recording. The benefit of 360° video recording is that the on-demand (offline) participants can choose the point of view they desire and zoom in or out on details of the meeting. The 360° video recording of the session was only made available upon request.

6 First Test and Feedback from Participants

6.1 Implementation Scenario

As testing ground for the TMS an internal meeting of the Chair for Ergonomics and Innovation at the Chemnitz University of Technology was selected. Before the meeting, five discussants were chosen. Three attended the session using a TPR, and two attended as online participants. The idea was to trigger an exciting discussion between the presenter/moderator (onsite), the TPR users, and all the online participants. The discussants using the TPR assume the role of TPR-Remote-User (person controlling the TPR onsite). The presenter and the online participants took the role as TPR-Local-Users (person(s) interacting with the TPR onsite) [36, 37, 54].

All five discussants had previously used a TPR. The average time driving a TPR of the discussants was 85 min. This average doesn't consider the training time on how to drive a TPR (approx. 20 min). The online participants didn't have to have any experience using a TPR to attend the session, and the total number of online participants was unlimited.

6.2 The First Test

22 members of the chair and 2 alumni participated in the meeting. The field of work of the participants was divided into five disciplines, Business Administration (3), Systems Engineering (6), Industrial Engineering (7), Automotive Engineering (1), Psychology (5), and Social Sciences (2). The meeting had a duration of approximately 1,5 h. Due to corona safety requirements, only one person (the presenter) was allowed in the conference room, 20 participants took part online, and 3 using a TPR.

Before the start of the meeting the TMS, the testing objectives, the agenda for the meeting (presentation, questions, and open discussion) and the role of each participant were explained. It was encouraged that the online participants take part during the open discussion (Fig. 4).

Fig. 4. Screenshot of the 360° recording

After the session was concluded, feedback from all participants was gathered to be later evaluated. The TPR-Remote-Users and the presenter took a brief tour (approx. 20 min) at the chair's office to gather some insights about the experience of using and talking through a TPR with other TPR-Remote-Users.

6.3   Results of the First TMS Prototype Testing

The TPR-Remote-Users said that attending the meeting using the TPR was more interesting due to how natural and easy the interaction with the other participants was, and the ability to move freely and explore the office was an aspect that the TPR-Remote-Users liked the most.

Online Participants said that the Setup encourages them to be more active during the meeting, and they would like to participate in future meetings as a TPR-Remote-User. They also suggest that the online participants could swap places with the TPR-Remote-Users during the meeting (e.g., during the coffee brakes). This could increase the level of interaction of all participants during hybrid meetings (Fig. 5).

Fig. 5. Screenshot of the TPR User Interface

All participants concluded that the TMS could be used at local and international conferences. The TMS should be further tested to create usage guidelines considering, for example, how big the online groups should be, the maximal duration of the meeting, the requirements of onsite participants, the role definition of the TPR-Remote-User(s), how many TPRs are needed, and how should they be used. After the quick tour, the TPR-Remote-Users found that interacting with other TPRs and exploring a location has considerable potential that should be explored in more depth.

The TMS could create a more interactive hybrid meeting setup in which all participants, whether online (using a video conferencing software or driving the Telepresence-Robot) or onsite, could communicate with each other better and improve the offline experience. They also feel more engaged in participating and starting discussions.

The recording of the meeting using a 360° Video offered the on-demand (offline) participants an interactive perspective of the meeting, especially during the questions and open discussion. The video gave a better insight into how the meeting developed without being present. The on-demand (offline) participants who watched the video said that a 360° video recording of the meeting was more entertaining and interesting than a conventional recording because they could focus on the person that was talking (presenter or participants) and zoom in on details of the presentation.

Due to the ongoing expansion and implementation of remote work and virtual meetings, creating a more interactive meeting environment is necessary, considering onsite, online, and on-demand (offline) participants. The Tribrid Meeting Setup (TMS) is the implementation of a Telepresence Robot (TPR) in hybrid meetings and was designed to counteract the negative aspects of remote work and virtual meetings, such as the lack of interaction during virtual meetings and the need to mitigate zoom fatigue.

7 Conclusions

A first test of the TMS prototype took place to assess its viability and outline how the setup should be put together and which aspects could be improved. We concluded that the TPR is a tool that could enhance the interaction during hybrid meetings and function as a bridge between the online and onsite participants. The TMS made participants more engaged to participate during the discussion session. The first set of requirements for the participants, a list of the components needed, and instructions on assembling and testing the TMS are given.

Further testing of the TMS is needed to determine other implementation scenarios (for example, digital learning at the workplace or in universities, presentation at conferences, trade fairs, etc.), the number of TPRs needed vs. the number of online and onsite participants, define the requirements for onsite participants, the duration of the meeting, the characteristics of the meeting room, and the limitations of the TMS. Exploring the interaction between TPRs in more detail would also be helpful. Further research is needed to determine the levels of zoom fatigue as a TPR-Remote-User.

Acknowledgments. This research was partially supported by the German Federal Ministry of Education and Research (Project PraeRI, 02L21B001 and Project SEAMLESS, 02K18D034). The sponsor had no role in the study design, the collection, analysis, and interpretation of the data, the writing of the report, or the submission of the paper for publication. We are very grateful to David Cann for his assistance and thank the two reviewers for their constructive comments.

References

1. Ellis, R., Goodacre, T., Mortensen, N., Oeppen, R.S., Brennan, P.A.: Application of human factors at hybrid meetings: facilitating productivity and inclusivity. Br. J. Oral Maxillofac. Surg. (2022). https://doi.org/10.1016/j.bjoms.2021.12.055
2. Mostafa, B.A.: Leveraging workforce insights to enhance employer attractiveness for young job seekers during pandemic era. Heliyon (2022). https://doi.org/10.1016/j.heliyon.2022.e09699
3. Kaiser, S., Suess, S., Cohen, R., Mikkelsen, E.N., Pedersen, A.R.: Working from home: findings and prospects for further research. German J. Hum. Resourc. Manag. (2022). https://doi.org/10.1177/23970022221106973
4. Appinio: Future of Work. Report 2022 (2022). https://de.statista.com/page/der-future-of-work-report-2022#dataBoxOptionsSalutation. Accessed 22 December 2022
5. Puccinelli, E., et al.: Hybrid conferences: opportunities, challenges and ways forward. Front. Mar. Sci. (2022). https://doi.org/10.3389/fmars.2022.902772
6. Sá, M.J., Ferreira, C.M., Serpa, S.: Virtual and Face-To-Face Academic Conferences: Comparison and Potentials, vol. 9 (2019). https://doi.org/10.2478/jesr-2019-0011
7. Shivananda, S., Doddawad, V.G.: The usefulness of hybrid platform meetings for research ethics committees review meetings. Oral Oncol. (2022). https://doi.org/10.1016/j.oraloncology.2022.105811
8. Nilles, J.M.: Making telecommuting happen. A guide for telemanagers and telecommuters/Jack M. Nilles. VNR computer library. Van Nostrand Reinhold; London: International Thomson Publishing [distributor], New York (1994)

9. Schumacher, D.: The 1973 Oil Crisis and its Aftermath. https://doi.org/10.1007/978-1-349-17797-4_2
10. Türkeş, M.C., Vuţă, D.R.: Telework: before and after COVID-19. Encyclopedia (2022). https://doi.org/10.3390/encyclopedia2030092
11. Allen, N.: The Pioneers of Modem Remote Work, 10 November 2020. https://wrkfrce.com/the-pioneers-of-modern-remote-work/. Accessed 1 July 2022
12. Gherini, A.: Would You Build an Office Without Walls? Building a remote work force is easier since technology has enabled us to virtually connect and communicate, 24 October 2017. https://www.inc.com/anne-gherini/would-you-build-an-office-without-walls.html. Accessed 1 July 2022
13. IBM: Technical Whitepaper: Challenging the modern myths of remote working (2014). ibm.com/downloads/cas/O90WYGXZ. Accessed 23 May 2023
14. Ferreira, R., Pereira, R., Bianchi, I.S., Da Silva, M.M.: Decision factors for remote work adoption: advantages, disadvantages, driving forces and challenges. JOItmC (2021). https://doi.org/10.3390/joitmc7010070
15. European Commission: Status Report on European Telework. TELEWORK 98 (1998). http://www.fim.uni-linz.ac.at/Research/telework/tw98.pdf. Accessed 21 Dec 2022
16. Gareis, K., Kordey, N.: The spread of telework in 2005. In: Stanford-Smith, B., Kidd, P.T. (eds.) E-Business. Key Issues, Applications and Technologies, pp. 83–90. IOS Press, Amsterdam, Washington, DC (2000)
17. Eurostat. Data Base: Employed persons working from home as a percentage of the total employment, by sex, age and professional status (%)(2022). https://ec.europa.eu/eurostat/databrowser/view/LFSA_EHOMP__custom_4290395/default/table?lang=en. Accessed 21 Dec 2022
18. Herrera, J., de las Heras-Rosas, C., Rodríguez-Fernández, M., Ciruela-Lorenzo, A.M.: Teleworking: The Link between Worker, Family and Company, vol. 10 (2022). https://doi.org/10.3390/systems10050134
19. United States Census Bureau: The Number of People Primarily Working From Home Tripled Between 2019 and 2021 (2022). https://www.census.gov/newsroom/press-releases/2022/people-working-from-home.html. Accessed 22 Dec 2022
20. Pelta, R.: FlexJobs survey finds employees want remote work post-pandemic. In: Work from Home and Remote Work (2022)
21. Buffer: 2022 state of remote work. In: Work from Home and Remote Work (2022)
22. Chew, D., Azizi, M.: The State of Video Conferencing 2022 (2022). https://www.dialpad.com/blog/video-conferencing-report/#:~:text=While%20meetings%20with%20three%20to,frequently%20last%20over%2070%20minutes!. Accessed 22 Dec 2022
23. Sharma, D.: The world of virtual conferencing: is the pandemic paving the path? J. Neurosurg. Anesthesiol. (2021). https://doi.org/10.1097/ANA.0000000000000737
24. Sethi, R.K., Nemani, V., Shaffrey, C., Lenke, L., Sponseller, P.: Reimagining Medical Conferences for a Virtual Setting (2020). https://hbr.org/2020/12/reimagining-medical-conferences-for-a-virtual-setting. Accessed 4 July 2022
25. Wiederhold, B.K.: Connecting through technology during the coronavirus disease 2019 pandemic: avoiding "zoom fatigue". Cyberpsychol. Behav. Soc. Network. (2020). https://doi.org/10.1089/cyber.2020.29188.bkw
26. Fauville, G., Luo, M., Queiroz, A.C.M., Bailenson, J.N., Hancock, J.: Zoom exhaustion & fatigue scale. SSRN J. (2021). https://doi.org/10.2139/ssrn.3786329
27. Fauville, G., Luo, M., Queiroz, A.C.M., Bailenson, J.N., Hancock, J.: Nonverbal mechanisms predict zoom fatigue and explain why women experience higher levels than men. SSRN J. (2021). https://doi.org/10.2139/ssrn.3820035
28. Hopf, N., Berger, E.: Zoom-fatigue – Ein Phänomen im Distance-Learning. R&E-SOURCE (2022). https://doi.org/10.53349/resource.2022.iS22.a1058

29. Jacks, T.: Research on remote work in the era of COVID-19. J. Glob. Inf. Technol. Manag. (2021). https://doi.org/10.1080/1097198X.2021.1914500
30. Slack: The great executive employee disconnect. Study of global knowledge workers shows the view of the office looks different from the top (2021). https://futureforum.com/wp-con tent/uploads/2021/10/Future-Forum-Pulse-Report-October-2021.pdf. Accessed 4 July 2022
31. Vellante, D.: Breaking analysis: enterprise technology predictions 2022. In: Work from Home and Remote Work (2022). https://wikibon.com/breaking-analysis-enterprise-technology-pre dictions-2022/. Accessed 23 May 2022
32. Inavero: Third Annual "Future Workforce Report" Sheds Light on How Younger Generations are Reshaping the Future of Work (2019). https://www.upwork.com/press/releases/third-ann ual-future-workforce-report. Accessed 22 December 2022
33. Rehak, M., Rehak, A., Lazzari, L.: The Tri-Brid Event Model (is better than hybrid!) (2020). https://matchboxvirtual.com/the-new-hybrid-event-model-designing-for-the-future/. Accessed 23 May 2022
34. McElnay, P.: 3 reasons why tribrid – not just hybrid -medical education is the future (2021). https://www.linkedin.com/pulse/3-reasons-why-tribrid-just-hybrid-medical-future-phil-mcelnay/. Accessed 12 Jan 2023
35. Bozelos, P.A., Vogels, T.P.: Talking science, online. Nat. Rev. Neurosci. (2021). https://doi.org/10.1038/s41583-020-00408-6
36. Hernandez, F., Waechter, M., Bullinger, A.C.: A first approach for implementing a telepres ence robot in an industrial environment. In: Nunes, I.L. (ed.) AHFE 2021. LNNS, vol. 265, pp. 141–146. Springer, Cham (2021). https://doi.org/10.1007/978-3-030-79816-1_18
37. Hernandez, F., Löffler, T., Schleicher, T., Bullinger, A.: Eignungeines Telepräsenz-Roboters für die Remote-instandhaltung. In: Biedermann, H. (ed.) Instandhaltung als Erfolgsfaktor. Strategie, Lebenszyklusorientierung und Digitalisierung. Reihe Praxiswissen für Ingenieure Instandhaltung, pp. 231–241. TÜV Media GmbH TÜV Rheinland Group, Köln (2021)
38. Kristoffersson, A., Coradeschi, S., Loutfi, A.: A review of mobile robotic telepresence. Adv. Hum.-Comput. Interact. (2013). https://doi.org/10.1155/2013/902316
39. Berri, R., Wolf, D., Osório, F.: From tele-operated robots to social robots with autonomous behaviors. In: Osório, F.S., Wolf, D.F., Castelo Branco, K., Grassi, V., Becker, M., Romero, R.A.F. (eds.) LARS/Robocontrol/SBR -2014. CCIS, vol. 507, pp. 32–52. Springer, Heidelberg (2015). https://doi.org/10.1007/978-3-662-48134-9_3
40. Kehl, C.: Robotik und assistive Neurotechnologien in der Pflege - gesellschaftliche Herausforderungen. Vertiefung des Projekts «Mensch-Maschine-Entgrenzung». Büro für Technikfolgen-Abschätzung beim Deutschen Bundestag (TAB) (2018). https://www.tab-beim-bundestag.de/de/pdf/publikationen/berichte/TAB-Arbeitsbericht-ab177.pdf. Accessed 22 July 2020
41. Frommeld, D., Haug, S., Currle, E., Weber, K.: Telepräsenzroboter in der Schlaganfall-rehabilitation. Pflegezeitschrift **75**(5), 52–55 (2022). https://doi.org/10.1007/s41906-022-1251-7
42. Minsky, M.: Telepresence. OMNI Mag. (1980)
43. Paulos, E., Canny, J.: Designing personal tele-embodiment. In: Proceedings of 1998 IEEE International Conference on Robotics and Automation (Cat. No. 98CH36146). IEEE International Conference on Robotics and Automation, Leuven, Belgium, 16–20 May 1998, pp. 3173–3178. IEEE (1998). https://doi.org/10.1109/ROBOT.1998.680913
44. Popp, C., Middel, L., Raptis, G.: Auswahlverfahrenfür Telepräsenzroboter für die Unter-stützung von Schlaganfallpatient*innen. https://doi.org/10.13140/RG.2.2.35546.00968
45. Björnfot, P., Bergqvist, J., Kaptelinin, V.: Non-technical users' first encounters with a robotic telepresence technology: an empirical study of office workers. Paladyn, J. Behav. Robot. (2018). https://doi.org/10.1515/pjbr-2018-0022

46. Lee, M.K., Takayama, L.: Now, I have a body. In: Tan, D., Fitzpatrick, G., Gutwin, C., Begole, B., Kellogg, W.A. (eds.) Proceedings of the 2011 Annual Conference on Human Factors in Computing Systems - CHI '11. the 2011 Annual Conference, Vancouver, BC, Canada, 07–12 May 2011, p. 33. ACM Press, New York (2011). https://doi.org/10.1145/1978942.1978950

47. Lee, W., Park, J., Park, C.H.: Acceptability of tele-assistive robotic nurse for human-robot collaboration in medical environment. In: Kanda, Ŝ.e.a. (ed.) Companion of the 2018 ACM/IEEE, pp. 171–172 (2018). https://doi.org/10.1145/3173386.3177084

48. Jungo, V.: Einsatz von Telepräsenzrobotern für ärztliche Konsultationen (2019)

49. Tischler, N.W.: "Assistive Social Robots" fürPersonen mit Demenz in der institutionellen Pflege (2017)

50. Fels, D.I., Waalen, J.K., Zhai, S., Weiss, P.: Telepresence under exceptional circumstances; enriching the connection to school for sick children (2001)

51. Herring, S.: Telepresence robots for academics (2013). https://doi.org/10.1002/meet.145050 01156

52. Wächter, M.: Gestaltung tangibler Mensch-Maschine-Schnittstellen. Springer Fachmedien Wiesbaden, Wiesbaden (2019). https://doi.org/10.1007/978-3-658-27666-9

53. Hevner, A.R., Chatterjee, S.: Design Research in Information Systems. Theory and Practice/ Alan Hevner, Samir Chatterjee; forewords by Paul Gray and Carliss Y. Baldwin. Integrated Series in Information Systems, vol. 22. Springer, New York (2010). https://doi.org/10.1007/978-1-4419-5653-8

54. Löffler, T., Hernandez, F., Kögel, A.: Telepräsenzroboter. Neue Potentiale für die Telearbeit. Nachgelesen - Mittelstand Digital Zentrum Chemnitz (2022). https://digitalzentrum-che mnitz.de/wissen/telepraesenzroboter-neue-potentiale-fuer-die-telearbeit/. Accessed 23 May 2022

Silent Delivery: Make Instant Delivery More Accessible for the DHH Delivery Workers Through Sensory Substitution

Shichao Huang[1], Xiaolong Li[1], Shang Shi[1], Haoye Dong[1], Xueyan Cai[1],
Kecheng Jin[1], Jiayi Wu[1], Weijia Lin[1], Jiayu Yao[1], Yuqi Hu[2], Fangtian Ying[3],
and Cheng Yao[4(✉)]

[1] School of Software Technology, Zhejiang University, Ningbo, China
{22251356,22251374}@zju.edu.cn
[2] University of Nottingham Ningbo, Ningbo, China
Yuqi.Hu@nottingham.edu.cn
[3] MACAU University of Science and Technology, Macau, China
[4] College of Computer Science and Technology, Zhejiang University, Hangzhou, China
yaoch@zju.edu.cn

Abstract. With the rapid development of the instant delivery industry in recent years, delivery jobs, have attracted many DHH (Deaf and Hard of Hearing) people because of their flexible working hours, predictable incoming, and low threshold. However, the delivery scenario is complicated. The existing aids for the DHH are not sufficiently targeted, and there are still many unresolved issues. Based on this, we propose Silent Delivery, an interactive system that assists the DHH delivery workers in instant delivering goods without barriers. The DHH delivery workers can feel the vibrating alert to get information through the smart haptic function provided by the system, instead of having to access the information visually through the mobile phone. With a between-subjects experiment (n = 24), we evaluated the efficiency, load factors, and experiences of participants. We verified the effectiveness of this system in improving efficiency, reducing the workload, and increasing the emotional experience of the DHH delivery workers during instant delivery. The results is positive and prove the system can help the DHH.

Keywords: the DHH · instant delivery · accessibility · sensory substitution

1 Introduction

The concept of accessibility emerged in the early 20th century, when the need for cities where all people, including the able-bodied and the disabled, can live and move freely together without barriers [1]. Sensory substitution design, a design for accessibility, aims at helping the disabled regain the ability to receive external information in order to work and live as well as the able-bodied people [2]. Sensory substitution is not only designed for the disabled such as the blind, the deaf, and the dumb, but also for situations in which the able-bodied have occasional sensory impaired.

N. A. Streitz and S. Konomi (Eds.): HCII 2023, LNCS 14037, pp. 362–379, 2023.
https://doi.org/10.1007/978-3-031-34609-5_27

The DHH usually have difficulty perceiving sound characteristics such as timbre [3], loudness [4], pitch, and location information [5], which means that the one-way transmission and two-way communication of information from the outside world toward the DHH is hindered. Previous studies have mainly focused on devices to assist the DHH in their daily lives. Most of the general assistive products use very few assistive technologies and digital information help the DHH [6]. And intelligent products are often expensive to be afforded by the general sensory-impaired people.

When the DHH are in a delivery scenario, the problems they face are multi-dimensional, multi-layered. Existing products focus on the technical aspects of communicating and information, but often ignore the difficulties that the DHH may encounter in actual usage scenarios and their emotional demands which weaken the important guiding significance of user experience in product design [7]. Existing hearing-impaired assistive tools are poorly targeted and most of the DHH delivery workers still communicate with users in a predominantly typed information [8]. In addition, how to race against time in a silent world is the biggest obstacle for the DHH. They can't hear the horn on road, thus they need to look in the rearview mirror frequently and confirm repeatedly before they can cross the road. The process of the DHH delivery workers from accepting the order to successful delivery contains many complex scenarios such as picking up, communicating with mobile phone, navigation, driving, etc. There are many issues that have not been resolved well.

This paper explores the difficulties and barriers faced by the DHH in the delivery industry such as learning, training, picking up, delivering goods, and communication. With the goal of providing accessible delivery experience through sensory substitution, this paper proposes an accessible delivery system for the DHH which help improve their work efficiency and satisfaction. Moreover, it provides the accessible design for the instant delivery industry.

We make the following three key contributions:

(1) By analyzing current hearing accessible design and current accessible design of instant delivery platform, we gain insights of the existing problems for the DHH in instant delivery work.
(2) In response to these challenges, we propose Silent Delivery, an instant delivery assistance system for the DHH delivery workers, which includes smart haptic hardware and software. We explored sensory substitution design using vibrative timeout reminders and vibrating-assisted visual navigation to reduce the visual load.
(3) We conducted two comparative experiments to verify the effectiveness of Silent Delivery in enhancing the reception of information for the DHH delivery workers, and we found that Silent Delivery was better than current methods. In the end, we made a discussion that focus on the innovations of Silent Delivery.

2 Related Work

2.1 Hearing Substitute System

Hearing impairment is a sensory dysfunction that is caused by injury or natural decline, resulting in damage and lesions to the hearing organs, making it difficult to obtain and discriminate between types of peripheral information [9]. The DHH can only rely on other senses such as sight, touch, and smell to receive information, which has a huge negative impact on their normal information perception and language communication.

Within the method of sensory substitution, most of the existing assistive approaches for the DHH use the visual and haptic senses to substitute for their hearing. To assist hearing-impaired people with more customized sound recognition, Dhruv Jain et al. proposed a sound training system——ProtoSound [10], which can be customized by users to record sounds and train their own sound recognition models. In addition to the communication of brief information, Suranga Nanayakkara et al. designed a Haptic Chair which in terms of making the DHH perceive complex musical information. The chair can vibrate to music and display corresponding visual effects on a screen, helping the DHH to perceive the melody and rhythm of the music [11]. Benjamin Petry et al. use MuSS-Bits++, a musical sensory substitution device that combines visual and vibrotactile sensations, to assist hearing-impaired children in rhythmic discrimination and reproduction [12]. They are mostly aided by visual and haptic means to compensate for their sense of hearing.

2.2 Accessible Communication Technology

Due to the limitation of hearing impairment, the DHH relies more on visual and haptic access to information, and sign language as a typical representative. Communication between DHH and DHH with able-bodied people is visual, written, gesture, and facial descriptions.

Different strategies have been developed to support communication between the DHH and the able-bodied [13], such as pen-talk [14] and sign language interpretation [15]. For face-to-face communication, there is a sign language translation glove built for deaf-hearing communication. When the DHH wear the glove for sign language communication, the APP connected to the glove can translate the sign language gestures into text and voice to the able-bodied people, solving the two-way communication barrier. Marianna Di Gregorio et al. designed ProSign, an application that helps the DHH to communicate fluently with able-bodied listeners in sign language, by using gesture recognition technology to inter-transfer sign language and speech text [16]. For online communication, Xiaomi phone can convert text to speech through virtual AI voice, and type a reply after understanding the converted text of the call. For instant communication, Buttussi et al. analyzed the typical communication patterns between the DHH patients and medics in a specific emergency scenario and developed an application to assist in making medical determinations in emergency situations [17].

3 Pre-design Investigation

The able-bodied delivery workers will encounter all kinds of difficulties in delivery, and the DHH delivery workers will encounter even more obstacles in distribution. Therefore, we conducted a pre-design study to understand the pain points, obstacles, and important contact points in the instant delivery process.

3.1 Method

We recruited a total of 9 people for interviews, including two DHH delivery workers, one accessible service expert, three operators who have helped the DHH many times with communication assistance, and three able-bodied people who have had contact with the DHH delivery workers.

- Online text interview: two DHH delivery workers
- Interview with sign language interpretation: an accessible service expert from a public service center for the disabled
- Semi-structured interview: three operators of service center who have helped the DHH delivery workers with communication assistance
- Open interview: three able-bodied people who had contact with the DHH delivery workers

Then, by combing the interview contents and analyzing the customer journey, the pain points, obstacles, and important contact points in the process of instant delivery for the DHH delivery were sorted out. According to the opportunity points summarized above, the two delivery workers entrusted with the interview distributed questionnaires to other DHH delivery workers who are engaged in or have engaged in the instant delivery industry. A total of 6 questionnaires were distributed. Through the form of KANO model scoring, the demand ranking and grading of eight opportunity points proposed by the research for the DHH delivery workers in the process of instant delivery were carried out. We spoke with a hearing-impaired expert with the help of a sign language interpreter (Fig. 1).

Fig. 1. Communicating with a hearing-impaired specialist with the help of a sign language interpreter

3.2 Key Findings and Design Implication

Customer Journey. According to the interview content, we established user portraits of the DHH delivery workers and drew a map of their experience in the process of instant delivery based on their behaviors in the four steps of receiving orders, picking up goods/buying on behalf of the DHH delivery workers, and receiving goods. And we sorted out the input and output of information blocked by the DHH delivery workers in each stage due to auditory channel obstacles. Therefore, the user pain points and contact points are summarized, and the opportunity points are proposed according to the theory of sensory compensatory design, as shown in Table 1.

Table 1. A customer journey of the instant delivery process for the DHH delivery workers

Step	Grab/Take orders	Pick up/Generation buy	Delivery	Goods receipt
Behavior	System online./Face verification Report within the group Grab/Take orders	Go to the merchant Inquire about shipment Buy goods on behalf of others Pick up goods	Drive a vehicle Go to the destination Lost/Mislocated	Order timeout warning Contact Customer Deposit / Deliver goods
Blocked message	Message tone	Interrogative discourse Merchant reply	Vehicle honk./Road environment sound Navigational sound Ask the way./The passer-by answers	Timeout alert Customer response
Pain point	Unable to hear a new message alert	Voiceless inquiry Unable to communicate with the merchant	Need to look at both navigation and road conditions Unable to communicate with passers-by	Can't hear timeout alert Unable to communicate with customers on the phone
Touch point	App, delivery group, prompt tone	Merchants and commodities	Road conditions, electric vehicles, passers-by, guides shipping software, goods	Customer, product, telephone, community, Security guard

(*continued*)

Table 1. (*continued*)

Step	Grab/Take orders	Pick up/Generation buy	Delivery	Goods receipt
Demand point	• Vibrate: indicate new orders	• Fuzzy input: selecting key words through preset voice phrases • Entrusting the merchant to take the goods through preset voice sentence patterns	• Vibration: alert turnaround and other instant information • Ask passers-by for directions through text • Provide emergency access to help	• Order timeout vibration strong alert • During telephone com- munication, discourses into words • Input words are answered by the voice agent

Opportunity Points. By combing the customer journey with the theory of sensory compensatory design, we proposed the opportunity points for the DHH delivery workers in the process of instant delivery summarized in Table 2.

Table 2. The opportunity points for the DHH delivery workers in the process of instant delivery

Code	Stage	Function
O1	Grab/Take orders	Send a new order by vibrating
O2	Distribution driving process	Visual navigation is aided by vibration, prompting turn corners, paying attention to traffic lights, destinations, and other key information
O3	Pick up/Generation buy	Through preset quick voice phrases and sentence patterns, instead of asking, entrusting the merchant to help replace the purchase of goods
O4	Order is about to run out	Give a strong alert to the DHH delivery workers through vibration
O5	The distribution has a positioning problem	Ask passers-by through an instant voice-to-text interchange

(*continued*)

Table 2. (*continued*)

Code	Stage	Function
O6	Communicate by phone upon completion of delivery	Can input text through the way of voice agents to inform each other, and immediately each other's discourses into words
O7	Input text	With the fuzzy input, the system automatically generates a soft and soothing statement to choose from when choosing key words and corresponding emotions
O8	Difficult to complete communication in case of emergency	Through the emergency help channel, in the most familiar way of sign language communication to the third-party personnel (such as sign language able-bodied person) to help solve the problem

Through the analysis with KANO model, the two delivery workers commissioned to interview distributed questionnaires to other DHH who are engaged in or have engaged in the instant delivery industry, a total of 6 questionnaires were distributed. Demand ranking and grading are conducted on eight opportunity points proposed by the study for the DHH delivery workers in the form of KANO model scoring. The results are shown in Table 3.

Table 3. KANO attributes and Better-Worse coefficients of eight opportunity points

Code	KANO attributes	Better coefficient	Worse coefficient
O2	Must-be Quality	50%	-66.67%
O4	Must-be Quality	33.33%	-50%
O8	Performance Quality	100%	-50%
O6	Performance Quality	83.33%	-66.67%
O1	Performance Quality	66.67%	-66.67%
O7	Attractive Quality	83.33%	-33.33%
O3	Attractive Quality	83.33%	-16.67%
O5	Attractive Quality	83.33%	0%

According to the data analysis of KANO model, the eight opportunity points proposed here have not been demonstrated as suspicious, reverse, and undifferentiated demands, so they are all positive design opportunity points that meet user requirements. According to the statistical results and the position of the opportunity point in the four

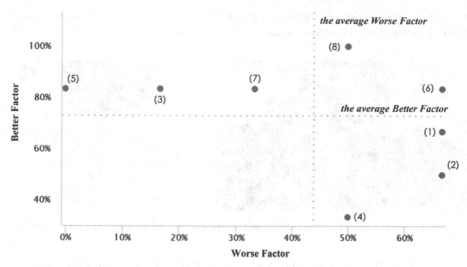

Fig. 2. Quadrants of Better-Worse coefficient analysis for eight opportunity points

quadrants of the better-worse coefficient value shown in Fig. 2 it can be seen that: (2) with a worse factor of 66.67% and (4) with a worse factor of 50% are basic user needs (M) that designer needs to satisfy first and foremost. (7), (3), and (5) all have a better coefficient of 83.33%. These three opportunity points are attractive needs (A), which are the entry points to establish product's innovation and advantage. The better and worse coefficients for (8), (6), and (1) are both above 50%. These three opportunities are aspirational needs (O), which are needs that can be satisfied after the most basic needs are met.

4   Vibration Module Design

Based on the analysis of the needs of DHH delivery workers in the process of instant delivery, we propose Silent Delivery, an instant delivery accessibility assistant system for DHH delivery workers, to help DHH delivery workers work more efficiently and with a better experience.

The system consists of a smart haptic hardware that fits around the delivery worker's neck, and accessibility assistant software. Design with sensory substitution, the smart haptic hardware is hung to the phone lanyard and fixed on the back of the neck when in use. Its main function is transmitting information through vibration. To investigate the relationship between different vibration modes and conveyed information, a focus group of other four expert users with more than five years learning experience of interaction design was organized. The discussion was divided into two modules which last 60 min.

The focus group focused on (1) the selection of the specific instruction content of the aided navigation, and (2) the correspondence between the content of the information conveyed and the vibration mode, through reviewing information, testing the vibration module, discussing and voting. As shown in Fig. 3 through the participants' analysis and interpretation of the existing maps, the instant navigation information can be divided into three main types: direction, distance and road conditions.

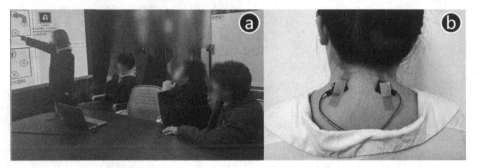

Fig. 3. (a) Focus Group Session; (b) Researchers try out the smart haptic hardware prototype

Considering that the vibration reminders in navigation scenarios only serve as assistance rather than a complete replacement of navigation applications, and in order not to increase the cognitive burden of hearing-impaired delivery workers, this study will only design an auditory haptic surrogate for the directional cues in four types of real-time navigation: left turn, left U-turn, right turn, and right U-turn. The participants then experienced two sets of vibration patterns: (1) vibrations of the same duration in different parts; and (2) vibrations of different durations in the same parts. The participants agreed that it was easier to perceive and judge the vibrations of different parts quickly than the vibrations of different durations. Therefore, the vibration mode with different parts was used for navigation information prompting, and the bilateral simultaneous vibration mode with different simultaneous lengths was used for order information. From the above work, we designed vibration patterns which were used on intelligent haptic hardware, as shown in Table 4.

Table 4. Correspondence table of conveyed information and vibration mode

Content of the message delivered	Vibration section	Vibration duration
New Order Alerts	Bilateral	Single vibration, lasting 1 s
Timeout warning		Single vibration, lasting 3 s
Left turn	Left side	Continuous vibration, continuous 0.5 s interval 0.5 s vibration 3 times
Left U-turn		Single vibration, lasting 3 s
Right turn	Right side	Continuous vibration, continuous 0.5 s interval 0.5 s vibration 3 times
Right U-turn		Single vibration, lasting 3 s

The hardware was developed using the Arduino IDE which consists of an ESP32 WROOM32 development board with embedded Wi-Fi and Bluetooth modules, two connected vibration motors, and a lithium battery. The hardware part is connected and controlled with Blinker app through cell phone's hotspot. To complete the simulation of the corresponding function, the experimental validation session later on was done directly by a research assistant who triggered the vibration switch according to the map navigation alerts. Thus, after completing the connection, the interface components for triggering the six vibration modes were set up through Blinker to facilitate the research assistant's control of its vibration alerts during the experiments. The overall packaging of the prototype is shown in Fig. 4.

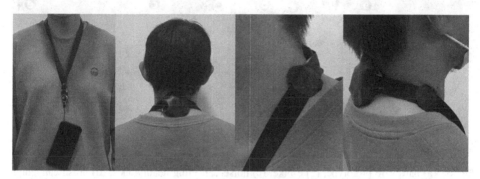

Fig. 4. The wearing status of smart haptic hardware prototype

5   Methods

In experiment, we identified vibration timeout reminders and vibration-assisted visual navigation to reduce the visual load as the core functions of the hardware system based on the ranking and grading of the eight opportunity points.

The smart haptic hardware proposed in this paper only addresses the characteristics of hearing impairment for sensory compensation without considering other differences between hearing impaired and able-bodied people. On the other hand, the group of DHH delivery workers is relatively niche, thus the experiments were conducted by blocking the hearing channel of the able-bodied users and simulating DHH delivery workers in the hardware part of the design verification.

5.1   Participants

Twenty-four able-bodied subjects (13 males and 11 females, aged 22–26 years, M = 23.75, SD = 1.48) were recruited for the study. All participants met the age requirements for driving an e-bike as stipulated in the Regulations for the Implementation of the Road Traffic Safety Law in China, and all 24 subjects had an e-bike driving experience.

5.2 Technical Apparatus and System

We prepared all the equipment for the experiment which included Arduino-based smart haptic hardware prototype (Fig. 5 (a)), Giant Island F6 electric bike (Fig. 5 (b)), Airpods Pro A2084 noise-canceling headphones (Fig. 5 (c)), DeltaPlus professional noise-canceling headphones (Fig. 5 (d)), mobile device and version 12.02.1 of the Gotoku navigation application (Fig. 5 (e)).

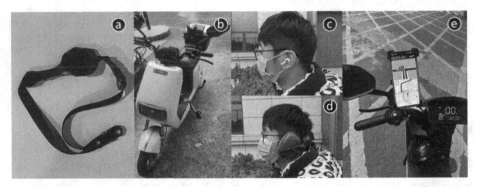

Fig. 5. (a) hardware prototype; (b) e-bike; (c) noise-canceling headphones; (d) noise-canceling earmuffs; (e) cell phone and navigation application

5.3 Procedure

The experiment requires participants to drive an e-bike who is guided by navigation from location A to location B, as presented in Fig. 6 (a). The total length of the journey is 1876 m, containing a total of 20 turns and 1 U-turn. After completing the driving task, a questionnaire will be completed and an interview will be conducted. The study was conducted as a between-group comparison experiment and participants were divided into two groups as shown in Fig. 6 (b). Group A wear the smart haptic hardware and drive with navigation alerts, while Group B does not wear the smart haptic hardware and drive with navigation alerts.

5.4 Experiment Procedure

After familiarizing themselves with the operation of the e-bike and adapting to the simulated significant hearing loss (Fig. 7), participants formally began the experiment. A research assistant sat in the back seat of the e-bike during the driving, recording the time consuming from departure to arrival at the destination and observing the subject's behavior. The research assistant was also in charge of the hardware module, which was operated by the cell phone software, to provide vibration alerts based on the real-time progress of the journey while Group A was conducting the experiment. This session lasted 10 min. After completing the driving task, participants were asked to complete the NASA-TLX [18] scale to assess the effectiveness of the smart haptic hardware in

Fig. 6. (a) Overview of the experimental task route; (b) Group A and Group B

reducing the load on the DHH delivery workers during the delivery. The SAM [19] scale was also completed to help assess the user's emotional experience after using the system, and participants in Group A were asked to complete an additional SUS scale questionnaire to assess the usability of the system. Afterward, all participants were interviewed for 15 min in a semi-structured interview about (1) their perceptions of the experiment and (2) the problems they encountered during the experiment.

6 Results

6.1 Quantitative Analysis

Our experiment evaluated the efficiency, load factors, and experience of participants when they wear and did not wear the hardware prototype by time-consuming records, NASA-TLX scale, and SAM scale. The data collected in the experiment are shown in Table 5. Furthermore, we invited participants from test Group A (with Silence delivery) to score the hardware system by SUS (System Usability Scale).

Firstly, based on the scale which users completed, we used the Shapiro-Wilk test to test the normality distribution of the data because the sample size of the experiment was 24, which is a small sample size. The results of the normality tests on the time consumed, the load factors assessed by the NASA-TLX scale, and the experience perception assessed by the SAM scale showed that the significant P values of the S-W test were 0.106, 0.614, and 0.785, which were higher than 0.05. Therefore, these P values satisfied the normal distribution. The results of the independent samples t-test for Group A-Silence delivery and Group B-None device are summarized in Table 6. In terms of data, we found that the three statistics ($p < .001$) in Group A were significantly greater

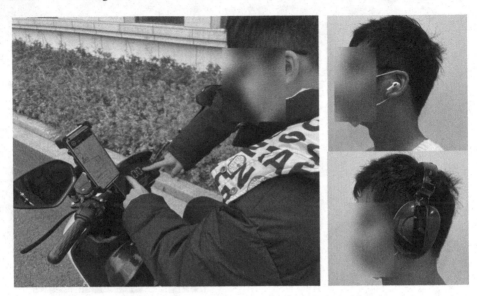

Fig. 7. Subjects familiarize themselves with the vehicle.

Table 5. Experimental data results

Number	Group	Consumption time (sec)	Load level	Emotional Experience
P1	1	495	44	11
P2	1	493	49	13
P3	1	526	51	13
P4	1	514	38	15
P5	1	506	41	12
P6	1	499	39	18
P7	1	536	44	16
P8	1	518	52	14
P9	1	539	47	9
P10	1	523	33	14
P11	1	517	59	13
P12	1	534	35	10
P13	2	573	66	19
P14	2	559	72	15
P15	2	576	78	18
P16	2	584	65	14

(*continued*)

Table 5. (*continued*)

Number	Group	Consumption time (sec)	Load level	Emotional Experience
P17	2	591	55	19
P18	2	546	77	17
P19	2	561	68	21
P20	2	578	62	19
P21	2	579	71	18
P22	2	586	57	22
P23	2	567	83	15
P24	2	594	64	14

than in Group B. The quantitative results indicate that there were significant differences between Group A and Group B in terms of time consumed (effect size of Cohen d = 5.653), load factors (effect size of Cohen d = 3.760), and experience perception (effect size of Cohen d = 1.560).

Table 6. Table of the results of the independent sample t-test analysis of the experiment

Variables	Group	Sample size	Average value	Standard deviation	t-value	p-value	Cohen's d
Time consuming	A	12	516.67	15.853	−9.427	0.000***	5.653
	B	12	574.5	14.152			
Load level	A	12	44.33	7.644	−7.245	0.000***	3.760
	B	12	68.17	8.451			
Emotions Experience	A	12	13.17	2.517	−4.191	0.000***	1.560
	B	12	17.58	2.644			

* p < .05, ** p < .01, *** p < .001

And then, we analyzed the scores of the hardware prototype by Group A to evaluate and calculated the SUS score (M = 86.125) of this smart haptic hardware prototype, and compared with the curve grading range of SUS scores, the usability prototype of the smart haptic hardware prototype proposed was assessed as A+, which proved it has a good user experience [20, 21].

6.2 Qualitative Analysis

We summarized and compiled the following conclusions in response to the semi-structured interview results of this experiment, combined with the analysis of observations made during the conduct of the experiment.

Availability. We found that, during driving the vehicle, the vibration effectively substituted for the auditory reception of information and was used to assist in reducing the visual load. As a result of wearing soundproofing devices, participants generally described a sense of insecurity while driving during the interview. However, the state of both groups began to change after driving for a period of time. "*I looked at the navigation during the first two shocks (to confirm whether I really needed to turn), but after getting used to it, I was very decisive and focused on driving and watching people, and I turned whichever way I felt the vibrations*" (P2). The participants in Group A were significantly more confident in driving after adapting to the driving condition and receiving the information. In contrast, the control Group B was different: "*Whenever I cross an intersection, I will struggle with whether to turn at the intersection or not*" (P16), "*When I see an intersection at the back of the road, I will drive a little slower and then look at the navigation to make sure I want to turn before accelerating*" (P21). We analyzed that the time consumed in Group A was less than that of Group B, which correlated with the participants' confidence levels. The participants agreed that the vibrations aided by the navigation cues could indeed reduce the visual load and make them focus more on the observation and driving of the road conditions. "*This thing (the smart haptic prototype) should work well, especially when there are a lot of people*" (P4).

Identifiability. The vibration modes we proposed were well perceived and recognized; however, the two vibration modes (the new message alert) still had learning costs and memory burdens. In terms of vibration-assisted navigation, participants in Group A unanimously agreed that the vibration mode of the smart haptic prototype is suitable for users' mental and behavioral habits. "*The vibration of the navigation alert is very direct*" (P3) and "*I almost feel it instinctively*" (P11). However, some participants mentioned that the timing of the vibration alert needs to be well-timed, "*it is best to cue 50 to 100 m before you are about to turn, not just after you are about to turn*" (P10). In the function of message alert, participants need more reaction time for the message content corresponding to the two vibration modes during the driving process. "*It takes some reaction in my head*", "*the new order reminder is a bit difficult to distinguish, and it needs to carefully correspond*", "*actually, the vibration of the strong reminder (order timeout alert) is still very strong*" (P1, P5, P8, P10, and P12). Combined with the good and accurate performance of the participants in the pre-experimental phase for the vibration pattern recognition, we analyzed that when the participants were driving, their attention was highly focused on the driving task, and the message alert was non-instant and low-priority information for them, so there would be a lag in the response. In combination with the fact that new order alert is more frequent in the actual situation, and if they occur frequently in the process of driving an e-bike, they may lead to driving distraction and other problems that affect driving safety. Therefore, we believe that only the strong vibration prompts with a higher priority and more urgent order timeout should be retained in the message alert vibration prompts during driving, in order to reduce the learning cost for DHH delivery workers using this hardware.

7 Discussion and Future Work

We presented Silent Delivery, an interactive system to make instant delivery more accessible to the DHH delivery workers. With the DHH delivery workers as the target users, focusing on the scenario of instant delivery, we aim to provide systematic solutions for their barrier-free delivery process. We conducted formative research, functional design, prototype implementation, and validity verification of the "Smart Haptic Alert" feature. Due to the ongoing impact of COVID-19 and the limitations in terms of researcher resource capacity, this study has the following limitations:

- A Number of target users. The salary of the delivery workers is closely related to their working hours, and their working hours are high, so they are less willing to accept interviews and experimental tests. This makes it difficult to conduct experiments with higher target precision and larger sample size during experimental validation. We can only use simulated DHH as much as possible and find similar DHH, combined with a small number of target user groups to carry out. Therefore, there may be some missing points in the effect validation.
- Prototype Development and Scene Simulation Effect. The systematic development involves the opening of existing instant delivery dispatching systems, navigation, and other multi-systems, as well as the purchase of various speech and word processing services. The experimental prototype at this stage is mainly development and production completed for the needs of functional effect seeking in validity verification, and its practical applicability is still low.
- Experimental target scene. The target scenario positioned for this study is the just-in-time delivery scenario. This scenario has many variables and many circumstances that are difficult to predict. It is also necessary to ensure the physical safety of the subjects. Thus, it is difficult to conduct in a 100% realistic environment.
- Timeliness of vibration feedback. Due to manual operation to complete the simulation of the vibration experiment, there is the problem of timeliness of feedback. The vibration function and the underlying interface of the navigation software should be integrated subsequently to achieve a fully automated vibration alert.

In the future, there are still many areas to be improved in this study. At the level of innovative functions, the future can continue to expand in the direction of intelligence. Smart haptic hardware can be extended to support user-defined vibration mode, be expanded to support richer navigation scenarios, and be set by the DHH delivery workers to set their specific application scenarios.

At the system service level, it can continue to be expanded in the direction of generalization in the future. The study in this paper is mainly proposed for the DHH delivery workers and oriented to their work process analysis, mainly to solve their visual overload and communication barriers. However, these problems also exist in different scenarios of life and work for the DHH. Thus, in further investigation, different vibration modes can be used to assist the communication of information in other high visual load scenarios, so that the system service can be adapted to more accessibility support for the work and life of the DHH.

In terms of system bidirectional interaction, the future should continue to optimize the intelligent word selection keyboard for the DHH delivery worker group. We will focus on its corpus content, candidate word recommendation mode, keyboard layout, and human-computer interaction features in complex scenarios, and conduct simulation experiments for the intelligent word selection keyboard in complex scenarios.

8 Conclusion

In this paper, combining the design means of sensory substitution, we proposed Silent Delivery, an interactive system to make instant delivery more accessible to the DHH delivery workers. The core innovation point proposed in this study is the smart haptic hardware vibration alert. We chose the experimental design method of between-group comparisons, combined SUS scales, and qualitative analysis to explore the feasibility of smart haptic hardware vibration alert and availability of the system. We verified the effectiveness of this system in improving efficiency, reducing the workload, and increasing the emotional experience of the DHH delivery workers during instant delivery. The results is positive and prove the system can help the DHH.

Acknowledgement. This research was funded by the Engineering Research Center of Computer Aided Product Innovation Design, Ministry of Education, National Natural Science Foundation of China (Grant No. 52075478), and National Social Science Foundation of China (Grant No. 21AZD056).

References

1. Li, Y.: Research on accessibility design of Internet products. Internet Weekly, 54–56 (2022)
2. Xiong, X., Li, S.: Application of sensory compensatory designs on products. Packag. Eng. **30**, 131–132+139 (2009). https://doi.org/10.19554/j.cnki.1001-3563.2009.10.042
3. Finn, C., Abbeel, P., Levine, S.: Model-agnostic meta-learning for fast adaptation of deep networks. In: Proceedings of the 34th International Conference on Machine Learning, vol. 70, pp. 1126–1135. JMLR.org, Sydney, NSW, Australia (2017)
4. Foggia, P., Petkov, N., Saggese, A., Strisciuglio, N., Vento, M.: Reliable detection of audio events in highly noisy environments. Pattern Recogn. Lett. **65**, 22–28 (2015). https://doi.org/10.1016/j.patrec.2015.06.026
5. Oreshkin, B., López, P.R., Lacoste, A.: TADAM: task dependent adaptive metric for improved few-shot learning
6. Wen, Y.: Analyses on the product design based on barrier-free concept: taking visual disabilities as an example. Des. Art Res. **3**, 45–48+57 (2013)
7. He, X.: Research on the design of accessible learning tools for hearing impaired students based on user experience. Ind. Des. 119–121 (2022)
8. Sogou Input Method-Homepage. https://shurufa.sogou.com/
9. Xu. R.: Interaction design research for the hearing impaired (2019). https://kns.cnki.net/kcms/detail/detail.aspx?dbcode=CMFD&dbname=CMFD202001&filename=1019191551.nh&uniplatform=NZKPT&v=4ZSvZHxmuA06zVdO-uFH5cs5KWPIamNaUHFc-oQ2CKtWdhnnjKS0caRZakkBH_FZ

10. Jain, D., et al.: ProtoSound: a personalized and scalable sound recognition system for deaf and hard-of-hearing users. In: CHI Conference on Human Factors in Computing Systems, pp. 1–16. ACM, New Orleans, LA, USA (2022)
11. Nanayakkara, S., Taylor, E., Wyse, L., Ong, S.H.: An enhanced musical experience for the deaf: design and evaluation of a music display and a haptic chair
12. Petry, B., Illandara, T., Elvitigala, D.S., Nanayakkara, S.: Supporting rhythm activities of deaf children using music-sensory-substitution systems. In: Proceedings of the 2018 CHI Conference on Human Factors in Computing Systems, pp. 1–10. ACM, Montreal, QC, Canada (2018)
13. Demorest, M.E., Erdman, S.A.: Scale composition and item analysis of the communication profile foil the hearing impaired (1986)
14. Hallam, R.S., Corney, R.: Conversation tactics in persons with normal hearing and hearing-impairment. Int. J. Audiol. **53**, 174–181 (2014). https://doi.org/10.3109/14992027.2013.852256
15. TyeMurray, N., Purdy, S.C.: Reported use of communication strategies by SHHH members: client, talker, and situational variables
16. Di Gregorio, M., Sebillo, M., Vitiello, G., Pizza, A., Vitale, F.: ProSign everywhere - addressing communication empowerment goals for deaf people. In: Proceedings of the 5th EAI International Conference on Smart Objects and Technologies for Social Good, pp. 207–212. ACM, Valencia, Spain (2019)
17. Buttussi, F., Chittaro, L., Carchietti, E., Coppo, M.: Using mobile devices to support communication between emergency medical responders and deaf people. In: Proceedings of the 12th International Conference on Human Computer Interaction with Mobile Devices and Services – MobileHCI'10, p. 7. ACM Press, Lisbon, Portugal (2010)
18. Hart, S.G.: Nasa-Task Load Index (NASA-TLX); 20 Years Later th Annual Meeting
19. Gugenheimer, J., et al.: The impact of assistive technology on communication quality between deaf and hearing individuals. In: Proceedings of the 2017 ACM Conference on Computer Supported Cooperative Work and Social Computing, pp. 669–682. ACM, Portland, Oregon, USA (2017)
20. Bangor, A.: Determining what individual SUS scores mean. **4** (2009)
21. Tullis, T., Albert, B.: Planning a usability study. In: Measuring the User Experience, pp. 45–62. Elsevier, Amsterdam (2008)

Augmented Reality Visual-Captions: Enhancing Captioning Experience for Real-Time Conversations

Jingya Li[✉]

Beijing Jiaotong University, Beijing, China
lijy1@bjtu.edu.cn

Abstract. Deaf and hard-of-hearing (DHH) individuals experience difficulties in engaging in conversations since they cannot access audio information effectively. People who speak different languages are hardly communicating with each others. Although assistive tools like captions and subtitles are developed specifically, people still have troubles to read or understand the textual information. To address this challenge, this paper develops an AR-based visual-captions, which aims to help people better receive information in live conversations. In this paper, we first collect existing studies on AR captions and analyze the design of these captions. Based on the identified design space, we design and implement a proof-of-concept demonstration of AR Visual-Captions, an AR interface that provides real-time speech-to-text captions that can be clearly presented to users and translates the recognized languages into targeted languages, displays the captions in 3D spatial space that automatically align with the speaker, and presents visual hints using the keywords that are automatically extracted from the recognized speech text, to connect people with different needs and improve their captioning experience. We describe the concept, design and implementation of our prototype, and discuss the potential application scenarios and future research directions.

Keywords: Augmented Reality · Accessibility · Translation · Captions · Speech Recognition

1 Introduction

Communicating with someone who speaks a different language, trying to follow the conversation with hearing individuals for deaf and hard of hearing (DHH) individuals, are real challenges which can create confusion and prevent people from understanding each other. With technologies such as Automatic Speech Recognition (ASR) and real-time machine translation, the speech could be recognized and converted into textual information and translated into targeted languages. Captions and subtitles are the most widely used methods to show the recognized and translated text [16, 17, 32]. However, these approaches can pose additional limitations. The captions that are shown on a shared large screen might split the user's visual attention between the screen and the speakers in the conversation, as well as other information in the surroundings such as slides [17,

24]. The privacy issue of showing the caption on a large screen is also not desired by the user [17]. This attention split might be more significant when speakers move around the environment but the caption stays at the fixed location [17]. Captioning on personal mobile devices [e.g., 25, 37, 39] enables people to understand conversations by looking at their own devices, while it also demands users to shift their attention away from the speaker or the environment to the devices [16].

Augmented Reality (AR) technology is changing the way of how information is presented to users by displaying virtual information in the real world without compromising users' natural vision [10, 28, 30, 41–43]. AR offers users the access to interactive and contextually relevant virtual content such as captions and visuals that also exists in the real environment [3, 5, 8], reducing the visual attention split and will not obstruct the objects in the real world [16, 17].

However, while previous work has proposed the idea of showing real-time captions on AR head-mounted display (HMD) (e.g., 18, 35), little work has specifically addressed on how to design captions properly, especially in live scenarios [7]. Commercial AR applications, such as *TranslatAR*, *Google Translate*, and the recently unveiled prototype of Google's latest AR glass, all overlay translated text on the screen while the real-world information is hidden from the user [33]. According to researchers [4], users might prefer placing captions in the environment rather than on the screen of AR glasses. The virtual captions should be moved or displayed around the real-world objects [33]. However, little work has explored positioning captions in 3D space using AR [17].

Besides, DHH individuals may have limited reading and comprehension skills for textual information [22, 26, 38], while sign language interpreter could be a more friendly way to convey information, it relies heavily on actor performance and advance recording [23]. RealityTalk [21] is a novel approach to displaying keywords and visual elements to facilitate interactive storytelling experience, while the system mainly focuses on the perspective of presenters creating presentations. Except for RealityTalk, no existing works have explored the approach of speech-driven augmented presentations [21].

Therefore, there is a gap in how to design AR captions for DHH individuals and for multilingual context. Our goal is to facilitate users a better captioning experience by displaying textual and visual elements in AR space for real-time conversations. In this paper, we first collect existing studies on AR captions and analyze the design of these captions. Based on our analysis, we identify the design space for AR visual-captions as the following three dimensions: 1) textual elements (text positions and appearances), 2) visual elements (associated images and positions), 3) interactions with the elements.

Based on the identified design space, we design and implement a proof-of-concept demonstration of AR Visual-Captions, an AR interface for real-time speech-to-text translation with visual hints to connect people with different needs. AR Visual-Captions provides real-time speech-to-text captions that can be clearly presented to users and translates the recognized languages into targeted languages, displays the captions in 3D spatial space that automatically align with the speaker, and presents visuals using the keywords that are automatically extracted from the recognized speech text, helping people understand the conversation and improve their captioning experience.

To achieve this, AR Visual-Captions leverages the components of Vosk API for speech recognition, Google Translation API for language translation, transformer-based natural language processing (NLP) engine for word extraction, GoogleImageCrawler for image obtain, and ARKit and AR Foundation for displaying AR elements in the real world. We describe how the AR interface can be applied in different scenarios and discuss research directions for future studies.

2 Related Work

2.1 Traditional Captions

Traditional captions allow users to understand videos or conversations without audio or in unfamiliar languages, which the text is often placed in static positions [15]. However, prior works have reported that using traditional captions requires users to quickly associate captions with on-screen content, which may negatively affect their viewing experience and easily miss information [12, 13, 32]. Traditional captioning systems on mobile devices such as *Microsoft Translator* and *Google Speech to Text*, making it easy to have a conversation while looking at the captions on the phone for live conversations. However, it still demands users to split their attention [16]. To make the overall viewing experience more immersive and less incoherent, prior studies have investigated dynamic captioning systems, which the position of captions is changing automatically [e.g., 6, 15]. However, these approaches use the existing text from media such as movies, TV shows, online videos, etc., which limit the freeform perspective of users and the usability for face-to-face spontaneous conversations [32]. Captioning approaches with tactile and visual-tactile feedback have also been explored and proved to bring significant benefits to DHH viewers [19], which also work for existing video content like TV shows and movies.

2.2 AR On-Screen Captions

Displaying real-time captions using AR is a promising approach for various real-world scenarios [33]. For example, Enssat [1] is a bilingual smartphone-based app that uses Google Glass to assist DHH people, which can perform real-time transcription, real-time translation, and alert management to users through the screen of the AR glass. Most of prior studies of AR captions have focused on investigating the text placement on AR devices [33]. Early in 2008, Tanaka et al. [36] have identified the difficulty in displaying information via AR HMD when the sight behind the display is too complex or too bright, and created a method to determine the ideal area to display text. Rzayev et al. [33] have conducted a study with 12 participants using AR to examine the placement of virtual content in a language learning context. In their study, participants have learned foreign words on the screen while viewing translations using HoloLens. The virtual translation is placed either on the top, on the right, or below the foreign words, which the one that placed on the top of foreign words is found to significantly decrease comprehension and increase users' task load [33]. They have also investigated how notifications should be displayed to users without negatively affecting their social interactions during face-to-face conversations by comparing the center and top-right positions in a study with 32 participants using HoloLens [34]. Similarly, Chua et al. [9] have investigated 9 different display positions with AR glasses for showing information in a dual-task scenario with 27 participants. They have found that although the notification displayed at the middle and bottom center positions are noticed quicker, the top and the peripheral positions provide better user experience [9].

The importance of text placement on the screen of AR devices has been identified by researchers and widely investigated in previous studies. However, researchers have found that users might prefer placing text in the environment rather than on the screen of AR glasses [31]. Therefore, we further investigate AR captions that are placed in the environment or provide spatial information in the next section.

2.3   AR Captions with Spatial Information

More recent AR interfaces have been proposed to improve users' experiences by displaying captions with spatial information. For example, SpeechBubbles [32] is an assistive interface for improving DHH individuals' experience of comprehending speech from hearing individuals in face-to-face group conversations using HoloLens. In this study, the captions are located on the right side of the speaker and moving together with the speaker's head. However, although the SpeechBubbles includes the spatial information of the source of the microphone (the directional information), the captions stay at the fixed distance on the screen without in-depth information.

Jain et al. [17] have explored AR Windows and AR Subtitles to display real-time captions for DDH individuals. In contrast to conventional captions which use external and fixed display, AR Windows allows users to manipulate the size or the placement of captions in 3D space with HoloLens. However, although the AR caption window could be moved by users, it could not automatically align with speakers in the depth space. Consequently, users might feel obtrusive when they have to resize and place the caption window by themselves [17]. AR Subtitles displays textual information placed at a fixed distance in front of the user and moves with the user's head without option to resize or place in different positions. According to their evaluations, users have described the AR Subtitles as would disconnect speakers and captions since it appears at a fixed distance [17].

Guo et al. [14] have proposed HoloSound in a poster paper, an AR prototype combining speech and sound feedback for DDH individuals. In addition to providing speech transcription, the prototype focuses more on non-spoken sound cues from users' surroundings for advancing sound awareness [14]. The system also has two types of views for the speech transcription: a normal subtitled view and a window view. In the window view, the user could place the text window on top of the speakers using the HoloLen's pinch gesture to reduce the visual split between the transcribed text and the speaker. In the subtitle view, similar to the study of Jain et al. [17], a single text block appears at a fixed distance in front of the speaker and moves together with the speaker's head. The findings have showed that both their solutions are effective to assist DDH users in daily lives [14].

These prior works mostly focus on presenting the textual captions and have not investigated visual elements to facilitate the understanding of conversations. The real-time translation is also not widely combined. Taking inspiration from prior works, we explore how we can combine speech-to-text recognition, visual elements, real-time translation, and with the expanding ubiquity of AR spatial interfaces for an optimized captioning visualizations and engaging a better captioning user experience.

3   Design Space

To better investigate the design space for AR captioning systems, we first collect nine existing works and analyze aspects in terms of textual elements, visual elements, and the interactions with the elements. The existing works are collected with a search in Google Scholar based on specific keywords like "AR captions". We only include works for real-time conversations and exclude the studies on TV shows or movies. We are not meant to provide a systematic literature review but to inform from the design space for AR designers who will develop AR captions in the future. The nine existing works are shown in Fig. 1. The design space analysis can be found in Table 1.

Fig. 1. Design space analysis with previous studies: a) SpeechBubbles [32] b) HoloSound windows view [14-1] c) HoloSound subtitles view [14-2] d) Wearable Subtitles [29] e) AR Windows [17-1] f) AR Subtitles [17-2] g) Speech Balloon [20] h) Mobile Captions [16] i) AR subtitle visualizations [27].

3.1   Textual Elements

Text Positions: One of the challenges for AR captions would be that the users might easily get distracted by looking through a screen and just focus on the screen but not surroundings in the real world [11]. Thus, for the AR interface, the text position is an important factor to consider during the design process.

Among the studies we analyzed, most of them (six studies) place the textual elements on the screen with the fixed distance. While AR Windows (Fig. 1-e) can be aligned with in-depth information by the control of users. HoloSound can be placed using HoloLens' 3D spatial mapping feature to recognize the environment automatically place the captions near the user's desired spatial position (Fig. 1-b). The captions can be automatically projected onto a surface in the surroundings in the real world without associating with the speakers in Mobile Captions (Fig. 1-h).

Users have suggested that captions should automatically align close to the speaker or background to reduce the visual attention split between captions and the environment. They would like the captions to be positioned above speakers (like speech bubbles) so the only way they could see captions is if they are looking at speakers [16]. Hence, the AR captions should be placed close to the speaker in the spatial location, which will move together with the speaker automatically. In the meantime, the captions should not obstruct users' view so they can pay attention to the surroundings [16, 17].

Out-of-View Text Positions: SpeechBubbles [32] has also provided the hint cues for out-of-view speakers at the relative locations. According to the DHH participants in their study, it is a major challenge for them to being aware of sounds that are out of their views since they barely hear sounds coming from behind them even with hearing aids [32]. Users can always receive the speech text without having speakers inside their field of view in another study [16]. For DHH users, they should be offered with the opportunity to receive information for out-of-view speakers as well. For other users, they can also choose from always looking at the speakers for the captions or they can pay more attention to the surroundings while still receiving the speech text on screen.

Appearances of Text: In prior studies, there is no unified design of the colors, size, fonts, etc. of the textual elements. In AR settings, the environment in the real world is changing in different situations. That might be the reason why the appearances of the text are different in different studies. Among the analyzed studies, five of them use white text with no background, two use transparent black (gray) background with white text, one uses gray background with black text, and one uses white background with black text. Besides, three of them enable users to configure the number of lines, length of each line, the font size, and the distance of captions from the eyes by themselves. All of previous studies use 2D text, the research on the effects between 2D and 3D text in AR captions is still a blank.

Thus, the user should be provided with different choices of colors and fonts of the text and can even customize by themselves. The size of the captions and visuals can be adjusted by their own needs via the AR device anytime they want. We can also make the captions in both 2D and 3D text.

Table 1. Design space analysis for various aspects.

Paper	Associate with the speaker	Cover the speaker's face	Text display type	Move with the speaker	In-depth position	Amount of content	Visual element	Translation	Interaction
[32]	Yes	No	Black background with 50% transparency and black text	Yes, automatically moving horizontal and vertical	No (fixed distance on screen)	2 lines	None	None	None
[14-1]	No	Yes	White text with no background, users can customize	No	Yes (automatically position the captions with HoloLens' 3D spatial mapping feature to recognize the environment)	2 lines, 60 characters	None	None	None
[14-2]	No	No	White text with no background, users can customize	Yes, automatically moving horizontal and vertical with speaker's head	No (fixed distance on screen)	2 lines, 60 characters	None	None	None
[29]	No	Yes	White text without background	No	No (fixed distance on screen)	Multiple lines with scrolling animations that would smoothly roll the text upwards as new lines are added	None	None	None

(continued)

Table 1. (*continued*)

Paper	Associate with the speaker	Cover the speaker's face	Text display type	Move with the speaker	In-depth position	Amount of content	Visual element	Translation	Interaction
[17-1]	Yes	Yes	Transparent black background with white text (web browser window)	Yes, but not automatically, by user's control	Yes (users can position the window in physical space)	Multiple lines, captions scroll up and disappear at the top of the window	None	None	HoloLens pinch gesture
[17-2]	Yes	No	White text with no background	Yes, automatically moving horizontal and vertical	No (fixed distance on screen)	1 line, 60 characters	None	None	None
[20]	Yes	No	Gray background with black text	Yes (face recognition)	No (fixed distance on screen)	1 line, users can look back past conversation with multi speech balloons	None	None	Users can look back conversation by looking up
[16]	No	No	White, Arial font, with no background. Users can customize	Follow the view of the viewer	Can be automatically projected onto a surface or at a fixed distance from the eye	2 lines, 60 characters per line, an angular font size of approximately 0.75 degree	None	None	None
[27]	Yes	No	White background with black text	Yes (face recognition)	No (fixed distance on screen)	One word	None	None	None

3.2 Visual Elements

Associated Image: None of analyzed prior work has displayed associated visuals such as images and pictures to the user. Previous works have demonstrated that DHH individuals have limited literacy skill and may have troubles in reading and comprehending the textual captions [22], which may in turn negatively affect the quality of their lives [20, 37]. Besides, the captioning speed is very likely to exceed the reading speed [23]. In the meantime, the feedback provided together with the caption, such as the visual cues and tactile feedback, have been demonstrated to bring significant benefits to DHH viewers for TV shows and movies [18]. The extra information offered by the visual cues are very helpful in guiding users attention towards immediately identifying the location of the sound [18]. Therefore, for real-time conversations, we will show visual information together with the textual information. We hope that the extra visual information can help users understand the speech content faster and facilitate them to read and understand the speech information.

Visual Positions: For AR captioning systems, we should reduce the attention split between the textual information and the visual sources as much as possible. Thus, the visual elements will be placed close to the textual elements placed on top of the speaker's head, either by the left of right side around the speaker. To not obstruct users to see the surroundings in the real world, the visual elements should also be placed in spatial positions. The size of the visuals can be customized by the user based on their own needs the same as the size of the textual elements.

3.3 Interactions with the Elements

Moving the Captions: In prior works, only one study allows the user to interact with the caption window with the HoloLens built-in gestures, to move the window to preferred positions. The rest of studies have not included any moving interaction, or the AR captions are following the speaker automatically.

Scaling the Captions: Similar to the moving interaction, the same study enables the user to resize the caption window with the built-in gestures as well. Other studies have not mentioned any scaling interaction.

Other Interactions: One study has also mentioned that the user could look up to look for the past conversations. Except for this study, prior work has not fully utilized the spatial affordances that AR provides.

Devices: Most prior works have used HoloLens as the AR device while issue has been identified that the current device HoloLens might not be an ideal form factor, which the device should be lighter, smaller, and would not obscure the wearer's eyes [16]. Mobile devices such as iPad or iPhone can also be alternative solutions.

4 Design and Implementation of AR Visual-Captions

4.1 Overview

Based on the above design space exploration, we design and develop AR Visual-Captions, a working proof-of-concept prototype that embeds textual and visual elements based on the real-time speech, and take the advantages of AR technology to display the virtual information in the real world environment for DHH people or multilingual context for enhanced captioning experience. The AR interface first provides real-time speech-to-text captions. Second, the AR interface presents real-time translation if required by the user. Third, visuals searched from Google Image using the keywords that are automatically extracted from the recognized speech text. The captions and the visuals will be continuously displayed around the speaker via AR devices. The virtual content is located in spatial position and will not block the user's view. For example, when the speaker is moving around the room, the captions and the visuals will follow his/her head/body.

AR Visual-Captions incorporate the following components: **Speech recognition:** Recognize and transcribe the speech into text in real-time with Vosk toolkit in Unity. **Speech translation:** Translate the recognized text into targeting languages using Google Translation API. **Word extraction:** Detect and extract the words based on NLP engine. **Visual search:** Based on the words extracted, the prototype searches for visuals using GoogleImageCrawler. **Visual display:** Display the captions and visual elements based on ARKit and AR Foundation in Unity.

Basic Setup: The goal of our prototype is to offer convenience to people in multilingual context or DHH people with minimal effort. The user might also include students in classroom settings. Hence, instead AR HMD, we intentionally use more accessible devices like iPhone or iPad. The devices can be put on top of the user's desk and face to the speaker, and the real-time augmented elements will be presented through the devices while the speaker is speaking.

4.2 Design

Positions of Textual and Visual Elements: AR Visual-Captions embeds transcribed textual elements and translated textual elements based on real-time speech recognition and real-time translation. Informed by the design space analysis, the captions should locate close to the speaker in the spatial position and move together with the speaker. Therefore, in our current prototype, the visual-captions will always follow the speaker and be displayed in spatial position. When the speaker is speaking, the captions will automatically show up on top of the speaker's head. See Fig. 2-a. If the translation is needed, the user can select the targeting languages from a drop-down list. See Fig. 2-c.

In the meantime, when the speaker is moving out of the user's field of view, the user should still receive the information as on-screen captions. Since we use mobile devices, the user can also hold the device and face the camera to the speaker if he/she is moving around in the physical space so that the user can always get the captioning information while looking at the speaker. If users do not want to hold the device, when the speaker walks out of the user's field of view, the captions and the visuals will be automatically transferred to on-screen subtitles and images, and will be changed back when the speaker is back to the user's field of view.

Appearance of Textual and Visual Elements: Informed by the design space above, in our prototype, we use a white background and black text for the text by default. In the meantime, the user is also provided with different choices of colors and fonts of the text and can customize by themselves according to the environment in the real world. See Fig. 2-b. The size of the captions and visuals can be adjusted by their own needs via the AR device. The textual elements will disappear with a certain duration according to the speaker's speaking speed. The staying duration should also be able to be specified according to users' needs.

Interactions with Textual and Visual Elements: To minimize the effort needed in using the AR interface, we apply the basic screen-touch gestures on mobile devices that users are familiar with. The visual-captions will follow the speaker automatically so that there is no need for the user to move these elements. The user can scale the textual and visual elements using pinch gestures: 1) place two fingers on the screen and spread them apart to scale up; 2) place two fingers on the screen and bring them together to scale down.

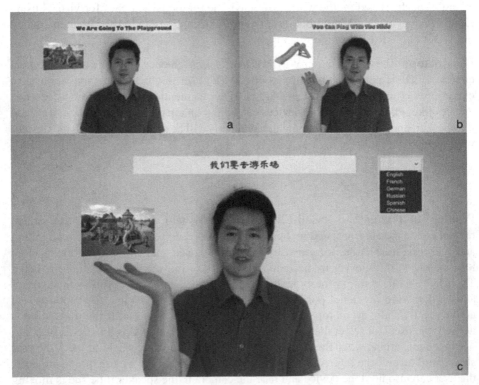

Fig. 2. a) AR Visual-Captions with textual and visual elements; b) AR Visual-Captions with different textual appearances; c) AR Visual-Captions with translation options (images are obtained from Google Image).

4.3 Implementation

Speech Recognition: We recognize and transcribe the speech of the speaker into text in real-time with Vosk toolkit in Unity, which provides the ability to detect and transcribe over 20 different languages from the microphone input on the device. The text transcriptions will be displayed as AR captions and used for word extraction in following steps.

Speech Translation: If the translation is needed, the user can choose the targeting language, and the transferred text will be translated using Google Translation API and displayed as AR captions.

Word Extraction: We use Python script on SpaCy to detect and extract the words from the speech text, using the pre-trained model based on the model of *en_core_web_md dataset*. Only nouns will be extracted, which will then be used for visual searching next.

Visual Search: The visuals are collected using icrawler.buitin.GoogleImageCrawler with the nouns extracted in the last step. The first result on Google Image will be obtained and can be used for displaying in Unity later.

Visual Display: We build the AR interface in Unity to display the captions and visual elements based on ARKit and AR Foundation around the speaker. The captions will be displayed on top of the speaker's head with the AR face tracking or AR body tracking and the visual elements will be displayed on the left or right side around the captions.

5 Discussion

5.1 Applications

Education for DHH Students: 430 million people (over 5% of the world's population) have hearing loss, among them, 34 million are children [39]. It is estimated that by 2050 the number of DHH individuals will reach 700 million [39]. DHH individuals are facing challenges that limit their ability to participate in areas such as education [2]. One of the educational challenges is the difficulty for DHH people to access audio information in the mainstream classroom in the same way as hearing individuals [22, 23]. Text-only AR captions are challenging for DHH students since they might have limited comprehension skills for textual information and the captioning speed is likely to exceed their reading speed, especially when the students are in primary school [22, 23]. AR Visual-Captions can be an aid for DHH students to receive information in classrooms.

Language Learning and Communicating for Hearing Individuals: For hearing individuals, the proposed prototype can be used for learning a different language such as learning vocabulary. For example, if the user does not understand the meaning of a word, the visual hint may help him/her understand and memorize the word. The user can also use the prototype when watching movies or videos and learn the meaning of unfamiliar language with the real-time machine translation. What's more, the prototype can also be used during a conference/conversation with people speaking different languages.

5.2 Future Directions

User Evaluation: Based on prior research and our own work, the following aspects should be further investigated and validated:

User Experience. We should evaluate the overall ratings with the AR Visual-Captions with both DHH individuals and hearing individuals, collecting feedback from them regarding the usability of the system and the user experience. Then, we should investigate the usefulness of the textual elements and the visual elements to figure out the effectiveness of the proposed prototype in helping users.

Design Implications. The textual and visual elements should be carefully designed to enhance the overall captioning experience, including their positions and appearances. To be more specific, the effects of captions automatically aligned to the speakers and captions statically stayed on the screen. The effects of customized appearances or fixed appearances such as text colors, fonts, and size.

Potential Use in Different Scenarios. The proposed prototype should be evaluated in different scenarios such as in classrooms, in conference meeting rooms, and in casual conversation scenarios, etc. Different targeted groups should also be addressed differently to identify a validated design guidelines.

Future Extensions: We also address further extensions of the current prototype, which are worth discussing in future studies:

Group Conversation. Previous studies have identified the importance to allow users participate in a group conversation [32]. The current prototype focuses on one speaker, which can be extended into group conversations. We can use the Netcode in Unity to connect different devices. The main device will start the server, and the other devices will join as a client. Each client device has the recognition function to receive the microphone source from the device.

Additional Information. Besides captions, AR can also convey information such as speakers' names, titles, speech emotions, tones, and environmental information. People use emotions and tones to express their moods during the conversation and engage in the communications more deeply [32]. Without being able to perceive these types of information, DHH users may misunderstand certain conversational context relying on the textural captions alone [32]. However, none of prior works has focused on displaying additional information. Therefore, we can expand the AR interface to convey people's emotions with the visual-captions, such as different caption colors and fonts that map to different emotions, or use stickers to express emotions.

Mutual Communication: We also plan to extend the current concept to provide opportunities for mutual communication. For example, we can collect the eye tracking data of the user following the captions and visuals, and give the feedback to speakers so that they can pay more attention to their speaking speed or their locations in the physical space. What's more, the user can also response to the speaker by typing textual elements or displaying visual elements. In this way, the speaker and the listener can communicate with each other regardless of the language barriers.

Spatial Information: The design space analysis shows that prior work has not fully utilized the spatial affordances that AR provides. In the future version, the speech can be retrospective by placing the captions in spatial space. The speakers could also leave a message in the spatial space for others.

5.3 Limitations

The current prototype still has limitations. First, we use automated approach as downloading the first result from Google Image search in the visual searching process. However, this approach may increase noise to the system due to the randomness of the obtained images. Besides, if there are multiple nouns in one sentence, it may be confusing for users to associate the visual to the word. The visuals also disappear too fast if multiple nouns are extracted in one sentence. We should refine the design to address above issues, such as highlighting the words with the visual hint, allowing users to click on the visual to show more results to eliminate randomness, etc. For improved device usage, we would like to explore smart-glasses with wider viewing areas instead of holding iPad/iPhone in our current case.

6 Conclusion

We present AR Visual-Captions, a visual captioning interface to facilitate DHH individuals and connect people speaking different languages with real-time speech recognition and translation. AR Visual-Captions enables users to receive real-time information of textual and visual elements in AR. Based on our analysis of existing works, we summarize the design space for AR interfaces. In the future, we would further test our design and expand our design perspectives.

References

1. Alkhalifa, S., Al-Razgan, M.: Enssat: wearable technology application for the deaf and hard of hearing. Multimedia Tools Appl. **77**(17), 22007–22031 (2018)
2. Alnafjan, A., Aljumaah, A., Alaskar, H., Alshraihi, R.: Designing "Najeeb": technology-enhanced learning for children with impaired hearing using Arabic sign-language ArSL Applications. In: 2017 International Conference on Computer and Applications (ICCA), pp. 238–273. IEEE, September 2017
3. Azuma, R.T.: A survey of augmented reality. Presence: Teleoper. Virtual Environ. **6**(4), 355–3851997
4. Basoglu, E.B., Akdemir, O.: A comparison of undergraduate students' English vocabulary learning: Using mobile phones and flash cards. Turk. Online J. Educ. Technol.-TOJET **9**(3), 1–7 (2010)
5. Billinghurst, M., Kato, H., Poupyrev, I.: The magicbook-moving seamlessly between reality and virtuality. IEEE Comput. Graph. Appl. **21**(3), 6–8 (2001)

6. Brown, A., et al.: Dynamic subtitles: the user experience. In: Proceedings of the ACM International Conference on Interactive Experiences for TV and Online Video, pp. 103–112, June 2015

7. Bowald, D.: AR Comic Chat. Rochester Institute of Technology (2020)

8. Breen, D.E., Rose, E.. Whitaker, R.T.: Interactive occlusion and collision of real and virtual objects in augmented reality. European Computer Industry Research Center, Munich, Germany (1995)

9. Chua, S.H., Perrault, S.T., Matthies, D.J., Zhao, S.: Positioning glass: investigating display positions of monocular optical see-through head-mounted display. In: Proceedings of the Fourth International Symposium on Chinese CHI, pp. 1–6, May 2016

10. Choi, J., et al.: Position- based augmented reality platform for aiding construction and inspection of offshore plants. Vis. Comput. J. **36**, 2039–2049 (2020)

11. Eksvärd, S., Falk, J.: Evaluating speech-to-text systems and AR-glasses: a study to develop a potential assistive device for people with hearing impairments (2021)

12. Gulliver, S.R., Ghinea, G.: Impact of captions on deaf and hearing perception of multimedia video clips. In: Proceedings. IEEE International Conference on Multimedia and Expo, vol. 1, pp. 753–756. IEEE, August 2002

13. Gulliver, S.R., Ghinea, G.: How level and type of deafness affect user perception of multimedia video clips. Univ. Access Inf. Soc. **2**(4), 374–386 (2003)

14. Guo, R., et al.: Holosound: combining speech and sound identification for deaf or hard of hearing users on a head-mounted display. In: The 22nd International ACM SIGACCESS Conference on Computers and Accessibility, pp. 1–4, October 2020

15. Hong, R., Wang, M., Xu, M., Yan, S., Chua, T.S.: Dynamic captioning: video accessibility enhancement for hearing impairment. In: Proceedings of the 18th ACM International Conference on Multimedia, pp. 421–430, October 2010

16. Jain, D., Franz, R., Findlater, L., Cannon, J., Kushalnagar, R., Froehlich, J.: Towards accessible conversations in a mobile context for people who are deaf and hard of hearing. In: Proceedings of the 20th International ACM SIGACCESS Conference on Computers and Accessibility, pp. 81–92, October 2018

17. Jain, D., Chinh, B., Findlater, L., Kushalnagar, R., Froehlich, J.: Exploring augmented reality approaches to real-time captioning: a preliminary autoethnographic study. In: Proceedings of the 2018 ACM Conference Companion Publication on Designing Interactive Systems, pp. 7–11, May 2018

18. Jain, D., et al.: Head-mounted display visualizations to support sound awareness for the deaf and hard of hearing. In: Proceedings of the 33rd Annual ACM Conference on Human Factors in Computing Systems, pp. 241–250, April 2015

19. Kushalnagar, R.S., Behm, G.W., Stanislow, J.S., Gupta, V.: Enhancing caption accessibility through simultaneous multimodal information: visual-tactile captions. In: Proceedings of the 16th International ACM SIGACCESS Conference on Computers and Accessibility, pp. 185–192, October 2014

20. Kurahashi, T., Sakuma, R., Zempo, K., Mizutani, K., Wakatsuki, N.: Retrospective speech balloons on speech-visible AR via head-mounted display. In: 2018 IEEE International Symposium on Mixed and Augmented Reality Adjunct (ISMAR-Adjunct), pp. 423–424. IEEE, October 2018

21. Liao J., Karim A., Jadon S.S., Kazi R.H., Suzuki R.: RealityTalk: real-time speech-driven augmented presentation for AR live storytelling. In: Proceedings of the 35th Annual ACM Symposium on User Interface Software and Technology, pp. 1–12, October 2002

22. Luckner, J.L., Handley, C.M.: A summary of the reading comprehension research undertaken with students who are deaf or hard of hearing. Am. Ann. Deaf **153**(1), 6–36 (2008)

23. Luo, L., Weng, D., Songrui, G., Hao, J., Tu, Z.: Avatar interpreter: improving classroom experiences for deaf and hard-of-hearing people based on augmented reality. In: CHI Conference on Human Factors in Computing Systems Extended Abstracts, pp. 1–5, April 2022

24. Marschark, M., Pelz, J.B., Convertino, C., Sapere, P., Arndt, M.E., Seewagen, R.: Classroom interpreting and visual information processing in mainstream education for deaf students: live or memorex®? Am. Educ. Res. J. **42**(4), 727–761 (2005)

25. Matthews, T., Carter, S., Pai, C., Fong, J., Mankoff, J.: Scribe4Me: evaluating a mobile sound transcription tool for the deaf. In: Dourish, P., Friday, A. (eds.) UbiComp 2006. LNCS, vol. 4206, pp. 159–176. Springer, Heidelberg (2006). https://doi.org/10.1007/11853565_10

26. Miller, A., Malasig, J., Castro, B., Hanson, V.L., Nicolau, H., Brandão, A.: The use of smart glasses for lecture comprehension by deaf and hard of hearing students. In: Proceedings of the 2017 CHI Conference Extended Abstracts on Human Factors in Computing Systems, pp. 1909–1915 (2017)

27. Moraru, O.A.: Real-time subtitle for the hearing impaired in augmented reality. Doctoral dissertation, Wien (2018)

28. Olbrich, M., et al.: Augmented reality supporting user-centric building information management. Vis. Comput. J. **29**, 1093–1105 (2013)

29. Olwal, A., et al.: Wearable subtitles: augmenting spoken communication with lightweight eyewear for all-day captioning. In: Proceedings of the 33rd Annual ACM Symposium on User Interface Software and Technology, pp. 1108–1120, October 2020

30. Ong, D.X., et al.: Smart captions: a novel solution for closed captioning in theatre settings with AR glasses. In: 2021 IEEE International Conference on Service Operations and Logistics, and Informatics (SOLI), pp. 1–5. IEEE, December 2021

31. Orlosky, J., Kiyokawa, K., Takemura, H.: Managing mobile text in head mounted displays: studies on visual preference and text placement. ACM SIGMOBILE Mob. Comput. Commun. Rev. **18**(2), 20–31 (2014)

32. Peng, Y.H., et al.: Speechbubbles: enhancing captioning experiences for deaf and hard-of-hearing people in group conversations. In: Proceedings of the 2018 CHI Conference on Human Factors in Computing Systems, pp. 1–10, April 2018

33. Rzayev, R., Hartl, S., Wittmann, V., Schwind, V., Henze, N.: Effects of position of real-time translation on AR glasses. In: Proceedings of the Conference on Mensch und Computer, pp. 251–257, September 2020

34. Rzayev, R., Korbely, S., Maul, M., Schark, A., Schwind, V., Henze, N.: Effects of position and alignment of notifications on AR glasses during social interaction. In: Proceedings of the 11th Nordic Conference on Human-Computer Interaction: Shaping Experiences, Shaping Society, pp. 1–11, October 2020

35. Suemitsu, K., Zempo, K., Mizutani, K., Wakatsuki, N.: Caption support system for complementary dialogical information using see-through head mounted display. In: 2015 IEEE 4th Global Conference on Consumer Electronics (GCCE), pp. 368–371. IEEE, October 2015

36. Tanaka, K., Kishino, Y., Miyamae, M., Terada, T., Nishio, S.: An information layout method for an optical see-through head mounted display focusing on the viewability. In: 2008 7th IEEE/ACM International Symposium on Mixed and Augmented Reality, pp. 139–142. IEEE, September 2008

37. TextHear Speech To Text Technologies for the Hearing Impaired. https://texthear.com/

38. Traxler, C.B.: The Stanford Achievement Test: National norming and performance standards for deaf and hard-of-hearing students. J. Deaf Stud. Deaf Educ. **5**(4), 337–348 (2000)

39. White, S.: Audiowiz: nearly real-time audio transcriptions. In: Proceedings of the 12th International ACM SIGACCESS Conference on Computers and Accessibility, pp. 307–308, October 2010

40. Wold Health Organization. Deafness and hearing loss (2021). https://www.who.int/news-room/fact-sheets/detail/deafness-and-hearing-loss

41. Xia, X., et al.: Towards a switchable AR/VR near-eye display with accommodation-vergence and eyeglass prescription support. IEEE Trans. Vis. Comput. Graph. (TVCG) **25**(11), 3114–3124 (2019)
42. Xia, X., et al.: Towards eyeglass-style holographic near-eye displays with statically expanded eyebox. Accepted for publishing in the Proceedings of IEEE ISMAR 2020 (2020)
43. Yu, K., Ahn, J., Lee, J., Kim, M., Han, J.: Collaborative SLAM and AR-guided navigation for floor layout inspection. Vis. Comput. **36**(10–12), 2051–2063 (2020). https://doi.org/10.1007/s00371-020-01911-8

Playful Learning: Promoting Immersive Learning Environment in Chinese Community

Yilin Liu[1]($\boxtimes$) and Xueying Niu[2]

[1] Boston College, Boston 02467, USA
elaine.liu@bc.edu
[2] Tsinghua University, Beijing 100084, People's Republic of China

Abstract. This paper is about the study of "Learning Landscape" in Chinese communities. The major goals of the present study include designing an adapted playful learning program in the Chinese community, assessing caregivers' attitudes toward this new form of learning (i.e., playful learning). We aimed to incorporate game mechanics and elements (e.g., stories design, jumping feet design, game board, and story dice) into the learning process with the main focus on children's math development. We expected to see that the playful learning program will create more opportunities for parent-child interactions and help children and families build connections with the spaces around them. The present study was designed to build our knowledge of Chinese caregivers' perspectives on playful learning. The results suggest that the majority of Chinese caregivers are positive about the construct of playful learning and are willing to take their children to visit learning landscapes. These results inform future studies to design and implement adaptive playful learning programs in Chinese communities and to examine the influence of learning landscapes on parent-child interactions and children's education outcomes.

Keywords: Playful learning · Learning landscapes · Immersive entertainment · Chinese community

1 Introduction

1.1 Gamification and Playful Learning

Gamification in education, known as the integration of game mechanics and components in a learning setting (Kiryakova et al. 2014), has increased in popularity in past few years because of its perceived capacity to increase children's motivation and interest in learning (Caponetto et al. 2014). Specifically, gamified learning environments could be composed of elements including points, badges, leaderboards, and storylines (Nah et al. 2014). So, why is it necessary to incorporate game elements into the learning process?

Prior research shows that children learn best in a stimulating, meaningful, engaged, and sociable environment (Hirsh-Pasek et al. 2015), thus making play a desirable setting for enhancing children's educational development (Weisberg et al. 2016). In addition, play experiences may also help build connections between individuals and their surroundings and rethink how to approach public space (Sumerling 2018). By integrating playful elements into public spaces children may grow more curious and eager to learn. This is critical because the physical environment can impact a child's internal-driven curiosity (Weisberg et al. 2014) and encourage parent-child interaction and participation in activities aimed to advance language, mathematics, and spatial development.

1.2 Learning Landscapes

Adopting the construct of playful learning, researchers in the United States cooperated with architects to design and launch major projects: learning landscapes. Learning Landscapes applies a strengths-based approach by utilizing families' enthusiasm in playing a bigger role in educating their children outside of school in an open-ended manner that occurs naturally and comfortably (Bustamante et al. 2019). The learning landscapes project, in particular, incorporates playful learning opportunities in public areas (e.g., community playgrounds) where kids and families frequently and naturally spend time together. Learning Landscapes aims to maximize learning during children's free time outside school, foster 21st-century learning skills (e.g., communication, critical thinking, and confidence; (Golinkoff & Hirsh-Pasek 2016), and prepare young children to become creative thinkers and global citizens (Bustamante et al. 2019).

1.3 The Guided Theory of Learning Landscapes: Theory of Change

The guided theoretical framework for learning landscapes is the theory of change. The theory of change emphasizes the need to adapt environments in a way that will promote changes in parenting beliefs and improve children's developmental outcomes (Hassinger-Das et al. 2018). Specifically, the theory of change suggests an influence of learning landscapes happens at multiple levels. According to the theory of change, the learning landscape project starts from various approaches including redesigning public space, promoting constructive use of the shared environment, incorporating game elements into the public setting, and embracing children, families, and residents. Particularly, learning landscapes focus on parental educational principles, reciprocal communications, and interactions in the landscape settings, along with community involvement, buy-in, and commitment (Hassinger-Das et al. 2018).

As for the outcomes, based on the theory of change, the long-term objectives of the learning landscapes are to integrate socially involved, active, meaningful, and engaged learning opportunities into public settings (Hassinger-Das et al. 2018). At the caregiver's level, learning landscapes focus on parental behavioral changes including more support for children's play and more self-assurance in creating meaningful interactions and conversations with their children. The goals of learning landscapes at the child level are to improve the play skills, school preparedness, socioemotional abilities, scientific curiosity, and academic performance of young learners (Hassinger-Das et al. 2018). At the dyad level, learning landscapes target promoting reciprocal communication and interaction between caregivers and children in public spaces and are not limited to landscape settings. As for the community level, the ultimate goal is to build environments that are purposefully constructed for learning and play. At the same time, moderators exist at every stage of the procedure. For instance, the frequency of family visits, the age of the kid, socioeconomic status, parenting beliefs, and the community aspects such as safety and support.

1.4   Implementation of Learning Landscapes

Implementation of learning landscapes includes multifaceted benefits for children and their families. First of all, installments of learning landscapes take low individual effort (Bustamante et al. 2019). That is, once set up, they don't further require staff or facilitators. Moreover, learning landscapes create an accessible place for all children and may promote educational outcomes for low-income children who often have fewer opportunities to participate in specialized electives, visit children's museums, and attend after-school programs. For example, the result of implementing Supermarkets Speak which is a learning landscapes project in Philadelphia shows a 33% increment in language interactions at the supermarket in a low-income community (Hassinger-Das et al. 2018). Besides enhancing language development, learning landscapes may promote children's math development. Research on Parkopolis which is a STEM-related learning landscape project indicates that children and caregivers utilized more numeracy, fraction, pattern, planning, and reasoning language while they are engaging in Parkopolis (Bustamante et al. 2018). In addition, children and caregivers who played Parkopolis took noticeably more turns in conversations and showed a greater level of math involvement (Bustamante et al. 2020).

However, compared to the United States, playful learning hasn't been widely accepted and generalized to populations in Asian countries. Learning Landscapes is also rare to see in Chinese neighborhoods. There are only a few projects and places designed based on the construct or similar idea of playful learning in Asia. For example, Anji Play is a large project launched in Zhejiang Province in China that aims to build an environment for true play which is the play that develops naturally from a child's own needs and interests using a bottom-up approach. The main objective of Anji Play is greatly resonant with the pursuit of learning landscapes. Furthermore, Anji Play is described as an "ecology of learning" by Ms. Cheng---- the designer of Anji Play. According to the Anji Play philosophy, children can take risks that are developmentally appropriate when they are in the play environment (Coffino & Bailey 2019). Specifically, those physical, emotional, social, and intellectual risks could promote joyful experiences for young children. The child becomes intensely involved in their own inquiry as a result of this adventure in playing. The reflection and insight of the child on these experiences establish the foundation for future learning and cultivates an interest in it (Coffino & Bailey 2019).

Another representative playful learning project in Asia is the Komazawa Harappa play park in Japan. This play park is also called the "mud park." Notably, in comparison to other learning landscapes, this play park is designed for "messy play." In addition, this park focuses more on creating opportunities for spontaneous interactions between generations. According to Amano Tomato, one of the founders of the Komazawa Harappa play park, "this is a place for all people, all generations." Eventually, the play park encourages everyone to progressively connect with each other by enabling them to both benefits from and contribute to improving the play park. Though there are a few playful learning programs across Asian countries, most of the early education programs are maintaining the traditional task-based teaching approach in which teachers give instructions and explanations as well as control the pace and students' motivation, attention, and actions.

There could be various reasons for the lack of similar applications of playful learning programs in China. For instance, the high-density housing architecture could be a major barrier to accomplishing learning landscape implementation. Meanwhile, there is a disparity in educational resources between communities in China. The issue of uneven educational resources is further exacerbated by the policy of school district houses which is a policy in China that public schools are required to only enroll students from designated areas. Another reason is that many Chinese communities are often managed in a relatively rudimentary manner, thus making it difficult to adapt community construction to local conditions.

Besides environment-related reasons, parental factors also lead to the limited application of playful learning. In China, the constructs of play and learning are almost always separated. The quote "work hard and play hard" is often introduced by Chinese parents to their children in a culturally unique way. That is, Chinese parents often want their children to learn with wholehearted devotion and ignore any distractions that may lead them to play. In addition, a lot of Chinese parents believe that play should only happen after the children complete the learning process. This interpretation of the quote to some extent can reflect Chinese parents' perspectives on playful learning. For many Chinese parents, the constructs of play and learning are so distinct, resulting in a potential difficulty in accepting playful learning programs.

Furthermore, there is a tendency in Asian countries to "over-occupy" and "over-organize" children's lives by having them participate in more indoor and adult-organized activities like athletics, music, homework, or tutoring (Malone 2010). Both environmental and parental factors may contribute to the lack of implementation of playful learning programs in China. Therefore, the first major goal of the present study is to assess current Chinese parental beliefs toward playful learning and learning landscapes.

1.5 Cross-Cultural Application of Playful Learning

Considering the existing cultural difference between American families and Chinese families, the design and implementation of learning landscapes in the present study will also take a cultural developmental perspective. According to Rogoff (2014), the cultural perspective places more emphasis on studying people's perspectives and experiences with various cultural practices rather than on forming generalizations based on categorical labels like race, ethnicity, or country of origin. Hence, while designing the learning landscapes, we aim to integrate with the existing features of the local community in China. In addition, we not only plan to add novel game mechanics (e.g., fraction dice & puzzle bench) which are adopted from Western cultures but also incorporate traditional Chinese game elements (e.g., Tangram & Aeroplane Chess) into the learning landscapes.

In addition to integrating Chinese distinctive factors, the current study targets Chinese families and populations in order to promote the generalization of findings in non-WEIRD (Western, Educated, Industrialized, Rich, and Democratic, (Henrich et al. 2010) subjects. According to (Henrich et al. 2010), in the context of education and psychology field, research on children and parents are often based on principles that have been created based on research from WEIRD subjects. Specifically, a survey of the top journals in six subdisciplines of psychology from 2003 to 2007 showed that about 68% of subjects were from the United States, and 96% were from Western industrialized nations (Arnett 2008). It is important to consider that the implications of findings and claims in the psychology and education field are not universal. Recognition of the limitations of research findings based on WEIRD populations is necessary. The current study aims to explore and create a cross-culture application of learning landscapes in the Chinese community and focus on the growth and development of Chinese families.

1.6 Current Study

The main goals of the present study include assessing caregivers' attitudes toward this new form of learning (i.e., playful learning) as well as designing an adapted playful learning program in the Chinese community. We aim to incorporate game mechanics and elements (e.g., puzzle bench, stories design, jumping feet design, fraction dice, game board, and story dice) into the learning process with the main focus on children's math development. We expect to see that the playful learning program will create more opportunities for parent-child interactions and help children and families build connections with the spaces around them.

2 Method

2.1 Participants

Researchers distributed an online survey and recruited 247 participants from mainland China. The majority of participants identified as female (64%). The highest proportion (31%) of overall participants are aged 31–40 years old. Overall, participants fall between the ages of 18 to 40. Most of the participants live in urban areas in the northern part of China. Participants' education attainments varied from less than a high school degree (4%), bachelor's degree or equivalent (73%), to above a bachelor's degree (23%). Among these participants, 155 of them reported having children ages varied from below 3 years old (14%), between 3 and 6 years old (19%), between 6 and 12 years old (31%), to above 12 years old (36%).

2.2 Design

In order to explore the development path of the "Learning Landscape" in Chinese communities, three games were designed in response to the situation of Chinese communities. A sign with introductory words is set up next to each game facility. These introductory words are specially designed for children so that they can understand the game rules more easily.

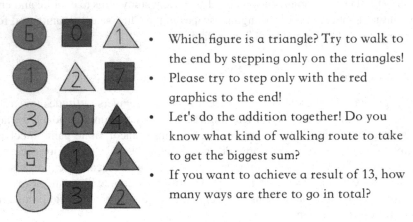

- Which figure is a triangle? Try to walk to the end by stepping only on the triangles!
- Please try to step only with the red graphics to the end!
- Let's do the addition together! Do you know what kind of walking route to take to get the biggest sum?
- If you want to achieve a result of 13, how many ways are there to go in total?

Fig. 1. "Jump Math"

Game 1: "Jump Math".

The first game is called Jump Math (See Fig. 1). In this game, drawings or stickers are used on the floor of a public space within the community. Children can play and learn about math-related problems such as geometric figure recognition, color recognition, and basic arithmetic through this game.

This game has three different ways to play. The first way is "Graph Identification". At the beginning of the game, children can choose a favorite figure, such as a circle, and jump from the circle in the first row to the circle in the second row, and so on until they reach the end. This game develops the child's ability to identify mathematical shapes. The second way is "Color Recognition". This method is similar to the previous one. The child chooses a favorite color before the game starts and jumps from the starting point to the color of his or her choice in the form of a jump. During the jumping process, the child cannot step on any color other than the color he/she has chosen. The third way is the "Mathematical Calculation". The geometric figures on the ground are marked with numbers. Children can choose to add the numbers they have stepped on one by one and calculate the sum of the numbers they have stepped on when they reach the end. This game can develop children's mathematical calculation skills.

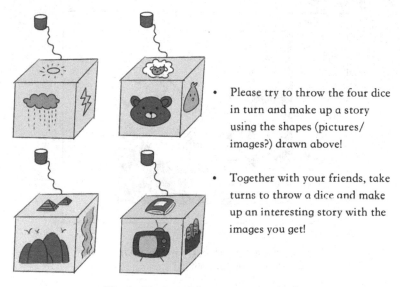

- Please try to throw the four dice in turn and make up a story using the shapes (pictures/ images?) drawn above!

- Together with your friends, take turns to throw a dice and make up an interesting story with the images you get!

Fig. 2. "Let's make up a story together"

Game 2: "Let's make up a story together".

The second game is called "Let's make up a story together" (See Fig. 2). The game is played with 4–5 story dice placed parallel to each other on the ground in a public activity area in the community and tethered to the ground (which cannot be easily moved or carried), where children can roll the dice in place. The height of the story dice will be at the knee of a 6 to 8-year-old child, and the material is planned to be made of plastic foam and other lightweight, non-breakable materials to ensure the safety of the child.

There are two ways to play this game. The first way applies to a single player. Children can use the story dice to roll the weather, time, place, and people to connect to a complete story. This game has the opportunity to exercise children's verbal and thinking skills, and adults can accompany children to complete it. The first method is suitable for multiple people. Many people work together in a solitaire format, each throwing a story die and telling a story based on the elements of the die roll, the content of the story told needs to be able to relate to the content of the previous die.

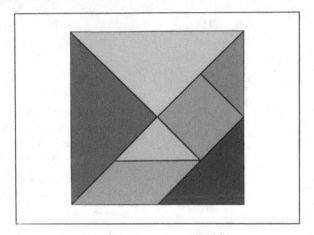

- Use your imagination and be creative! Try out how to form different shapes with Tangram!

- Do you know how many kinds of triangles can be combined using Tangram? Let's try it together!

Fig. 3. "Wall Tangram"

Game 3: "Wall Tangram".

Tangram is a traditional Chinese intellectual toy. It can spell not only geometric figures but also many different figures such as animals, people, and buildings. The "Wall Tangram" game plan replaces ordinary Tangram with magnetic materials and places them in the middle of a wall or wire fence at the boundary of a public area in the community (See Fig. 3). Children can shape, identify colors, or create shapes according to the diagram. Tangram can also be arranged into various geometric shapes to explore mathematical problems.

2.3 Measures

An online survey was administered to examine how people in the Chinese community perceive children playing games, playful learning, and learning landscapes. The survey included three major parts asking participants' perspectives plus two examples of the learning landscapes.

Perspective on Games. We assessed participants' attitudes toward children playing games on a 10-point Likert scale. Participants were asked to indicate how much (1 = strongly disagree, 10 = strongly agree) they endorse the idea that playing games can change education, and how much they believe that playing games would only impede CHILDren's learning. The second question was reversed-coded, and the mean was taken for two items. Higher numbers reflected that parents have more positive attitudes toward CHILDren's playing.

Beliefs About Playful Learning. Participants' attitudes toward playful learning were examined by 5 items (e.g., "DO You view CHildren's playing as opportunities for learning?") using a 10-point Likert scale and 1 item (i.e., "What type of knowledge and skill do you think children can learning from playing?") asking participants to indicate their opinion. The mean was taken for the 5 items, with a higher number reflecting a more positive viewpoint on playful learning. The options to the opinion question were classified into five categories including consciousness growth (e.g., rule consciousness), specialized knowledge in a certain domain (e.g., science knowledge), holistic education (e.g., emotion management strategies), other types of knowledge, and a viewpoint of children are not able to learn from playing.

Attitude Toward Learning Landscapes. Participants' perspectives on learning landscapes were measured by 11 items on a 10-point Likert scale and 2 items asking participants' specific view of the learning landscapes and the reasons for why they may or may not take their children to visit learning landscapes in their community. The total 13 items were designed to have participants rate 3 aspects of the learning landscapes including the overall design of learning landscapes (e.g., "How accessible do you think the learning landscapes are?"), the guiding prompts for activities (e.g., "How helpful are the guiding prompts provided in learning landscape examples in facilitating playing and learning interactions?"), and the influence of learning landscapes (e.g., "How confident are you that the learning landscapes will do a good job in the future of having children learning math or language from playing?"). The mean was taken for each group, with a higher number reflecting a more positive attitude toward one aspect of learning landscapes.

3   Results

In the current study, a confirmatory factor analysis (CFA) was conducted first to investigate the factor structure and validity of the scale which measures participants' perspectives on playing games (PG), playful learning (PL), and learning landscapes (LL). Our final model contained three latent factors as listed above. The results suggest that the model provided a good fit to the data, TLI $= .951$, CFI $= .961$, RMSEA $= .074$, SRMR $= .040$.

The descriptive statistics and bivariate correlations between major study variables are presented in Table 1.

About 95% of the sample believed that children's playing behavior is meaningful, with 91% reporting that they would actively take their children to the community facilities if playful learning elements were added to the current playground equipment. In comparison, about 85% of the participants reported a strong positive attitude when asking if they will take their children to the community playground once learning landscape facilities were implemented in their communities, suggesting a more conservative perspective on building learning landscapes in their communities. Among participants who answered willingness to visit learning landscapes, 96% of them answered that they would expect to take children to visit there at least once a week.

Table 1. Descriptive statistics and correlations matrix

Variables	M	SD	α	PG	PL	LL	Age	Sex	Education
PG	8.281	1.785	.756	-					
PL	8.385	1.466	.824	.772**	-				
LL	8.197	1.375	.956	.552**	.769**	-			
Age	2.866	1.446	-	.033	.029	.132*	-		
Sex	-	-	-	-.016	-.052	-.039	-.163*	-	
Education	3.045	.706	-	.002	.043	-.052	-.301**	-.048	-

Note. M = mean. SD = standard deviation. All means and standard deviations were rounded to three decimal places. ** p < 0.01. * p < 0.05

Results suggest that the majority (92%) of the participants believed that children could have consciousness development (e.g., the spirit of competition) through playing, with 64% of the sample believing that children could learn certain knowledge in a specific domain while playing. 85% of the respondents reported they believed that playing behavior facilitates holistic education (e.g., cooperative ability) for children.

Notably, when asking participants' perceptive of the existing facilities in their communities, only 74% of them reported a positive attitude toward the facilities and 10% of them reported strong dissatisfaction. In contrast, 92% of the participants reported a very positive attitude to the question asking whether learning landscapes meet their expectations for community facilities that are designed for children. Respondents' positive attitude toward learning landscapes may be related to their belief that learning landscapes may support children's development as 93% of them align with this idea. In addition, about 94% of respondents believed that learning landscapes could facilitate parent-child interaction.

Results on items about guiding prompts for the learning landscape also reflected a positive attitude, with 90% of the sample recognizing the accessibility and usefulness of the guiding prompts presented in the learning landscape example in the survey. About 92% of respondents also reported satisfaction with the security of the learning landscape facilities. In addition, when asking participants' perspectives on the design of the learning landscapes, 78% of them reported viewing learning landscapes as useful and 67% of the sample reported learning landscapes as accessible.

In this survey, we also set two open-ended questions. For question 14, "What do they think of children's play? What are the purposes of play?" The total number of responses for this question was 247. The overall response was very positive. In the survey, 236 people thought that children's play behavior was meaningful, and 155 people wrote their opinion. Parents are generally concerned about the effects of play on health and brain development. The survey showed that 29% mentioned the importance of play behavior to exercise/move the body, including the concern for children's physical and mental health. 27% said play helps to develop the brain and intelligence, while 7% said play helps to broaden the mind and understand the world. Notably, there was a significant overlap between those who focused on brain and intellectual development and those who focused on exercise and physical and mental health. Parents are also concerned that "play" plays an important role in "learning through fun". In the survey, 10% mentioned playful learning. One of them pointed out that "finding one's interest can be transformed into a driving force for learning" In addition, 25% of parents believe that play can improve children's ability, such as social ability, cooperation ability, practical ability, coordination ability, thinking ability, creativity, etc. In addition, 8%of parents agreed that the pleasure brought by play itself has some positive significance. They agree that play is the nature of children and that a happy childhood is conducive to the construction of character and personality.

From the results obtained so far, it seems that parents' attitude towards children's play behavior is very positive. They generally believe that play can promote children's physical and mental health, brain development, edutainment, ability improvement, emotional value, parent-child interaction, and other positive significance.

For question 32, "What are the three main reasons you are likely/not likely to return to the learning landscapes site in the future" In general, the answer is very positive. There are 92% of people willing to take their children to the "Learning Landscape" facilities to play, and 8% will not take their children to play. Among those willing to take their children, 156 gave the main reason. Among them, the most important reason is the learning and ability cultivation of children. 24% think that "learning through fun" or "playful learning" is the main reason for them to go. 15% believed that "learning landscape" could increase knowledge and cultivate interest, especially raise awareness of a certain subject (such as mathematics) in a targeted way; 12% believed that "learning landscape" was helpful to strengthen children's exercise, socialization, and teamwork. Some reasons focus on the features of "learning landscape" facilities. For example, 17% proposed the convenience, diversity, playability, and safety of the "learning landscape", which is novel and close to home, can enhance the game experience, and is very convenient for children to play. "Learning landscape" as a "playful learning" new situation in the community, has been recognized by many parents. Among them, 15 parents believed that "learning landscape" can promote parent-child interaction and enhance parent-child relationships. Some parents also raised concerns about the "learning landscape" sites. The reasons for their reluctance to take their children to the facilities focused on the balance between play and learning, community sanitation problems, and road safety issues.

Overall, results indicate a strong positive perspective on children's playing behavior, playful learning, and learning landscapes.

4 Discussion

The major goals of the current study were to examine participants' perspectives on children's playing behavior, playful learning, and learning landscapes, and to design an adapted playful learning program in the Chinese community. The results suggest that participants who live in the Chinese community have strong positive attitudes toward this new form of learning and strongly recognize the usefulness and accessibility of learning landscapes. The present study also proposed three learning landscape designs with considerations of the traditional Chinese games and the feasibility of implementation in Chinese communities.

The value of this study is threefold. First, this study explored the cross-cultural application of playful learning in the Chinese community. To our knowledge, there is little research on studying and designing learning landscapes in China. The present study took the first step and provided a general image of Chinese caregivers' perspectives on playful learning. Secondly, this study introduced three learning landscape designs that may support parent-child interactions and children's language and mathematical development. Third, this study targets Chinese families and thus provides us with a better understanding of an underrepresented group in the psychology and education research field. Taken together, the current study sheds light on implementing learning landscapes in the Chinese community and contribute to our knowledge of Chinese caregivers' attitude toward playful learning.

Some limitations of this study should be noted. First, the current study was an exploratory study. Even though the reliability of the items is acceptable, the design of the survey contains flaws. In future studies, a more valid and concrete survey should be administrated. Another limitation is that the current study only has descriptive results due to the descriptive research design. Specifically, this study only examines "what" are the participants' perspectives on playful learning but not "why" they have either a positive or negative perspective. Third, because of the exploratory nature of the study, the cross-cultural application of the learning landscape was not implemented in a Chinese community but only discussed the feasibility. Future study could consider implementing the learning landscape design and investigate whether learning landscapes has a positive effect on children's learning outcomes. Lastly, the latent factors in the model have high correlation coefficients suggesting the possibility of a 2-factor model. Future research could consider reducing a factor or modifying items to measure each latent factor more accurately.

The present study was designed to build our knowledge of Chinese caregivers' perspectives on playful learning. The results suggest that the majority of Chinese caregivers are positive about the construct of playful learning and are willing to take their children to visit learning landscapes. These results inform future studies to design and implement adaptive playful learning programs in Chinese communities and to examine the influence of learning landscapes on parent-child interactions and children's education outcomes.

References

Arnett, J.: The neglected 95%: Why American psychology needs to become less American. Am. Psychol. **63**(7), 602–614 (2008)

Bustamante, A.S., Hassinger-Das, B., Hirsh-Pasek, K., Golinkoff, R.M.: Learning landscapes: Where the science of learning meets architectural design. Child Dev. Perspect. **13**(1), 34–40 (2019)

Bustamante, A.S, et al.: More than just a game: transforming social interaction and STEM play with Parkopolis. Developmental psychology, **56**(6), 1041(2020)

Coffino, J.R., Bailey, C.: The Anji Play ecology of early learning. Child. Educ. **95**(1), 3–9 (2019)

Caponetto, I., Earp, J.,S Ott, M.: Gamification and education: a literature review. In European Conference on Games Based Learning 1, p. 50). Academic Conferences International Limited (2014)

Golinkoff, R.M., Hirsh-Pasek, K.: Becoming brilliant: What science tells us about raising successful children. American Psychological Association (2016)

Henrich, J., Heine, S.J., Norenzayan, A.: The weirdest people in the world? Behav. brain sci. **33**(2–3), 61–83s (2010)

Hassinger-Das, B., Bustamante, A.S., Hirsh-Pasek, K., Golinkoff, R.M.: Learning landscapes: Playing the way to learning and engagement in public spaces. Education Sciences, 8(2), 74(2018).

Hirsh-Pasek, K., Zosh, J.M., Golinkoff, R.M., Gray, J.H., Robb, M.B., Kaufman, J.: Putting education in "educational" apps: Lessons from the science of learning. Psychol. Sci. Public Interest **16**(1), 3–34 (2015)

Kiryakova, G., Angelova, N., Yordanova, L.: Gamification in education. In: Proceedings of 9th International Balkan Education and Science Conference (2014)

Malone, K.A.: Freeing children to contribute: Building child-friendly cities in the Asia Pacific region. Childhood Matters **115**, 20–25 (2010)

Nah, F.F.H., Zeng, Q., Telaprolu, V.R., Ayyappa, A.P., Eschenbrenner, B.: Gamification of education: a review of literature. In International conference on hci in business (pp. 401–409). Springer, Cham (2014)

Rogoff, B.: Learning by observing and pitching in to family and community endeavors: an orientation. Hum. Dev. **57**(2–3), 69–81 (2014)

Sumerling, B.: A place to play: An exploration of people's connection to local greenspace in East Leeds. Conscious Cities, 2 (2017)

The Tokyo Playpark: A landscape for all ages. ToyProject.net.: Retrieved December 6, 2022, from http://www.toyproject.net/2018/06/tokyo-playpark-landscape-ages/(2018

Weisberg, D.S., Hirsh-Pasek, K., Golinkoff, R.M., McCandliss, B.D.: Mise en place: Setting the stage for thought and action. Trends Cogn. Sci. **18**(6), 276–278 (2014)

Weisberg, D.S., Hirsh-Pasek, K., Golinkoff, R.M., Kittredge, A.K., Klahr, D.: Guided play: Principles and practices. Curr. Dir. Psychol. Sci. **25**(3), 177–182 (2016)

Augmented Social Meal via Multi-sensory Feedback Modulated by Bodily-In-Coordinated Measures

Yanjun Lyu[✉] and Xin Wei Sha

Synthesis Center, School of Arts Media and Engineering, Arizona State University,
Tempe 85281, USA
ylyu16@asu.edu

Abstract. We study how people can affectively engage with one another, using the everyday social setting of an informal meal augmented by media fields sensitive to measurement of coordination. Our contributions are (1) to extend the study of social engagement from dyadic one-to-one interactions to *ensemble activity*, in which joint intention and coordinated activity of three or more people cannot be reduced to dyadic interaction, and (2) to create computational media techniques, *social wearables*, that enhance our bodily ability to communicate and empathize with others, to express with additional layers of social signaling that uses responsive haptic, sonic and visual media that are modulated by measures of ensemble togetherness such as group movement coordination. Our findings as design insights may inspire those particularly focused on the experimental design and development of technology intended to support co-located, embodied interaction.

Keywords: Affect engagement · Social coordination · Participatory sense-making · Embodiment · Intersubjectivity · Multi-sensory technology

1 Introduction

1.1 Research Questions

Our project explores ensemble coordinated movement [12, 16] as a means to promote affective engagement via computational responsive media and wearable technology. We choose to modulate affective engagement as a field of felt meaning [13] primordial to social connectedness. We use multimodal responsive media modulated by measures of interpersonal synchrony which has been found to play a crucial role in social development.

Our contribution simultaneously (1) extends the study of social engagement from dyadic one-to-one interactions to ensemble activity, meaning the joint intention and coordinated activity of three or more people that cannot be reduced to dyadic interaction, and (2) creates computational media techniques for augmenting everyday social situations using responsive haptic and sonic and visual media that are modulated by measures of

© The Author(s), under exclusive license to Springer Nature Switzerland AG 2023
N. A. Streitz and S. Konomi (Eds.): HCII 2023, LNCS 14037, pp. 410–425, 2023.
https://doi.org/10.1007/978-3-031-34609-5_30

ensemble togetherness (e.g. group movement coordination). Our motivating questions include:

1. How people coordinate and interleave their interventions using tableware, gestures, sensory signals;
2. How social experience can be enhanced through improvisatory multi-sensory togetherness;
3. How the method of "interactive synchrony" can create affective social engagement through performing the coordinated actions;
4. How sensorimotor reciprocity influences the transition from individual to ensemble coordination;

Specifically, we design media techniques that exploit perception-guided [14] multi-modal motor action supporting the tacit [15, 27] aspects of embodied, ensemble coordination. This is informed by the extensive work done in sensorimotor [9, 10] and embodied, embedded, extended and enactive (4E) experience—[10, 26, 38].

1.2 Affective Engagement and Relational Interplay

As Massumi describes it: "affect is basically a way of coupling to other people through relational interaction [22]...". In our work we replace interaction with interplay, thus removing the unintended reductive analogy to a unidimensional arc joining two zero-dimensional nodes. By contrast with emotion, affect actually transcends the individual and rather emphasizes a mutual attunement and the "relation" between people and time, space, architecture, environments, objects, cultural circumstances and situations...etc. Furthermore, affect is conceived not simply as "cognitive, or mental phenomena" [8, 35], nor as a property of an isolated individual, nor as a unidimensional dyadic relation between specific individuals, but rather as a dynamically evolving, potential field in which and out of which social and emotional relations and relata emerge [33]. Our practical and empirical method is to exploit this understanding of affect as a field by creating fields of computational media (sound, haptic, visual) that evolve in concert with distributed activity in particular social and physical settings.

Affective engagement refers to processes of social interaction that dynamically shape the entanglement of moving (agent) and being-moved (patient), of affecting and being-affected. Relational interplay, thus, is a key characteristic of affective engagement, and we explore the concept of relational interplay from two aspects: 1) the relationship between the ambience and participants; 2) ensemble synchrony rather than a sum of individual actions or dyadic interactions. Throughout our paper, where we use the term relation or interaction, we wish to avoid the abstraction of a unidimensional join (arc) between two entities (nodes), but instead replace it by the richer and less geometrically reductive notion of ensemble.

1.3 Ensemble Synchrony

Ensemble coordination or ensemble synchrony is the study of how people "get together" and synchronize with one another in a social context [4, 29, 32]. As Bernieri [4] defined it, it is the degree to which the behavior in an interaction is nonrandom, patterned, or

synchronized in both time and form [4]; and has been categorized into three components: rhythm, simultaneous movement, and the smooth meshing of interaction [4, 29].
Inspired by Freed's taxonomy of synchrony cited in Sha & Johnson[1][32], we set out to
investigate what is meant by connectedness as a relational measurement in the domain
of social interaction. These examples furnish us with our conception of ensemble coordination which extends beyond coordination/ synchronization (timekeeping) to a world
in which relations are as real as relata. The inspired terms are, Syntonic (together in frequency), Synchronic (together in phase); Simultaneous (together in time), or Consequent
(following) [32]. We formed and analyzed the data based on our designed social behavior studies, one being a dialogue-based (rehearsal) event, and another a *para-theatrical
social meal* (more formal).

Table 1. The synchronized social behaviors that appear in studies 1 and 2, and corresponding
terminology.

Taxonomy	These collective acts occur in both dialogue-based(study1) and social meal(study2) experiments
Syntonic	Three participants nod their heads with a similar frequency; Eating pace (take food with a fork, then put food in the mouth);
Synchronic	Toasting; Drinking;
Simultaneous	When participants show changes in movement that start, stop, change speed, or change directions suddenly; participants raise up champagne glasses at the same time; two participants took food with a fork, at the same time, the third participant took a glass; drinking; 3) look down at the wearable device as a vibration produced from it;
Posture similarity	Participants sit upright; Dinking; Hands are worn device overlap on chair handle;
Consequent	Following doesn't require perfect matching or time similarity. Leader-followers, one raises a champagne glass, the rest of them follow;

2 Related Study

A literature review of how researchers, designers, and artists apply the idea to social
related projects to measure coordination (synchronization) including experiences in
which the participants were present and on site for example, [1–3, 5, 19, 21, 25, 34,
37] as well as those in which participants were remote, [7, 23, 24, 30]. They include the
synchronizing of participants' breathing to fuel the growth of a visual effect [34] and
the using of phones to measure the acceleration through strapping arm and leg together,
resulting in a musical experience [3], and participants coordinating their movement

---

[1] See semblance typology of entrainments based on etymologies by Adrian Freed, cited by
Sha and Johnson in "Rhythm and Textural Temporality", in Rhythm and Critique: Technics,
Modalities, Practices, eds. Paola Crespi and Sunil Manghani, 2014, p111.

through a mutual internal self-paced rhythm remotely, (the feedback being an ocean wave sound generated in real-time), leading to the sensation of being "in the same boat," as well as scenarios where two remote players synchronize their breathing rates and facial expressions to steer a virtual canoe, avoiding obstacles along the way: all these experimental results from artists and researchers suggest the importance that embodied coordination has in the research of social closeness [30]. Additionally, and interestingly, the number of experiments that highlight acoustic feedback as a relatively important element to motivate more interaction is significant; relatively fewer projects arc considering visual-tactile effect by comparison [6, 23]. Interpersonal coordination is considered one of the core aspects of contributing to effective and smooth social coordination [29]. Researchers interested in the matching-of-behavior aspect of interpersonal coordination are primarily concerned with the correspondence of interactive internal states and attitudes [28]. Interpersonal coordination suggests that the congruence of mental states between interactants is reflected in their physical behavior toward each other [8, 31]. Trust, collaboration, a willingness to help, as well as feelings of closeness, connectedness and similarity have all been reported after people perform synchronized actions.

In recent years technologies have been developed and used to measure social interactions in order to understand the impact of social dynamics and non-verbal behaviors which in turn establish and maintain rapport and facilitate the feeling of togetherness. One of the notable research approaches is: social bowl [20], a centerpiece on which participants can focus their attention, and this coordinated attention in turn makes participants form cooperative awareness, guided by acoustic feedback. A number of art-research experiments has shown the importance of information exchanges (e.g., intonation, speed, tempo and voice quality) within conversations. However, an additional important approach includes participatory embodied sense-making [3, 10, 35] and perceptual-guided experience, as we create technical-support experiments that involve the body-centered and multi-modal/sensory motivation. Telematic wearable device [36] by Thorn explores an embodied approach with a movement-responsive, collectively wearable instrument. The wearable devices greatly activate embodied sense-making in the telematic classroom learning environment, but it also brings more group awareness to collaborative improvisation via Zoom. Another example is by Fantauzza et al. [11] from Topological Media Lab. This work builds on research streams in augmented places and clothing from Synthesis and its predecessor and exploits fabric textiles as a continuous haptic medium and exploits social norms of greeting / engagement.

Connectivity Cafe by Barun, Lyu [2] event was a previous version— an augmented multimodal engagement. It centers around the idea of social meal setting as a way to explore relational measurement by amplifying coordinated movement (relational measure) and also exploring whether the haptic/visual stimuli are effective in social contexts. Tableware [21] by first author Lyu, which examines the impact of sound on participants' dynamic social interaction by augmenting human daily social behaviors and encouraging improvised social expression. Kryztzaniak et al. [18], displayed a good example of togetherness measures. KEY: (1) continuous measures of continuous collective movement mapping to continuous sound (musical) feedback; (2) ensemble (three or more people in concerted, concurrent activity (MORE THAN dyadic interaction); (3) sense-making that is MORE THAN verbal (dancers).

3 Research Methodology

Instead of leveraging a typical HCI research approach that relies primarily on interviewing and observing participants' activities in an abstract laboratory-based workshop using computational technology; we highlight thick[2]([33], *in situ* settings - that is, ordinary, open-ended social contexts rather than abstract academic theoretical research methodology). We study commonplace events, such as having an informal conversation while sharing refreshment, or having dinner together; or perhaps a studio in which people are making or prototyping something together. To this end, Sha has established the antecedents Topological Media Lab[3] and Synthesis Center[4] to study how ordinary gesture-mapping and the augmentation of environments through various socio/technological/artistic means may reveal or add a sense and meaning or an affective relation in the course of ad hoc ordinary or rehearsed activity. This *in situ* experiential approach aligns with the scientific methodology of observing how people and technical wearable devices, and ambient displays enact social-aesthetic experiences [33]. However, it differs from scientific practice in one key respect: the experimentalist by design is also an active participant in the creation of the event. We exploit responsive media techniques that are developed enough and robust enough for theatrical live performance but adapt them to modulate qualities of the environment. This also differs from theater in that there is no distinction between performer and actor, and there is no script for the event. It would be more appropriate to call it a para-theatrical event.

Gill [15] develops the idea of an engagement space, a body-centered approach to studying collaborative acts. Among other virtues it recognizes that participants' body movements affect and enact the way in which people are present to each other; they influence people's degree of closeness and their commitment to engage in action and they physically demonstrate this [15].

3.1 Study Design

The primary aim of this study was to investigate whether multimodal feedback, responding to relational interaction, such as interactional synchrony, has the potential to help initiate a relationship, convey acceptance, encourage self-awareness, and build a coordinated rapport. To explore these questions, we use a meal as the social context of the experimental event. Also, we provided a couple of ostensive motivations for the event: (1) to discuss how social engagement has become more challenging in the age of Covid and ubiquitous videoconferencing in place of in-person encounter; (2) to get together and make fresh acquaintances in an everyday event that was augmented by poetic media. (The

---

[2] "By 'thickness' I refer not only to perceptual thickness—density of video and sound textures—but also to the rich magma of social, imaginative, and erotic fields within which people play even in ordinary situations, situations in which we perform without first analyzing and cutting up our experiences into analytic layers....I say "thick" mindful of Clifford Geertz's sociological and anthropological approach to describing culture in all of its rich social patterns and dynamics without orthogonalizing it a priori into categories and schemata that we would bring to bear on that culture." ([33], p. 72).

[3] Topological Media Lab, http://topologicalmedialab.net/

[4] Synthesis Center, http://synthesis.ame.asu.edu/

additional media was calibrated to provide a balance between the ordinary setting and a responsive environment used in this para-theatrical way (See Synthesis techniques).

A key aspect of the design is to explore various measures of synchrony that are functions, NOT of individual action, but of dyadic relational (e.g., the degree of difference between the ego and one other person's activity) and ensemble activity (e.g. ego feels the sum of activity of all the other people involved). (Described below in Responding to the non-verbal Manifestations in distributed (field of) media of togetherness measures). Another key aspect of the design is the incorporation of feedback media that are NOT pictures with conventionally coded semantic content, but instead are fields of continuously varying intensity. We call these real-time mappings of continuous fields of movement into continuous fields of media dense mappings. By real-time, we mean the latency between a user's action and felt response under the threshold of human perception of immediacy for that sensory modality. (For a visual sense of coupling, the delay has to be under O (50 ms), but for haptic/mechanical coupling the threshold is much lower (1 ms). We emphasize dense media and dense mapping in order to explore motor entrainment and affective engagement, both of which work via dynamically varying sub-representational (sub-linguistic) fields of media.

We invited eight adults (four women and four men) who did not know each other before participating in the event. Four of them are just participants, the other four are both observers *and* participants. These two observer-participants were primed since they were both already familiar with the concept from prior participations. Their main role was to take notes from a given criterion measure. One trained observer had also taken part in the first experiment one week ago, which was a 50 min dialogue-based workshop where only drinks had been served. Both trained and untrained observers were asked to write down their observations about the awkwardness/togetherness of the scene and also their opinions on how/what they think would move the dialogue smoothly forward at different points. Their observations are primarily from three angles: 1) make note of the different types of synchronization they witness 2) mark the time and the 3) conditions (conditions could be scenario-based and/or Stimulus-based).

Participants were recruited via the general university mailing list. Each participant was compensated with a gift card for their time. Throughout the event, participants were given freedom to playfully improvise gestures, to collectively or individually react through responsive sound or movement to the visual and haptic patterns they experience. The observers' responsibilities are simply to see if the multimodal feedback induced more collective acts and to provide insight into how this tendency might result from asking, for example, whether individuals tend to attune their acts /tempo to others especially while the haptic/visual feedback was happening, and it further raises the question whether the responsive media can amplify nonverbal behaviors linked to rapport. This is an embodied participatory sense-making [35, 38] experiment through three designed perceptual-guided phases. At the start of the session, they were asked to spend several minutes simply introducing themselves to the other participants.

Para-theatrical Social Meal. Although the setup is staged for live self-consciously marked conversation in a socially heightened occasion, it is essential to understand that we define sensing policies and real-time mappings to multimodal responsive media as conditioning but not determining sense-perceptions, actions and thoughts – this is not a

Fig. 1. Observer is placing wearable devices and explaining how to initiate them.

scripted event that can be repeated more or less identically. The structured event passes through a sequence of "scenes" inviting and enabling progressively more improvised and expressive activity. Below we describe the scenes' characteristic features in terms of characteristic actions, props—objects as affordances for meaningful activity, visual feedback, audio feedback, and haptic feedback.

Before starting, the visual cues projected on the table cue the participants to put the champagne glass, the plate, and the spoon on their expected respective locations. The first phase is named SIP: Getting acquainted. A server pours drinks into each cup, which causes a bubbling-like acoustic feedback to be heard, and ripples then suddenly appear and display under the bottom of each champagne cup, their depth and intensity depending on the volume of the drink in the glass. Through this experiment, we are not only supposed to convey a sense of enchanted instruments to participants, but also to entice a sense of relationship between the participants, the unfamiliar atmosphere, the various objects on the table, and, ultimately, with the others via the table objects. Phase 2 is named TASTE. We projected a visual video to cue what they're going to eat at this session. Then we serve real food (as media) to them. We observe their eating pace and synchronized movement involving all verbal and non-verbal movement (such as head nods, direct eye contacts). In Phase 3, DIP, we took away the plate, the food, and the silverware, and only kept the glass there as another type of social scenario. We served a shared small plate with chopped bread and dipping and put it at the center of the table. This aims to focus their joint attention and actions on a common object. All media feedback produced is because of synchronized movement, which may or may not happen during the entire experiment. (Below is a sequence with corresponding medias).

3.2 Responding to the Non-verbal Manifestations in Distributed (Field of) Media of Togetherness Measures

Anticipation and Retrospection. On a note orthogonal to measuring ensemble coordination, we point out that an important, but incompletely exploited aspect of the event design was the projection of moving images and animated patterns that suggest past provenance: how the food came to be prepared before it arrived at the table, and future potential: suggesting an open range of what the participants may be able to do in the proximate future.

Table 2. The sequence of para-theatrical social meal

Time	Scene	Actions	Visual	Audio	Haptic
5:00 SIP		Participants help each other to set the table, placing utensils on the expected shadow projected on the table	light	None	None
5: 05		To wear the device and initiate it	Beam Angle	None	None
5:10	Mutual awareness is made by noticing how the different haptic patterns, ambient sounds, and visual ripples change over time	Shake glass collectively Toasting together Spin the glass collectively Move the glass to follow the ripples; and mimic each other's movement Head nods at the same time *Asynchronized actions:* Leader and followers Actively share opinions Verbal gestures Utterances showing agreement / listening such as "uh ah Direct eye contact	Each glass has vibrant, lively ripples at the bottom	The higher pitched sound is, the greater the wave size, and color changes	Haptic feedback brought on by motion (Moving at a faster speed gives you a stronger sense of vibration)

(*continued*)

Table 2. (*continued*)

Time	Scene	Actions	Visual	Audio	Haptic
5:20 TASTE	Video projected on each plate to cue what they were able to eat by displaying how the food came to be prepared before it arrived at the table	Watch a "past" video Serve Drinks Freely play the forks	The "past" dynamic video draw participants' attention	None	None
5: 23	Real food serving; the wearable tracked right-hand movement	Eat with forks Share tasty experiences Talk ideas about the "past" video; Toast togetherness Drink togetherness	Food	None	Haptic feedback brought on by motion)
5: 45 DIP	Take away forks, plate, then serve a "shared plate" with chopped bread and dipping sauce	Take the bread by hand; Dip; Eat; Drink; Toast; four people take bread simultaneously Back channel responses: Share Opinions Head nods; Utterances showing agreement / listening such as "uh ah" Direct eye gaze	Each glass has vibrant, lively ripples at the bottom	The higher pitched sound is, the greater the wave size, and color changes	Haptic feedback brought on by motion)

Mapping. Before the meal-as-event started, all participants were asked to wear a wrist-band (see Fig. 2) - a wearable device as an expressive instrument. The electronic kit was made up of a 3D printed container involving ESP32 Microcontroller, a 3.7v battery, DRV2605L Motor Driver, flat-type linear motor, and an adjustable wrist strap to hold it in place. A wireless 3-axis fusion sensor (accelerometer, gyroscope, and orientation) and haptic driver and actuators are connected to a Feather M0 microcontroller and embedded into the wristband. The microcontroller is programmed to simultaneously convert raw data into an Open Sound Control (OSC) data stream and send it via WIFI to a computer running Max/MSP, which maps sensor data to several digital synthesizers, and sends featured data to Arduino code to program vibration patterns.

Vibrotactile Perception. An individual's perceived haptic feedback is not generated by their own acts. Instead, it is caused by others' movements. Thus, this design allows participants to perceive the dynamic intensity as other people move and interact. Different speeds of motion can reflect different vibrotactile textures of duration or intensity. Importantly, the measure of relational impact is, the sum of actions from three individuals collectively generating the type of haptic feedback for a fourth person to experience. E.g., Hapticperson1 = ActionXperson2 + ActionXperson3 + ActionXperson 4. This idea supports the scenario of ActionX being defined as a function of IMU's accelerometer where orientation sensors measure an aggregate of shaking, tilting and translational movement simultaneously Specifically, we used an accelerometer xyz value and gyroscope roll, yaw and pitch values. This way, each person can feel the resultant of the n-1 fellow participants, and directly sense any correlation to her own activity and intention during the interaction /experience.

   We supplement the sensors tracking movement of the glasses and the participant's limbs with additional sensors (BNO055). The place-based sensor (FSR). It fixes on a tracking location when an object has been placed on that location or has changed state -indicated by changing its weight.

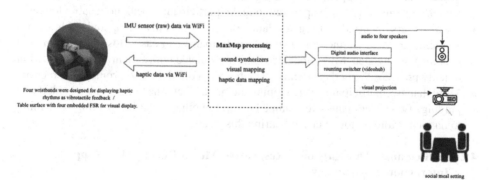

Fig. 2. The diagram of system architecture.

4 Findings

This section provides an analysis of the relationship between the multimodal responses, coordinated movement, and observers' judgements, and a themed analysis of the interview data.

4.1 The Relationship Between Observers' Judgements of Coordinated Behaviors and the Responsive Medias

This section mainly describes some differences and insight based on the two different experiments, one with no responsive media and fewer props and the other involving responsive ambient media, props, refreshments and drinks and wearable technology. Both observers are familiar with the concept, one is the author, the other is one of the previous participants from experiment study 1. They both took notes and conferred after the workshop. We compiled a summarized report from their common perspectives.

- The responsive media which amplified nonverbal manifestations of rapport did appear to influence the overall level of ensemble synchronization as reported by observers and participants. Although the vibrotactile/visual responses associated with coordinated movement aren't always obvious or fully perceived in participants' reports, observers did notice the engaged, close encounters (they were laughing together at 28:00; openly sharing opinions at 13:05, nodding their heads together more than three times, uttering things such as "uh ah" at 15:20, and sustaining direct eye contact) after Phase1, SIP, and during Phase 2, TASTE.
- Amplifying media through bodily- motion encourages improvised interactions in which they subconsciously jointly create relations with others. When they sensed a relation between a technological device and multimodal feedback, they were actively trying to explore more improvised expressions, such as quickly finishing a drink, just to see what would happen, then pouring drinks back and forth from cup to cup, to see what *that* would do; it also appeared to make participants speak noticeably louder.
- As observers reported, during the latter phase (especially compared with a non-ambient pervasive technological study), participants can easily lose connection and become less engaged. Multimodal feedback modulated with synchronized interaction quickly provides themed encounters which open a dialogue and promote interaction.
- More than two participants were tapping the plate where the "provenance" video was playing. Two participants even jumped to tap the other's plate, expecting something to happen. More dialogue ensued during this phase.

4.2 Participants' Thoughts on a Responsive Media Display that Supports Interactional Synchrony

A semi-structured interview was conducted with each participant at the end, which was around 25 min in duration in the same room. It was recorded with a camera placed in the back of the room. A qualitative inductive analysis was applied to the data with themes identified by the authors based on both a deep video watching and the research questions. Here we provide an overview of the interview data around three main themes:

relational movement sensing; degree of understanding the relationship between synchronized movement and responsive media; and techniques issues and thoughts on future development.

Four participants were asked to share their understanding of what caused variable vibration patterns and ripples (only four participants wore the devices; the other three did not). These four participants agree there are three different types of vibration patterns, but they fail to catch up with the idea of the impact of synchronized behaviors or the impact. Only one participant reported that he seems to have a sense of simultaneous movement, a sense of togetherness with the toasting action concurrently, driving a high intensity vibrotactile feedback. When I put forward the idea of the impact of synchronized movement, one of them replied to me with a sense of identity, as participant 3 described. Participant 4 indirectly suggested that his sense of connectedness is caused by synchronized vibrotactile feedback, which focused their joint attention and motivated more improvised actions, inducing collective motion at some point.

Participant 1: *"I could sense the changes in frequency, intensity, and also sound. I thought it was a connection with a type of movement when I first wore it, then I tried to find the connection by freely moving, raising up the glass, holding it still ...etc., ... It doesn't seem to follow my thoughts. Or I speak too much?"*.

Participant 2: *"It seems that drinking simultaneously drives one type of vibration but I'm not sure because the different vibration confuses me."*

Participant 3: *"Yes, There were several movements where I sensed a strong vibration: toasting, picking up bread..etc."*.

Participant 4 (referring to participant 1): *"I found more connected with you! You suddenly looked down at the device, same as me!"* (Laughing) Participant 1 replies: *"I thought, 'ok he's gonna confuse this, and me too.' That's why I was finishing the drinks, starting it and stopping...etc., cause I was wondering if it was because of continually moving."*

We then asked the participants to share their experience of how the responsive ripple/visual responses impacted their coordination, asking if they were trying to attune their acts with those of the others to jointly create ripples. The size of the ensemble ripples is different from the four individual ripples. Participant 5(untrained observer): *"I was playing with the champagne glass. I expected to see a reflective ripple tracking path, which is somehow entangled with other ripples."*

Participants 4: *"I was trying to find a connection between ripples and ... that... Since I noticed it changed color textures, grew and became entangled with other ripples, and dissipated ...etc., but I didn't find a synchronized connection with it; but I realized the ensemble ripples were produced by similar movement."*

Participant 3: *"I like the "past video", which really engages my motivation. if it appears in the center place instead of an individual plate, a shared video is displayed on the table."*

Some participants have an interest in communicational technology applied to telematic social meals as a much more meaningful research direction. As Participant 5 (untrained observer) said: *"As for the communication technology, I can't understand the value of the application to face-to-face interaction, since he/she sits next to me.*

Some participants suggested certain scenarios for people who are over speaking or under speaking during a social context. All responsive media depend on human social movement. Without human movement, the technology is unable to be applied. Thus, we shouldn't only consider synchronized scenarios with potential media, but should also consider how to motivate human action especially in an awkward/unfamiliar scene. As Participant 6 said: *"Until you moved the glass to the white board, when I noticed there is a sensor— maybe a table mat, or a cup mat, or a table napkin—all these allow for embedded sensors, but also allow us to put the silverware into expected locations."* Participant 3: *"Multimodal display is useful to "break the ice" at the beginning. The latter half section should keep the ripping-like sound (ambient sound) off, which somewhat distracts my attention."*

5   Conclusion

Authors Balaam et al. [2], Valdesolo et al. [37] have theorized about the relative importance of three nonverbal components of rapport, which are positivity, mutual attentiveness, and coordination. In our model, positivity is considered to be particularly important to feelings of rapport in initial encounters among strangers, and coordination becomes more important to the evaluation of rapport in later phases. It successfully motivated their interests in phase 1, Sip, where pouring drinks in a glass triggers ripples and sound. It hopefully motivating them. During phase2, Taste, although some relational responses to stimulate more synchronized movement are not as expected, participants still have a sense of trying to attune their movement. In phase3, Dip, participants 3 and 1 and 2, showed a consequent matching and posture similarity of behaviors in this section and participant 2 was following participants 1 and 3 with eye gaze. As some reported, it is sometimes hard for them to sense synchronized behavior by only receiving visual-haptic perception. One reason is that without synchronized movement, the design is not useful. People won't receive any perceptual feedback if there are no collective acts at the beginning of a social context. We designed different types of synchronization and four different corresponding types of vibration feedback, which only confused them. Thus, it required more accurate and logical designing work to make it more intuitive; We appreciated the idea, from participant 6, who suggested incorporating sensor/controllers into ordinary tableware such as placemats or cup mats and use them even for telematic interaction.

Another problem we experienced was that signal processing measure Approximate Entropy did not work as well as simpler measures of togetherness because the sensor data rate (approx 15–30 fps) was slow and noisy.

Our most important findings were:.

- Drawing people's attention to a common object (e.g. host pouring drink into a demonstration glass), or even allowing people to physically co-manipulate a common object (a pitcher) automatically constitutes joint attention and enables ensemble coordination and group intention. There is no need to measure individual activity or derive some measures based on dyadic differences (e.g. difference between tilts of orientations of two people's right hands), and then map that to a media synthesis parameter for feedback to individuals. In a pilot session, we found that individualized augmentations tended to atomize attention and encourage each participant to focus only on their own media-enriched gestures, ignoring everyone else, the opposite of what we intended.

- Ambient sound had the least effect, since it could easily be masked by noise, and people readily ignored it once visual and haptic responses appeared. Vibrotactile and visual feedback can produce more social reciprocity and inter-corporeal movement fluidity. Vibrotactile cues contribute more than visual and sound cues for engaging joint activity.
- Human hosts are part of the responsive environment and just as important as the algorithmic parts of the technical ensemble in eliciting responses to the situation and promoting social affective engagement. (As when observer intervened at 05:46 to ask people to introduce themselves, or 14:10 filled a glass with drink demonstrating how to play the instrumented tableware; or when one of trained observer at 12:40 engaged with one of the three un-instrumented "wall-flower" participants, handed her a drink and invited her to take his place at the table.)
- To enable ensemble interplay and social play it may suffice to pass the sensor stream to the media synthesis without classification into semantic categories.
- It is not necessary, and often less effective to classify sensor data under some human-interpretable labels like "happy" "sad" "tilting glasses in a toast". Instead, it is most effective to map real-time functions (filters) of the data streams into media synthesis. Even degrees of togetherness or synchrony need not be identified if the point is to enable and encourage ensemble coordination and interplay. We only need to classify the sensor streams when the experimentalist / researcher needs to tokenize it and classify it in the abstract away from the event.
- When we foreshadowed food with projected "provenance" videos and then introduced real drink and food (16:10 in the video), people markedly livened up and begin to engage and play with each other.
- Participants in a social-meal setting exhibit more polite and socially-distanced behavior because of physical constraints, in contrast to participants in an open-ended space, who tend to more active, even context-breaking behavior.

6 Future Work

Finer- and coarser-grained sensing of activity may open up richer sets of measures of synchrony. For example, our more powerful real-time signal processing tools like approximate entropy may become relevant if we use sensor data at much higher rates via for example tethered devices or acoustic sensing. At the larger scale, we propose to refine the social framing of the event by designing more compelling ostensive motivations and event structures. The retrospective and prospective hinting we described in 4.2.1 are examples of how the multimodally augmented tableware conditions how the participants account for past activity and how they intend to enact subsequent social action, in other words how they narrativize the event. Thus, we can further develop this paratheatrical approach.

Acknowledgments. The authors thank Synthesis for hosting this work: Connor Rawls for support on the installing of the experimental workshop, and Andrew Robinson for technical assistance.

References

1. Alavesa, P., Schmidt, J., Fedosov, A., Byrne, R., & Mueller, F. F. (2015). Air tandem: A collaborative bodily game exploring interpersonal synchronization. In Proceedings of the 2015 Annual Symposium on Computer-Human Interaction in Play, London, UK. https://doi.org/10.1145/2793107.2810311
2. Balaam, M., Fitzpatrick, G., Good, J., Harris, E.: Enhancing interactional synchrony with an ambient display. In: Proceedings of the SIGCHI Conference on Human Factors in Computing Systems, 867–876 (2011)https://doi.org/10.1145/1978942.1979070
3. Barua, S; Lyu,Y.: Connectivity Café: Prototyping the Dining Event" EASST-4S virPrague (2020) https://vimeo.com/synthesiscenter/connectivitycafe (password: Synthesis)
4. Benford, S., Höök, K., Marshall, J., Mueller, F., Svanes, D.: Body-Centric Computing (Dagstuhl Reports 17392). In Dagstuhl Reports Schloss Dagstuhl-Leibniz-Zentrum fuer Informatik 7(9). (2018)
5. Bernieri, F.J., Rosenthal, R.: Interpersonal coordination: Behavior matching and interactional synchrony. In: Feldman, R.S., Rimé, B. (eds.) Fundamentals of nonverbal behavior, pp. 401–432. Cambridge University Press; Editions de la Maison des Sciences de l'Homme (1991)
6. Borovoy, R., Martin, F., Resnick, M., Silverman, B. GroupWear: nametags that tell about relationships. In CHI 98 conference summary on Human factors in computing systems (pp. 329–330) (1998)
7. Burke, J., Prewett, M.S.: Comparing the effects of Visual-Auditory and visual-tactile feedback on user performance.
8. Hummels, C., Dijk, J.V.: Seven Principles to Design for Embodied Sensemaking. In: Proceedings of the 9th International Conference on Tangible, Embedded, and Embodied Interaction - TEI '14. ACM Press, Stanford, California, USA, 21–28.(2015) https://doi.org/10.1145/2677199.2680577
9. Colombetti, G.: The feeling body: Affective science meets the enactive mind. MIT press (2014)
10. Condon, W.S., Sander, L.W.: Neonate movement is synchronized with adult speech: Interactional participation and language acquisition. Science 183(4120), 99–101 (1974)
11. Degenaar, J., O'Regan, J.K.: Sensorimotor theory of consciousness. Scholarpedia 10(5), 4952 (2015)
12. Fantauzza, J., Berzowska, J., Dow, S., Iachello, G., Wei, S.X.: Greeting dynamics using expressive softwear. In Ubicomp 2003 Adjunct Proceedings.(2003)
13. Fitzpatrick, P., et al.: Social Motor Synchronization: Insights for Understanding Social Behavior in Autism. J. Autism Dev. Disord. 47(7), 2092–2107 (2017). https://doi.org/10.1007/s10803-017-3124-2
14. Gendlin, E.T.: Thinking Beyond Patterns.The Presence of Feeling in Thought. eds Ouden, B.D., Moen, M., New York: Peter Lang, 21–151 (1992)
15. Gibson, J.J.: The Ecological Approach to Visual Perception. Psychology Press, New York, N.Y. (2015)
16. Gill, Satinder. (2016). Tacit Engagement: beyond interaction. Springer International Pu
17. Isbister, K., Abe, K., Karlesky, M.: Interdependent Wearables (for Play): A Strong Concept for Design. In (2017)
18. Sha, X.W.: Writing in water: dense responsive media in place of relational interfaces. AI & Soc. , 1–9 (2021). https://doi.org/10.1007/s00146-021-01185-1
19. Krzyzaniak, M., Anirudh, R., Venkataraman, V., Turaga, P., Sha, X.W.: Towards realtime measurement of connectedness in human move- ment. In MOCO '15 In: Proceedings of the 2nd International Workshop on Movement and Computing, pp. 120–123 (2015)

20. Lakin, J.L., Chartrand, T.L.: Using nonconscious behavioral mimicry to create affiliation and rapport. Psychol. Sci. **14**(4), 334–339 (2003)
21. Leong, J., Wang, Y., Sayah, R., Pappa, S.R., Perteneder, F., Ishii, H.: SociaBowl: a Dynamic Table Centerpiece to Mediate Group Conversations. In Extended Abstracts of the 2019 CHI Conference on Human Factors in Computing Systems, pp. 1–6 (2019)
22. Lyu, Y., Mechtley, B., Hayes, L., Sha, X.W.: Tableware: Social Coordination Through Computationally Augmented Everyday Objects Using Auditory Feedback. In HCI International 2020–Late Breaking Papers: Digital Human Modeling and Ergonomics, Mobility and Intelligent Environments: 22nd HCI International Conference, HCII 2020, Copenhagen, Denmark, July 19–24, 2020, Proceedings 22, pp. 332–349 Springer International Publishing (2020). https://doi.org/10.1007/978-3-030-59987-4_24
23. Massumi, B.: Politics of Affect. Polity Press, Germany (2015)
24. Mullenbach, J., Shultz, C., Colgate, J.E., Piper, A. M.: Exploring affective communication through variable-friction surface haptics. In: Proceedings of the SIGCHI Conference on Human Factors in Computing Systems, pp. 3963–3972 (2014)
25. Nakanishi, H., Tanaka, K., Wada, Y.: Remote handshaking: touch enhances video-mediated social telepresence. In: Proceedings of the SIGCHI conference on human factors in computing systems, pp. 2143–2152 (2014)
26. O'Brien, S., Mueller, F.: Jogging the distance. In: Proceedings of the SIGCHI Conference on Human Factors in Computing Systems, San Jose, USA, pp. 523–526 (2007) https://doi.org/10.1145/1240624.1240708
27. O'Regan, J.K., Noë, A.: A sensorimotor account of vision and visual consciousness. In Behavioral and Brain Sciences 24 (5), pp. 883–917 (2001)
28. Polauyi, M.: The Tacit Dimension. Garden City, N.Y., Doubleday (1966)
29. Ramseyer, F., Tschacher, W.: Nonverbal synchrony in psychotherapy: coordinated body movement reflects relationship quality and outcome. J. Consult. Clin. Psychol. **79**(3), 284 (2011)
30. Rinott, M., Tractinsky, N.: Designing for interpersonal motor synchronization. Human–computer interactions, 1–48.(2021) https://doi.org/10.1080/07370024.2021.1912608
31. Robinson, R.B., Reid, E., Fey, J.C., Depping, A.E., Isbister, K., Mandryk, R.L.: April). Designing and Evaluating'in the Same Boat', a Game of Embodied Synchronization for Enhancing Social Play. In Proceedings of the 2020 CHI conference on human factors in computing systems, pp. 1–14 (2020)
32. Scheflen, A.E.: The significance of posture in communication systems. Psychiatry **27**, 316–331 (1964)
33. Sha., Johnson.: Rhythm and Textural Temporality. in Rhythm and Critique: Technics, Modalities, Practices, eds. Paola Crespi and Sunil Manghani, (2014)
34. Sha, X.W.: Poiesis and Enchantment in Topological Matter. MIT Press (2013)
35. Stepanova, E.R., Desnoyers-Stewart, J., Pasquier, P., & Riecke, B. E., JeL: Breathing together to connect with others and nature. DIS 2020 In: Proceedings of the 2020 ACM Designing Interactive Systems Conference, Eindhoven, Netherlands, pp. 641–654 (2020) https://doi.org/10.1145/3357236.3395532
36. Thompson, E.: Mind in life. Harvard University Press (2010)
37. Thorn, S.: Telematic Wearable Music: remote Ensembles and Inclusive Embodied Education. In Audio Mostly, pp. 188–195 (2021)
38. Valdesolo, P., Ouyang, J., Desteno, D., Ramseyer, F.: The rhythm of joint action: Synchrony promotes cooperative ability. **46**, 693–695 (2010). https://doi.org/10.1016/j.jesp.2010.03.004.
39. Varela, F. J., Thompson, E., & Rosch, E. The embodied mind: Cognitive science and human experience. MIT, 1991

Ambient Information Design for a Work Environment

Jan Torpus[1]([⊠]) [iD], Toni Kovacevic[2] [iD], and José Navarro[1] [iD]

[1] FHNW Academy of Art and Design, Freilager-Platz 1, 4002 Basel, Switzerland
{jan.torpus,jose.navarro}@fhnw.ch
[2] FHNW School of Applied Psychology, Riggenbachstrasse 16, 4600 Olten, Switzerland
toni.kovacevic@fhnw.ch

Abstract. To empirically investigate the impact of ambient information systems in a work environment, we developed a sensor-actuator system, designed a data mapping choreography, and set up a responsive office to be evaluated by experimental participants. 22 subjects were asked to work in the setting for 90 min and to give feedback by means of an online questionnaire and a follow-up interview. Their behavioral and arousal signals were measured and recorded as well as transmitted in real time to office equipment such as lamps, speakers, and a fan to control parameters such as brightness, hue, saturation, volume, speed, etc. to convey ambient information. The focus was on user experience, appropriation processes, well-being, productivity, and design principles for embedded ambient interfaces. The acquired sensor data was used to validate the data collected through the online questionnaire and the qualitatively analyzed interview. The study provides insights into the implications and benefits of embedded environmental information and data mapping design strategies. The paper concludes with experimental design considerations and an outlook on further research approaches.

Keywords: Design research · Work psychology · Sensor actuator system · Ambient information system · Responsive environment · Internet of things

1 Introduction

This article is based on the experiment *Periphery* of the running research project *Paradigms of Ubiquitous Computing* funded by the *Swiss National Science Foundation* (2019–2023). The project investigates user experience in technologically enhanced responsive environments, and the *Periphery* experiment focuses on their applicability in work situations. We studied responses of the participants of the experiment in an interactive work environment that reflects personal behavior and arousal in real time. We wanted to find out how the ambient display of personal data is perceived and processed, how it influences the work process, and when it is considered to be disruptive or helpful. We examined how participants interacted, adjusted their behavior, and which design approaches and conditions were rated most promising for improving well-being and productivity.

N. A. Streitz and S. Konomi (Eds.): HCII 2023, LNCS 14037, pp. 426–443, 2023.
https://doi.org/10.1007/978-3-031-34609-5_31

The appearance of the physical environment was restrained and consisted of an arrangement of classic office furniture that offered different work modes. The focus of the design was more on the Ambient Information System (AIS), the mapping design, on how the measured data is translated into spatially integrated physical representations. We developed a Sensor-Actuator System to measure participant behavior and arousal signals and transmit the data to technical devices integrated into the office space. The signals were recorded through positional tracking, detection of head and wrist movement, and heart rate. The data were collected, processed, and assigned in real time to various physical parameters of devices such as lamps (brightness, color, saturation, frequency), loudspeakers (type of sound, volume, audio effects), contact speakers (vibration intensity, interval) and a fan (strength, interval of airflow).

The immersive research facility was evaluated with 22 participants taking into account diversity of age and gender. They were introduced and calibrated following a standard protocol, asked to put on a sensoric wristband and cap for data collection, and to consent to the use of anonymized data collection. Thereafter, we asked them to enter the research facility and to follow their daily business on their personal laptop computers for one and a half hours. In addition to quantitative sensor data, we also collected qualitative data by asking participants to keep an online diary during the experiment and to complete a short interview afterwards. We heuristically analyzed the collected sensor data sets by contextualizing the data curves with the video tracking camera recordings. The interviews were analyzed using Qualitative Data Analysis (MaxQDA) and the patterns found were verified with the results of the online diary and the quantitative datasets.

The study presents findings on user experiences, appropriation processes, well-being, productivity, and data mapping strategies in a work environment with an integrated ambient information system. The paper concludes with experimental design considerations and an outlook on further research approaches.

2 Related Work and Theoretical Background

In this section, we introduce relevant theories and studies in the field of tension between **Science & Technology Studies** (Ubiquitous Computing, HCI), **Design Research** (User Experience, Ambient Information Systems), and **psychology** (Sense-Making, Work Psychology). Throughout this paper, we refer to these terms, concepts, and research approaches.

UbiComp calls for new interaction paradigms that structure the experiences with technologically augmented environments much "more like the way humans interact with the physical world" [1]. For this purpose, it is necessary for computing processes to become "invisible," which means that they successively merge with the environment. "Invisibility of computing, from the human perspective, can start when we are able to determine an individual's identity, location, affect, or activity through her mere presence and natural interactions within an environment" [1]. For our experiment, we made the necessary technology as invisible as possible by building it into normal office furniture and turning it into data displays in the appropriate situations.

Ambient Information Systems (AIS) are described as physical, tangible representations of information in the environment [19] and Ambient Displays as architectural spaces turned into interfaces between people and digital information [26]. An inspiration for our experiment was Wisneski et al. [26] presentation of the ambientROOM, a personal interface environment designed to provide information through room interfaces. In addition to those ambient media, such rooms use graspable objects, which pass on information to the users via technical systems such as sound [17], light, or via messages on the phone [11]. Many experiments are already further in the past. Today's technology makes it possible to include reliable measuring devices and systems for experiments at low cost. Some of these ambient media displays are attributable by natural forces such as wind, sunlight, or the sounds of a rainforest.

In 1995, Natalie Jeremijenko [7] developed "The Dangling String" at Xerox PARC, a physical plastic rope that represented tracked network traffic through whirling motion, which is considered to be the first ambient representation of a data flow. Information mediated in this way, is not asking for full user control but occasionally shifts from the periphery to attention [19, 24]. Furthermore, there are already research approaches that examine the individual environment, so-called **Ambient Assisted Living systems**. Such systems are mainly used and researched in the medical environment for the care of elderly people to increase autonomy and support activities of daily living with the help of smart products. Jara et. al. [6] evaluated NFC communication to perform continuous monitoring of electrocardiogram (ECG). However, it is not only in the context of people in need of support that such devices can be applied.

eHealth devices, wearables and health-apps on the phone can provide personalized biodata in real time and are already on the market and scientifically studied [18]. Such devices have been a big fitness trend in recent years [23] and have been widely used in all age groups [22, 23]. It is no wonder that scientists and professionals are very interested in the potential to provide users with wearable devices to promote physical activity [9, 13]. Rapid advances in technology have led to the automation of real-time activity tracking based on individual goals and public health recommendations, allowing users to self-monitor their activity over time [10, 20]. Further studies confirm that such information can be used for personal interventions to change behavior, increase well-being [8] and, with the right signal, also enhance productivity during work.

In comparison to these mobile devices, that are based on graphic data visualizations and ask for conscient information retrieval, we propose to weave the information into the environment with design qualities. The study provides insights into the users' assessment and allows the derivation of some design principles.

Sense-making refers to a social interpretative process that structures human experience. It is closely connected to the narrative structure of social understanding: past experiences become the basis on which new information, gathered in the present, is categorized and used for the anticipation of the future. According to McCarthy & Wright [14], the cyclical sense-making process consists of six individual phases, namely *anticipating, connecting, interpreting, reflecting, appropriating,* and *recounting.* In our study, the sense-making approach comes into play when we analyze participants' learning, habituation, and judgment processes.

Over the last 20 years, several **HCI** studies have investigated user behavior in artistic interactive installations [5, 16] and UbiComp research settings [3, 21]. Linda Candy and Sam Ferguson [2] give an overview of methods for evaluating interactive art experiences and propose frameworks to identify the corresponding contextual situations, that were useful for our mixed methods evaluation approach.

3   Research Interests

To investigate **user experience** and **cognitive interpretation** processes of test subjects in a work environment with an embedded AIS, we developed a responsive office space. One focus of the study was on the impact on everyday work, a second on the design approaches of data mapping.

We were interested in finding out to what extent the technologically enhanced environment had an influence on the participants' state of mind, whether they perceived it as pleasant or disturbing or even **attributed characteristics** to it. The ninety-minute experiment also allowed us to examine **learning processes** to determine what ambient information the participants recognized without introduction and whether they became accustomed to it.

In terms of work psychology, we wanted to gain insights into the **usability** or possible **implications**, the potential for improved **well-being** or increased **productivity** in everyday work. Because the experiment was conducted in a semi-public space, we were also able to investigate whether participants were uncomfortable that others in the room might perceive their personal state of mind as indicated by the AIS (**data privacy**).

To draw conclusions about the **design of embedded interfaces**, we examined how the different forms of data representation were perceived, comprehended and accepted. Since the responsive office space was staged according to a **data mapping** choreography with different design means, such as light, sound, vibration, and ventilation, we were able to compare concrete design approaches. We asked the participants how they interpreted the different situations, which causal connections they could recognize between their behavior and the space, what forms of interaction and types of media they preferred, and whether they also perceived temporal changes.

4   Research Setting

To study the impact of the AIS on the work environment, we set up a Responsive Work Environment (4.1), developed a Sensor-Actuator System (4.2) and designed an Ambient Information System (4.3).

4.1   Responsive Work Environment

In the *Critical Media Lab* of the *Academy of Art and Design FHNW*, we set up a research facility for the *Periphery* experiment. The name periphery comes from Marc Weiser's concept of **Calm Technologies** [24] which remain in the periphery of attention and come to the fore only when needed in the right context. The staged office space was designed low-key and composed of classic office furniture and some plants. It was shaped by partition walls and curtains that allowed the participants to isolate without losing audible connectivity with the rest of the media lab. The office space was divided into a work area and a rest area, offering different work modes. The work area consisted of a table, a table lamp, and an office chair and the rest area of a small sofa and a little sideboard. The technical output devices (actuators) of the AIS were subtly woven into the work environment. Colored light of three longitudinal RGBW LED lamps was reflected by the white partition walls and the table lamp was also accessible for data representation. Sound came from two speakers fixed to the partition walls but was also perceivable through vibration by contact speakers mounted underneath the table and the sofa. A ventilator placed on the floor was also technically controllable to emit information via airstream. To shift the perception of environmental information from the periphery to the center of participant attention, the activities of the technical devices faded in and out, **transforming from incidental office furniture to tools of data representation**.

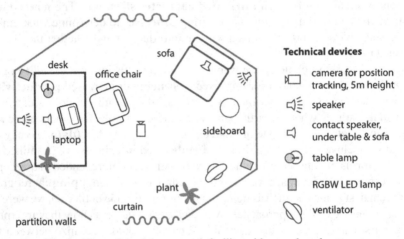

Fig. 1. Floor plan of the research facility with a work and rest area.

4.2 Sensor-Actuator System

To design an AIS for the representation of human behavior and arousal, we developed a Sensor-Actuator System. Using the software MaxMSP, we set up a technical environment that allowed the **acquired data streams to be mapped to physical parameters in real time** and the signals to be recorded for later analysis. Behavior and arousal were captured by **sensor measurements** of:

- position tracking (camera-based color tracking of red hat: x, y coordinates),
- head movement (3-axis accelerometer fixed to red hat: sum of delta values),
- wrist movement (3-axis accelerometer sensor in *E4 Empatica* wristband: sum of delta values),
- heart rate (pulse sensor in *E4 Empatica* wristband: beats per minute (bpm).

Some sensors were wired, others transmitted data via xBee or bluetooth wireless protocols. The measured data was processed, and different **actuator parameters** were controlled according to a rule-based system:

- light by different types of lamps (brightness, hue, saturation, interval),
- sound by speakers (source, volume, audio effects),
- vibration by contact speakers (source, intensity, interval),
- and airflow by a ventilator (strength, interval).

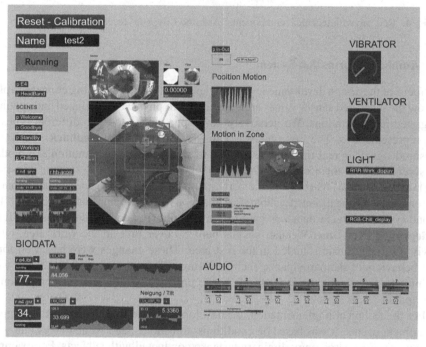

Fig. 2. Screenshot of MaxMSP control interface with camera tracking view, input signals and output controls.

Fig. 3. *Empatica E4* wrist sensor for measurement of heartbeat and acceleration.

Fig. 4. Red cap with technical components: Arduino Lilypads, accelerometer, and battery.

4.3 Ambient Information System

The focus of the design developments was on the AIS, the **data mapping choreography**, on how the measured sensor values are translated into physically mediated and spatially integrated representations. We iteratively developed and tested two different types of data representations. The first type was **causally recognizable feedback**, displaying measured signals in real-time. It was applied to signals of physical motion and biodata measurements and therefore an indicator of physical activity and somatic (possibly psychophysiological) reactions of the participants. We used it to generate participants' awareness of physical and psychological reactions to different work processes. The second type of ambient data was based on **atmospheric compositions that built up or degraded over time**: Weather sounds built up over time in the work area, while slowly decaying music sounded in the rest area. These changes were based on long-term behaviors of the participants, such as sitting still for a longer period. They were not intended to provide direct feedback, but to proactively influence or even patronize participants.

For the technical implementation, we developed a **rule-based system** that triggers the ambient events. It was based on conditions, thresholds, and value ranges that were defined or scaled based on preliminary tests we conducted with subjects. For example:

Fig. 5. Participant wearing the red cap in the work area with colored light displays.

If the participant is in the work area and the heart rate is above 85 bpm, start to increase the intensity of the contact speaker according to the bpm (85+).

Fig. 6. Participant wearing the red cap in the rest area with colored light display, fan and plant.

The AIS was divided into different spatial areas: entrance areas, work area, rest area, and intermediate area. The **entrance areas**, in combination with the intermediate area, were used to determine whether the participant was present in the room. Accordingly, a greeting tone was triggered when the participant arrived and a farewell tone when s/he left. Upon entering the **intermediate area**, the participant only triggered quiet city sounds slowly fading in. It was offered as a hidden area without AIS features.

In the **work area**, the heartbeat was presented in the form of colored light (two RGBW LED wall lamps behind the table), heartbeat sounds, and vibration of the table. The light pulsed in blue-green color at low heart rates and turned red as the frequency increased, with faster flashing intensified by an increase in color saturation. The heartbeats also became increasingly audible, and the vibrations of the table became increasingly noticeable as the frequency increased. Pretests with different subjects were necessary to adjust the parameter settings to a middle ground between detectability and tolerability. This approach represented the current pulse, thus acted as "positive feedback" and was not intended to have a calming effect on the person. Over a period of twenty minutes, a thunderstorm built up hardly noticeable: It started with soft wind sounds, increased with rain sounds, culminated with lightning and thunder, and remained at this intensity level until the person left the work area. The lightning was accentuated by the flickering of the table lamp and the gusts of wind were physically felt through the fan. If the participant left the work area early, the absence time (multiplied by a factor of 12) was subtracted from the presence time and the buildup of the thunderstorm was reset accordingly. This staging served as a patronizing request from the room for the participant to finally take a break. Regardless of heartbeat and dwell time, arm movements and head movements triggered different water sounds that integrated with the rainy weather sounds.

In the **rest area** meditative music was played, different pieces of music in varying order. Each piece of music was visually underlaid with the RGBW LED wall lamps by a different color spectrum (e.g., green-blue, orange-yellow). The heartbeat was represented by color changes between the poles of each color spectrum, with colors slowly fading at low bpm and flashing without progression at high pbm. We implemented this alternative pulse representation to compare with that in the work area. Like the building thunderstorm in the work area, a temporal change came into play: After ten minutes, the music became increasingly distorted by a sound effect and the fan began to blow if the participant did not move. This staging patronized the participants by asking them not to remain idle in the quiet zone. Participants were to realize that they could stop the increasing process by moving their head and arms. The contact speaker mounted under the sofa was activated by the movements to make causality more apparent.

5   Evaluation Design and Data Analysis

To evaluate the research setting, we developed a **mixed-methods approach** following a standardized evaluation process with invited participants. Quantitative sensor data (biofeedback and camera image) were collected, visualized, and used to validate qualitative data, which is the main source of knowledge production in this work. In order to capture subjective experiences, the participants were asked to complete an online questionnaire during the experiment followed by an interview. The interviews were analyzed using Qualitative Data Analysis (MaxQDA) and the patterns were reviewed with the online diary.

We invited **22 participants**, taking into account diversity as much as possible. The gender sampling was equal (11 females and 11 males) and the age groups – which were divided into blocks of 10 years each – were sufficiently covered by the selection of participants: 3 participants of the age group 15–24, 7x 25–34, 5x 35–44, 3x 45–54, and 4x 55–64. Diversity of professional background was neglected as we mainly tested with colleagues from our university who are mainly working in the fields of culture, design and humanities. All participants were asked to give consent to the use of **anonymized data collection** and camera recording. The anonymized data is stored on the database SWITCH, based on the Data Management Plan agreed on with the Swiss National Science Foundation.

All participants were introduced to the experiment according to a **standardized protocol**. To level personal somatic and psychophysiological variations, they were calibrated with a three-part exercise wearing the wristband. To determine the physical state of relaxation, they had to lie down to yoga music. To reach climax, they had to do some fitness exercises and to measure psychophysiological arousal, they had to watch a thrilling video sequence. The duration of the experiment was set at **one and a half hours** and was designed to allow habituation and learning processes to occur. To be able to investigate the shifts of attention for the AIS, we asked participants to perform **everyday tasks on their personal laptop**. They should be busy with something, but also perceive feedback, be disturbed, or pointed to something in different situations and phases of concentration. We also asked them to use both the work and rest area and allowed them to talk on the phone or leave the room for short breaks.

To be able to investigate which embedded interfaces and AIS designs were recognized by the participants themselves, Test Group A was not given any **explanations about the features and functionalities** of the AIS beforehand. Test Group B was told that the colored wall lights, speaker sounds, and vibrations of the table in the work area represented their heartbeat, and that the movement of their left arm and head produced water sounds. They were also made aware that the vibrator under the sofa and the fan in the rest area were responding to them. Nobody was made aware of staged temporal changes that depended on the length of stay or other behaviors. The division into these two groups made it possible to elicit the influence of prior knowledge on experimentation and sense making processes.

Since the experimental facility was spatially separated from the rest of the lab only by partition walls, the participants were not completely isolated from other people working in the lab. This allowed us to study whether they considered the display of their somatic signals in the semi-public space to be problematic in terms of **data privacy**.

The camera image used for position tracking was recorded as well as the heartbeat. The sensor values were visualized in a dashboard and synchronized with the video recordings. However, these **quantitative methods** were not statistically evaluated in this experiment, but only used heuristically to contextualize and verify the subjects' statements about their user experience.

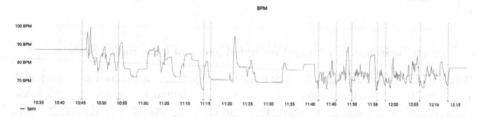

Fig. 7: Data set of a participant's heart rate during the 90-min experiment, including markers for diary entry assignment.

To obtain feedback during the experiment, participants were asked by an acoustic signal to make an entry in an **online diary**. This was triggered at 20-min intervals and for particular behaviors, for example, if the participant did not move for a long time or if his heart rate exceeded 90 bpm. It contained three standard questions about their mood, the environmental influence on their mood and their productivity, that could be rated with a 5-point Likert scale. The repeated questioning served to generate a quantitative picture of the course of the dimensions surveyed (pulse survey).

Finally, we conducted guideline-based **interviews** that allowed us to gain insight into the reality of the subjects. The questions covered topics such as the condition of the day, tasks performed, influence of the responsive environment on the state of mind, characterization of the environment, the perception of the AIS interaction modes, and the use of the setting as a workplace. The questionnaire as well as the interviews were conducted and recorded in German, transcribed and translated into English at the time of analysis. The translations were validated by means of the 4-eyes principle in order to avoid translation errors and later prepared for qualitative data analysis using the MaxQDA software. Category-based content coding [12] was initially deductive, with inductive categories adding to the system as the process progressed. The topics of the interview questions were expanded by the following constructs: affection, possible areas of application, privacy, description of room functions. To ensure that no narratives were lost, all interviews were re-coded in an iterative process. A compiling summary of each category was provided for the final rendition of the reactants' realities. For the comparison of Test Group A and B and demographic factors such as age and gender, the corresponding categories were also assigned and the content summarized per group. To find key statements, keywords such as space, character, productivity, well-being, system and design were searched across all transcripts.

6 Findings and Discussion

The study has produced interesting findings, which we would like to present and discuss in this section. According to the defined focus areas, we divide it into the general part Work Environment with an Embedded Ambient Information System (6.1) on the one hand, and the design-oriented part Embedded Ambient Interfaces & Data Mapping Design (6.2) on the other hand. Quotations from the transcripts are reproduced below in parentheses with the initials of the interviewee and the paragraph number, e.g. (TK; 13).

6.1 Work Environment with an Embedded Ambient Information System

We asked the participants how they felt before the experiment and what they anticipated. They mostly came without great expectations and wanted to use the time to work. Participants who were very focused on their work hardly perceived correlations between their actions and the environment and were even able to **mentally escape** the patronizing temporal developments (storm and distorted music). Even though most participants were doing administrative computer work, they were very immersed and an AIS for a work environment must therefore be designed with appropriate emphasis. Since we did not want to adjust the sometimes subtle design appearance of the AIS during the experiment - e.g., by using more intense light and louder sounds - we decided to inform a second Test Group B in advance about the features and functions of the AIS. In addition to insights into the recognition of the AIS, this should lead to findings about the **willingness to experiment**, use and acceptance during the work process. **Learning and habituation processes** therefore occurred at different times depending on the group: Participants in Test Group B already used interaction and reaction patterns in the first half of the experiment, whereas about half of Test Group A did not notice them until later in the second half. It would be good to repeat the experiment over a longer period of time to check the presence of the AIS across work processes with different concentration phases.

Due to the discrete integration of the sensor technology in the cap and wristband, the test subjects hardly perceived the wearables as measuring instruments. As intended, the majority of participants described the Office Space as clean and neutral. The AIS was mostly classified as an ambient tool at the beginning. However, as the experiment progressed and the stimuli intensified, participants increasingly **characterized the space** as uncomfortable, noisy or repulsive: *"The room, it wants to get rid of me now. It just wants to annoy me"* (BT; 21). Four participants had already worked with sound tools to increase their productivity and were therefore open to the basic strategies of the installation. The feedback was probably also unexpectedly positive for this reason and there was less spontaneous reflection on the artistic concepts than on possible applicability. Since we conducted the research with colleagues from our university, the familiar environment certainly also had an influence on **acceptance**: *"But it's also, it's also special as a laboratory arrangement somehow. But it also doesn't matter what I do in it. It's still somehow within the bounds of what's okay"* (LF; 83).

The approach of increasing one's own **productivity** with an AIS was mostly rated positively. *"B: I can imagine using acoustics or light or basically colors or space, climate, atmosphere, to create a room in which one can perhaps learn better or work more concentrated in any case"* (SH; 55–59). However, about three-quarters of the participants wished to be able to **customize** the AIS individually and situationally, for example, to be able to activate only the sound or to use an intelligent version: *"And I guess at a certain point, you can also maybe it could be more personalized, and like kind of, it could also be some sort of a, how do you say, some machine learning system that is a little bit more organic, the way in which those breaks are set, rather than being fixed on some certain parameters"* (JP: 44). The dubbing of one's own heartbeat was rated as a potentially valuable tool but was also criticized in terms of **sensitivities**: *"And I think, I don't know, I find the sound of heartbeat something fundamentally not calming, but something that tends to stress me out"* (NS; 11). One participant noted that certain tasks could also be completed more successfully under stress, depending on the situation, and that in terms of productivity it is not always just a matter of feeling particularly good.

The analysis of the online diary (pulse survey) also yielded interesting results concerning mood and productivity. Given the sample size, it is difficult to draw meaningful conclusions, but the tendencies observed could be compared to the qualitative data of the interviews. **Mood and environment mood** did not show much of a variance in the purely descriptive statistics. After the first measurement point, productivity showed slightly increased values at the second and third measurement points and decreased again at the fourth. In the interviews, participants also retrospectively reported higher productivity in the middle of the experiment than at the beginning and end. Many participants stated that they had to get used to the situation at the beginning, which would make the lower value in the figures plausible. The noisy environment, often described as annoying, could be understood as the reason for the lower productivity scores at the end of the experiment.

Table 1. Descriptive statistics of the total values of the online diary (pulse survey).

Online Diary (N = 21)	*M*	*SD*
Mood 1	3.9524	.97346
Mood 2	3.8095	.81358
Mood 3	3.8571	.85356
Mood 4	3.6667	.65828
Environment Mood 1	3.2381	.94365

(continued)

Table 1. (*continued*)

Online Diary (N = 21)	M	SD
Environment Mood 2	3.5238	1.07792
Environment Mood 3	3.3810	.92066
Environment Mood 4	3.4286	.74642
Productivity Level 1	3.4286	.74642
Productivity Level 2	3.4762	1.07792
Productivity Level 3	3.4762	.87287
Productivity Level 4	3.3810	.74001

Notes. Numbers 1–4 show the measuring time of the pulse survey

Since the experimental setting was shaped by partition walls and curtains only, the audio biofeedback of the participants was perceivable for the rest of the media lab's staff. When being asked, most participants were not worried about their data being audible for others. It was hardly considered critical, since they did not expect others to understand their **semi-publicly displayed biofeedback**. However, there were also situations in which the acoustic feedback was experienced as unpleasant in a social context: One participant recognized the increase in her biofeedback when preparing for an uneasy phone call. She was uncomfortable that other people in the media lab and, depending on the situation, even the person on the other end of the phone line could detect her arousal.

6.2 Embedded Ambient Interfaces & Data Mapping Design

In this section, we would like to focus on the design-based aspects, highlighting the effect of the different AIS media, their parameter settings, and distinguishing findings about subjects' perception and interpretation of spatio-temporal and causal interactions.

Furnishing as Information Mediator
As **physical components** for the AIS, we chose a table lamp, three wall lamps, two speakers, two contact speakers, and a fan. The furniture and devices were used as channels to display information about the position, movement, and personal heartbeat of the participants. They could also be **combined and compared.** The heartbeat, for example, was represented in the work area by colored lamps, speakers and a fan and allowed to compare the user experience of the different channels. Nevertheless, the patricians of Test Group A hardly perceived this multimedia biofeedback or did not identify with it. Once recognized, the acoustic data representation was perceived as most pleasant. The vibration transmitted by the contact speaker under the tabletop was also rated positively, as it was applied very discreetly. In comparison, the data visualization via colored light with the wall lamps was perceived as rather disturbing and was not judged to be purposeful. Four participants, however, reported that they were able to mentally block out the lights very well even though they were located behind their computer screen.

The physical AIS components were also **used scenically**. The flickering of the table lamp during the thunderclap and the gusts of the fan during violent wind noises supported the immersive experience of the acoustically represented thunderstorm. These interventions were designed to explore strategies to influence participant behavior and were not primarily intended to improve well-being. The choreographic interplay was understood as intended by most participants and contributed to the intensification of the narrative. As mentioned above, the reactions varied: some were so engrossed in their work that they could even block out a thunderstorm, for others it felt very cozy, and still others were annoyed and looked for a non-responsive place.

In terms of **interactions with the devices,** women were more eager to experiment than men. Even plants, which were understood as possible electronically enhanced interfaces, were investigated:

AM: *"Exactly. So, I also moved my hand in the middle of the room or looked under the table or touched the plant."*

I: *"Did you also play?"*.

AM: *"Yes, but I don't think anything changed there. There's nothing connected to the plant like that. But yes, I wanted to see if maybe something is hidden somewhere."* (AM; 37–39).

Although detailed group comparisons were made among age groups, we could not identify any differences of behavior and attitudes based on age groups.

Mapping Choreography: Parametric Information Design
The development of the research setting required many design decisions and iterative optimization processes. After choosing the appropriate tools for conveying information, we had to design their parameter settings. Pretests with different people were necessary to adjust them to a **middle ground between detectability and tolerability.** The vibrator under the chair, for example, was perceived as unbearable at high intensity, but as pleasant and supportive after the right dosage. In the end it was set so subtly that the participants were sometimes not sure whether the vibration was transmitted via the furniture or the air.

The design potential when dealing with parameter settings can also be illustrated by the data visualization of the heartbeat using colored light. We implemented two different pulse displays in the rest area and the work area to compare them. In the work area, faster blinking for higher pulse was accentuated by increasing the color saturation (white-color), in the rest area by increasing the length of the fade between two colors. Such design nuances were never consciously perceived during the timespan of the experiment and the computer work. However, these types of design considerations are valuable tools to **improve the aesthetics** of the user experience and to scale the presence of data distribution.

The **information mediator fan** would probably have been better camouflaged in a hotter environment but would also have made itself noticeable there by independently changing the speed. The intense wind gusts emitted during the storm were perceived as very disturbing and contributed significantly to the participants leaving the work area. The gradual increase in wind flow after a period of physical inactivity in the resting area was also found to be disturbing, and no one could see the causal relationship between their head and arm movements and fan activity.

Interpretation of Spatio-Temporal Assignments

Based on personal preferences and according to the work to be done, the participants decided to work at the desk or on the sofa with background music or to alternate. The medial change of mood in the two areas was recognized by all test persons. Some participants became aware of the intentions and patronizing attitudes of the **room's dramaturgy**: *"The room wanted me to go!"* (JB:23). In one case, the scenic change was judged as too fast and causal, indicating that the parameters "responsivity timing" and "intensity of responsivity" are important design issues. *"When you're just looking out for a moment or just going here or there for a moment, the switch, so it's great that that works, but then it's a bit unnecessary that it switches immediately like that and then a second later it switches back again."* (FG; 32–35). In general, the **atmospheric sounds** of nature in the workspace were found to be more pleasant and conducive to productivity than music. We received feedback that the *"rain sounds from outside"* made people feel like they were in a protected, cozy place, and thus immersed in the staged narrative. *"But when the thunderstorm was, I kind of already imagined myself in a mountain hut like that."* (JS; 15).

The responsive staging of the areas sometimes led to discomfort and frequent changes of location: Three participants discovered the intermediate zone with the quiet city background sounds as a place of rest for themselves. They avoided the patronizing character of the installation and customized their situation: *"Yes, or even when I have to think big thoughts that I can have very quiet, for example. Then I go back to the table, but that was too exhausting for me. Then I looked for something quiet in the middle of the room"* (LF; 27).

Interpretation of Causal Relationships

The experiment began with us telling participants that the room responded to them, but not how (Test Group A). We wanted to find out what causalities they could identify in their interactions. The implemented biofeedback for the heartbeat was partially suspected, but not confidently related to itself. *"I just always found this heartbeat a bit strange, because there I didn't know if it was me or is it someone else."* (NB; 5) In Test Group B, some attention was paid to it and the tool was considered quite interesting, as an occasional, somewhat unconscious form of control of one's own psychophysiological state.

In the work area real-time sound effects of head and arm movement were designed to indicate restlessness. They were meant to make people aware of (strange or unnecessary) movements they perform during the work process. No participant detected this form of causal feedback, unless they were told (Group B). Even in Group B, they did **barely consciously interact** with it. We assume that it was a design issue, that the triggered water noises were too neatly integrated into the weather background sounds. Design adjustments would be interesting to be studied in a follow-up experiment. One participant from Group B however stated that she had used the arm and head movement to express outrage. Instead of screaming she used the tool to unload frustration during the work process. This kind of participant feedback is very valuable to create new design approaches.

In the rest area we implemented that the staging of the increasing music distortion can be stopped by moving arm and head. It was a form of **paternalism** that asked participants to move more (not fall asleep). Since we did not explicitly mention this precise form of interaction even in Group B, no one recognized it. Such forms of interaction would have to be observed and functionally adapted over a longer period.

7 Conclusions and Outlook

With this study, we present results on user experiences, appropriation processes, well-being, productivity, and data mapping strategies in a work environment with an ambient information system embedded in the furnishing. The paper concludes with suggestions for **adapting the experimental setup** and an **outlook** on further research approaches.

The quantitative methods were not evaluated statistically in this experiment but were used to verify the participants' statements. We made this decision because we had collected little information about the **participants' activities** and could not assign their influence on the biodata. In a follow-up experiment, participants could play a game in which different situations are trackable and measurements and behaviors can be contextually assigned. Also, the experiment length of 90 min turned out to be rather short for appropriation processes. We suggest developing a mobile sensor-actuator setting that could simply be set up at test subjects' home offices and studied over a longer period of time. Although the **sampling of participants** was sufficiently heterogeneous in gender and age, we mainly recruited colleagues for the survey. In order to obtain more valid results, participants from outside the university with different backgrounds should be recruited. To study to what extent **data privacy** would become more critical if all persons in an open-plan office could understand each other's biofeedback, we suggest equipping several workstations with the same AIS and have several participants work in them at the same time.

In order to derive further **design principles** for the AIS, the different media and their parametric settings would have to be examined individually in a next step and a distinction would have to be made between direct biofeedback and influencing strategies. Although acoustics were judged best as spatially distributed feedback, vibration in everyday objects also seems promising. However, with the right parametric settings and situational integrations of information into furnishing, we continue to see opportunities to work with lamps and fans. The contextualized recognition of ambient information, on the one hand, and the disruptive influence during the work process, on the other, requires fine-tuned design and handling adjusted over time. In order to identify the critical features and contexts and to identify standard settings for different work situations, a Graphical User Interface for customization could be provided to the participants in a follow-up project.

The *Periphery* experiment was created as part of the *Paradigms of UbiComp* artistic research project. It is partly playful and challenging, but partly has a claim to concrete applicability. Because the AIS under study encompasses multiple approaches in parallel and the results are based on feedback from only 22 participants, follow-up projects are needed to produce quantifiable results. Nonetheless, the results open up an exciting field of perspectives for designers and work psychologists, and detailed insights into design processes and strategies for embedding an AIS into furnishing.

Acknowledgements. We would like to thank the rest of the research team: Cedric Spindler (data collection), Sophie Kellner (physical setup) and Jonas Kellermeyer (media theory). A big thank you also goes to our colleagues who spent time at our research facility.

References

1. Abowd, G., Mynatt, E.D.: Designing for the human experience in smart environments. In: Cook, D., Das, S. (eds.) Technology, Protocols, and Applications, pp. 153–174. John Wiley & Sons Inc., Hoboken, NJ (2005)
2. Candy, L., Ferguson, S.: Interactive Experience in the Digital Age: Evaluating New Art Practice. Springer, Cham (2014). https://doi.org/10.1007/978-3-319-04510-8
3. Heibach, C., Torpus, J., Simon, A.: Immersion und Irritation: Emotionale und kognitive Aneignungsprozesse in der physischen Technosphäre. In: Breyer, T., Kasprowicz, D. (eds.) Immersion: Grenzen und Metaphorik des digitalen Subjekt, Navigationen – Zeitschrift für Medien- und Kulturwissenschaften, Jg. 19, Heft 1. University, Siegen (2019)
4. Arrue, M., Vigo, M., Abascal, J.: Including heterogeneous web accessibility guidelines in the development process. In: Gulliksen, J., Harning, M.B., Palanque, P., van der Veer, G.C., Wesson, J. (eds.) DSV-IS/EHCI/HCSE -2007. LNCS, vol. 4940, pp. 620–637. Springer, Heidelberg (2008). https://doi.org/10.1007/978-3-540-92698-6_37
5. Höök, K., Sengers, P., Andersson, G.: Sense and sensibility: evaluation and interactive art. In: Proceedings of the SIGCHI Conference on Human Factors in Computing Systems, pp. 241–248. ACM, New York (2003)
6. Jara, A.J., Zamora, M.A., Skarmeta, A.F.: An Internet of Things—based personal device for diabetes therapy management in ambient assisted living (AAL). Personal Ubiquitous Comput. **15**(4), 431–440 (2011). https://doi.org/10.1007/s00779-010-0353-1
7. Jeremijenko, N.: https://news.ycombinator.com/item?id=28351064. Accessed 05 Feb 2023
8. Lukan, J., Bolliger, L., Pauwels, N.S., Lustrek, M., De Bacquer, D., Clays, E.: Work environment risk factors causing day-to-day stress in occupational settings: a systematic review. BMC Public Health **22**, 240 (2022)
9. Lupton, D.: Health promotion in the digital era: a critical commentary. Health Promot Int. **30**(1), 174–83 (2015) https://doi.org/10.1093/heapro/dau091
10. Maher, C., Ryan, J., Ambrosi, C., Edney, S.: Users' experiences of wearable activity trackers: a cross-sectional study. BMC Public Health **17**(1), 880 (2017)
11. Matthews, T., Rattenbury, T., Carter, S., Dey, A., Mankoff, J.: A Peripheral Display Toolkit. Tech Report IRB TR-03–018. Intel Research, Berkeley (2002)
12. Mayring, P.: Qualitative Inhaltsanalyse. In: Mey, G., Mruck, K. (eds.) Handbuch Qualitative Forschung in der Psychologie. VS Verlag für Sozialwissenschaften, Wiesbaden (2010). https://doi.org/10.1007/978-3-531-92052-8_42
13. McCallum, C., Rooksby, J., Gray, C.M.: Evaluating the impact of physical activity apps and wearables: interdisciplinary review. JMIR, mHealth uHealth **6**(3) (2018). https://doi.org/10.2196/mhealth.9054
14. McCarthy, J., Wright, P.: Technology as Experience. The MIT Press, Cambridge (2004)
15. Moere, A.V.: Towards designing persuasive ambient visualization. In: Pervasive 2007 Workshop: W9 - Ambient Information Systems, Toronto (2007)
16. Morreale, F., De Angeli, A.: Evaluating visitor experiences with interactive art. In: Proceedings of the 11th Biannual Conference on Italian SIGCHI, chapter, pp. 50–57. ACM, New York (2015)
17. Mynatt, E.D., Back, M., Want, R., Ellis, J.B.: Designing audio aura. In: Proceedings of CHI 1998, pp. 566–573. ACM, New York (1998)

18. Papaa, A., Mital, M., Pisano, P., Del Giudice, M.: E-health and wellbeing monitoring using smart healthcare devices: an empirical investigation. Technol. Forecast. Soc. Change **153**, 119226 (2020). https://doi.org/10.1016/j.techfore.2018.02.018

19. Pousman, Z., Stasko, J.: A taxonomy of ambient information systems: four patterns of design. In: Proceedings of the Working Conference on Advanced Visual Interfaces, pp. 67–74. ACM, New York (2006). https://doi.org/10.1145/1133265.1133277

20. Ridgers, N.D., McNarry, M.A., Mackintosh, K.A.: Feasibility and effectiveness of using wearable activity trackers in youth: a systematic review. JMIR mHealth uHealth **4**(4), e129 (2016). https://doi.org/10.2196/mhealth.6540

21. Simon, A., Torpus, J., Heibach, C., Navarro, J.: Affect and atmosphere in controlled responsive environments. In: Streitz, N., Markopoulos, P. (eds.) DAPI 2016. LNCS, vol. 9749, pp. 350–361. Springer, Cham (2016). https://doi.org/10.1007/978-3-319-39862-4_32

22. Statistica: Wearable technology - Statistics & Facts (2017). https://www.statista.com/topics/1556/wearable-technology/. Accessed 08 Feb 2018

23. Thompson, W.R.: Worldwide survey of fitness trends for 2020. ACSMs Health Fit J. **23**(6), 10–18 (2019). https://doi.org/10.1249/FIT.0000000000000526

24. Weiser, M., Brown, J.S.: Designing calm technology. PowerGrid J. **1**, 1 (1996)

25. Weiser, M.: The Computer for the 21st Century. In: Scientific American special issue on Communications, Computers, and Networks, vol. 265, no. 3, pp. 94–104 (1991)

26. Wisneski, C., et al.: Ambient displays: turning architectural space into an interface between people and digital information. In: Streitz, N.A., Konomi, S., Burkhardt, H.-J. (eds.) CoBuild 1998. LNCS, vol. 1370, pp. 22–32. Springer, Heidelberg (1998). https://doi.org/10.1007/3-540-69706-3_4

Card Type Device to Support Acquirement of Card Techniques

Koji Tsukada[✉], Kenki Tsuda, and Maho Oki

Future University Hakodate, Hokkaido, Japan
{tsuka,okimaho}@acm.org

Abstract. Recently, the development of methods that use sensors and computer technology to evaluate how people learn and use skills in sports or performance art has become a subject of active research; and various tools, such as balls used in sports games, have been equipped with sensors to detect motion. However, the acquisition of card techniques, such as shuffling and cutting, has rarely been studied. Therefore, we propose a system based on a device with a form factor resembling a common playing card to support computational measurement and analysis of users' skills acquisition related to card manipulation. We designed thin sensors with patterns of conductive ink to maintain the thickness and shape of common playing cards. We also implemented the proposed system as a prototype card device to measure users' manipulations of a deck of cards. Further, we measured and compared three common card techniques using the prototype system. The results of our analysis demonstrate the possibility of using the proposed system to learn card techniques.

Keywords: Cards · Acquirement of Techniques · Conductive ink

1 Introduction

Many studies have been conducted on methods to collect data on human activities in various fields such as performance art and sports [1,5,8]. However, relatively few studies have considered collecting such data on card manipulation techniques (hereafter referred to as card techniques) in card games and magic, although classic movements such as shuffling or cutting a deck of playing cards are well-known in popular culture. Hence, existing methods of learning card techniques are quite traditional, and mainly include activities such as watching skilled people perform the technique and practicing repeatedly with reference to literature. In addition, because the population of skilled people who are familiar with card techniques is smaller than that of common popular sports, learning techniques directly from people who have the skill can be difficult. Considering this background, we propose an electronic device with a form factor resembling a common playing card designed to collect analyze, and quantitatively evaluate a users' application of card techniques.

N. A. Streitz and S. Konomi (Eds.): HCII 2023, LNCS 14037, pp. 444–455, 2023.
https://doi.org/10.1007/978-3-031-34609-5_32

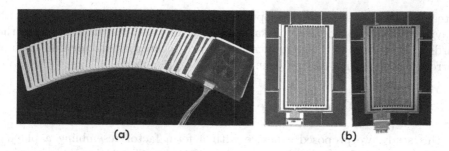

Fig. 1. Prototype of a card device. (a) Usage example. (b) Designed patterns (left) and implemented flexible printed circuit board (right).

2   Related Work

2.1   Magic Augmentation with Digital Technology

In this study, we focus on card techniques commonly used to perform magic with playing cards. In the field of magic, various attempts have been made to adopt computer technology to create novel tricks and performances. Many magicians, including Marco Tempest [10], used iPads, AR, and drones to create magic tricks. In addition, new magic shows that integrate mixed reality and augmented reality [2] as well as the use of humanoid robots [7,9] have been recently proposed. Although their project is still in a technical validation stage, Koretake et al. [4] proposed a robot magician designed to perform card magic with four fingers, with an ability to manipulate cards like a human. In contrast to these approaches that incorporate digital technology into specific tricks and shows, in the present work, we developed a system designed to support the acquisition of card manipulation skills used in card games and magic.

2.2   Skill Acquisition Support System

Various systems have been proposed to support effective practices to help users learn to do activities, such as playing sports and musical instruments, or dancing, by detecting user actions and providing feedback [1,5,8]. Such systems use sensors and motion capture to collect information on movements and timings from video, sound, vibration data, numerical values, etc. The SwingTracer [6] device, which is designed to be attached to a baseball bat, and the Adidas Smart Ball [3], which incorporates a sensor in a soccer ball, have been marketed as products for sports analysis. In contrast, card techniques in magic are mostly practiced and learned using classical methods, such as watching skilled players or repeating exercises by referring to literature. Many instructional books have been published on magic techniques, and card techniques are also widely described on the web with photos, text, and videos on wiki sites and YouTube. However, in terms of actual practice, the only approach is to repeat the exercise independently, but it is challenging to recognize the reasons for good or poor performances without a teacher. In this study, we developed a card-shaped sensing device for use with playing cards and a software package for recording and viewing data from the cards to contribute to the quantification of card techniques and identification of correct actions, which has not been explored in prior works.

3   Design of Card Device

In this study, we proposed a device with a form factor resembling a playing card to support the acquisition of card techniques. The device is designed to collect data on a user's performance of card techniques using integrated sensors to enable a quantitative analysis and comparison. In the design of the sensor in the proposed device, we aimed to measure physical changes related to the execution of card techniques while retaining the shape of a standard playing card as much as possible.

Regarding the former, one of the authors is an experienced magician with some proficiency with card techniques, and we determined the properties to be measured by the system based on that experience. As a result, we designed the device to measure where the user's fingers are touching and the extent to which the card is bent while in use, which are important for basic card techniques, such as shuffling and cutting a deck. Regarding the latter, we designed capacitive touch and bending sensors using a thin flexible substrate with a special pattern. The device is designed to be placed at the top or bottom of a deck of cards. We also attached the device to a real playing card, which was thinned down with sandpaper to retain the approximate shape and thickness of a standard playing card.

4   Implementation

In this section, we describe the implementation of the prototype device and the feedback application.

4.1   Card Device

Figure 1 shows the prototype device. The card part was implemented as a P-Flex-brand flexible circuit board for conductive ink[1] to closely resemble the shape and feel of a standard playing card. The card was $73\,\mu m$ thick, and its face was the same size as that of a common playing card ($63 \times 89\,mm$).

The capacitive touch and bending sensors were designed using the pattern printed on the flexible circuit board (Fig. 1-b). The eight polygon areas arranged along the edge of the card comprised capacitive touch sensors, and a single line pattern across the center comprised a bend sensor. Each pattern was connected to the control circuit and a microcontroller (an Arduino Pro Mini) via a cable. For the design of the bend sensor, we referred to Vadgama's method [11].

---

[1] https://info.elephantech.co.jp/en/p-flex-fpc.

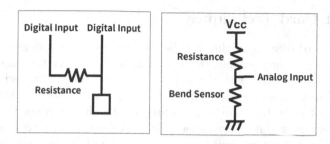

Fig. 2. Control circuit for touch sensor (left) and bending sensor(right).

The capacitance touch sensor was implemented using the CapacitiveSensor library[2], and the delay time between the digital input and output was measured as shown in Fig. 2. When the user touches the capacitive touch sensor with their finger, the delay time increases, and the length of the delay time is used to determine whether a finger is touching. When the microcontroller detects a change in the sensor values, it normalizes the data and sends it to the computer via serial communication.

4.2 Feedback Application

The feedback application records sensor data along with a video from a camera connected to a computer. After recording the execution of a technique, the user can view their video and a graph of the sensor data. Figure 3 shows the overall system configuration and a screen of the feedback application displaying sensor data.

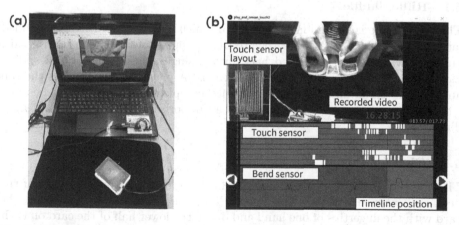

Fig. 3. (a) System configuration used to record data when users perform card techniques. (b) Screenshot of the feedback application.

---

[2] https://www.arduino.cc/reference/en/libraries/capacitivesensor/.

5   Target Card Techniques

The types of card techniques that can be measured with this device are limited owing to the need for a connector and cable and the fact that not all cards in a deck can be replaced with the device. However, some card techniques can be measured using the proposed approach. Among these, we selected the most commonly used basic techniques, including a riffle shuffle, a spring technique, and a Charlier cut, and measured users attempting to perform these techniques. The procedure for each technique is shown in Fig. 4 and described in detail below.

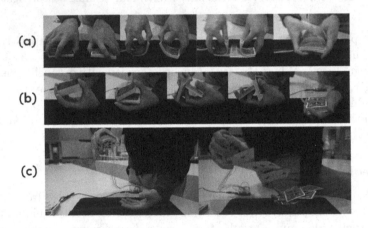

Fig. 4. (a) Riffle shuffle, (b) Charlier cut, and (c) card spring.

5.1   Riffle Shuffle

The riffle shuffle is a shuffling technique in which a deck of cards is first divided into two piles. Both stacks of cards are then popped together with both hands, and the two piles are combined back into a single stack with a quick sliding motion that rearranges the order of the cards. A player always touches the top and bottom cards until all movements are completed. The degree of bending when flipping the cards is also considered an important factor in successful shuffling.

5.2   Charlier Cut

The Charlier cut is a cut technique in which the top and bottom halves of the deck are swapped using a single hand. First, the player holds the deck of the card with the fingertips of one hand and drops the lower half of the card on their palm. Subsequently, the dropped lower half of the deck is pressed with the index finger, the upper half is replaced, and the card is merged into a single stack. In this technique, the fingers always touch the top and bottom cards of the deck, and it is important to know where to place ones' fingers to support the cards when replacing them.

5.3 Spring

The spring is a technique in which the player holds a deck of cards in one hand and bends the cards so that they fly one by one into the other hand. The bending of the cards is considered critical for the success of this technique.

6 Evaluation

We performed two evaluations, first considering the basic performance of the system and then the measurement of card techniques performed by users.

6.1 Evaluation of Basic Performance

The detection accuracy of each sensor was evaluated using the card device.

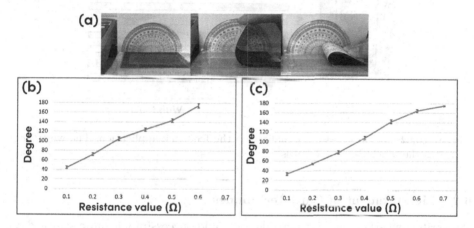

Fig. 5. (a) Experimental method for evaluating bending sensors (from left to right: 0°, 104°, 176°). (b) Results of bending the sensor in the front direction. (c) Results of bending the sensor in the back direction.

Bending Sensor. We verified how many steps could be measured and the amount of change in the angle per step. The experiment was conducted as follows. The card-type device was gradually bent in front of a protractor (Fig. 5(a)) and the angles at which the resistance measured by the tester changed by 0.1Ω was recorded. This was performed five times each for the front (side with the connector) and back. Figure 5(b) shows the measured values when the device was bent in the front direction and Fig. 5(c) shows the measured values when it was bent in the back direction. These are the average values of the angles for a 0.1Ω change. Bending angles of approximately 44–174° in six steps on the front side and approximately 33–175° in seven steps on the back side could be measured. This difference in the number of steps was presumably caused by the fact that the back of the device was covered with a thinly shaved playing card. Thus, the device was able to measure bending in six to seven steps.

Touch Sensor. The accuracy of the touch detection was verified for each of the eight touch sensors. In the experiment, we graphed the data obtained by touching each touch sensor with an index finger for approximately 5 s using the feedback application. The results are shown in Fig. 6. All of the touch sensors were able to detect the input. There were two to five discontinuous areas where the touch was not detected; however, we believe that these brief detection failures could be eliminated with a smoothing filter.

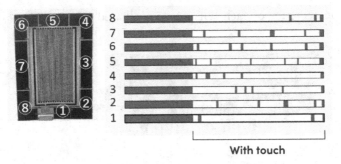

With touch

Fig. 6. Touch detection results visualized in the feedback application. The white area indicates the touch detection status.

6.2 Measurement of Card Techniques

We verified whether the prototype device could successfully acquire sensor data using the card technique. In addition, data from skilled and novice players were collected, analyzed, and compared to determine the essential characteristics of successful execution of each card technique.

Method. The initial state of this experiment is shown in Fig. 3(a), with a deck of playing cards on a magic mat and the card device on top of the deck. The card device was connected to a laptop computer running the feedback application, and sensor data and video were recorded when the subjects performed the card techniques. At the beginning of the experiment, an experimenter (who was skilled in card techniques) explained and demonstrated the basic procedure of each technique. The subject was asked to practice several times to confirm that they understood the procedure, and then the main experiment was conducted. The tasks examined in the experiment involved the riffle shuffle, spring, and

Charlier cut, in that order. Three subjects were skilled (with four to eight years of experience with magic using playing cards) and six were novices.

The data obtained from the experiments were visualized using the feedback application to compare skilled users with successful novices and successful with unsuccessful subjects.

Result for the Riffle Shuffle. All the skilled subjects succeeded in performing the riffle shuffle technique, and one of the six novices succeeded. When two separate piles of cards were completely combined into a single pile, the shuffle was judged to be successful. In the successful case shown in Fig. 7, the deck of cards was combined into one stack; however, in the failure case, the cards are disorganized.

There was no noticeable difference between the skilled and successful novice participants other than the time they took to complete the shuffle. The difference in time was owing to the difference in familiarity with shuffling. The finding that no other differences were observed is attributed to the fact that the riffle shuffle is a relatively easy technique; and as long as the correct method is used, shuffling can be performed successfully.

The results of the comparison of the data of the successful and failed subjects are described. The data for the successful subjects all showed two bending steps from the previous state during shuffling. However, all failed subjects bent the cards in only one step. Figure 8 shows examples of the data from the bending sensor obtained from a successful subject and a failed subject. The interval under "shuffling" in the figure was later added in red to the graph visualized in the feedback application. The results of this experiment for the task shown in Fig. 5, suggest that bending the card more than 70° is key to successfully performing a riffle shuffle.

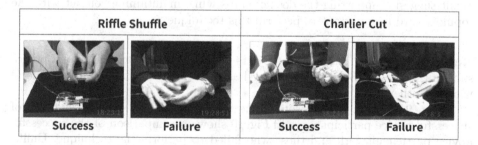

Fig. 7. Examples of successful and failed executions of the riffle shuffle and Charlier cut techniques.

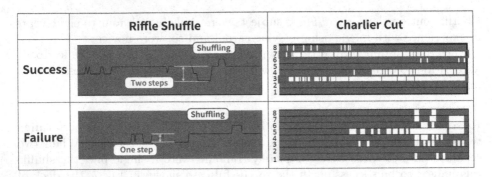

Fig. 8. Comparison of bending sensor data from successful and failed attempts to perform a riffle shuffle and touch sensor data from successful and failed attempts to perform a Charlier cut.

Result of Charlier Cut. All of the skilled subjects succeeded, and three of the six novices succeeded. The technique was considered successful if the top and bottom halves of a stack of cards could be swapped without significantly disrupting the deck.

Figure 7 shows examples of successes and failures. As in the riffle shuffle, there was no noticeable difference between the skilled subjects and successful novice subjects.

A comparison of the touch sensor data of successful and unsuccessful subjects is shown in Fig. 8, showing that successful subjects commonly touched their fingers at locations 3 and 7 in Fig. 8 when performing the Charlier cut, and they held and supported this area firmly to prevent the upper half of the card from falling out of their hands. In contrast, subjects who failed to perform the technique did not touch these locations but only held the card together. This result suggests supporting the deck of cards while maintaining contact with the topmost card is important to perform this technique.

Result of Spring. All skilled subjects succeeded, and one of the six novice subjects succeeded. Success was defined as catching all cards flung by one hand with the other hand.

Figure 9 shows a comparison of the results of skilled users with those of successful novice participants, and Fig. 10 shows a comparison of the successful novice participant with and those who failed to perform the technique. Unlike the other techniques, differences were observed between the two groups.

Regarding the comparison between skilled and successful novice subjects, the data from the bending sensor showed that both increased their bending in the second half of the spring motion. The change in the touch sensor differed between skilled and novice subjects. Skilled subjects touched only the areas corresponding to touch sensors 4 and 8 with their fingertips and hardly touched other areas, whereas most novice subjects touched many parts of the touch sensor and held the card deck in their hands as if they were grasping it, including the novice subject who performed the technique successfully.

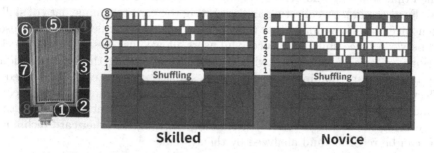

Fig. 9. Comparison of skilled/novice data on the spring.

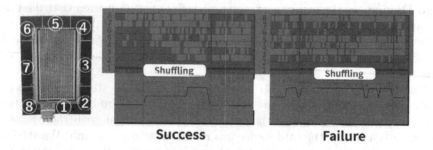

Fig. 10. Comparison of successful/failure data on the spring.

Next, we compared the successful and unsuccessful novice users. The successful novice subject increased the degree of bending in the second half of the spring, whereas the data from unsuccessful subjects included parts where bending was weakened. Regardless of the success or failure of the touch sensor, the novice participants touched many parts of the card. These results suggest that to perform the spring technique successfully, strengthening the bending of the cards while executing the movement is important, and the skilled users held only the positions marked as four and eight.

7 Discussion

In this section, we discuss the availability of the system and some issues noted by users.

7.1   Availability

Through performance evaluation experiments on the prototype system, we confirmed that touching and bending could be detected with a certain level of accuracy. Furthermore, by collecting and analyzing the card technique data of skilled and novice players, we found that the differences between skilled and novice users and between successful and unsuccessful users allowed us to estimate the specific motions or "tricks" associated with successfully executing the card techniques like a skilled card manipulator. This suggests that the system can be used to collect and analyze data on card techniques. The availability of the system could be increased by verifying the effectiveness of the tricks identified in this study in acquiring the technique and by examining the range of other card techniques that can be recorded and analyzed by the system.

7.2   Issues

Card Device. In the experiment, some participants commented that the thickness and hardness of the device was not a problem, but the cable was in the way, and that the cable was hard and the card sometimes moved unintentionally. To solve these problems, we considered integrating the card and microcontroller parts.

The current card device also has a problem with the strength of the card itself. After several measurements in the experiment, we found that the electrical connection was faulty. Some other problems also occurred with the prototype device, and each time the card device was replaced with a new unit. We attribute this outcome to the fact that the board and connector of the card section were bonded only by solder. This electrical connection should be reinforced to improve the connection method or the strength of the connector.

Feedback Application. In this study, one of the author with skill in card techniques compared the graphed data and organized the features, differences, and commonalities of the data. The tricks required to perform the techniques were also examined. However, novice users may not be able to discover the features of such data on their own. Therefore, a more user-friendly feedback method that enables novice users to understand the features of the recorded data should be developed and implemented.

8   Conclusion

In this study, we have proposed a card device to support users in learning to perform card techniques. A prototype of the card device equipped with bending and touch sensors was developed with shape and stiffness almost identical to that of a standard playing card. We also developed a feedback application to record and analyze the sensor data and video of the user performing the card techniques. By measuring, comparing, and analyzing three different card techniques, we found notable differences and similarities between successful and failed attempts and between users with and without skill in performing the techniques. The results demonstrate the possibility of gaining knowledge that could help a user to learn to perform card techniques. Therefore, the usefulness and reliability of this device should be increased by verifying the effectiveness of this knowledge in acquiring skills, investigating the range of applicable card techniques, and improving the feedback application.

Acknowledgments. This work was partly supported by JST-Mirai Program Grant Number JPMJMI21J6, Japan.

References

1. Cannavò, A., Prattico, F.G., Ministeri, G., Lamberti, F.: A movement analysis system based on immersive virtual reality and wearable technology for sport training (2018)
2. Carreras, A., Sora, C.: Coupling digital and physical worlds in an AR magic show performance: lessons learned. In: 2009 IEEE International Symposium on Mixed and Augmented Reality - Arts, Media and Humanities, pp. 25–28 (2009). https://doi.org/10.1109/ISMAR-AMH.2009.5336729
3. Foundry: Adidas micoach smart ball. https://www.foundrycollaborative.com/. Accessed 21 Oct 2022
4. Koretake, R., Kaneko, M., Higashimori, M.: The robot that can achieve card magic. In: 2014 IEEE/ASME International Conference on Advanced Intelligent Mechatronics, pp. 1249–1254 (2014). https://doi.org/10.1109/AIM.2014.6878253
5. van der Linden, J., Schoonderwaldt, E., Bird, J.: Towards a real-time system for teaching novices correct violin bowing technique. In: 2009 IEEE International Workshop on Haptic Audio visual Environments and Games, pp. 81–86 (2009). https://doi.org/10.1109/HAVE.2009.5356123
6. Mizuno Corporation: Swingtracer. https://www.mizuno.jp/baseball/swingtracer/. (in Japanese). Accessed 21 Oct 2022
7. Morris, K.J., Samonin, V., Anderson, J., Lau, M.C., Baltes, J.: Robot magic: a robust interactive humanoid entertainment robot. In: Mouhoub, M., Sadaoui, S., Ait Mohamed, O., Ali, M. (eds.) Recent Trends and Future Technology in Applied Intelligence (2018)
8. Nakamura, A., Tabata, S., Ueda, T., Kiyofuji, S., Kuno, Y.: Multimodal presentation method for a dance training system (2005)
9. Nuñez, D., Tempest, M., Viola, E., Breazeal, C.: An initial discussion of timing considerations raised during development of a magician-robot interaction. In: ACM/IEEE International Conference on Human-Robot Interaction (HRI) Workshop on Timing in HRI (2014)
10. Tempest, M.: TED Conferences. https://www.ted.com/speakers/marco_tempest. Accessed 13 Jan 2022
11. Vadgama, N., Steimle, J.: Flexy: Shape-customizable, single-layer, inkjet printable patterns for 1D and 2D flex sensing (2017)

E-Reminder: A Mindfulness-Based Interactive Eating Reminder Device to Improve Emotional Eating

Xiaoqian Xie[1], Liyi Zhang[1], Yumeng Cao[1], Sining Xue[2], Mengru Xue[3], Yuqi Hu[3], and Cheng Yao[4(✉)]

[1] Polytechnic Institute, Zhejiang University, Hangzhou, China
{xiexiaoqian,22260398}@zju.edu.cn
[2] Social Sciences, University of Southampton, Southampton, UK
sx7n22@soton.ac.uk
[3] Ningbo Research Institute, Zhejiang University, Ningbo, China
{Mengruxue,yuqihu}@zju.edu.cn
[4] College of Computer Science and Technology, Zhejiang University, Hangzhou, China
yaoch@zju.edu.cn

Abstract. Obesity has become a health problem that plagues people worldwide, and emotional eating is a significant cause of obesity. It is essential to reduce the frequency of emotional eating. We innovatively put forward E-Reminder: an interactive mindfulness-based eating reminder system. Based on mindful eating, E-Reminder encourages users to reduce the frequency of emotional eating and establish normal eating behavior by reminding them to focus on their feelings and the characteristics of the food itself. E-Reminder includes a wearable mindfulness interactive device and a mobile application. The system can be used during eating to improve emotional eating problems and establish normal eating behavior. The results of user experiments show that E-Reminder can effectively improve users' emotional eating in the short term and implant weight loss ideas in them.

Keywords: Mindfulness · Emotional eating · Interactive system

1 Introduction

In the past 40 years, the prevalence of obesity in the world has increased dramatically [1]. It has become a global health problem, bringing many health risks, such as hyperlipidemia, stroke, cancer, sleep apnea, hepatobiliary diseases, etc., and tremendous psychological and social pressure. The stigma of body shape and obesity is increasingly recognized [2]. Therefore, obesity will harm the physical and psychosocial quality of life, especially among severely obese people [3].

Previous studies have shown that as a risk factor for obesity, emotional eating has received particular attention. Emotional eating is defined as overeating in response to negative emotions [4]. When emotional eating occurs, people always choose energy-intensive and delicious food [5]. According to studies, psychotherapy strategies must be

© The Author(s), under exclusive license to Springer Nature Switzerland AG 2023
N. A. Streitz and S. Konomi (Eds.): HCII 2023, LNCS 14037, pp. 456–469, 2023.
https://doi.org/10.1007/978-3-031-34609-5_33

formulated to address emotional eating issues [6] to prevent obesity in the long run. And some other studies show that Mindfulness-based methods are effective ways to solve this problem [7].

As a concept based on Buddhism, mindfulness has attracted more and more attention from psychologists and researchers [8]. In terms of diet, mindfulness is described as a non-judgemental psychological awareness of physical and emotional feelings related to diet [9]. Mindful eating has been proven effective in reducing emotional eating [10]. It focuses on the moment observation of visual stimulation, taste, satiety, and private events (such as thoughts) related to the eating experience [11]. In recent years, mindfulness intervention for eating behavior has become increasingly popular [12]. Studies have shown that mindful eating has been used for emotional eating management and can also be used as a part of an obesity treatment plan [13]. Moreover, mindfulness-based programs may also have beneficial effects on the increase of happiness [14]. The research results of Aileen Pidgeon et al. support the effectiveness of mindfulness intervention in treating the emotional eating habits of individuals with anxiety, stress, and lower depression [15]. Some other studies show that mindfulness practice is related to reducing pain intensity, reducing emotional exhaustion, and helping individuals to reduce their reactions to negative thoughts and emotions when trying to engage in healthy behaviors [8, 16, 17].

Mindfulness intervention has the characteristics of "paying attention in a specific way, purposefully, in the present moment and without judgment" [18], which means that mindfulness intervention requires users to cultivate conscious awareness and attention all the time [19]. In the fast-paced contemporary society, such a request is undoubtedly difficult. A systematic review shows that mindfulness-based intervention focusing on eating behavior (that is, eating consciously) is more effective in weight loss than general mindfulness intervention [10]. Mindfulness-based food awareness training [20] was developed to treat bulimia. Its practice involves paying attention to eating foods usually included in overeating, such as biscuits and cakes, focusing on eating behavior, emotions related to eating, and the texture and taste of the food eaten.

We have expanded our efforts to improve emotional eating through mindfulness intervention and innovatively combined wearable sensor technology with mindfulness intervention, which is expected to improve emotional eating. This paper presents E-Reminder: an interactive eating reminder system based on mindfulness, which includes a mobile application and a wearable device. The wearable device is hung on the user's ear, and it consists of a heart rate sensor and an electromyographic sensor. The system detects whether the user is in an emotional eating state through sensor data. When it is detected that the user is in an emotional eating status, the device gives a mindfulness intervention prompt to guide users to feel the attributes of food itself, such as shape, taste, and color, and also the users' emotions in the process of emotional eating. Past emotional eating behaviors will be recorded in mobile applications to help users understand their eating behaviors. The results of user experiments show that E-Reminder can effectively improve users' emotional eating in the short term and implant weight loss ideas in them.

2 Related Work

2.1 Mindfulness Therapy for Emotional Eating

Emotional eating can be seen as a way to escape negative emotions [21, 22]. At present, several methods have been proposed to solve emotional eating, including mindfulness, Acceptance and Commitment Therapy (ACT), Cognitive Behavioral Therapy (CBT), and Analytical Behavioral Therapy (DBT) [23]. Among these methods, a large number of research results support that mindfulness intervention is particularly effective in changing obesity-related eating behaviors, especially for emotional eating problems [12]. Mindfulness is usually described as non-judgemental awareness of the current experience and acceptance of the moment of experience [8]. After reviewing 14 studies, the evaluation showed that mindfulness-based interventions effectively reduced people's emotional eating behaviors and food cravings [10, 24, 25]. The current evidence shows that mindful eating can significantly improve eating behavior and reduce or maintain weight [26, 27]. Other research results show that mindfulness-based diet courses can effectively reduce calorie intake and encourage children to choose healthier diets [28].

2.2 Sensors Detect Emotions

With the development and progress of sensors and technologies for detecting human emotions, it is now possible to quickly and effectively detect various human emotions through sensor technologies [29]. Now specially designed wearable devices, such as wristbands and smart watches with sensors such as Electrical Skin Reaction (GSR) and Electromyography (EMG) sensors, can inconspicuously detect certain physiological signals. And identify emotions through the collected data [30]. For example, Andreas Haag Et al. Described a program to train computers to use multiple signals from many different biosensors to recognize emotions [31]. Hua Wang et al. put forward a chat system that can obtain the emotional state of chat users through physiological sensors attached to users' bodies [32]. And Bohdan Myroniv et al. proposed using ready-made wearable sensors, including heart rate, skin electrochemical reaction, and body temperature sensors, to read users' physiological signals and apply machine learning technology to identify the emotional state of users [33].

2.3 Application of Sensors in Diet Detection

Presently, there have been studies on the application of sensors in diet detection. For example, Edward Sazonov et al. developed a method to study ingestion behavior by non-invasive monitoring of swallowing and chewing with sensors. The purpose is to study the behavior pattern of food consumption and generate estimates of the volume and weight of energy ingested by people [34]. There are studies to predict the risk of users' emotional diet by evaluating the heart rate variability data collected by users wearing Empatica E4 sensors [35]. In addition, research has been done to obtain physiological data through customized sensing devices placed in bras, and to detect emotions based on machine learning methods, to establish an emotional approximate real-time support system [36].

After summarizing the above work, we found that the research of combining sensing technology with mindful eating intervention to improve emotional eating has received little attention.

3   Design Concept

We propose E-Reminder: an interactive eating reminder system based on mindfulness, which includes a wearable mindfulness interactive device and a mobile application (Fig. 1). E-Reminder aims to help users improve their emotional eating problems in daily life, thus helping them to establish healthy eating habits. E-Minder detects whether the user is in an emotional eating state through sensor data, and when it is detected that the user is in an emotional eating state, it gives a mindfulness intervention prompt through the device, such as paying attention to the taste and color of food, and the current emotions of people. Past emotional eating behaviors will be recorded in mobile applications to help users understand their eating behaviors.

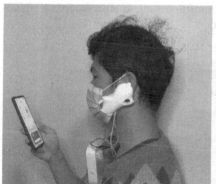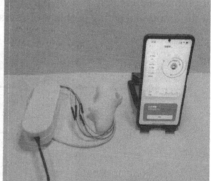

Fig. 1. Users use E-Reminder (left) and E-Reminder (right)

The wearable mindfulness interactive device consists of Arduino nano integrated with Bluetooth module, heart rate blood oxygen sensor, dry electrode electromyography sensor, and Bluetooth headset (Fig. 2). The data communicated between the wearable interactive device and mobile application is transmitted through the Bluetooth module in Arduino nano, realizing data intercommunication. It is used to detect users' EMG and heart rate changing data and transmit the analyzed data through Bluetooth to guide users' mindful eating behavior.

That is, to guide users to feel the attributes of food itself, such as shape, taste, and color, and also the users' emotions in the process of emotional eating. During eating, we can experience the psychological process of eating and switch users' concerns to improve users' emotional eating habits.

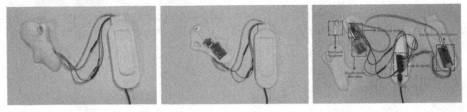

Fig. 2. Front view of the device (left), back view of the device (middle), and disassembly view of the device (right)

4 Wearable Mindfulness System

Our wearable mindfulness interactive device includes the functions of emotional eating detection and mindfulness guidance. The device is equipped with a dry electrode electromyography sensor and a heart rate blood oxygen sensor to detect emotional eating. The primary procedure (Fig. 3) is to integrate the data of two sensors through data analysis and feature extraction, judge the emotional eating of users, and guide users to mindfulness eating behavior by playing mindfulness audio after receiving signals to adjust the emotional eating problem of users.

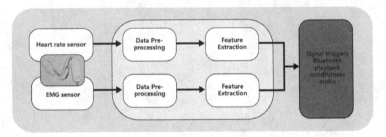

Fig. 3. Overview of functions of wearable mindfulness system

A dry EMG sensor detects the EMG signal of the human body surface, and then reflects the activity of human muscles and nerves. The dry electrode electromyography sensor which integrates filtering and amplifying circuits amplifies the weak human surface electromyography signal in the range of +1.5 mV by 1000 times and effectively suppresses the noise by differential input and analog filtering circuit. The output signal is an analog signal, with 1.5 V as the reference voltage and a 0–3.0 V range. The magnitude of the output signal depends on the selected muscle's activity, and the output signal's waveform can significantly indicate the condition of the subcutaneous muscle at the observed position. The EMG sensor in this device needs to be attached directly to the specific muscle position of the user's face for detection, and it is used to capture the EMG signal of the masseter muscle contraction of the user to judge the chewing and eating behavior of the user. With the user's test, the data of the EMG sensor has good sensing quality on the graph (Fig. 4), and the noise is slight, which can accurately detect the chewing behavior of users.

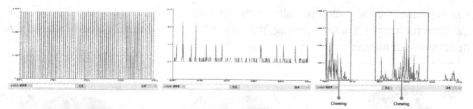

Fig. 4. EMG sensor standby data (left) sensor wearing but not recognizing chewing signal (middle) EMG sensor recognizing chewing signal (right)

The heart rate and blood oxygen sensor used to detect the user's emotions measures the pulse and blood oxygen saturation by using the difference of light transmittance caused by human tissues when blood vessels beat. The sensor consists of a light source and a photoelectric converter, which need to be fixed on the finger, wrist, or earlobe of the user. Generally, the light source adopts a light-emitting diode with a specific wavelength that is selective to oxygenated hemoglobin and hemoglobin in arterial blood. When the light beam passes through the human body's peripheral blood vessels, the light beam's light transmittance changes due to the change in arterial pulse congestion volume. At this time, the photoelectric converter receives the light reflected by the human tissue, converts it into an electrical signal, and amplifies and outputs it. When the device is used, it needs to be attached to the user's earlobe, and the heart rate data can be obtained by detecting the time interval between heartbeats and taking the average value of multiple times of data. The change of this data can reflect the heart rate variability through images, thus reflecting the emotional change of the user. We enlarge the heart rate by ten times to facilitate the observation of heart rate variability and better adapt to the waveform of the EMG signal. In this paper, we use the data combination of EMG and heart rate sensor signals (Fig. 5) to detect users' emotional eating. In the figure, we can observe noticeable sensor signal changes to judge emotional eating.

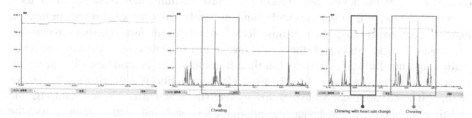

Fig. 5. The sensor does not recognize the chewing signal and the heart rate is stable (left) the sensor recognizes the chewing signal and the heart rate is stable (middle) the sensor recognizes the chewing signal and sends the heart rate abnormality (right)

The main body is divided into two parts: the ear prototype and the chest prototype (Fig. 6). The prototype is fixed to the user's ear through a Bluetooth headset, equipped with sensors and Bluetooth headset, which are used to detect user data and guide mindfulness. The chest prototype is fixed on the user's clothes by clips, mainly equipped with a processor and sensor elements, which do not have direct contact with the user.

During usage, the ear prototype collects data and transmits the data to the processor of the chest prototype. After processing, the data is fed back to the Bluetooth headset for mindfulness guidance.

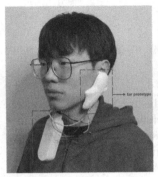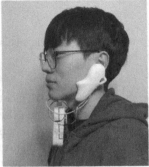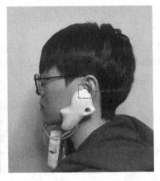

Fig. 6. Device Wearing Figure (left) Device Wearing Side A (middle) Device Wearing Side Figure B (right)

5   Auxiliary Mobile Application

Our software (Fig. 7) identifies and connects with the wearable mindfulness interaction device through Bluetooth, and cooperates with the devices to have a process of mindfulness intervention and guidance during emotional eating. The mobile application is designed to regulate the behavior activation in treatment for mindfulness, and record the emotional eating events of users. After the user connects the application with the device via Bluetooth, the device can be configured and controlled by the application. And the data collected by the device can be recorded to provide immediate feedback to the user.

Users can record information quickly and discretely in real-time using the application matching device. Through the real-time detection of relevant data, whether the user has emotional eating events outside the regular meal time can be recorded, and the user can be guided into mindfulness adjustment in time to improve the emotional eating problem, record it in time, and respond to the user. Users may find it difficult to self-monitor challenging and unpopular behaviors, so they avoid these activities. However, through the real-time monitoring of the device, the automatic feedback and encouragement from the system will quickly follow up and establish a positive connection with self-monitoring activities. After receiving positive feedback, users will further build confidence and establish a virtuous circle. Therefore, the application program can effectively reduce the burden on users. Many features considered therapeutic value are identified as part of the application, including reminders, encouraging feedback and warnings, community communication, sharing relevant coping strategies, and summary charts.

The following are the three core functions of the application.

Mindfulness regulation: The application program provides the auxiliary function of mindfulness regulation. When the device detects the emotional eating behavior of

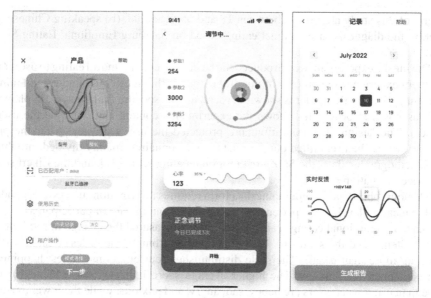

Fig. 7. Hardware Matching Interface (left) Mindfulness Adjustment Interface (middle) Hardware Matching (right)

the user, it immediately enters the mindfulness guidance state for real-time intervention. The application program provides an active intervention mode based on different users and scenes. Users can directly enter mindfulness adjustment through the application program, set the adjustment degree by themselves, and record the user's eating habits, etc., to improve the applicability. It also urges the user to know the target behavior, current emotional state, diet, current adjustment mode, and adjustment record. And record each index parameter for analysis so that users can know their state, adjust in time, and plan the next stage according to the records.

Feedback record: This application feeds back the emotional eating events of users through real-time changes in their heart rate, electromyography, and other data, and makes an inductive analysis of these events This way, users can know their state in real-time, adjust coping strategies in time, and improve intervention efficiency.

Community communication: This application provides opportunities for people of the same kind to communicate with each other. By providing community communication channels to create a sense of belonging, users can exchange experiences and feelings through community friends and supervise each other's company, thus better-motivating users to adhere to mindful eating interventions.

6   User Study

This study aims to investigate whether E-Reminder is effective in improving users' emotional eating problems. To test E-Reminder, we set up a user study and collected the questionnaire data. In this study, we recruited 34 participants from an eating disorder community in Weibo, where most people have emotional eating problems. The inclusion criteria of this study are (a) age between 18 and 55 years old, (b) speaking Chinese (c) meeting the diagnosis of emotional eating based on Salzburg Emotional Eating Scale [37].

During the experiment, we introduced the basic concept of mindful eating to users and had them experience the process of mindful eating so that they could understand mindful eating. Then, E-Reminder is shown to users, and its specific functions are explained. Each user was informed and shown the experiment's content and obtained the user's consent. The design of the questionnaire protected the user's privacy. After the preliminary work, the users filled out the related questionnaires, mainly divided into three parts: demographic data, the Salzburg emotional eating scale [37], and the Likert scale of device evaluation.

Demographic data, Demographic data form requires information such as age, gender, BMI, education level, the experience of mindfulness eating, etc. of participants.

Salzburg emotional eating scale (SEES), SEES measured the change in food intake with 20 items, and the scores of these items ranged from 1 (eating less than usual) to 5 (eating more than usual). The scale distinguishes four emotional states: happiness, sadness, anger, and anxiety. The higher average score indicates the tendency to eat more than usual when users are happy, sad, angry, and anxious, while the lower average score indicates that users are more inclined to eat less than usual when experiencing these emotions. A moderate score (the average total score is about 3 points) indicates that these emotions will not change a person's food intake. In the validation study, the internal reliability is acceptable or good.

The Likert scale of the evaluation device is a commonly used scale of scoring and summation. In this study, a five-component scale is used. Each respondent's attitude score is obtained by his or her answers to each question. The scale score can indicate his attitude or his different state. The higher the score, the better the user feedback. In this study, this scale was applied to evaluate devices by users.

All 34 participants' data were included in the analysis. Table 1 introduces all participants' demographic data and the emotional eating scale results. In the whole sample, the average age of participants was 24.8(SD = 8.95, range 18–45). Most participants are undergraduates (70.5%) and full-time students (91.1%). More than half of the participants (61.7%) have experience with mindful eating and hope to improve their emotional eating problems through mindful eating. The Emotional Eating Scale screened all participants before the experiment. Most users' emotional food intake increased significantly in anxiety (M = 3.6 SD = 1.53) and happiness (M = 3.3 SD = 1.08) emotions, but in sadness (M = 2.9 SD = 1.38) and anger (M = 3.1 SD = 1.17).

Table 1. Demographic data of participants and results of emotional eating scale

N = 34	M(SD)	N
Age(years)	24.8(8.95)	
Gender		
Male		3(8.8%)

(continued)

Table 1. (*continued*)

N = 34	M(SD)	N
Female		31(91.2%)
BMI	20.4(2.59)	
Education		
High School or less		1(2.9%)
Associate Degree		2(6.0%)
Undergraduate College Degree		24(70.5%)
Graduate Degree		7(20.6%)
Salzburg Emotional Eating Scale		
Happiness	3.3(1.08)	
Sadness	2.9(1.38)	
Anger	3.1(1.17)	
Anxiety	3.6(1.53)	
Experience of mindfulness eating		21(61.7%)

In the questionnaire (Table 2), the first four questions collected users' experience data on mindfulness eating. After a single mindfulness experience, most users had a good psychological experience and thought that the taste eating experience (M = 3.6 SD = 0.97) and abdominal breathing (M = 3.7 SD = 0.78) had a good effect on emotional eating, and users insisted on mindfulness eating for a long time. The last five questions investigated users' views and expectations of the device. The result shows that users can accept the guidance of mindful eating and the records of emotional eating with E-Reminder (M = 3.5 SD = 0.95) and think that sensor technology combined with mindful eating intervention can improve the effect of emotional eating (M = 3.4 SD = 1.09). Users think that mindfulness eating with this device can effectively alleviate emotional eating problems (M = 3.7 SD = 1.09) and the device is comfortable to wear (M = 3.3 SD = 0.92), but users lack firm confidence (M = 3.1 SD = 1.06) in persisting in using this device for a long time.

Table 2. Likert scale of device evaluation

Questions	N	M(SD)
How do you experience the act of looking closely at the external features of food before eating?	34	3.4(0.88)
How do you experience the act of carefully tasting the taste characteristics of food while eating?	34	3.6(0.97)
What is your experience with abdominal breathing after eating?	34	3.7(0.78)

(*continued*)

Table 2. (*continued*)

Questions	N	M(SD)
Do you think the above methods of mindfulness will solve your emotional eating problem?	34	3.3(0.92)
How receptive are you to using a device for mindfulness and using software to record emotional eating?	34	3.5(0.95)
Do you think sensor technology combined with mindfulness eating can better improve this situation?	34	3.4(1.03)
Do you think this device that detects emotional eating and conducts mindfulness guidance can alleviate the problem of emotional eating?	34	3.7 (1.09)
Do you think you can persist in using the device to solve emotional eating problems?	34	3.1(1.06)
How comfortable do you think the device is to wear on your ears?	34	3.3(0.92)

7 Discussion

The primary purpose of E-Reminder is to provide a tool for emotional eating users, to improve their emotional eating problems, and to provide them with ideas to lose weight. It collects the physiological data of the user through the mindfulness interaction device fixed on the user's ear, and after analyzing the data, if the user is in an emotional eating state, it uses the device to guide the user to mindful eating, that is, to keep the awareness of food and emotions. Then, the emotional eating events will be recorded in the application. Of course, users can also spontaneously use the app for mindful eating behavior when eating.

The wearable mindfulness interactive device can monitor in real time whether the user has emotional eating problems and give mindfulness guidance in time. During mindful eating, users can keep their awareness of food and emotions in their eating process so that users can know and accept their current eating status, then calm down and reduce anxiety and stress. In the long run, this will help to follow a balanced diet. At the same time, users with emotional eating behaviors often fall into a negative cycle uncontrollably, and users may find it difficult to self-monitor some challenging and unpopular behaviors. Therefore, they will keep themselves away from these activities, and they will repeatedly fall into feelings of remorse and evasion. Moreover, this kind of eating behavior is usually sporadic and concealed, making it difficult to intervene in the outside world [38]. Suppose feedback or encouragement can be provided immediately when the intervention process is completed. In that case, the automatic feedback and encouragement in the self-monitoring record will be followed up quickly to reduce possible disharmony and encourage users to persist in treatment to form a virtuous circle.

Still, our research has several limitations. Firstly, it is impossible to conduct long-term user observation experiments and research due to the epidemic. We need long-term research to determine whether E-Reminder can improve users' emotional eating problems and whether users can persist in using equipment remains to be studied. Secondly, the problems of the physical device, such as the device's volume and the sensor's recognition, still need to be optimized. The device should have a compact volume and more accurate recognition ability to improve the user's wearing and using experience.

In future work, we plan to find more participants to conduct long-term user research and conduct controlled trials to verify the long-term improvement effect of the device on emotional eating problems. At the same time, it is necessary to conduct further research on the technical level of the device, such as reducing the device's volume, and improving the detection accuracy of emotional eating by studying the cooperation of multiple sensors, to ensure users' use in daily life.

8 Conclusion

In this paper, we propose an E-Reminder --an interactive eating reminder system for emotional eating based on mindfulness. The system includes a wearable mindfulness interactive device and a mobile application program, and we combine sensor technology and mindful eating intervention to improve emotional eating problems. We optimized the experience of mindfulness therapy through an E-Reminder, detected emotional eating problems through sensors, and then guided users with mindful eating intervention so that the process of mindful eating can be integrated into users' daily lives, emotional eating problems can be improved, and regular eating behaviors can be established. E-Reminder will effectively improve users' emotional eating and give them weight loss ideas.

Acknowledgement. This research was funded by the Engineering Research Center of Computer Aided Product Innovation Design, Ministry of Education, National Natural Science Foundation of China (Grant No. 52075478), and National Social Science Foundation of China (Grant No. 21AZD056).

References

1. Jaacks, L.M., et al.: The obesity transition: stages of the global epidemic. Lancet Diabetes Endocrinol. **7**, 231–240 (2019)
2. Williams, E.P., Mesidor, M., Winters, K., Dubbert, P.M., Wyatt, S.B.: Overweight and obesity: prevalence, consequences, and causes of a growing public health problem. Curr. Obes. Rep. **4**, 363–370 (2015)
3. Kushner, R.F., Foster, G.D.: Obesity and quality of life. Nutrition **16**, 947–952 (2000)
4. Ford, T., Lee, H., Jeon, M.: The emotional eating and negative food relationship experiences of obese and overweight adults. Soc. Work Health Care **56**, 488–504 (2017)
5. Konttinen, H.: Emotional eating and obesity in adults: The role of depression, sleep and genes. Proc. Nutrition Soc. **79**, 283–289 (2020)
6. Koenders, P.G., van Strien, T.: Emotional eating, rather than lifestyle behavior, drives weight gain in a prospective study in 1562 employees. J. Occup. Environ. Med. **53**(11), 1287–1293 (2011)

7. Warren, J.M., Smith, N., Ashwell, M.: A structured literature review on the role of mindfulness, mindful eating and intuitive eating in changing eating behaviours: effectiveness and associated potential mechanisms. Nutr. Res. Rev. **30**, 272–283 (2017)

8. Bishop, S.R., et al.: Mindfulness: a proposed operational definition. Clin. Psychol. Sci. Pract. **11**, 230 (2004)

9. Framson, C., Kristal, A.R., Schenk, J.M., Littman, A.J., Zeliadt, S., Benitez, D.: Development and validation of the mindful eating questionnaire. J. Am. Diet. Assoc. **109**, 1439–1444 (2009)

10. Katterman, S.N., Kleinman, B.M., Hood, M.M., Nackers, L.M., Corsica, J.A.: Mindfulness meditation as an intervention for binge eating, emotional eating, and weight loss: a systematic review. Eat. Behav. **15**, 197–204 (2014)

11. Hendrickson, K.L., Rasmussen, E.B.: Mindful eating reduces impulsive food choice in adolescents and adults. Health Psychol. **36**, 226 (2017)

12. O'Reilly, G.A., Cook, L., Spruijt-Metz, D., Black, D.S.: Mindfulness-based interventions for obesity-related eating behaviours: a literature review. Obes. Rev. **15**, 453–461 (2014)

13. Gizem, K.: Can mindful eating help us when we struggle with eating? Mindful eating replaces diets. Turkish J. Sport Exerc. **22**, 72–77 (2020)

14. Sarto, H.M., et al.: Efficacy of a mindful-eating programme to reduce emotional eating in patients suffering from overweight or obesity in primary care settings: a cluster-randomised trial protocol. BMJ Open **9**, e031327 (2019)

15. Pidgeon, A., Lacota, K., Champion, J.: The moderating effects of mindfulness on psychological distress and emotional eating behaviour. Aust. Psychol. **48**, 262–269 (2013)

16. Roemer, L., Williston, S.K., Rollins, L.G.: Mindfulness and emotion regulation. Curr. Opin. Psychol. **3**, 52–57 (2015)

17. Hülsheger, U.R., Alberts, H.J., Feinholdt, A., Lang, J.W.: Benefits of mindfulness at work: the role of mindfulness in emotion regulation, emotional exhaustion, and job satisfaction. J. Appl. Psychol. **98**, 310 (2013)

18. Kabat-Zinn, J.: Wherever You Go, There You Are: Mindfulness Meditation in Everyday Life. Hachette Books (2009)

19. Academic Mindfulness Interest Group, M.: Mindfulness-based psychotherapies: a review of conceptual foundations, empirical evidence and practical considerations. Austr. New Zealand J. Psychiatry. **40**, 285–294 (2006)

20. Kristeller, J.L., Hallett, C.B.: An exploratory study of a meditation-based intervention for binge eating disorder. J. Health Psychol. **4**, 357–363 (1999)

21. Altheimer, G., Urry, H.L.: Do emotions cause eating? The role of previous experiences and social context in emotional eating. Curr. Direct. Psychol. Sci. **28**(3), 234–240 (2019). https://doi.org/10.1177/0963721419837685

22. Van Strien, T., Frijters, J.E., Bergers, G.P., Defares, P.B.: The Dutch eating behavior questionnaire (DEBQ) for assessment of restrained, emotional, and external eating behavior. Int. J. Eat. Disord. **5**, 295–315 (1986)

23. Frayn, M., Knäuper, B.: Emotional eating and weight in adults: a review. Key Topics Health Nature Behavior 1–10 (2022)

24. Alberts, H.J.E.M., Thewissen, R., Raes, L.: Dealing with problematic eating behaviour. The effects of a mindfulness-based intervention on eating behaviour, food cravings, dichotomous thinking and body image concern. Appetite **58**(3), 847–851 (2012)

25. Corsica, J., Hood, M.M., Katterman, S., Kleinman, B., Ivan, I.: Development of a novel mindfulness and cognitive behavioral intervention for stress-eating: a comparative pilot study. Eat. Behav. **15**, 694–699 (2014)

26. Kearney, D.J., Milton, M.L., Malte, C.A., McDermott, K.A., Martinez, M., Simpson, T.L.: Participation in mindfulness-based stress reduction is not associated with reductions in emotional eating or uncontrolled eating. Nutr. Res. **32**, 413–420 (2012)

27. Miller, C.K., Kristeller, J.L., Headings, A., Nagaraja, H., Miser, W.F.: Comparative effectiveness of a mindful eating intervention to a diabetes self-management intervention among adults with type 2 diabetes: a pilot study. J. Acad. Nutr. Diet. **112**, 1835–1842 (2012)
28. Gayoso, L., de Tomas, I., Téllez, R., Maiz, E., Etxeberria, U.: Mindfulness-based eating intervention in children: effects on food intake and food-related behaviour during a mid-morning snack. Mindfulness **12**, 1185–1194 (2021)
29. Pal, S., Mukhopadhyay, S., Suryadevara, N.: Development and progress in sensors and technologies for human emotion recognition. Sensors **21**, 5554 (2021)
30. Shu, J., Chiu, M., Hui, P.: Emotion sensing for mobile computing. IEEE Commun. Mag. **57**, 84–90 (2019)
31. Haag, A., Goronzy, S., Schaich, P., Williams, J.: Emotion recognition using bio-sensors: first steps towards an automatic system. In: André, E., Dybkjær, L., Minker, W., Heisterkamp, P. (eds.) ADS 2004. LNCS (LNAI), vol. 3068, pp. 36–48. Springer, Heidelberg (2004). https://doi.org/10.1007/978-3-540-24842-2_4
32. Wang, H., Prendinger, H., Igarashi, T.: Communicating emotions in online chat using physiological sensors and animated text. In: CHI 2004 Extended Abstracts on Human Factors in Computing Systems, pp. 1171–1174 (2004)
33. Myroniv, B., Wu, C.-W., Ren, Y., Christian, A., Bajo, E., Tseng, Y.-C.: Analyzing user emotions via physiology signals. Data Sci. Pattern Recognit. **1**, 11–25 (2017)
34. Sazonov, E., et al.: Non-invasive monitoring of chewing and swallowing for objective quantification of ingestive behavior. Physiol. Meas. **29**, 525 (2008)
35. Juarascio, A.S., Crochiere, R.J., Tapera, T.M., Palermo, M., Zhang, F.: Momentary changes in heart rate variability can detect risk for emotional eating episodes. Appetite **152**, 104698 (2020)
36. Carroll, E.A., et al.: Food and mood: Just-in-time support for emotional eating. In: 2013 Humaine Association Conference on Affective Computing and Intelligent Interaction, pp. 252–257. IEEE (2013)
37. Meule, A., Reichenberger, J., Blechert, J.: Development and preliminary validation of the Salzburg emotional eating scale. Front. Psychol. **9**, 88 (2018)
38. Loro, A.D., Jr., Orleans, C.S.: Binge eating in obesity: preliminary findings and guidelines for behavioral analysis and treatment. Addict. Behav. **6**, 155–166 (1981)

Detecting Hand Hygienic Behaviors In-the-Wild Using a Microphone and Motion Sensor on a Smartwatch

Haoyu Zhuang[1]([✉]), Liqiang Xu[1], Yuuki Nishiyama[2], and Kaoru Sezaki[1,2]

[1] Institute of Industrial Science, The University of Tokyo, Tokyo, Japan
{zhuanghaoyu,xuliqiang}@mcl.iis.u-tokyo.ac.jp
[2] Center for Spatial Information Science, The University of Tokyo, Tokyo, Japan
{yuukin,sezaki}@iis.u-tokyo.ac.jp

Abstract. In recent years, the emergence of the COVID-19 pandemic has led to new viral variants, such as Omicron. These variants are more harmful and impose more restrictions on people's daily hygiene habits. Therefore, during the COVID-19 pandemic, it is logical to automatically detect epidemic protective behaviors without user intent. In this study, we used multiple sensor data from an off-the-shelf smartwatch to detect several defined behaviors. To increase the utility and generalizability of the research results, we collected audio and inertial measurement unit (IMU) data from eight participants in real environments over a long period. In the model-building process, we first created a binary classification between hand hygiene behaviors(hand washing, disinfection, and face-touching) and daily behavior. Then, we distinguished between specific hand hygiene behaviors based on audio and IMU. Ultimately, our model achieves 93% classification accuracy for three behaviors(Hand washing, face touching, and disinfection). The results prove that the accuracy of the classification of behaviors has improved remarkably, which also emphasizes the feasibility of recognizing hand hygiene behaviors using inertial acoustic data.

Keywords: Multimodal Fusion · Wearable device · Hygiene behaviors detection · IMU · Audio

1 Introduction

Currently, the COVID-19 epidemic has developed in recent years and produced new variants of the virus, such as Delta, Omicron, etc. These variants have been proven to be more infectious and have had a widespread impact on human society. Improving personal daily hygiene habits is one of the effective solutions to slow down the spread of the epidemic [1]. However, it is difficult for people to be aware of their hygiene habits, such as hand washing and disinfection. In order to help improve individual daily habits and reduce the rate of transmission of COVID-19 and other infectious diseases such as influenza [2], firstly it is necessary to know human specific protective awareness and daily habits. By automatically detecting epidemic protective behaviors without a user's intention, we could objectively evaluate human awareness and the condition of self-protection. Then, we could use some strategies, like persuasive technology, to encourage humans to improve their daily hygiene habits [3]. In addition, automatic recognition of a wide range of human activities plays a key role in realizing many compelling applications in health, personal assistance, and human-computer interaction [4]. Over the last decade, smart devices are more popular in people's daily life. Along with this rise are the increasing amount of data and ubiquitous computing. Existing environmental sensors are the basis for real-time data collection and identification of human activity, especially portable smart devices [5]. The development of smartwatch technology and applications has led researchers to conduct many studies regarding human behavior detection based on smartwatches because the smartwatch contains multiple sensors with low-energy consumption [4–6]. The data that smart devices could collect is diverse and not limited to sensing data, but also includes audio, as well as image data. The information obtained from a single source is usually inadequate, which limits the accuracy of many tasks. By combing various sensors on smart devices, we could collect human daily data and accurately predict human behavior patterns by analyzing these data.

In this paper, we utilize a smartwatch to collect IMU and sound data from ten subjects in an unsupervised environment for a long period of time and propose a behavioral classification model based on IMU and sound data. The model can effectively identify three hand hygiene behaviors (hand washing, sanitizing and face touching) in daily life, and the optimal model has a classification accuracy of 93% and an F1 score of 97%. By classifying user behaviors with this model, the smartwatch can effectively help users count and record hand hygiene behaviors, which can contribute to people's health.

The remainder of the paper is organized as follows. Section 2 introduces previous related work, including hand behavior recognition, behavior recognition by multimodality, and experiments based on real environments. Section 3 presents the research objectives of this article based on previous related studies. Section 4 describes the data collection as well as the pre-processing process. Section 5 describes the whole training process, including the purpose of designing two classification starts, the model of data processing, and the method of data fusion. Section 6 presents the classification performance of the models by comparison and selects the model with the best performance for discussion. Section 7 discusses the classification results of the models and analyzes and speculates on the limitations of the models in terms of applications and experiments.

2 Related Work

This section presents related work from three perspectives: human activity recognition based on inertial sensors, human activity recognition based on multidimensional data, and human activity recognition based on in-the-wild datasets. This section illustrates the origins and expectations of experiment-related techniques and ideas.

2.1 Hand Behaviors Detection Based on Inertial Data

Various behavior detection models based on smartwatches have been proposed. Behavioral detection of sports-related human activities such as running, cycling, stair climbing, and squatting has been widely used in several applications and is beneficial to personal health [2,5,7].

For example, using hand motion data to detect social distance has yielded promising results [8]. Recently, some studies on face-touching behavior recognition have been proposed [6,9], and the accuracy of these models is impressive. In addition, exploring the detection of mask wearers using smartwatches during epidemics is conducted [10].

Innovative classification methods for handwashing that rely on smartwatches have been proposed [2]. In this study, the researchers utilized the output from the penultimate layer of a neural network for behavior recognition. This approach saved computational resources but yielded an F1-score of approximately 0.78. This accuracy is not sufficient because of the complicated real world situations in which hand washing behavior needs to be detected, particularly during the pandemic. In some studies, researchers have used traditional machine learning methods to classify hand washing with other behaviors, such as SVM with KNN [11]; however, this study divided the dataset into three categories only: hand washing, hand rubbing, and other activities, which is not sufficiently effective in the utilization of the data; we expect to fully utilize the collected data to identify most of the daily hand hygiene activities successfully.

2.2 Human Activity Recognition Based on Multi-sensor

Research on the use of acoustic data for human activity recognition has not been developed recently. Stork *et al.* identified 22 activities by using acoustic data [12]. A number of studies on human behavior recognition based on multi-dimensional data have been conducted. Siddiqui *et al.* realized human gesture recognition based on an IMU and acoustic datasets [13]. Furthermore, another study recently proposed a more accurate and realistic approach [4]. By exploring the application of inertial sensors and acoustic sensors on off-the-shelf commodity smartwatches for daily activity recognition, a model using multi-sensor data to classify daily activities performed well on the in-the-wild dataset. In this study, we attempted two approaches combining IMU and acoustic data and focused on the classification of hand hygiene behaviors in anticipation of obtaining better classification performance.

2.3 Human Activity Recognition in the Wild

Most studies on human hand behavior recognition have been conducted in laboratory settings, which means that the dataset contains minimal noise and a small amount of data. However, some researchers have collected data in real environments. The study by Bhattacharya *et al.* presented a procedure for multiple daily behavior recognition using smartwatches. Recently, Dittakavi *et al.* conducted studies on posture correction in the wild [14]. Conducting experiments in an unsupervised environment results in the dataset containing more noise and the efficiency of data collection being lower. Therefore, most experiments are done in the laboratory. However, in order to improve the robustness of the model, collecting data in the wild is necessary.

3   Motivation

Existing studies have primarily utilized only laboratory sensor data to detect hand behaviors. Most researchers have collected and analyzed IMU from experimenters and developed models to detect specific behaviors [2, 15]. The collection and analysis of experimenter IMU alone is insufficient because IMU characteristics have similarities for some activities, such as hand washing and disinfection. Therefore, it is difficult to distinguish these behaviors successfully using a classification model based only on IMU. Acoustic signals generated by practical activities are often distinctive and enable accurate recognition of human activity. Adding the dimension of acoustic data to the collection of IMU can improve the classification accuracy of specific behaviors, and more behaviors can be defined in the experiments. In addition, although the sensors used to collect data in several experiments included both acoustic and IMU [16, 17], the limitations of the laboratory environment resulted in the data being less than comprehensive, and the models were susceptible to overfitting.

Sensor data collected in the real world often differ significantly from data collected in a laboratory environment. Data from real world environments can contain considerable noise, and user behavior cannot be strictly defined. These differences can cause models trained on laboratory data to be less robust or practical. When testing data from real environments, the model's classification results are often unreliable to the extent that the model, although passing the test on data from the laboratory environment, cannot be deployed practically.

This method eliminates the limitations of a single dimension of data and increases the upper limit of the classification results by combining IMU and acoustic data to increase the amount of information in a single dimension of data, thus increasing the number of features extracted from the data by the model. The collected data in-the-wild contain both ambient noise and human voice, which has a higher complexity than the laboratory data. Therefore, we designed two classifiers in the training process to reduce the overall complexity of the data and improve classification efficiency.

4   Dataset

This section describes the process of collecting original data and creating a dataset for training. We first discuss the hardware and software used for the experiments, and then the process of collecting and labeling the experimental data; finally, we briefly describe the dataset in general and the related methods for data preprocessing.

4.1   Data Collection and Annotation

To ensure that our research results could identify behaviors related to the pandemic with other daily behaviors, we selected the following three behaviors as our identification targets: hand washing, daily disinfection, and face-touching. The first two behaviors are significantly effective in preventing viral infections, whereas touching the face renders people more susceptible to infection.

The hardware devices used in the experiment were an Apple Watch and a wearable action camera(GoPro). The experiment collected target data using the IMU and microphone on the smartwatch, and recorded behavior by the GoPro as reference video data. In addition, the transmission of data was performed using the software of Apple Watch that collects and transmits data [18].

Our experiments were unsupervised; however, to ensure efficient experimental collection, the researchers informed the experimenters prior to the start of the experiment that they would perform the target behavior at least once during the experiment. For each participant, the duration of the experiment was at least 50 min. During the experiment, participants' hand behavior was monitored by GoPro cameras, which recorded video and served as the basis for data labeling. The data labels of the original dataset were manually labeled by the researchers based on the video content and timestamps captured using GoPro. Figure 1 includes three types of specific behaviors and a type of daily behavior.

Fig. 1. View of a particular participant while performing the three types of hand hygiene behaviors(hand washing, face-touching, and disinfection) and other daily behaviors.

4.2   Data Processing

The three-axis accelerometer and gyroscope data were sampled 100 Hz, whereas acoustic data were sampled using a microphone on the smartwatch at a sampling frequency of 22.05 KHz. Both audio and motion data were segmented using several frame sizes of seconds with 50% overlap. According to previous studies, the frame size in human activity recognition has a significant impact on the classification performance of a model [19]. Based on the timestamps contained in the acoustic data in the original dataset, we filled in the missing data in the IMU. This method enables the IMU and acoustic data to be synchronized to ensure that each data block corresponds to the same time period when input to the model.

4.3   Data Augmentation

As shown in Fig. 2, because the experiment simulates human behavior in a real environment, hand washing, disinfection, and face-touching behaviors occupy an extremely low proportion of daily time, enabling us to collect data on daily behaviors for a long period, which is not only our target for classification but also leads to an unbalanced data distribution. Data augmentation techniques were applied [20,21], and we increased the amount of data in the target class by injecting Gaussian noise, scaling the time and frequency domains, and rotating the matrix to minimize the impact of data imbalance on the model performance. After data augmentation, about twelve hours of IMU and acoustic data were utilized for model training and evaluation.

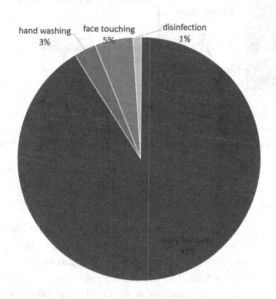

Fig. 2. Distribution of different behaviors in the raw data

5   Methods

This section describes the process of training our model using IMU and acoustic datasets. We first present the training process from the input data to the specific behavior labels, then describe the models applied to the specific processing data and the techniques for acoustic data feature extraction, and finally describe two methods for combining IMU with acoustic data.

5.1   Training Flow

Owing to the imbalance of the data samples, we opted to dichotomize the raw data by filtering out the hand hygiene behaviors (hand washing, disinfecting, and face-touching) as a whole and then training the model to explicitly classify the prevention-related behaviors. Hand hygiene behaviors were specifically defined in the study, enabling these behaviors to possess regularity in IMU and acoustic features, whereas daily behaviors possess chaotic and disordered features. The model can discriminate the relevant features of hand hygiene behaviors and classify them accurately using binary classification training. We expect that this step can indirectly improve the classification accuracy of the model for specific prevention-related behaviors. Figure 3 shows the specific training process.

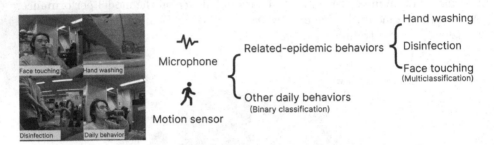

Fig. 3. Classification process (first, collecting acoustic and IMU from daily activities based on the smartwatch; second, distinguishing hand hygiene or other daily behaviors; finally, distinguishing specific hand hygiene behavior such as washing hands and disinfection)

5.2   Inertial and Acoustic Model

In this study, we used multiple sensor data from an off-the-shelf smartwatch to detect several defined behaviors. To increase the utility and generalizability of the research results, we collected audio and IMU from eight participants in real environments over a long period. During data processing, we increased inter-user data variability by data augmentation, a method that has been proven to help improve the imbalance of the raw dataset and the overall model classification accuracy.

Considering the inertial sensory data as input, we explored two models to establish a baseline performance on our dataset: (1) Long Short-Term Memory (LSTM) and (2) ECAPA-TDNN. LSTM is a classical neural network model based on recurrent neural networks and hidden states. We adopted the LSTM model as the primary model for processing inertial and acoustic data in our experiments because of its excellent performance in acoustic processing and time-series data processing [19,22]. The ECAPA-TDNN is a type of TDNN-based acoustic model that places more emphasis on channel attention, propagation, and aggregation [23]. The incorporation of multiscale Res2Net features and channel-dependent attentive statistics pooling enabled the model to capture more data features during the training process. Owing to the time-series similarity between the acoustic and IMU, we expect that the model can perform better in the time-series data processing.

For acoustic classification, we extracted features from the log-Mel spectrograms that have been proven effective in previous studies. By computing the short-time Fourier transform, we extracted the spectrograms of our audio data using a Hanning window of 1024 samples and a hop size of 512 samples. Examples of log-Mel spectrograms for each activity class are shown in Fig. 4.

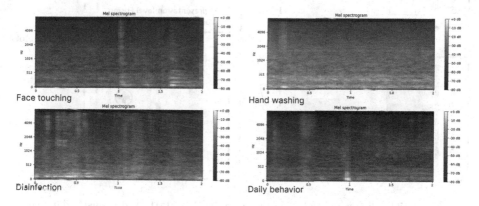

Fig. 4. Mel spectrograms of a particular participant while performing the three types of hand hygienic behaviors(hand washing, face-touching, and disinfection and one type of daily behavior

5.3   Fusion Methods

Traditional fusion strategies for data fusion include representation-level fusion [17] and score-level fusion [22]. We believe that the data fusion strategy should be able to combine the motion features represented by IMU with the acoustic features represented by acoustic data, resulting in a more accurate output from the framework. The entire framework is shown in Fig. 5. We used the following two data fusion techniques:

(1) Simple concatenation of the feature maps: In this method, the feature maps from the penultimate layer of the inertial and acoustic data modules are concatenated and classified using the SoftMax layer. This method can reduce the impact of interclass similarity on classification accuracy in a single dimension by concatenating features.
(2) Score-level fusion: This method classifies the inertial and acoustic data modules separately and averages the class probabilities to obtain the final probabilities. This is more straightforward and can combine the outputs of the two models to achieve better classification results.

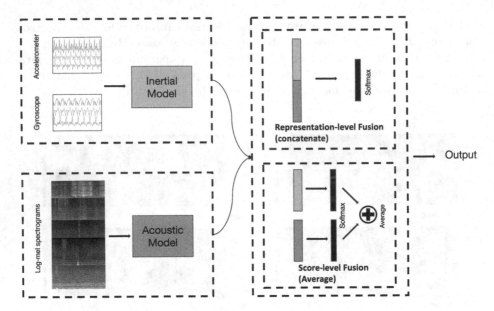

Fig. 5. This figure presents two fusion methods of IMU and acoustic data.

6   Evaluation

This section presents the evaluation and analysis of the performance of our inertial acoustic data processing on a classification task using the collected data. First, we evaluated the performance of different data and different models in distinguishing between daily and prevention-related behaviors. We then analyzed the performance of the models in distinguishing specific prevention-related behaviors (hand washing, sanitizing, and face washing) and described the advantages of combining IMU with acoustic data in terms of model performance. During the evaluation phase of the model training, we use cross-validation method to divide the data that 80% for training set and 20% for test set. We used the PyTorch framework and trained the network via the Adam optimizer.

6.1   Binary Classification: Distinguishing Hand Hygienic Behaviors and Daily Behaviors

In the binary classification stage of the model, we trained the IMU and acoustic data with LSTM and ECAPA-TDNN models, respectively, and obtained the following results. Table 1 lists the detailed classification results. From the above table, we can observe that the binary classification model trained with IMU has a significantly better classification performance than the binary classification model trained with acoustic data. Among them, the best-performing ECPA model trained with IMU achieved a 35% higher classification accuracy than that trained with acoustic data. The worst-performing IMU model was approximately 20% more accurate than the best-performing acoustic model.

Table 1. Evaluation of the binary classification. IMU-ECPA represents the model based on the ECAPA-TDNN model with the IMU. IMU-LSTM represents the model based on the LSTM model with the IMU dataset. VOI-ECPA represents the model based on the ECAPA-TDNN model with the acoustic dataset. VOI-LSTM represents the model based on the LSTM model with the acoustic dataset.

Data-model	Precision	Recall	F1-score
IMU-ECPA	**0.98**	**0.96**	**0.97**
IMU-LSTM	0.77	0.72	0.74
VOI-ECPA	**0.64**	**0.63**	**0.63**
VOI-LSTM	0.57	0.60	0.58

6.2 Multi-classification: Distinguishing the Specific Hand Hygienic Behaviors

After the binary classification, we filtered the behavioral data related to prevention but still required a model to classify specific behaviors. At this stage, we fed the processed IMU and acoustic datasets into the LSTM and ECAPA-TDNN models, respectively, to obtain classification results for a single type of data under different models(see Table 2). Then, we combined the two types of data in one dataset and output better classification results by the concatenation or score-level method.

Evidently, the classification model using both IMU and acoustic data has a higher classification accuracy than the model using single dimension data. The ECAPA-TDNN model achieved a higher accuracy than LSTM with the same data input. Moreover, among the two multimodal data combination methods, the concatenation method achieved a higher accuracy than the score-level method.

Table 2. Evaluation of the multiclassification. In this model, AVE represents a score-level data fusion method, and CON represents the concatenation data fusion method.

Data-model	Precision	Recall	F1-score
IMU-ECPA	0.82	0.82	0.82
IMU-LSTM	0.77	0.72	0.74
VOI-ECPA	0.76	0.75	0.76
VOI-LSTM	0.56	0.56	0.56
IMUVOI-ECPA-AVE	**0.93**	**0.96**	**0.94**
IMUVOI-LSTM-AVE	0.89	0.90	0.89
IMUVOI-ECPA-CON	**0.90**	**0.90**	**0.90**
IMUVOI-LSTM-CON	0.86	0.87	0.86

As shown in Fig. 6, nearly all face-touching behaviors in the test set are correctly recognized by the model, with only a 7% error occurring between handwashing and sanitizing behaviors. Eleven percent of the disinfection behaviors are misidentified as hand washing, and we conjecture this misidentification to be because of interclass similarity between hand washing and disinfection behaviors at the IMU level.

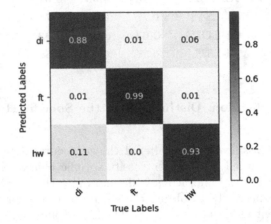

Fig. 6. Figure showing the classification results of IMUVOI-ECPA-AVE listed in Table 2. The IMU and acoustic data were input at the same time, which were processed using the ECAPA-TDNN model, and score-level fusion was performed based on the output from the IMU module and acoustic module. The word "di" in this figure represents disinfection. The "hw" in this figure represents hand washing. The "ft" in this figure represents face touching.

7   Discussion

The evaluation of the model training results demonstrated a 10% increase in the accuracy of the classification model after combining acoustic data, indicating that acoustic data are critical for complementing behavioral features related to prevention. Although acoustic data from real environments are noisier than those from laboratory environments, they still contain features that cannot be expressed by IMU. Evaluation of the training results of the dichotomous classification model demonstrated that the IMU dataset contained more features than the acoustic data in distinguishing between daily and hand hygiene behaviors. This suggests that, in most cases, the model can determine whether the current behavior is relevant to vaccination without the user activating the microphone. Both the energy consumption problems associated with activating a microphone for long periods of time were reduced, and the privacy risks associated with human voice conversations in everyday scenarios were avoided. Our results highlight the feasibility of using inertial acoustic data from practical off-the-shelf wrist-worn devices to identify the relevant epidemic behaviors. The model can be mounted on a widely used portable device, the smartwatch, to enable the detection and recording of user behavior.

Our study has some limitations. First, even though we allowed participants to conduct the experiment in an unsupervised environment as much as possible, the dataset still cannot cover most of the daily behaviors because of the limitation of the number of participants and the duration of the experiment, rendering the model less robust. Second, after analyzing the GoPro video data, we found that most of the time the participants chose to stay indoors, a more quiet and orderly space, rendering the model unable to detect and record behaviors from features from acoustic data in outdoor or noisy environments.

8   Conclusion

In summary, this study explored the possibility of monitoring hand washing, disinfection, and face-touching in a real environment based on the acoustic and inertial sensing elements of a smartwatch. We collected datasets that included IMU and acoustic data from eight people over a 50-minute period through smart-watches. In this study, an LSTM model was used to classify different behaviors using the IMU and acoustic data. Combining acoustic and inertial data, we also explored connection fusion and fraction fusion to illustrate the significantly improved classification performance of the model obtained by training with acoustic data compared to that with the regular LSTM network. Although our proposed method has achieved some progress in classification results by combining acoustic and inertial data, some biases exist in experimental data collection; for example, nearly all experiments were conducted indoors, resulting in models that are not sufficient to resist outdoor noise. Second, because of the limitation of the camera range, the experiments lacked long-term data collection, and we believe that the data imbalance will be more pronounced over a longer time scale. Therefore, we will continue to advance this study by developing a framework to achieve higher accuracy in health behavior classification by combining IMU and acoustic data through other methods and conducting future experiments based on other network structures, such as transformers.

Acknowledgment. This work was partly supported by National Institute of Information and Communications Technology (NICT), Japan.

References

1. Głąbska, D., Skolmowska, D., Guzek, D.: Population-based study of the influence of the COVID-19 pandemic on hand hygiene behaviors-polish adolescents' COVID-19 experience (place-19) study. Sustainability **12**(12), 4930 (2020)
2. Mondol, M.A.S., Stankovic, J.A.: Hawad: hand washing detection using wrist wearable inertial sensors. In: 2020 16th International Conference on Distributed Computing in Sensor Systems (DCOSS), pp. 11–18. IEEE (2020)

3. Xu, L., Nishiyama, Y., Sezaki, K.: Enhancing self-protection: what influences human's epidemic prevention behavior during the COVID-19 pandemic. In: Distributed, A., Interactions, P. (eds.) HCII 2022, Part II. LNCS, vol. 13326, pp. 336–351. Springer, Proceedings (2022). https://doi.org/10.1007/978-3-031-05431-0_23

4. Bhattacharya, S., Adaimi, R., Thomaz, E.: Leveraging sound and wrist motion to detect activities of daily living with commodity smartwatches. Proc. ACM Interact. Mob. Wearable Ubiquit. Technol. 6(2), 1–28 (2022)

5. Weiss, G.M., Timko, J.L., Gallagher, C.M., Yoneda, K., Schreiber, A.J.: Smartwatch-based activity recognition: a machine learning approach. In: 2016 IEEE-EMBS International Conference on Biomedical and Health Informatics (BHI), pp. 426–429. IEEE (2016)

6. Chen, X.: Faceoff: detecting face touching with a wrist-worn accelerometer. arXiv preprint arXiv:2008.01769 (2020)

7. Ellis, K., Godbole, S., Chen, J., Marshall, S., Lanckriet, G., Kerr, J.: Physical activity recognition in free-living from body-worn sensors. In: Proceedings of the 4th International SenseCam and Pervasive Imaging Conference, pp. 88–89 (2013)

8. Wang, X., et al.: Social distancing alert with smartwatches. arXiv preprint arXiv:2205.06110 (2022)

9. Kwok, Y.L.A., Gralton, J., McLaws, M.-L.: Face touching: a frequent habit that has implications for hand hygiene. Am. J. Infect. Control 43(2), 112–114 (2015)

10. Duan, Y., et al.: Predicting hand washing, mask wearing and social distancing behaviors among older adults during the COVID-19 pandemic: an integrated social cognition model. BMC Geriatr. 22(1), 91 (2022)

11. Lattanzi, E., Calisti, L., Freschi, V.: Automatic unstructured handwashing recognition using smartwatch to reduce contact transmission of pathogens (2022)

12. Stork, J.A., Spinello, L., Silva, J., Arras, K.O.: Audio-based human activity recognition using non-Markovian ensemble voting. In: IEEE RO-MAN: The 21st IEEE International Symposium on Robot and Human Interactive Communication, pp. 509–514. IEEE (2012)

13. Siddiqui, N., Chan, R.H.: Multimodal hand gesture recognition using single IMU and acoustic measurements at wrist. PLoS ONE 15(1), e0227039 (2020)

14. Dittakavi, B., et al.: Pose tutor: an explainable system for pose correction in the wild. In: Proceedings of the IEEE/CVF Conference on Computer Vision and Pattern Recognition, pp. 3540–3549 (2022)

15. Samyoun, S., Shubha, S.S., Mondol, M.A.S., Stankovic, J.A.: iWash: a smartwatch handwashing quality assessment and reminder system with real-time feedback in the context of infectious disease. Smart Health 19, 100171 (2021)

16. Mollyn, V., Ahuja, K., Verma, D., Harrison, C., Goel, M.: Samosa: sensing activities with motion and subsampled audio. Proc. ACM Interact. Mob. Wearable Ubiquit. Technol. 6(3), 1–19 (2022)

17. Becker, V., Fessler, L., Sörös, G.: Gestear: combining audio and motion sensing for gesture recognition on smartwatches. In: Proceedings of the 2019 ACM International Symposium on Wearable Computers, pp. 10–19 (2019)

18. Nishiyama, Y., et al.: IOS crowd–sensing won't hurt a bit!: AWARE framework and sustainable study guideline for iOS platform. In: Streitz, N., Konomi, S. (eds.) HCII 2020. LNCS, vol. 12203, pp. 223–243. Springer, Cham (2020). https://doi.org/10.1007/978-3-030-50344-4_17

19. Gers, F.A., Eck, D., Schmidhuber, J.: Applying LSTM to time series predictable through time-window approaches. In: Dorffner, G., Bischof, H., Hornik, K. (eds.) ICANN 2001. LNCS, vol. 2130, pp. 669–676. Springer, Heidelberg (2001). https://doi.org/10.1007/3-540-44668-0_93
20. Wen, Q., et al.: Time series data augmentation for deep learning: a survey. arXiv preprint arXiv:2002.12478 (2020)
21. Um, T.T., et al.: Data augmentation of wearable sensor data for Parkinson's disease monitoring using convolutional neural networks. In: Proceedings of the 19th ACM International Conference on Multimodal Interaction, pp. 216–220 (2017)
22. Guan, Y., Plötz, T.: Ensembles of deep LSTM learners for activity recognition using wearables. Proc. ACM Interact. Mob. Wearable Ubiquit. Technol. 1(2), 1–28 (2017)
23. Desplanques, B., Thienpondt, J., Demuynck, K.: Ecapa-TDNN: emphasized channel attention, propagation and aggregation in TDNN based speaker verification. arXiv preprint arXiv:2005.07143 (2020)

Author Index

Printed in the United States
by Baker & Taylor Publisher Services